PRENTICE HALL
THE AMERICAN NATION
Civil War to the Present

Dr. James West Davidson
Author

IN ASSOCIATION WITH
American Heritage®

PEARSON
Prentice
Hall

Dr. Michael B. Stoff
Author

Dr. Herman J. Viola
Senior Consultant

Upper Saddle River, New Jersey
Glenview, Illinois
Needham, Massachusetts

Collections of the Fort Ticonderoga Museum

ISBN 0-13-058849-0
4 5 6 7 8 9 10   07 06 05 04 03

Authors

Dr. James West Davidson is coauthor of *After the Fact: The Art of Historical Detection* and *Nation of Nations: A Narrative History of the American Republic.* Dr. Davidson has taught at both the college and high school levels. He has also consulted on curriculum design for American history courses. Dr. Davidson is an avid canoeist and hiker. His published works on these subjects include *Great Heart,* the true story of a 1903 canoe trip in the Canadian wilderness.

Dr. Michael B. Stoff received his Ph.D. from Yale University and teaches history at the University of Texas at Austin. He is the author of *Oil, War, and American Security: The Search for a National Policy on Foreign Oil, 1941–1947,* coauthor of *Nation of Nations: A Narrative History of the American Republic,* and coeditor of *The Manhattan Project: A Documentary Introduction to the Atomic Age.* Dr. Stoff has won numerous grants, fellowships, and teaching awards.

Senior Consultant

Dr. Herman J. Viola, curator emeritus with the Smithsonian Institution, is a distinguished historian and author. Dr. Viola received his Ph.D. in American history from Indiana University. He founded the scholarly journal *Prologue* at the National Archives. Dr. Viola also served as director of the National Anthropological Archives at the Smithsonian Institution. A nationally recognized authority on American Indians, the history of the American West, and the Civil War, Dr. Viola is the author of many historical works for both adults and young readers.

AmericanHeritage® **American Heritage** magazine was founded in 1954, and it quickly rose to the position it occupies today: the country's preeminent magazine of history and culture. Dedicated to presenting the past in entertaining narratives underpinned by scrupulous scholarship, *American Heritage* today goes to more than 300,000 subscribers and counts the country's very best writers and historians among its contributors.

Program Reviewers

Nancy Foss
Social Studies Teacher
Glenn Hills Middle School
Augusta, Georgia

Mike Harter
Social Studies Teacher
Austin Middle School
Amarillo, Texas

Beverly Hooper
Social Studies Teacher
Dartmouth Middle School
San Jose, California

Patricia Mymbs
Social Studies Teacher
Edward H. Cary Middle School
Dallas, Texas

Denis O'Rourke
Social Studies Teacher
Hommocks Middle School
Larchmont, New York

David Peterson
Social Studies Teacher
Fairmont Junior High School
Boise, Idaho

Lauri Rule
Social Studies Teacher
Shackelford Junior High School
Arlington, Texas

Dana Sanders
Social Studies Teacher
Knox County High School
Edina, Missouri

W. David Scott
Social Studies Teacher
Havenview Middle School
Memphis, Tennessee

Bill Speer
Social Studies Teacher
Albright Middle School
Houston, Texas

Donna Wenger
Social Studies Teacher
Wilson Middle School
Plano, Texas

Pamela West
Social Studies Teacher
Greshman Middle School
Birmingham, Alabama

Reading Specialist

Bonnie Armbruster, Ph.D.
Professor of Education
University of Illinois at Urbana-Champaign
Champaign, Illinois

Curriculum and Assessment Specialist

Jan Moberley
Dallas, Texas

Accuracy Panel

Esther Ratner
Greyherne Information Services
Lynn D. Hoover, The Hoover Associates
Jane B. Malcolm, Professional Research Services
Alice Radosh, Ph.D., Academy of Educational
  Development
Lorrain Rosenberg, Baldwin School District, New York
  (Ret.)
Cathy S. Zazueta, California State University, Los
  Angeles

Program Advisors

Pat Easterbrook
Social Studies Consultant
Cary, North Carolina

Michal Howden
Social Studies Consultant
Zionsville, Indiana

Kathy Lewis
Social Studies Consultant
Fort Worth, Texas

Rick Moulden
Social Studies Consultant
Federal Way, Washington

Sharon Pope
Social Studies Consultant
Houston, Texas

Joe Wieczorek
Social Studies Consultant
Baltimore, Maryland

The 54th Massachusetts Regiment in battle, 1863

Contents

A Plains family and livestock

Theodore Roosevelt leading a charge in Cuba

UNIT 7 — A NEW ROLE FOR THE NATION — 626

A Teddy bear, named for
President Theodore Roosevelt

Best-selling novel from the 1920s

MAIN STREET

SINCLAIR LEWIS

UNIT ⭐ 8 PROSPERITY, DEPRESSION, AND WAR 714

Hard times during the Great Depression

The Vietnam Veterans Memorial, Washington, D.C.

Special Features

Master skills you will use all your life.

A baseball game in 1886

Connecting With...

See how history has fascinating links with other subjects.

Special Features

The Kennedy Space Center

Special Features/Primary Sources

An American Profile

Meet fascinating history makers.

Mary McLeod Bethune

Primary Sources

Relive history through eyewitness accounts, literature, and documents.

President Bush addresses Congress

Primary Sources

In-text Primary Sources

> **❝** This momentous question, like a fire bell in the night, awakened and filled me with terror. I considered it at once as the knell of the Union…. We have the wolf by the ears, and we can neither hold him, nor safely let him go. **❞**
>
> —Thomas Jefferson, Letter to John Holmes, April 22, 1820

> **❝** A cloud of smoke hangs over it by day. The glow of scores of furnaces lights the riverbanks by night. It stands at the junction of two great rivers, the Monongahela which flows down today in a [slow] yellow stream, and the Allegheny which is blackish. **❞**
>
> —Charles Philips Trevelyan, *Letters from North America and the Pacific,* April 15, 1898

(continued)

Primary Sources

> **66**This great nation will endure as it has endured, will revive and will prosper. So, first of all, let me assert my firm belief that the only thing we have to fear is fear itself...**99**
>
> —Franklin D. Roosevelt, Inaugural Address, March 4, 1933

Maps

Chapter Maps

Reference Section Maps

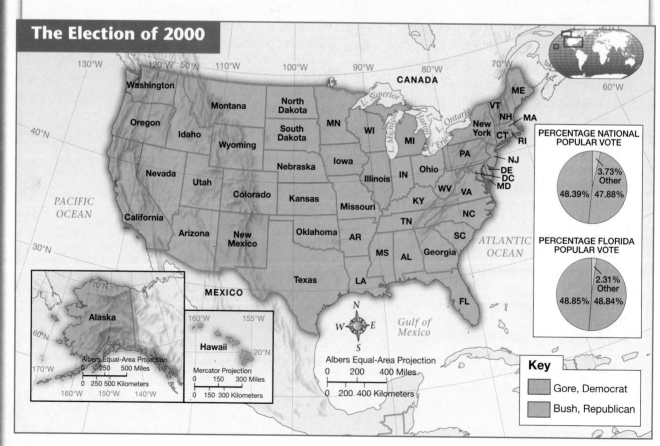

The Election of 2000

Political Cartoons

Political Cartoons

Theodore Roosevelt and the Muckrakers

President Clinton and Congress

Charts and Graphs

Charts and Graphs

Immigrants: Push and Pull Factors

Push Factors:	Pull Factors:
• Scarce land	• Promise of freedom
• Farm jobs lost to new machines	• Family or friends already settled in the United States
• Political and religious persecution	• Factory jobs available
• Revolution	
• Poverty and hard lives	

Charts and Graphs

Cause and Effect

Graphic Organizers

Should the United States Declare War on Germany?

YES BECAUSE:

- Many Americans are outraged by German submarine warfare.
- Many Americans favor Britain and France.
- The Zimmermann telegram angered many Americans.
- American trade with the Allies is growing.

NO BECAUSE:

- The United States has a tradition of neutrality.
- Some Americans sympathize with the Central Powers.
- Wilson opposes the alliance with the Russian czar.
- Pacifists are opposed to joining the war.

A Changing American Culture

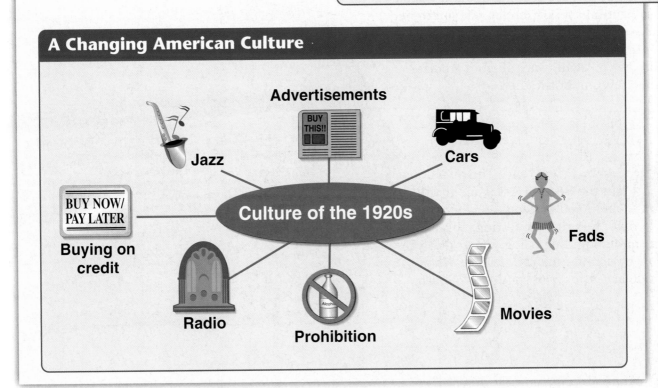

Advertisements

Jazz

Cars

BUY NOW/ PAY LATER

Buying on credit

Culture of the 1920s

Fads

Radio

Prohibition

Movies

Use This Book for Success

You can use this book as a tool to master American history. Spend a few minutes becoming familiar with the way the book is set up, and see how you can unlock the secrets of American history.

Read for Content Mastery

BEFORE YOU READ **Before You Read** The sections in this book begin with Reading Focus questions. These questions point out important ideas in the section. They give you a purpose for reading. Another helpful aid is the Taking Notes exercise at the beginning of each section. It will help you take notes as you read.

AS YOU READ **As You Read** This book also helps you while you are reading. From time to time, you will see a question or thinking activity beside a paragraph in the text. If you are reading about the Civil War, it might ask you to predict which side will win. If you are reading about a wagon train heading west, it might ask you to list what you already know about transportation in the 1800s. By stopping to really think as you read, you will gain a better understanding of the text.

AFTER YOU READ **After You Read** The questions in the Section Assessment will help you understand what you have read. Use these questions to assess your understanding. Then, show what you know by completing the activity. When you do activities, you continue to learn.

2 No Easy Victory

BEFORE YOU READ

Reading Focus
- What strategies did each side adopt to win the war?
- How did early encounters dispel hopes for a quick end to the war?
- What victories did the Confederates achieve?
- What victories did the Union achieve?

Key Terms
Battle of Bull Run
Virginia
Monitor
Battle of Antietam
Battle of Fredericksburg
Battle of Chancellorsville
Battle of Shiloh

Taking Notes
As you read, prepare an outline of the section. Use roman numerals to indicate major headings, capital letters for subheadings, and numbers for supporting details. The sample below will help you get started.

> I. Strategies for Victory
>   A. Union plans
>   1.
>   2.
>   3.
>   B. Confederate plans
>   1.
>   2.
> II. Early Encounters

Main Idea Despite hopes for a quick victory, both northerners and southerners soon learned that they were in for a long, difficult struggle.

Setting the Scene At first, the armies of the North and the South marched proudly off to war. Each side expected a quick and painless victory. The reality of war soon shattered this expectation. Over and over, soldiers wrote home describing the awful face of battle:

> 66 I never saw so many broken down and exhausted men in all my life. I was sick as a horse, and as wet with blood and sweat as I could be. . . . Our tongues were parched and cracked for water, and our faces blackened with powder and smoke. 99
> —quoted by Shelby Foote in *The Civil War: A Narrative*

It soon became clear that there would be no quick end to the struggle. Both sides began to dig in for a long, difficult war.

AS YOU READ **Bullet caught in shoulder plate**
Predict What effect would improved weapons have upon the war?

AFTER YOU READ ★ ★ **Section 2 Assessment** ★ ★ ★

Recall
1. **Identify** Explain the significance of (a) Stonewall Jackson, (b) Battle of Bull Run, (c) George McClellan, (d) *Virginia*, (e) *Monitor*, (f) Battle of Antietam, (g) Battle of Fredericksburg, (h) Battle of Chancellorsville, (i) Ulysses S. Grant, (j) Battle of Shiloh.

Comprehension
2. **Describe** (a) the North's three-part plan for defeating the South, (b) the South's plan to defeat the North.
3. What did both sides learn from the Battle of Bull Run?

4. Why was the Confederate victory at Fredericksburg critical?
5. How did Union victories at New Orleans and Memphis affect the South?

Critical Thinking and Writing
6. **Exploring the Main Idea** Review the Main Idea statement at the beginning of this section. Make a list of five events and their results during the first two years of the war.
7. **Analyzing Ideas** Analyze the meaning of this statement: "The South could win the war by not losing, but the North could win only by winning."

ACTIVITY
Take It to the NET
Connecting to Today
Both the Union and Confederate navies developed ironclad ships during the Civil War. Use the Internet to research technological advances in modern naval vessels. Prepare an oral class presentation including pictures. Visit *The American Nation* section of www.phschool.com for help in completing the activity.

494 ★ Chapter 17 *The Civil War*

Develop Your Skills

Each chapter has a Skills for Life feature. Use these features to learn and practice social studies skills. These skills will help you be successful in understanding American history. Complete the Skills Assessment at the end of every chapter to apply the skills that you have learned.

Use the Internet to Explore

At the click of a mouse, the Internet offers you access to a wealth of American history resources. Use the Take It to the NET activities to research and learn more about key concepts in American history. The Virtual Field Trips in the American Heritage® History Happened Here feature let you go online to explore historic sites.

Prepare for Tests

This book helps you prepare for tests. Start by answering the questions at the end of every section and chapter. Go to www.phschool.com at the end of each chapter to take the practice Chapter Self-Test. Then, use the Test Preparation pages at the end of the unit to check yourself further.

Success in social studies comes from doing three things well—reading, testing, and writing. The following pages present strategies to help you read for meaning, understand test questions, and write well for social studies.

Reading for Meaning

Do you have trouble remembering what you read? Here are some tips from experts that will improve your ability to recall and understand what you read:

▶ Before You Read

Preview the text to identify important information.
Like watching the coming attractions at a movie theater, previewing the text helps you know what to expect. Study the questions and strategies below to learn how to preview what you read.

Ask yourself these questions:	Use these strategies to find the answers:
• What is the text about?	Read the headings, subheadings, and captions. Study the photos, maps, tables, or graphs.
• What do I already know about the topic?	Read the questions at the end of the text to see if you can answer any of them.
• What is the purpose of the text?	Turn the headings into *who, what, when, where, why,* or *how* questions. This will help you decide if the text compares things, tells a chain of events, or explains causes and effects.

▶ As You Read

Organize information in a way that helps you see meaningful connections or relationships.

Taking notes as you read will improve your understanding. Use graphic organizers like the ones below to record the information you read. Study these descriptions and examples to learn how to create each type of organizer.

Sequencing

A **flowchart** helps you see how one event led to another. It can also display the steps in a process.

Use a flowchart if the text—
- tells about a chain of events.
- explains a method of doing something.

TIP▶ List the events or steps in order.

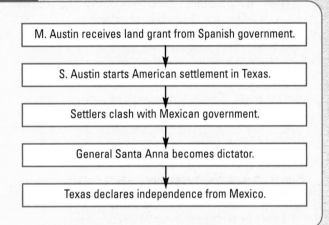

Comparing and Contrasting

A **Venn diagram** displays similarities and differences.

Use a Venn diagram if the text—
- compares and contrasts two individuals, groups, places, things, or events.

TIP▶ Label the outside section of each circle and list differences.
Label the shared section and list similarities.

Student *Success* Handbook

Categorizing Information

A **table** organizes information in categories.

Use a table if the text—
- lists similar facts about several places or things.
- presents characteristics of different groups.

TIP▶ Write an appropriate heading for each column in the table to identify its category.

COLONY	FOUNDED	LEADERS
Massachusetts	1620	William Bradford John Winthrop
New Hampshire	1623	John Wentworth
Connecticut	1636	Thomas Hooker
Rhode Island	1636	Roger Williams

Identifying Main Ideas and Details

A **concept web** helps you understand relationships among ideas.

Use a concept web if the text—
- provides examples to support a main idea.
- links several ideas to a main topic.

TIP▶ Write the main idea in the largest circle.
Write details in smaller circles and draw lines to show relationships.

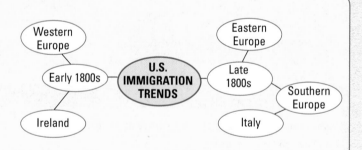

Organizing Information

An **outline** provides an overview, or a kind of blueprint for reading.

Use an outline to organize ideas—
- according to their importance.
- according to the order in which they are presented.

TIP ▶ Use roman numerals for main ideas, capital letters for secondary ideas, arabic numerals for supporting details.

I. Differences Between the North and the South
- **A.** Views on slavery
    - **1.** Northern abolitionists
    - **2.** Southern slave owners
- **B.** Economies
    - **1.** Northern manufacturing
    - **2.** Southern agriculture

Identifying Cause and Effect

A **cause-and-effect** chart shows the relationship between what happened (effect) and the reason why it happened (cause).

Use a cause-and-effect chart if the text—
- lists one or more causes for an event.
- lists one or more results of an event.

TIP ▶ Label causes and effects. Draw arrows to indicate how ideas are related.

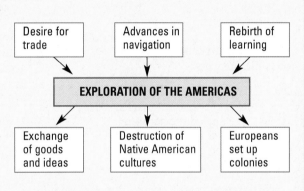

▶ After You Read

Test yourself to find out what you learned from reading the text.

Go back to the questions you asked yourself before you read the text. You should be able to give more complete answers to these questions:
- What is the text about?
- What is the purpose of the text?

You should also be able to make connections between the new information you learned from the text and what you already knew about the topic.

Study your graphic organizer. Use this information as the *answers*. Make up a meaningful *question* about each piece of information.

Taking Tests

Do you panic at the thought of taking a standardized test? Here are some tips that most test developers recommend to help you achieve good scores.

▶ Multiple-Choice Questions

Read each part of a multiple-choice question to make sure you understand what is being asked.

Many tests are made up of multiple-choice questions. Some multiple-choice items are **direct questions.** They are complete sentences followed by possible answers, called distractors.

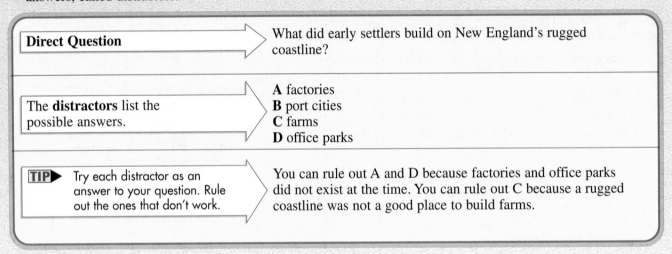

Direct Question	What did early settlers build on New England's rugged coastline?
The **distractors** list the possible answers.	A factories B port cities C farms D office parks
TIP▶ Try each distractor as an answer to your question. Rule out the ones that don't work.	You can rule out A and D because factories and office parks did not exist at the time. You can rule out C because a rugged coastline was not a good place to build farms.

Other multiple-choice questions are **incomplete sentences** that you are to finish. They are followed by possible answers.

The **stem** tells you what the question is looking for	New England's rugged coastline was a good place for early settlers to build
Distractors	A factories B port cities C farms D office parks
TIP▶ Turn the stem into a direct question, using *who, what, when, where,* or *why.*	What did early settlers build on New England's rugged coastline?

▶ What's Being Tested?

Identify the type of question you are being asked.

Social studies tests often ask questions that involve reading comprehension. Other questions may require you to gather or interpret information from a map, graph, or chart. The following strategies will help you answer different kinds of questions.

Reading Comprehension Questions

What to do:	How to do it:
1. Determine the content and organization of the selection.	Read the **title.** Skim the selection. Look for key words that indicate time, cause-and-effect, or comparison.
2. Analyze the questions. Do they ask you to *recall facts?*	Look for **key words** in the stem: <u>According to</u> the selection . . . The selection <u>states</u> that . . .
Do they ask you to *make judgments?*	The <u>main idea</u> of the selection is. . . The author <u>would likely</u> agree that. . .
3. Read the selection.	Read quickly. Keep the questions in mind.
4. Answer the questions.	Try out each distractor and choose the best answer. Refer back to the selection if necessary.

Example:

The Dust Bowl During the 1930s, an area of the southern Great Plains became known as the "Dust Bowl." Climate and farming methods combined to cause one of the worst environmental disasters in United States history. As a result of a severe drought, the soil was dry. When farmers plowed the land, they removed the prairie grasses that held the soil in place. When strong winds swept the region, the soil was easily eroded and carried hundreds of miles away. A series of destructive dust-storms brought economic ruin to farmers.

What caused the soil to become dry?
A strong winds
B plowing
C drought
D high temperatures

TIP ▶ The key words <u>as a result</u> tell why the soil was dry.

(The correct answer is C.)

▶ What's Being Tested? *(continued)*

Map Questions

What to do:

1. Determine what kind of information is presented on the map.

2. Read the question. Determine which component on the map will help you find the answer.

3. Look at the map and answer the question in your own words.

4. Choose the best answer.

How to do it:

Read the map **title.** It will indicate the purpose of the map.
Study the **map key.** It will explain the symbols used on the map.
Look at the **scale.** It will help you calculate distance between places on the map.

Look for **key words** in the stem.
About <u>how far</u> . . . [use the scale]
<u>What crops</u> were grown in . . . [use the map key]

Do not read the distractors yet.

Decide which distractor agrees with the answer you determined from the map.

Example

Which of the southern colonies produced ship supplies, tobacco, rice, and indigo?

A New Jersey
B North Carolina
C Virginia
D South Carolina

TIP▶ Read the labels and the key to understand the map.

(The correct answer is B.)

Graph Questions

What to do:

1. Determine the purpose of the graph.

2. Determine what information on the graph will help you find the answer.

3. Choose the best answer.

How to do it:

Read the graph **title**. It indicates what the graph represents.

Read the **labels** on the graph or on the key. They tell the units of measurement used by the graph.

Decide which distractor agrees with the answer you determined from the graph.

Example

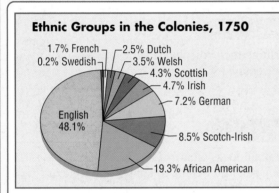

A **circle graph** shows the relationship of parts to the whole in terms of percentages.

After the English, the next largest ethnic group in the colonies was
A French   **C** German
B Irish   **D** African American

TIP ▶ Compare the percentages listed in the labels.
(The correct answer is D.)

A **line graph** shows a pattern or change over time by the direction of the line.

Between 1940 and 1943, unemployment
A decreased a little   **C** stayed about the same
B decreased greatly   **D** increased a little

TIP ▶ Compare the vertical distance between the two points on the line graph.
(The correct answer is B.)

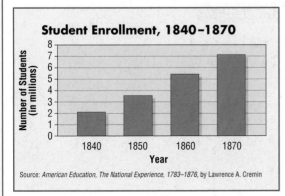

Source: *American Education, The National Experience, 1783–1876,* by Lawrence A. Cremin

A **bar graph** compares differences in quantity by showing bars of different lengths.

Between 1850 and 1860, school enrollment increased by about
A 1 million   **C** 3 million
B 2 million   **D** 4 million

TIP ▶ Compare the heights of the bars to find the difference.
(The correct answer is B.)

Writing for Social Studies

When you face a writing assignment, do you think, "How will I ever get through this?" Here are some tips to guide you through any writing project from start to finish.

▶ The Writing Process

Follow each step of the writing process to communicate effectively.

Step 1. Prewrite

- Establish the purpose.
- Define the topic.
- Determine the audience.
- Gather details.

Step 2. Draft

- Organize information logically in an outline or graphic organizer.
- Write an introduction, body, and conclusion.
- State main ideas clearly.
- Include relevant details to support your ideas.

Step 3. Revise

- Edit for clarity of ideas and elaboration.

Step 4. Proofread

- Correct any errors in spelling, grammar, and punctuation.

Step 5. Publish and Present

- Copy text neatly by hand, typewriter, or word processor.
- Illustrate as needed.
- Create a cover if appropriate.

► Types of Writing for Social Studies

Identify the purpose for your writing.

Each type of writing assignment has a specific purpose, and each purpose needs a different plan for development. The following descriptions and examples will help you identify the three purposes for social studies writing. The lists of steps will help you plan your writing.

Writing to Inform

Purpose: to present facts or ideas

Example

During the 1960s, research indicated the dangers of the insecticide DDT. It killed insects but also had long-term effects. When birds and fish ate poisoned insects, DDT built up in their fatty tissue. The poison also showed up in human beings who ate birds and fish contaminated by DDT.

 TIP ▶ Look for these **key terms** in the assignment: explain, describe, report, narrate

How to get started:
- Determine the topic you will write about.
- Write a topic sentence that tells the main idea.
- List all the ideas you can think of that are related to the topic.
- Arrange the ideas in logical order.

Writing to Persuade

Purpose: to influence someone

Example

Teaching computer skills in the classroom uses time that could be spent teaching students how to think for themselves or how to interact with others. Students who can reason well, express themselves clearly, and get along with other people will be better prepared for life than those who can use a computer.

TIP ▶ Look for these **key terms** in the assignment: convince, argue, request

How to get started:
- Make sure you understand the problem or issue clearly.
- Determine your position.
- List evidence to support your arguments.
- Predict opposing views.
- List evidence you can use to overcome the opposing arguments.

Writing to Provide Historical Interpretation

Purpose: to present the perspective of someone in a different era

Example

The crossing took a week, but the steamship voyage was hard. We were cramped in steerage with hundreds of others. At last we saw the huge statue of the lady with the torch. In the reception center, my mother held my hand while the doctor examined me. Then, my father showed our papers to the official, and we collected our bags. I was scared as we headed off to find a home in our new country.

 TIP ▶ Look for these **key terms** in the assignment: go back in time, create, suppose that, if you were

How to get started:
- Study the events or issues of the time period you will write about.
- Consider how these events or issues might have affected different people at the time.
- Choose a person whose views you would like to present.
- Identify the thoughts and feelings this person might have experienced.

Student Success Handbook

▶ Research for Writing

Follow each step of the writing process to communicate effectively.

After you have identified the purpose for your writing, you may need to do research. The following steps will help you plan, gather, organize, and present information.

Step 1. Ask Questions

Ask yourself questions to help guide your research.	What do I already know about the topic? What do I want to find out about the topic?

Step 2. Acquire Information

Locate and use appropriate sources of information about the topic.	Library Internet search Interviews
Take notes.	Follow accepted format for listing sources.

Step 3. Analyze Information

Evaluate the information you find.	Is it relevant to the topic? Is it up to date? Is it accurate? Is the writer an authority on the topic? Is there any bias?

Step 4. Use Information

Answer your research questions with the information you have found. (You may find that you need to do more research.)	Do I have all the information I need?
Organize your information into the main points you want to make. Identify supporting details.	Arrange ideas in outline form or in a graphic organizer.

Step 5. Communicate What You've Learned

Review the purpose for your writing and choose an appropriate way to present the information.

Purpose	Presentation
inform	formal paper, documentary, multimedia
persuade	essay, letter to the editor, speech
interpret	journal, newspaper account, drama

Draft and revise your writing, then evaluate it.   Use a rubric for self-evaluation.

▶ Evaluating Your Writing

Use the following rubric to help you evaluate your writing.

	Excellent	Good	Acceptable	Unacceptable
Purpose	Achieves purpose—to inform, persuade, or provide historical interpretation—very well	Informs, persuades, or provides historical interpretation reasonably well	Reader cannot easily tell if the purpose is to inform, persuade, or provide historical interpretation	Lacks purpose
Organization	Develops ideas in a very clear and logical way	Presents ideas in a reasonably well-organized way	Reader has difficulty following the organization	Lacks organization
Elaboration	Explains all ideas with facts and details	Explains most ideas with facts and details	Includes some supporting facts and details	Lacks supporting details
Use of Language	Uses excellent vocabulary and sentence structure with no errors in spelling, grammar, or punctuation	Uses good vocabulary and sentence structure with very few errors in spelling, grammar, or punctuation	Includes some errors in grammar, punctuation, and spelling	Includes many errors in grammar, punctuation, and spelling

The Emerging Nation

1 One Land, Many Peoples

Key Facts

- Over the centuries, different groups of people have settled in the Americas.
- Many European settlers came seeking religious and political freedom.
- Reform movements in the 1800s led to improved education, demands for women's rights, and a movement to end slavery.

Early encounter between a European and Native American

"Here is not merely a nation, but a teeming nation of nations," wrote poet Walt Whitman. The people of the United States came from all over the world to form a "nation of nations." They brought with them different customs, religions, and languages. Yet today they form a single nation. The history of the United States is the story of how people from many nations and cultures formed one nation with its own heritage and traditions.

A Diverse Nation

From the beginning, the American land was open to not one but many peoples. Some scientists believe the first people came to North America thousands of years ago by crossing a land bridge that joined Asia to Alaska in North America. Other scientists believe people traveled along coastal routes by boat from Asia. Over thousands of years, they spread throughout North and South America. When Christopher Columbus crossed the Atlantic Ocean from Europe in 1492, millions of Native Americans lived in the Americas.

Spain sent the first European settlers to the Americas in the 1500s. Other Europeans followed, as did many Africans. By 1775, the 13 English colonies on the Atlantic Coast were the most densely settled section of North America. Nearly 3 million people lived there. About half were English or had English ancestors. About a fifth were nonwhite.

These settlers came to North America for many reasons. Some were looking for rich farmland at low cost. Others came to escape fierce religious wars in Europe. Most Africans came against their will. They had been captured in Africa and shipped to the colonies as slaves.

During the 1800s, immigrants continued to arrive. A great famine in Ireland in 1845 sparked a wave of newcomers. Others arrived after a failed revolution in Germany in 1848. In Texas, the Southwest, and California, hundreds of thousands of Mexicans and Native Americans became residents of the United States after the Mexican War of 1846–1848. Many Chinese immigrants arrived after gold was discovered in California in 1848.

The Religious Tradition

Many European settlers fled to the colonies in search of religious freedom. The Pilgrims and the Puritans came to Massachusetts because the Church of England would not let them worship in their own way. Maryland was founded by Lord

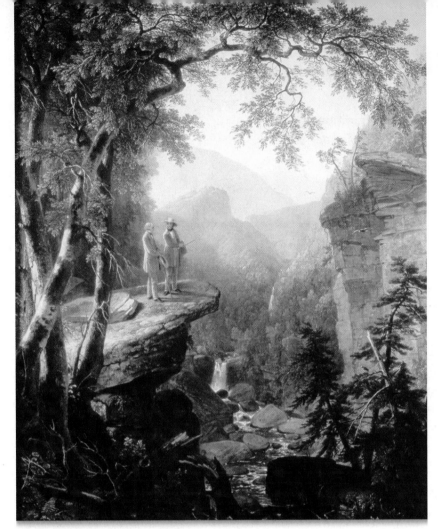

A view of the Catskill Mountains from Asher B. Durand's painting, *Kindred Spirits*

Baltimore to give Roman Catholics a place safe from persecution. At first, most colonies had their own established churches, or churches officially supported by the government. But there were many different religious groups in the colonies and established churches, in time, tolerated those with other beliefs.

After the Revolutionary War, most states did away with established churches. Freedom of religion became one of the fundamental rights in the Constitution of the United States.

The Reforming Spirit

In a democracy, people have the right to speak out to bring about change. During the mid-1800s, many reformers spoke out. They had different goals, but they all hoped to improve the quality of American life.

Religious reformers encouraged people to take personal responsibility for their faith and to lead holy lives. Many held revivals, meetings that stirred a religious spirit in those who attended.

Other reformers concentrated on changing the institutions of American society. Some, like Horace Mann, offered ideas for improving education. Through the efforts of Mann and others, many states had created free public elementary schools by the 1850s.

Reformers like Elizabeth Cady Stanton demanded more rights for women. In 1848, she and other feminists met in Seneca Falls, New York. Launching the women's rights movement, they declared, "All men and women are created equal."

Another crusade of the 1800s was the movement to abolish slavery. Americans known as abolitionists called for an immediate end to slavery. William Lloyd Garrison led the way, founding *The Liberator,* an antislavery newspaper, in 1831. Free African Americans like Frederick Douglass were active in the cause.

An American Culture

As the young nation developed, American artists and writers began to celebrate the new American culture that was flowering around them.

Ralph Waldo Emerson reflected the optimism and individualism that were typical of the new nation. In his essay "Self-Reliance," Emerson advised his readers to depend on themselves rather than follow others. Henry David Thoreau revealed his own kind of individualism in *Walden,* the story of his solitary life by Walden Pond in Massachusetts.

Perhaps more than anyone else, poet Walt Whitman captured the idealistic spirit of the republic. In *Leaves of Grass,* published in 1855, Whitman describes the people of the nation.

66 In all people I see myself, none more and not one barleycorn less,

And the good or bad I say of myself I say of them. 99

—Walt Whitman, "Song of Myself"

2 Building a Republic

Key Facts

- American democracy is rooted in English tradition.
- The United States Constitution provides the framework for American government.
- American democracy has developed over time.

Following the Revolutionary War, Americans began a dramatic political experiment. They decided to create a federal republic. Under this system, voters elect representatives to govern the country.

The plan was especially bold because the United States included many different peoples, spread out over a vast region. Few republics in history had survived for more than a few years. No republic so large had ever been created.

The English Heritage

Americans did have democratic traditions that they used to guide them. For hundreds of years,

the power of English monarchs had been limited by charters, or documents, such as the Magna Carta, that guaranteed certain rights and privileges to English citizens. The English Parliament, or legislature, wrote the charters. It also helped create the laws that governed England.

English settlers brought this tradition of representative government with them. In 1619, the Virginia colony received a charter that allowed eligible voters to elect a legislature. The Virginia House of Burgesses became the first representative assembly in the Americas.

The 13 colonies were founded at different times and under different circumstances but all

The Battle of Bunker Hill, 1775, during the American Revolution

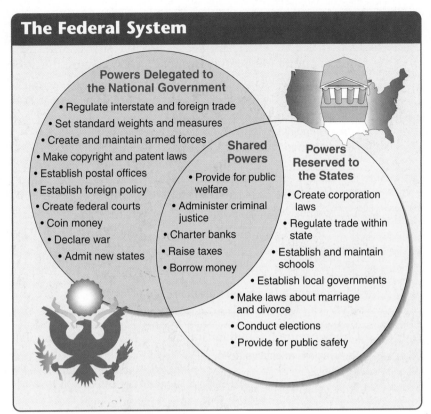

The Federal System

Powers Delegated to the National Government
- Regulate interstate and foreign trade
- Set standard weights and measures
- Create and maintain armed forces
- Make copyright and patent laws
- Establish postal offices
- Establish foreign policy
- Create federal courts
- Coin money
- Declare war
- Admit new states

Shared Powers
- Provide for public welfare
- Administer criminal justice
- Charter banks
- Raise taxes
- Borrow money

Powers Reserved to the States
- Create corporation laws
- Regulate trade within state
- Establish and maintain schools
- Establish local governments
- Make laws about marriage and divorce
- Conduct elections
- Provide for public safety

Federalism is the dividing of power between the national government and the states

eventually set up elected legislatures. Representative government became a part of colonial life.

Independence

The colonies' break with England began in the 1760s. Britain had spent large sums of money to protect the colonies during a war with France. Afterward, Parliament decided to control the colonies more closely, particularly to collect taxes. The colonists protested that they did not elect representatives to Parliament. A free people, they argued, could be taxed only by its own legislature.

Parliament refused to back down. During ten years of colonial protests, it imposed harsh measures on the colonies. The colonists responded by sending representatives to a Continental Congress in Philadelphia. In 1776, Congress issued the Declaration of Independence.

Written by Thomas Jefferson, the Declaration became a landmark in American political thought. It proclaimed that all people were "endowed by their creator with certain unalienable rights," including "life, liberty, and the pursuit of happiness."

After independence, the new nation first governed itself under a set of rules that were called the Articles of Confederation. But the Articles gave most of the power to the states and little to the national government. Congress found it very difficult to solve crucial economic, political, and foreign policy questions. It could not collect taxes or enforce the laws that it passed.

In the summer of 1787, a special convention met in Philadelphia. Working behind closed doors, it drew up a new Constitution designed to replace the Articles of Confederation. In 1789, the new government went into effect.

A Federal System

The Constitution set up a system of government called federalism. Under federalism, the states and the federal government share the power of governing. The Constitution gives certain powers entirely to the federal government. But all powers that the Constitution does not grant specifically to the federal government are reserved for the individual states.

System of Checks and Balances

Executive Branch (President carries out laws)	**Checks on the Legislative Branch**	**Checks on the Judicial Branch**
	• Can propose laws • Can veto laws • Can call special sessions of Congress • Makes appointments • Negotiates foreign treaties	• Appoints federal judges • Can grant pardons to federal offenders

Legislative Branch (Congress makes laws)	**Checks on the Executive Branch**	**Checks on the Judicial Branch**
	• Can override President's veto • Confirms executive appointments • Ratifies treaties • Can declare war • Appropriates money • Can impeach and remove President	• Creates lower federal courts • Can impeach and remove judges • Can propose amendments to overrule judicial decisions • Approves appointments of federal judges

Judicial Branch (Supreme Court interprets laws)	**Check on the Executive Branch**	**Check on the Legislative Branch**
	• Can declare executive actions unconstitutional	• Can declare acts of Congress unconstitutional

Checks and balances help to limit the power of each branch of government

The Constitution also put in place three separate branches of national government. The executive branch is headed by the President, whose job is to enforce the laws of the land. Congress forms the legislative branch, which makes the laws. The judicial branch, a system of federal courts, decides cases that involve federal law. It also settles disputes between the states.

To further strengthen this basic principle of separation of powers, the Constitution also established a system of checks and balances. Under this system, each branch of government can check, or limit, the power of the other two.

A Growing Democracy

Even after the Constitution went into effect, many details of the political system remained to be worked out over time. The Constitution itself may be altered if enough people and enough states agree to a proposed amendment, or change. The process can take months or years to complete. Over the past 200 years, 27 amendments have been adopted.

As the nation gained experience in governing itself, Americans developed new ideas about how a democracy should work. They came to believe that political parties were an effective way for people to organize in order to achieve change. Many states also dropped property requirements that limited who was allowed to vote. They permitted white male suffrage, or voting by all adult white men.

During the presidency of Andrew Jackson (1829–1837), Americans could take pride in living in the most democratic country in the world at that time. Even so, that democracy had serious limits. Women, Native Americans, and most African Americans could not vote.

Even more disturbing was the institution of slavery in the South. Slaves had none of the basic liberties that other Americans cherished. As the nation expanded toward the Pacific Ocean, the debate increased over what a free society should do about slavery.

3 The Nation Expands

Key Facts

- The United States was rich in people and resources.
- The Industrial Revolution dramatically changed the American economy.
- The belief in Manifest Destiny drove American territorial expansion to the Pacific Ocean.

Alexis de Tocqueville, a French visitor to the United States in 1831, was amazed at the bustling activity he saw. "The Americans arrived but yesterday on the territory which they inhabit and they have already changed the whole order of nature for their own advantage."

Tocqueville's observation was accurate. By the time of his travels, the United States was in the midst of a period of growth.

Colonial Economies

The booming economy of Tocqueville's day was very different from the way Americans made their living during the colonial period. Before the 1800s, most trade involved sending raw materials from colonies to the parent countries in Europe.

In Spain's colonies, for example, silver was mined by Indian laborers and shipped to Europe. The English colonies along the Atlantic coast sent timber, tobacco, furs, and fish to England. There, manufacturers turned the raw materials into finished products like ships, hats, and cloth. English merchants then sold the products around the world.

This type of economic system was called mercantilism. It was meant to benefit the parent country more than it did the American colonies. To strengthen control over the colonies, England passed laws to regulate colonial trade.

Samuel Slater's textile mill in Pawtucket, Rhode Island

Lewis and Clark with
Native American translator
Sacagawea

Even after independence, most American products were sold abroad.

An Enterprising People

During the 1800s, the economic system changed. American merchants and manufacturers began to sell more products to other Americans, not just to Europe. Encouraging its own industries, the young nation gradually built a strong, independent economy.

The economy grew for several reasons. Americans possessed a bountiful land. It had rich farmland, vast mineral deposits, fine forests, and good waterways for transportation. The population of the United States doubled about every 23 years in the 1800s, due to large families and immigration. Merchants and manufacturers had more customers to whom they could sell American goods.

The expanding economy also reflected the democratic character of the nation. In Europe, rigid social divisions made it difficult for anyone to rise out of poverty. However, the situation was different for Americans. Many wanted the opportunity to advance. In the United States, that was possible. Tocqueville noted, "in America most of the rich men were formerly poor," and "any man's son may become the equal of any other man's son."

An Industrial Revolution

The American economy also grew because of a revolution in the way goods were manufactured. Before machines were introduced, most goods were produced by hand. By the late 1700s, steam engines had been developed in England and were used to run machines in English textile mills, spinning cotton thread and weaving it into cloth.

Americans learned how to build similar machines in the early 1800s. New England became the center of a thriving textile industry.

The Industrial Revolution led to a new way of producing goods. With the new factory system, workers and machinery were together in one place. Workers earned weekly or daily wages and worked a set number of hours each day.

The steam engine revolutionized American life in other ways. Two Americans, John Fitch and Robert Fulton, put steam engines on boats. Using these steamboats, merchants could ship freight upstream even against strong currents.

When the cost of shipping goods dropped, the American economy benefited. By the 1840s, engines were also put to work hauling cars along iron rails, or railroads.

Machines had far-reaching effects on farming, too. In 1793, Eli Whitney invented the cotton gin—short for "engine"—a machine that removed seeds from cotton. With a cotton gin, one person could clean as much cotton as it had taken 50 people to clean before. Cotton production in the South spread rapidly. By the 1840s, the South was supplying 60 percent of the world's cotton.

From the Atlantic to the Pacific

As the economy grew, so did the nation itself. Between 1803 and 1853, the United States expanded westward from the Mississippi River to the Pacific Ocean.

President Thomas Jefferson bought the Louisiana Territory from France for $15 million in 1803. Overnight, the Louisiana Purchase doubled the size of the nation. Jefferson had the team of Meriweather Lewis and William Clark explore the vast new lands.

The nation grew again when Texas joined the Union. Since 1821, groups of settlers from the United States had moved to Texas, which was then part of Mexico. As a result of disputes with the Mexican government, Texans declared their independence in 1836 and set up a new nation called the Republic of Texas. Sam Houston became commander of the Texan army. Texas defeated the Mexican army in the war that followed. In 1845, Congress passed a joint resolution **annexing,** or adding, Texas to the United States.

The United States and Britain agreed to divide the Oregon Country in 1846. That same year, the United States went to war with Mexico over the location of the Texas border. Victory in the war gave the United States control of a large new section of territory in the Southwest. The land included the present-day states of California, Nevada, and Utah as well as parts of Arizona, New Mexico, Colorado, and Wyoming.

Many Americans were proud of their country and wanted to expand its borders. By 1853, the United States had fulfilled what many believed was its clear mission, or **Manifest Destiny.** Americans believed they had a right to extend their boundaries to the Pacific Ocean.

By 1853, the United States stretched from the Atlantic Ocean to the Pacific Ocean

Growth of the United States to 1853

BRITISH TERRITORY

(Ceded by Britain, 1818)

OREGON COUNTRY
(Agreement with Britain, 1846)

L. Superior

L. Michigan
L. Huron
L. Ontario
L. Erie

LOUISIANA PURCHASE
(Purchased from France, 1803)

THE UNITED STATES, 1783

Albers Equal-Area Projection
0   200   400 Miles
0   200   400 Kilometers

MEXICAN CESSION
(Treaty of Guadalupe-Hidalgo, 1848)

ORIGINAL 13 STATES

ATLANTIC OCEAN

Key
Present-day state boundaries

TEXAS ANNEXATION
(Annexed by Congress, 1845)

GADSDEN PURCHASE
(Purchased from Mexico, 1853)

PACIFIC OCEAN

(Annexed, 1810)

(Annexed, 1812)

FLORIDA
(Ceded by Spain, 1819)

MEXICO

Gulf of Mexico

120°W   110°W   100°W   90°W   80°W   70°W

40°N   30°N

4 The Union Splits in Two

Key Facts

- The issue of slavery divided Americans in the 1800s.
- Congress passed compromises in an effort to avoid civil war.
- The war to return the South to the Union became a war to end slavery.

In 1850, an old and grizzled Senator John Calhoun of South Carolina gave his last speech in the Senate. Calhoun warned that "the cords which bind these states together in one common union" were breaking one by one. He predicted that if the disagreements between the North and the South did not end, the Union would fall apart.

John C. Calhoun

Andrew Jackson

Congress decided that slavery would be permitted in Missouri. But it banned slavery everywhere else in the Louisiana Purchase north of latitude 36°30'.

The debate flared once again after the United States conquered new lands in the Southwest but, during the Mexican War. But, once more, members of Congress managed to work out their differences. They approved the Compromise of 1850.

Calhoun's warning was prophetic. During the 1850s, a series of dramatic events brought the nation, step by step, to civil war. As Abraham Lincoln said in 1858, "A house divided against itself cannot stand." What most divided that house was the issue of slavery.

Half Slave, Half Free

The issue of slavery had long caused tension between the North and South. Even during the Constitutional Convention of 1787, the question stirred bitter debate.

As settlers moved west during the 1800s, the controversy over slavery continued. Each time a new territory was organized, Congress had to decide whether to allow slavery there and admit it as a slave state, or to ban slavery and admit it as a free state. Many northerners wanted Congress to ban slavery in all the territories. Many southerners argued that all territories should be open to slavery.

For a time, it seemed that the North and South could work out their differences. A crisis over how Missouri would enter the Union was settled by the Missouri Compromise of 1820.

The End of Compromise

These agreements began to unravel when Congress organized the territories of Kansas and Nebraska. At that time, Senator Stephen A. Douglas tried to satisfy both North and South with his proposal of "popular sovereignty." Under popular sovereignty, Kansas and Nebraska would be allowed to decide for themselves whether to permit slavery. In 1856, however, bloody fighting broke out in Kansas between proslavery and antislavery settlers.

A year later, the Supreme Court handed down the Dred Scott decision. To the surprise of most northerners, the Court ruled that Congress had no power to outlaw slavery in any territory. It seemed to support the extreme southern position that slavery could be permitted in all territories. Northerners were outraged. They hoped that slavery could at least be confined to the South.

Tensions rose further in 1859 when a northerner named John Brown raided the federal arsenal in Harpers Ferry, Virginia. Brown hoped to lead slaves in an armed uprising. He was captured, tried, and hanged. Many outraged southerners considered Brown's raid a northern plot to destroy the South.

Secession

As these events divided the nation, a new political party, called the Republican party, formed in the North. Its main goal was to oppose the spread of slavery. The Republican candidate for president, Abraham Lincoln of Illinois, won the election of 1860.

Lincoln's victory convinced southerners that only by seceding, or withdrawing, from the Union could they hope to save their way of life. In December 1860, South Carolina became the first of 11 southern states to secede. Banding together, they formed the Confederate States of America. In April 1861, Confederate forces bombarded federal troops at Fort Sumter in Charleston harbor. War had begun.

War and Emancipation

The Civil War continued for four terrible years. At first, it seemed that the Confederacy might prevent a Union victory. White southerners, after all, were defending their homeland. The Confederacy's distinguished military leaders included Robert E. Lee and Thomas "Stonewall" Jackson.

It took the North several years to find a general as skilled as Lee. In the end, the dogged Ulysses S. Grant wore down southern armies. Equally as important to the North were its greater resources: more soldiers, better weapons, many more factories, and a larger railroad network to transport soldiers and supplies.

As the war dragged on, calls for abolition grew stronger. On January 1, 1863, President Lincoln issued the Emancipation Proclamation, freeing all slaves behind Confederate lines. The proclamation changed the character of the war. It became a fight for the freedom of slaves as well as for union.

During the war, over 200,000 African Americans fought for the Union. Furthermore, the war's end came sooner because hundreds of thousands of slaves fled southern plantations and crossed Union lines.

On April 9, 1865, Lee surrendered to Grant at Appomattox Court House, Virginia. The "House divided" by slavery had fallen in a ghastly war. The new house—the Union made whole and free—would face new storms.

The 1876 presidential election hinged on the disputed votes of three southern states.

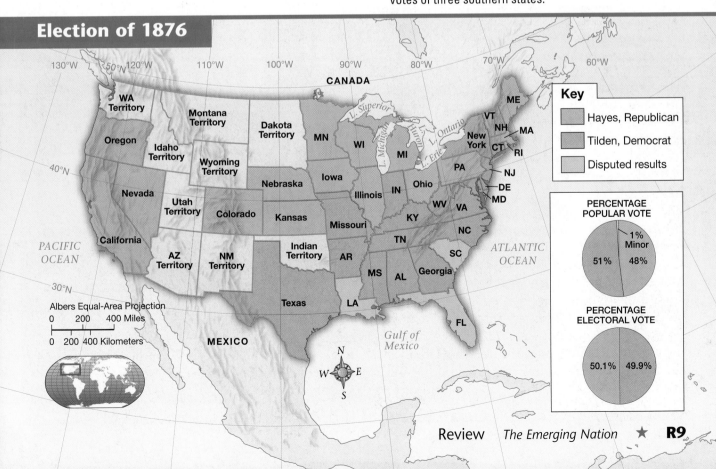

Election of 1876

Key
- Hayes, Republican
- Tilden, Democrat
- Disputed results

PERCENTAGE POPULAR VOTE
51% 48% 1% Minor

PERCENTAGE ELECTORAL VOTE
50.1% 49.9%

Events in American History, 1492–1788

1492–1606   **An Age of Exploration**

1492	Columbus reaches America
1513	Balboa sights Pacific Ocean
1517	Protestant Reformation begins in Europe
1587	English colonists settle at Roanoke

1607–1762   **The Early Colonial Period**

1607	Jamestown, first successful colony, founded
1619	First Africans arrive at Jamestown; Virginia House of Burgesses meets
1620	Puritans sign Mayflower Compact and establish Plymouth Colony
1630	Puritans establish Massachusetts Bay Colony
1673	Joliet and Marquette explore Mississippi River
1690s	Spanish missions established in Arizona and California
1754	French and Indian War begins

1763–1788   **The Revolutionary Era**

1763	Treaty of Paris ends French and Indian War
1765	Parliament passes Stamp Act; Stamp Act Congress meets
1773	Parliament passes Tea Act; Boston Tea Party takes place
1774	Parliament passes Intolerable Acts; First Continental Congress meets
1775	Shots fired at Lexington and Concord; Second Continental Congress meets; Battle of Breed's Hill and Bunker Hill fought
1776	Colonists declare independence from Britain
1781	British surrender at Yorktown; Articles of Confederation ratified
1783	Treaty of Paris ends Revolutionary War
1788	Constitution of the United States ratified

Presenting the Declaration of Independence to the Continental Congress

Events in American History, 1789–1865

President	Term	Events
George Washington	1789–1797	1789 Judiciary Act organizes Supreme Court 1791 Bill of Rights adopted 1793 Eli Whitney invents cotton gin
John Adams	1797–1801	1798 XYZ affair encourages war fever; Alien and Sedition Acts passed
Thomas Jefferson	1801–1809	1803 Louisiana Territory purchased from France 1804–1806 Lewis and Clark explore Louisiana Purchase
James Madison	1809–1817	1811 Battle of Tippecanoe fought 1812 War of 1812 breaks out with Great Britain 1814 Treaty of Ghent ends war with England
James Monroe	1817–1825	1820 Missouri Compromise adopted 1823 Monroe Doctrine issued
James Quincy Adams	1825–1829	1825 Erie Canal Opens 1828 Tariff of Abominations passed
Andrew Jackson	1829–1837	1830 Congress passes Indian Removal Act 1939 Indians forced west on Trail of Tears
Martin Van Buren	1837–1841	1837 Panic affects nation
William Henry Harrison	1841	1841 Harrison is first President to die in office
John Tyler	1841–1845	1842 Massachusetts court allows workers' strikes
James K. Polk	1845–1849	1845 Florida and Texas enter Union 1846 Mexican War begins 1847 Mexican War ends; United States receives California and New Mexico territories
Zachary Taylor	1849–1850	1849 California Gold Rush begins
Millard Fillmore	1850–1853	1850 Compromise of 1850 achieved 1851 Uncle Tom's Cabin published
Franklin Pierce	1853–1856	1854 Congress passes Kansas-Nebraska Act
James Buchanan	1857–1861	1857 Supreme Court issues Dred Scott decision 1858 John Brown raids Harpers Ferry 1860 South Carolina secedes from the Union
Abraham Lincoln	1861–1865	1861 Confederate States of America formed 1862 Homestead Act grants land to farmers 1863 Lincoln issues Emancipation Proclamation; construction of transcontinental railroad begins 1864 Civil War ends; Lincoln is assassinated

Tea chest from the
Boston Tea party

The American Flag

The Flag That Inspired Our National Anthem

During the War of 1812, Mary Young Pickersgill was hired to make a new flag for Fort McHenry in Baltimore harbor. She was told to make a huge flag.

Pickersgill's flag was so large that, when it was hung at Fort McHenry, it could be seen far and wide. In fact, Francis Scott Key could see the flag from eight miles away during the bombardment of the fort by British warships. Its "broad stripes and bright stars" inspired him to write the poem, "The Star-Spangled Banner." The poem was later set to music. In 1931, Congress made "The Star-Spangled Banner" the national anthem of the United States.

Today, the original Star-Spangled Banner hangs at the Smithsonian Institution in Washington, D.C.

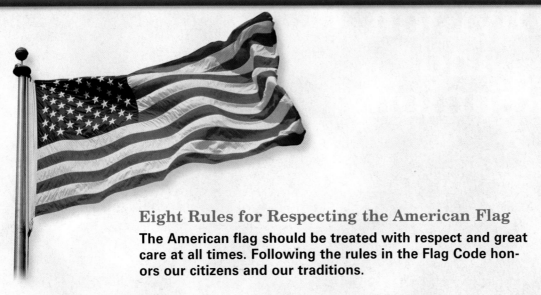

Eight Rules for Respecting the American Flag

The American flag should be treated with respect and great care at all times. Following the rules in the Flag Code honors our citizens and our traditions.

1. The flag should be treated courteously, as if it were a person.
2. The flag of the United States of America should be at the center and at the highest point of the group when a number of flags of states or localities are displayed.
3. The flag is usually displayed in the open from sunrise to sunset.
4. When a flag is displayed at half-staff, the flag should first be hoisted briskly to the peak of the staff and then lowered slowly.
5. The flag should never be used as wearing apparel, bedding, or drapery.
6. The flag should never be displayed, used, or stored in such a way that would permit it to be easily torn, soiled, or damaged.
7. The flag should never be used for advertising purposes. It should not be embroidered on such articles as cushions or handkerchiefs.
8. When a flag is no longer in good enough condition to be displayed, it should be destroyed in a dignified way, preferably by burning.

—Adapted from the Federal Flag Code

The Pledge of Allegiance

The Pledge of Allegiance should be said standing at attention, facing the flag, with the right hand over the heart.

I pledge allegiance to the Flag of the United States of America, and to the Republic for which it stands, one nation under God, indivisible, with liberty and justice for all.

The High School Student Who Changed Our Flag

Our present 50-star flag was designed by a 17-year-old high school student. In 1958, Robert Heft was a shy high school junior in Lancaster, Ohio. At the time, the United States had 48 states. However, talk of Alaska and Hawaii becoming states led him to design a 50-star flag as a school project. He arranged the 50 stars in alternating rows of six stars and five stars. His teacher was not impressed. He gave Robert a B-minus grade for the project but said he would improve the grade if Heft could get Congress to accept the design. Heft took on the challenge. He sent the flag to his representative in Congress. In 1960, President Dwight D. Eisenhower phoned Heft to tell him that his design had been selected to be the nation's new flag. And Heft's grade? True to his promise, the teacher changed the grade to an A!

Unit 5

Division and Reunion

The Soldiers of the Civil War
In *A Rainy Day in Camp* by Winslow Homer, Civil War soldiers find time to gather around a campfire.

"Union! I can more easily conceive of the Lion and Lambs lying down together, than of a union of the North and South."

—Sarah Chase, Massachusetts teacher in the South (1866)

Slavery Divides the Nation

1820–1861

1 **Slavery in the Territories**
2 **The Compromise of 1850**
3 **The Crisis Deepens**
4 **The Republican Party Emerges**
5 **A Nation Divides**

Family escaping slavery

RAN AWAY!

FROM THE SUBSCRIBER. My Mulatto Boy, GEORGE. Said George is 5 feet 8 inches in height, brown curly Hair, dark coat. I will give $400 for him alive, and the same sum for satisfactory proof that he has been killed.
Vide ANTHONY & ELLIS' MAMMOTH "UNCLE TOM'S CABIN." WM. HARRIS.

Fugitive slave poster

1820

The Missouri Compromise maintains the balance of free and slave states in the Union.

John Quincy Adams	1825–1829
Andrew Jackson	1829–1837
Martin Van Buren	1837–1841
William Henry Harrison	1841

Congress passes the Compromise of 1850. One new law requires all Americans to help recapture fugitive slaves.

1850

1848

The Free-Soil party is formed to oppose the extension of slavery in the West.

AMERICAN EVENTS

Presidential Terms: James Monroe 1817–1825   John Tyler 1841–1845   James K. Polk 1845–1849   Zachary Taylor 1849–1850

1820   **1845**   **1850**

WORLD EVENTS

▲ **1833**
Slavery is abolished in the British Empire.

1850 ▲
Civil war breaks out in China.

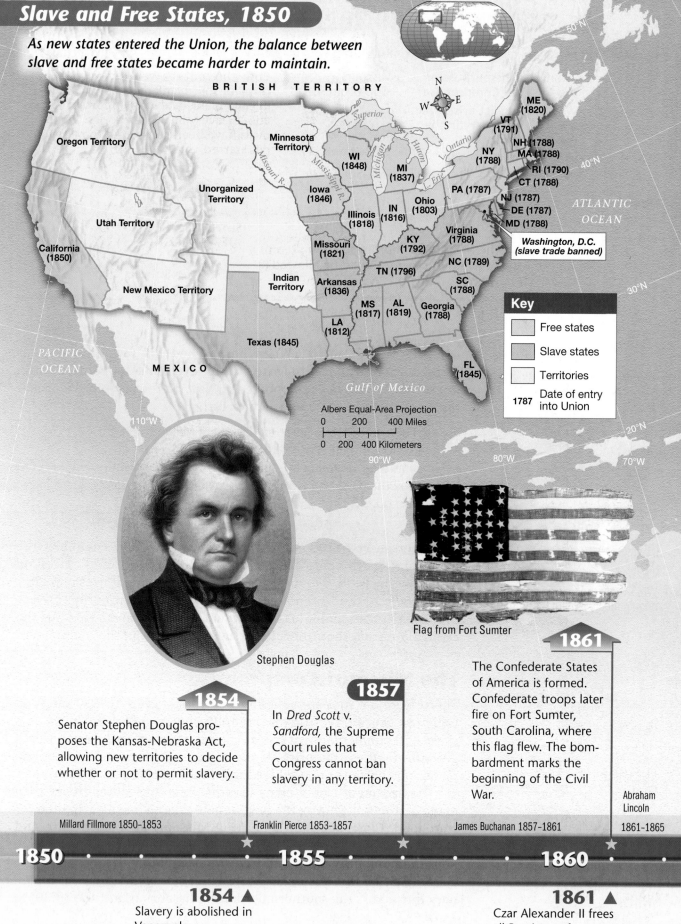

Slave and Free States, 1850

As new states entered the Union, the balance between slave and free states became harder to maintain.

BRITISH TERRITORY

Oregon Territory

Minnesota Territory

WI (1848)

MI (1837)

ME (1820)

VT (1791)

NH (1788)

MA (1788)

NY (1788)

RI (1790)

CT (1788)

PA (1787)

NJ (1787)

DE (1787)

MD (1788)

Unorganized Territory

Iowa (1846)

Ohio (1803)

IN (1816)

Illinois (1818)

Utah Territory

California (1850)

Missouri (1821)

KY (1792)

Virginia (1788)

NC (1789)

Washington, D.C. (slave trade banned)

ATLANTIC OCEAN

New Mexico Territory

Indian Territory

Arkansas (1836)

TN (1796)

SC (1788)

MS (1817)

AL (1819)

Georgia (1788)

LA (1812)

Texas (1845)

FL (1845)

PACIFIC OCEAN

MEXICO

Gulf of Mexico

Albers Equal-Area Projection

0   200   400 Miles

0   200   400 Kilometers

Key

Free states

Slave states

Territories

1787 Date of entry into Union

Stephen Douglas

Flag from Fort Sumter

1854

Senator Stephen Douglas proposes the Kansas-Nebraska Act, allowing new territories to decide whether or not to permit slavery.

Millard Fillmore 1850–1853

1857

In *Dred Scott* v. *Sandford,* the Supreme Court rules that Congress cannot ban slavery in any territory.

Franklin Pierce 1853–1857

1861

The Confederate States of America is formed. Confederate troops later fire on Fort Sumter, South Carolina, where this flag flew. The bombardment marks the beginning of the Civil War.

James Buchanan 1857–1861

Abraham Lincoln

1861–1865

1850 · · · **1855** · · · **1860** · · ·

1854 ▲
Slavery is abolished in Venezuela.

1861 ▲
Czar Alexander II frees all Russian serfs.

1 Slavery in the Territories

BEFORE YOU READ

Reading Focus

- What was the purpose of the Missouri Compromise?
- Why did conflict arise over the issue of slavery in the western territories?
- Why was the Free-Soil party founded?

Key Terms

Missouri Compromise

Wilmot Proviso

popular sovereignty

Free-Soil party

Taking Notes

Copy the concept web below. Include three or four blank ovals. As you read, fill in each blank oval with important facts about slavery in the territories. Some ovals have been completed to help you get started.

Disagreements over Missouri entering Union

SLAVERY IN THE TERRITORIES

Free-Soil party opposes extension of slavery

Main Idea The Missouri Compromise attempted to settle the issue of whether slavery should be allowed in the western territories.

AS YOU READ **Jefferson at 78**
Use Prior Knowledge
Why would the failure of the Union be especially painful for Jefferson?

Setting the Scene When he reached his seventies, Thomas Jefferson vowed "never to write, talk, or even think of politics." Still, in 1820 at the age of 77, he broke this vow. Jefferson voiced alarm at the fierce debate going on in Congress:

> 66 This momentous question, like a fire bell in the night, awakened and filled me with terror. I considered it at once as the [funeral bells] of the Union. . . . We have the wolf by the ears, and we can neither hold him, nor safely let him go. 99
>
> —Thomas Jefferson, Letter to John Holmes, April 22, 1820

Jefferson knew the "wolf," or the issue of slavery, could tear the North and South apart. As settlers moved west, Congress faced an agonizing decision. Should it ban slavery in the territories and later admit them to the Union as free states? Or should it permit slavery in the territories and later admit them as slave states? This was the critical question that filled Jefferson with terror in the night.

The Missouri Compromise

There were 11 free states and 11 slave states in 1819. That year, Congress considered Missouri's application to join the Union as a slave state. Immediately, a crisis erupted. Missouri's admission would give the South a majority in the Senate. Determined not to lose power, northerners opposed letting Missouri enter as a slave state.

The argument lasted many months. Finally, Senator Henry Clay made a proposal. During the long debate, Maine had also applied for statehood. Clay suggested admitting Missouri as a slave state and Maine as a free state. His plan, called the Missouri Compromise, kept the number of slave and free states equal.

As part of the Missouri Compromise, Congress drew an imaginary line across the southern border of Missouri at latitude 36°30′ N.

Slavery was permitted in the part of the Louisiana Purchase south of that line. It was banned north of the Missouri Compromise line. The only exception to this was Missouri itself.

Slavery in the West

The Missouri Compromise applied only to the Louisiana Purchase. In 1848, the Mexican War added vast western lands to the United States. Once again, the question of slavery in the territories arose.

Wilmot Proviso Many northerners feared that the South would extend slavery into the West. David Wilmot, a member of Congress from Pennsylvania, called for a law to ban slavery in any territories won from Mexico. Southern leaders angrily opposed this Wilmot Proviso. They said that Congress had no right to ban slavery in the West.

The House passed the Wilmot Proviso in 1846, but the Senate defeated it. As a result, Americans continued to argue about slavery in the West even while their army fought in Mexico.

Opposing Views As the debate heated up, people found it hard not to take sides. Abolitionists wanted slavery banned throughout the country. They insisted that slavery was morally wrong.

Southern slaveholders thought that slavery should be allowed in any territory. They also demanded that slaves who escaped to the North be returned to them. Even white southerners who did not own slaves generally agreed with these ideas.

Between these two extreme views were more moderate positions. Some moderates argued that the Missouri Compromise line should be extended across the Mexican Cession to the Pacific. Any new state north of the line would be a free state. Any new state south of the line could

Viewing History

A Family for Sale

Southern States

As Americans debated the issue of slavery, slave auctions continued in the South. The family members on the auction block here might never see each other again.
Drawing Inferences *What do the poster (above) and the painting (left) suggest about the attitude of slaveholders toward slaves?*

allow slavery. Other moderates supported the idea of popular sovereignty, or the right of people to create their government. Under popular sovereignty, voters in a new territory would decide for themselves whether or not to allow slavery.

The Free-Soil Party

The debate over slavery led to the birth of a new political party. By 1848, many northern Democrats and Whigs opposed the spread of slavery. However, the leaders of both parties refused to take a stand. They did not want to lose any southern votes. Some also feared that the slavery issue would split the nation.

In 1848, antislavery members of both parties met in Buffalo, New York. There, they founded the Free-Soil party. The main goal of the Free-Soil party was to keep slavery out of the western territories. Only a few Free-Soilers were abolitionists who wanted to end slavery in the South.

In the 1848 presidential campaign, Free-Soilers named former President Martin Van Buren as their candidate. Democrats chose Lewis Cass of Michigan. The Whigs selected Zachary Taylor, a hero of the Mexican War.

For the first time, slavery was an important election issue. Van Buren called for a ban on slavery in the Mexican Cession. Cass supported popular sovereignty. Taylor did not speak on the issue. However, because he was a slave owner from Louisiana, many southern voters assumed that he supported slavery.

Zachary Taylor won the election. Still, Van Buren took 10 percent of the popular vote, and 13 other Free-Soil candidates won seats in Congress. The success of the new Free-Soil party showed that slavery had become a national issue.

 Predict What does the success of the Free-Soil party suggest about the future of the slavery issue?

AFTER YOU READ

Section 1 Assessment

Recall

1. **Identify** Explain the significance of **(a)** Missouri Compromise, **(b)** Wilmot Proviso, **(c)** Free-Soil party, **(d)** Zachary Taylor.
2. **Define** popular sovereignty.

Comprehension

3. What was the Missouri Compromise?
4. Describe three conflicting views on slavery in the West.
5. Why did voters leave the Whig and Democratic parties to join the Free-Soil party in 1848?

Critical Thinking and Writing

6. **Exploring the Main Idea** Review the Main Idea statement at the beginning of this section. Then, write a paragraph explaining whether the Missouri Compromise settled the issue of slavery in the western territories.
7. **Drawing Conclusions** The goals of the Free-Soil party pleased some northerners but not others. Write a paragraph explaining why some northerners were pleased and others displeased by the Free-Soil party.

ACTIVITY

Drawing a Political Cartoon With a partner, plan and sketch a political cartoon about the issue of slavery in the western territories. Assume one of the opposing viewpoints described in this section: southern slaveholder, abolitionist, supporter of extending the Missouri Compromise line across the country, or supporter of popular sovereignty. Then, create a cartoon that represents your point of view.

2 The Compromise of 1850

BEFORE YOU READ

Reading Focus

- Why did the slavery debate erupt again in 1850?
- What was the impact of the Compromise of 1850?
- How did *Uncle Tom's Cabin* affect attitudes toward slavery?

Key Terms

secede

fugitive

civil war

Compromise of 1850

Fugitive Slave Act

Uncle Tom's Cabin

Taking Notes

As you read, complete the chart at right to show some of the causes and effects of the Compromise of 1850.

CAUSES
I. California seeks statehood
2.
3.

COMPROMISE OF 1850

EFFECTS
I. North reacts to Fugitive Slave Act
2.
3.

Main Idea The Compromise of 1850, which was supposed to save the Union, only inflamed tensions.

Setting the Scene Tempers in Congress had reached the boiling point. California had applied to be admitted to the Union as a free state in 1850. Senator Thomas Hart Benton of Missouri supported California's request. He denounced Senator Henry Foote of Mississippi for opposing California's admission.

In response, Senator Foote rose angrily, picked up a pistol, and aimed it at Benton. As other senators watched in horror, Benton turned toward Foote and roared, "Let him fire. Stand out of the way and let the assassin fire!"

No blood was shed in the Senate that day. However, even as Congress tried to reach a new compromise, many Americans began to fear that a peaceful solution to the slavery issue was impossible.

The Slavery Debate Erupts Again

For a time after the Missouri Compromise, both slave and free states entered the Union peacefully. However, when California requested admission to the Union as a free state in 1850, the balance of power in the Senate was once again threatened.

California's Impact In 1849, there were 15 slave states and 15 free states in the nation. If California entered the union as a free state, the balance of power would be broken. Furthermore, it seemed quite possible that Oregon, Utah, and New Mexico might also join the Union as free states.

Many southerners feared that the South would be hopelessly outvoted in the Senate. Some even suggested that southern states might want to secede, or remove themselves, from the United States. Northern congressmen, meanwhile, argued that California should enter the Union as a free state because most of the territory lay north of the Missouri Compromise line.

It was clear that the nation faced a crisis. Many in Congress looked to Senator Henry Clay for a solution.

AS YOU READ **Violence threatens in the Senate**

Ask Questions Write one question you would have asked Senator Benton and one question you would have asked Senator Foote if you had been on the floor of the Senate on the day of the conflict.

Balance of Free and Slave States

Free States	Slave States
California (1850)	
Wisconsin (1848)	Texas (1845)
Iowa (1846)	Florida (1845)
Michigan (1837)	Arkansas (1836)
Maine (1820)	Missouri (1821)
Illinois (1818)	Alabama (1819)
Indiana (1816)	Mississippi (1817)
Ohio (1803)	Louisiana (1812)
Vermont (1791)	Tennessee (1796)
Rhode Island	Kentucky (1792)
New York	Virginia
New Hampshire	North Carolina
Massachusetts	South Carolina
Connecticut	Maryland
New Jersey	Georgia
Pennsylvania	Delaware

John C. Calhoun

Daniel Webster   Henry Clay

☐ Original 13 states

Viewing History

Crisis in the Senate

The admission of California to the Union threatened to upset the delicate balance of slave and free states. The issue led to the final showdown in Congress for Henry Clay, Daniel Webster, and John C. Calhoun. **Analyzing Primary Sources** *Why do you think the gallery was filled with spectators to hear this debate?*

AS YOU READ **Find Main Ideas** What were the main differences between the views of Henry Clay and those of John C. Calhoun?

Clay vs. Calhoun Clay had won the nickname "the Great Compromiser" for working out the Missouri Compromise. Now, nearly 30 years later, the 73-year-old Clay was frail and ill. Still, he pleaded for the North and South to reach an agreement. If they failed to do so, Clay warned, the nation could break apart.

Senator John C. Calhoun of South Carolina replied to Clay. Calhoun was dying of tuberculosis and could not speak loudly enough to address the Senate. He stared defiantly at his northern foes while Senator James Mason of Virginia read his speech.

Calhoun refused to compromise. He insisted that slavery be allowed in the western territories. In addition, Calhoun demanded that fugitive, or runaway, slaves be returned to their owners. He wanted northerners to admit that southern slaveholders had the right to reclaim their "property."

If the North rejected the South's demands, Calhoun told the Senate, "let the states . . . agree to part in peace. If you are unwilling that we should part in peace, tell us so, and we shall know what to do." Everyone knew what Calhoun meant. If an agreement could not be reached, the South would use force to leave the Union.

Webster Calls for Unity Daniel Webster of Massachusetts spoke next. He supported Clay's plea to save the Union. Webster stated his position clearly:

> 66 I speak today not as a Massachusetts man, nor as a northern man, but as an American. . . . I speak today for the preservation of the Union. . . . There can be no such thing as a peaceable secession. 99
>
> —Daniel Webster, Speech in the U.S. Senate, July 17, 1850

Webster feared that the states could not separate without starting a bloody civil war. A civil war is a war between people of the same country.

Like many northerners, Webster viewed slavery as evil. The breakup of the United States, however, he believed was worse. To save the Union, Webster was willing to compromise. He would support southern demands that northerners be forced to return fugitive slaves.

Compromise of 1850

In 1850, as the debate raged, Calhoun died. His last words reportedly were "The South! The poor South! God knows what will become of her now!" President Taylor also died in 1850. The new President was Millard Fillmore. Unlike Taylor, he supported Clay's compromise plan.

The Compromise Passes Henry Clay gave more than 70 speeches in favor of a compromise. At last, however, he became too sick to continue. Stephen Douglas, of Illinois, took up the fight for him and guided Clay's plan, the Compromise of 1850, through Congress.

The Compromise of 1850 had five parts. First, it allowed California to enter the Union as a free state. Second, it divided the rest of the Mexican Cession into the territories of New Mexico and Utah. Voters in each would decide the slavery question according to popular sovereignty. Third, it ended the slave trade in Washington, D.C., the nation's capital. Congress, however, declared that it had no power to ban the slave trade between slave states. Fourth, it included a strict fugitive slave law. Fifth, it settled a border dispute between Texas and New Mexico.

Fugitive Slave Act The Fugitive Slave Act of 1850 required all citizens to help catch runaway slaves. People who let fugitives escape could be fined $1,000 and jailed. The new law also set up special courts to handle the cases of runaways. Suspects were not allowed a jury trial. Judges received $10 for sending an accused runaway to the South but only $5 for setting someone free. Lured by the extra money, some judges sent African Americans to the South whether or not they were runaways.

Reaction The Fugitive Slave Act enraged antislavery northerners. By forcing them to catch runaways, the law made northerners feel as if they were part of the slave system. In several northern cities, crowds tried to rescue fugitive slaves from their captors.

Despite the compromise, tensions remained high because neither side got everything that it wanted. The new Fugitive Slave Act was especially hard for northerners to accept. Each time the act was

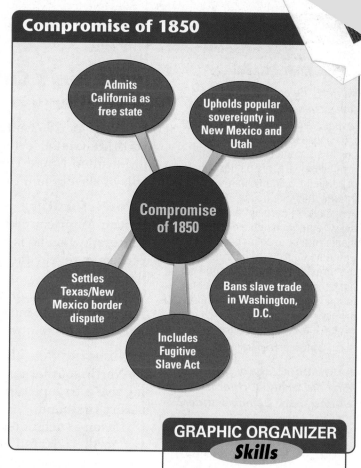

Compromise of 1850

- Admits California as free state
- Upholds popular sovereignty in New Mexico and Utah
- Compromise of 1850
- Settles Texas/New Mexico border dispute
- Bans slave trade in Washington, D.C.
- Includes Fugitive Slave Act

GRAPHIC ORGANIZER
Skills

The Compromise of 1850 was a desperate attempt to save the Union.

1. **Comprehension** Which parts of the Compromise would have been favored by the South?

2. **Critical Thinking Identifying Points of View** Would an abolitionist approve of the Compromise of 1850? Why or why not?

Civics

enforced, it convinced more northerners that slavery was immoral and evil.

Uncle Tom's Cabin: An Antislavery Bestseller

An event in 1852 added to the growing antislavery mood of the North. Harriet Beecher Stowe, a New England woman, published a novel called *Uncle Tom's Cabin.* Stowe wrote the novel to show the evils of slavery and the injustice of the Fugitive Slave Act.

A Powerful Story Stowe told the story of Uncle Tom, an enslaved African American noted for his kindness and piety. Tom's world is shattered when he is bought by the brutal Simon Legree. When Tom refuses to reveal the whereabouts of two runaways, Legree whips him to death.

Uncle Tom's Cabin had wide appeal among northern readers. The first printing sold out in just two days. Eventually, the book sold millions of copies and was translated into dozens of languages.

Nationwide Reaction Although *Uncle Tom's Cabin* was popular in the North, southerners objected to the book. They claimed that it did not give a true picture of slave life. Indeed, Stowe had seen little of slavery firsthand.

Despite such objections, *Uncle Tom's Cabin* helped to change the way northerners felt about slavery. No longer could they ignore slavery as a political problem for Congress to settle. More and more northerners now saw slavery as a moral problem facing every American. For this reason, *Uncle Tom's Cabin* was one of the most important books in American history.

AFTER YOU READ

Section 2 Assessment

Recall

1. **Identify** Explain the significance of **(a)** Stephen Douglas, **(b)** Compromise of 1850, **(c)** Fugitive Slave Act, **(d)** Harriet Beecher Stowe, **(e)** *Uncle Tom's Cabin.*
2. **Define (a)** secede, **(b)** fugitive, **(c)** civil war.

Comprehension

3. How did the issue of admitting California to the Union in 1850 again raise the debate over slavery?
4. How did Americans respond to the Compromise of 1850?
5. What was the impact of *Uncle Tom's Cabin?*

Critical Thinking and Writing

6. **Exploring the Main Idea** Review the Main Idea statement at the beginning of this section. Then, write a letter to a newspaper editor explaining whether you think the Compromise of 1850 was a success or a failure. Give reasons for your answer.
7. **Summarizing** For each of the following leaders, write one sentence summarizing his attitude toward the need for a compromise in 1850: **(a)** Calhoun, **(b)** Webster, **(c)** Clay.

ACTIVITY

Making a Decision You are a northerner during the 1850s. There is a knock at your door. It's a fugitive slave! Will you help the runaway, or will you turn the person in to the authorities? Write a brief statement explaining the reasons for your decision.

Uncle Tom's Cabin

Harriet Beecher Stowe saw the horrors of slavery while living in Cincinnati. Across the Ohio River was Kentucky, a slave state. Her hatred of slavery led her to write *Uncle Tom's Cabin*. The novel had an impact that lasted long after slavery ended.

Harriet Beecher Stowe

Uncle Tom Defies Simon Legree

"Well, Tom!" said Legree, walking up and seizing him grimly by the collar of his coat, and speaking through his teeth, in a paroxysm of determined rage, "do you know I've made up my mind to KILL you?"

"It's very likely, Mas'r," said Tom, calmly.

"I have," said Legree, with grim terrible calmness, "done—just—that—thing, Tom, unless you tell me what you know about these yer gals!"

Tom stood silent.

"D'ye hear?" said Legree, stamping with a roar like that of an incensed lion. "Speak!"

"I han't got nothing to tell, Mas'r," said Tom with a slow, firm deliberate utterance.

"Do you dare to tell me, ye old black Christian, ye don't know?"…

"I know, Mas'r; but I can't tell anything. I can die!"

— Harriet Beecher Stowe,
Uncle Tom's Cabin, Chapter 40

In this poster for a stage version of *Uncle Tom's Cabin*, the fugitive slave Eliza flees across an icy river.

Fast Facts

- The character of Tom was inspired by Josiah Henson, a Methodist preacher who had escaped slavery.
- Some southerners wrote "anti-Tom" novels to defend slavery.
- The first movie of *Uncle Tom's Cabin* was made in 1903.

Simon Legree and Uncle Tom

ACTIVITY

You are hosting a dinner honoring Harriet Beecher Stowe. Prepare a brief speech introducing Stowe. Explain how her book reflects divisions in the United States.

3 The Crisis Deepens

Reading Focus

- What was the goal of the Kansas-Nebraska Act?
- Why did violence erupt in Kansas and in the Senate?
- What impact did the Dred Scott case have on the nation?

Key Terms

Kansas-Nebraska Act

Border Ruffians

guerrilla warfare

lawsuit

Dred Scott v. *Sandford*

Taking Notes

As you read, complete the following chart to show some of the causes that directly led the United States to become a more divided nation.

Main Idea In the 1850s, violence in Kansas and the Dred Scott decision inflamed tensions over slavery.

Setting the Scene Americans had hoped that the Compromise of 1850 would end the debate over slavery in the West. Before long, though, proslavery and antislavery forces were battling for control of the territory of Kansas. An observer described election day in one Kansas district in 1855:

> 66 On the morning of the election, before the polls were opened, some 300 or 400 Missourians and others were collected in the yard . . . where the election was to be held, armed with bowie-knives, revolvers, and clubs. They said they came to vote, and whip the . . . Yankees, and would vote without being sworn. Some said they came to have a fight, and wanted one. 99
>
> —Report of the Congressional Committee, July 1, 1856

AS YOU READ An election in Kansas

Ask Questions Based on this picture and the description at right, write one question you would ask these Kansas voters.

Hearing of events in Kansas, Abraham Lincoln, then a young lawyer in Illinois, predicted that "the contest will come to blows, and bloodshed." Once again, the issue of slavery in the territories divided the nation.

Kansas-Nebraska Act

The Compromise of 1850 dealt mainly with lands that were part of the Mexican Cession. It did not resolve the issue of slavery in lands that had been part of the Louisiana Purchase. In January 1854, Senator Stephen Douglas introduced a bill to set up a government for the Nebraska Territory. This territory stretched from Texas north to Canada, and from Missouri west to the Rockies.

Douglas knew that white southerners did not want to add another free state to the Union. He proposed that the Nebraska Territory be divided into two territories, Kansas and Nebraska. The settlers living in each territory would then be able to decide the issue of slavery by popular sovereignty. Douglas's bill was known as the Kansas-Nebraska Act.

Support for the Act The Kansas-Nebraska Act seemed fair to many people. After all, the Compromise of 1850 had applied popular sovereignty in New Mexico and Utah. Southern leaders especially supported the Kansas-Nebraska Act. They were sure that slave owners from neighboring Missouri would move with their slaves across the border into Kansas. In time, they hoped, Kansas would become a slave state.

President Franklin Pierce, a Democrat elected in 1852, also supported the bill. With the President's help, Douglas pushed the Kansas-Nebraska Act through Congress. He did not realize it at the time, but he had lit a fire under a powder keg.

Northern Outrage Many northerners were unhappy with the new law. The Missouri Compromise had already banned slavery in Kansas and Nebraska, they insisted. In effect, the Kansas-Nebraska Act would repeal the Missouri Compromise.

The northern reaction to the Kansas-Nebraska Act was swift and angry. Opponents of slavery called the act a "criminal betrayal of precious rights." Slavery could now spread to areas that had been free for more than 30 years. Some northerners protested by openly challenging the Fugitive Slave Act.

The Crisis Turns Violent

Kansas now became a testing ground for popular sovereignty. Stephen Douglas hoped that settlers would decide the slavery issue peacefully on election day. Instead, proslavery and antislavery forces sent settlers to Kansas to fight for control of the territory.

GEOGRAPHY
Skills

The issue of whether to allow slavery in the territories created tension between the North and the South.

1. **Location** On the map, locate (a) Missouri Compromise Line, (b) Kansas Territory, (c) Nebraska Territory.

2. **Region** (a) Which territories were open to slavery after 1854? (b) Which territories were closed to slavery?

3. **Critical Thinking Making Predictions** How would the balance of power in the Senate change if western territories became slave states?

Slavery After the Kansas-Nebraska Act

Key
- Free states and territories
- Slave states and territories
- Open to slavery by popular vote, Compromise of 1850
- Open to slavery by popular vote, Kansas-Nebraska Act, 1854

Most of the new arrivals were farmers from neighboring states. Their main interest in moving to Kansas was to acquire cheap land. Few of these settlers owned slaves. At the same time, abolitionists brought in more than 1,000 settlers from New England.

Proslavery settlers moved into Kansas as well. They wanted to make sure that antislavery forces did not overrun the territory. Proslavery bands from Missouri often rode across the border. These Border Ruffians, as they were called, battled the antislavery forces in Kansas.

Two Governments In 1855, Kansas held elections to choose lawmakers. Hundreds of Border Ruffians crossed into Kansas and voted illegally. They helped to elect a proslavery legislature.

The new legislature quickly passed laws to support slavery. One law said that people could be put to death for helping slaves escape. Another made speaking out against slavery a crime punishable by two years of hard labor.

Antislavery settlers refused to accept these laws. They elected their own governor and legislature. With two rival governments, Kansas was in chaos. Armed gangs roamed the territory looking for trouble.

"Bleeding Kansas" A band of proslavery men raided the town of Lawrence, an antislavery stronghold, in 1856. The attackers destroyed homes and smashed the press of a Free-Soil newspaper.

John Brown, an abolitionist, decided to strike back. Brown had moved to Kansas to help make it a free state. He claimed that God had sent him to punish supporters of slavery.

Brown rode with his four sons and two other men to the town of Pottawatomie (paht uh WAHT uh mee) Creek. In the middle of the night, they dragged five proslavery settlers from their beds and murdered them.

The killings at Pottawatomie Creek led to even more violence. Both sides fought fiercely and engaged in guerrilla warfare, or the use of hit-and-run tactics. By late 1856, more than 200 people had been killed. Newspapers started calling the territory "Bleeding Kansas."

Violence in the Senate

Even before John Brown's attack, the battle over Kansas had spilled into the Senate. Charles Sumner of Massachusetts was the leading abolitionist senator. In one speech, the sharp-tongued Sumner denounced the proslavery legislature of Kansas. He then viciously criticized his southern foes, singling out Andrew Butler, an elderly senator from South Carolina.

Butler was not in the Senate on the day Sumner spoke. A few days later, however, Butler's nephew, Congressman Preston Brooks, marched into the Senate chamber. Using a heavy cane, Brooks beat Sumner until he fell down, bloody and unconscious, to the floor. Sumner did not fully recover from the beating for three years.

Many southerners felt that Sumner got what he deserved for his verbal abuse of another senator. Hundreds of people sent canes to

Brooks to show their support. To northerners, however, the brutal act was more evidence that slavery led to violence.

The Dred Scott Case

With Congress in an uproar, many Americans looked to the Supreme Court to settle the slavery issue and restore peace. In 1857, the Court ruled on a case that involved an enslaved person named Dred Scott. Instead of bringing harmony, however, the Court's decision further divided the North and the South.

Dred Scott had been enslaved for many years in Missouri. Later, he moved with his owner to Illinois and then to the Wisconsin Territory, where slavery was not allowed. After they returned to Missouri, Scott's owner died. Antislavery lawyers helped Scott to file a **lawsuit,** a legal case brought to settle a dispute between people or groups. Scott's lawyers argued that, because Scott had lived in a free territory, he had become a free man.

The Supreme Court's Decision In time, the case reached the Supreme Court as *Dred Scott* v. *Sandford.* The Court's decision shocked and dismayed Americans who opposed slavery. First, the Court ruled that Scott could not file a lawsuit because, as an enslaved person, he was not a citizen. Also, the Court's written decision clearly stated that slaves were considered to be property.

The Court's ruling did not stop there. Instead, the Justices went on to make a sweeping decision about the larger issue of slavery in

Viewing History

Bleeding Kansas

In 1856, the slavery issue sparked bloodshed in Kansas. Here, Border Ruffians attack antislavery settlers. Abolitionists like John Brown also committed acts of violence. **Identifying Bias** *What details in the picture suggest that the artist favored the antislavery settlers?*

the territories. According to the Court, Congress did not have the power to outlaw slavery in any territory. The Court's ruling meant that the Missouri Compromise was unconstitutional.

AS YOU READ **Use Prior Knowledge** Why did the Dred Scott decision make the Missouri Compromise unconstitutional?

The Nation Reacts White southerners rejoiced at *Dred Scott* v. *Sandford*. It meant that slavery was legal in all the territories. This was just what white southerners had been demanding for years.

African Americans responded angrily to the Dred Scott decision. In the North, many held public meetings to condemn the ruling. At one meeting in Philadelphia, a speaker hoped that the ruling would lead more whites to "join with us in our efforts to recover the long lost boon of freedom."

White northerners were also shocked by the ruling. Many had hoped that slavery would eventually die out if it were restricted to the South. Now, however, slavery could spread throughout the West. Even northerners who disliked abolitionists felt that the ruling in *Dred Scott* v. *Sandford* was wrong. A newspaper in Cincinnati declared, "We are now one great . . . slaveholding community."

Abolitionist Frederick Douglass also spoke out against *Dred Scott* v. *Sandford*: "This infamous decision," he declared, "maintains that slaves . . . are property in the same sense that horses, sheep, and swine are property . . . that [people] of African descent are not and cannot be citizens of the United States." He told his listeners:

> 66 All I ask of the American people is that they live up to the Constitution, adopt its principles, [take in] its spirit, and enforce its provisions. When this is done . . . liberty . . . will become the inheritance of all the inhabitants of this highly favored country. 99
>
> —Frederick Douglass, *Collected Speeches*, 1857

 Section 3 Assessment

AFTER YOU READ

Recall

1. **Identify** Explain the significance of **(a)** Kansas-Nebraska Act, **(b)** Franklin Pierce, **(c)** Border Ruffians, **(d)** Charles Sumner, **(e)** *Dred Scott* v. *Sandford*.
2. **Define** **(a)** guerrilla warfare, **(b)** lawsuit.

Comprehension

3. Why did Stephen Douglas propose the Kansas-Nebraska Act?
4. How did the Kansas-Nebraska Act lead to violence?
5. How did white southerners, African Americans, and white northerners react to the Dred Scott decision?

Critical Thinking and Writing

6. **Exploring the Main Idea** Review the Main Idea statement at the beginning of this section. Then, make a list of five statements from this section that support the main idea.
7. **Analyzing Primary Sources** After the Kansas-Nebraska Act was passed, Stephen Douglas stated: "The struggle for freedom was forever banished from the halls of Congress to the western plains." Rewrite Douglas's statement in your own words. Then, explain why you agree or disagree with it.

ACTIVITY

 Take It to the NET
Connecting to Today
Use the Internet to find out more about a recent Supreme Court decision involving the rights of workers, minorities, or students. Write a brief summary describing both sides of the issue and what the court decided. Visit *The American Nation* section of **www.phschool.com** for help in completing the activity.

4 The Republican Party Emerges

FORE YOU READ

Reading Focus

- Why did the Republican party come into being in the mid-1850s?
- What events lay behind the rapid emergence of Abraham Lincoln as a Republican leader?
- How did Americans react to John Brown's raid on Harpers Ferry?

Key Terms

Republican party

arsenal

treason

martyr

Taking Notes

As you read, complete this table listing the conflicting views of Abraham Lincoln and Stephen Douglas. Add as many rows as needed to finish the table.

LINCOLN'S VIEWS	DOUGLAS'S VIEWS
• Slavery was morally wrong	•
•	• Western territories should decide slavery issue by popular sovereignty
•	•

Main Idea Abraham Lincoln emerged as a leader of the new Republican party, which was dedicated to halting the spread of slavery.

Setting the Scene The tall lawyer stood before a political convention in Springfield, Illinois. People in the packed hall listened carefully as he addressed the number one issue of the day—slavery:

> 66 A house divided against itself cannot stand. I believe this government cannot endure permanently half slave and half free. I do not expect the Union to be dissolved—I do not expect the house to fall—but I do expect it will cease to be divided. It will become all one thing, or all the other. 99
>
> —Abraham Lincoln, Speech, June 16, 1858

Few people outside of Illinois had heard of Abraham Lincoln. Yet, his speech became famous. Many northerners were soon repeating his prediction about the "house divided." Lincoln and the new party he represented—the Republican party—moved to the forefront of the debate over slavery.

The Republican Party

By the mid-1850s, people who opposed slavery in the territories sought a new political voice. Neither Whigs nor Democrats, they argued, would take a strong stand against slavery. "We have submitted to slavery long enough," an Ohio Democrat declared.

A group of Free-Soilers, northern Democrats, and antislavery Whigs gathered in Michigan in 1854. There they formed the Republican party. Its main goal was to keep slavery out of the western territories. A few Republicans were abolitionists. They hoped to end slavery in the South as well. Most Republicans, however, wanted only to stop the spread of slavery.

The new party grew quickly. By 1856, it was ready to challenge the older parties for power. Republicans selected John C. Frémont to run for President. Frémont was a frontiersman who had fought for

AS YOU READ
Figure of Abraham Lincoln

Use Prior Knowledge
Freewrite a list of 3–5 things that you already know about Abraham Lincoln.

California's independence. He had little political experience, but he opposed the spread of slavery.

Frémont's main opponent was Democrat James Buchanan of Pennsylvania. Many Democrats saw Buchanan as a "northern man with southern principles." They hoped that he would attract voters in both the North and the South. Former President Millard Fillmore also ran as the candidate of the American, or "Know-Nothing," party. A strong supporter of the Union, Fillmore feared that a Republican victory would split the nation apart.

Buchanan won the election with support from a large majority of southerners and many northerners. Still, the Republicans made a strong showing in the election. Without the support of a single southern state, Frémont won one third of the popular vote. Southerners worried that their influence in the national government was fading.

Abe Lincoln of Illinois

The next test for the Republican party came in 1858 in Illinois. Abraham Lincoln, a Republican, challenged Democrat Stephen Douglas for his seat in the Senate. Because most Americans expected Douglas to run for President in 1860, the race captured the attention of the whole nation.

 Predict What might happen to the nation if the Republican party wins a presidential election?

From the Backwoods of Kentucky Abraham Lincoln was born on the Kentucky frontier. Like many frontier people, his parents moved often to find better land. The family lived in Indiana and later in Illinois. As a child, Lincoln spent only a year in school. Still, he taught himself to read, poring over his books by firelight.

After Lincoln left home, he opened a store in Illinois. There, he studied law on his own and launched a career in politics. He served eight years in the state legislature and one term in Congress. Bitterly opposed to the Kansas-Nebraska Act, he decided to run for the Senate in 1858.

When the race began, Lincoln was not a national figure. Still, people in Illinois knew him well and liked him. To them, he was "just folks"—someone who enjoyed picnics, wrestling contests, and all their favorite pastimes. His honesty, wit, and plain-spoken manner made him a good speaker.

Lincoln-Douglas Debates During the Senate campaign, Lincoln challenged Douglas to a series of debates. Douglas was not eager to accept, but he did. During the campaign, the two debated seven times. Slavery was the important issue.

Douglas wanted to settle the slavery question by popular sovereignty. He personally disliked slavery, but stated that he did not care whether people in the territories voted "down or up" for it.

Lincoln, like nearly all whites of his day, did not believe in "perfect equality" between blacks and whites. He did, however, believe that slavery was wrong:

> 66 There is no reason in the world why the negro is not entitled to all the natural rights [listed] in the Declaration of Independence, the right to life, liberty, and the pursuit of happiness. . . . In the right to eat the bread, without the leave of anybody else, which his own hand earns, he is my equal and the equal of Judge Douglas, and the equal of every living man. 99
>
> —Abraham Lincoln, Speech at Ottawa, Illinois, August 21, 1858

Since slavery was a "moral, social, and political wrong," said Lincoln, Douglas and other Americans should not treat it as an unimportant question to be voted "down or up." Lincoln was totally opposed to slavery in the territories. Still, he was not an abolitionist. He had no wish to interfere with slavery in the states where it already existed.

A Leader Emerges Week after week, both men spoke nearly every day to large crowds. Newspapers reprinted their campaign speeches. The more northerners read Lincoln's words, the more they thought about the injustice of slavery.

In the end, Douglas won the election by a slim margin. Still, Lincoln was a winner, too. He was now known throughout the country. Two years later, the two rivals would again meet face to face—both seeking the office of President.

John Brown's Raid

In the meantime, more bloodshed inflamed divisions between the North and the South. In 1859, the radical abolitionist John Brown carried his antislavery campaign from Kansas to the East. He led a group of followers, including five African Americans, to the town of Harpers Ferry, Virginia.

Primary Source

Douglas Debates Lincoln

In his first debate with Lincoln, Stephen Douglas defended the principle of popular sovereignty: "We have settled the slavery question as far as we are concerned; we have prohibited it in Illinois forever, . . . but when we settled it for ourselves, we exhausted all our power over that subject. We must leave each and every other state to decide for itself the same question. . . . Now, my friends, if we will only act conscientiously and rigidly upon this great principle of popular sovereignty, we will continue at peace, one with another."

—Stephen Douglas, Speech at Ottawa, Illinois, August 21, 1858

Analyzing Primary Sources
How might an abolitionist respond to Douglas?

There, Brown planned to raid a federal *arsenal,* or gun warehouse. He thought that enslaved African Americans would flock to him at the arsenal. He would then give them weapons and lead them in a revolt.

Sentenced to Death Brown quickly gained control of the arsenal. No slave uprising took place, however. Instead, troops under the command of Robert E. Lee killed ten raiders and captured Brown.

Most people, in both the North and the South, thought that Brown's plan to lead a slave revolt was insane. After all, there were few enslaved African Americans in Harpers Ferry. Furthermore, after seizing the arsenal, Brown did nothing further to encourage a slave revolt. At his trial, however, Brown seemed perfectly sane. He sat quietly as the court found him guilty of murder and *treason,* or actions against one's country. Before hearing his sentence, he gave a moving defense of his actions. He showed no emotion as he was sentenced to death.

Hero or Villain? Because he conducted himself with such dignity during his trial, John Brown became a hero to many northerners. Some considered him a *martyr* because he was willing to give up his life for his beliefs. On the morning he was hanged, church bells rang solemnly throughout the North. In years to come, New Englanders would sing a popular song with the chorus: "John Brown's body lies a mold'ring in the grave, but his soul is marching on."

To white southerners, the northern response to John Brown's death was outrageous. People were singing the praises of a man who had tried to lead a slave revolt! Many southerners became convinced that the North wanted to destroy slavery—and the South along with it. The nation was poised for a violent clash.

 AS YOU READ **Summarize** Using information from this section and Section 3, write a sentence summarizing the influence of John Brown on the slavery debate.

 AFTER YOU READ ★ ★ ★ **Section 4 Assessment** ★ ★ ★

Recall

1. **Identify** Explain the significance of **(a)** Republican party, **(b)** John C. Frémont, **(c)** James Buchanan, **(d)** Abraham Lincoln, **(e)** Harpers Ferry.
2. **Define** **(a)** arsenal, **(b)** treason, **(c)** martyr.

Comprehension

3. What issue led to the founding of the Republican party?
4. How did Abraham Lincoln emerge as a Republican leader?
5. How did northerners and southerners respond to John Brown's raid?

Critical Thinking and Writing

6. **Exploring the Main Idea** Review the Main Idea statement at the beginning of this section. Then, write a paragraph explaining how the views of the Republican party differed from the views of earlier parties.
7. **Supporting a Point of View** Lincoln said the nation could not "endure permanently half slave and half free." Do you agree that slavery was too important an issue to allow differences among the states? Write a paragraph explaining the reasons for your opinion.

ACTIVITY

Take It to the NET
Writing a Profile
Use the Internet to find out more about the Lincoln-Douglas debates. Use the information to prepare a profile of either Douglas or Lincoln for a TV news report on the debates. Visit *The American Nation* section of **www.phschool.com** for help in completing the activity.

Was John Brown a hero or a villain? That depends on your point of view. To evaluate historical evidence correctly, you must be able to identify *bias*, strong beliefs that prejudice someone's point of view.

A North Carolina newspaper ran this editorial after the execution of John Brown:

The Execution of Brown

" We give to-day full accounts of the scenes attending the execution of the traitor, murderer, and thief, John Brown. He died, as he lived, a hardened criminal. [When] his wretched confederates shall have paid the penalty of their crimes, we hope that their allies and sympathizers at the North will realize the fact that the South has the power to protect her soil and property, and will exercise it in spite of all the measures which can be leveled at her by the abolitionists and their [supporters]. "

—Raleigh, North Carolina, *Register*, December 9, 1859

In this abolitionist painting, John Brown pauses on his way to his execution to kiss an enslaved woman's baby.

Learn the Skill *To identify bias, use the following steps:*

1. **Identify the sources.** Knowing a person's background helps you evaluate that person's attitudes.

2. **Identify main ideas.** What is the main point that is being made?

3. **Distinguish facts from opinions.** Remember, facts are statements that can be proven, while opinions are someone's beliefs.

4. **Look for emotion-packed words or images.** How information is presented is an important clue to the point of view.

5. **Identify bias.** How do the writer's or artist's feelings and beliefs affect his or her presentation?

Practice the Skill *Answer the following questions about the editorial and picture above:*

1. Where was the newspaper published?

2. What are the points of view of the editorial and the painting?

3. (a) Which statements made by the writer can be proven as facts? (b) Which are opinions?

4. (a) Evaluate the language the writer uses to describe John Brown. (b) What emotions do the images in the painting create?

5. (a) What bias does the editorial show? (b) What bias does the painting show?

Apply the Skill *See the Chapter Review and Assessment.*

5 A Nation Divides

BEFORE YOU READ

Reading Focus

- How did the election of 1860 reflect sectional divisions?
- How did the South react to the election results?
- How did the Civil War begin in 1861?

Taking Notes

As you read, prepare an outline of this section. Use roman numerals to indicate the major headings, capital letters for the subheadings, and numbers for the supporting details. The sample at right will help you get started.

> I. The Election of 1860
> A. Candidates and political parties
>   1.
>   2.
>   3.
>   4.
> B. Results of the election
>   1.
>   2.
> II. The South Reacts
> A. Secession
>   1.
>   2.
> B. The Confederacy

Main Idea The election of Abraham Lincoln as President in 1860 led a number of southern states to secede from the Union.

Setting the Scene Thousands of people swarmed into Chicago, Illinois, for the 1860 Republican national convention. They filled all of the city's 42 hotels. When beds ran out, people slept on billiard tables. All were there to find out one thing: Who would win the Republican nomination for President—William Seward of New York or Abraham Lincoln of Illinois?

On the third day of the convention, a delegate rushed to the roof of the hall. There, a man stood waiting next to a cannon. "Fire the salute," ordered the delegate. "Old Abe is nominated!" Amid the celebration, though, a delegate from Kentucky struck a somber note. "Gentlemen, we are on the brink of a great civil war."

The Election of 1860

The Democrats held their convention in Charleston, South Carolina. Southerners wanted the party to support slavery in the territories. However, northern Democrats refused to do so. In the end, the party split in two. Northern Democrats chose Stephen Douglas to run for President. Southern Democrats picked John Breckinridge of Kentucky.

Some Americans tried to heal the split between the North and the South by forming a new party. The Constitutional Union party chose John Bell of Tennessee to run for President. Bell was a moderate who wanted to keep the Union together. He got support only in a few southern states that were still seeking a compromise.

Douglas was sure that Lincoln would win. However, he believed that Democrats "must try to save the Union." He urged southerners to stay with the Union, no matter who was elected.

When the votes were counted, Lincoln had carried the North and won the election. Southern votes did not affect the outcome at all. Lincoln's name was not even on the ballot in 10 southern states. Northerners outnumbered southerners and outvoted them.

AS YOU READ

Lincoln campaign badge

Use Prior Knowledge Why would some people view Lincoln's nomination as a step toward civil war?

The South Reacts

Lincoln's election brought a strong reaction in the South. A South Carolina woman described how the news was received:

❝ The excitement was very great. Everybody was talking at the same time. One . . . more moved than the others, stood up saying . . . 'No more vain regrets—sad forebodings are useless. The stake is life or death—.' ❞

—Mary Boykin Chesnut, *A Diary From Dixie,* 1860

To many southerners, Lincoln's election meant that the South no longer had a voice in national government. They believed that the President and Congress were now set against their interests—especially slavery. Even before the election, South Carolina's governor had written to other southern governors. If Lincoln won, he wrote, it would be their duty to leave the Union.

Secession Senator John Crittenden of Kentucky made a last effort to save the Union. In December 1860, he introduced a bill to extend the Missouri Compromise line to the Pacific. Crittenden also proposed an "unamendable" amendment to the Constitution that would guarantee forever the right to hold slaves in states south of the compromise line.

The compromise bill received little support. Slavery in the West was no longer the issue. Many southerners believed that the North had put an abolitionist in the White House. They felt that secession was their only choice. Most Republicans also were unwilling to surrender what they had won in the national election.

GEOGRAPHY
Skills

Abraham Lincoln won the election of 1860 with less than 40 percent of the popular vote.

1. **Location** On the map, locate **(a)** Kentucky, **(b)** Illinois, **(c)** South Carolina.

2. **Region** **(a)** Which political party did the northern states support? **(b)** Which party did most southern states support?

3. **Critical Thinking Drawing Conclusions** Did the results of the popular vote weaken or strengthen Lincoln's chances of effectively leading the nation? Explain.

Election of 1860

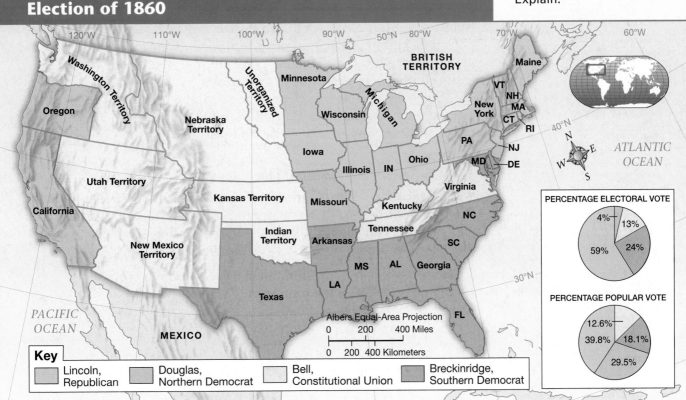

Key
- Lincoln, Republican
- Douglas, Northern Democrat
- Bell, Constitutional Union
- Breckinridge, Southern Democrat

PERCENTAGE ELECTORAL VOTE
4% | 13% | 59% | 24%

PERCENTAGE POPULAR VOTE
12.6% | 39.8% | 18.1% | 29.5%

Fort Sumter

The Civil War began in 1861 when Confederate forces bombarded and captured Fort Sumter in Charleston Harbor, South Carolina. Later in the war, Union gunships reduced Sumter to rubble. The fort was rebuilt, and it remained part of the seacoast defenses until 1947. Today, Fort Sumter is a national monument. Tour boats to the fort leave regularly from downtown Charleston.

Charleston, South Carolina

 Take It to the NET

Virtual Field Trip For an interactive look at Fort Sumter, visit *The American Nation* section of **www.phschool.com**.

On December 20, 1860, South Carolina became the first state to secede. By late February, 1861, Alabama, Florida, Georgia, Louisiana, Mississippi, and Texas had also seceded.

The Confederacy Most southerners believed that they had every right to secede. After all, the Declaration of Independence said that "it is the right of the people to alter or to abolish" a government that denies the rights of its citizens. Lincoln, they believed, would deny white southerners the right to own slaves.

At a convention in Montgomery, Alabama, the seven states formed a new nation, the Confederate States of America. Jefferson Davis of Mississippi became the first president of the Confederacy.

The Civil War Begins

When Lincoln took the oath of office on March 4, 1861, he faced a dangerous situation. In his inaugural address, Lincoln warned that "no state . . . can lawfully get out of the Union." Still, he pledged that there would be no war unless the South started it:

AS YOU READ **Draw Inferences** What did Lincoln mean by the statement "In your hands, . . .is the momentous issue of civil war"?

66 In YOUR hands, my dissatisfied fellow-countrymen, and not in MINE, is the momentous issue of civil war. . . . We are not enemies, but friends. We must not be enemies. Though passion may have strained, it must not break our bonds of affection. 99

— Abraham Lincoln, First Inaugural Address

Lincoln's Difficult Decision Jefferson Davis, however, had already ordered Confederate forces to begin seizing federal forts in the South. President Lincoln faced a difficult decision. Should he let the Confederates take over federal property? If he did, he would seem to be admitting that states had the right to leave the Union. On the other hand, if he sent troops to hold the forts, he might start a civil war. He might also lose the support of the eight slave states that had not seceded from the Union.

In April, the Confederacy forced Lincoln to make up his mind. By then, Confederate troops controlled nearly all forts, post offices, and other federal buildings in the South. The Union held only three forts off the Florida coast and Fort Sumter in South Carolina. Fort Sumter was important to the Confederacy because it guarded Charleston Harbor.

Bombardment of Fort Sumter President Lincoln learned that food supplies at Fort Sumter were running low. He notified the governor of South Carolina that he was going to ship food to the fort. Lincoln promised not to send troops or weapons.

The Confederates, however, felt that they could not leave the fort in Union hands. On April 11, 1861, they demanded that Fort Sumter surrender. Major Robert Anderson, the Union commander, refused to give in until he had run out of food or was ordered to surrender by the United States government. Confederate guns then opened fire. The Union troops quickly ran out of ammunition. On April 13, Anderson surrendered the fort.

When Confederate troops shelled Fort Sumter, people in Charleston gathered on their rooftops to watch. To many, it was like a fireworks show. No one knew that the fireworks marked the start of a civil war that would last four terrible years.

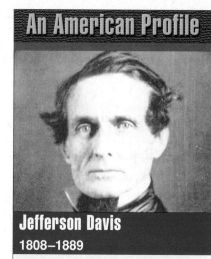

An American Profile

Jefferson Davis
1808–1889

After service in the Mexican War, Jefferson Davis became a United States Senator from Mississippi. Here, he championed states' rights. Then, as secretary of war, he influenced President Pierce to sign the Kansas-Nebraska Act. But Davis opposed splitting the Union. As tensions grew between the South and the North, he urged southern states not to secede.

They disregarded his advice. When Mississippi left the Union in 1861, Davis left the Senate and became president of the Confederacy.

Why do you think Jefferson Davis opposed secession?

Section 5 Assessment

Recall

1. **Identify** Explain the significance of **(a)** John Breckinridge, **(b)** John Bell, **(c)** John Crittenden, **(d)** Jefferson Davis.

Comprehension

2. How did the four candidates for President in 1860 reflect the nation's sectional differences?
3. Why did many southerners support secession after Lincoln won the presidency in 1860?
4. What happened at Fort Sumter in 1861 to begin the Civil War?

Critical Thinking and Writing

5. **Exploring the Main Idea** Review the Main idea statement at the beginning of this section. Then, write a newspaper editorial about Lincoln's election that might have appeared in a southern newspaper in November 1860.
6. **Solving Problems** Write an outline for a compromise plan that tries to save the Union in 1861. Your plan should offer advantages to both the North and the South.

ACTIVITY

Planning a Political Campaign You are a political campaign manager in 1860. Write a campaign slogan for each of the four candidates in the presidential election of 1860. Or, choose one of the candidates and design a campaign poster for that candidate.

Review and Assessment

CREATING A CHAPTER SUMMARY

On a sheet of paper, draw a flow-chart like this one. Include 6–8 boxes. Fill in each box with a key event or development in the growing conflict between the North and the South. For each event, include the date as well as one important result of the event. Some information has been filled in to help you get started.

1819: Missouri Compromise
Result: temporarily settled issue of slavery in territories

1857:
Result: undid Missouri Compromise

1860: Lincoln elected President
Result:

For additional review and enrich-ment activities, see the interactive version of *The American Nation*, available on the Web and on CD-ROM.

Take It to the NET

Chapter Self-Test For prac-tice test questions for Chapter 16, visit *The American Nation* section of **www.phschool.com**.

Building Vocabulary

Review the chapter vocabulary words listed below. Then, use the words and their definitions to create a matching quiz. Exchange quizzes with another student. Check each other's answers when you are finished.

1. popular sovereignty
2. fugitive
3. civil war
4. guerrilla warfare
5. lawsuit
6. arsenal
7. treason
8. martyr
9. Missouri Compromise
10. Kansas-Nebraska Act

Reviewing Key Facts

11. Describe three positions on slavery held by Americans in the 1840s. (Section 1)
12. What were the five parts of the Compromise of 1850? (Section 2)
13. How did Kansas gain the nickname "Bleeding Kansas"? (Section 3)
14. What groups combined to form the Republican party? (Section 4)
15. Why did South Carolina secede from the Union? (Section 5)

Critical Thinking and Writing

16. **Connecting to Geography: Regions** Study the map of the election of 1860 in Section 5.
(a) From which regions did Lincoln draw his support? **(b)** Which candidate was most popu-lar in the upper south? **(c)** Does the map show from what regions Douglas drew most of his support? Why or why not?
17. **Supporting a Point of View** Many northerners condemned Daniel Webster for supporting the Fugitive Slave Act. Write two brief statements summarizing one argument for and one argu-ment against Webster's position.
18. **Identifying Causes and Effects** **(a)** List two causes for the split in the Democratic party in the 1860 election. **(b)** List two effects of the election.
19. **Identifying Alternatives** **(a)** Write a paragraph suggesting one alternative to secession that the slave states could have chosen in 1860–1861. **(b)** Why do you think they chose secession?

This drawing appeared in northern newspapers in 1856. Look at the drawing and answer the questions that follow.

20. How is Sumner defending himself in the drawing?
21. What is the attitude of the other senators?
22. Which side does the artist support? Explain your answer.
23. What does the artist's view of the incident tell you about the mood of the country in 1856?

The election of 1860 outraged white southerners. They were especially upset that a President had been elected without any southern electoral votes. According to an Augusta, Georgia, newspaper editor, the Republican party:

❝ stands forth today, hideous, revolting, loathsome, a menace not only to the Union of these states, but to Society, to Liberty, and to Law. It has drawn to it the corrupt, the vile, and [immoral], the [wasteful], the lawless. . . . It is a fiend, the type of lawless Democracy, a law unto itself, its only Lord King Numbers, its decrees but the will of a wild mob. ❞

—Augusta, Georgia, *Chronicle,* November 1860, quoted in "Michael Holt, the Political Crisis of the 1850s"

24. Which of the following titles best reflects the viewpoint of the editorial writer?
   A A Tribute to the Republicans
   B A Loathsome Menace
   C Separation of Powers
   D Dangers of the Party System
25. What does this editorial tell you about the state of relations between the North and the South in November 1860?

ACTIVITIES

Connecting With . . . Economics

Transferring Information to Charts By 1861, the North had 65 percent of the farmland, 71 percent of the railroad track, 85 percent of the factories, 92 percent of the industrial workers, and 63 percent of the population of the United States. Use this information to create a series of pie charts comparing the resources of the North and the South. One pie chart has already been completed. After making the charts, use them to make two generalizations about the economic situation of the Confederate States.

35%
65%
■ Farmland in North
□ Farmland in South

Take It to the NET

Connecting to Today

Creating a Fact Sheet Like the Free-Soil party, new political parties often form in response to specific issues. Use the Internet to find out about a current "third party." Create a fact sheet describing the third party. For help in starting this activity, visit *The American Nation* section of **www.phschool.com**.

Researching a Biography

Ranking Lincoln Web Sites Use the Internet to find sites relating to Abraham Lincoln. Write a report listing the resources you found on these sites that make them valuable for a Lincoln biography. List five sites, and rank them in order of usefulness. For help in starting this activity, visit *The American Nation* section of **www.phschool.com**.

The Civil War

1861–1865

1 **The Conflict Takes Shape**
2 **No Easy Victory**
3 **A Promise of Freedom**
4 **Hardships of War**
5 **The War Ends**

The Battle of Bull Run

1861

The first major battle of the war takes place at Bull Run on July 21.

1862

Union gunboats capture New Orleans and Memphis.

1863

The Battle of Gettysburg ends the Confederate drive into the North.

AMERICAN EVENTS

Presidential Terms:　　Abraham Lincoln 1861–1865

1861　　　　　　　　　**1862**　　　　　　　　　**1863**

WORLD EVENTS

▲ **1861**
The Russian czar frees the serfs.

▲ **1862**
Great Britain refuses to recognize the Confederacy.

Choosing Sides

In April 1861, eight slave states were still in the Union. These states would have to decide whether to remain in the Union or join the Confederacy.

Key

- Union states
- Confederate states
- Border states that stayed in the Union
- States that joined the Confederacy after April 1861
- Territories
- Confederate States of America

* West Virginia separated from Virginia in 1861 and was admitted to the Union in 1863.

Albers Equal-Area Projection

0 · 300 · 600 Miles
0 · 300 · 600 Kilometers

The Emancipation Proclamation

The surrender at Appomattox Court House

1863
Abraham Lincoln issues the Emancipation Proclamation.

1864
General Grant becomes commander of the Union Army.

1865
General Lee surrenders at Appomattox Court House.

1863 · 1864 · 1865

▲ **1863**
The first Red Cross societies are established in Europe.

▲ **1864**
Archduke Maximilian of Austria becomes emperor of Mexico.

1 The Conflict Takes Shape

BEFORE YOU READ

Reading Focus

- What issues divided the nation when the war began?
- What were the primary strengths and weaknesses of the North and the South at the beginning of the war?
- Who were the leaders of each side in the war?

Key Terms

border state

martial law

Taking Notes

Copy the table below. As you read the section, fill in the table with the strengths of the North and the South at the start of the war and their reasons for fighting. Add as many entries as you need.

NORTH	SOUTH
Strengths	**Strengths**
•	•
•	•
Reasons for fighting	**Reasons for fighting**
•	•
•	•

Main Idea Although both sides believed that their cause was just, the North had important advantages at the start of the war.

AS YOU READ
A poster calling for volunteers

Draw Inferences Why would volunteers be eager to enlist?

Setting the Scene President Abraham Lincoln called for 75,000 volunteers to serve as soldiers in a campaign against the South. The term of enlistment was only 90 days—most northerners believed that the war would be over quickly. In the words of one confident Union supporter, "We shall crush out this rebellion as an elephant would trample on a mouse."

Southerners were just as convinced that a Confederate victory would be quick. A Confederate in North Carolina predicted, "Just throw three or four [bomb]shells among those blue-bellied Yankees and they'll scatter like sheep."

With flags held high, both northerners and southerners marched off to war. Most felt certain that a single, gallant battle would bring a quick end to the conflict. Few suspected that the Civil War would last four terrible years. By the time the fighting was over, every part of American society would be affected by the Civil War.

A Nation Divided

When the war began, each side was convinced that its cause was just. Southerners believed that they had the right to leave the Union. In fact, they called the conflict the War for Southern Independence. Southerners wanted independence so that they could keep their traditional way of life—including the institution of slavery.

Northerners, meanwhile, believed that they had to fight to save the Union. At the outset of the war, abolishing slavery was not an official goal of the North. In fact, many northerners, guided by feelings of racism, approved of slavery. Racism is the belief that one race is by nature superior to another.

In April 1861, eight slave states were still in the Union. As the war began, they had to make the difficult decision of which side to join. Their decision would greatly affect the outcome of the war. These states had more than half of the South's population and food crops. In addition, many of the South's factories were in these states.

Four of these states—Virginia,* North Carolina, Tennessee, and Arkansas—quickly joined the Confederacy. However, after some wavering between the North and South, the four border states—Kentucky, Missouri, Maryland, and Delaware—decided to remain in the Union. Maryland was especially critical to the Union cause since it bordered the nation's capital at Washington, D.C.

Still, there were some citizens of the border states who supported the South. In April 1861, pro-Confederate mobs attacked Union troops in Baltimore, Maryland. In response, President Lincoln declared martial law, or rule by the army instead of the elected government. Many people who sided with the South were arrested.

Strengths and Weaknesses

Both sides in the conflict had strengths and weaknesses as the war began. The South had the strong advantage of fighting a defensive war. "We seek no conquest," said Confederate President Jefferson Davis. "All we ask is to be let alone." If the North did not move its forces into the South, the Confederacy would remain a separate country.

The South White southerners believed that they were fighting a war for independence, similar to the American Revolution. Defending their homeland and their way of life gave them a strong reason to fight. "Our men must prevail in combat," one Confederate said, "or they will lose their property, country, freedom—in short, everything."

Confederate soldiers also enjoyed an advantage because they knew the southern countryside better. Friendly civilians often guided soldiers along obscure roads that did not appear on maps. Much of the South was wooded, too. Confederate forces used the woods for cover as they defended themselves against invading Union troops.

The South, however, had serious economic weaknesses. It had few factories to produce weapons and other vital supplies. It also had few railroads to move troops and supplies. The railroads that it did have often did not connect to one another. Tracks simply ran between two points and then stopped.

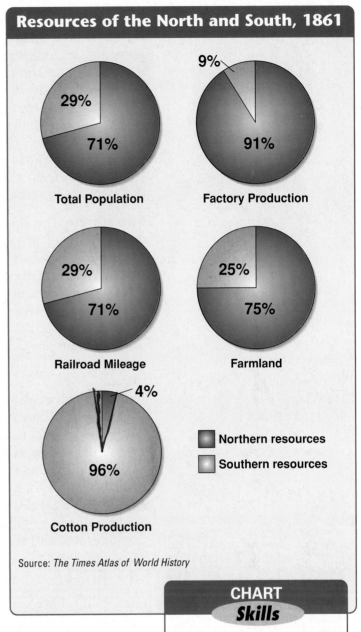

Resources of the North and South, 1861

Total Population: 29% / 71%

Factory Production: 9% / 91%

Railroad Mileage: 29% / 71%

Farmland: 25% / 75%

Cotton Production: 4% / 96%

Northern resources
Southern resources

Source: *The Times Atlas of World History*

CHART
Skills

As the Civil War began, the North had a number of economic advantages over the South.

1. **Comprehension** (a) How much farmland did each side have? (b) What percentage of the nation's factories did the South have?

2. **Critical Thinking**
Making Predictions
(a) Which side had more railroad track? (b) How would this affect the war?

Economics

---

*In western Virginia, where there were few slave owners, many people supported the Union. When Virginia seceded, westerners formed their own government. West Virginia became a state of the Union in 1863.

The South also had political problems. The Confederate constitution favored states' rights and limited the authority of the central government. As a result, the Confederate government often found it difficult to get things done. On one occasion, for example, the governor of Georgia insisted that only Georgian officers should command Georgian troops.

Finally, the South had a small population. Only about 9 million people lived in the Confederacy, compared with 22 million in the Union. More than one third of the southern population were enslaved African Americans. As a result, the South did not have enough people to serve as soldiers and to support the war effort.

The North The North had almost four times as many free citizens as the South. Thus, it had a large source of volunteers. It also had many people to grow food and to work in factories making supplies.

Industry was the North's greatest resource. Before the war, northern factories produced more than 90 percent of the nation's manufactured goods. Once the war began, these factories quickly began making guns, bullets, cannons, boots, uniforms, and other supplies for the Union army. In addition, the North had more than 70 percent of the nation's rail lines, which it used to transport both troops and supplies.

The North benefited from a strong navy and a large fleet of trading ships. With few warships and only a small merchant fleet, the South was unable to compete with the North at sea.

Despite these advantages, the North faced a difficult military challenge. To bring the South back into the Union, northern soldiers had to conquer a huge area. Instead of defending their homes, they were invading unfamiliar land. As Union armies marched into the South, their lines of supply would be much longer than those of the Confederates and thus more open to attack.

The War's Leaders

Leadership was a crucial factor in the Civil War. President Jefferson Davis of the Confederacy, President Abraham Lincoln of the Union, and military leaders on both sides played key roles in determining the war's outcome.

President Jefferson Davis Many people thought that Davis was a stronger leader than Lincoln. Davis's experience prepared him for the position. However, he did not want it. As one observer stated:

> 66 Mr. Davis's military instincts still predominate, and his eager wish was to have joined the army instead of being elected President. 99
>
> —Arthur James Freemantle, from *The Freemantle Diary*

Davis had attended the United States Military Academy at West Point. He had served as an officer in the Mexican War. Later, he served as Secretary of War under President Franklin Pierce. Furthermore, Davis was widely respected for his honesty and courage.

Davis, however, did not like to turn over to others the details of military planning. As a result, he spent much time worrying about small matters and arguing with his advisers.

President Abraham Lincoln At first, some northerners had doubts about Abraham Lincoln's ability to lead. He did not have much experience in national politics or military matters. However, Lincoln proved to be a patient but strong leader and a fine war planner.

Day by day, Lincoln gained the respect of those around him. Many liked his sense of humor. They noted that Lincoln even accepted criticism with a smile. When Secretary of War Edwin Stanton called Lincoln a fool, Lincoln commented, "Did Stanton say I was a fool? Then I must be one, for Stanton is generally right and he always says what he means."

Military Leaders As the war began, army officers in the South had to decide whether to stay in the Union army and fight against their home states, or join the Confederate forces.

Robert E. Lee of Virginia faced this dilemma when Lincoln asked him to command the Union army. He explains in a letter to a friend:

> 66 If Virginia stands by the old Union, so will I. But if she secedes . . . , then I will still follow my native State with my sword and, if need be, with my life. 99
>
> —Robert E. Lee, quoted in Carl Sandburg, *Abraham Lincoln*

Virginia did secede and Lee refused Lincoln's offer. Later, Lee became commander of the Confederate army.

Many of the army's best officers served the Confederacy. As a result, President Lincoln had trouble finding generals to match those of the South.

AFTER YOU READ

Section 1 Assessment

Recall

1. **Identify** Explain the significance of **(a)** Abraham Lincoln, **(b)** Jefferson Davis, **(c)** Robert E. Lee.
2. **Define** **(a)** border state, **(b)** martial law.

Comprehension

3. What were the goals of each side as the war began?
4. Describe two advantages that the North had over the South at the start of the Civil War.
5. Describe one strength and one weakness of **(a)** President Abraham Lincoln, **(b)** President Jefferson Davis.

Critical Thinking and Writing

6. **Exploring the Main Idea** Review the Main Idea statement at the beginning of this section. Then, list five statements from the section that support the main idea.
7. **Making Decisions** Imagine that you are an army officer from the South at the beginning of the war. Would you side with the Union or with the Confederacy? Give at least two reasons for your decision.

ACTIVITY

Analyzing a Chart
Study the chart on page 487. Then, use the information on the chart to write a report analyzing the strengths and weaknesses of each side at the start of the Civil War. Based on your analysis, which side do you think will win the war? Explain.

2 No Easy Victory

BEFORE YOU READ

Reading Focus

- What strategies did each side adopt to win the war?
- How did early encounters dispel hopes for a quick end to the war?
- What victories did the Confederates achieve?
- What victories did the Union achieve?

Key Terms

Battle of Bull Run

Virginia

Monitor

Battle of Antietam

Battle of Fredericksburg

Battle of Chancellorsville

Battle of Shiloh

Taking Notes

As you read, prepare an outline of the section. Use roman numerals to indicate major headings, capital letters for subheadings, and numbers for supporting details. The sample below will help you get started.

> I. Strategies for Victory
>   A. Union plans
>   1.
>   2.
>   3.
>   B. Confederate plans
>   1.
>   2.
> II. Early Encounters

Main Idea Despite hopes for a quick victory, both northerners and southerners soon learned that they were in for a long, difficult struggle.

AS YOU READ
Bullet caught in a shoulder plate

Predict What effect would improved weapons have on the war?

Setting the Scene At first, the armies of the North and the South marched proudly off to war. Each side expected a quick and painless victory. The reality of war soon shattered this expectation. Over and over, soldiers wrote home describing the awful face of battle:

> 66 I never saw so many broken down and exhausted men in all my life. I was sick as a horse, and as wet with blood and sweat as I could be. . . . Our tongues were parched and cracked for water, and our faces blackened with powder and smoke. 99
>
> —quoted by Shelby Foote in *The Civil War: A Narrative*

It soon became clear that there would be no quick end to the struggle. Both sides began to dig in for a long, difficult war.

Strategies for Victory

The North and South had different strategies for victory. The Union planned an aggressive campaign against the South. The South, meanwhile, planned to hold tight until the North lost the will to fight.

Union Plans First, the Union planned to use its navy to blockade southern ports. This would cut off the South's supply of manufactured goods from Europe.

In the East, Union generals aimed to seize Richmond, Virginia, the Confederate capital. They thought that they might end the war quickly by capturing the Confederate government.

In the West, the Union planned to seize control of the Mississippi River. This would prevent the South from using the river to supply its troops. It would also separate Arkansas, Texas, and Louisiana from the rest of the Confederacy.

Confederate Plans The South's strategy was simpler: The Confederate army would fight a defensive war until northerners tired of fighting. If the war became unpopular in the North, President Lincoln would have to stop the war and recognize the South's independence.

The Confederacy counted on European money and supplies to help fight the war. Southern cotton was important to the textile mills of England and other countries. Southerners were confident that Europeans would recognize the Confederacy as an independent nation and continue to buy southern cotton for their factories.

Early Encounters

"Forward to Richmond! Forward to Richmond!" Every day for more than a month, the influential *New York Tribune* blazed this war cry across its front page. At last, responding to popular pressure, President Lincoln ordered an attack.

Battle of Bull Run On July 21, 1861, Union troops set out from Washington, D.C., for Richmond, about 100 miles away. Hundreds of Washingtonians, in a festive mood, rode out along with them to watch the battle.

The Union troops had not gone far when they met up with Confederate soldiers. A battle quickly followed. It took place near a small Virginia stream known as Bull Run.

At first, Union forces succeeded in breaking up Confederate battle lines. "The war is over!" yelled some soldiers from Massachusetts. But General Thomas Jackson rallied the Virginia troops on a nearby hill. "Look!" cried a Confederate officer to his men, "There is Jackson standing like a stone wall! Rally behind the Virginians!" From that day on, the general was known as "Stonewall" Jackson.

In the end, it was the Union troops who panicked and ran. "Off they went," reported one observer, "across fields, toward the woods, anywhere, everywhere, to escape." For most of the soldiers, the retreat did not stop until they reached Washington, D.C.

The Battle of Bull Run showed both the Union and the Confederacy that their soldiers needed training. It also showed that the war would be long and bloody.

Caution, Delay, and Retreat After the shocking disaster at Bull Run, President Lincoln appointed General George McClellan as commander of the Union army of the East, known as the Army of the Potomac. McClellan, a superb organizer, transformed inexperienced recruits into an army of trained soldiers prepared for battle.

GEOGRAPHY
Skills

Early in the war, Union armies were unsuccessful in their attempts to capture Richmond, the Confederate capital.

1. **Location** On the map, locate (a) Washington, D.C., (b) Richmond, (c) Bull Run, (d) Chancellorsville.

2. **Movement** Describe the route that General McClellan took when he tried to capture Richmond in 1862.

3. **Critical Thinking Making Decisions** Do you think that the Confederacy made a wise decision in locating its capital at Richmond? Explain.

The Civil War in the East

Key
← Union troops
← Confederate troops
⭐ Union victories
⭐ Confederate victories

McClellan, however, was very cautious. He delayed leading his troops into battle. Newspapers reported "all quiet along the Potomac" so often that the phrase became a national joke. Finally, President Lincoln lost patience. "If General McClellan does not want to use the army," the President snapped, "I would like to borrow it."

At last, in March 1862, McClellan and most of his troops left Washington and sailed down the Potomac River. After landing south of Richmond, McClellan began inching slowly toward the Confederate capital.

Learning of the Union approach, General Robert E. Lee launched a series of counterattacks. At the same time, Lee sent General Stonewall Jackson north to threaten Washington. As a result, Lincoln was prevented from sending the rest of the Union army to help McClellan. Cautious as usual, McClellan abandoned the attack and retreated.

AS YOU READ **Draw Inferences** Before you read this section, think about why the Union wanted to blockade southern ports. Then, read to find the reason.

Naval Action Early in the war, Union ships blockaded southern ports. At first, some small, fast ships slipped through the blockade. These "blockade runners" brought everything from matches to guns to the Confederacy.

In time, however, the blockade became more effective. Trade through southern ports dropped by more than 90 percent. The South desperately needed a way to break the Union blockade. One method it tried was the ironclad ship.

Confederates took over an abandoned Union warship, the USS *Merrimack.* They covered it with iron plates and renamed it the *Virginia.* On its first day out in March 1862, the *Virginia* destroyed two Union ships and drove three more aground. Union cannonballs bounced harmlessly off the *Virginia's* metal skin.

The Union countered with its own ironclad, the *Monitor.* The two ships clashed in the waters off Hampton Roads, Virginia. Despite an exhausting battle, neither vessel seriously damaged the other, and both withdrew. Two months later Confederates had to sink the *Virginia* when the Union captured Norfolk. The Union eventually built more than 50 ironclads.

Ironclad ships changed naval warfare. However, the South was never again able to mount a serious attack against the Union navy. The Union blockade held throughout the war.

Antietam In September 1862, General Lee took the offensive and marched his troops north into Maryland. He believed that a southern victory on northern soil would be a great blow to northern morale.

Luck was against Lee, however. At an abandoned Confederate campsite, a Union officer found a copy of Lee's battle plan. It was wrapped around three cigars, left behind by a careless general. General McClellan was overjoyed to have the information. "If I cannot whip 'Bobbie Lee,' I will be willing to go home," he boasted.

However, McClellan was slow to act. Finally, after a few days, he attacked Lee's main force at Antietam (an TEE tuhm) on September 17. In the day-long battle that followed, more than 23,000 Union and Confederate soldiers were killed or wounded.

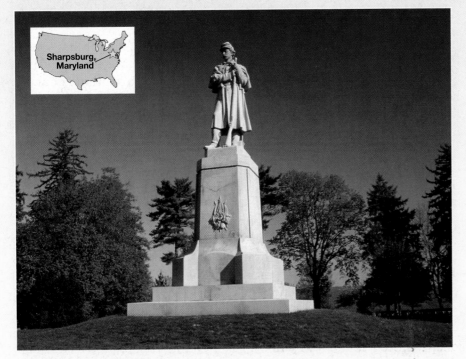

Sharpsburg, Maryland

Antietam National Battlefield

On September 17, 1862, Union and Confederate troops faced one another at Antietam Creek near Sharpsburg, Maryland.

Today, 103 monuments at Antietam honor those who fought there. Most of the monuments were built by Civil War veterans. The barrels of 500 cannons, which were used in the Civil War, are on the battlefield. These mark the location of artillery during the battle.

 Take It to the NET

Virtual Field Trip For an interactive look at the Antietam battle site, visit *The American Nation* section of **www.phschool.com**.

On the night of September 18, Lee ordered his troops to slip back into Virginia. The Confederates breathed a sigh of relief when they saw that McClellan was not pursuing them.

Neither side was a clear winner at the Battle of Antietam. The North was able to claim victory, though, because Lee had ordered his forces to withdraw. As a result, northern morale increased. Still, President Lincoln was keenly disappointed. General McClellan had failed to follow up his victory by pursuing the Confederates. In November, Lincoln appointed General Ambrose Burnside to replace McClellan as commander of the Army of the Potomac.

Confederate Victories in the East

Two stunning victories for the Confederacy came in late 1862 and 1863. In December 1862, Union forces set out once again toward Richmond.

Meeting Burnside's army outside Fredericksburg, Virginia, Lee's forces dug into the crest of a hill. There, in a strong defensive position, Confederate guns mowed down wave after wave of charging Union troops. The Battle of Fredericksburg was one of the Union's worst defeats. (See page 495.)

Half a year later, in May 1863, Lee, aided by Stonewall Jackson, again outmaneuvered Union forces. The Battle of Chancellorsville took place on thickly wooded ground near Chancellorsville, Virginia. Lee and Jackson defeated the Union troops in three days. Victory came at a high price for the South, however. During the battle, nervous

Confederate sentries fired at what they thought was an approaching Union soldier. The "Union soldier" was General Stonewall Jackson. Several days later, Jackson died as a result of his injuries.

Union Victories in the West

In the West, Union forces met with better success. As you have read, the Union strategy was to seize control of the Mississippi River. General Ulysses S. Grant began moving toward that goal. In February 1862, Grant attacked and captured Fort Henry and Fort Donelson in Tennessee. These Confederate forts guarded two important tributaries of the Mississippi.

Grant now pushed south to Shiloh, a village on the Tennessee River. There, on April 6, he was surprised by Confederate forces. By the end of the day, the Confederates had driven the Union troops back toward the river.

Grant now showed the toughness and determination that would enable him to win many battles in the future. That night, one of Grant's soldiers approached him. The officer thought Union forces should retreat. But, seeing Grant's stubborn face, the officer only said, "Well, Grant, we've had the devil's own day, haven't we?"

"Yes," Grant replied. "Lick 'em tomorrow, though."

And they did. With the aid of reinforcements, Grant beat back the Confederates and won the **Battle of Shiloh.** It was, however, one of the bloodiest encounters of the Civil War.

While Grant was fighting at Shiloh, the Union navy moved to gain control of the Mississippi River. In April 1862, Union gunboats captured New Orleans. Other ships seized Memphis, Tennessee. By capturing these two cities, the Union controlled both ends of the Mississippi. The South could no longer use the river as a supply line.

Ulysses S. Grant 1822–1885

General Ulysses S. Grant's troops had the Confederates surrounded at Fort Donelson. Confederate General Simon Bolivar Buckner wanted to discuss terms of surrender.

Grant's response was to the point: "No terms except an unconditional and immediate surrender can be accepted." Buckner immediately surrendered the fort. Grant's victory caused great celebration in the North. It also earned him the nickname "Unconditional Surrender" Grant.

What characteristics did Grant reveal by his actions at Fort Donelson?

AFTER YOU READ

Section 2 Assessment

Recall

1. **Identify** Explain the significance of **(a)** Stonewall Jackson, **(b)** Battle of Bull Run, **(c)** George McClellan, **(d)** *Virginia,* **(e)** *Monitor,* **(f)** Battle of Antietam, **(g)** Battle of Fredericksburg, **(h)** Battle of Chancellorsville, **(i)** Ulysses S. Grant, **(j)** Battle of Shiloh.

Comprehension

2. Describe **(a)** the North's three-part plan for defeating the South, **(b)** the South's plan to defeat the North.
3. What did both sides learn from the Battle of Bull Run?

4. Why was the Confederate victory at Fredericksburg critical?
5. How did Union victories at New Orleans and Memphis affect the South?

Critical Thinking and Writing

6. **Exploring the Main Idea** Review the Main Idea statement at the beginning of this section. Make a list of five events and their results during the first two years of the war.
7. **Analyzing Ideas** Analyze the meaning of this statement: "The South could win the war by not losing, but the North could win only by winning."

ACTIVITY

Take It to the NET
Connecting to Today
Both the Union and Confederate navies developed ironclad ships during the Civil War. Use the Internet to research technological advances in modern naval vessels. Prepare an oral class presentation including pictures. Visit *The American Nation* section of **www.phschool.com** for help in completing the activity.

The Battle of Fredericksburg

Fredericksburg, Virginia, was located between Washington, D.C., and Richmond, the Confederate capital. Taking Fredericksburg was a step toward capturing Richmond.

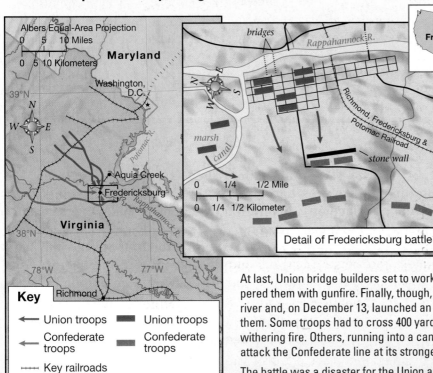

Detail of Fredericksburg battle

Key

- ← Union troops
- ← Confederate troops
- ┄┄┄ Key railroads
- ▬ Union troops
- ▬ Confederate troops

In the fall of 1862, General Ambrose Burnside began moving his Union army toward Fredericksburg. They were stopped by the Rappahannock River. While the Union troops waited for engineers to bridge the river, General Robert E. Lee's Confederate forces occupied the city and the high ground behind it. They took up a strong position, overlooking a large, open field.

At last, Union bridge builders set to work, but Confederate snipers peppered them with gunfire. Finally, though, the Union army got across the river and, on December 13, launched an attack. The terrain was against them. Some troops had to cross 400 yards of open ground in the face of withering fire. Others, running into a canal and a marsh, were forced to attack the Confederate line at its strongest point—the top of a hill.

The battle was a disaster for the Union army. For hours, soldiers marched up the hill only to be mowed down by gunfire. Finally, Burnside halted the attack. His army had lost 13,000 men, compared with only 5,000 for Lee's.

ACTIVITY

You are a correspondent for a northern or southern newspaper, and you saw the Battle of Fredericksburg. Write a description of the battle that explains how geography affected the outcome.

3 A Promise of Freedom

Reading Focus

- What was Lincoln's primary goal in the war?
- What were the effects of the Emancipation Proclamation?
- How did African Americans contribute to the war effort both in the Union army and behind Confederate lines?

Key Terms

emancipate

Emancipation Proclamation

54th Massachusetts Regiment

Fort Wagner

Taking Notes

Copy the chart. As you read, complete the chart to show the causes and effects of the Emancipation Proclamation. Add as many entries as you need.

CAUSES
1.
2. Lincoln wanted to weaken the Confederacy's ability to fight

EMANCIPATION PROCLAMATION

EFFECTS
1. Union fighting to end slavery
2.

Main Idea By issuing the Emancipation Proclamation, Lincoln expanded the goals of the war to include the ending of slavery.

AS YOU READ African American soldier

Draw Inferences Why were the Union lines a symbol of freedom to the enslaved African Americans?

Setting the Scene

John Finnely heard the news first thing in the morning: Ten slaves had run off the night before. Finnely, a twelve-year-old slave on a plantation in Alabama, had a pretty good idea where the escapees had gone. Most certainly, they had headed for Union troops camped a few miles to the north—and freedom.

Finnely, too, began to "think and think 'bout gittin' freedom." At last, with a mixture of hope and fear, he decided to make the break:

> 66 I makes up my mind to go and I leaves with a chunk of meat and cornbread . . . half skeert to death. I sure have my eyes open and my ears forward, watchin' for the [Confederate slave patrols]. I step off the road in the night, at the sight of anything, and in the day I take to the woods. 99
>
> —John Finnely, quoted in *Remembering Slavery*

At first, the Civil War was not a war against slavery. But as thousands of slaves like John Finnely rushed into the arms of Union troops with the hope of freedom, some northerners began to rethink the aims of the war.

Lincoln's Goal

The Civil War began as a war to restore the Union, not to end slavery. President Lincoln made this point clear in a letter that was widely distributed:

> 66 If I could save the Union without freeing any slave, I would do it; and if I could save it by freeing all the slaves, I would do it; and if I could do it by freeing some and leaving others alone, I would also do that. 99
>
> —Abraham Lincoln, August 22, 1862, quoted in Carl Sandburg, *Abraham Lincoln*

Lincoln had a reason for handling the slavery issue cautiously. As you have read, four slave states remained in the Union. The President did not want to do anything that might cause these states to shift their loyalty to the Confederacy. The resources of the border states might allow the South to turn the tide of the war.

The Emancipation Proclamation

By mid-1862, Lincoln came to believe that he could save the Union only by broadening the goals of the war. He decided to emancipate, or free, enslaved African Americans living in the Confederacy. In the four loyal slave states, however, slaves would not be freed. Nor would slaves be freed in Confederate lands that had already been captured by the Union, such as the city of New Orleans.

Motives and Timing Lincoln had practical reasons for his emancipation plan. At the start of the Civil War, more than 3 million slaves labored for the Confederacy. They helped grow the food that fed Confederate soldiers. They also worked in iron and lead mines that were vital to the South's war effort. Some served as nurses and cooks for the army. Lincoln knew that emancipation would weaken the Confederacy's ability to carry on the war.

However, Lincoln did not want to anger slave owners in the Union. Also, he knew that many northerners opposed freedom for enslaved African Americans. Lincoln hoped to introduce the idea of emancipation slowly, by limiting it to territory controlled by the Confederacy.

The President had another motive. As you read in Chapter 16, Lincoln believed that slavery was wrong. When he felt that he could act to free slaves without threatening the Union, he did so.

Lincoln was concerned about the timing of his announcement. The war was not going well for the Union. He did not want Americans to think he was freeing slaves as a desperate effort to save a losing cause. He waited for a victory to announce his plan.

On September 22, 1862, following the Union victory at Antietam, Lincoln issued a preliminary proclamation. He issued the formal Emancipation Proclamation on January 1, 1863.

Impact of the Proclamation Because the rebelling states were not under Union control, no slaves actually gained their freedom on January 1, 1863. Still, the Emancipation Proclamation changed the purpose of the war. Now, Union troops were fighting to end slavery as well as to save the Union.

The opponents of slavery greeted the proclamation with joy. In Boston, African American abolitionist Frederick Douglass witnessed one of the many emotional celebrations that took place:

> 66 The effect of this announcement was startling . . . and the scene was wild and grand. . . . My old friend Rue, a Negro preacher, . . . expressed the heartfelt emotion of the hour, when he led all voices in the anthem, 'Sound the loud timbrel o'er Egypt's dark sea, Jehovah hath triumphed, his people are free!' 99

—Frederick Douglass, *Life and Times of Frederick Douglass*

Primary Source

The Emancipation Proclamation

On January 1, 1863, President Lincoln issued the Emancipation Proclamation. The document declared the following:
"On the 1st day of January, in the year of our Lord 1863, all persons held as slaves within any state or . . . part of a state [whose] people . . . shall then be in rebellion against the United States, shall be then, thenceforward, and forever free."

Analyzing Primary Sources
Were all enslaved African Americans freed? Explain.

AS YOU READ **Visualize** Form a mental picture of how slaves would have reacted to hearing about the Emancipation Proclamation.

Viewing History

Assault on Fort Wagner

Fort Wagner

In this painting by Tom Lovell, African American soldiers of the 54th Massachusetts Regiment charge Confederate troops at Fort Wagner. Nearly half the regiment died in the failed attack, including the regiment's commander, Colonel Robert Gould Shaw. **Applying Information** *Why did African Americans have their own regiments?*

In the South, Lincoln's proclamation was seen as a "fiend's act" that destroyed expensive property. The proclamation won the sympathy of Europeans, especially workers. As a result, it became less likely that Britain or any other European country would come to the aid of the South.

African American Contributions

When the war began, thousands of free blacks volunteered to fight for the Union. At first, federal law forbade African Americans to serve as soldiers. When Congress repealed that law in 1862, however, both free African Americans and escaped slaves enlisted in the Union army.

In the Union Army The army assigned African American volunteers to all-black units, commanded by white officers. At first, the black troops served only as laborers. They performed noncombat duties such as building roads and guarding supplies. Black troops received only half the pay of white soldiers.

African American soldiers protested against this policy of discrimination that denied them the same treatment as other soldiers. Gradually, conditions changed. By 1863, African American troops were fighting in major battles against the Confederates. In 1864, the United States War Department announced that all soldiers would receive equal pay. By the end of the war, about 200,000 African Americans had fought for the Union. Nearly 40,000 lost their lives.

Acts of Bravery One of the most famous African American units in the Union army was the 54th Massachusetts Regiment. The 54th accepted African Americans from all across the North. Frederick Douglass helped recruit troops for the regiment, and two of his sons served in it.

On July 18, 1863, the 54th Massachusetts Regiment led an attack on Fort Wagner near Charleston, South Carolina. Under heavy fire, troops fought their way into the fort before being forced to withdraw. In the desperate fighting, almost half the regiment was killed.

The courage of the 54th Massachusetts and other regiments helped to win respect for African American soldiers. Sergeant William Carney of the 54th Massachusetts was the first of 16 African American soldiers to win the Medal of Honor in the Civil War. Such soldiers had "proved themselves among the bravest of the brave," Secretary of War Edwin Stanton told Lincoln.

Behind Confederate Lines Despite the Emancipation Proclamation, African Americans still worked in the South as slaves on plantations. However, many slaves slowed down their work or refused to work at all. In this way, they hoped to weaken the South's war effort. They knew that when victorious Union troops arrived in their area, they would be free.

Thousands of enslaved African Americans took direct action to free themselves. Whenever a Union army appeared, slaves from all over the area would flee their former masters. They crossed the Union lines to freedom. By the end of the war, about one fourth of the South's enslaved population had escaped to freedom.

Section 3 Assessment

Recall
1. **Identify** Explain the significance of **(a)** Emancipation Proclamation, **(b)** 54th Massachusetts Regiment, **(c)** Fort Wagner.
2. **Define** emancipate.

Comprehension
3. Why was President Lincoln cautious about making the abolition of slavery a goal of the war?
4. How did the Emancipation Proclamation affect the status of enslaved African Americans?
5. How did enslaved African Americans help to hurt the Confederate war effort?

Critical Thinking and Writing
6. **Exploring the Main Idea** Review the Main Idea statement at the beginning of this section. Write a newspaper article explaining why Lincoln issued the Emancipation Proclamation.
7. **Analyzing Primary Sources** In 1861, Frederick Douglass said, "This is no time to fight with one hand when both hands are needed. This is no time to fight with only your white hand, and allow your black hand to remain tied!" **(a)** What did Douglass mean by this statement? **(b)** Did the United States Congress agree with Douglass? Explain.

ACTIVITY

Writing a Poem A monument is being built to honor the courageous African American soldiers of the Civil War. Write a poem to be inscribed on the monument, mentioning some of the facts you learned in this section.

4 Hardships of War

BEFORE YOU READ

Reading Focus

- What was life like for Confederate and Union soldiers?
- What problems did each side face at home?
- How did the war affect the economy of the North and the South?
- What role did women play in the war?

Key Terms

Copperhead

draft

habeas corpus

income tax

inflation

profiteer

Taking Notes

Copy this incomplete Venn diagram. As you read, fill in key facts about conditions in the North and South during the Civil War. Write common characteristics in the overlapping section.

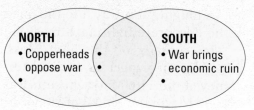

NORTH
- Copperheads oppose war
-

SOUTH
- War brings economic ruin
-

Main Idea The demands of the war hurt civilians as well as soldiers on both sides, but the problems were worse in the Confederate States.

AS YOU READ

Homecoming
Summarize Why did the war cause more damage in the South?

Setting the Scene John Jones knew that he was not alone in the hardships he experienced. All he had to do was look around in the Confederate capital of Richmond. Some of the city's residents, he noted, looked "like vagabonds . . . gaunt and pale with hunger." As for his own family:

> 66 My daughter's cat is staggering today, for want of animal food. Sometimes I fancy I stagger myself. We do not average two ounces of meat daily; and some do not get any for several days together. 99
> —John B. Jones, *A Rebel War Clerk's Diary*

The Civil War caused hardships not only for soldiers but for people at home as well. Southerners were especially hard hit, because most of the fighting took place in the South. But for both North and South, the war affected every area of life.

The Hard Life of Soldiers

On both sides, most soldiers were under the age of 21. War, however, quickly turned gentle boys into tough men. Soldiers drilled and marched for long hours. They slept on the ground even in rain and snow. In combat, boys of 18 learned to stand firm as cannon blasts shook the earth and bullets whizzed past their ears.

As the death toll rose, the age restrictions for soldiers were relaxed. The South drafted boys as young as 17 and men as old as 50.

New technology added to the horror of war. Cone-shaped bullets made rifles twice as accurate. Improved cannons hurled exploding shells several miles. The new weapons had deadly results. In most battles, one fourth or more of the soldiers were killed or wounded.

Sick and wounded soldiers faced other horrors. Medical care on the battlefield was crude. Surgeons routinely amputated injured arms and legs. At the time, doctors did not know how germs cause infection and disease. As a result, minor wounds often became infected. In addition, poor sanitary conditions in the army camps allowed diseases to spread rapidly. Diseases such as pneumonia and malaria killed more men than guns or cannons did.

On both sides, prisoners of war faced horrifying conditions. At Andersonville, a prison camp in Georgia, many Union prisoners died of disease or starvation.

The difficult life of soldiers led many to desert. One out of every seven Union soldiers and one out of every nine Confederate soldiers deserted.

Opposition to War in the North

Some northerners opposed using force to keep the South in the Union. Supporters of the war called these people Copperheads, after the poisonous snake. Other northerners supported the war but opposed the way Lincoln was conducting it.

The Draft Law As the war dragged on, public support dwindled. When the war began, the North offered men money to enlist. However, some men abused the system. They would sign up, collect the money, and then desert. Soon, however, there was a shortage of volunteers to serve in the Union army.

LINKING PAST AND PRESENT

▲ Past

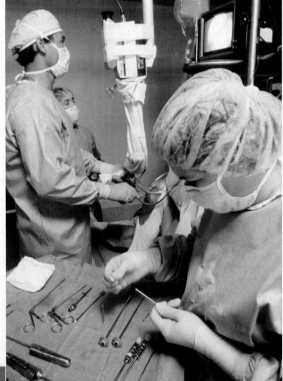

▲ Present

Congress passed a **draft** law in 1863. It required all able-bodied males between the ages of 20 and 45 to serve in the military if they were called. Under the law, a man could avoid the draft by paying the government $300 or by hiring someone to serve in his place. This angered many people, who began to see the Civil War as "a rich man's war and a poor man's fight."

Riots in the Cities Opposition to the draft law led to riots in several northern cities. The law had gone into effect soon after Lincoln issued the Emancipation Proclamation. Some white northerners, especially recent immigrants in the cities, believed that they were being forced to fight to end slavery. They also worried that they would have to compete with free African Americans for jobs.

The worst riot took place in New York City during July 1863. For four days, white workers attacked free blacks. Rioters also attacked rich New Yorkers who had paid to avoid serving in the army. At least 74 people were killed during the riot.

President Lincoln moved to stop the riots and other "disloyal practices." Several times, he suspended **habeas corpus** (HAY bee uhs KOR puhs), the right to be charged or have a hearing before being jailed. Lincoln argued that the Constitution allowed him to deny people their rights "when in the cases of rebellion or invasion, the public safety may require it." The President also said that those arrested could be tried under the stricter rules of a military court. Eventually, nearly 14,000 people were arrested. However, most were never charged with a specific crime or brought to trial.

Problems in the South

President Davis, meanwhile, struggled to create a strong federal government for the Confederacy. Many southerners firmly believed in states' rights. They resisted paying taxes to a central government. At one point, Georgia even threatened to secede from the Confederacy!

Like the North, the South was forced to pass a draft law to fill its army. However, men who owned or supervised more than 20 slaves did not have to serve. Southern farmers who had few or no slaves resented this law.

Near the end of the war, the South no longer had enough white men to fill the ranks. Robert E. Lee urged that enslaved African Americans be allowed to serve as soldiers. Desperate, the Confederate congress finally agreed. The war ended, however, before any enslaved people put on Confederate uniforms.

AS YOU READ **Summarize** Write two or three sentences summarizing how the Civil War affected the northern economy.

The Northern Economy

The Civil War cost far more than any previous war. The Union had to use several strategies to raise money. In some ways, however, war helped the North's economy.

Taxation and Inflation To pay for the war, Congress established the nation's first **income tax,** or tax on people's earnings, in 1861. A new agency, the Internal Revenue Bureau, oversaw the collection process. The Union also issued bonds worth millions of dollars. Still, taxes and bonds did not raise enough money. To get the funds it needed, the North printed more than $400 million in paper money.

As the money supply increased, each dollar was worth less. In response, businesses charged more for their goods. The North was experiencing inflation, a rise in prices and a decrease in the value of money. During the war, prices for goods nearly doubled in the North.

Economic Benefits The war helped the North's economy in several ways. Since many farmers went off to fight, there was a greater need for machines to plant and harvest crops. The purchase of reapers rose to nearly 165,000 during the war. As a result, farm production actually went up during the war.

The wartime demand for clothing, shoes, guns, and other goods helped many northern industries. Some manufacturers made fortunes by profiteering. Profiteers charged excessive prices for goods that the government desperately needed for the war.

The Southern Economy

For the South, war brought economic ruin. The South had to struggle with the cost of the war, the loss of the cotton trade, and severe shortages brought on by the Union blockade.

The Economy Suffers To raise money, the Confederacy imposed an income tax and a tax-in-kind. The tax-in-kind required farmers to turn over one tenth of their crops to the government. The government took crops because it knew that southern farmers had little money.

Like the North, the South printed paper money. It printed so much that wild inflation set in. By 1865, one Confederate dollar was worth only two cents in gold. Prices were especially high in Richmond, where a barrel of flour was $275 in early 1864, potatoes were $25 a bushel, and butter was $15 a pound.

The war did serious damage to the cotton trade, the South's main source of income. Early in the war, President Davis halted cotton shipments to Britain. He hoped to force Britain to side with the South in return for renewed shipments of cotton. The tactic backfired. Britain simply bought more cotton from Egypt and India. Davis succeeded only in cutting the South's income.

Effects of the Blockade The Union blockade created severe shortages in the South. Confederate armies sometimes had to wait weeks for supplies of food and clothing. With few factories of its own, the South bought many of its weapons in Europe. However, the

Cause and Effect

Causes

- Issue of slavery in the territories divides the North and South
- Abolitionists want slavery to end
- South fears it will lose power in the national government
- Southern states secede after Lincoln's election
- Confederates bombard Fort Sumter

THE CIVIL WAR

Effects

- Lincoln issues the Emancipation Proclamation
- Northern economy booms
- South loses its cotton trade with Britain
- Total war destroys the South's economy
- Hundreds of thousands of Americans killed

Effects Today

- Disagreements over states' rights persist
- African Americans have equal protection under the Constitution
- Millions of Americans visit Civil War battlefields each year

GRAPHIC ORGANIZER
Skills

The Civil War was a major turning point in the history of the United States.

1. **Comprehension** How did the war affect the northern and southern economies?

2. **Critical Thinking** **Identifying Causes and Effects** Describe another cause or effect that could be added to this chart.

blockade cut off most deliveries from across the Atlantic. To acquire goods, the government began building and running factories. Private manufacturers were offered contracts and draft exemptions for their workers if they started making war goods.

For civilians, the blockade brought food shortages. The production of food became critical to the economy. Many plantations switched from growing cotton to raising grain and livestock, or animals raised for food. In some states, cotton production was limited.

Women in the War

Women of both the North and the South played vital roles during the war. As men left for the battlefields, women took jobs in industry and on farms.

Women's aid societies helped supply the troops with food, bedding, clothing, and medicine. Throughout the North, women held fairs and other fundraising events to pay for supplies.

Nursing the Wounded Women on both sides worked as nurses. At first, doctors were unwilling to permit even trained nurses to work in military hospitals. When wounded men began to swamp army hospitals, however, this attitude soon changed. In fact, women performed so well that nursing became an accepted occupation for women after the war.

Dorothea Dix, famous for her work reforming prisons and mental hospitals, and Clara Barton, who later founded the American Red Cross, both became nurses for the Union army. Sojourner Truth, the African American antislavery leader, worked in Union hospitals and in camps for freed slaves. In the South, Sally Tompkins set up a hospital in Richmond, Virginia.

Section 4 Assessment

Recall

1. **Identify** Explain the significance of (a) Copperhead, (b) Dorothea Dix, (c) Clara Barton, (d) Sojourner Truth, (e) Sally Tompkins.
2. **Define** (a) draft, (b) habeas corpus, (c) income tax, (d) inflation, (e) profiteer.

Comprehension

3. Describe three hardships faced by soldiers during the Civil War.
4. (a) Why did some northerners oppose the war? (b) How did the blockade affect the southern economy?

5. Describe three ways in which women contributed to the war effort.

Critical Thinking and Writing

6. **Exploring the Main Idea** Review the Main Idea statement at the beginning of this section. Then, write a diary entry describing conditions in the South during the later days of the Civil War.
7. **Linking Past and Present** (a) What advances in technology made Civil War battles deadly? (b) In what ways would war today be even more deadly?

ACTIVITY

Take It to the NET
Writing a Report
Use the Internet to find out more about Civil War medicine. Among the topics you might research are nurses, surgeons, field hospitals, battle wounds, and disease. Then, use what you find to write a report about battlefield medicine during the Civil War. Visit *The American Nation* section of **www.phschool.com** for help in completing the activity.

5 The War Ends

BEFORE YOU READ

Reading Focus

- Why were the Union victories at Vicksburg and Gettysburg important?
- What plan did Grant have for ending the war with the South?
- After his reelection, what hopes did Lincoln have for the Union?
- Why was the Civil War a major turning point in American history?

Key Terms

siege

Battle of Gettysburg

Pickett's Charge

Gettysburg Address

total war

Appomattox Court House

Taking Notes

Copy the flowchart. As you read the section, fill in the boxes with information about the conclusion of the war. Add as many boxes and bullets as you need.

Vicksburg
- Grant makes many attempts to capture
- Grant has brilliant plan
-

Gettysburg
-
-

 Main Idea Under the leadership of General Ulysses S. Grant, Union armies used their resources and manpower to defeat the Confederacy.

Setting the Scene

To General Ulysses S. Grant, every problem had a solution. For example, he needed telegraph lines to coordinate the march of his Union troops into the South. So, he had them strung as his troops advanced. Some of Grant's operators even learned to receive messages without a telegraph station. Touching the ends of the bare wires to their tongues, these resourceful men picked up the faint spark of the Morse Code signals.

In 1864, President Lincoln had appointed Ulysses S. Grant commander in chief of the Union army. "The art of war is simple," Grant said. "Find out where your enemy is, get at him as soon as you can and strike him as hard as you can, and keep moving on." It seemed the President had finally found the general who could lead the Union to victory.

The Fall of Vicksburg

As you have read, Confederate armies won major battles at Fredericksburg in December 1862 and at Chancellorsville in May 1863. These were gloomy days for the North. Then, in July 1863, the tide of war turned against the South as Union forces won major victories in both the East and the West.

In the West, Union triumph came along the Mississippi River. The Union, which had captured New Orleans and Memphis, already controlled both ends of the Mississippi River. Still, the Confederates held Vicksburg, Mississippi. Vicksburg sat on a cliff high above the river.

Early in 1863, Grant's forces tried again and again to seize Vicksburg. The Confederates held out bravely. At last, Grant devised a brilliant plan. Marching his troops inland, he launched a surprise attack on Jackson, Mississippi. Then, he turned west and attacked Vicksburg from the rear. (See the map on page 507.)

AS YOU READ **Civil War soldier on a telegraph pole**

Summarize How was the telegraph used in the war?

For more than six weeks, Grant's forces lay siege to Vicksburg. A **siege** is a military encirclement of an enemy position and blockading or bombarding it in order to force it to surrender. Finally, on July 4, 1863, the Confederates surrendered Vicksburg.

On July 9, Union forces also captured Port Hudson, Louisiana. The entire Mississippi was now under Union control. The Confederacy was split into two parts. Texas, Arkansas, and Louisiana were cut off from the rest of the Confederate states.

Union Victory at Gettysburg

Meanwhile, in the East, after his victory at Chancellorsville, General Lee moved his army north into Pennsylvania. He hoped to take the Yankees by surprise. If he succeeded in Pennsylvania, Lee planned to swing south and capture Washington, D.C.

On June 30, 1863, a Union force under General George C. Meade met part of Lee's army at the small town of Gettysburg, Pennsylvania. Both sides quickly sent in reinforcements. The three-day **Battle of Gettysburg** that followed was one of the most important battles of the Civil War.

On the first day of battle, July 1, the Confederates drove the Union forces out of Gettysburg. The Yankees, however, took up strong positions on Cemetery Ridge, overlooking the town.

The next day, Lee ordered an attack on both ends of the Union line. Southern troops fought hard, but the Union army was well prepared for Lee's offensive. At the end of a day of savage fighting, Lee's forces had suffered heavy casualties but failed to dislodge the Union army from its strong position.

Pickett's Charge Despite his losses, Lee decided to attack again. He wanted to "create a panic and virtually destroy the [Union] army." On July 3, he ordered General George Pickett to lead 15,000 men in a daring charge against the center of the Union line. To reach their target, Pickett's men would have to march 1,000 yards across open ground and climb up a steep slope within clear view of the enemy.

This last attack led by Pickett is known as **Pickett's Charge.** Pickett gave the order to charge. As the men rushed forward, Union guns opened fire. Row after row of soldiers fell to the ground, dead. The battle noise, one soldier recalled, was "strange and terrible, a sound that came from thousands of human throats . . . like a vast mournful roar."

Pickett's Charge failed. The steady barrage of bullets and shells kept all but a few Confederate soldiers from reaching the Union lines. The next day, a Union officer trying to ride over the battlefield could not because "the dead and wounded lay too thick to guide a horse through them."

As the survivors limped back, Lee rode among them. "It's all my fault," he admitted humbly. Lee had no choice but to retreat. After they were defeated at Gettysburg, the Confederates would never invade the North again.

Geography and History

The Vicksburg Campaign

Set on high bluffs overlooking the Mississippi River, Vicksburg was a major strategic target during the Civil War. If Union forces captured Vicksburg, they would control the river and split the Confederacy into two parts. "Vicksburg is the key!" said President Lincoln.

The swamps, rivers, and bluffs around Vicksburg made a direct attack almost impossible. At the same time, Confederate artillery, perched high above the Mississippi, could easily blast Union ships attempting to sail past the city.

In the end, General Grant determined that the only way to subdue Vicksburg was to lay siege to the city. After 48 days of being cut off from all supplies and of constant hammering by cannon fire, the Confederates finally surrendered.

Analyze the effect of geography on the Battle of Vicksburg.

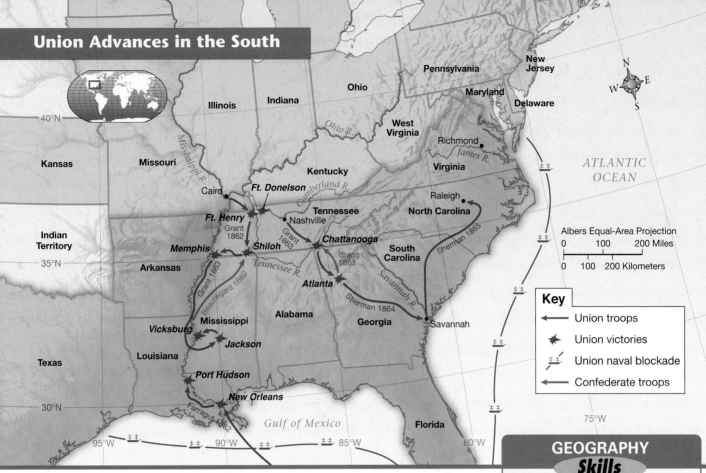

Union Advances in the South

General Meade was proud of the victory. Lincoln, however, was disappointed. He felt that the Union army had once again allowed the Confederate troops to get away.

The Union victories at Vicksburg and Gettysburg marked the turning point of the Civil War. It seemed just a matter of time before the Confederacy would fall. However, the South was still determined to fight. The war would last another two years.

The Gettysburg Address

The Battle of Gettysburg left more than 50,000 dead or wounded. On November 19, 1863, there was a ceremony to dedicate a cemetery to the memory of those soldiers who died in the battle. President Lincoln attended the ceremony. He delivered a speech now known as the Gettysburg Address. Lincoln said that the Civil War was a test of whether or not a democratic nation could survive. He reminded Americans that their nation was founded on the belief that "all men are created equal." Lincoln told the audience:

> 66 We here highly resolve that these dead shall not have died in vain—that this nation, under God, shall have a new birth of freedom—and that government of the people, by the people, for the people, shall not perish from the earth. 99
>
> —Abraham Lincoln, Gettysburg Address, November 19, 1863

GEOGRAPHY Skills

As the Civil War dragged on, Union armies advanced deeper and deeper into the South. General Sherman marched his troops through Georgia and the Carolinas.

1. **Location** On the map, locate **(a)** Vicksburg, **(b)** Atlanta, **(c)** Savannah.

2. **Place** What three Confederate states were cut off from the rest of the Confederacy after Union forces gained control of the Mississippi River?

3. **Critical Thinking Applying Information** Based on the map, why would the South suffer more damage than the North—no matter who won the war?

Lincoln's entire speech was only ten sentences long and took about three minutes to deliver, but it is honored as a profound statement of American ideals.

Grant's Plan for Total War

Since the beginning of the war, Lincoln had searched for a general who could lead the Union to victory. More and more, he thought of Ulysses S. Grant. After capturing Vicksburg, Grant continued to win battles in the West. In 1864, Lincoln appointed him commander of the Union forces.

Some questioned the choice, but President Lincoln felt that "Unconditional Surrender" Grant was the general who would end the war in the Union's favor. "I can't spare this man," Lincoln said. "He fights."

Grant had a plan for ending the war. He wanted to destroy the South's ability to fight. To achieve this, Grant ordered his generals to wage total war against the South. He wanted the Union army to destroy food, equipment, and anything else they found that might be useful to the enemy. In the past, war had been restricted to soldiers. Total war, however, did not make any distinctions. Civilians in the South suffered the same hardships as the army.

Sheridan in the Shenandoah To set his plan in motion, Grant sent General Philip Sheridan and his cavalry into the rich farmland of Virginia's Shenandoah Valley. He instructed Sheridan:

> 66 Leave nothing to invite the enemy to return. Destroy whatever cannot be consumed. Let the valley be left so that crows flying over it will have to carry their rations along with them. 99
> —Ulysses S. Grant, quoted in Bruce Catton, *Grant Takes Command*

Sheridan obeyed. In the summer and fall of 1864, he marched through the valley, destroying farms and livestock. During the campaign, Sheridan's troops burned 2,000 barns filled with grain. There was nothing left for Lee's troops or for southern civilians.

Sherman's March to the Sea Grant also ordered General William Tecumseh Sherman to capture Atlanta, Georgia, and then march to the Atlantic coast. Like Sheridan, Sherman had orders to destroy everything useful to the South.

Sherman's troops captured Atlanta in September 1864. They began their campaign by turning the people of Atlanta out of their homes and burning a large part of the city. Then, Sherman began his "march to the sea."

As they marched through Georgia, Sherman's troops ripped up railroad tracks, built bonfires from the ties, then heated and twisted the rails. They killed livestock and tore up fields. They burned barns, homes, bridges, and factories.

Lincoln Is Reelected

Lincoln ran for reelection in 1864. At first, his defeat seemed, in his own words, "exceedingly probable." Before the capture of Atlanta,

AS YOU READ **Find Main Ideas** As you read, look for specific examples of Grant's strategy for waging total war.

Union chances for victory looked bleak. Lincoln knew that many northerners were unhappy with his handling of the war. He thought that this might cost him the election.

The Democrats nominated General George McClellan to oppose Lincoln. They adopted a resolution demanding the immediate "cessation of hostilities" against the South. Although he had commanded the Union army, McClellan was willing to compromise with the Confederacy. If peace could be achieved, he was ready to restore slavery.

Then, in September, Sherman took Atlanta, and the North rallied around Lincoln. Sheridan's smashing victories in the Shenandoah Valley in October further increased Lincoln's popular support. In the election in November, the vote was close, but Lincoln remained President.

In his second Inaugural Address, Lincoln looked forward to the coming of peace:

66 With malice toward none, with charity for all . . . let us strive . . . to bind up the nation's wounds . . . to do all which may achieve a just and a lasting peace among ourselves and with all nations. 99

—Abraham Lincoln, Second Inaugural Address

The Civil War Ends

Grant had begun a drive to capture Richmond in May 1864. Throughout the spring and summer, he and Lee fought a series of costly battles.

Northerners read with horror that 60,000 men were killed or wounded in a single month at the battles of the Wilderness, Spotsylvania, and Cold Harbor. Still, Grant pressed on. He knew that the Union could replace men and supplies. The South could not.

Lee dug in at Petersburg, near Richmond. Here, Grant kept Lee under siege for nine months. At last, with a fresh supply of troops, Grant took Petersburg on April 2, 1865. The same day, Richmond fell.

Lee and his army withdrew to a small Virginia town called Appomattox Court House. There, a week later, they were trapped by Union troops. Lee knew that his men would be slaughtered if he kept fighting. On April 9, 1865, Lee surrendered.

At Appomattox Court House, Grant offered generous terms of surrender to the defeated Confederate army. Soldiers were required to turn over their rifles, but officers were allowed to keep their pistols. Soldiers who had horses could keep them. Grant knew that southerners would need the animals for spring plowing. Finally, ordered Grant, "each officer and man will be allowed to return to his home, not to be disturbed by the United States authorities."

The Final Battles

Key

← Union troops

✶ Union victories

← Confederate troops

✶ Confederate victories

Albers Equal-Area Projection

0   25   50 Miles

0   25   50 Kilometers

GEOGRAPHY Skills

The final battles of the Civil War pitted Grant against Lee in Virginia. Finally, on April 9, 1865, Lee surrendered at Appomattox Court House.

1. **Location** On the map, locate (a) Richmond, (b) Petersburg, (c) Appomattox Court House.

2. **Place** Where did Grant lay siege to Lee's forces for nine months?

3. **Critical Thinking Applying Information** Which battle took place first: Cold Harbor or Spotsylvania? Explain.

As the Confederates surrendered, Union soldiers began to cheer. Grant ordered them to be silent. "The war is over," he said. "The rebels are our countrymen again."

A Turning Point in American History

The toll of the Civil War was immense. More than 360,000 Union soldiers and 250,000 Confederate soldiers lost their lives. No war has ever resulted in more American deaths. In dollars, the war's cost was about 20 billion. That was more than 11 times the entire amount spent by the federal government between 1789 and 1861!

The Civil War was a major turning point in American history. The balance of power was changed. The Democratic party lost its influence and the Republicans were in a commanding position. No longer would Americans speak of the nation as a confederation of states. Before the war, Americans referred to "*these* United States." After, they began speaking of "*the* United States." The idea that each state might secede, if it chose, was dead. As a result, the power of the federal government grew.

The war also put an end to slavery in the United States. For years, Americans had debated whether slavery could exist in a nation dedicated to the ideals of liberty and equality. By the war's end, millions of African Americans had gained their freedom. Millions more Americans, both North and South, began to think about what it meant to be free and equal.

To be sure, a long and difficult struggle for equality lay ahead. Yet, Lincoln's words at Gettysburg were prophetic: "We here highly resolve . . . that this nation, under God, shall have a new birth of freedom." From out of a cruel, bitter, often heart-rending war, the United States did indeed emerge a stronger, freer nation.

Section 5 Assessment

Recall

1. **Identify** Explain the significance of **(a)** Battle of Gettysburg, **(b)** Pickett's Charge, **(c)** Gettysburg Address, **(d)** Ulysses S. Grant, **(e)** William Tecumseh Sherman, **(f)** Appomattox Court House.
2. **Define** **(a)** siege, **(b)** total war.

Comprehension

3. Which Union victories were a turning point?
4. What was Grant's plan for ending the war?
5. What ideals did Lincoln express in the Gettysburg Address and his Second Inaugural Address?
6. How did the Civil War change the United States?

Critical Thinking and Writing

7. **Exploring the Main Idea** Review the Main Idea statement at the beginning of this section. Then, make a list of the major events of the years 1863–1865 of the Civil War. Indicate the importance of each.

8. **Supporting a Point of View** Some people believe that Grant's decision to wage total war on the South was wrong because it caused great suffering among civilians. Do you agree or disagree? Explain.

ACTIVITY

Writing a Speech
Suppose that you are President of the United States at the end of the Civil War. Write a speech summarizing the important events of the war and explaining what you believe the Union victory accomplished.

Analyzing Photographs

When the Civil War began, photography was just beginning. Pioneer photographers shouldered their bulky cameras and followed armies into battle. The result was the first detailed photographic record of a war.

These Civil War photographs, like all photographs, are valuable primary source documents. Just as with other primary sources, however, we must learn to evaluate them for accuracy and bias.

In this photograph, a family gathers at a Union Army camp in 1862.

Learn the Skill *To analyze a photograph, use the following steps:*

1. **Identify the subject.** What does the photograph show?

2. **Look for details.** What evidence does the photograph include about people, daily life, the weather, events, or the environment?

3. **Analyze the photographer's intent.** Why did the photographer take this picture? How did the photographer feel about the subject?

4. **Draw conclusions.** What can you learn from this photograph? How does it add to your understanding of history?

Practice the Skill *Answer the following questions about the photograph above:*

1. **(a)** Who are the people in the photograph? **(b)** Where are they?

2. **(a)** What tools, utensils, and furniture do you see? **(b)** Where are the people living? **(c)** What other details do you see?

3. **(a)** Why do you think the photographer took this picture? **(b)** How do you think the photographer felt about families and war?

4. What did you learn from this photograph?

Apply the Skill *See the Chapter Review and Assessment.*

CREATING A CHAPTER SUMMARY

Copy the timeline below. As you read, add information about the events and issues of the Civil War. Add as many entries as you need.

BATTLE OF BULL RUN
North and South realize war will be long and hard

1861   1862   1865

For additional review and enrichment activities, see the interactive version of *The American Nation,* available on the Web and on CD-ROM.

Take It to the NET

Chapter Self-Test For practice test questions for Chapter 17, visit *The American Nation* section of **www.phschool.com**.

Building Vocabulary

Review the meaning of the vocabulary words listed below. Then, write a sentence for each word in which you define the word and describe its relationship to the Civil War.

1. border state
2. martial law
3. emancipate
4. draft
5. habeas corpus
6. inflation
7. profiteer
8. total war

Reviewing Key Facts

9. Why did each side go to war? (Section 1)
10. Why was President Lincoln unhappy with General McClellan? (Section 2)
11. (a) What did the Emancipation Proclamation provide? (b) How did it change the nature of the war? (Section 3)
12. (a) Why did some northerners object to the draft law? (b) What was the response to the draft law in the South? (Section 4)
13. How did the Union wage total war on the South in 1864 and 1865? (Section 5)

Critical Thinking and Writing

14. **Making Generalizations** Make a generalization about the strengths and weaknesses of the North and South at the start of the war. List three facts to support your generalization.
15. **Summarizing** Write one or two sentences summarizing Lincoln's attitudes toward slavery and the war.
16. **Making Comparisons** How did the North's General Grant and the South's General Lee compare as military leaders?
17. **Connecting to Geography: Movement** Describe the effects of the Union blockade of southern ports.
18. **Synthesizing Information** Review the excerpt from Lincoln's Second Inaugural Address on page 509. How did Grant's treatment of the defeated Confederate army at Appomattox Court House reflect the ideas in the Inaugural Address?

The Union blockade caused great difficulty for southern families. Dr. Paul Barringer recalls how his family managed. Read the excerpt, then answer the questions that follow:

66 Almost at once we began to feel the pinch of war. White sugar disappeared immediately; not only were there no more lumps for gun-shy horses, but there was no sugar for the table. There was, however, an unlimited quantity of sorghum syrup, and around the barrels of sorghum, a thick crust of brown sugar often formed. This was carefully scraped off to be served with coffee and berries, the fluid product going to the slaves. 99

—Dr. Paul B. Barringer, *The Natural Bent: The Memories of Dr. Paul Barringer*

19. According to Barringer, how soon were southerners affected by the blockade?
20. How was sugar used?
21. What substitute was used for sugar?
22. How did southerners meet the challenges posed by the blockade?

Mathew Brady took this picture of Abraham Lincoln and his son, Tad, in 1864. Look at the picture. Then, answer the questions that follow.

23. What details are emphasized in the photograph?
   A Lincoln's position in the chair.
   B His son's lack of interest in the book.
   C The concentration of Lincoln and his son.
   D Tad's hand resting on his father's chair.
24. What can you learn about Lincoln from this photograph?

ACTIVITIES

Connecting With . . . Economics

Making a Chart You are the graphic illustrator for an economics magazine. Create a flowchart to illustrate how the high cost of the Civil War led to inflation.

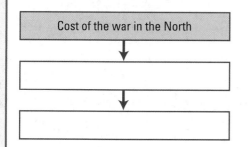

Cost of the war in the North

Take It to the NET

Connecting to Today

Planning a TV Documentary The Civil War ended slavery for African Americans. Use the Internet to find out how African Americans fight for equality today. Choose a leader in the civil rights movement. Use what you learn to write an outline for a TV documentary on the person of your choice. For help in starting this activity, visit *The American Nation* section of **www.phschool.com**.

Researching Civil War Photos

Creating a Photo Essay Photographers like Mathew Brady took thousands of pictures documenting the Civil War. Use the Internet to find photographs taken of the war. Then, download selected pictures to create a photo essay of the war. Write a caption for each photograph that you include. For help in starting this activity, visit *The American Nation* section of **www.phschool.com**.

Reconstruction and the Changing South

1863–1896

1 **Early Steps to Reunion**
2 **Radical Reconstruction**
3 **The South Under Reconstruction**
4 **The End of Reconstruction**

Reward poster (left) and chair in which Lincoln was shot (right)

Thaddeus Stevens

1865

Lincoln is assassinated five days after the war ends. As the nation mourns, the issue of readmitting southern states remains unresolved.

1863

President Abraham Lincoln proposes a mild Reconstruction plan for readmitting southern states after the Civil War.

1867

Radical Reconstruction begins. Republican leaders in Congress like Thaddeus Stevens call for harsh measures against the South.

AMERICAN EVENTS

Presidential Terms:	Abraham Lincoln 1861–1865	Andrew Johnson 1865–1869	Ulysses S. Grant 1869–1877

1860 · · · · · · **1865** · · · · · · **1870**

WORLD EVENTS

1867 ▲
The Dominion of Canada is formed.

1870 ▲
Italy becomes a unified nation.

The South After the Civil War

One by one, southern states rejoined the Union after the Civil War.

MEXICO

ATLANTIC OCEAN

Gulf of Mexico

CUBA (Sp.)

Albers Equal-Area Projection

0   200   400 Miles

0   200   400 Kilometers

Key

Former Confederate states

(1868) Date of readmission to the Union

States labeled on map:
- Virginia (1870)
- North Carolina (1868)
- Tennessee (1866)
- SC (1868)
- Georgia (1870)
- Alabama (1868)
- MS (1870)
- LA (1868)
- Arkansas (1868)
- Texas (1870)
- FL (1868)

Hayes campaign poster

1870
Voting during Reconstruction

The Fifteenth Amendment is ratified. It forbids states to deny citizens the right to vote because of race.

1876
Rutherford B. Hayes runs against Samuel Tilden in a disputed election. In time, Hayes becomes President and ends Reconstruction.

James A. Garfield	1881
Chester A. Arthur	1881–1885
Grover Cleveland	1885–1889
Benjamin Harrison	1889–1893
Grover Cleveland	1893–1897
William McKinley	1897–1901

Rutherford B. Hayes 1877–1881

1896
In *Plessy* v. *Ferguson*, the Supreme Court rules that it is legal for a state to create separate facilities for blacks and whites.

1870 — 1875 — 1900

1873 ▲
Slave markets are abolished in Zanzibar.

▲ **1876**
Porfirio Díaz becomes the leader of Mexico.

1 Early Steps to Reunion

BEFORE YOU READ

Reading Focus

- Why were postwar problems more severe in the South than in the North?
- What early steps were taken toward reconstruction?
- How did the assassination of Lincoln and the inauguration of a new President lead to conflict?

Key Terms

freedmen

Reconstruction

Ten Percent Plan

amnesty

Wade-Davis Bill

Freedmen's Bureau

Thirteenth Amendment

Taking Notes

Copy this flowchart. As you read, fill in the boxes with information about the early years of Reconstruction. Two boxes have been completed to help you get started. Add as many boxes as you need.

1863
- Lincoln proposes Ten Percent Plan

↓

↓

1865
- Civil War ends
-

↓

Main Idea After the Civil War, the country had to repair the damage done by the fighting and find a way to rebuild.

AS YOU READ
Ruined plantation house

Use Prior Knowledge Why were many southern plantations in the condition described in the quotation by Smedes?

Setting the Scene At the end of the Civil War, the future looked bleak to many southerners. Susan Dabney Smedes described the scene facing her father, once a wealthy planter:

> 66 My father had come home to a house stripped of nearly every article of furniture and to a plantation stripped of the means of cultivating . . . it. A few mules and one cow were all that were left of the stock. 99
> —Susan Dabney Smedes, *Memorials of a Southern Planter*

Across the South, cities and farms lay in ruins. All southerners, black or white, faced an unfamiliar new world. At the same time, a shattered nation had to find a way to become whole again.

Postwar Problems

After four years of war, both northerners and southerners had to adjust to a changed world. The adjustment was far more difficult in the South.

The Victorious North Despite their victory, northerners faced a number of economic problems. Some 800,000 returning Union soldiers needed jobs. The government was canceling its war orders, and factories were laying off workers. Still, the North's economic disruption was only temporary. Boom times quickly returned.

The North lost more soldiers in the war than the South did. However, only a few battles had taken place on northern soil. Northern farms and cities were hardly touched. One returning Union soldier remarked, "It seemed . . . as if I had been away only a day or two, and had just taken up . . . where I had left off."

The Defeated South Confederate soldiers had little chance of taking up where they had left off. In some areas, every house, barn, and bridge had been destroyed. Two thirds of the South's railroad tracks had been turned into twisted heaps of scrap. The cities of

Columbia, Richmond, and Atlanta had been leveled.

The war wrecked the South's financial system. After the war, Confederate money was worthless. People who had loaned money to the Confederacy were never repaid. Many southern banks closed, and depositors lost their savings.

The war changed southern society forever. Almost overnight, there was a new class of nearly four million people known as freedmen—men and women who had been slaves. Under slavery, they had been forbidden to own property and to learn to read and write. What would become of them? How could the South cope with this sudden, drastic change?

Early Steps Toward Reconstruction

President Lincoln was worried about Reconstruction, or the rebuilding of the South. He wanted to make it fairly easy for southerners to rejoin the Union. The sooner the nation was reunited, Lincoln believed, the faster the South would be able to rebuild.

Lincoln's Reconstruction Plan As early as 1863, Lincoln outlined his Ten Percent Plan for Reconstruction. Under this plan, a southern state could form a new government after 10 percent of its voters swore an oath of loyalty to the United States. The new government had to abolish slavery. Voters could then elect members of Congress and take part in the national government once again.

Lincoln's plan also offered amnesty, or a government pardon, to Confederates who swore loyalty to the Union. Amnesty would not apply to the former leaders of the Confederacy, however.

A Rival Proposal Many Republicans in Congress felt that the Ten Percent Plan was too generous toward the South. In 1864, they passed the Wade-Davis Bill, a rival plan for Reconstruction. It required a majority of white men in each southern state to swear loyalty to the Union. It also denied the right to vote or hold office to anyone who had volunteered to fight for the Confederacy. Lincoln refused to sign the Wade-Davis Bill because he felt it was too harsh.

The Freedmen's Bureau Congress and the President did agree on one proposal. One month before Lee surrendered, Congress passed a bill creating the Freedmen's Bureau, a government agency to help former slaves. Lincoln signed the bill.

The Freedmen's Bureau gave food and clothing to former slaves. It also tried to find jobs for freedmen. The bureau helped poor whites as well. It provided medical care for more than one million people.

Viewing History

Richmond in Ruins After the Civil War, some of the South's most important cities lay in ruins. This picture shows the devastation in Richmond, Virginia. **Drawing Conclusions** *What effect do you think this kind of devastation had on southerners?*

Ford's Theatre

On April 14, 1865, John Wilkes Booth crept into Abraham Lincoln's box at Ford's Theatre. As the President watched the comedy Our American Cousin, *Booth shot him. Today, park rangers at the restored theatre recount the story of the tragic assassination. You can visit a museum devoted to Lincoln's death—and even attend a play.*

Take It to the NET

Virtual Field Trip For an interactive look at Ford's Theatre, visit *The American Nation* section of **www.phschool.com**.

Washington, D.C.

AS YOU READ **Find Main Ideas** As you read, identify the major goals and accomplishments of the Freedmen's Bureau.

One of the bureau's most important tasks was to set up schools for freedmen. Most of the teachers were volunteers, often women, from the North. Grandparents and grandchildren sat side by side in the classroom. Charlotte Forten, an African American volunteer from Philadelphia, wrote:

> 66 It is wonderful how a people who have been so long crushed to the earth . . . can have so great a desire for knowledge, and such a capacity for attaining it. 99
> —Charlotte Forten, article in the *Atlantic Monthly*

The Freedmen's Bureau laid the foundation for the South's public school system. It also created colleges for African Americans, including Howard, Morehouse, and Fisk. Many of the graduates of these schools became teachers themselves. By the 1870s, African Americans were teaching in grade schools throughout the South.

Lincoln Is Assassinated

President Lincoln hoped to persuade Congress to accept his Reconstruction plan. However, he never got the chance.

On April 14, 1865, just five days after Lee's surrender, the President attended a play at Ford's Theatre in Washington, D.C. A popular actor from the South, John Wilkes Booth, crept into the President's box and shot Lincoln in the head. Lincoln died the next morning. Booth was later caught and killed in a barn outside the city.

The nation was plunged into grief. Millions who had been celebrating the war's end now mourned Lincoln's death. "Now he belongs to the ages," commented Secretary of War Edwin Stanton.

The New President

Vice President Andrew Johnson was now President. Johnson had represented Tennessee in Congress. When his state seceded, Johnson had remained loyal to the Union.

Johnson's Plan Republicans in Congress believed Johnson would support a strict Reconstruction plan. But his plan was much milder than expected. It called for a majority of voters in each southern state to pledge loyalty to the United States. Each state also had to ratify the Thirteenth Amendment, which Congress had approved in January 1865. It banned slavery throughout the nation. (As you read, the Emancipation Proclamation did not free slaves in states loyal to the Union.)

Congress Rebels The southern states quickly met Johnson's conditions. As a result, the President approved their new state governments in late 1865. Voters in the South then elected representatives to Congress. Many of those elected had held office in the Confederacy. For example, Alexander Stephens, the former vice president of the Confederacy, was elected senator from Georgia.

Republicans in Congress were outraged. The men who had led the South out of the Union were being elected to the House and Senate. Also, no southern state allowed African Americans to vote.

When the new Congress met, Republicans refused to let southern representatives take their seats. Instead, they set up a Joint Committee on Reconstruction to form a new plan for the South. The stage was set for a showdown between Congress and the President.

Section 1 Assessment

Recall

1. **Identify** Explain the significance of **(a)** Reconstruction, **(b)** Ten Percent Plan, **(c)** Wade-Davis Bill, **(d)** Freedmen's Bureau, **(e)** John Wilkes Booth, **(f)** Andrew Johnson, **(g)** Thirteenth Amendment.
2. **Define** **(a)** freedmen, **(b)** amnesty.

Comprehension

3. Describe two problems faced by the South after the Civil War.
4. What early Reconstruction measure did Lincoln and Congress agree upon?

5. Why did Republicans in Congress oppose Johnson's Reconstruction plan?

Critical Thinking and Writing

6. **Exploring the Main Idea** Review the Main Idea statement at the beginning of this section. Then, write a letter to President Lincoln supporting or opposing his Reconstruction plan.
7. **Drawing Inferences** One teacher said that freedmen "will starve themselves in order to send their children to school." Write a paragraph explaining why you think education meant so much to the freedmen.

Solving Problems

Learning how to solve problems is an important skill for both citizens and government leaders. Just as the solutions to problems of the past affect the present, the solutions you choose today will have consequences in the future.

African American writer W.E.B. DuBois described some of the problems faced by the Freedmen's Bureau:

> **"**Here, at a stroke of the pen, was erected a government of millions of men,—and not ordinary men, either, but black men [weakened] by a peculiarly complete system of slavery, centuries old; and now, suddenly, violently, they come into a new birthright, at a time of war and passion, in the midst of the stricken, embittered population of their former masters. Any man might well have hesitated to assume charge of such a work, with vast responsibilities, indefinite powers, and limited resources . . . for Congress had appropriated no money for salaries and expenses.**"**
>
> —W.E.B. DuBois, "The Freedmen's Bureau"

As it set up new schools throughout the South, the Freedmen's Bureau faced the problem of finding enough teachers for so many eager new students.

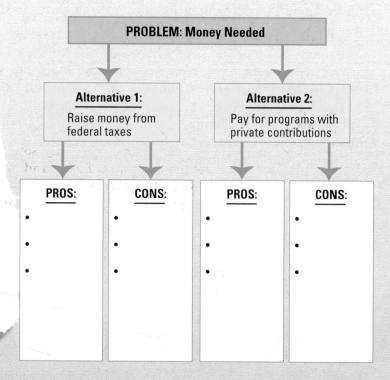

Learn the Skill *To learn problem-solving skills, use the following steps:*

1. **Identify the problem.** State the problem you want to solve as simply and completely as possible.

2. **List possible solutions.** There is usually more than one way to solve a problem. Identify your alternatives.

3. **Review the alternatives.** What resources would be needed to implement the solution? What would the consequences be?

4. **Choose a course of action.** Decide how you will resolve the problem.

Practice the Skill *Use the information above to answer the following questions:*

1. According to DuBois what was one problem that the Freedmen's Bureau faced?

2. **(a)** What two alternatives are shown on the chart? **(b)** Can you think of a third alternative? Explain.

3. **(a)** What might be some of the pros and cons of Alternative 1? **(b)** What might be some of the pros and cons of Alternative 2?

4. What solution to the problem would you have favored? Why?

Apply the Skill *See the Chapter Review and Assessment.*

2 Radical Reconstruction

BEFORE YOU READ

Reading Focus

- How did Congress react to the passage of black codes in the South?
- How did Radical Republicans gain power in Congress?
- Why was President Johnson impeached?

Key Terms

black codes

Radical Republican

Fourteenth Amendment

Radical Reconstruction

Reconstruction Act

impeach

Fifteenth Amendment

Taking Notes

Copy the chart below. As you read, complete the chart to show some of the effects of the rise of Radical Republicans in Congress. Add as many boxes as you need.

RISE OF RADICAL REPUBLICANS

Congress passes Fourteenth Amendment

Main Idea Angered by the South's response to President Johnson's Reconstruction program, Republicans in Congress put in place a harsher plan.

Setting the Scene In New Orleans, Confederate flags were being sold in the streets. In Mississippi, the governor refused to fly the American flag over the state capitol. Many southerners were singing, "I'm a good old rebel, that's what I am / And I don't want no pardon for anything I done." Hearing such reports in 1866, Republicans decided to take harsh measures against the South.

Black Codes Anger Congress

After the war, most southern states promptly ratified the Thirteenth Amendment. However, southern legislatures also passed black codes, laws that severely limited the rights of freedmen.

Rights and Restrictions The black codes did grant some rights. For example, African Americans could marry legally and own some kinds of property. Still, the codes were clearly meant to keep freedmen from gaining political or economic power.

Black codes forbade freedmen to vote, own guns, or serve on juries. In some states, African Americans were permitted to work only as servants or farm laborers. In others, they had to sign contracts for a year's work. Those without contracts could be arrested and sentenced to work on a plantation.

Congress Reacts Republicans charged that Johnson's lenient Reconstruction plan had encouraged southern legislatures to pass the black codes. Republicans were also outraged by reports of violence against freedmen. In 1866, angry whites burned homes, churches, and schoolhouses in a black section of Memphis, Tennessee. More than 40 African Americans were killed. Similar riots broke out in New Orleans when freedmen met to support the right to vote.

A report by the Joint Committee on Reconstruction accused the South of trying to "preserve slavery . . . as long as possible." When

AS YOU READ
Confederate flag
Draw Inferences What do these incidents suggest about the mood of many southerners at this time?

Rival Plans for Reconstruction

Plan	Ten Percent Plan	Wade-Davis Bill	Johnson Plan	Reconstruction Act
Proposed by	President Abraham Lincoln (1863)	Republicans in Congress (1864)	President Andrew Johnson (1865)	Radical Republicans (1867)
Conditions for Former Confederate States to Rejoin Union	• 10 percent of voters must swear loyalty to Union • Must abolish slavery	• Majority of white men must swear loyalty • Former Confederate volunteers cannot vote or hold office	• Majority of white men must swear loyalty • Must ratify Thirteenth Amendment • Former Confederate officials may vote and hold office	• Must disband state governments • Must write new constitutions • Must ratify Fourteenth Amendment • African American men must be allowed to vote

GRAPHIC ORGANIZER
Skills

In the early years of Reconstruction, federal leaders debated several plans for readmitting southern states to the Union.

1. **Comprehension** (a) Identify one similarity between the Wade-Davis Bill and President Johnson's plan. (b) Identify one difference.

2. **Critical Thinking** **Evaluating Information** Which of the plans shown here seems to be the harshest toward the South? Explain.

Civics

President Johnson ignored the report, members of Congress called Radical Republicans vowed to take control of Reconstruction.

Rise of the Radicals

The Radicals were led by Thaddeus Stevens of Pennsylvania in the House and Charles Sumner of Massachusetts in the Senate. Radical Republicans had two main goals. First, they wanted to break the power of wealthy planters who had long ruled the South. Second, they wanted to ensure that freedmen received the right to vote.

Republican Control Radicals needed the support of moderate Republicans, the largest group in Congress. Moderates and Radicals disagreed on many issues, but they shared a strong political motive. Most southerners were Democrats. With southerners barred from Congress, Republicans could control both houses.

To combat the black codes, Congress passed the Civil Rights Act in April 1866. It gave citizenship to African Americans. When Johnson vetoed the bill, Congress overrode the veto.

Fourteenth Amendment Republicans feared that the Supreme Court might use its power of judicial review to declare the Civil Rights Act unconstitutional. In the Dred Scott decision of 1857, the Court had ruled that African Americans were not citizens.

To avoid a similar ruling, Republicans proposed the Fourteenth Amendment. It defined citizens as "all persons born or naturalized in the United States." (The amendment did not apply to most Native Americans.) It guaranteed citizens "equal protection of the laws" and forbade states to "deprive any person of life, liberty, or property without due process of law." Thus, states could not legally discriminate against a citizen on unreasonable grounds, such as race.

Under the Fourteenth Amendment, any state that denied any male citizen age 21 or older the right to vote would have its representation in Congress reduced. Republicans believed that freedmen would be able to defend their rights if they could vote.

Republicans hoped the amendment would secure basic political rights for African Americans in the South. That goal would take a century to achieve. In the 1950s, the Fourteenth Amendment became a powerful tool in the struggle for citizenship rights.

AS YOU READ **Summarize** Explain why the Fourteenth Amendment was a powerful tool in the struggle for citizenship rights.

Radicals in Power

President Johnson encouraged former Confederate states to reject the Fourteenth Amendment. He also decided to make the amendment an issue in the 1866 congressional elections.

Election of 1866 Across the North, Johnson urged voters to reject the Radicals. When a heckler yelled for Johnson to hang Jefferson Davis, Johnson shouted, "Why not hang Thad Stevens?" Many northerners criticized the President for losing his temper.

In July, white mobs in New Orleans killed 34 African Americans. The violence convinced many northerners that stronger measures were needed. In the end, the elections were a disaster for Johnson. Republicans won majorities in both houses of Congress.

The Radical Program In 1867, Republicans in Congress prepared to take charge of Reconstruction. With huge majorities in both houses, Congress could easily override a veto. The period that followed is often called Radical Reconstruction.

Congress passed the first Reconstruction Act in March 1867. It threw out the state governments that had refused to ratify the Fourteenth Amendment—all the former Confederate states except Tennessee. The act also divided the South into five military districts. Army commanders were given broad powers to enforce Reconstruction. Many southerners bitterly resented the imposition of military rule.

To rejoin the Union, former Confederate states had to write new constitutions and ratify the Fourteenth Amendment. The Reconstruction Act also required that southern states allow African Americans to vote.

With the new constitutions in place, reconstructed states held elections to set up new state governments. Former Confederate officials were barred from voting. Many other white southerners stayed away from the polls in protest. Protected by the army, freedmen proudly exercised their new right to vote. As a result, Republicans gained control of all of the new southern state governments.

Impeachment and a New President

Congress passed other Reconstruction acts over Johnson's veto. As President, Johnson had a duty to execute the new laws. However, Johnson did what he could to limit their effect. He fired several military commanders who supported Radical Reconstruction. Republicans in Congress decided to remove Johnson from office.

Trial On February 24, 1868, the House of Representatives voted to impeach, or bring formal charges against, Johnson. According to the Constitution, the House may impeach a President for "treason,

Primary Source

The Impeachment of Andrew Johnson

At the impeachment trial of President Johnson, Senator James Grimes of Iowa voted against conviction. Here, he explains why:
"Nor can I suffer my judgment of the law governing this case to be influenced by political considerations. I cannot agree to destroy the harmonious working of the Constitution for the sake of getting rid of an unacceptable President. Whatever may be my opinion of [Johnson], I cannot consent to trifle with the high office he holds. I can do nothing which, by implication, may be [seen as] an approval of impeachment as a part of future political machinery."

—James Grimes, quoted in *Trial of Andrew Johnson* (Poore)

Analyzing Primary Sources

Write a sentence summarizing the main reason that Grimes voted against the removal of President Johnson.

bribery, or other high crimes and misdemeanors." The President is removed from office if found guilty by two thirds of the Senate.

During Johnson's trial, it became clear that he was not guilty of high crimes and misdemeanors. Even Charles Sumner, Johnson's bitter foe, admitted that the charges were "political in character."

Despite intense pressure, seven Republican senators refused to vote for conviction. The Constitution, they said, did not allow Congress to remove a President just because they disagreed with him. In the end, the vote was 35 to 19—one vote shy of the two thirds needed to convict.

AS YOU READ **Use Prior Knowledge** Review what you have learned about Ulysses S. Grant. Why would Republicans find him an attractive candidate?

A New President Johnson served out the few remaining months of his term. In 1868, Republicans nominated the Union's greatest war hero, Ulysses S. Grant, for President.

By election day, most southern states had rejoined the Union. As Congress demanded, the southern governments allowed African American men to vote. About 500,000 blacks voted—nearly all of them for Grant. He easily won the election.

Fifteenth Amendment In 1869, Congress proposed the Fifteenth Amendment. It forbade any state to deny any citizen the right to vote because of "race, color, or previous condition of servitude."

Republicans had moral and political reasons for supporting the Fifteenth Amendment. They remembered the great sacrifices made by African American soldiers in the Civil War. They also felt it was wrong to let African Americans vote in the South but not in the North. In addition, Republicans knew that if African Americans could vote in the North, they would help Republicans win elections there.

The Fifteenth Amendment was ratified in 1870. At last, all African American men over age 21 had the right to vote.

  AFTER YOU READ

 Section 2 Assessment

Recall

1. **Identify** Explain the significance of (a) Radical Republicans, (b) Thaddeus Stevens, (c) Charles Sumner, (d) Fourteenth Amendment, (e) Radical Reconstruction, (f) Reconstruction Act, (g) Fifteenth Amendment.
2. **Define** (a) black codes, (b) impeach.

Comprehension

3. Why did the black codes anger Republicans in Congress?
4. How did Radical Republicans win control of Congress?

5. Why did Congress impeach President Johnson?

Critical Thinking and Writing

6. **Exploring the Main Idea** Review the Main Idea statement at the beginning of this section. Then, write two sentences evaluating the Reconstruction Act— one from Andrew Johnson's viewpoint, the other from a Radical Republican's viewpoint.
7. **Supporting a Point of View** Write a note from one member of Congress to another explaining why you think the Fourteenth or Fifteenth Amendment is necessary.

ACTIVITY

Drawing a Political Cartoon Draw a political cartoon that might have appeared during the congressional elections of 1866. Your cartoon should express a point of view about the conflict between Radical Republicans and the President over control of Reconstruction.

The Power of the Fourteenth Amendment

The Fourteenth Amendment was originally intended to grant citizenship to former slaves and to ensure their rights. As society changed, the Court's interpretation of the Fourteenth Amendment changed as well.

> "...No State shall make or enforce any law which shall abridge the privileges or immunities of citizens of the United States; nor shall any State deprive any person of life, liberty, or property, without due process of law; nor deny to any person within its jurisdiction the equal protection of the laws."
>
> —Fourteenth Amendment

1905

Lochner v. New York

The Supreme Court strikes down a law regulating working hours. The Court rules that **equal protection** means that employers have the right to make contracts with workers freely. This ruling is later reversed.

1954

Brown v. Board of Education of Topeka

The Supreme Court rules that having separate schools for white and black students discriminates against African Americans and is a violation of **equal protection.** The ruling ends school segregation and becomes a landmark in the fight for equal rights.

1963

Gideon v. Wainwright

The Supreme Court rules that **due process** means that all people accused of a crime have the right to an attorney. If a person cannot afford an attorney, the state must provide one for her or him.

1971

Reed v. Reed

The Supreme Court strikes down an Idaho law giving men automatic preference over women in certain situations. The Court rules that **equal protection** means that men and women must be treated equally before the law.

ACTIVITY

The Fourteenth Amendment has affected every citizen's life in some way. List two ways in which your life has been or might be affected by the Fourteenth Amendment.

3 The South Under Reconstruction

BEFORE YOU READ

Reading Focus

- What groups of people made up the new forces in southern politics?
- How did southern Conservatives resist Reconstruction?
- What challenges did Reconstruction governments face?
- How did many southerners become locked into a cycle of poverty?

Key Terms

scalawag

carpetbagger

Conservatives

Ku Klux Klan

sharecropper

Taking Notes

As you read, prepare an outline of this section. Use roman numerals to indicate the major headings, capital letters for the subheadings, and numbers for the supporting details. The sample at right will help you get started.

> I. New Forces in Southern Politics
>   A. White southern Republicans
>   1. Opposed secession
>   2.
>   B. Northerners
>   1.
>   2.
>   C.
> II. Conservatives Resist
>   A.
>   B.

Main Idea Reconstruction governments tried to rebuild the South despite sometimes fierce opposition.

AS YOU READ Meeting of a southern legislature

Visualize Picture the scene as freedmen crowded in to watch the debate. How would you describe the mood?

Setting the Scene

White superintendents in Virginia's tobacco factories were puzzled. Suddenly, many of their black workers were absent from their jobs. White households experienced the same problem. With their servants missing, they were forced "to cook their own dinners or content themselves with a cold lunch."

What was going on? In 1867, as southern states began writing new constitutions, African American delegates took an active part. On days when important issues were debated, freedmen from all around flocked to watch. In Alabama, a political convention of freedmen declared, "We claim exactly the same rights, privileges and immunities as are enjoyed by white men."

Before the Civil War, a small group of rich planters had dominated southern politics. During Reconstruction, however, new groups tried to reshape southern politics.

New Forces in Southern Politics

The state governments created during Radical Reconstruction were different from any governments the South had known before. The old leaders had lost much of their influence. Three groups stepped in to replace them.

White Southern Republicans Some white southerners supported the new Republican governments. Many were businesspeople who had opposed secession in 1860. They wanted to forget the war and get on with rebuilding the South.

Many whites in the South felt that any southerner who helped the Republicans was a traitor. They called the white southern Republicans **scalawags,** a word used for small, scruffy horses.

Northerners Northerners who came to the South after the war were another important force. White southerners accused the new arrivals of hoping to get rich from the South's misery. Southerners claimed that these northerners were in such a hurry they had time only to fling a few clothes into cheap suitcases, or carpetbags. As a result, they became known as carpetbaggers.

In fact, northerners went south for various reasons. A few did hope to profit as the South was being rebuilt. Many more, however, were Union soldiers who had grown to love the South's rich land. Others, both white and black, were teachers, ministers, and reformers who sincerely wanted to help the freedmen.

African Americans African Americans were the third major new group in southern politics. Before the war, they had no voice in southern government. During Reconstruction, they not only voted in large numbers, but they also ran for and were elected to public office in the South. African Americans became sheriffs, mayors, and legislators in the new state and local governments. Sixteen African Americans were elected to Congress between 1869 and 1880.

Two African Americans, both representing Mississippi, served in the Senate. Hiram Revels, a clergyman and teacher, became the nation's first black senator in 1870. He completed the unfinished term of former Confederate president Jefferson Davis. In 1874, Blanche K. Bruce became the first African American to serve a full term in the Senate.

Freedmen had less political influence than many whites claimed, however. Only in South Carolina did African Americans win a majority in one house of the state legislature. No state elected a black governor.

Conservatives Resist

Most white southerners who had held power before the Civil War resisted Reconstruction. These Conservatives resented the changes imposed by Congress and enforced by the military. They wanted the South to change as little as possible. Conservatives were willing to let African Americans vote and hold a few offices. Still, they were determined that real power would remain in the hands of whites.

A few wealthy planters tried to force African Americans back onto plantations. Many small farmers and laborers wanted the government to take action against freedmen, who now competed with them for land and power.

Most of these white southerners were Democrats. They declared war on anyone who cooperated with the Republicans. "This is a white man's country," declared one southern senator, "and white men must govern it."

Spreading Terror Some white southerners formed secret societies to help them regain power. The most dangerous was the Ku Klux Klan, or KKK. The Klan worked to keep African Americans and white Republicans out of office.

Dressed in white robes and hoods to hide their identities, Klansmen rode at night to the homes of African American voters, shouting threats and burning wooden crosses. When threats did not work, the Klan turned to violence. Klan members murdered hundreds of African Americans and their white allies.

An American Profile

Hiram Revels 1822–1901

Hiram Revels was born to free parents in North Carolina. Yet, he had to learn to read in secret because the law banned education for free blacks as well as slaves. Moving north, he became a minister and educator with the African Methodist Episcopal Church. He recalled, "I was imprisoned in Missouri in 1854, for preaching the gospel to Negroes, though I was never subjected to violence." During the Civil War, he helped recruit the first two black regiments in Maryland. This life of service paved the way for Revels to become the first African American in the Senate.

How might his previous experience have prepared Hiram Revels for service in the Senate?

POLITICAL CARTOON
Skills

The Ku Klux Klan
The KKK used terror and violence to keep African Americans from voting. Northern cartoonist Thomas Nast attacked the Klan and other secret societies in this cartoon.

1. **Comprehension** Identify two Klan activities shown in this cartoon.

2. **Understanding Main Ideas** How does Nast show the impact of the Ku Klux Klan and similar groups on African Americans?

3. **Critical Thinking Identifying a Point of View** What details in this cartoon show Nast's view of the Ku Klux Klan?

Congress Responds Many moderate southerners condemned the violence of the Klan. Yet, they could do little to stop the Klan's reign of terror. Freedmen turned to the federal government for help. In Kentucky, African American voters wrote to Congress:

66 We believe you are not familiar with the Ku Klux Klan's riding nightly over the country spreading terror wherever they go by robbing, whipping, and killing our people without provocation. 99

— Records of the U.S. Senate, April 11, 1871

In 1870, Congress made it a crime to use force to keep people from voting. Although Klan activities decreased, the threat of violence remained. Some African Americans continued to vote and hold office, but others were frightened away from the ballot box.

The Challenge of Rebuilding

Despite political problems, Reconstruction governments tried to rebuild the South. They built public schools for both black and white children. Many states gave women the right to own property. In addition, Reconstruction governments rebuilt railroads, telegraph lines, bridges, and roads. Between 1865 and 1879, the South put down 7,000 miles of railroad track.

Rebuilding cost money. Before the war, southerners paid low taxes. Reconstruction governments raised taxes sharply. This created discontent among many southern whites.

Southerners were further angered by widespread corruption in the Reconstruction governments. One state legislature, for example, voted $1,000 to cover a member's bet on a horse race. Other items billed to the state included hams, perfume, and a coffin.

Corruption was not limited to the South. After the Civil War, dishonesty plagued northern governments, as well. Most southern officeholders, however, served their states honestly.

A Cycle of Poverty

In the first months after the war, freedmen left the plantations on which they had lived and worked. They found few opportunities, however.

AS YOU READ **Draw Inferences** What does the phrase "cycle of poverty" suggest to you?

"Nothing but Freedom" Some Radical Republicans talked about giving each freedman "40 acres and a mule." Thaddeus Stevens suggested breaking up big plantations and distributing the land. Most Americans opposed the plan, however. In the end, former slaves received—in the words of a freedman—"nothing but freedom."

Through hard work or good luck, some freedmen were able to become landowners. Most, however, had little choice but to return to where they had lived in slavery. At the same time, some large planters found themselves with land but nobody to work it.

Sharecropping During Reconstruction, many freedmen and poor whites went to work on the large plantations. These sharecroppers rented and farmed a plot of land. Planters provided seed, fertilizer, and tools in return for a share of the crop at harvest time. To many freedmen, sharecropping offered a measure of independence. Many hoped to own their own land one day.

In fact, most sharecroppers and small landowners became locked in a cycle of poverty. Each spring, they received supplies on credit. In the fall, they had to repay what they had borrowed. If the harvest did not cover what they owed, they sank deeper into debt. Many farmers lost their land and became sharecroppers themselves.

AFTER YOU READ

Section 3 Assessment

Recall

1. **Identify** Explain the significance of **(a)** Hiram Revels, **(b)** Blanche K. Bruce, **(c)** Conservatives, **(d)** Ku Klux Klan.
2. **Define (a)** scalawag, **(b)** carpetbagger, **(c)** sharecropper.

Comprehension

3. What role did freedmen play in Reconstruction governments?
4. What was the goal of groups like the Ku Klux Klan?
5. Describe two economic problems faced by Reconstruction governments in the South.

6. Why did many farmers become sharecroppers?

Critical Thinking and Writing

7. **Exploring the Main Idea** Review the Main Idea statement at the beginning of this section. Then, list two accomplishments of Reconstruction governments. Evaluate the impact of each on the South.
8. **Making Decisions** If you had been an African American during Reconstruction, would you have tried to vote despite threats? Write a paragraph explaining your reasons.

ACTIVITY

Writing a Welcoming Speech You are a Republican member of Congress in 1870. You have been asked to write a brief speech welcoming one of the first African Americans elected to the House of Representatives. Your speech should highlight the importance of this occasion.

4 The End of Reconstruction

BEFORE YOU READ

Reading Focus

- What events led to the end of Reconstruction?
- How were the rights of African Americans restricted in the South after Reconstruction?
- What industries flourished in the "New South"?

Key Terms

poll tax

literacy test

grandfather clause

segregation

Jim Crow laws

Plessy v. Ferguson

"New South"

Taking Notes

Copy the concept web below. As you read, fill in the blank ovals with information about the aftermath of Reconstruction. Add as many ovals as you need.

Main Idea When the North lost interest in protecting the goals of Reconstruction, the era came to an end.

Frederick Douglass

AS YOU READ
Use Prior Knowledge
What have you already learned about Frederick Douglass?

Setting the Scene Americans flocked to the great Centennial Exposition held in Philadelphia in 1876. Fairgoers gazed at the latest wonders of modern industry—the elevator, a giant steam engine, and the telephone ("Of what use is such an invention?" asked the New York *Tribune*).

At the opening ceremony, Frederick Douglass was invited to sit on the platform. But when the famed abolitionist tried to take his place, a policeman barred the way. The officer could not believe that a black man belonged on stage. Finally, a United States Senator persuaded the policeman to let Douglass pass.

By 1876, Americans were looking ahead to a bright future. Eager to put the past behind them, many northerners lost interest in Reconstruction. For African Americans in the South, the end of Reconstruction meant a slow erosion of their hard-won rights.

The End of Reconstruction

By the 1870s, Radical Republicans were losing power. Many northerners grew weary of trying to reform the South. It was time to let southerners run their own governments, they said—even if it meant that African Americans in the South might lose their rights.

Radicals in Decline Disclosure of widespread corruption also hurt Republicans. President Grant had appointed many friends to government offices. Some used their position to steal large sums of money from the government. Grant won reelection in 1872, but many northerners lost faith in Republicans and their policies.

Congress passed the Amnesty Act in 1872. It restored the right to vote to nearly all white southerners. They voted solidly Democratic. At the same time, threats of violence kept many African Americans from voting. By 1876, only three southern states—South Carolina, Florida, and Tennessee—remained under Republican control.

Election of 1876 The end of Reconstruction came with the election of 1876. The Democrats nominated Samuel Tilden, governor of New York, for President. The Republicans chose Ohio governor Rutherford B. Hayes. Both candidates vowed to fight corruption.

Tilden won the popular vote. However, he had only 184 electoral votes, one short of the number needed to win. The outcome of the election hung on 20 disputed votes. All but one came from the three southern states still controlled by Republicans.

As inauguration day drew near, the nation still had no one to swear in as President. Congress set up a special commission to settle the crisis. The commission, made up mostly of Republicans, decided to give all the disputed electoral votes to Hayes.

Southern Democrats could have fought the decision. Hayes, however, had privately agreed to end Reconstruction. Once in office, he removed all remaining federal troops from Louisiana, South Carolina, and Florida. Reconstruction was over.

Impact of Reconstruction Reconstruction had a deep and lasting impact on southern politics. White southerners had bitter memories of Radical Republican policies and military rule. For the next hundred years, the South remained a stronghold of the Democratic party. At the same time, black southerners steadily lost most of their political rights.

Restricted Rights

As Conservatives tightened their grip on southern governments, states found new ways to keep African Americans from exercising their rights. Many of these laws restricted the right to vote.

GEOGRAPHY Skills

The 1876 presidential election hinged on the disputed votes of three southern states. Although Samuel Tilden won the popular vote, Rutherford B. Hayes was declared the winner of the election.

1. **Location** On the map, locate **(a)** Florida, **(b)** Louisiana, **(c)** South Carolina.

2. **Regions** Which candidate carried the southern states where the vote was not disputed?

3. **Critical Thinking Drawing Inferences** Based on this map, do you think the Civil War ended sectionalism in the United States? Explain.

Election of 1876

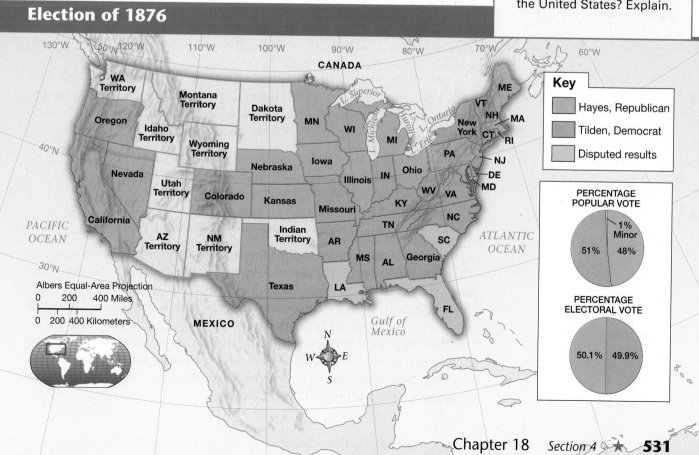

Key
- Hayes, Republican
- Tilden, Democrat
- Disputed results

PERCENTAGE POPULAR VOTE
51% | 48% | 1% Minor

PERCENTAGE ELECTORAL VOTE
50.1% | 49.9%

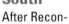

Viewing History

A Port in the New South

Shreveport

After Reconstruction, the economy of the South slowly began to recover. This print, made in the 1870s, shows the port of Shreveport, Louisiana. **Analyzing Information** *How does this picture suggest that the South was recovering from the effects of the war?*

Voting Restrictions Over time, many southern states passed poll taxes, requiring voters to pay a fee each time they voted. As a result, poor freedmen could rarely afford to vote. States also imposed literacy tests that required voters to read and explain a section of the Constitution. Since most freedmen had little education, such tests kept them away from the polls.

Many poor whites could not pass the literacy test. To increase the number of white voters, states passed grandfather clauses. These laws stated that if a voter's father or grandfather had been eligible to vote on January 1, 1867, the voter did not have to take a literacy test. Since no African Americans in the South could vote before 1868, grandfather clauses ensured that only white men could vote.

Segregation After 1877, segregation, or legal separation of races, became the law of the South. Laws separated blacks and whites in schools, restaurants, theaters, trains, streetcars, playgrounds, hospitals, and even cemeteries. These Jim Crow laws, as they were known, trapped southern blacks in a hopeless situation. Louisiana novelist George Washington Cable described segregation as:

> ❝ A system of oppression so rank that nothing could make it seem small except the fact that [African Americans] had already been ground under it for a century and a half. ❞
>
> — George Washington Cable, "The Freedman's Case in Equity"

African Americans brought lawsuits to challenge segregation. In 1896, in the case of *Plessy* v. *Ferguson,* the Supreme Court ruled that segregation was legal so long as facilities for blacks and whites were equal. In fact, facilities were rarely equal. For example, southern states spent much less on schools for blacks than for whites.

Despite such setbacks, the Constitution now recognized African Americans as citizens. Laws passed during Reconstruction—especially the Fourteenth Amendment—would become the basis of the civil rights movement almost 100 years later.

Industry in the "New South"

During Reconstruction, the South made some progress toward rebuilding its economy. Cotton production, long the basis of the South's economy, slowly recovered. By 1880, planters were growing as much cotton as they had in 1860.

A new generation of southern leaders worked to expand the economy. In stirring speeches, Atlanta journalist Henry Grady described a "New South" that used its vast natural resources to build up its own industry instead of depending on the North.

Agricultural Resources In 1880, the entire South still produced fewer finished textiles than Massachusetts. In the next decade, more and more communities started building textile mills to turn cotton into cloth.

The tobacco industry also grew. In North Carolina, James Duke used new machinery to revolutionize the manufacture of tobacco products. Duke's American Tobacco Company eventually controlled 90 percent of the nation's tobacco industry.

New Industries The South also tapped its mineral resources. With its large deposits of iron ore and coal, Alabama became a center of the steel industry. Oil refineries sprang up in Louisiana and Texas. Other states produced copper, granite, and marble.

By the 1890s, many northern forests had been cut down. The southern yellow pine competed with the northwestern white pine as a lumber source. Southern factories turned out cypress shingles and hardwood furniture.

The South had developed a more balanced economy by 1900. "We find a South wide awake with business," wrote a visitor, "eagerly laying lines of communication, rapidly opening mines, building furnaces, foundries, and all sorts of shops." Still, the South could not keep up with even more rapid growth in the North and the West.

AS YOU READ **Find Main Ideas** What was new about the "New South"?

AFTER YOU READ

Section 4 Assessment

Recall

1. **Identify** Explain the significance of **(a)** Rutherford B. Hayes, **(b)** Jim Crow laws, **(c)** *Plessy* v. *Ferguson*, **(d)** Henry Grady, **(e)** "New South," **(f)** James Duke.
2. **Define** **(a)** poll tax, **(b)** literacy test, **(c)** grandfather clause, **(d)** segregation.

Comprehension

3. Why did the Radical Republicans lose their power?
4. Describe two ways in which African Americans in the South lost political rights.

5. How did the southern economy change after Reconstruction?

Critical Thinking and Writing

6. **Exploring the Main Idea** Review the Main Idea statement at the beginning of this section. Then, evaluate the ways in which Reconstruction was both a success and a failure.
7. **Making Predictions** Write a paragraph predicting how the Supreme Court decision in *Plessy* v. *Ferguson* might affect later efforts by African Americans to achieve equality.

ACTIVITY

Take It to the NET
Connecting to Today
Choose one of the former Confederate states. Then, use the Internet to find out what the major industries and resources of that state are. Use this information to create a chart. Visit *The American Nation* section of **www.phschool.com** for help in completing the activity.

CREATING A CHAPTER SUMMARY

Copy the chart below. Fill in the boxes with key events and developments of the different stages of Reconstruction. Some boxes have been partially filled in to help you get started.

1863–1865 (Lincoln)
• Ten Percent Plan • Wade-Davis Bill
1865–1867 (Johnson versus Congress)
• Johnson's Reconstruction plan •
1867–1876 (Radical Reconstruction)
• • •
1877–1896 (After Reconstruction)
• •

For additional review and enrichment activities, see the interactive version of *The American Nation,* available on the Web and on CD-ROM.

 Take It to the NET

Chapter Self-Test For practice test questions for Chapter 18, visit *The American Nation* section of **www.phschool.com**.

Building Vocabulary

Review the meaning of the chapter vocabulary words listed below. Then, write a sentence for each word in which you define the word and describe its relation to the postwar South.

1. freedmen
2. amnesty
3. black codes
4. scalawag
5. carpetbagger
6. sharecropper
7. poll tax
8. literacy test
9. grandfather clause
10. segregation

Reviewing Key Facts

11. Describe Lincoln's plan for Reconstruction. (Section 1)
12. Describe two accomplishments of the Freedmen's Bureau. (Section 1)
13. What did the Fifteenth Amendment state? (Section 2)
14. Why did many northerners go to the South during Reconstruction? (Section 3)
15. What were the results of the presidential election of 1876? (Section 4)

Critical Thinking and Writing

16. **Drawing Conclusions** If Abraham Lincoln had lived, do you think he would have supported Radical Reconstruction? Write a paragraph explaining your answer and giving reasons.

17. **Supporting a Point of View** Do you think former Confederate officeholders should have been barred from serving in Congress? Write a position statement giving reasons for your point of view.

18. **Identifying Causes and Effects** Analyze the causes and effects of the passage of the Fourteenth Amendment.

19. **Linking Past and Present** (a) What action did the federal government take to stop violence by groups like the Ku Klux Klan? (b) List two ways governments and individuals work to end hate crimes today.

20. **Connecting to Geography: Place** Analyze the effect of geographic factors on the rise of the "New South." List at least three specific examples.

Analyzing Primary Sources

In an 1876 speech, Senator Blanche K. Bruce of Mississippi discussed the hopes that African Americans had for the future:

> 66 Although many of us are uneducated in the schools, we are informed and advised as to our duties to the government, our state, and ourselves. . . . With scrupulous respect for the rights of others, and with the hopefulness of political youth, we are determined that the great government that gave us liberty and rendered its gift valuable by giving us the ballot shall not find us wanting in a sufficient response to any demand that humanity or patriotism may make upon us. 99

—Blanche K. Bruce, Record of the 44th Congress, 1876

21. What statement does Bruce make about the education of African Americans at the time?
22. What does he mean by the phrase "political youth"?
23. What actions of the federal government does Bruce praise in this speech?
24. How would you describe the tone of this speech? Explain.

Solving Problems

Examine the chart below, and answer the questions that follow.

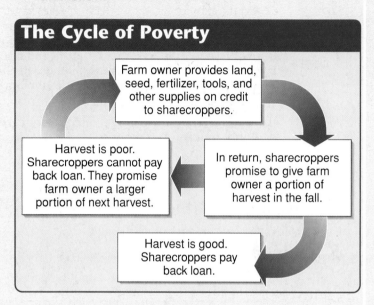

The Cycle of Poverty

Farm owner provides land, seed, fertilizer, tools, and other supplies on credit to sharecroppers.

In return, sharecroppers promise to give farm owner a portion of harvest in the fall.

Harvest is good. Sharecroppers pay back loan.

Harvest is poor. Sharecroppers cannot pay back loan. They promise farm owner a larger portion of next harvest.

25. What problem is the main topic of this chart?
    A Poor harvest
    B Scarcity of supplies
    C Sharecroppers' rising debt
    D Inability to get credit
26. Suggest and evaluate one possible solution to the problem shown on the chart.

ACTIVITIES

Connecting With . . .
Government and Citizenship

Creating a Poster Choose one of the three Civil War amendments to the Constitution discussed in this chapter. With a partner, create a poster that expresses the key ideas of that amendment and its importance to Americans. Include both images and words. You may include modern images that reflect the importance of the amendment today.

Take It to the NET

Connecting to Today

Giving a Report Many of the colleges created by the Freedmen's Bureau are still in operation today. Use the Internet to find out about the nation's Historically Black Colleges and Universities (HBCUs). Report to the class on the location, history, and current goals of one of these schools. For help in starting this activity, visit *The American Nation* section of **www.phschool.com**.

Researching

Preparing a News Magazine Use the Internet to find more information about the impeachment of Andrew Johnson. With a group of partners, use this information to prepare a segment about the impeachment for a television newsmagazine. Include interviews with major figures, as well as graphics. For help in starting this activity, visit *The American Nation* section of **www.phschool.com**.

Leaves of Grass
Walt Whitman

Introduction One of the best-loved of all American poets, Walt Whitman served as a Union nurse in the Civil War. The following poems were written in response to the end of the war and the death of Abraham Lincoln. In the most famous, "O Captain! My Captain!" Whitman compares Lincoln to the captain of a ship.

Vocabulary Before you read the selections, find the meanings of these words in a dictionary: **reconciliation, carnage, incessantly, exulting, mournful, ceaseless.**

Walt Whitman

RECONCILIATION

Word over all, beautiful as the sky,

Beautiful that war and all its deeds of carnage must in time be utterly lost,

That the hands of the sisters Death and Night incessantly softly wash again, and ever, this soil'd world;

For my enemy is dead, a man divine as myself is dead,

I look where he lies white-faced and still in the coffin—I draw near,

Bend down and touch lightly with my lips the white face in the coffin.

O CAPTAIN! MY CAPTAIN!

O Captain! My Captain! our fearful trip is done,

Our ship has weather'd every rack,* the prize we sought is won,

The port is near, the bells I hear, the people all exulting,

While follow eyes the steady keel, the vessel grim and daring;

But O heart! heart! heart!

O the bleeding drops of red,

Where on the deck my Captain lies,

Fallen cold and dead.

O Captain! My Captain! rise up and hear the bells;

Rise up—for you the flag is flung—for you the bugle trills,

For you bouquets and ribbon'd wreaths—for you the shores a-crowding,

For you they call, the swaying mass, their eager faces turning;

Here Captain! dear father!

This arm beneath your head!

It is some dream that on the deck

You've fallen cold and dead.

My Captain does not answer, his lips are pale and still,

My father does not feel my arm, he has no pulse nor will,

The ship is anchor'd safe and sound, its voyage closed and done,

From fearful trip the victor ship comes in with object won;

Exult O shores, and ring O bells!

But I with mournful tread,

Walk the deck my Captain lies,

Fallen cold and dead.

****rack**: storm

HUSH'D BE THE CAMPS TO-DAY
(MAY 4, 1865)

Hush'd be the camps to-day,

And soldiers let us drape our war-worn
   weapons,

And each with musing soul retire to celebrate

Our dear commander's death.

No more for him life's stormy conflicts,

Nor victory, nor defeat—no more time's dark
   events,

Charging like ceaseless clouds across the sky.

But sing poet in our name,

Sing of the love we bore him—because you,
   dweller in camps, know it truly.

As they invault the coffin there,

Sing—as they close the doors of earth upon
   him—one verse,

For the heavy hearts of soldiers.

Statue at the Lincoln Memorial

Analyzing Literature

1. In "Reconciliation," how would you describe the speaker's attitude toward the enemy?
   - **A** Triumphant
   - **B** Forgiving
   - **C** Vengeful
   - **D** Fearful

2. In "Oh Captain! My Captain!" the people are rejoicing because
   - **A** Lincoln is dead
   - **B** Lincoln has issued the Emancipation Proclamation
   - **C** the Union has been preserved
   - **D** the South has been destroyed

3. **Critical Thinking and Writing** **Applying Information** How does Whitman's depiction of Abraham Lincoln reflect what you have learned about his role as a leader during the Civil War? Refer to at least two lines from Whitman's poems.

TEST PREPARATION

Use the map **and** your knowledge of social studies to answer the following question.

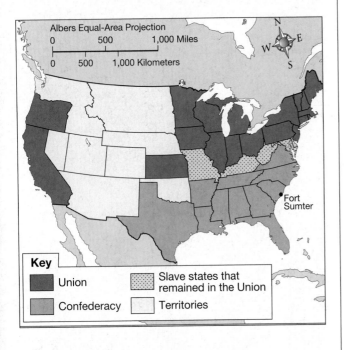

Albers Equal-Area Projection

0   500   1,000 Miles

0   500   1,000 Kilometers

Fort Sumter

Key
- Union
- Confederacy
- Slave states that remained in the Union
- Territories

1 Which conclusion can you draw from this map?

A More people lived in the Union than in the Confederacy.

B The Confederacy occupied most of the Atlantic Coast.

C Most of the fighting in the Civil War took place in the South.

D All slave states seceded from the Union.

2 Which of the following was not a goal of Radical Reconstruction?

A Break the power of southern planters

B Guarantee the vote to freedmen

C End slavery

D Strengthen Republican control of Congress

3 In which of the following pairs was the first event a cause of the second?

A Fort Sumter is fired upon; South Carolina secedes

B California applies for statehood; Compromise of 1850 passed

C Fighting erupts in Kansas; Kansas-Nebraska Act passed

D John Brown leads raid on Harpers Ferry; Republican party is formed

4 What was one major effect of the Emancipation Proclamation?

A It immediately freed slaves in the North.

B It immediately freed slaves in the South.

C It allowed African Americans to enlist in the Union army.

D It increased support for the Union cause in Europe.

5 With which of these statements would both Abraham Lincoln and Stephen Douglas have agreed?

A "The Kansas-Nebraska Act will help save the Union."

B "The Union must be preserved."

C "The people of each state have the right to decide whether to allow slavery."

D "The nation cannot survive half-slave, half-free."

Use the statements below **and** your knowledge of social studies to answer the following question.

- "All persons formerly held as slaves shall have the right to own, sell, purchase, and inherit property."

- "No one other than white men shall be permitted to serve on juries, hold office, or vote in any election."

---

6 Where would you be most likely to find *both* of the above statements?

   A The Wade-Davis Bill

   B The Reconstruction Act

   C One of the black codes

   D The Supreme Court decision in *Plessy* v. *Ferguson*

7 Which of the following individuals would have been most likely to agree with the Dred Scott decision?

   A Harriet Beecher Stowe

   B Frederick Douglass

   C John C. Calhoun

   D John Brown

8 Which of the following explained which people were considered to be American citizens?

   A Thirteenth Amendment

   B Fourteenth Amendment

   C Fifteenth Amendment

   D Gettysburg Address

Use the table **and** your knowledge of social studies to answer the following question.

Casualties of Selected Civil War Battles

Battle Site	Union Casualties	Confederate Casualties
Gettysburg	23,053	28,063
Antietam	12,410	10,316
Shiloh	13,047	10,694
Fredericksburg	12,653	5,309

Source: *The Civil War,* Time-Life Books

9 Which battle had the largest percentage of Union casualties?

   A Antietam

   B Gettysburg

   C Shiloh

   D Fredericksburg

Writing Practice

10 "Slavery was the chief cause of the Civil War." Agree or disagree with this statement. Give reasons for your answer.

11 Describe one social, one political, and one economic effect of the Civil War on the South. Explain which effect you think had the greatest impact.

Transforming the Nation

An American Steel Mill
The manufacture of stronger steel,
as shown in Peter Kroyer's *The
Biermeister and Main Steel Forge,*
helped spark rapid industrial growth.

The manufacturers of this country, with our wonderful stores of raw materials at hand, [have] become the successful rivals . . . of any country that desires to compete with them. "

—Carroll D. Wright, United States labor commissioner (1882)

The New West

1865–1914

1 **Indian Peoples of the Great Plains**
2 **Mining and Railroading**
3 **The Cattle Kingdom**
4 **Indian Peoples in Retreat**
5 **Farming**

Battle at Little Bighorn

Sioux warrior's bow and arrow case

AMERICAN EVENTS

1869
The first transcontinental railroad is completed.

1876
The Lakota Sioux, Arapahos, and Cheyenne, led by Chief Crazy Horse, defeat General Custer at the Battle of Little Bighorn.

1887
The Dawes Act encourages Native Americans to become farmers.

James A. Garfield 1881

	Andrew Johnson		Rutherford B. Hayes	Chester A. Arthur	Grover Cleveland
Presidential Terms:	1865–1869	Ulysses S. Grant 1869–1877	1877–1881	1881–1885	1885–1889

1860   **1875**   **1890**

 WORLD EVENTS

1869 ▲
The Suez Canal opens in Egypt.

1885 ▲
The first transcontinental railroad is completed in Canada.

New States in the West

As settlers flooded into the West, towns and cities quickly grew. Between 1865 and 1914, eight western territories became states.

1896 campaign poster shows William Jennings Bryan and his family

1896

Populist candidate William Jennings Bryan and Republican candidate William McKinley run for President.

1913

States ratify the income tax amendment to the Constitution.

Benjamin Harrison	Grover Cleveland	William McKinley	Theodore Roosevelt 1901–1909	William H. Taft	Woodrow Wilson 1913–1921
1889–1893	1893–1897	1897–1901		1909–1913	

1890   **1905**   **1920**

1896 ▲
Klondike gold rush begins in Canada.

▲ **1910**
China abolishes slavery.

1 Indian Peoples of the Great Plains

BEFORE YOU READ

Reading Focus

- What was life like for the Plains Indians?
- Why did the Plains Indians follow herds of buffalo?
- How did the roles of men and women differ in the Plains Indian society?

Key Terms

tepee

travois

corral

jerky

Taking Notes

As you read, prepare an outline of this section. Use roman numerals to indicate the major headings, capital letters for the subheadings, and numbers for the supporting details. The sample, at right, will help you get started.

> I. The Plains Indians
>   A. Life on the Plains
>   1. Different cultures
>   2.
>   B. The arrival of horses
>   1.
>   2.
> II. Following the Buffalo

Main Idea Different Indian peoples lived on the Great Plains, and many relied on the horse and the buffalo as they developed their varied cultures and traditions.

AS YOU READ **Kiowa warrior's shield**

Find Main Ideas How did the Plains Indians use the buffalo?

Setting the Scene Looking back years later, Old Lady Horse of the Kiowa nation remembered well her childhood days when huge herds of buffalo roamed the Plains. The Kiowa, she explained, could not have survived without them:

> 66 Everything the Kiowas had came from the buffalo. Their tipis were made of buffalo hides, so were their clothes and moccasins. They ate buffalo meat. Their containers were made of hide, or of bladders or stomachs. The buffalo were the life of the Kiowas. 99
>
> —Old Lady Horse, quoted in Alice Marriott and Carol K. Rachlin, *American Indian Mythology*

Indian peoples had been living for centuries on the Great Plains. The many uses of the buffalo provide just one example of how the Indians adapted their ways of life to the region. They created well-ordered societies that divided work between men and women and made the most of the resources on hand.

The Plains Indians

Many different Native American nations lived on the Great Plains. A number of them, such as the Arikaras, had lived on the Plains for hundreds of years. Others, like the Lakotas, did not move to the Plains until the early 1700s.

Life on the Plains Plains Indians had rich and varied cultures. They were skilled artists. They also had well-organized religions and warrior societies. Each nation had its own language. People from different nations used sign language to talk to one another.

At one time, most Plains Indians were farmers who lived in semi-permanent villages. From there, they sent out hunting parties that pursued on foot herds of buffalo and other animals. Agriculture, however, was their main source of food.

The Arrival of Horses During the 1600s, the Plains Indians' way of life changed as they learned about horses from neighboring tribes.

The Spanish had brought horses to the Americas in the late 1400s. At first, Indians were not allowed to own horses, but they did learn how to care for and how to ride them. After the Pueblo Indians revolted against the Spaniards in 1680, the Pueblos were left with thousands of horses. They started trading these horses to neighboring tribes. Eventually, the horses reached the tribes of the northern plains.

Plains Indians used horses while hunting. They also used horses when moving their villages and going on raids.

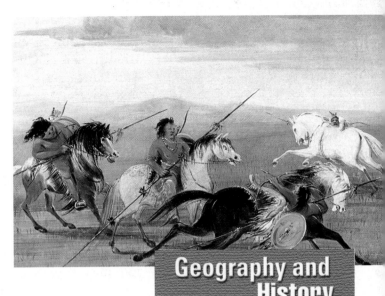

Following the Buffalo

The buffalo served as a living grocery store for Plains Indians. After acquiring horses, they followed the huge herds that had roamed their homeland for centuries. They began to live in tepees (TEE pees), or tents made by stretching buffalo skins on tall poles. The tepees could easily be carried on a travois (truh VOI), or sled pulled by a dog or horse.

The migration of the Plains Indians mirrored the movement of the buffalo. In winter, small groups of buffalo moved to protected valleys and forests. In summer, huge buffalo herds gathered on the Plains where the grass was plentiful. In the same way, Plains Indians spent the winter in small bands and gathered in large groups during the summers.

The Buffalo Hunt There were different ways to hunt buffalo. Before horses came to the Plains, a group of hunters would shout and wave colored robes at the buffalo. The hunters would gradually drive a herd of buffalo into a corral, or enclosure. There they killed the trapped buffalo. When the hunt was over, the women and children joined the hunters in cutting up the buffalo and taking it back to camp. Once they had horses, hunters would ride the horses right into the herd and kill the buffalo with bows and arrows.

Uses of the Buffalo Although the Plains Indians also hunted deer and elk, they depended on the buffalo for food, clothing, and shelter. Buffalo meat, rich in protein, was a main item of the Indians' diet. Women cut up and dried the meat on racks. The dried meat was called jerky.

Women also tanned buffalo hides to make sleeping robes and tepee covers. They wove buffalo fur into coarse, warm cloth. The cloth was used as an outer covering for a tepee.

Tradition and Ceremony Many Native American groups met on the Plains. They hunted together and attended special events.

Summer gatherings were the time for councils. At the councils, the elders were consulted about the problems that affected the whole nation.

Geography and History

Wild Horses in the West

At the first sight of horses, the Plains Indians believed them to be mysterious, magical animals. They called them "sacred dogs." These "sacred dogs" forever changed the life of Plains Indians. Before the horse, tribes lived at the edge of the plains, venturing out to hunt buffalo on foot during the summer. Horses made them mobile, allowing them to live on the Plains year round and to follow the buffalo herds. The Comanches, one of the first tribes to ride horses, became skilled and feared warriors who moved swiftly over long distances. With horses, the Comanches could expand their territory and defend it from neighboring tribes. A man on foot was no match for the "sacred dog."

 Why did the Plains Indians refer to horses as "sacred dogs"?

The most important religious ceremony was the Sun Dance. Hundreds of people attended the four-day ceremony to thank the Great Spirit for blessings, good hunts, and help in times of trouble. Sun Dancers also asked the Great Spirit for good fortune in the coming year.

Ask Questions What questions would you have asked the Plains Indians about the roles of men and women?

The Roles of Women and Men

Women and men usually had specific roles in Indian society. In some tribes, women helped men with the hunting and governing. A Blackfoot woman, Running Eagle, led many hunting parties herself.

The Role of Women Women oversaw life in the home. They gathered food and prepared meals for their families. The women not only made the tepees, but they were also responsible for raising and taking down tepees. Women cared for the children and, along with the men, passed along the traditions of their people.

Women also engaged in many crafts. They made the baskets and blankets. Their work often showed great artistic skill and design. In fact, a woman's ability in crafts established her rank in society.

The Role of Men The men of the Plains Indians had important responsibilities too. They hunted and protected the women, children, and the elders. They passed on their valuable skills and knowledge to the boys. They supervised the spiritual life of the community by leading religious ceremonies.

Another important responsibility of the men was to provide military leadership. They waged war to defend or extend territory, to gain horses and other riches, or to seek revenge. More than anything else, however, men waged war to protect their people and to prove their bravery and ability. The most successful warriors gained great respect from the members of their nation.

Section 1 Assessment

AFTER YOU READ

Recall
1. **Define** (a) tepee, (b) travois, (c) corral, (d) jerky.

Comprehension
2. How did the arrival of the horse change the life of the Plains Indians?
3. Why did the Plains Indians depend on the buffalo?
4. (a) What were the responsibilities of women in the society? (b) What were the responsibilities of men?

Critical Thinking and Writing
5. **Exploring the Main Idea** Review the Main Idea statement at the beginning of this section. Then, write a paragraph describing how the dependence on buffalo hunting affected the lives of the men and the women.
6. **Making Generalizations** Based on what you know about the Sun Dance ceremony, what were some religious beliefs of the Plains Indians?

ACTIVITY

 Take It to the NET
Connecting to Today
The buffalo was important to the Plains Indians. Use the Internet to find out about the status of the buffalo today. Work with a partner to prepare a museum exhibit about the buffalo in the past and today. Visit *The American Nation* section of **www.phschool.com** for help in completing the activity.

2 Mining and Railroading

Reading Focus

- How did the boom in gold and silver change the West?
- What problems arose on the mining frontier?
- How did railroads help the West develop?

Key Terms

lode

vigilante

transcontinental railroad

subsidy

Taking Notes

Copy this flowchart. As you read, fill in the boxes with some of the events described in this section that led up to completion of the first transcontinental railroad. The first and last boxes have been filled in to help you get started. Add as many boxes as you need.

Mining towns need supplies

↓

↓

↓

Transcontinental railroad is completed in 1869

Main Idea A mining boom changed the West, bringing people and a new means of transportation to the region.

Setting the Scene Late in 1859, a pack train of 80 mules made its way across the Sierra Nevada mountains into California. The mules bore tons of silver ore fresh from a new strike in the Washoe Valley east of the Sierras. At $5,000 a ton, this single load was enough to make a man rich beyond his dreams. Later, glittering white bars of silver made from the ore were put on exhibit in the window of a San Francisco bank. Passersby gazed in amazement at the sight of so much wealth.

The lure of instant riches drew tens of thousands west. Miners came from all over the globe to strike it rich in the new West.

A Boom in Gold and Silver

The western mining boom had begun with the California gold rush of 1849. When the gold rush ended, miners looked for new opportunities. A mere rumor sent them racing east in search of new strikes.

The Comstock Lode Two prospectors struck gold in the Sierra Nevada in 1859. Then, another miner, Henry Comstock, appeared. "The land is mine," he cried, demanding to be made a partner. From then on, Comstock boasted about "his" mine. The strike became known as the Comstock Lode. A lode is a rich vein of gold or silver.

Comstock and his partners often complained about the heavy blue sand that was mixed in with the gold. It clogged the devices used for separating out the gold and made the gold hard to reach. When Mexican miners took the "danged blue stuff" to an expert in California, tests showed that it was loaded with silver. Comstock had stumbled onto one of the richest silver mines in the world.

Miners moved into many other areas of the West. Some found valuable ore in Montana and Idaho. Others struck it rich in Colorado. In the 1870s, miners discovered gold in the Black Hills of South Dakota. In the late 1890s, thousands rushed north to Alaska after major gold strikes were made there.

AS YOU READ Men with a pile of silver bars

Draw Inferences What were the difficulties of silver mining?

From Boomtown to Ghost Town Gold and silver strikes attracted thousands of prospectors. Towns sprang up almost overnight near all the major mining sites.

First, miners built a tent city near the diggings. Then, people came to supply the miners' needs. Traders brought mule teams loaded with tools, food, and clothing. Merchants hauled in wagonloads of supplies and set up stores.

Soon, wood-frame houses, hotels, restaurants, and stores replaced the tents. For example, it took less than a year for the mining camp at the Comstock Lode to become the boomtown of Virginia City, Nevada.

Most settlers in the boomtowns of the mining frontier were men. However, enterprising women also found ways to profit. Some women ran boardinghouses and laundries. Others opened restaurants, where miners gladly paid high prices for home-cooked meals.

Many boomtowns lasted for only a few years. When the gold or silver ore was gone, the miners moved away. Without the miners for customers, businesses often had to close. In this way, a boomtown could quickly go bust and turn into a ghost town.

Still, some boomtowns survived and prospered even after the mines shut down. In these towns, miners stayed and found new ways to make a living.

Problems Along the Mining Frontier

The surge of miners in the West created problems, as did the arrival of cattle ranchers and homesteaders. Mines and towns polluted clear mountain streams. Miners cut down forests to get wood for buildings. They also forced Native Americans from the land.

GEOGRAPHY Skills

The discovery of gold, the Homestead Act, and the arrival of railroad builders, ranchers, and other settlers contributed to the population growth of the West.

1. **Location** On the map, locate **(a)** Comstock Lode, **(b)** Central Pacific Railroad, **(c)** Promontory, **(d)** Chisholm Trail.

2. **Interaction** How did mining affect nearby soil, water, and other natural resources?

3. **Critical Thinking**
   Applying Information
   How do you think the railroad lines affected the cattle ranchers in Colorado?

The Changing West

Growth of Colorado and Nebraska, 1860–1890

Source: *Statistical Abstract of the United States*

Foreign miners were often treated unfairly. In many camps, mobs drove Mexicans from their claims. Chinese miners were heavily taxed or forced to work claims abandoned by others.

Few miners ever got rich. Much of the gold and silver lay deep underground. It could be reached only with costly machinery. Eventually, most mining in the West was taken over by large companies that could afford to buy this equipment. Furthermore, independent prospectors like Henry Comstock largely disappeared. They were replaced by paid laborers who worked for the large companies.

Territorial Government Lawlessness and disorder often accompanied the rapid growth of a town. Stories have exaggerated the number of fights and killings that took place in these towns, but some towns actually were violent places. In response, miners sometimes resorted to organizing groups of vigilantes, or self-appointed law enforcers. Vigilantes tracked down outlaws and punished them, usually without trials. A common punishment was lynching.

Occasionally, vigilante groups did not form to fight crime. At least one San Francisco group organized to take political control of the city.

Informal methods of governing gradually gave way to more formal arrangements. In 1861, Colorado, Dakota, and Nevada were organized into territories. Idaho and Arizona followed in 1863 and Montana, in 1864. The process of permanent settlement and government had begun.

The Railroads

To the Indians, the railroad was a terrifying monster, an "iron horse" belching black smoke and moving at stunning speeds. However, for the people of mining towns, railroads meant supplies, new townsfolk, and a rapid means of transporting their gold and silver. The West needed a transportation system that could carry heavy loads over great distances at a cost low enough to guarantee a profit. It is no wonder, then, that railroad companies raced to lay track to the mines and boomtowns.

A Transcontinental Railroad In 1863, two companies began a race to build the first transcontinental railroad. A transcontinental railroad is one that stretches across a continent from coast to coast. The Union Pacific Railroad started building a rail line westward from Omaha, Nebraska. The Central Pacific Railroad began in Sacramento, California, and built eastward. A local paper reported:

Boom and Bust

Gold or Silver Strike
↓
Miners arrive and build a tent city
↓
Merchants arrive to supply miners
↓
Wood-frame structures replace tents
↓
Boomtown
↓
Gold or silver production falls
↓
Miners move on
↓
Stores close and merchants leave
↓
Town is abandoned
↓
Ghost Town

GRAPHIC ORGANIZER
Skills

A gold or silver strike often led to the building of a boomtown. However, many boomtowns quickly became ghost towns.

1. **Comprehension** (a) Why did merchants often follow miners? (b) What caused large numbers of miners to suddenly leave a boomtown?

2. **Critical Thinking Analyzing Information** Based on this chart and on the map on page 548, why do you think there are more ghost towns today in Idaho than there are in Texas?

Economics $

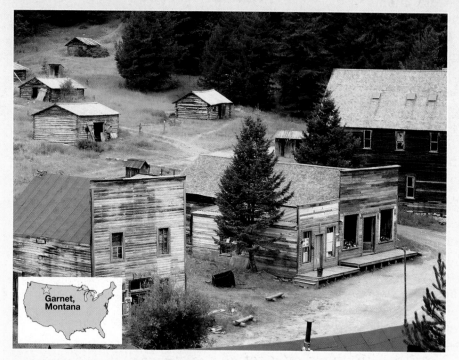

Garnet, Montana

Bustling boomtowns became abandoned ghost towns once the mines no longer yielded gold or silver. Garnet, Montana, now a ghost town, was founded in 1895 and swelled to nearly 1,000 people by 1898. Aside from the saloons found in all boomtowns, Garnet also had a school, barbershops, a union hall, and a doctor's office. It even claimed to have a low crime rate. By 1905, the population had fallen to 150.

 Take It to the NET

Virtual Field Trip For an interactive look at Garnet, Montana, visit *The American Nation* section of **www.phschool.com**.

66 With rites appropriate to the occasion . . . ground was formally broken at noon for the commencement of the Central Pacific Railroad—the California link of the continental chain that is to unite American communities now divided by thousands of miles of trackless wilderness. 99

—Sacramento *Union*, January 8, 1863

The federal government helped the railroad companies because it felt that rail lines in the West would benefit the entire nation. The government's aid came in the form of subsidies. A subsidy is financial aid or a land grant from the government. Congress lent money to the railroad companies and gave them land. For every mile of track completed, the railroad companies received twenty sections of land in the states along the route and forty sections per mile in the territories. By the time the Central Pacific and Union Pacific railroads were completed, they had received about 45 million acres of land. Often, both business and government ignored the fact that Native Americans lived on the land.

Working on the Railroad Both companies had trouble getting workers. Labor was scarce during the Civil War. Also, the work was backbreaking and dangerous and the pay was low.

The railroad companies hired immigrant workers, who accepted low wages. The Central Pacific brought in thousands of workers from China. The Union Pacific hired newcomers from Ireland. African Americans and Mexican Americans also worked for each line.

The workers faced a daunting task. The Central Pacific had to carve a path through the rugged Sierra Nevada. The Union Pacific had to cut through the towering Rocky Mountains. Snowstorms and avalanches killed workers and slowed progress. At times, crews cutting tunnels through rock advanced only a few inches a day.

Railroads Promote Growth   The Central Pacific and Union Pacific met at Promontory, Utah, on May 10, 1869. Leland Stanford, president of the Central Pacific, dropped a solid-gold spike into a pre-drilled hole in the rail. In doing so, he joined the two tracks and united the country. The nation's first transcontinental railroad was complete.

With the Civil War fresh in their minds, people cheered this new symbol of unity. The words that were engraved on the golden spike expressed their feelings:

> 66 May God continue the unity of our Country as the Railroad unites the two great Oceans of the world. 99

Before long, other major rail lines linked the West and the East. The railroads brought growth and new settlement all across the West. They enabled people, supplies, and mail to move quickly and cheaply across the plains and mountains. Wherever rail lines went, settlements sprang up along the tracks. The largest towns and cities developed where major railroad lines met. Cities where sea and land transportation met, such as Seattle, San Francisco, and Los Angeles, experienced huge population growth with the coming of the Southern Pacific and Santa Fe railroads. Western cities, such as Denver, Cheyenne, and Wichita, grew when railroads were joined to the great cattle trails.

Because of their rapid growth, western territories began to apply for statehood. Nevada became a state in 1864; Colorado, in 1876; North Dakota, South Dakota, Montana, and Washington, in 1889; Idaho and Wyoming in 1890.

Primary Source

Roughing It

In 1861, Mark Twain traveled west to prospect for gold. Here he describes some of the hardships of the journey:
"On the nineteenth day, we crossed the Great American Desert—forty memorable miles of bottomless sand. . . . We worked our passage most of the way across. That is to say, we got out and walked. It was a dreary pull and a long thirsty one, for we had no water. From one extremity of this desert to the other, the road was white with the bones of oxen and horses. . . . we could have walked forty miles and set our feet on a bone every step! The desert was one [large] graveyard. And the log-chains, wagon tyres, and rotting wrecks of vehicles were almost as thick as the bones."

Analyzing Primary Sources
Why do you think Twain and the other prospectors were willing to endure such hardships?

Section 2 Assessment

AFTER YOU READ

Recall

1. **Identify** Explain the significance of (a) Comstock Lode, (b) Union Pacific Railroad, (c) Central Pacific Railroad, (d) Leland Stanford.
2. **Define** (a) lode, (b) vigilante, (c) transcontinental railroad, (d) subsidy.

Comprehension

3. How did mining encourage the growth of towns in the West?
4. Describe three problems that occurred in mining towns.
5. How did railroads change the West?

Critical Thinking and Writing

6. **Exploring the Main Idea** Review the Main Idea statement at the beginning of this section. Then, prepare a cause-and-effect chart that gives information on how mining changed the West. The first "cause" entry can be: Silver discovered in Sierra Nevada in 1859. The first "effect" entry can be: Huge numbers of people rush to Nevada.
7. **Linking Past and Present** Are railroads as important today as they were in the late 1800s? Explain.

ACTIVITY

Writing a Speech You are a railroad official in 1869. Write a short speech to celebrate the completion of the first transcontinental railroad. In your speech, explain how you think the railroad will benefit the entire nation.

3 The Cattle Kingdom

BEFORE YOU READ

Reading Focus

- What was the Cattle Kingdom?
- What was life like for a cowhand?
- Why were cow towns important during the cattle boom?

Key Terms

cattle drive

vaquero

cow town

Taking Notes

Copy the chart below. As you read, complete the chart to show other causes that led to the end of the Cattle Kingdom. Add as many boxes as you need.

Sheepherders move onto the Plains → → → → **CATTLE KINGDOM ENDS**

Main Idea Cattle ranching boomed on the open range in the 1870s, producing a Cattle Kingdom of ranchers, cowboys, cattle drives, and cow towns.

AS YOU READ

A pair of spurs
Use Prior Knowledge
In addition to spurs, what clothes did cowhands wear?

Setting the Scene Andy Adams was a cattleman on a "long drive" from Texas to the rail stations in the North. Adams reported that the cattle had been under the blistering sun for three days. Crazed with thirst, the steers were out of control. Then, Adams made a terrible discovery:

❝ In a number of instances wild steers deliberately walked against our horses, and then for the first time a fact dawned on us that chilled the marrow in our bones—the herd was going blind. ❞

—Andy Adams, *The Log of a Cowboy*, 1903

There was little for the cowhands to do now. "Nothing short of water would stop the herd and we rode aside and let them pass," Adams explained. Eventually the herd found water, and with it "their eyesight would gradually return."

In the 1860s a new group of Americans began arriving on the Plains. Along with miners, these newcomers created a new way of life on the Great Plains.

Creating a Cattle Kingdom

Before the arrival of settlers from the United States, the Spanish, and then the Mexicans, set up cattle ranches in the Southwest. Over the years, strays from these ranches, along with American breeds, grew into large herds of wild cattle. These wild cattle were known as longhorns. They roamed freely across the grassy plains of Texas.

After the Civil War, the demand for beef increased. People in the growing cities in the East needed more meat. Miners, railroad crews, farmers, and growing communities in the West added to the demand. The Texas longhorns were perfect for the commercial market. They could travel far on little water, and they required no winter feeding.

Cattle Drives In response, Texas ranchers began rounding up herds of longhorns. They drove the animals hundreds of miles north to railroad lines in Kansas and Missouri on trips called **cattle drives.**

The Chisholm Trail Jesse Chisholm blazed one of the most famous cattle trails. Chisholm was half Scottish and half Cherokee. In the late 1860s, he began hauling goods by wagon between Texas and the Kansas Pacific Railroad. His route crossed rivers at the best places and passed by water holes. Ranchers began using the Chisholm Trail in 1867. Within five years, more than one million cattle had walked the road.

The Life of a Cowhand

Ranchers employed cowhands to tend their cattle and drive herds to market. These hard workers rode alongside the huge herds in good and bad weather. They kept the cattle moving and rounded up strays. After the Civil War, veterans of the Confederate Army made up the majority of the cowhands who worked in Texas. However, it is estimated that nearly one in three cowhands was either Mexican American or African American. Some cowhands dreamed of setting aside enough money to start a herd of their own. Most, in the end, just worked to earn wages.

Spanish Heritage American cowhands learned much about riding, roping, and branding from Spanish and Mexican vaqueros (vah KYEHR ohs). **Vaqueros** were skilled riders who herded cattle on ranches in Mexico, California, and the Southwest.

The gear used by American cowhands was modeled on the tools of the vaquero. Cowhands used the leather lariat to catch cattle and horses. "Lariat" comes from the Spanish word for rope. Cowhands wore wide-brimmed hats like the Spanish *sombrero*. Their leather leggings, called "chaps," were modeled on Spanish *chaparreras* (chap ah RAY rahs). Chaps protected a rider's legs from the thorny plants that grow in the Southwest.

On the Trail A cattle drive was hot, dirty, tiring, and often boring work. A cowboy's day could last for nearly 18 hours. The work was so strenuous that cowhands usually brought a number of horses so that each day a fresh one would be available. Cowhands worked in all kinds of weather and faced many dangers, including prairie dog holes, rattlesnakes, and fierce thunderstorms. They had to prevent nervous cattle from drowning while crossing a fast-flowing river. They had to fight raging grass fires. They also faced attacks from cattle thieves who roamed the countryside.

One of the cowhand's worst fears on a cattle drive was a stampede. A clap of thunder or a gunshot could set thousands of longhorns off at a run. Cowhands had to avoid the crush of hoofs and horns while attempting to turn the stampeding herd in a wide circle.

Most cowhands did not work for themselves. Instead, they were hired hands for the owners of large ranches. For all their hard work, cowhands were fed, housed, and lucky to earn $1 a day! Even in the 1870s, this was low pay.

AS YOU READ **Find Main Ideas** Use the heading and subheadings to start an outline of the main ideas in this section.

▲ Past

▲ Present

The Cow Towns

Cattle drives ended in cow towns that had sprung up along the railroad lines. The Chisholm Trail, for example, ended in Abilene, Kansas. Other cow towns in Kansas were Wichita, Caldwell, and Dodge City. In cow towns, cattle were held in great pens until they could be loaded into railroad cars and shipped to markets in the East.

In Abilene and other busy cow towns, dance halls, saloons, hotels, and restaurants catered to the cowhands. Sheriffs often had a hard time keeping the peace. Some cowhands spent wild nights drinking, dancing, and gambling.

Cow towns also attracted settlers who wanted to build stable communities where families could thrive. Doctors, barbers, artisans, bankers, and merchants helped to turn cow towns into communities.

The main street of a town was where people conducted business. Almost every town had a general store that sold groceries, tools, clothing, and all sorts of other goods. The general store also served as a social center where people could talk and exchange the latest news. As a town grew, drugstores, hardware stores, and even ice-cream parlors lined its main street.

Religion also played an important role for the townspeople. Throughout the West, places of worship grew in number and membership. They served as spiritual and social centers and as symbols of progress and stability. "A church does as much to build up a town as a school, a railroad, or a fair," noted one New Mexico newspaper.

The Cattle Boom

In the 1870s, ranching spread north from Texas and across the grassy Plains. Soon, cattle grazed from Kansas to present-day Montana. Ranchers had built a Cattle Kingdom in the West. They came to expect high profits. Millions of dollars poured into the West from people in the East and in foreign countries who wanted to earn money from the cattle boom. However, the boom did not last.

The Open Range Ranchers let their cattle run wild on the open range. To identify cattle, each ranch had its own brand that was burned into a cow's hide.

Sometimes, there were conflicts on the range. When sheepherders moved onto the Plains, ranchers tried to drive them out. The ranchers complained that sheep nibbled the grass so low that cattle could not eat it. To protect the range, which they saw as their own, ranchers sometimes attacked sheepherders and their flocks.

The End of the Cattle Kingdom In the 1870s, farmers began moving onto the range. They fenced their fields with barbed wire, which kept cattle and sheep from pushing over fences and trampling plowed fields. As more farmers bought land, the open range began to disappear. Large grants of land to the railroads also limited it.

Nature imposed limits on the cattle boom. After a time, there just was not enough grass to feed all the cattle that lived on the plains. The need to buy feed and land pushed up the costs. Diseases such as "Texas fever" sometimes destroyed entire herds. Then, the bitterly cold winters of 1886 and 1887 killed entire herds of cattle. In the summer, severe heat and drought dried up water holes and scorched the grasslands.

Cattle owners began to buy land and fence it in. Soon, farmers and ranchers divided the open range into a patchwork of large fenced plots. The days of the Cattle Kingdom were over.

Section 3 Assessment

Recall

1. Identify Explain the significance of (a) Chisholm Trail, (b) Cattle Kingdom.

2. Define (a) cattle drive, (b) vaquero, (c) cow town.

Comprehension

3. How did the Cattle Kingdom begin?

4. Describe the life of a cowhand.

5. Why did cow towns develop?

Critical Thinking and Writing

6. Exploring the Main Idea Review the Main Idea statement at the beginning of this section. Then, write several paragraphs describing the cattle industry in the 1870s and 1880s.

7. Analyzing Information How do you think the growth of the Cattle Kingdom affected the Plains Indians? Explain.

ACTIVITY

Take It to the NET
Connecting to Today
Where do boomtowns exist today? Use the Internet to find out about boomtowns such as those in Silicon Valley. How do they compare with earlier boomtowns? Write a brief report. Visit *The American Nation* section of **www.phschool.com** for help in completing the activity.

Evaluating Written Sources

What was the "Old West" really like? As you have learned, historical evidence comes from many sources. Evaluating the validity of written sources is important in putting together a picture of the past.

In his novel *The Big Sky*, the newspaperman and author A. B. Guthrie, Jr. (1901–1991) wrote the following description of life in the West in the 1800s. *The Big Sky* was published in 1947:

66 This was the way to live. . . . A body got so's he felt everything was kin to him, the earth and sky and buffalo and beaver and the yellow moon at night. It was better than being walled in by a house, better than breathing in spoiled air and feeling caged like a varmint. 99

The following passage was written by Teddy Blue Abbott, a famous cowboy in the 1880s. Here, he describes a blizzard in Montana in 1887. Abbott's account was published in 1939 in a book called *We Pointed Them North: Recollections of a Cowpuncher.*

66 The cattle drifted down on all the rivers. . . . On the Missouri we lost I don't know how many that way. They would walk out on the ice and the ones behind would push the front ones in. The cowpunchers worked like slaves to move them back in the hills, but as all the outfits cut their forces down every winter, they were shorthanded. No one knows how they worked but themselves. They saved thousands of cattle. Think of riding all day in a blinding snow storm, the temperature fifty and sixty below zero, and no dinner. 99

Learn the Skill *To evaluate written sources, use the following steps:*

1. **Identify the sources.** Knowing the background of a writer helps you evaluate that person's account.

2. **Note the context.** When was the account written? In what form did it appear? What was the purpose of the account?

3. **Analyze the point of view.** What is the message? How does the writer feel about the subject?

4. **Evaluate the validity of the material.** How true is this account? Why do you think so?

Practice the Skill *Answer the following questions about the passages above:*

1. **(a)** Who was A. B. Guthrie? **(b)** Who was Teddy Blue Abbott? **(c)** Which passage is from a firsthand account?

2. **(a)** When did each account appear? **(b)** In what form did it appear? **(c)** What was the purpose of each account?

3. **(a)** What message does Guthrie's passage give? **(b)** What is the message in Abbott's account? **(c)** How does each writer feel about his subject?

4. Which account is more accurate? Why do you think so?

Apply the Skill *See the Chapter Review and Assessment.*

4 Indian Peoples in Retreat

Reading Focus

- What promises did the government make to Indians?
- Why did the buffalo begin to disappear?
- How did the movement west help end the Indian way of life?
- Why did reformers fail?

Taking Notes

Copy the concept web at right. As you read, fill in the blank ovals with events that show the effects of western settlement on Native American life. Add as many ovals as you need.

Settlers ask for protection

THE EFFECTS OF WESTERN SETTLEMENT

4

Settlers continue to go west

Main Idea Despite government promises to protect their land, Indian peoples found their way of life threatened as white settlers invaded their territory.

Setting the Scene
In 1883, Sitting Bull, a Lakota war chief and holy man, addressed a group of senators from Washington.

> 66 If a man loses anything and goes back and looks carefully for it he will find it, and that is what the Indians are doing now when they ask you to give them the things that were promised them in the past. And I do not think they should be treated like beasts, and that is the reason I have grown up with the feelings I have. 99
>
> —Tatanka Iyotanka (Sitting Bull), Report to the Senate Committee, 1883

As settlers moved into the West after the Civil War, the government promised to protect Indian hunting grounds. However, the government soon broke its promises, as more settlers pushed westward. When Indians resisted white settlement, wars erupted. The result was tragedy for the Indian peoples.

AS YOU READ **Sitting Bull**
Find Main Ideas
What is Sitting Bull asking of the senators?

Promises Made and Broken

Conflict began as early as the 1840s, when settlers and miners began to cross Indian hunting grounds. The settlers and miners asked for government protection from the Indians.

Fort Laramie Treaty The government built a string of forts to protect settlers and miners. In 1851, federal government officials met with Indian nations near Fort Laramie in Wyoming. The officials asked each nation to keep to a limited area. In return, they promised money, domestic animals, agricultural tools, and other goods. Officials told the Native Americans that the lands that were reserved for them would be theirs forever.

Native American leaders agreed to the terms of the Fort Laramie Treaty. However, in 1858, gold was discovered at Pikes Peak in Colorado. A wave of miners rushed to land that the government had promised to the Cheyennes and Arapahos. Federal officials forced

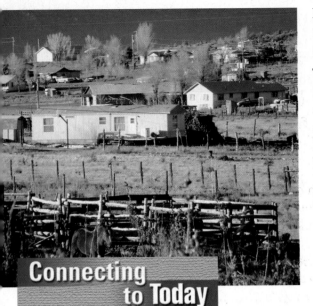

Connecting to Today

Housing on Indian Reservations

Since the late 1800s, many Native Americans in the West have lived a dreary existence on reservations. Today, one of the biggest problems on the reservations is housing. Homes are crowded and often lack adequate plumbing. Older people, especially, have been known to freeze to death in the cold, drafty shacks. The government is trying to help by offering home mortgage loans. Other help comes from the Red Feather Development Group, which teaches the straw-bale construction technique. This is an efficient and economical method of building. The first home, built on the Crow Reservation, is now a model for buildings being constructed by Native Americans on other reservations in the West.

How can the new building technique help the housing problem?

Indian leaders to sign a new treaty giving up the land around Pikes Peak. Some Native Americans refused to accept the agreement. They attacked white settlers.

The Chivington Massacre The settlers struck back. In 1864, Colonel John Chivington led his militia against a Cheyenne village whose leaders had come to a fort asking for protection. When Chivington attacked, the Indians raised both a white flag of surrender and the flag of the United States. Chivington ignored the flags. He ordered his men to destroy the village and take no prisoners. In the Chivington Massacre, the militia slaughtered more than 200 men, women, and children.

People throughout the United States were outraged at the brutality and the bloodshed. "When the white man comes in my country he leaves a trail of blood behind him," said Lakota War Chief Red Cloud. Across the Plains, soldiers and Indians went to war.

Learning "American" Ways In 1867, federal officials established a peace commission to end the wars on the Plains so that settlers would be safe. The commission urged Native Americans to settle down and live as white farmers did. It also urged them to send their children to white schools to learn "American" ways.

Forced Onto Reservations In 1867, the Kiowas, Comanches, and other southern Plains Indians signed a new treaty with the government. They promised to move to Indian Territory in present-day Oklahoma. The soil there was poor. Also, most Plains Indians were hunters, not farmers. The Indians did not like the treaty but knew they had no choice.

The Lakotas and Arapahos of the northern Plains also signed a treaty. They agreed to live on reservations in present-day South Dakota. A reservation is a limited area set aside for Native Americans.

End of the Buffalo

The Plains Indians suffered from lost battles and broken treaties. Even worse for them, however, was the destruction of the buffalo.

The decline of the buffalo began before the arrival of white settlers. Herds of buffalo lived in areas east of the Mississippi and west of the Rockies. However, with disease, drought, and destruction of the areas in which they lived, the herds were slowly growing smaller. As the market demand for buffalo robes increased during the 1830s and 1840s, professional buffalo hunters killed more buffalo. In addition, buffalo hunting became a pleasure sport where railroads cut through the areas in which buffalo lived. Indian people themselves learned to hunt more efficiently. Some Indian tribes, such as the Pawnees, continued to hunt buffalo even though they recognized that the number of buffalo was decreasing. The buffalo hunt was a part of their culture that they did not want to give up. As the buffalo disappeared, so did the Plains Indians' way of life.

The War for the West

Settlers and miners continued to move into the West. They wanted more and more land for themselves. Even on reservations, the Indians were not left in peace.

Custer's Last Stand In 1874, prospectors found gold in the Black Hills region of the Lakota, or Sioux, reservation. Thousands of miners rushed to the area. Led by Sitting Bull, Crazy Horse, and other Lakota chiefs, the Indians fought back in what became known as the Sioux War of 1876.

In June 1876, Colonel George A. Custer led a column of soldiers into the Little Bighorn Valley. They were sent by the federal government to protect the miners. A group of 600 men under Custer's command prepared to attack. Indian scouts warned Custer that there were many Lakotas and Cheyennes camped ahead. Nearly 2,000 warriors awaited Custer and his men. Custer divided his troops and attacked with only 225 men. Custer and all his men died in the Battle of Little Bighorn.

The Indian victory at the Little Bighorn was short-lived. The army soon defeated the Lakotas and Cheyennes. Then, Congress ordered that no food rations be distributed to the Indians until they agreed to the government's demands. To avoid starvation, the Lakotas gave up most claims to the Black Hills and other territory. In this way, they surrendered about one third of the lands that the United States government had guaranteed them with the Fort Laramie Treaty.

Sitting Bull and Crazy Horse had taken their few remaining followers to Canada. Eventually, both men returned.

Chief Joseph Flees The Nez Percé lived in the Snake River valley, at the place where Oregon, Washington, and Idaho meet. In 1855, some Nez Percé signed a treaty with the United States government in which they relinquished part of their land.

In the 1860s, gold strikes brought miners onto Nez Percé land. The government ordered the Nez Percés to move to a reservation in Idaho. Those who had not signed the treaty refused. Led by Chief Joseph, about 500 Nez Percés fled north to Canada. Army troops followed close behind.

In the months that followed, the Nez Percés fought off or eluded pursuing army units. Finally, after a tragic journey of more than 1,000 miles, Chief Joseph decided that he must surrender. Of the approximately 800 Nez Percés who had set out with him, fewer than 450 remained.

The Apache Wars In the arid lands of the Southwest, the Apaches fiercely resisted the loss of their lands. One leader, Geronimo, continued fighting the longest. In 1876, he assumed leadership of a band of Apache warriors when the government tried to force his people onto a reservation.

Geronimo waged war off and on for the next 10 years. From Mexico, he led frequent raids into Arizona and New Mexico. His surrender in 1886 marked the end of formal warfare between Indians and whites.

An American Profile

Geronimo (1829–1909)

Geronimo was an Apache warrior, revered for his wisdom. He was also one of the fiercest and most courageous warriors the United States army ever pursued. When his family was killed by whites, Geronimo vowed vengeance and led his band of warriors in fierce raids against whites. More than once, he was captured, only to escape. In the last campaign, his small, ragged band was pursued by over 5,000 United States troops. Finally, in 1886, Geronimo was forced to surrender.

Why was Geronimo willing to fight against such great odds to remain free?

Native American Territory, 1850–1890

GEOGRAPHY Skills

Fighting between Native Americans and the United States government went on for years, until most Indians were forced onto reservations.

1. **Location** On the map, locate (a) Fort Laramie, (b) Little Bighorn, (c) Apache reservations, (d) Wounded Knee.

2. **Region** In which areas of the country did Native Americans still retain much of their land in 1870?

3. **Critical Thinking Drawing Inferences** Why do you think the Apaches of the desert Southwest were one of the last Indian nations to lose their land?

The Indian Way of Life Ends

Many Indians longed for their lost way of life. On the reservations, the Lakotas and other Plains Indians turned to a religious ceremony called the Ghost Dance. It celebrated the time when Native Americans lived freely on the Plains.

The Ghost Dance In 1889, word spread that a prophet named Wovoka had appeared among the Paiute people of the southern Plains. Wovoka said that the Great Spirit would make a new world for his people, free from whites and filled with plenty. To bring about this new world, all the Indians had to do was to dance the Ghost Dance.

In their ceremonies, Ghost Dancers joined hands in a large circle in which they danced, chanted, and prayed. As they danced, some felt a "growing happiness." Others saw a glowing vision of a new world.

Settlers React Many settlers grew alarmed. The Ghost Dancers, they said, were preparing for war. The settlers persuaded the government to outlaw the Ghost Dance.

In December 1890, police officers entered a Lakota reservation to arrest Sitting Bull, who had returned from Canada and was living on the reservation. They claimed that he was spreading the Ghost Dance among the Lakotas. In the struggle that followed, Sitting Bull was accidentally shot and killed.

Massacre at Wounded Knee Upset by Sitting Bull's death, groups of Lakotas fled the reservations. Army troops pursued them to Wounded Knee Creek, in present-day South Dakota. On December 29, the Indians were preparing to surrender. As nervous troops watched, the Indians began to give up their guns.

Suddenly, a shot rang out. The army opened fire. By the time the shooting stopped, nearly 300 Native American men, women, and children lay dead. About 25 soldiers had also died. The fighting at Wounded Knee marked the end of the Ghost Dance religion.

Reformers Fail

The Native Americans were no longer able to resist the government. During the late 1800s, more Indians were forced onto reservations.

Reformers Speak Out Many people, Indian and white, spoke out against the tragedy that was occurring. One reformer, Susette La Flesche, was the daughter of an Omaha chief. She wrote and lectured about the destruction of the Native American way of life.

Another reformer, Helen Hunt Jackson, published *A Century of Dishonor* in 1881. The book recounts the long history of broken treaties between the United States and the Native Americans.

A New Federal Policy Calls for reform led Congress to pass the Dawes Act in 1887. The act encouraged Native Americans to become farmers. Some tribal lands were divided up and given to individual Native American families.

The Dawes Act was unsuccessful. To Native Americans, land was an open place for riding and hunting. As a result, Indians often sold their shares of land to whites for low prices.

Life on the reservations changed Native American culture. The federal government took away the power of Indian leaders. In their place, it appointed government agents to make most decisions.

AS YOU READ **Predict** Before reading this section, predict what the reformers wanted to accomplish.

Section 4 Assessment

Recall

1. **Identify** Explain the significance of **(a)** Sitting Bull, **(b)** Fort Laramie Treaty, **(c)** Chivington Massacre, **(d)** Battle of Little Bighorn, **(e)** Chief Joseph, **(f)** Geronimo, **(g)** Ghost Dance, **(h)** Susette La Flesche, **(i)** Helen Hunt Jackson, **(j)** Dawes Act.

Comprehension

2. What promises to Native Americans did the government break?
3. How did the loss of the buffalo affect Native Americans?
4. Describe two conflicts between Native Americans and settlers.

5. How did reformers try to help Native Americans?

Critical Thinking and Writing

6. **Exploring the Main Idea** Review the Main Idea statement at the beginning of this section. Then, write a paragraph describing what you think the government could have done to avoid wars with the Native Americans in the West.
7. **Making Inferences** Why do you think the religious movement called the Ghost Dance became so popular among Native Americans?

ACTIVITY

Writing Editorials As a reformer supporting the cause of Native Americans, you feel the Dawes Act is significant. Write an editorial giving your reasons for supporting it. Then, write an editorial that a Native American might have composed in response to the Dawes Act.

5 Farming

Reading Focus

- Why did farmers and other settlers move west?
- What was the Oklahoma land rush?
- Why was life hard for Plains farmers?
- Why did farmers help form the Populist Party?

Key Terms

sod house

sodbuster

cooperative

wholesale

inflation

Taking Notes

Copy this incomplete Venn diagram. As you read, write key facts about the National Grange and the Farmers' Alliance. Write common characteristics in the overlapping section.

NATIONAL GRANGE
- Organized in 1867
-

• Farmers unite
•

FARMERS' ALLIANCE
- Organized in the 1870s
-

Main Idea The Homestead Act opened the West to farmers who struggled to survive the harsh environment of the Great Plains.

A farmer hoping for rain

Summarize Write two or three sentences describing the challenges Plains farmers faced.

Setting the Scene No matter what he did, W. M. Taylor could not get ahead. He planted his crops in the rich Nebraska soil and tended them carefully. Sometimes the weather or grasshoppers ruined his harvest. However, in 1891, it was a human agent that was destroying his livelihood. Wrote Taylor:

> 66 We are cursed, many of us financially, beyond redemption, not by the hot winds so much as by the swindling games of the bankers and money loaners, who have taken the money and are now after the property, leaving the farmer moneyless and homeless. 99
>
> —W. M. Taylor, Letter to Editor, *Farmers' Alliance*,
> January 10, 1891

Like the miners and ranchers who came before them, farmers faced many challenges, including deals with "bankers and money loaners" who charged high interest rates, then laid their own claims to the land of farmers who could not pay their debts.

Farmers Move West

Congress passed the Homestead Act in 1862. The law promised 160 acres of free land to anyone who paid a small filing fee and farmed it for five years.

Problems With Homesteading Many immigrants and easterners rushed to accept the offer of free land. They planted their 160 acres with wheat and corn. By 1900, half a million Americans had set up farms under the Homestead Act. Under the Homestead Act the land was free, but many people did not have the money to move west and start a farm. Also, only about 20 percent of the homestead land went directly to small farmers. Land-owning companies took large areas of land illegally and resold it to farmers at a high price.

Exodusters African Americans joined the rush for homestead land. The largest group moved west at the end of Reconstruction, when the freedoms blacks had gained after the Civil War were slipping away.

In 1879, a group of African Americans moved to Kansas. They called themselves Exodusters, after Exodus, the book of the Bible that tells about the Jews escaping from slavery in Egypt. Between 40,000 and 70,000 African Americans had moved to Kansas by 1881.

Los Mexicanos Easterners who moved to the Southwest met a large Spanish-speaking population there. As you recall, the United States had gained much of the Southwest through the Mexican War. Spanish-speaking southwesterners called themselves Mexicanos. White Americans who lived in the region were known as Anglos.

Most Mexicanos lived in small villages, where they farmed and raised sheep. A few wealthy Mexicanos were large landowners and merchants.

As more Anglos settled in the Southwest, they acquired the best jobs and land. Often, Mexicanos found themselves working as low-paid laborers on Anglo farms. In New Mexico, in the 1880s, angry farmers known as *Las Gorras Blancas*, or "White Caps," demanded fair treatment. Other Mexicanos in Arizona founded the Hispanic-American Alliance in 1894 to protect and fight for their rights.

The Oklahoma Land Rush

As settlers spread across the West, free land began to disappear. The last major land rush took place in Oklahoma. Several Indian nations

Viewing History

The Rush for Land

In 1889, at the stroke of noon, thousands of hopeful home-steaders rushed across the Okla-homa border to claim a piece of farmland. **Drawing Inferences** *What type of people do you think these homesteaders were?*

lived there, but the government forced them to sell their land. The government then announced that farmers could claim free homesteads in Oklahoma. They could not stake their claims, however, until noon on April 22, 1889.

On the appointed day, as many as 100,000 land seekers lined up at the Oklahoma border. At noon, a gunshot rang out. The "boomers" charged into Oklahoma, but they found that others were already there. "Sooners" had sneaked into Oklahoma before the official opening and had staked out much of the best land.

Hard Life on the Plains

Farmers on the western plains faced many hardships. The first problem was shelter. Because wood was scarce on the Great Plains, many farmers built houses of sod—soil held together by grass roots. Rain was a serious problem for sod houses. One pioneer woman complained that her sod roof "leaked two days before a rain and for three days after."

Sodbusting The fertile soil of the Great Plains was covered with a layer of thick sod that could crack wood or iron plows. A new sodbusting plow made of steel reached the market by 1877. It enabled sodbusters, as Plains farmers were called, to cut through the sod to the soil below.

Technology helped farmers in other ways. On the Great Plains, water often lay hundreds of feet underground. Farmers built windmills to pump the water to the surface. New reapers, threshing machines, and binders helped farmers to harvest crops.

Surviving the Climate The dry climate was a constant threat. When too little rain fell, the crops shriveled and died. Dry weather also brought the threat of fire. A grass fire traveled "as fast as a horse could run."

The summers often brought swarms of grasshoppers that ate everything in their path—crops, food, tree bark, even clothing.

Pioneers dreaded the winters most. With few trees or hills to block the wind, icy gusts built huge snowdrifts. The deep snow buried farm animals and trapped families inside their homes.

Women on the Plains Women had to be strong to survive the hardships of life on the Great Plains. Since there were few stores, women made clothing, soap, candles, and other goods by hand. They also cooked and preserved food needed for the long winter.

Women served their communities in many ways. Most schoolteachers were women. When there were no doctors nearby, women treated the sick and injured.

Pioneer families usually lived miles apart. They relaxed by visiting with neighbors and gathering for church services. Picnics, dances, and weddings were eagerly awaited events.

More Crops, Less Money Despite the harsh conditions, farmers began to thrive in the West. Before long, they were selling huge amounts of wheat and corn in the nation's growing cities and even in Europe.

Then, farmers faced an unexpected problem. The more they harvested, the less they earned. In 1881, a bushel of wheat sold for $1.19. By 1894, the price had plunged to 49 cents. Western farmers were hurt most by low grain prices. They had borrowed money during good times to buy land and machinery. When wheat prices fell, they could not repay their debts.

Farmers Take Action

As early as the 1860s, farmers began to work together. They learned that they could improve their condition through economic cooperation and political action.

The Grange In 1867, farmers formed the National Grange. Grangers wanted to boost farm profits and reduce the rates that railroads charged for shipping grain.

Grangers helped farmers set up cooperatives. In a cooperative a group of farmers pooled their money to buy seeds and tools wholesale. Wholesale means buying or selling something in large quantities at lower prices. Grangers built cooperative warehouses so that farmers could store grain cheaply while waiting for better selling prices.

Leaders of the Grange urged farmers to use their vote. In 1873, western and southern Grangers pledged to vote only for candidates who supported their aims. They elected officials who understood the farmers' problems. As a result, several states passed laws limiting what could be charged for grain shipment and storage. Nevertheless, crop prices continued to drop. Farmers sank deeper into debt.

Farmers' Alliance Another group, the Farmers' Alliance, joined the struggle in the 1870s. Like the Grange, the Alliance set up cooperatives and warehouses. The Farmers' Alliance spread from Texas through the South and into the Plains states. Alliance leaders also tried to join with factory workers and miners who were angry about their treatment by employers.

Some women were active in the group. One of the most popular speakers was Kansas lawyer Mary Elizabeth Lease.

The Populists

In 1892, farmers and labor unions joined together to form the Populist party. At their first national convention, the Populists demanded that the government help to raise farm prices and to regulate railroad rates. They also called for an income tax, an eight-hour workday, and limits on immigration.

Another Populist party demand was "free silver." Populists wanted all silver mined in the West to be coined into money. They said that farm prices dropped because there was not enough money in circulation. Free silver would increase the money supply and make it easier for farmers to repay their debts.

Eastern bankers and factory owners disagreed. They argued that increasing the money supply would cause inflation, or increased prices. Business people feared that inflation would wreck the

An American Profile

Mary Elizabeth Lease
(1853–1933)

Mary Elizabeth Lease's father and two brothers died in the Civil War. Since she held the Democratic party responsible for the war, she opposed the Democrats throughout her political career. Lease joined the Farmers' Alliance of the Populist Party. She quickly became its most influential speaker, making over 160 speeches for the 1890 campaign. One newspaper alleged that she told farmers in Kansas to "raise less corn and more hell." Lease also helped to defeat the Kansas senator, Democrat John Ingalls, a big victory for the Farmers' Alliance.

What did Mary Lease mean when she told the farmers to "raise less corn and more hell"?

Primary Source

"The Cross of Gold"

On July 9, 1896, William Jennings Bryan spoke at the Democratic National Convention:

"You come to us and tell us that the great cities are in favor of the gold standard; we reply that the great cities rest upon our broad and fertile prairies. Burn down your cities and leave our farms, and your cities will spring up again . . . but destroy our farms and the grass will grow in the streets of every city in the country . . . we will answer [the] demand for a gold standard by saying . . . You shall not press down upon the brow of labor this crown of thorns, you shall not crucify mankind upon a cross of gold."

—William Jennings Bryan, speech to the Democratic National Convention, July 9, 1896

Analyzing Primary Sources

What does Bryan mean when he says that grass will grow in the cities if the farms are destroyed?

economy. They favored the gold standard with which the government backs every dollar with a certain amount of gold. Since the supply of gold is limited, there would be less money in circulation. Prices would drop.

Election of 1896 The Populist candidate for President in 1892 won one million votes. The next year, a severe depression brought the Populists new support. In 1894, they elected six senators and seven representatives to Congress.

The Populists looked toward the election of 1896 with high hopes. Their program had been endorsed by one of the great orators of the age: William Jennings Bryan.

A young Democratic congressman from Nebraska, Bryan was called the "Great Commoner" because he championed the cause of common people. Like the Populists, he believed that the nation needed to increase the supply of money. At the Democratic convention in 1896, Bryan made a powerful speech against the rich and for free silver.

Both Democrats and Populists supported Bryan for President. However, bankers and business people feared that Bryan would ruin the economy. They supported William McKinley, the Republican candidate.

Bryan narrowly lost the election of 1896. He carried the South and West, but McKinley won the heavily populated states of the East.

The End of the Populist Party The Populist party broke up after 1896. One reason was that the Democrats adopted several Populist causes. Also, prosperity returned in the late 1890s. People worried less about railroad rates and free silver.

Section 5 Assessment

Recall

1. **Identify** Explain the significance of **(a)** Homestead Act, **(b)** Exodusters, **(c)** Hispanic-American Alliance, **(d)** National Grange, **(e)** Farmers' Alliance, **(f)** Populist Party, **(g)** William Jennings Bryan, **(h)** William McKinley.
2. **Define** **(a)** sod house, **(b)** sodbuster, **(c)** cooperative, **(d)** wholesale, **(e)** inflation.

Comprehension

3. **(a)** What was the Homestead Act? **(b)** What was the Oklahoma land rush?
4. Describe the life of a Plains farmer.
5. How did the National Grange help farmers?
6. What was the purpose of the Populist party?

Critical Thinking and Writing

7. **Exploring the Main Idea** Review the Main Idea statement at the beginning of this section. Then, discuss the following questions: What geographic features of the Great Plains created a need for new kinds of machinery? How were these needs met?
8. **Analyzing Information** Discuss the reasons why the Populist party became popular.

ACTIVITY

Drawing a Political Cartoon You are a cartoonist during the late 1800s. Draw a political cartoon to illustrate one of the problems that farmers faced during this period.

Sodbusting *on the Plains*

The earliest settlers of the West quickly grabbed the fertile land near rivers and streams. Later homesteaders were forced to settle on outlying lands that had much less moisture. Out on the Great Plains, these settlers faced enormous challenges.

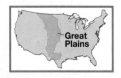

The Great Plains that were settled by homesteaders covered a huge portion of the middle part of the continent, as this map shows. The plains were covered with a variety of prairie grasses, the most common of which was buffalo grass. The grass was difficult to cut through. Its roots were densely inter-twined. This was the sod that the farmers had to break up in order to plant their crops.

A sod house
Wood was scarce on the prairie, so the farmers invented a new kind of shelter: a sod house, or soddy. The long rows of sod turned over by the farmer's plow were cut into bricks with an ax. These blocks of sod were stacked in layers to make the walls. Timber—or twigs, branches, and bushes—was used to make a roof support, which was then covered with more sod. The dirt floor was packed down and smoothed. Settlers used dried buffalo chips as fuel to heat their homes.

A Plains farm family

Inside, the sod house was warm in winter and cool in summer. Occupants often had to deal with unwanted "guests," however, such as mice and—worst of all—prairie rattlesnakes. Outside, the family of settlers had to cope with insects—grasshoppers often invaded and ate entire crops. There was a lack of water, lack of schools and medical services, and above all, the terrible isolation of the western prairies. Despite all the difficul-ties, most sodbusters were determined to stay.

ACTIVITY

Suppose you could travel back in time to 1880 and visit a sodbuster family. You are able to take one mod-ern invention with you to help make life easier for the farmer. Write a para-graph describing what item you would take and why.

CREATING A CHAPTER SUMMARY

Copy the concept web below. As you read, fill in the blank ovals with important events that shaped the West in the late 1800s. Add as many ovals as you need.

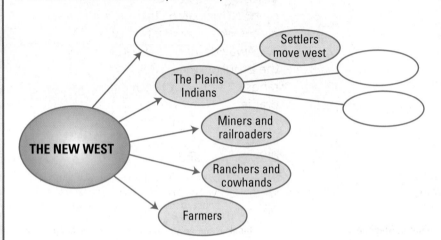

THE NEW WEST

The Plains Indians

Settlers move west

Miners and railroaders

Ranchers and cowhands

Farmers

For additional review and enrichment activities, see the interactive version of *The American Nation,* available on the Web and on CD-ROM.

Take It to the NET

Chapter Self-Test For practice test questions for Chapter 19, visit *The American Nation* section of **www.phschool.com**.

Building Vocabulary

Review the meaning of the chapter vocabulary words listed below. Then, write a sentence for each word in which you define the word and describe its relation to the events that changed the West from 1865 to 1914.

1. travois
2. lode
3. vigilante
4. transcontinental railroad
5. cattle drive
6. cow town
7. sod house
8. cooperative
9. wholesale
10. inflation

Reviewing Key Facts

11. How did the Plains Indians rely on the horse and the buffalo? (Section 1)
12. Discuss the effects of mining on the West. (Section 2)
13. (a) What caused the cattle boom of the 1870s? (b) Why did the Cattle Kingdom end? (Section 3)

14. How did life change for the Plains Indians between the 1860s and the 1880s? (Section 4)
15. (a) What problems did farmers face? (b) How did farmers in the late 1800s unite? (Section 5)

Critical Thinking and Writing

16. **Connecting to Geography: Regions** Settlers crossing the Great Plains saw it as a vast land of grass. Yet, Native Americans survived on the Great Plains for nearly 200 years. Discuss the ways in which the geography of the region offered opportunities and challenges to the Native Americans and then to the new settlers.
17. **Evaluating Information** Near the end of the nineteenth century, Native American Black Elk wrote, "We are prisoners of war." Do you agree with this statement? Explain.
18. **Drawing Inferences** Why do you think settlers stayed in spite of the hardships of life on the Great Plains?
19. **Applying Information** (a) What is inaccurate in the way movie westerns show the life of the American cowhand? (b) Why do you think the stories of cowhands live on today?

Analyzing Primary Sources

In 1890, Washington Gladden, a Congregational minister, spoke about the farmer. Read the excerpt and answer the questions that follow:

66The business of farming has become, for some reasons, extremely unprofitable. With the hardest work and with the sharpest economy, the average farmer is unable to make both ends meet; every year closes with debt, and the mortgage grows . . . The Labor Bureau of Connecticut . . . by an investigation of 693 representative farms, [shows] that the average annual reward of the farm proprietor of that state . . . is $181.31, while the average annual wage of the ordinary hired man is $368.36.**99**

—Washington Gladden,
Congregational Minister, 1890

20. How does Gladden feel about farming?
21. What statistics does the Labor Bureau show about a farmer's earnings?
22. Do you think Gladden would support the Populist platform? Explain.

Evaluating Written Sources

On April 22, 1889, Oklahoma was opened for settlement. Pioneers waited for the signal to start the race to stake their claims. Read the following passage and answer the questions.

66Here was a contest in which thousands participated. Truly an historical event! We, . . . witnessed the spectacle. . . . Away dashed the thoroughbreds, the broncos, the pintos, and the mustangs at a breakneck pace across the prairie. . . . It was amazing to witness the recklessness of those cow-boy riders; they jumped obstacles; they leaped ditches; . . . and when they came to a ravine too wide to leap, down they would go with a rush, and up the other side with a spurt of energy. . . .**99**

—Hamilton S. Wicks, "The Opening of Oklahoma," 1889

23. How would you describe the riders?
   A Eager but careful as they raced
   B Skilled riders who raced wildly
   C Skilled riders who jumped pools and fences
   D Eager but not skilled riders
24. How true is this account? Explain.

ACTIVITIES

Connecting With . . . Government and Citizenship

Dangerous Jobs Workers who built the transcontinental railroad were subjected to hazardous conditions. Mining was another dangerous occupation. Should the government be responsible for imposing restrictions on dangerous occupations? Write your opinion in a persuasive essay.

 Take It to the NET

Connecting to Today

Preparing a Report Today, groups of people still meet to buy supplies wholesale. This helps lower the prices of goods for each person. Use the Internet to research cooperatives. List the advantages and disadvantages of cooperatives. For help in starting this activity, visit *The American Nation* section of **www.phschool.com**.

Honoring Native Americans

Writing a Speech Use the Internet to find out about the large sculpture of Chief Crazy Horse that is being carved into a mountain near Custer, South Dakota. Then, write a speech that might be given at a ceremony honoring Chief Crazy Horse and other Native Americans. For help in starting this activity, visit *The American Nation* section of **www.phschool.com**.

Dragon's Gate
Laurence Yep

Introduction When Charles Crocker, the head of the Central Pacific Railroad, needed workers, he at first dismissed the idea of using Chinese laborers. However, in the end, nearly 10,000 Chinese laborers picked and chipped a route for the transcontinental railroad through the Sierra Nevada. In *Dragon's Gate,* Laurence Yep uses the experience of the Chinese workers to tell the story of Otter, a Chinese boy who joins his father and uncle in California, where they are working as railroad laborers.

Vocabulary Before you read the selection, find the meaning of these words in a dictionary: **pickax, goad.**

Laurence Yep

As we got ready to leave the next day, I said to Uncle Foxfire, "I want to use a pickax today." When he hesitated, I insisted. "I need to hit something."

Curly looked at me sympathetically. "He could use Doggy's today."

With a thoughtful nod, Uncle Foxfire got the pickax from the stack in the corner and handed it to me.

That day, I felt like I was marching with the others through the snow tunnels to a battle. Glancing around, I saw the same grim look on all the others' faces, and I realized they felt as much grief as I did and were determined to do something about it. Bright Star glanced at me and nodded as if he understood my thoughts. The loss of Doggy's music had bound us even more tightly together than the initial loss of his moon guitar.

Once we reached the tunnel, everyone sprang willingly into action. No one hesitated. No one held back or complained that someone else was doing more work. A few quick orders sent drill teams to the end under Father's command. The others began scraping and clawing at the rock while Uncle Foxfire tried again to teach me to use a pickax.

He swung it, twisting from the waist with his whole torso and shoulders, aiming a blow that would have crushed a water buffalo's skull. He did it effortlessly, ready to deliver one crushing blow after another for twelve hours if he had to. The pickax rang as it bit into the rock; and yet despite all the noise and the force, he hardly seemed to have scraped the rock at all.

Then he had me try the motion without the pickax, correcting a few things. When I finally picked up the pickax, it felt heavy as I lifted it over my shoulder and swung, trying to copy Uncle Foxfire. I let the motion itself bring the weight of my body into the blow. The pickax hit the wall with a clink. As before, my forearms felt numb.

"Good," Uncle Foxfire grunted. "Now get into a rhythm."

I swung the pickax again with all my strength; but the point hardly seemed to dent the hard granite.

"Hit it," Uncle Foxfire goaded me. "Don't pat it."

I aimed the pickax at the wall, and the point landed with a clank.

"I thought you were angry." He pretended to look disgusted.

"I am." This time when I hit the wall, I could feel the vibrations shake my whole body.

"Attack it," Uncle Foxfire urged. "Lazy monkey. Monkey! Monkey!"

Chinese laborers working on the railroad

I could feel anger and fear swell up inside me and explode, and I began to pound the pickax in rhythm to his chant. I hated the slab of stone in front of me—hated it for being hard, hated it for being in the way of the westerners, hated it for making me come here to this crazy place, hated it for a lot of reasons that didn't make any real sense.

I hated the mountain for being so hard. I hated the pickax for not being sharper. My whole world narrowed to a sharp point. I wanted to drive it right through the heart of the Tiger.

Then, as if from a great distance, I heard Uncle Foxfire saying to me, "Easy. That's it. Get into a steady rhythm now." And I became aware of his hand on my shoulder.

I looked to the side. He smiled as if he knew just how much I'd needed to hit something. Then he stepped back so I could begin to swing the pickax in an easier, steadier rhythm. Each blow was still solid; but the stone was so hard, it felt like it was hammering back. . . .

Next to me, Uncle Foxfire had gotten a pickax and was swinging it just as hard. What had seemed like a wide enough space for one became very narrow as we swung our pickaxes in wide arcs that seemed just to miss one another.

Analyzing Literature

1. Why are the workers unhappy as they leave for the tunnel?

   A Their tools are too heavy.

   B They miss Doggy's music.

   C They are tired of marching.

   D They resent Doggy's presence.

2. How does Uncle Foxfire help Otter learn to use the pickax?

   A He guides Otter's arms and shoulders.

   B He quickly hands Otter the pickax.

   C He tries to make Otter angry.

   D He tells Otter to watch the other workers.

3. **Critical Thinking** **Drawing Conclusions** What does Otter experience as he works on the rock?

CHAPTER 20
Industrial Growth

1865–1914

1 Railroads Spur Industry
2 The Rise of Big Business
3 Inventions Change the Nation
4 The Rise of Organized Labor

Vanderbilt towering over his railroad empire

The Haymarket Riot

1869
Cornelius Vanderbilt gains control of the largest railroad empire in the United States.

1886
An explosion during a workers' protest in Chicago's Haymarket Square leads to a wave of antilabor feeling.

1890
Congress passes the Sherman Antitrust Act, which bans trusts and monopolies.

AMERICAN EVENTS

Presidential Terms:	Abraham Lincoln 1861–1865	Andrew Johnson 1865–1869	Ulysses S. Grant 1869–1877	Rutherford B. Hayes 1877–1881	James A. Garfield 1881 · Chester A. Arthur 1881–1885	Grover Cleveland 1885–1889

1860   1875   1890

WORLD EVENTS

▲ **1866**
Swedish chemist Alfred Nobel invents dynamite.

▲ **mid-1880s**
Germany provides sickness, accident, and old age insurance.

Industrial Centers, 1865–1914

Large population centers grew up as American industry boomed.

Key

Meat packing		Auto industry		Coal mines	
Textile industry		Steel industry		Iron mines	
Clothing industry		Pullman cars and locomotives		Oil	

CANADA

Mesabi Ra.

MN · WI · MI · ME · VT · NH · Lowell · Schenectady · NY · MA · CT · RI · Detroit · Chicago · Titusville · Bethlehem · New York · IA · IN · Pittsburgh · PA · NJ · Philadelphia · NE · IL · OH · MD · DE · WY · WV · VA

PACIFIC OCEAN

NV · UT · CO · KS · St. Louis · MO · KY · NC · ATLANTIC OCEAN

CA · AZ · NM · OK · AR · TN · SC · MS · AL · GA

TX · LA · FL

Gulf of Mexico

MEXICO

Albers Equal-Area Projection

0 — 250 — 500 Miles
0 — 250 — 500 Kilometers

Inside Carnegie's steelworks

On the Ford assembly line

1890

The huge Carnegie Steel Company produces more steel than does all of Britain.

Benjamin Harrison	Grover Cleveland	William McKinley
1889–1893	1893–1897	1897–1901

1903

Orville Wright makes the first airplane flight.

Theodore Roosevelt	William Howard Taft
1901–1909	1909–1913

1913

Henry Ford introduces the assembly line in his Highland Park, Michigan, automobile plant.

Woodrow Wilson 1913–1921

1890 · · 1905 · · 1920

1900 ▲

The Labour party is founded in Britain.

1914 ▲

The Panama Canal opens, linking the Caribbean Sea with the Pacific Ocean.

1 Railroads Spur Industry

Reading Focus

- What factors led to the construction of a network of railroads after the Civil War?
- How did railroad executives eliminate competition?
- How did railroad building encourage the growth of the American economy?

Key Terms

gauge

network

consolidate

rebate

pool

Taking Notes

Copy the concept web below. As you read, fill in the blank ovals with information about the age of railroad building after the Civil War. Add as many ovals as you need.

AGE OF RAILROAD BUILDING

Knitting the nation together

Eliminating competition

Pools

Main Idea A boom in railroad building encouraged American industry to grow but gave vast amounts of power to a few railroad owners.

Vanderbilt ignores the public

Draw Inferences Do you think many American people of the time agreed with William Vanderbilt?

Setting the Scene William Vanderbilt knew how to make money. His father, Cornelius, had created a railroad empire worth millions. After the death of Cornelius, William doubled the family fortune. Cornelius had ruthlessly crushed competitors and ignored protests from the public. William followed much the same path. He kept his goal clear, telling reporters:

> 66 The railroads are not run for the benefit of the dear public. That cry is all nonsense. They are built for men who invest their money and expect to get a fair percentage on the same. 99
>
> —William H. Vanderbilt (to reporters), 1882

Railroad men like the Vanderbilts might ignore the public, but no one could ignore the vast changes that railroads had brought. The railroad was a breakthrough in transportation. For the first time, human beings could travel overland without relying on animals. Just as important, railroads were the single most significant spur to the amazing growth of industry in the United States.

A Network of Rails

The Civil War showed the importance of railroads. Railroads carried troops and supplies to the battlefields. They also moved raw materials to factories. After the war, railroad companies began to build new lines all over the country.

Knitting the Nation Together Early railroads were short lines that served local communities. Many lines ran for no more than 50 miles. When passengers and freight reached the end of one line, they had to move to a train on a different line to continue their journey.

Even if the lines had been connected, the problem would not have been eliminated. Different lines used tracks of different gauges, or widths. As a result, the trains from one line could not run on the tracks of another line. In general, the tracks of northern lines used different gauges from those of southern lines.

In 1886, railroads in the South decided to adopt the northern gauge. On May 30, southern railroads stopped running so that work could begin. Using crowbars and sledgehammers, crews worked from dawn to dusk to move the rails a few inches farther apart. When they had finished, some 13,000 miles of track had been changed.

Once the track was standardized, American railroads formed a network, or system of connected lines. The creation of a rail network brought benefits to shippers. Often, rail companies arranged for freight cars on one line to use the tracks of another. For example, goods loaded in Chicago could stay on the same car all the way to New York, instead of being transferred from one car to another. As a result, the shipper had to pay only one fare for the whole distance.

New rails knit the sprawling nation together. By 1900, there were more miles of tracks in the United States than in Europe and Russia combined.

Improving Rail Travel New inventions helped make railway travel safer and faster. On early trains, each railroad car had its own brakes and its own brake operator. If different cars stopped at different times, serious accidents could result. In 1869, George Westinghouse began selling his new air brake. Westinghouse's air brake allowed a locomotive engineer to stop all the railroad cars at once. The air brake increased safety and allowed for longer, faster trains.

Long distance travel also became more comfortable. In 1864, George Pullman designed a railroad sleeping car. Pullman cars had convertible berths for sleeping as well as lavatories. Rail lines also added dining cars. Porters, conductors, and waiters attended to the needs of passengers.

Consolidation Brings Efficiency As railroads grew, they looked for ways to operate more efficiently. Small lines were often costly to run, so many companies began to consolidate, or combine. Larger companies bought up smaller ones or forced them out of business. The Pennsylvania Railroad, for example, consolidated 73 companies into its system.

Tough-minded business people led the drive for consolidation. Cornelius Vanderbilt was among the most powerful of these leaders. The son of a poor farmer, Vanderbilt earned one fortune in steamship lines. He then began to buy up railroad lines in New York State.

Vanderbilt sometimes used ruthless tactics to force smaller owners to sell to him. In the early 1860s, he decided to buy the New York Central Railroad. The owners refused to sell. Vanderbilt then announced that New York Central passengers would not be allowed to transfer to his trains. With their passengers stranded and business dropping sharply, the New York Central owners gave in and sold their line to Vanderbilt.

Vanderbilt then bought up most of the lines between Chicago and Buffalo. By the time of his death in 1877, his companies controlled 4,500 miles of track and linked New York City to the Great Lakes region.

Geography and History

Why Are There Time Zones?

Our system of time zones is a result of the railroad boom of the late 1800s. At that time, many towns kept their own time. When the sun was highest over the town, it was noon. But 100 miles west, where the sun was still rising, the time was a few minutes before noon. Thus, for example, there were 27 local times in Illinois, 23 in Indiana, and 38 in Wisconsin.

To simplify train schedules, railroads established their own uniform time standard. On November 18, 1883, all railway clocks were set to the new standard. In 1918, Congress enacted the Standard Time Act, which was based on time zones in use by railroads.

Why was the old system of keeping time risky for railroad passengers?

POLITICAL CARTOON
Skills

Farmers vs. Railroads

In this 1873 cartoon, Thomas Nast portrayed the railroad as a monster snaking through American farmland.

1. **Comprehension** Whom does the figure with the club represent?

2. **Finding the Main Idea** In the background, the monster has its coils wrapped around a building. What building is it? What point is Nast making?

3. **Critical Thinking** **Analyzing Primary Sources** What devices does Nast use to portray railroads as evil and farmers as good?

Civics

Other consolidations were soon underway. Before long, the major railroads of the United States were organized into a number of systems directed by a handful of wealthy and powerful men.

Building New Lines Railroad builders raced to create thousands of miles of new tracks. In the years after completion of the first transcontinental rail line in 1869, Americans built three more. James Hill, a Canadian-born owner, finished the last major cross-country line in 1893. His Great Northern Railway wound from Duluth, Minnesota, to Everett, Washington.

Unlike other rail lines, the Great Northern was built without financial aid from Congress. To make his railroad succeed, Hill had to turn a profit from the start. He encouraged farmers and ranchers to move to the Northwest and settle near his railroad. He gave seed to farmers and helped them buy equipment. He imported special bulls in order to breed hardier cattle. Not only was Hill's policy generous, it also made good business sense.

Eliminating the Competition

With builders rushing to share in the profits of the railroad boom, overbuilding occurred. Soon, there were too many rail lines in some parts of the country. Between Atlanta and St. Louis, for example, 20 different lines competed for business. There was not nearly enough rail traffic to keep all these lines busy.

Rebates and Pools In the West, especially, there were too few people for the railroads to make a profit. Competition was fierce. Rate wars broke out as rival railroads slashed their fares to win customers. Usually, all the companies lost money as a result.

Often, railroads were forced to grant secret rebates, or discounts, to their biggest customers. This practice forced many small companies out of business. It also hurt small shippers, such as farmers, who still had to pay the full price.

Railroad owners soon realized that cutthroat competition was hurting even their large lines. They looked for ways to end the competition. One method was pooling. In a pool, several railroad companies agreed to divide up the business in an area. They then fixed their prices at a high level.

Extra Burdens for Farmers Railroad rebates and pools angered small farmers in the South and the West. Both practices kept shipping prices high for them. Indeed, rates were so high that at times farmers burned their crops for fuel rather than ship them to market.

As you have read in Chapter 19, many farmers joined the Populist party. Populists called for government regulation of rail rates. Some Populists even called for a government takeover of the railroads. Congress and several states passed laws regulating railroad companies. However, the laws did not end abuses. Railroad owners sometimes bribed officials to keep the laws from being enforced.

Railroads Fuel the Economy

Although railroads caused certain problems, they also made possible the rapid growth of industry after 1865. Building rail lines created thousands of jobs. Steelworkers turned millions of tons of iron into steel for tracks and engines. Lumberjacks cut down whole forests to supply wood for railroad ties. Miners sweated in dusty mine shafts digging coal to fuel railroad engines. The railroad companies themselves employed thousands of workers. They laid tracks, built trestles across rivers, carved tunnels through mountains, and built countless railroad stations.

The large railroads also pioneered new ways of managing business. Rail companies created special departments for shipping and accounting and for servicing equipment. Expert managers headed each department, while chains of command ensured that the organization ran smoothly. Other big businesses soon copied these management techniques.

Railroads opened every corner of the country to settlement and growth. They brought people together, especially in the West. New businesses sprang up, and towns sprouted where rail lines crossed. With rail lines in place, the United States was ready to become the greatest industrial nation the world had ever seen.

 Find Main Ideas As you read, look for the main ways in which the railroad "fueled" the economy.

★ Section 1 Assessment ★

Recall

1. **Identify** Explain the significance of **(a)** William Vanderbilt, **(b)** George Westinghouse, **(c)** Cornelius Vanderbilt.
2. **Define (a)** gauge, **(b)** network, **(c)** consolidate, **(d)** rebate, **(e)** pool.

Comprehension

3. How did a broad network of railroads develop in the years after the Civil War?
4. What tactics did railroad owners use to eliminate competition?
5. How did American industry benefit from the widespread railroad building?

Critical Thinking and Writing

6. **Exploring the Main Idea** Review the Main Idea statement at the beginning of the section. Then, write at least four questions that you would ask a railroad owner or a western farmer to help decide whether the growth and consolidation of railroads were good for the country.
7. **Analyzing Information** After the Civil War, railroads consolidated as large railroad companies took over smaller ones. **(a)** What were the advantages of consolidation? **(b)** What were the disadvantages?

2 The Rise of Big Business

BEFORE YOU READ

Reading Focus

- What factors were responsible for the growth of huge steel empires after the Civil War?
- What benefits did corporations and bankers provide to the growing economy?
- How did John D. Rockefeller amass his huge oil holdings?
- What were the arguments for and against trusts?

Key Terms

Bessemer process
vertical integration
corporation
stock
dividend
trust
monopoly
free enterprise system
Sherman Antitrust Act

Taking Notes

Copy the concept web below. Include three or four blank ovals. As you read, fill in each blank oval with a major development associated with the rise of big business during the late 1800s. Two ovals have been completed to help you get started.

Corporations develop → STEEL INDUSTRY THRIVES ← Carnegie builds huge empire

Main Idea As industry boomed, American businesses grew and developed new ways of organizing and limiting competition.

AS YOU READ
Steel-mill pollution
Find Main Ideas How did Charles Trevelyan's attitude toward Pittsburgh both match and differ from this picture?

Setting the Scene

In the spring of 1898, an Englishman named Charles Trevelyan visited Pittsburgh. Trevelyan found Pittsburgh to be a rough town dominated by the steel business.

> 66 A cloud of smoke hangs over it by day. The glow of scores of furnaces lights the riverbanks by night. It stands at the junction of two great rivers, the Monongahela which flows down today in a [slow] yellow stream, and the Allegheny which is blackish. 99
>
> —Charles Philips Trevelyan, *Letters From North America and the Pacific,* April 15, 1898

Trevelyan met some of Pittsburgh's wealthiest people. He thought they were "a good breed and shrewd and friendly."

Pittsburgh was one of many cities that drew its energy from business and industry in the late 1800s. Its wealthiest citizens were a new breed of American business leaders. They were bold, imaginative, sometimes generous, and sometimes ruthless. By the end of the 1800s, they had made their businesses big beyond imagining.

Growth of the Steel Industry

The growth of railroads after the Civil War spurred the growth of the steel industry. Early trains ran on iron rails that wore out quickly. Railroad owners knew that steel rails were much stronger and not as likely to rust as iron. Steel, however, was costly and difficult to make.

Making Steel a New Way In the 1850s, William Kelly in the United States and Henry Bessemer in England each discovered a new way to make steel. The Bessemer process, as it came to be called, enabled steel makers to produce strong steel at a lower cost. As a result, railroads began to lay steel rails.

Other industries also took advantage of the cheaper steel. Manufacturers made steel nails, screws, needles, and other items. Steel girders supported the great weight of the new "skyscrapers"— the new tall buildings going up in the cities.

Thriving Steel Mills Steel mills sprang up in cities throughout the midwest. Pittsburgh became the steel-making capital of the nation. Nearby coal mines and good transportation helped Pittsburgh's steel mills to thrive.

The boom in steel making brought jobs and prosperity to Pittsburgh and other steel towns. It also caused problems. The yellow-colored river that Charles Trevelyan saw on his visit to Pittsburgh in 1898 was the result of years of pouring industrial waste into waterways. Steel mills belched thick black smoke that turned the air gray. Soot blanketed houses, trees, and streets.

Andrew Carnegie's Steel Empire

Many Americans made fortunes in the steel industry. Richest of all was a Scottish immigrant, Andrew Carnegie. Carnegie's ideas about how to make money—and how to spend it—had a wide influence.

Controlling the Steel Industry During a visit to Britain, Carnegie had seen the Bessemer process in action. Returning to the United States, he borrowed money and began his own steel mill. Within a short time, Carnegie was earning huge profits. He used the money to buy out rivals. He also bought iron mines, railroad and steamship lines, and warehouses.

Soon, Carnegie controlled all phases of the steel industry— from mining iron ore to shipping finished steel. Gaining control of all the steps used to change raw materials into finished products is called **vertical integration.** Vertical integration gave Carnegie a great advantage over other steel producers. By 1900, Carnegie's steel mills were turning out more steel than was produced in all of Great Britain.

The "Gospel of Wealth" Like other business owners, Carnegie drove his workers hard. Still, he believed that the rich had a duty to help the poor and to improve society. He called this idea the "gospel of wealth." Carnegie gave millions of dollars to charities. After selling his steel empire in 1901, he spent his time and money helping people.

The Corporation and the Bankers

Before the railroad boom, nearly every American town had its own small factories. They produced goods for people in the area. By the late 1800s, however, big factories were producing goods more cheaply than small factories could. Railroads distributed these goods to nationwide markets. As demand for local goods fell, many small factories closed. Big factories then increased their output.

Expanding factories needed capital, or money, for investment. Factory owners used the capital to buy raw materials, pay workers, and cover shipping and advertising costs. To raise capital, Americans adopted new ways of organizing their businesses.

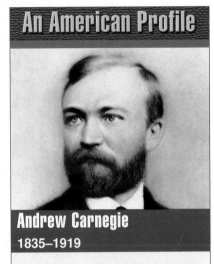

An American Profile

Andrew Carnegie
1835–1919

When Andrew Carnegie was 12, his family left Scotland to immigrate to the United States. He first worked in a cotton factory for $1.20 a week. Then, he worked as a telegram messenger. Carnegie worked long hours during the day and studied Morse code at night.

Luck favored Carnegie when Thomas Scott, superintendent of the Pennsylvania Railroad, hired the young man as his telegrapher. Scott introduced Carnegie to other industrial leaders and helped him invest his savings. Although Carnegie earned only a modest salary, shrewd investment made him a millionaire. By the 1890s, he was one of the world's richest men.

How did Carnegie take advantage of his good luck?

The Rise of the Corporation Many expanding businesses became corporations. A **corporation** is a business that is owned by investors. A corporation sells **stock,** or shares in the business, to investors, who are known as stockholders. The corporation can use the money invested by stockholders to build a new factory or buy new machines.

In return for their investment, stockholders hope to receive **dividends,** or shares of a corporation's profit. To protect their investment, stockholders elect a board of directors to run the corporation.

Stockholders face fewer risks than owners of private businesses do. If a private business goes bankrupt, the owner must pay all the debts of the business. By law, stockholders cannot be held responsible for a corporation's debts.

Banks and Industry In the years after the Civil War, corporations attracted large amounts of capital from American investors. Corporations also borrowed millions of dollars from banks. These loans helped American industry grow at a rapid pace. At the same time, bankers made huge profits.

The most powerful banker of the late 1800s was J. Pierpont Morgan. Morgan's influence was not limited to banking. He used his banking profits to gain control of major corporations.

During economic hard times in the 1890s, Morgan and other bankers invested in the stock of troubled corporations. As large stockholders, they easily won seats on the boards of directors. They then adopted policies that reduced competition and ensured big profits. "I like a little competition, but I like combination more," Morgan used to say.

AS YOU READ **Draw Inferences** Why did Morgan prefer "combination" to "competition"?

Between 1894 and 1898, Morgan gained control of most of the nation's major rail lines. He then began to buy up steel companies, including Carnegie Steel, and to merge them into a single large corporation. By 1901, Morgan had become head of the United States Steel Company. It was the first American business worth more than $1 billion.

Rockefeller's Oil Empire

Industry could not have expanded so quickly in the United States without the nation's rich supply of natural resources. Iron ore was plentiful, especially in the Mesabi Range of Minnesota. Pennsylvania, West Virginia, and the Rocky Mountains had large deposits of coal. The Rockies also contained minerals, such as gold, silver, and copper. Vast forests provided lumber for building.

In 1859, Americans discovered a valuable new resource: oil. Drillers near Titusville, Pennsylvania, made the nation's first oil strike. An oil boom quickly followed. Hundreds of prospectors rushed to western Pennsylvania ready to drill wells in search of oil.

Rockefeller and Standard Oil Among those who came to the Pennsylvania oil fields was young John D. Rockefeller. Rockefeller, however, did not rush to drill for oil. He knew that oil had little value until it was refined, or purified, to make kerosene. Kerosene was used as a fuel in stoves and lamps. So Rockefeller built an oil refinery.

Rockefeller believed that competition was wasteful. He used the profits from his refinery to buy up other refineries. He then combined the companies into the Standard Oil Company of Ohio.

Rockefeller was a shrewd businessman. He was always trying to improve the quality of his oil. He also did whatever he could to get rid of competition. Standard Oil slashed its prices to drive rivals out of business. It pressured its customers not to deal with other oil companies. It forced railroad companies eager for his business to grant rebates to Standard Oil. Lower shipping costs gave Rockefeller an important advantage over his competitors.

The Standard Oil Trust To tighten his hold over the oil industry, Rockefeller formed the Standard Oil trust in 1882. A trust is a group of corporations run by a single board of directors.

Stockholders in dozens of smaller oil companies turned over their stock to Standard Oil. In return, they got stock in the newly created trust. The trust paid the stockholders high dividends. However, the board of Standard Oil, headed by Rockefeller, managed all the companies that had previously been rivals.

The Standard Oil trust created a monopoly of the oil industry. A monopoly controls all or nearly all the business of an industry. The Standard Oil trust controlled 95 percent of all oil refining in the United States.

Other businesses followed Rockefeller's lead. They set up trusts and tried to build monopolies. By the 1890s, monopolies and trusts controlled some of the nation's most important industries.

The Case For and Against Trusts

Some Americans charged that the leaders of giant corporations were abusing the free enterprise system. In a free enterprise system, businesses are owned by private citizens. Owners decide what products to make, how much to produce, where to sell products, and what prices to charge. Companies compete to win customers by making the best product at the lowest price.

The Case Against Trusts Critics argued that trusts and monopolies reduced competition. Without competition, there was no reason for companies to keep prices low or to improve their products. It was also hard for new companies to compete with powerful trusts.

Critics were also upset about the political influence of trusts. Some people worried that millionaires were using their wealth to

Cause *and* Effect

Causes

- Railroad boom spurs business
- Businesses become corporations
- Nation has rich supply of natural resources
- New inventions make business more efficient

THE RISE OF INDUSTRY

Effects

- Steel and oil become giant industries
- Monopolies and trusts dominate important industries
- Factory workers face harsh conditions
- Membership in labor unions grows

Effects Today

- United States is world's leading economic power
- American corporations do business around the world
- Government laws regulate monopolies

GRAPHIC ORGANIZER
Skills

American industry boomed after the Civil War. The effects of industrial growth are still being felt today.

1. **Comprehension** List two causes for the rise of industry.

2. **Critical Thinking Drawing Conclusions** Why do you think the government now tries to regulate monopolies?

Economics

buy favors from elected officials. John Reagan, a member of Congress from Texas, said:

> 66 There were no beggars till Vanderbilts . . . shaped the actions of Congress and molded the purposes of government. Then the few became fabulously wealthy, the many wretchedly poor. 99
>
> —John Reagan, *Austin Weekly Democratic Statesman*, 1877

Under pressure from the public, the government slowly moved toward controlling giant corporations. Congress approved the Sherman Antitrust Act in 1890, which banned the formation of trusts and monopolies. However, it was too weak to be effective. Some state governments passed laws to regulate business, but the corporations usually sidestepped them.

The Case for Trusts Naturally, some business leaders defended trusts. Andrew Carnegie published articles arguing that too much competition ruined businesses and put people out of work. In an article titled "Wealth and Its Uses," he wrote:

> 66 It will be a great mistake for the community to shoot the millionaires, for they are the bees that make the most honey, and contribute most to the hive even after they have gorged themselves full. 99
>
> —Andrew Carnegie, "Wealth and Its Uses"

Defenders of big business argued that the growth of giant corporations brought lower production costs, lower prices, higher wages, and a better quality of life for millions of Americans. They pointed out that by 1900, Americans enjoyed the highest standard of living in the world.

  Section 2 Assessment

Recall

1. **Identify** Explain the significance of **(a)** Andrew Carnegie, **(b)** Bessemer process, **(c)** John D. Rockefeller, **(d)** Sherman Antitrust Act.
2. **Define** **(a)** vertical integration, **(b)** corporation, **(c)** stock, **(d)** dividend, **(e)** trust, **(f)** monopoly, **(g)** free enterprise system.

Comprehension

3. Why did the steel industry grow so quickly after the Civil War?
4. How did corporations and banking help the United States economy to expand?

5. How did John D. Rockefeller monopolize the oil industry?
6. What arguments did supporters and opponents of trusts each use?

Critical Thinking and Writing

7. **Exploring the Main Idea** Review the Main Idea statement at the beginning of the section. Then, list the ways that the need for capital led to new ways of running businesses.
8. **Applying Information** Andrew Carnegie once said of people who held onto their fortunes, "The man who dies thus rich, dies disgraced." How did Carnegie follow this philosophy?

ACTIVITY

Creating an Advertisement It is 1875, and you have been given the job of designing a one-page advertisement for the financial pages of a newspaper. The assignment: Explain the advantages of a corporation to a public that is not familiar with it. The goal: to get people to invest in corporations.

ADVERTISING in the *Industrial Age*

Although ads had appeared in newspapers since colonial times, there was a boom in advertising after 1870. The growth of industry and the expansion of railroads made it possible to sell goods all over the country. At first, there were few limits on what an ad could claim. Many promised happiness, popularity, and a life of ease—if only the consumer bought the product being advertised.

Elegance for the Wealthy

The Stevens-Duryea was so classy that its advertisement did not even need words. The spacious car and the well-dressed group of six adults—plus their chauffeur—said everything about luxury. The price for this 1914 model: $4,500 to $5,950—a huge amount for the times.

65 Cents Each!

That's what it cost for one of these 12-inch, double-sided records. The 1914 ad says: "If you think you have danced to the best dance music that your talking machine can produce, have your dealer play any one of these. Tangos, . . . One Steps and Turkey Trots, . . . Boston and Hesitation Waltzes. You will never be too tired when these waltzes are played."

Through the Wringer

Fashionable women tend to the laundry in this 1869 poster. It all seems very dignified in this spotless, well-stocked kitchen. However, before the days of electric-powered washing machines, doing the laundry was hard and messy work. Not a hint of this appears in the poster.

ACTIVITY

Ask your school media specialist for old magazines with advertisements. Select one ad and study it. To what emotion or hope does the ad appeal? Share your ideas with your classmates.

3 Inventions Change the Nation

Reading Focus

- What new devices speeded up communications after the Civil War?
- How did Thomas Edison and other inventors bring new technologies to Americans at work and at home?
- What changes did the automobile and airplane make in American life?

Key Terms

patent

transatlantic

moving assembly line

mass production

Taking Notes

As you read, complete this table listing the advances that transformed American life in the last half of the 1800s. Add as many bullets as you need to complete the table.

ADVANCES IN COMMUNI- CATION	ADVANCES IN TRAVEL	ADVANCES IN HOME AND OFFICE
• Transatlantic cable	• Air brakes	• Typewriters
•	•	•
•	•	•

Main Idea New technologies transformed American industry and life in the late 1800s.

AS YOU READ
An early washing machine

Use Prior Knowledge What developments paved the way for the success of such inventions as the early washing machine?

Setting the Scene

The Patent Office had never seen a year like 1897. An average of nearly 60 patents, or licenses for new inventions, were being granted every day. By year's end, Americans had registered some 21,000 patents. This was more than the total recorded in the entire 1850s.

The United States had become a land of invention. Between 1870 and 1900, patent officers issued more than 500,000 new patents. Some went to lone inventors like William Blackstone of Indiana. In 1874, he built a machine that washed away dirt from clothes. It was the first washing machine designed for use in the home. Other inventors, like the legendary Thomas Edison, filed patent request after patent request with the government. Thousands of inventions poured from his laboratory.

A flood of invention swept the United States in the late 1800s. Some inventions helped industry to grow and become more efficient. Others made daily life easier in many American homes.

Speeding Up Communications

Better communication was vital to growing American businesses. Some remarkable new devices filled the need for faster communication. The telegraph, which had been in use since 1844, helped people around the nation stay in touch. For example, a steel maker in Pittsburgh could instantly order iron ore from a mine in Minnesota.

Communicating Across the Atlantic The telegraph speeded up communication within the United States. It still took weeks, however, for news from Europe to arrive by ship.

Cyrus Field had the idea of laying a cable under the ocean so that telegraph messages could go back and forth between North

A Time of Invention

INVENTOR	DATE	INVENTION
Elisha Otis	1852	Passenger elevator brake
George Pullman	1864	Sleeping car
George Westinghouse	1869	Air brake
Elijah McCoy	1872	Automatic engine-oiling machine
Andrew S. Hallidie	1873	Cable streetcar
Stephen Dudley Field	1874	Electric streetcar
Alexander Graham Bell	1876	Telephone
Thomas Alva Edison	1877	Phonograph
Anna Baldwin	1878	Milking machine
Thomas Alva Edison	1879	First practical incandescent light bulb
James Ritty	1879	Cash register
Jan E. Matzeliger	1883	Shoemaking machine
Lewis E. Waterman	1884	Fountain pen
Granville T. Woods	1887	Automatic air brake
Charles and J. Frank Duryea	1893	Gasoline-powered car
King C. Gillette	1895	Safety razor with throwaway blades
John Thurman	1899	Motor-driven vacuum cleaner
Leo H. Baekeland	1909	Improved plastic

A 1908 vacuum cleaner

GRAPHIC ORGANIZER
Skills

New inventions transformed daily life in the United States. They also helped the American economy grow.

1. **Comprehension**
(a) What did George Westinghouse invent? In what year? (b) Who improved on Westinghouse's invention? In what year?

2. **Critical Thinking**
Applying Information Which of the inventions on the chart might be found in a home today?

America and Europe. He began working in 1854, making five attempts to lay the cable. Each time, the cable snapped. In 1858, two American ships managed to lay a cable between Ireland and Newfoundland. Field then arranged for Britain's Queen Victoria in London to send the first transatlantic, or across the Atlantic, message to President James Buchanan in Washington, D.C. For three weeks, Field was a hero. Then, the cable broke. But Field would not give up. In 1866, the ship *Great Eastern* succeeded in laying the cable. Field's transatlantic cable brought the United States and Europe closer together and made him famous. He marveled at his success:

66 In five months . . . the cable had been manufactured, shipped . . . stretched across the Atlantic, and was sending messages . . . swift as lightning from continent to continent. 99

—Cyrus Field, speech, 1866

Bell's "Talking Machine" The telegraph sent only dots and dashes over the wire. Several inventors were looking for a way to transmit voices. One of them was Alexander Graham Bell, a Scottish-born teacher of the deaf.

Bell had been working on his invention since 1865. In March 1876, he was ready to test his "talking machine." Bell sat in one room and spoke into his machine. His assistant, Thomas Watson, sat in another room with the receiver. "Mr. Watson, come here. I want to see you," Bell said. Watson heard the words faintly and rushed to

Menlo Park

Bell's side. "Mr. Bell," he cried, "I heard every word you said!" The telephone worked.

Bell's telephone aroused little interest at first. Scientists praised the invention. Most people, however, saw it as a toy. Bell offered to sell the telephone to the Western Union Telegraph Company for $100,000. The company refused—a costly mistake. In the end, the telephone earned Bell millions.

Bell formed the Bell Telephone Company in 1877. By 1885, he had sold more than 300,000 phones, mostly to businesses. With the telephone, the pace of business speeded up even more. People no longer had to go to a telegraph office to send messages. Business people could find out about prices or supplies by picking up the telephone.

Edison: "The Wizard of Menlo Park"

In an age of invention, Thomas Edison was right at home. In 1876, he opened a research laboratory in Menlo Park, New Jersey. There, Edison boasted that he and his co-workers created a "minor" invention every 10 days and "a big thing every six months or so." By the end of his career, Edison had earned worldwide fame as the greatest inventor of the age.

Turning Invention Into a System The key to Edison's success lay in his approach. He turned inventing into a system. Teams of experts refined Edison's ideas and translated them into practical inventions. The work was long and grueling. "Genius," Edison said, "is one percent inspiration and ninety-nine percent perspiration."

The results were amazing. Edison became known as the "Wizard of Menlo Park" for inventing the light bulb, the phonograph, and hundreds of other devices.

One invention from Edison's laboratory launched a new industry: the movies. In 1893, Edison introduced his first machine for showing moving pictures. Viewers watched short films by looking through a peephole in a cabinet. Later, Edison developed a motion picture projector, making it possible for many people to watch a film at the same time. By 1908, thousands of silent-movie houses had opened in cities across the United States.

The Power of Electricity One of Edison's most important creations was the electric power plant. He built the first power plant in New York City in 1882 and wired the business district first in hopes of attracting investors. With the flip of a switch, Edison set the district ablaze with light.

Within a year, Edison's power plant was supplying electricity to homes as well as businesses. Soon, more power plants were built. Factories replaced steam-powered engines with safer, quieter, electric engines. Electric energy powered streetcars in cities and lighted countless homes. The modern age of electricity had begun.

Technology Takes Command

Almost every day, it seemed, American inventors were creating new devices. As technology took command, businesses became more efficient, and life became easier and more pleasant.

AS YOU READ **Ask Questions** Form a question from the heading "Technology Takes Command." Then, read to find the answer to your question.

The Refrigerated Railroad Car In the 1880s, Gustavus Swift came up with an idea that transformed the American diet. Swift introduced refrigeration to the meatpacking industry. In the past, cattle, pigs, and chickens had been raised and sold locally. Meat spoiled quickly, so it could not be shipped over long distances.

Swift set up a meatpacking plant in Chicago, a railroad hub midway between the cattle ranches of the West and the cities of the East. Cattle were shipped by train to Chicago. At Swift's plant, the animals were slaughtered and carved up into sides of beef. The fresh beef was quickly loaded onto refrigerated railroad cars and carried to market. Even in summer, Swift sent fresh meat to eastern cities.

New Technologies at the Office and at Home New inventions also affected life at home and in the office. Christopher Sholes perfected the typewriter in 1868. This invention speeded up communication between businesses.

In 1888, George Eastman introduced the lightweight Kodak camera. No longer did photography require bulky equipment and chemicals. After 100 snaps of the shutter, the owner returned the camera to Kodak. The company developed the pictures and sent them back, along with a reloaded camera. Taking pictures became a popular pastime.

African American Inventors African Americans contributed to the flood of inventions. In 1872, Elijah McCoy created a special device that oiled engines automatically. It was widely used on railroad engines and in factories. Another inventor, Granville T. Woods, found a way to send telegraph messages between moving railroad trains.

Jan Matzeliger invented a machine that could perform almost all the steps in shoemaking that had previously been done by hand. Patented in 1883, Matzeliger's machine was eventually used in shoe factories across the country.

Many African American inventors had trouble getting patents for their inventions. Even so, in 1900, an assistant in the patent office compiled a list of patents issued to African American inventors. The list, together with drawings and plans of all the inventions, filled four huge volumes.

Automobiles and the Assembly Line

No single person invented the automobile. Europeans had produced motorized vehicles as early as the 1860s. By 1890, France led the world in automaking. In the 1890s, several Americans began building cars. Still, only the wealthy could afford them.

Ford's Moving Assembly Line It was Henry Ford who made the auto a part of everyday American life. In 1913, Ford introduced the

Dearborn, Michigan

Henry Ford Museum

Not far from his Detroit auto plant, Henry Ford built a place to display "every household article, every kind of vehicle, every sort of tool." Today at the Henry Ford Museum in Dearborn, Michigan, you can explore the world's largest transportation collection, from giant locomotives to classic cars.

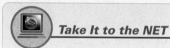

Take It to the NET

Virtual Field Trip For an interactive look at the Henry Ford Museum, visit *The American Nation* section of **www.phschool.com**.

moving assembly line. With this method of production, workers stay in one place as products edge along on a moving belt. At Ford's auto plant, one group of workers would bolt seats onto a passing car frame, the next would add the roof, and so on. The assembly line greatly reduced the time needed to build a car. Other industries soon adopted the method.

Ford's assembly line allowed mass production of cars. **Mass production** means making large quantities of a product quickly and cheaply. Because of mass production, Ford could sell his cars at a lower price than other automakers.

Cars for the Public It took a number of years for the automobile to catch on. At first, most people laughed at it. Some thought the "horseless carriage" was a nuisance. Others thought it was dangerous. A backfiring auto engine could scare a horse right off the road. Towns and villages across the nation posted signs: "No horseless carriages allowed." In Tennessee, a person planning to drive a car had to advertise the fact a week ahead of time. This warning gave others time to prepare for the danger!

Over time, attitudes toward the automobile changed. No other means of travel offered such freedom. As prices dropped, more people could afford to buy cars. In 1900, only 8,000 Americans owned cars. By 1917, more than 4.5 million autos were chugging along American roads.

Automobiles were at first regarded as machines for men only. Automakers soon realized, however, that women could drive—and buy—cars. Companies began to direct advertisements to women, stressing the comfort and usefulness of automobiles. Driving gave women greater independence.

The First Flight

Meanwhile, two Ohio bicycle mechanics, Orville and Wilbur Wright, were experimenting with another new method of transportation: flying. The Wright brothers owned a bicycle shop in Dayton, Ohio. During the 1890s, they read about Europeans who were experimenting with glider planes. The brothers were soon caught up in the dream of flying.

After trying out hundreds of designs, the Wright brothers tested their first "flying machine" on December 17, 1903, at Kitty Hawk, North Carolina. Orville made the first flight. The plane, powered by a small gasoline engine, stayed in the air for 12 seconds and flew a distance of 120 feet. Orville flew three more times that day. His longest flight lasted 59 seconds.

Improvements came quickly after the first flight. By 1905, the Wrights had built a plane that could turn, make figure-eights, and remain in the air for up to half an hour.

Surprisingly, the first flights did not attract much interest. No one could see any practical use for the flying machine.

It was the United States military that first saw a use for airplanes. In 1908, the Wrights demonstrated how planes could fly over battlefields to locate enemy positions. Then, they produced an airplane for the military that could reach the amazing speed of 40 miles per hour!

In time, the airplane would achieve its vast potential. It would change the world by making travel quicker and trade easier.

Section 3 Assessment

Recall

1. **Identify** Explain the significance of **(a)** Cyrus Field, **(b)** Alexander Graham Bell, **(c)** Thomas Edison, **(d)** Gustavus Swift, **(e)** Elijah McCoy, **(f)** Henry Ford.
2. **Define (a)** patent, **(b)** transatlantic, **(c)** moving assembly line, **(d)** mass production.

Comprehension

3. How did the transatlantic cable and the telephone speed up communications?
4. Name five other inventions that changed the way Americans lived and worked in the late 1800s.

5. How did the auto and the airplane change American life?

Critical Thinking and Writing

6. **Exploring the Main Idea** Review the Main Idea statement at the beginning of the section. Then, make a list of the five most important inventions of this period. Rank the five inventions in order of importance, and write a paragraph explaining your choices.
7. **Drawing Conclusions** Why might inventors be more creative working in an invention factory, such as Edison's, than working on their own?

ACTIVITY

Take It to the NET

Inventions for the Twenty-first Century
Use the Internet to find Web sites that predict inventions likely to make an impact on American homes in 2050. Choose one invention, and write a description for a newspaper advertisement. Visit *The American Nation* section of **www.phschool.com** for help in completing the activity.

4 The Rise of Organized Labor

BEFORE YOU READ

Reading Focus

- How did workplace changes lead to the rise of labor organizations such as the American Federation of Labor?
- What progress and problems affected women in the workplace during the late 1800s?
- Why did organized labor face hard times after 1870?

Key Terms

sweatshop
Knights of Labor
strikebreaker
anarchist
Haymarket Riot
AFL
trade union
collective bargaining
ILGWU
Triangle Fire

Taking Notes

As you read, prepare an outline of this section. Use roman numerals to indicate the major headings, capital letters for the subheadings, and numbers for the supporting details. The sample below will help you get started.

> I. New Workplace
>   A. Children at work
>   B.
> II. The Rise of Organized Labor
>   A.
>   B. Trouble in Haymarket Square

Main Idea As workers lost power over their working conditions, they began to organize into unions and fight for better conditions.

AS YOU READ

In the steel mills
Draw Inferences What do the picture and the quotation from James Davis tell you about the qualities required to be an old-time steelworker?

Setting the Scene

As James Davis looked back on his life, he recalled his youth working in a steel mill in the 1880s. Davis worked as a "puddler," the person who mixed the molten metals. Standing near white-hot furnaces, he learned to mix the right brew of metals at the right temperatures to produce fine steel. He noted with pride:

> 66 This process was handed down from father to son and in the course of time came to my father and so to me. None of us ever went to school and learned the chemistry of it from books. We learned the trick by doing it, standing with our faces in the scorching heat. . . . 99
>
> —James Davis, *The Iron Puddler*, 1922

But machines were taking over what people had done in the past. Giant converters could automatically mix the metals, cook them at the right temperatures, and produce excellent steel. Skilled puddlers like Davis were being transformed into mere tenders of those machines.

The growth of these huge machine-driven factories affected all workers. By the late 1800s, a growing sense of powerlessness led workers to join together.

A New Workplace

Workers had to adjust to the new kinds of factories of the late 1800s. Before the Civil War, most factories were small and family run. Bosses knew their workers by name and chatted with them about their families. Because most workers had skills that the factory needed, they could bargain with the boss for wages.

By the 1880s, the relationship between worker and boss had changed. People worked all day tending machines in a large, crowded, noisy room. Because their skills were easily replaced, many workers were forced to work for low wages. In the garment trade and other industries, sweatshops became common. A sweatshop is a workplace where people labor long hours in poor conditions for low pay. Most sweatshop workers were young women, or children.

Children at Work The 1900 census reported nearly 2 million children under age 15 at work throughout the country. Boys and girls labored in hazardous textile mills, tobacco factories, and garment sweatshops. In coal mines, they picked stones out of the coal for 12 hours a day, 6 days a week. Working children had little time for schooling. Lack of education reduced their chance to build a better life as adults.

Hazards of Work Factories were filled with hazards. Lung-damaging dust filled the air of textile mills. Cave-ins and gas explosions plagued mines. In steel mills, vats of molten metal spilled without warning. Some workers had their health destroyed. Others were severely injured or killed in industrial accidents. In one year, 195 workers died in the steel mills of Pittsburgh.

The Rise of Organized Labor

Many workers found ways to fight back. Some workers slowed their work pace. Others went on strike. Strikes were usually informal, organized by workers in individual factories.

Sometimes, workers banded together to win better conditions. However, most early efforts to form unions failed.

Knights of Labor In 1869, workers formed the Knights of Labor. At first, the union was open to skilled workers only. The members held meetings in secret because employers fired workers who joined unions.

In 1879, the Knights of Labor elected Terence Powderly as their president. Powderly worked to strengthen the union by opening its membership to immigrants, African Americans, women, and unskilled workers.

Powderly did not believe in strikes. Rather, he relied on rallies and meetings to win public support. Goals of the Knights included a shorter workday, an end to child labor, and equal pay for men and women. Most important, Powderly wanted workers and employers to share ownership and profits.

In 1885, some members of the Knights of Labor launched a strike that forced the Missouri Pacific Railroad to restore wages that it had previously cut. The Knights did not officially support the strike. Still, workers everywhere saw the strike as a victory for the union. Membership soared to 700,000, including 60,000 African Americans.

Trouble in Haymarket Square The following year, the Knights of Labor ran into serious trouble. Workers at the McCormick Harvester Company in Chicago went on strike. Again, the Knights did not endorse the strike.

Like many companies at the time, the McCormick company hired strikebreakers, or replacements for striking workers. On

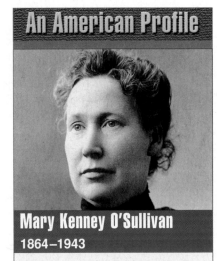

Growth of Labor Unions

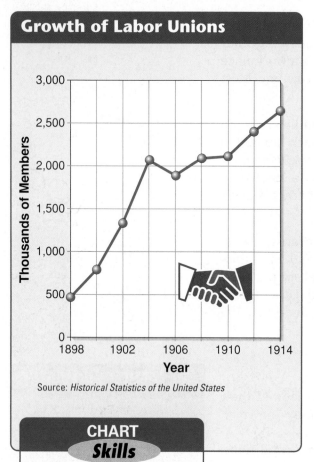

Thousands of Members

3,000
2,500
2,000
1,500
1,000
500
0

1898 1902 1906 1910 1914

Year

Source: *Historical Statistics of the United States*

CHART Skills

A growing number of workers joined unions in the late 1800s and early 1900s.

1. **Comprehension**
   (a) How much did union membership increase between 1898 and 1914?
   (b) What years showed a decrease in membership?

2. **Critical Thinking**
   Drawing Conclusions
   In which time period on this chart do you think a recession hit the economy?

Economics $

 Find Main Ideas As you read, look for sentences that describe the conditions that women workers faced during this period.

May 3, 1886, workers clashed with strikebreakers outside the factory. Police opened fire, and four workers were killed.

The next day, thousands of workers gathered in Haymarket Square to protest the killings. The rally was led by **anarchists,** people who oppose all forms of organized government. Suddenly, a bomb exploded, killing seven police officers.

Eight anarchists were arrested for their part in the Haymarket Riot, as the incident was called. No real evidence linked these men to the bombing, but four were tried, convicted, and hanged. A wave of antilabor feeling swept the nation. Many Americans thought that the unions were controlled by anarchists. As a result, membership in the Knights of Labor dropped sharply.

American Federation of Labor

Despite the failure of the Knights of Labor, the labor movement continued to grow. In 1886, an immigrant cigar maker named Samuel Gompers organized a new union in Columbus, Ohio. The American Federation of Labor (AFL) was open to skilled workers only.

Workers did not join the AFL directly. Rather, they joined a trade union, a union of persons working in the same trade. For example, a typesetter joined a typesetter's union. The union then joined the AFL. Thus, the AFL was a large organization made up of many different unions.

Unlike the Knights of Labor, the AFL stressed practical goals. It focused on higher wages, shorter hours, and improved working conditions. It led the fight for collective bargaining, the right of unions to negotiate with management for workers as a group. The AFL also supported the use of strikes to achieve its goals.

Its practical approach helped the AFL become the most powerful labor organization in the nation. Between 1886 and 1910, membership in the AFL swelled from 150,000 to more than one and a half million. However, because African Americans, immigrants, and unskilled workers were barred from most trade unions, they could not join the AFL.

Women at Work

By 1890, one million women worked in American factories. In the textile mills of New England and the tobacco factories of the South, women formed the majority of workers. In New York City, women outnumbered men in the garment industry.

During the 1800s, some women formed their own unions. A few, like the all-black Washerwomen's Association of Atlanta, struck for higher wages. None of these unions succeeded, however.

Mother Jones Organizes The best-known woman in the labor movement was Irish-born Mary Harris Jones, known as Mother Jones. Jones devoted much of her adult life to the cause of workers.

Jones spoke out about the hard lives of children in textile mills, "barefoot . . . reaching thin little hands into the machinery." By calling attention to such abuses, Mother Jones helped pave the way for reform.

Organizing Garment Workers In 1900, garment workers organized the International Ladies' Garment Workers Union (ILGWU). More than 20,000 women and men in the ILGWU walked off their jobs in 1909. After a few weeks, employers met union demands for better pay and shorter hours. The ILGWU became a key member of the AFL.

Despite the efforts of the ILGWU and other labor groups, most women with factory jobs did not join unions. They continued to work long hours for low pay. Many labored under unsafe conditions. Then, a tragic event focused attention on the dangers faced by women workers.

Tragedy at Triangle The workday was just ending on a cool March day in 1911, when a fire broke out in the Triangle Shirtwaist Factory, a sweatshop in New York City. Within minutes, the upper stories were ablaze. Hundreds of workers raced for the exits, only to find them locked. The company had locked the doors to keep workers at their jobs. In their panic, workers ran headlong into the doors, blocking them with their bodies.

Fire trucks arrived almost immediately, but their ladders could not reach the upper floors. One after another, workers trying to escape the flames leaped to their deaths. One reporter wrote:

> 66 As I looked up . . . there, at a window, a young man was helping girls to leap out. Suddenly one of them put her arms around him and kiss[ed] him. Then he held her into space and dropped her. He jumped next. Thud . . . dead. Thud . . . dead. 99
>
> —*The New York Times,* March 26, 1911

Nearly 150 people, mostly young women, lost their lives in the Triangle Fire. The deaths shocked the public. As a result, New York and other states approved new safety laws to help protect factory workers.

Hard Times for Organized Labor

The new era of industry led to vast economic growth. At the same time, it created economic strains. In the rush for profits, many industries expanded too fast. As goods flooded the market, prices dropped. To cover their losses, factory owners often fired workers. In time, factories geared up again, and the cycle was repeated.

The economy swung wildly between good times and bad. Between 1870 and 1900, two major depressions and three smaller recessions rocked the country. In such hard times, workers lost their jobs or faced pay cuts.

Primary Source

The Triangle Fire

The day after the fire, this story appeared in The New York Times: "Cecilia Walker, 20 years old, . . . slid down the cable at the Washington Place elevator and escaped with burned hands and body bruises. She was on the eighth floor of the building when the fire started. Running over to the elevator shaft she rang for the car, but it did not come. As she passed the sixth floor sliding on the cable she became unconscious, . . . and does not know what happened until she reached St. Vincent's Hospital, where she is now.

"'A girl and I, . . . were on the eighth floor, and when I ran for the elevator shaft my girl friend started for the window on the Washington Street side. I looked around to call her but she had gone.'"

—*The New York Times,* March 26, 1911

Analyzing Primary Sources
How do you think the public reacted to stories of the fire?

Strike! During a severe depression in the 1870s, railroad workers were forced to take several cuts in pay. In July 1877, workers went on strike, shutting down rail lines across the country. Riots erupted in many cities as workers burned rail yards and ripped up track.

Violent strikes also broke out in the West. In the 1870s, miners in Idaho tried to shut down two large mines. In 1893, after another bitter strike, miners formed the Western Federation of Miners. This union gained great strength in the Rocky Mountain states. Between 1894 and 1904, it organized strike after strike.

Government Sides With Owners The federal government usually sided with factory owners. Several Presidents sent in troops to end strikes. Courts usually ruled against strikers, too.

In 1894, a Chicago court dealt a serious blow to unions. A year earlier, George Pullman had cut the pay of workers at his railroad car factory. Yet, he did not reduce the rents he charged them for company-owned houses. Workers walked off the job in protest.

A federal judge ordered the Pullman workers to stop their strike. Leaders of the strike were jailed for violating the Sherman Antitrust Act. This act had been meant to keep trusts from limiting free trade. The courts, however, said that the strikers were limiting free trade.

Slow Progress Union workers staged thousands of strikes during the late 1800s. However, few Americans supported the strikes. Many were afraid that unions were run by foreign-born radicals. Because unions were unpopular, owners felt free to try to crush them.

Workers did make some gains. Overall, wages rose slightly between 1870 and 1900. Still, union growth was slow. In 1910, only one worker in 20 belonged to a union. Some 30 years would pass before large numbers of unskilled workers were able to join unions.

 Section 4 Assessment

Recall

1. **Identify** Explain the significance of (a) Knights of Labor, (b) Haymarket Riot, (c) American Federation of Labor, (d) ILGWU, (e) Triangle Fire.
2. **Define** (a) sweatshop, (b) strikebreaker, (c) anarchist, (d) trade union, (e) collective bargaining.

Comprehension

3. How did changing factory conditions promote the rise of labor unions in the late 1800s?
4. What advances did women make in the workplace, and what problems still remained in the late 1800s?

5. Why did the labor movement suffer a number of major defeats after 1870?

Critical Thinking and Writing

6. **Exploring the Main Idea** Review the Main Idea statement at the beginning of this section. Then, write five statements of fact that support the main idea.
7. **Making Generalizations** Why do you think that it often takes a tragedy to spur people to make reforms?

Creating Compound Words During times of technological change, many new words are created. Some of them are compound words—words invented by combining two existing words. There are two examples of these words in the Key Terms for this section. Find these words and tell what they mean. Then, create five compound words of your own from the content of this chapter.

You can increase your understanding of history by asking questions about what you see and read. Formulating, or drafting, questions is a critical-thinking process that helps you become a more effective learner. The better your questions, the more you will learn.

Child labor became a common practice in the United States during the 1800s. These photographs show boys and girls in work situations about a century ago.

Learn the Skill *To formulate questions, use the following steps:*

1. **Examine the material.** Ask basic questions to help summarize what you are seeing or reading. Formulate questions that begin with *who, what, when, where*, and *how much*.

2. **Think of analytical questions.** These are questions that reflect a thoughtful approach to the information. They might begin with *how* or *why*.

3. **Ask questions that evaluate.** These call for judgments and opinions based on evidence.

4. **Formulate hypothetical questions.** Hypothetical questions involve the word *if*. They suggest possible outcomes, such as *if this happens, would such and such occur?*

Practice the Skill *Answer the following questions about the photographs above:*

1. **(a)** What kind of work are the people in each photograph doing? **(b)** Ask and answer a basic question of your own.

2. **(a)** How are the people dressed? **(b)** Form an analytical question of your own.

3. **(a)** Are the working conditions healthful or harmful? Explain. **(b)** Create an evaluative question.

4. **(a)** If young people work and don't go to school, what might happen? **(b)** Ask and answer a hypothetical question about the workers.

Apply the Skill *See the Chapter Review and Assessment.*

CREATING A CHAPTER SUMMARY

On a sheet of paper, draw a timeline like this one. Include six to eight boxes. Fill in each box with a key event or development of this period of rapid economic growth. For each event, include its date.

For additional review and enrichment activities, see the interactive version of *The American Nation,* available on the Web and on CD-ROM.

Take It to the NET

Chapter Self-Test For practice test questions for Chapter 20, visit *The American Nation* section of **www.phschool.com**.

Building Vocabulary

Write sentences that use the chapter vocabulary words listed below, leaving blanks where the vocabulary words would go. Exchange your sentences with another student, and fill in the blanks in each other's sentences.

1. network
2. consolidate
3. rebate
4. corporation
5. stock
6. dividend
7. patent
8. transatlantic
9. strikebreaker
10. trade union

Reviewing Key Facts

11. What methods did railroad companies use to limit competition? (Section 1)
12. What advantages did the corporation offer to investors? (Section 2)
13. What was the assembly line, and how did it transform manufacturing? (Section 3)
14. How was factory work in the late 1800s different from factory work before the Civil War? (Section 4)

15. How did the Triangle Fire influence public opinion? (Section 4)

Critical Thinking and Writing

16. **Connecting to Geography: Location** Study the map of industrial centers of the United States at the beginning of this chapter. Then, write a paragraph explaining why Pittsburgh's location helped it to become the steel-making capital of the United States.
17. **Identifying Causes and Effects** Suppose you were asked to create a graphic organizer in the shape of a pyramid showing the growth of American industry in the last half of the 1800s. At the bottom you plan to write three developments that caused this growth. What three developments would you choose?
18. **Summarizing** Summarize the arguments for and against monopolies and trusts.
19. **Identifying Bias** During the late 1800s, many people connected labor unions with violence and foreign influences. Why might people have associated these things with labor unions?

Analyzing Primary Sources

One of John D. Rockefeller's favorite sayings was "Every right implies a responsibility. Every opportunity, an obligation. Every possession, a duty." Late in life, Rockefeller wrote his only known poem. It summed up his approach to life so well that he had it printed on cards and distributed to many friends. It read:

> I was early taught to work as well as play;
>
> My life has been one long, happy holiday—
>
> Full of work, and full of play—
>
> I dropped the worry on the way—
>
> And God was good to me every day.
>
> —John D. Rockefeller, quoted in his obituary in *The New York Times*, May 24, 1937

20. According to Rockefeller, what was he taught early in life?

21. What does Rockefeller mean when he says "Every possession [implies] a duty"?

22. What is the tone of Rockefeller's poem?

23. Does the philosophy of the poem differ from that of the statement that begins "Every right implies a responsibility"? Explain.

Formulating Questions

The cartoon above criticizes monopolies by showing Standard Oil as a huge octopus.

24. Which of the following is an analytical question you might ask the cartoonist?
  A What is the building in the grip of the octopus?
  B Why did you select the octopus as the main symbol of the cartoon?
  C Who are the people at the bottom?
  D When did you draw this cartoon?

25. Formulate an evaluative question about the cartoon.

ACTIVITIES

Connecting With . . . Economics

Advertising Catalog You work for the largest advertising agency in Chicago. Your boss has given you a challenging assignment: You are to create advertisements for a mail-order catalog that contains the new inventions discussed in this chapter. Write a one-paragraph description of the main features of three new inventions, and draw pictures for your ads. Then, organize your ads into a catalog.

Take It to the NET

Connecting to Today

Writing a Proposal Use the Internet to find sites dealing with the Rockefeller Foundation or the Carnegie Foundation for the Advancement of Teaching. Then, write a proposal for a project that you think deserves foundation support. For help in starting this activity, visit *The American Nation* section of **www.phschool.com**.

Collecting Data for a Project

Creating a Comic Strip Many of the business leaders who grew immensely wealthy during this period led fascinating and colorful lives. Use the Internet to find information about Jay Gould, Daniel Drew, William Vanderbilt, or Leland Stanford. Choose one of these people and draw a comic strip illustrating an interesting event in his life. For help in starting this activity, visit *The American Nation* section of **www.phschool.com**.

A New Urban Culture

1865–1914

1 **New Immigrants in a Promised Land**
2 **An Age of Cities**
3 **Life in the Changing Cities**
4 **Public Education and American Culture**

Mark Twain

The Statue of Liberty

1865

Mark Twain publishes "The Celebrated Jumping Frog of Calaveras County." Twain becomes one of the best-loved American writers.

1873

The first American kindergarten opens in St. Louis.

1886

The Statue of Liberty is dedicated in New York harbor. It becomes a symbol of welcome to new immigrants.

AMERICAN EVENTS

	Andrew Johnson	Ulysses S. Grant	Rutherford B. Hayes	James A. Garfield 1881	Grover Cleveland
				Chester A. Arthur	
Presidential Terms:	1865–1869	1869–1877	1877–1881	1881–1885	1885–1889

1860   **1875**   **1890**

WORLD EVENTS

▲ 1865
The Salvation Army is founded in London.

1881 ▲
The czar steps up persecution of Russian Jews.

Largest Cities in the United States, 1900

In 1900, there were 32 American cities with populations over 100,000—four times as many as before the Civil War.

Key

- • 100,000–500,000 people
- ■ Over 500,000 people

CANADA

Syracuse
Rochester   Worcester   Boston
Buffalo   Providence
Minneapolis   St. Paul   Scranton   Fall River
Milwaukee   Detroit   Newark   New Haven
Toledo   Pittsburgh   New York
Chicago   Cleveland   Jersey City
Omaha   Philadelphia
Columbus   Baltimore
Indianapolis   Cincinnati   Washington, D.C.
St. Joseph   St. Louis   Louisville
Kansas City
San Francisco
Denver
Memphis

Los Angeles

PACIFIC OCEAN

ATLANTIC OCEAN

New Orleans

MEXICO

Albers Equal-Area Projection
0   250   500 Miles
0   250   500 Kilometers

Boston subway station

1891

James Naismith invents basketball.

1897

The first subway system in the United States opens in Boston.

1910

Angel Island becomes processing center for Asian immigrants.

| Benjamin Harrison | Grover Cleveland | William McKinley | | William H. Taft | |
| 1889–1893 | 1893–1897 | 1897–1901 | Theodore Roosevelt 1901–1909 | 1909–1913 | Woodrow Wilson 1913–1921 |

1890 ● ★ ● **1905** ● ★ ● **1920** ●

▲ **1892**
Arthur Conan Doyle publishes *Adventures of Sherlock Holmes.*

1910 ▲
The Mexican Revolution begins.

1 New Immigrants in a Promised Land

BEFORE YOU READ

Reading Focus

- Why did millions of immigrants decide to make the difficult journey to the United States?
- What problems did the "new immigrants" face in adapting to American life?
- Why were some Americans opposed to increased immigration?

Key Terms

push factor
pull factor
pogrom
steerage
Statue of Liberty
acculturation
nativist
Chinese Exclusion Act

Taking Notes

Copy this flowchart. As you read, fill in the boxes with stages in the process of immigration. The first box has been partly filled in. Add as many boxes as you need.

- Immigrant decides to leave home
- Seeks freedom
-

Main Idea In the late 1800s, millions of "new immigrants" came to the United States in search of economic opportunity and freedom.

AS YOU READ Immigrants in New York

Ask Questions Read the passage by Abraham Cahan. Then, write three questions you would like to ask the immigrants about coming to the United States.

Setting the Scene For millions of immigrants, nothing quite matched their first sight of the "Promised Land"—America. Abraham Cahan, a Lithuanian-born journalist, wrote:

> 66 Imagine a new-born babe in possession of a fully developed intellect. Would it ever forget its entry into the world? Neither does the immigrant ever forget his entry into a country which is, to him, a new world . . . in which he expects to pass the rest of his life. 99
>
> —Abraham Cahan, *The Rise of David Levinsky*

Not all immigrants who came to the United States planned to remain. Pulled by the promise of work in industry, many hoped to make their fortunes and return home. But millions did end up staying. As new Americans, they helped to transform the nation.

Why Immigrants Came

Between 1865 and 1915, more than 25 million immigrants poured into the United States. They were part of a great network of some 60 million workers in search of jobs in industrial countries. As you have read, an industrial boom had created a huge need for workers.

Both push and pull factors played a part in this global migration. Push factors are conditions that drive people from their homes. Pull factors are conditions that attract immigrants to a new area.

Push Factors European immigrants were often small farmers or landless farmworkers. As European populations grew, land became scarce. Small farms could barely support the families that worked them. In some areas, new farm machines replaced farmworkers.

Political or religious persecution drove many people from their homes. In Russia, the czar supported pogroms (POH grahmz), or

Immigrants: Push and Pull Factors

Push Factors:	Pull Factors:
• Scarce land • Farm jobs lost to new machines • Political and religious persecution • Revolution • Poverty and hard lives	• Promise of freedom • Family or friends already settled in the United States • Factory jobs available

organized attacks on Jewish villages. Persecution and violence also pushed Armenian Christians out of the Ottoman Empire (present-day Turkey).

Political unrest was another push factor. After 1910, a revolution erupted in Mexico. Thousands of Mexicans crossed the border into the southwestern United States.

Pull Factors Industrial jobs were the chief pull factor for immigrants. American factories needed labor. Factory owners sent agents to Europe and Asia to hire workers at low wages. Steamship companies offered low fares for the ocean crossing. Railroads posted notices in Europe advertising cheap land in the American West.

Often, one family member—usually a young, single male—made the trip. Once settled, he would send for family members to join him. As immigrants wrote home describing the "land of opportunity," they pulled other neighbors from the "old country." For example, one out of every ten Greeks immigrated to the United States in the late 1800s.

The promise of freedom was another pull factor. Many immigrants were eager to live in a land where police could not arrest or imprison you without a reason and where freedom of religion was guaranteed to all by the Bill of Rights.

A Difficult Journey

Leaving home required great courage. The voyage across the Atlantic or Pacific was often miserable. Most immigrants could afford only the cheapest berths. Shipowners jammed up to 2,000 people in steerage, the airless rooms below deck. On the return voyage, cattle or cargo filled the same spaces.

In such close quarters, disease spread rapidly. An outbreak of measles infected every child on one German immigrant ship. The dead were thrown into the water "like cattle," reported a horrified passenger.

GRAPHIC ORGANIZER
Skills

Push factors drove many people to leave their native countries. Pull factors drew them to the United States.

1. **Comprehension** Identify one push factor and one pull factor related to economics.

2. **Critical Thinking Linking Past and Present** Choose one push factor or pull factor listed here. Explain how that factor still brings immigrants to the United States.

Ellis Island

Ellis Island

On tiny Ellis Island, millions of immigrants first set foot on American soil. Across the harbor was New York City, where many would soon make their homes. For years, Ellis Island was in disrepair. Now restored, the main building houses a museum of immigration. At the Ellis Island Web site, you can also search for individual immigrants by name.

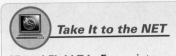

Take It to the NET

Virtual Field Trip For an interactive look at Ellis Island, visit *The American Nation* section of **www.phschool.com**.

On the East Coast For most European immigrants, the voyage ended in New York City. Sailing into the harbor, they were greeted by the giant **Statue of Liberty.** Dedicated in 1886, it became a symbol of hope and freedom. A poem of welcome was carved on the base:

AS YOU READ **Use Prior Knowledge** How does the poem by Emma Lazarus relate to "push" and "pull" factors? Which lines reflect "push" factors and which reflect "pull" factors?

> 66 Give me your tired, your poor,
> Your huddled masses yearning to breathe free,
> The wretched refuse of your teeming shore.
> Send these, the homeless, tempest-tossed to me:
> I lift my lamp beside the golden door! 99
>
> —Emma Lazarus, "The New Colossus"

In 1892, a new receiving station opened on Ellis Island. Here, immigrants had to face a dreaded medical inspection. Doctors watched newcomers climb a long flight of stairs. Anyone who limped or appeared out of breath might be stopped. Doctors also examined eyes, ears, and throats. The sick had to stay on Ellis Island until they got well. A small percentage who failed to regain full health were sent home.

With hundreds of immigrants to process each day, officials had only minutes to check each new arrival. To save time, they often changed names that they found hard to spell. Krzeznewski became Kramer. Smargiaso ended up as Smarga. Even the first name of one Italian immigrant was changed, from Bartolomeo to Bill.

Lucky immigrants went directly into the welcoming arms of friends and relatives. Many others stepped into a terrifying new land whose language and customs they did not know.

On the West Coast After 1910, many Asian immigrants were processed on Angel Island in San Francisco Bay. Because Americans wanted to discourage Asian immigration, new arrivals often faced long delays. One Chinese immigrant scratched these lines on the wall:

66 Imprisoned in the wooden building day after day,
My freedom withheld; how can I bear to talk about it? 99

—Anonymous, quoted in *Strangers From a Different Shore* (Takaki)

Despite such obstacles, many Asians were able to make a home in the United States. Like European immigrants in the East, Asians on the West Coast faced a difficult adjustment.

"Old" and "New" Immigrants

Immigration patterns changed in the late 1800s. Most earlier immigrants had been Protestants from Northern and Western Europe. Those from England and Ireland already spoke English. The early wave of English, Irish, Germans, and Scandinavians became known as "old immigrants." At first, Irish Catholics and other groups faced discrimination. In time, they were drawn into American life.

After 1885, millions of "new immigrants" arrived from Southern and Eastern Europe. They included Italians, Poles, Greeks, Russians, and Hungarians. On the West Coast, a smaller but growing number of Asian immigrants arrived, mostly from China and, later, from Japan. There were also a few immigrants from Korea, India, and the Philippines.

Few of these new immigrants spoke English. Many of the Europeans were Catholic, Jewish, or Eastern Orthodox. Immigrants from Asia might be Buddhist or Daoist. Set apart by language and religion, they found it harder to adapt to a new life.

Adapting to American Life

Many immigrants had heard stories that the streets in the United States were paved with gold. Once they arrived, they had to adjust to reality. "First," reported one immigrant, "the streets were not paved with gold. Second, they were not paved at all. Third, they expected me to pave them."

Newcomers immediately set out to find work. European peasants living off the land had had little need for money, but it took cash to survive in the United States. Through friends, relatives, labor contractors, and employment agencies, the new arrivals found jobs.

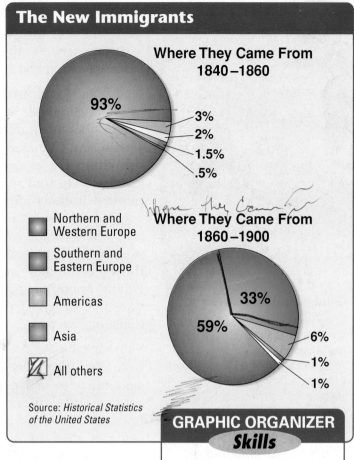

The New Immigrants

Where They Came From
1840–1860

93%
3%
2%
1.5%
.5%

■ Northern and Western Europe
■ Southern and Eastern Europe
□ Americas
■ Asia
▨ All others

Where They Came From
1860–1900

59%
33%
6%
1%
1%

Source: *Historical Statistics of the United States*

GRAPHIC ORGANIZER
Skills

In the late 1800s, patterns of immigration to the United States began to shift.

1. **Comprehension** What percentage of immigrants came from Eastern and Southern Europe between 1840 and 1860? Between 1860 and 1900?

2. **Critical Thinking Drawing Inferences** Why would many immigrants who arrived between 1860 and 1900 find it harder to adapt than did earlier immigrants?

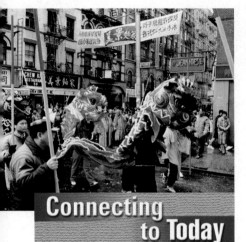

Connecting to Today

Celebrating Our Heritage

Firecrackers boom. Rockets flare. A dragon is snaking through the city streets! What is going on?

You are watching a Chinese New Year's parade. For hundreds of years, people in China shot off fireworks when the new year began. Today, the custom is alive and well in the United States.

Other immigrants also brought their holiday traditions to the United States. Irish Americans march in St. Patrick's Day parades. Italian Americans enjoy outdoor food festivals on the Feast of Saint Anthony. Mexican Americans mark Cinco de Mayo with parades, barbecues, and music. And you don't have to be Chinese, Irish, Italian, or Mexican to join in the fun.

In what other ways do Americans celebrate their ethnic heritage?

Most immigrants stayed in the cities where they landed. Cities were the seat of industrial work. City slums soon became packed with poor immigrants. By 1900, one neighborhood on New York's lower east side had become the most crowded place in the world.

Immigrant Neighborhoods Immigrants eased into their new lives by settling in their own neighborhoods. Large American cities became patchworks of Italian, Irish, Polish, Hungarian, Greek, German, Jewish, and Chinese neighborhoods.

Within these neighborhoods, newcomers spoke their own language, celebrated special holidays, and prepared foods as in the old country. Italians joined clubs such as the Sons of Italy. Hungarians bought and read Hungarian newspapers.

Religion stood at the center of immigrant family life. Houses of worship both united and separated ethnic groups. Catholics from Italy worshipped in Italian neighborhood parishes. Those from Poland worshipped in Polish parishes. Jewish communities divided into the older Orthodox or Reform branches and the newer Conservative wing.

Learning to Be American As newcomers struggled to adjust, they were often torn between old traditions and American ways. The first generation to arrive acculturated. Acculturation is the process of holding on to older traditions while adapting to a new culture. Immigrants learned how to use American institutions such as schools, factories, and the political system. At the same time, they tried to keep their traditional religions, family structures, and community life.

In their effort to adapt, immigrants blended old and new ways. For example, some newcomers mixed their native tongues with English. Italians called the Fourth of July "Il Forte Gelato," a phrase that actually means "the great freeze." In El Paso, Texas, Mexican immigrants developed *Chuco*, a blend of English and Spanish.

Children adapted to the new culture more quickly than their parents. They learned English in school and then helped their families to speak it. Because children wanted to be seen as Americans, they often gave up customs that their parents honored. They played American games and dressed in American-style clothes.

Nativists Oppose Immigration

Even before the Civil War, Americans known as nativists sought to limit immigration and preserve the country for native-born white Protestants. As immigration boomed in the late 1800s, nativist feelings reached a new peak.

Nativists argued that immigrants would not fit into American culture because their languages, religions, and customs were too different. Many workers resented the new immigrants because they took jobs for low pay. Others feared them because they were different. One magazine described all immigrants as "long-haired, wild-eyed, bad-smelling, atheistic, reckless foreign wretches, who never did an honest hour's work in their lives."

Wherever new immigrants settled, nativist pressure grew. Nativists targeted Jews and Italians in the Northeast and Mexicans in the Southwest. On the West Coast, nativists worked to end immigration from China.

Chinese Exclusion Since the California Gold Rush, Chinese immigrants had helped build the West. Most lived in cities, in tight-knit communities called "Chinatowns." Others farmed for a living.

Most Americans did not understand Chinese customs. Also, some Chinese did not try to learn American ways. Like many other immigrants, they planned to stay only until they made a lot of money. They hoped to then return home, to live out their lives as rich and respected members of Chinese society. When that dream failed, many Chinese settled in the United States permanently.

As the numbers of Chinese grew, so did the prejudice and violence against them. Gangs attacked and sometimes killed Chinese people, especially during hard times.

Congress responded to this anti-Chinese feeling by passing the **Chinese Exclusion Act** in 1882. It barred Chinese laborers from entering the country. In addition, no Chinese person who left the United States could return.

The Chinese Exclusion Act was the first law to exclude a specific national group from immigrating to the United States. Congress renewed the original 10-year ban several times. It was finally repealed in 1943.

Restricting Immigration In 1887, nativists formed the American Protective Association. The group campaigned for laws to restrict immigration. Congress responded by passing a bill that denied entry to people who could not read their own language.

President Grover Cleveland vetoed the bill. It was wrong, he said, to keep out peasants just because they had never gone to school. Three later Presidents vetoed similar bills. Finally, in 1917, Congress overrode President Woodrow Wilson's veto, and the bill became law.

Section 1 Assessment

Recall
1. **Identify** Explain the significance of (a) Statue of Liberty, (b) Ellis Island, (c) Angel Island, (d) Chinese Exclusion Act.
2. **Define** (a) push factor, (b) pull factor, (c) pogrom, (d) steerage, (e) acculturation, (f) nativist.

Comprehension
3. Describe two push factors and two pull factors for immigration.
4. (a) Where did the new immigrants come from? (b) What problems did they face adjusting to life in the United States?

5. Why did nativists resent and distrust the new immigrants?

Critical Thinking and Writing
6. **Exploring the Main Idea** Review the Main Idea statement at the beginning of this section. Then, write a letter from an immigrant explaining your hopes and fears.
7. **Identifying Points of View** Write 2 or 3 sentences describing the process of acculturation from the viewpoint of immigrant parents. Then, write 2 or 3 sentences describing the same process from the children's viewpoint.

ACTIVITY

Take It to the NET
Connecting to Today
Choose one of the groups of new immigrants mentioned in this section. Use the Internet to find out how that group helped shape modern American life and culture. Use your findings to give an oral report or create a poster. Visit *The American Nation* section of **www.phschool.com** for help in completing the activity.

2 An Age of Cities

BEFORE YOU READ

Reading Focus

- Why did cities experience a population explosion?
- How did city settlement patterns change?
- How did settlement house workers and other reformers work to solve city problems?

Key Terms

urbanization

tenement

building code

Social Gospel

Salvation Army

Young Men's Hebrew Association

settlement house

Hull House

Taking Notes

Copy the concept web below. As you read, fill in the blank ovals with information about the growth of American cities. Add as many ovals as you need.

Main Idea Vast numbers of people migrated to cities, changing urban landscapes and creating new problems.

AS YOU READ

The Chicago Fire

Draw Inferences What conditions allowed the Chicago Fire to spread so rapidly?

Setting the Scene "The dogs of hell were upon the housetops ... bounding from one to another," wrote Chicago journalist Horace White. He watched in horror as flames engulfed his city:

66 Billows of fire were rolling over the business palaces of the city and swallowing their contents. Walls were falling so fast that the quaking of the ground under our feet was scarcely noticed. 99

—Horace White, Report to the *Cincinnati Commercial*, October 14, 1871

Fires were a constant danger in cities. Still, Americans agreed that they had never seen anything like the great Chicago Fire of 1871. Whipped by strong, dry winds, the blaze raced across the city, sometimes faster than a person could run. It killed nearly 300 people, left almost 100,000 homeless, and destroyed the entire downtown. Covered with factory grease and oil, even the Chicago River caught fire.

Yet, from the ashes, a new city rose. By the end of the century, Chicago was the fastest growing city in the world, with a population of over one million. Other American cities also underwent rapid population growth. For new and old Americans alike, the golden door of opportunity opened into the city.

Urban Populations Boom

"We cannot all live in cities," declared newspaper publisher Horace Greeley, "yet nearly all seem determined to do so." Urbanization, the movement of population from farms to cities, began slowly in the early 1800s. As the nation industrialized, the pace quickened. In 1860, only one American in five lived in a city. By 1890, one in three did.

Jobs drew people to cities. As industries grew, so did the need for workers. New city dwellers took jobs in steel mills, meatpacking plants, and garment factories. Others worked as salesclerks, waiters, barbers, bank tellers, and secretaries.

Immigrants and In-migrants The flood of immigrants swelled city populations. So, too, did migrations from farm to city within the country. As the frontier closed, fewer pioneers went west to homestead. In fact, many Americans left farms and migrated to cities to find a better life. One young woman summed up the feelings of many farmers toward their backbreaking work:

> 66 If I were offered a deed to the best farm . . . on the condition of going back to the country to live, I would not take it. I would rather face starvation in town. 99
>
> —quoted in *The Good Old Days—They Were Terrible!* (Bettmann)

African Americans Move to Cities African Americans, too, sought a better life in the cities. Most lived in the rural South. When hard times hit or prejudice led to violence, some headed to northern cities. By the 1890s, the south side of Chicago had a thriving African American community. Detroit, New York, Philadelphia, and other northern cities also had growing African American neighborhoods. The migration to the north began gradually, but increased rapidly after 1915.

As with overseas immigration, black migration usually began with one family member moving north. Later, relatives and friends followed. Like immigrants from rural areas in Europe, many African Americans faced the challenge of adjusting to urban life.

Patterns of City Settlement

Cities grew outward from their old downtown sections. Before long, many cities took on a similar shape.

The Urban Poor Poor families crammed into the city's center, the oldest section. They struggled to survive in crowded slums. The streets were jammed with people, horses, pushcarts, and garbage.

Because space was so limited, builders devised a new kind of house to hold more people. They put up buildings six or seven stories high. They divided the buildings into small apartments, called tenements. Many tenements had no windows, heat, or indoor bathrooms. Often, 10 people shared a single room.

Crowding increased as factory owners moved into the city centers to take advantage of low rents and cheap labor. They took over buildings for use as factories, thus forcing more and more people into fewer and fewer apartments.

The Growth of Cities

Population Growth in Ten Selected Cities

City	Population in 1870	Population in 1900
New York	1,478,103	3,437,202
Chicago	298,977	1,698,575
Philadelphia	674,022	1,293,697
St. Louis	310,864	575,238
Boston	250,526	560,892
San Francisco	149,473	342,782
New Orleans	191,418	287,104
Denver	4,759	140,472
Los Angeles	5,728	104,266
Memphis	40,226	102,647

Rural and Urban Population in the United States, 1860–1920

Year	Rural population	Urban population
1860	80%	20%
1870	74%	26%
1880	72%	28%
1890	65%	35%
1900	60%	40%
1910	54%	46%
1920	49%	51%

Sources: *Historical Statistics of the United States* and *Statistical Abstract of the United States*

GRAPHIC ORGANIZER
Skills

The population of American cities grew rapidly after the Civil War.

1. **Comprehension** Between 1870 and 1900, which cities more than doubled in population?

2. **Critical Thinking** **Making Generalizations** Based on the bar graph, make one generalization about changes in the population of the United States.

Typhoid and cholera raged through the tenements. Tuberculosis, a lung disease, was the biggest killer, accounting for thousands of deaths each year. Babies, especially, fell victim to disease. In one Chicago slum, around 1900, more than half of all babies died before they were one year old. Despite the poor conditions, the populations of slums grew rapidly.

The Urban Middle Class Beyond the slums stood the homes of the new middle class, including doctors, lawyers, business managers, skilled machinists, and office workers. Rows of neat houses lined tree-shaded streets. Here, disease broke out less frequently than in the slums.

Leisure activities gave middle-class people a sense of community and purpose. They joined clubs, singing societies, bowling leagues, and charitable organizations. As one writer said, the clubs "bring together many people who are striving upward, trying to uplift themselves."

The Rich On the outskirts of the city, behind brick walls or iron gates, lay the mansions of the very rich. In New York, huge homes dotted Fifth Avenue, which was then on the city's outskirts. In Chicago, 200 millionaires lived along the exclusive lakefront by the 1880s. In San Francisco, wealthy residents built their mansions nearer the center of the city, in the exclusive Nob Hill area.

Rich Americans modeled their lives on European royalty. They filled their mansions with priceless artwork and gave lavish parties. At one banquet, the host handed out cigarettes rolled in hundred-dollar bills.

Solving City Problems

As more and more people crowded into cities, problems grew. Garbage rotted in the streets. Factories polluted the air. Crime flourished. Thieves and pickpockets haunted lonely alleys, especially at night.

Tenement buildings were deathtraps if a fire broke out. News reporter Jacob Riis brought readers into the tenements in his startling expose, *How the Other Half Lives*. He wrote:

> 66 Step carefully over this baby—it is a baby, spite of its rags and dirt—under these iron bridges called fire-escapes, but loaded down . . . with broken household goods, with washtubs and barrels, over which no man could climb from a fire. 99

—Jacob Riis, *How the Other Half Lives*

Urban Reforms By the 1880s, reformers pressured city governments for change. **Building codes** set standards for construction and safety. New buildings were required to have fire escapes and decent plumbing. Cities also hired workers to collect garbage and sweep the streets. To reduce pollution, zoning laws kept factories out of neighborhoods where people lived.

Safety improved when cities set up professional fire companies and police forces. Gas—and later electric—lights made streets less dangerous at night. As you will read, many cities built new systems of public transportation as well.

Pushed by reformers, city governments hired engineers and architects to design new water systems. New York City, for example, dug underground tunnels to the Catskill Mountains, 100 miles to the north. The tunnels brought a clean water supply to the city every day.

Religious Organizations Help the Poor Religious groups worked to ease the problems of the poor. The Catholic Church ministered to the needs of Irish, Polish, and Italian immigrants. An Italian-born nun, Mother Cabrini, helped found dozens of hospitals for the poor.

In cities, Protestant ministers began preaching a new **Social Gospel.** They called on their well-to-do members to do their duty as Christians by helping society's poor. One minister urged merchants and industrialists to pay their workers enough to enable them to marry and have families. He also proposed that they grant their workers a half day off on Saturdays.

In 1865, a Methodist minister named William Booth created the **Salvation Army** in London. It expanded to the United States by 1880. In addition to spreading Christian teachings, the Salvation Army offered food and shelter to the poor.

In Jewish neighborhoods, too, religious organizations provided community services. The first **Young Men's Hebrew Association** (YMHA) began in Baltimore in 1854. The YMHA provided social activities, encouraged good citizenship, and helped Jewish families preserve their culture. In the 1880s, the Young Women's Hebrew Association (YWHA) grew out of the YMHA.

The Settlement House Movement

Some people looked for ways to help the poor. By the late 1800s, individuals began to organize **settlement houses,** community centers that offered services to the poor. The leading figure of the settlement house movement was a Chicago woman named Jane Addams.

AS YOU READ **Visualize** Form a mental image of the scene described by Jacob Riis. Describe two additional things that you see or hear.

An American Profile

Jane Addams 1860–1935

Jane Addams developed her strong sense of duty early. Her father, a wealthy abolitionist, taught her that people should respect others and live moral lives. She also learned to value education. She wanted to become a doctor, but her own poor health ended that dream.

Recovering from an illness, Jane Addams traveled to Europe in 1888. There, she visited a settlement house in London. She and a friend decided to create such a place in Chicago. She devoted the rest of her life to making a better life for the poor.

How did Jane Addams's life reflect the values taught to her by her father?

Hull House Addams came from a well-to-do family but had strong convictions about helping the poor. After college, she moved into one of the poorest slums in Chicago. There, in an old mansion, she opened a settlement house, named Hull House, in 1889.

Other idealistic young women soon joined Addams. They took up residence in Hull House so that they could experience firsthand some of the hardships of the slum community in which they worked. These women dedicated their lives to service and to sacrifice—"like the early Christians," in the words of one volunteer.

Hull House volunteers offered a wide variety of services. To help immigrants acculturate, they taught classes in American government and the English language. Other volunteers gave instruction in health care or operated day nurseries for children whose mothers worked outside the home. In addition, Hull House provided recreational activities for young people, such as sports, a choral group, and a theater.

Over the years, the settlement house movement spread. By 1900, about 100 such centers had opened in cities across the United States.

Pressing for Reform Addams and her staff were an important influence in bringing about reform legislation. They studied the slum neighborhoods where they worked and lived. They realized that the problems were too big for any one person or group, and they urged the government to act.

Alice Hamilton, a Hull House doctor, campaigned for better health laws. Florence Kelley worked to ban child labor. Jane Addams herself believed that reform legislation would be speeded if women were allowed to vote. She joined the continuing campaign for women's suffrage.

Section 2 Assessment

Recall
1. **Identify** Explain the significance of **(a)** Mother Cabrini, **(b)** Social Gospel, **(c)** Salvation Army, **(d)** Young Men's Hebrew Association, **(e)** Jane Addams, **(f)** Hull House.
2. **Define (a)** urbanization, **(b)** tenement, **(c)** building code, **(d)** settlement house.

Comprehension
3. Why did American cities grow rapidly in the late 1800s?
4. Describe the settlement pattern of a typical American city.
5. **(a)** Identify two problems of growing cities. **(b)** How did reformers work to ease these problems?

Critical Thinking and Writing
6. **Exploring the Main Idea** Review the Main Idea statement at the beginning of this section. Then, draw a two-column chart. In the left column, list reasons for moving to the city from a poor farm. In the right column, list reasons for staying on the farm.
7. **Linking Past and Present** Write a paragraph comparing some of the problems faced by city dwellers in the late 1800s with problems faced by city dwellers today.

> **ACTIVITY**
>
> **Writing a Proposal**
> You want to start a settlement house in a major American city in the late 1800s. Outline a proposal asking a wealthy contributor or a charity for funds to help you get started. Explain what services you plan to offer and how you will use the money.

Comparing Maps Over Time

History is the story of changes over time. By comparing maps from different time periods, you can see how historical changes affected a country, state, or city. The two maps below show settled areas (with at least one house per acre) in Kansas City, Missouri, at different times.

As a nation constantly on the move, Americans traveled West to build new lives. Small farm settlements became cities. Eventually, many cities—including Pittsburgh, Cincinnati, St. Louis, Louisville, Memphis, and St. Paul—appeared. Among the new crop of cities was the Town of Kansas, which became a city in 1853.

Kansas City, 1855

Key
- Settled areas—1855
- Kansas City, MO—today
- River

Missouri R.
Kansas
Kansas R.
Missouri
Missouri R.

Lambert Conic Projection
0   5   10 Miles
0   5   10 Kilometers

Kansas City, 1917

Key
- Settled areas—1917
- Kansas City, MO—today
- River

Missouri R.
Kansas
Kansas R.
Missouri
Missouri R.

Lambert Conic Projection
0   5   10 Miles
0   5   10 Kilometers

Learn the Skill *To learn to compare maps, use the following steps:*

1. **Check the subject and area shown on each map.** What do the title and labels tell you? Is the same area shown on each map?

2. **Study the map key.** Determine what symbols are used to present specific information.

3. **Compare the maps.** Use the data on the maps to make comparisons and note changes over time.

4. **Interpret the maps.** Think over what you already know about this period. Draw conclusions or make predictions.

Practice the Skill *Use the two maps above to answer the following questions:*

1. **(a)** What area is shown on both maps? Are they the same? **(b)** What is the date of each map?

2. **(a)** Do the two map keys give the same information? **(b)** What do their colors represent?

3. **(a)** Which were the settled areas in Kansas City in 1855? **(b)** How do the settled areas in 1917 differ from those in 1855?

4. **(a)** Based on the evidence shown on the maps, what conclusion can you reach about Kansas City during this time? **(b)** What changes would you expect to see on a later map of the same area?

Apply the Skill *See the Chapter Review and Assessment.*

3 Life in the Changing Cities

BEFORE YOU READ

Reading Focus

- How did the building boom affect city life?
- Why were sports so popular?
- What forms of entertainment did city dwellers enjoy?

Key Terms

skyscraper

suburb

department store

vaudeville

ragtime

Taking Notes

Copy the table below. As you read, fill in the boxes with additional information about changes in city life.

CHANGING LANDSCAPE	NEW ACTIVITIES
• Skyscrapers • Streetcars • •	• Baseball • • •

Main Idea A building boom, new technology, and new leisure activities changed the way city dwellers lived.

AS YOU READ
Early elevator
Use Prior Knowledge
What other inventions from 1865–1915 have you learned about that might affect how people lived in cities?

Setting the Scene The first one appeared in Boston on the eve of the Civil War. Soon new "apartment hotels" were springing up all over the country. Some, like the Ansonia in New York, covered whole square blocks. They featured all the marvels of modern living—hot-water heating, kitchens, flush toilets, telephone service, and by the 1880s, electric lighting and appliances.

Of all these new conveniences, none was more amazing than the elevator. Elevators whisked residents to the top floors in a matter of seconds. Raved one character in a popular play:

> 66 It's the ideal way of living. All on one floor. No stairs. Nothing. All these apartment hotels have them. 99
>
> —William Dean Howells, *The Elevator*

By the early 1900s, less grand, one-room, "efficiency" apartments had begun to spring up in San Francisco and to spread eastward. New apartment buildings were but one sign of the changing landscape of American cities.

A Building Boom

A building boom changed the face of American cities. Cities like Chicago and New York gradually began to run out of space in their downtown areas. Resourceful city planners and architects decided to build up instead of out.

Building Upward After fire leveled downtown Chicago in 1871, planners tried out many new ideas as they rebuilt the city. Using new technology, they designed **skyscrapers,** tall buildings with many floors supported by a lightweight steel frame. The first skyscraper, only nine stories tall, was built in Chicago in 1885. As technology improved, builders competed to raise taller and taller skyscrapers.

Newly invented electric elevators, like those installed in larger apartment buildings, carried residents and workers to upper floors.

Elevators moved so quickly, according to one rider, that "the passenger seems to feel his stomach pass into his shoes."

Moving People As skyscrapers crowded more people into smaller spaces, they added to a growing problem: traffic. Downtown streets were jammed with horse-drawn buses, carriages, and carts.

Electricity offered one solution. Frank Sprague, an engineer from Richmond, Virginia, designed the first electric streetcar system in 1887. Streetcars, or trolleys, were fast, clean, and quiet. Many trolley lines ran from the center of a city to the outlying countryside, creating the first suburbs. A **suburb** is a residential area on or near the outskirts of a city.

Other cities built steam-driven passenger trains on overhead tracks. In 1897, Boston built the first American subway, or underground electric railway. Subways and elevated railroads carried workers rapidly to and from their jobs.

Some cities needed ways to move masses of people across rivers or bays. In 1874, James B. Eads designed and built a three-arched bridge across the Mississippi River at St. Louis. The Eads Bridge was more than a quarter of a mile long. Nine years later, New York City completed the Brooklyn Bridge linking Manhattan Island and Brooklyn. Over a mile long, it contained a footpath and two railroad lines. The bridge was soon carrying 33 million people a year.

Public Parks While cities grew up and out, some planners wanted to preserve open spaces. They believed that open land would calm busy city dwellers.

In the 1850s, landscape architect Frederick Law Olmsted planned spacious Central Park in New York City. Other cities followed this model. They set aside land for public parks that contained zoos and gardens, so that city people could enjoy green grass and trees during their leisure time.

Shopping Shopping areas also got a new look. In the past, people had bought shoes in one store, socks in another, and dishes in a third. The new **department stores** sold all kinds of goods in different sections or departments.

In New York, R. H. Macy opened a nine-story department store in 1902. Its motto stated, "We sell goods cheaper than any house in the world." Soon, other cities had department stores. Shopping became a popular pastime. People browsed through each floor, looking at clothes, furniture, and jewelry. On the street, "window-shoppers" paused to view elaborate displays behind enormous new plate-glass windows.

Viewing History

A Street in Chicago This photograph shows State Street in Chicago in the 1890s. Among the buildings shown here is Marshall Field's, Chicago's largest department store. **Applying Information** *Review the subsection A Building Boom. What other new features of cities can you identify in this photograph?*

Americans at Play

The rise of the factory split the worlds of work and play more sharply than ever. With less chance to socialize on the job, there was more interest in leisure. Sports provided a great escape from the pressures of work.

"Play Ball!" Baseball was the most popular sport in the nation. The game was first played in New York. During the Civil War, New York soldiers showed other Union troops how to play. By the 1870s, several cities had professional baseball teams and the first professional league was organized.

Early baseball was somewhat different from today's game. Pitchers threw underhanded. Catchers caught the ball after one bounce. Fielders did not wear gloves. As a result, high scores were common. One championship baseball game ended with a score of 103 to 8!

At first, African Americans played professional baseball. In time, though, the major leagues barred black players. In 1885, Frank Thompson organized a group of waiters into one of the first African American professional teams, the Cuban Giants of Long Island. They took the name "Cuban," not because they were from Cuba, but in hopes that all-white teams might be willing to play them.

Viewing History

The Days of Vaudeville

United States

Audiences loved the ridiculous costumes and rowdy horseplay of comics such as Weber and Fields (top). A vaudeville program, or "bill," might also include a magician, an animal act, or even dancing "drummer girls" (bottom). **Drawing Conclusions** *Why might sight gags and physical humor be popular with immigrant audiences?*

Football Football grew out of European soccer, which Americans had played since colonial times. Early football called for lots of muscle and little skill. On every play, the opposing teams crashed into each other like fighting rams. The quarterback ran or jumped over the tangle of bodies.

Players did not wear helmets and were often hurt. In 1908 alone, 33 college football players died from injuries. Some colleges banned the sport or drew up stricter rules of play for the game.

Basketball In 1891, James Naismith invented basketball. Naismith taught physical education at a Young Men's Christian Association (YMCA) in Springfield, Massachusetts. He wanted a sport that could be played indoors in winter. He nailed two bushel baskets to the gym walls. Players tried to throw a soccer ball into the baskets.

Basketball caught on quickly. It spread to other YMCAs and then to schools and colleges around the country.

A New World of Theater and Music

By the late 1800s, American cities supported a wide variety of cultural activities. Talented immigrants contributed to a new world of music and theater.

Music and other kinds of entertainment brought Americans together. People from different cultures sang the same songs and enjoyed the same shows. As railroads grew, circuses, acting companies, and "Wild West" shows toured the country. These traveling groups helped spread American culture beyond the cities to the small towns.

Variety Shows Many large cities organized symphony orchestras and opera companies. Generally, only the wealthy attended the symphony or the opera. For other city dwellers, an evening out often meant a trip to a vaudeville house. Vaudeville (VAWD vihl) was a variety show that included comedians, song-and-dance routines, and acrobats.

Vaudeville provided opportunities for people from many ethnic backgrounds, such as Irish American dancer-singer George M. Cohan and Jewish comedians like the Marx Brothers. Will Rogers, a performer of Cherokee descent, was one of the best-loved entertainers in the nation. Wearing a cowboy hat and twirling a rope, Rogers used gentle wit to comment on American life. "Everybody is ignorant," he said, "only on different subjects."

Popular Music Songwriters produced many popular tunes, such as "Shine On, Harvest Moon." Later, Thomas Edison's phonograph sparked a new industry. By 1900, millions of phonograph records had been sold.

Ragtime was a new kind of music with a lively, rhythmic sound. Scott Joplin, an African American composer, helped make ragtime popular. His "Maple Leaf Rag" was a nationwide hit.

In towns and cities, marching bands played the military music of John Philip Sousa. Sousa wrote more than 100 marches, including "The Stars and Stripes Forever." His marches became favorites at Fourth of July celebrations.

An American Profile

Scott Joplin 1868–1917

Growing up in Texas, Scott Joplin showed his musical talent at an early age. He was a fine singer and a skilled pianist. From his piano teacher, a German immigrant, Joplin learned to love classical music.

Joplin's popular rags combined bouncy ragtime rhythms with elements of European music. He wrote a textbook about ragtime, hoping that it would be recognized as a form of serious music. He even wrote ballets and operas, but they were rarely performed. Today, Joplin is most widely honored as the "King of Ragtime."

Why do you think Joplin wanted to use ragtime to write ballets and operas?

AFTER YOU READ

Section 3 Assessment

Recall

1. **Identify** Explain the significance of **(a)** Frank Sprague, **(b)** Frederick Law Olmstead, **(c)** R. H. Macy, **(d)** James Naismith, **(e)** Will Rogers, **(f)** Scott Joplin, **(g)** John Philip Sousa.
2. **Define** **(a)** skyscraper, **(b)** suburb, **(c)** department store, **(d)** vaudeville, **(e)** ragtime.

Comprehension

3. How did new technology change the face of American cities? Give three examples.
4. What sports became popular in the late 1800s?

5. How did entertainment unite Americans?

Critical Thinking and Writing

6. **Exploring the Main Idea** Review the Main Idea statement at the beginning of this section. Then, list what you think were the three most important developments mentioned in this section. Give reasons for your ranking.
7. **Identifying Causes and Effects** Write one sentence explaining the cause-and-effect relationship between population growth and the development of the skyscraper.

ACTIVITY

Designing a Poster
With a partner, create an illustrated poster advertising one of the following: the opening of a new subway or bridge, a new department store, a sporting event, a vaudeville show.

The Early Days of Baseball

As early as the American Revolution, George Washington's men played a game they called Base Ball. Not until 1834, however, did someone write a book of rules. At first, baseball was a hobby for those wealthy enough to have afternoons free. But by 1900, baseball had become "the national pastime."

Written in 1888, "Casey at the Bat" is one of the most popular American poems. It shows the devotion that fans felt toward home team heroes like the mighty Casey.

"Oh! Somewhere in this favored land the sun is shining bright;
The band is playing somewhere, and somewhere hearts are light.
And somewhere men are laughing, and somewhere children shout;
But there is no joy in Mudville—mighty Casey has Struck Out."
—Ernest Thayer, "Casey at the Bat"

Pitcher Cy Young was an early superstar. From 1890 to 1911, he won 511 games out of 749. Today, the Cy Young Award is given to the outstanding pitcher in each league.

Fast Facts

- Technology helped baseball grow more popular. Railroads made it easier for teams to travel from city to city. The telegraph carried game scores at lightning speed.
- In 1903, Boston played Pittsburgh in the first World Series.
- It took songwriter Jack Norworth 15 minutes to write "Take Me Out to the Ball Game" in 1909.

This picture shows the opening game between New York and Boston in 1886. Six other cities had National League teams that season: Chicago, Detroit, Kansas City, Philadelphia, St. Louis, and Washington.

ACTIVITY

Baseball and other sports have affected the way Americans talk. For example, if somebody surprises you, you might say he "threw you a curve." With a partner, think of five other words or phrases that come from sports. Write a definition for each.

4 Public Education and American Culture

BEFORE YOU READ

Reading Focus

- How did public education grow after the Civil War?
- How did newspapers, magazines, and dime novels reflect changes in reading habits?
- Why did writers and painters turn to everyday life for subjects?

Key Terms

compulsory education

parochial

Chautauqua Society

yellow journalism

dime novel

realist

local color

Taking Notes

As you read, prepare an outline of this section. Use roman numerals to indicate the major headings, capital letters for the subheadings, and numbers for the supporting details. The sample at right will help you get started.

> I. Educating Americans
>   A. Public schools
>   1. First kindergartens
>   2.
>   B. The school day
>   1.
>   2.
> II. Newspaper Boom
>   A.
>   B.

Main Idea The growth of public education was closely linked to other changes in American culture.

Setting the Scene

The city of St. Louis tried a novel experiment in 1873. Following the lead of schools in Germany, the city opened the first American kindergarten. Children as young as three and four would be brought to school for part of the day. There, gentle teachers would help them to express themselves and learn to reason through songs, stories, and games. Educators believed that such creative play would give youngsters a head start on their education.

At the same time, children learned how to behave. Kindergartens taught cleanliness, politeness, and obedience. As public education spread, schools became centers of both learning and discipline.

Educating Americans

Before 1870, fewer than half of American children went to school. Many who did attended one-room schoolhouses, with only one teacher. Often, several students shared a single book.

Public Schools As industry grew, the nation needed an educated work force. As a result, states improved public schools at all levels. By 1900, there were 4,000 kindergartens across the nation.

In the North, most states passed compulsory education laws that required children to attend school, usually through sixth grade. In the South, which had no tradition of public schools, the Freedmen's Bureau had built grade schools for both African American and white students. By 1900, most southern schools were segregated.

In cities such as Boston and New York, public schools taught English to young immigrants. Children also learned about the duties and rights of citizens. In the 1880s, Catholics became worried that public schools stressed Protestant teachings. They opened their own parochial, or church-sponsored, schools.

The School Day The typical school day lasted from 8:00 A.M. to 4:00 P.M. Pupils learned the "three Rs": reading, 'riting, and 'rithmetic. Students memorized and recited passages from the most widely

AS YOU READ Kindergarten class
Find Main Ideas
What were the main goals of kindergartens?

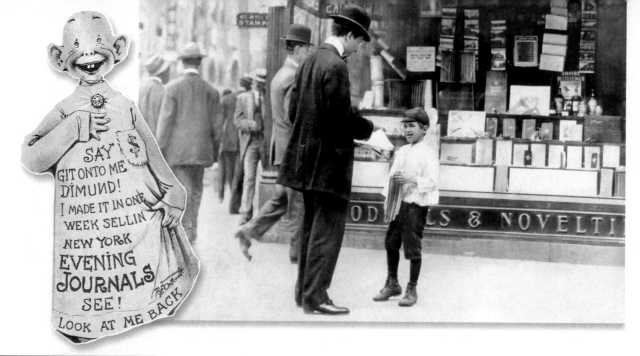

Viewing History

A City Newsboy

United States

Introduced in 1895, the Yellow Kid (left) became the first popular comic strip character. Here, the Kid encourages other boys to sell the New York *Journal*. **Drawing Conclusions** *Why might selling newspapers on the street be an appealing job for young city boys?*

used textbook, *McGuffey's Eclectic Reader.* With titles like "Waste Not, Want Not," the poems and stories taught not only reading but also religion, ethics, and values.

Schools emphasized discipline and obedience. Students had to sit upright in their seats, often with their hands folded in front of them. Punishment was swift and severe—a cuff on the head for whispering, or a paddling for arriving late.

Higher Learning After the Civil War, many cities and towns built public high schools. By 1900, there were 6,000 high schools in the country. Higher education also expanded. New private colleges for both women and men opened. Many states built universities that offered free or low-cost education.

To help meet the need for trained workers, the Chicago Manual Training School opened in 1884. It offered courses in "shop work," such as electricity and carpentry, as well as in a few academic subjects. Soon, most public schools in the nation had programs to prepare students for jobs in business and in industry.

Family Learning In 1874, a Methodist minister opened a summer school for Bible teachers along Lake Chautauqua in New York. The next year, the camp was opened to the general public. Mostly middle-class men and women of all ages gathered at Chautauqua each summer. In addition to receiving spiritual guidance, they enjoyed lectures about art, politics, philosophy, and other subjects.

In 1903, the Chautauqua Society began to send out traveling companies. Before long, Chautauquas were reaching as many as 5 million people in 10,000 American towns every year.

A Newspaper Boom

"Read all about it!" cried newsboys on city street corners. As education spread, people read more, especially newspapers. The number of newspapers grew dramatically. By 1900, half the newspapers in the world were printed in the United States.

The newspaper boom was linked to the growth of cities. In towns and villages, neighbors shared news face to face. In the crowded and busy cities, people needed newspapers to stay informed.

Newspapers reported on major events of the day. Most of them featured stories about local government, business, fashion, and sports. Many immigrants learned to read English by spelling their way through a daily paper. They also learned about American life.

Two Newspaper Giants Joseph Pulitzer, a Hungarian immigrant, created the first modern, mass-circulation newspaper. In 1883, Pulitzer bought the New York *World*. He set out to make it lively and "truly democratic." To win readers, Pulitzer slashed prices and added comic strips. Pictures and bold "scare" headlines attracted reader attention. The *World* splashed crimes and political scandals across its front page.

William Randolph Hearst challenged Pulitzer. Hearst's New York *Journal* began to outdo the *World* in presenting scandals, crime stories, and gossip. Critics complained that the papers offered less news and more scandal every day. They coined the term yellow journalism for the sensational reporting style of the *World* and the *Journal*.

Women as Readers and Reporters Newspapers competed for women readers. They added special sections on fashion, social events, health, homemaking, and family matters. Newspapers rarely pushed for women's rights, however. Most were afraid to take bold positions that might anger some readers.

A few women worked as reporters. Nellie Bly of the *World* pretended to be insane in order to find out about treatment of the mentally ill. Her articles about cruelty in mental hospitals led to reforms.

New Reading Habits

Americans also read more books and magazines. New printing methods lowered the cost of magazines. Magazines also added eye-catching pictures to attract readers.

Each magazine had its special audience. *The Ladies' Home Journal* appealed mostly to middle-class women. By 1900, it had one million readers. Other magazines, such as *Harper's Monthly* and *The Nation*, specialized in politics or current events.

Low-priced paperbacks, known as dime novels, offered thrilling adventure stories. Many told about the "Wild West." Young people loved dime novels, but parents often disapproved. "Stories for children used to begin, 'Once upon a time . . . ,' a critic complained. "Now they begin, 'Vengeance, blood, death,' shouted Rattlesnake Jim.'"

Horatio Alger wrote more than 100 dime novels for children. Most told of poor boys who became rich and respected through hard work, luck, and honesty. "Rags-to-riches" stories offered the hope that even the poorest person could succeed in the United States.

New American Writers

In the 1880s, a new crop of American writers appeared. For the first time, Americans were reading more books by American authors than by British authors.

PAUL THE PEDDLER

HORATIO ALGER JR.

Primary Source

Rags to Riches

Paul the Peddler *is a typical Horatio Alger story. Below, Alger describes the book's hero:*
". . . He knew there were plenty of ways in which he could earn something. He had never tried [shining shoes], but still he could do it in case of emergency. He had sold papers, and succeeded fairly [well] in that line, and knew he could again. He had pitted himself against other boys, and the result had been to give him a certain confidence in his own powers and business abilities. . . .

Paul had learned to rely upon himself; [and] the influence of a good, though humble, home, and a [wise] mother had kept him aloof from the bad habits into which many street boys are led."

—Horatio Alger, *Paul the Peddler*

Analyzing Primary Sources
Based on this passage, what qualities and values would help Paul succeed?

Viewing History

A Realist Painting Philadelphia painter Thomas Eakins often depicted sports scenes. This 1873 painting, *The Biglin Brothers Racing,* shows two famous rowers of the time. **Drawing Conclusions** *How would his study of anatomy have helped Eakins create this painting?*

Philadelphia

Realists One group of writers, called realists, tried to show the harsh side of life as it was. Many realists had worked as newspaper reporters. They had seen poverty and wanted to make people aware of the costs of urbanization and industrial growth.

Stephen Crane was best known for his Civil War novel, *The Red Badge of Courage.* Crane also wrote about the shattered lives of young city slum dwellers in novels like *Maggie: A Girl of the Streets.* Jack London, born in California, wrote about miners and sailors on the West Coast who put their lives at risk in backbreaking jobs.

Kate Chopin found an audience in women's magazines for her short stories about New Orleans life. Chopin's stories showed women breaking out of traditional roles.

Paul Laurence Dunbar was the first African American to make a living as a writer. He wrote poems, such as "We Wear the Mask," in a serious, elegant style. In other poems, he used everyday language to express the feelings of African Americans of the time.

Mark Twain The most famous and popular author of this period was Mark Twain, the pen name of Samuel Clemens. Twain had his first success in 1865 with his comical short story "The Celebrated Jumping Frog of Calaveras County."

Like many other writers, Twain used local color to make his stories more realistic. Local color refers to the speech and habits of a particular region. Twain captured the speech patterns of southerners who lived and worked along the Mississippi River.

In novels like *Huckleberry Finn,* Twain used homespun characters to poke fun at serious issues. Huck, a country boy, and Jim, an escaped slave, raft down the Mississippi River together in the days before the Civil War. Huck comes to respect Jim and to view slavery as wrong. Here, Huck talks about Jim's love for his family:

❤ He was saying how the first thing he would do when he got to a free state he would go to saving up money, . . . and when he got enough he would buy his wife, which was owned on a farm close to where Miss Watson lived; and then they would both work to buy the two children, and if their master wouldn't sell them, they'd get an Ab'litionist to go and steal them. **"**

—Mark Twain, *The Adventures of Huckleberry Finn*

AS YOU READ **Use Prior Knowledge** How does this passage show the use of local color? How does it reflect what you know about slavery before the Civil War?

Although *Huckleberry Finn* became a classic, some schools and libraries refused to buy the book. They claimed that Huck was a crude character who would have a bad influence on "our pure-minded lads and lasses."

Painting Everyday Life

Like writers of the period, many artists sought to capture local color and the gritty side of modern life. In the late 1800s, leading artists painted realistic everyday scenes.

During the Civil War, Winslow Homer drew scenes of brutal battles for magazines. Later, he gained fame for realistic paintings of the New England coast. Thomas Eakins learned anatomy and dissected dead bodies to be able to portray the human form accurately. Many of his paintings depicted sports scenes or medical operations. Henry Tanner, an African American student of Eakins, won fame for pictures of black sharecroppers. Later, Tanner moved to Paris to enjoy greater freedom.

Other American artists preferred to work in Europe, too. James Whistler left Massachusetts for Paris and London. His use of color and light influenced young European artists. Mary Cassatt (kuh SAT) also carved out a place for herself in the French art world. Cassatt painted bright, colorful scenes of people in everyday situations, especially mothers with their children.

Section 4 Assessment

Recall

1. **Identify** Explain the significance of **(a)** Chautauqua Society, **(b)** Joseph Pulitzer, **(c)** William Randolph Hearst, **(d)** Horatio Alger, **(e)** Stephen Crane, **(f)** Kate Chopin, **(g)** Paul Laurence Dunbar, **(h)** Mark Twain, **(i)** Thomas Eakins, **(j)** Mary Cassatt.
2. **Define** **(a)** compulsory education, **(b)** parochial, **(c)** yellow journalism, **(d)** dime novel, **(e)** realist, **(f)** local color.

Comprehension

3. How did American education change in the late 1800s?

4. Why did the number of American newspapers grow rapidly?
5. Identify three themes explored by realists in literature or art.

Critical Thinking and Writing

6. **Exploring the Main Idea** Review the Main Idea statement and the Setting the Scene story at the beginning of this section. Then, write a paragraph explaining the connection between education and new reading habits.
7. **Supporting a Point of View** Write a letter to Pulitzer or Hearst. Explain your views on his methods to increase newspaper circulation.

ACTIVITY

Take It to the NET
Writing a Museum Guide Use the Internet to find other examples of American painting from 1865–1915. Choose one work, and prepare a write-up that might appear in a museum guide. Include the title, artist, and date, plus a description of the subject matter. Visit *The American Nation* section of **www.phschool.com** for help in completing the activity.

CREATING A CHAPTER SUMMARY

Copy the concept web below. Fill in the blank ovals with important facts and developments relating to the growth of cities. Add as many ovals as you need to complete the table.

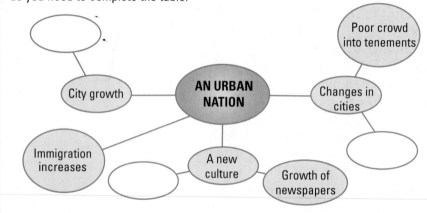

i TEXT

For additional review and enrichment activities, see the interactive version of *The American Nation,* available on the Web and on CD-ROM.

Take It to the NET

Chapter Self-Test For practice test questions for Chapter 21, visit *The American Nation* section of **www.phschool.com**.

Building Vocabulary

Use the chapter vocabulary words listed below to create a crossword puzzle. Exchange puzzles with a classmate. Complete the puzzles, and then check each other's answers.

1. **push factor**
2. **pull factor**
3. **acculturation**
4. **urbanization**
5. **tenement**
6. **skyscraper**
7. **suburb**
8. **vaudeville**
9. **ragtime**
10. **yellow journalism**

Reviewing Key Facts

11. Describe immigrant neighborhoods in American cities. (Section 1)
12. Why did cities set up building codes? (Section 2)
13. What services did religious organizations provide for the urban poor? (Section 2)
14. How did city planners deal with traffic problems? (Section 3)
15. How did schools prepare people for jobs in business and industry? (Section 4)

Critical Thinking and Writing

16. **Connecting to Geography: Regions** For each of the following factors, write a sentence explaining how it influenced the development of different neighborhoods within American cities: **(a)** ethnic makeup, **(b)** economic level, **(c)** transportation.
17. **Sequencing** Place the following developments in logical sequence: American cities boom, city governments do not provide adequate services, immigrants book passage on steamships, reforms help cities work better, peasants in Europe and Asia face economic hardships. Write a paragraph explaining how each development contributed to the next.
18. **Making Decisions** If you had been a city planner, would you have favored using city land and money to build public parks? List pros and cons. Then, explain your decision.
19. **Synthesizing Information** Make a diagram showing how the building of tenements, improvements in public education, and the move toward realism in literature were all linked to industrial growth.

Analyzing Primary Sources

Mary Antin, a Russian Jewish immigrant, came to the United States in 1890. Here, she speaks of the opportunities in her new home:

> ❝Education was free. That subject my father had written about repeatedly, as comprising his chief hope for us children, the essence of American opportunity, the treasure that no thief could touch, not even misfortune or poverty. It was the one thing that he was able to promise us when he sent for us; surer, safer than bread or shelter. . . . No application made, no questions asked, no examinations, rulings, exclusions. . . . The doors stood open for every one of us.❞
>
> —Mary Antin, *The Promised Land*

20. **(a)** Why do you think Antin's father wanted to take his family out of Russia? **(b)** Who came to the United States first? Why?
21. How do Antin and her father value wealth in comparison to education?
22. **(a)** Why do you think immigrants valued education so highly? **(b)** Do you think Americans value education in the same way today? Why or why not?

Comparing Maps Over Time

Eastern American Cities, 1870

Compare this map with the one on page 599. Then, answer the questions that follow.

23. Which city's population passed the 100,000 mark between 1870 and 1900?
    A Philadelphia   C Albany
    B Detroit   D Baltimore
24. What changes would you expect to see on a later map of the same area?

ACTIVITIES

Connecting With . . . Culture

Planning a Story With a partner, outline the plot for a "rags-to-riches" story like those written by Horatio Alger. Your main character is a young immigrant or a farmer who comes to live in the city in the late 1800s. Consider your character's hardships and how he or she becomes successful.

Take It to the NET

Connecting to Today
Comparing News Media Today, most newspapers operate their own Web sites. Use the Internet to find the Web site for a local newspaper. Compare the Web site with an edition of the newspaper. Then, write a letter to the editor explaining which is the best method for citizens to stay informed and why. For help in starting this activity, visit *The American Nation* section of **www.phschool.com**.

Researching
Preparing a News Report Use the Internet to find out more about the Chicago Fire of 1871. Then, with a small group, prepare a news report on the fire. Focus on the causes of the fire and its impact on the city. Include interviews with witnesses and an editorial on what the city should do in the future. Visit *The American Nation* section of **www.phschool.com** for help in completing this activity.

1 Which urban innovation was most closely linked to the growth of suburbs?

   A Apartment buildings

   B Streetcars

   C Skyscrapers

   D Department stores

Use the map and your knowledge of social studies to answer the following question.

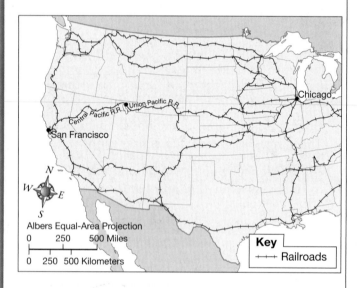

2 Which of the following questions would this map not help you answer?

   A Where was the first transcontinental railroad completed?

   B What railroad routes could a company use to ship goods from the Pacific Ocean to the Great Lakes?

   C What geographic obstacles did western railroad builders have to overcome?

   D What was the length of the shortest railway route from Chicago to San Francisco?

3 Which statement is true of both the Knights of Labor and the American Federation of Labor?

   A It officially supported the use of strikes.

   B It was open to both skilled and unskilled workers.

   C Its goals included a shorter workday.

   D Its goals included equal pay for men and women.

4 Which of the following was not a goal of the Populist party?

   A Free silver

   B Regulation of railroad rates

   C Open immigration

   D An income tax

Use the quotations and your knowledge of social studies to answer the following question.

John H. Vincent, 1886 [adapted]

"No man has a right to neglect his personal education, whether he be prince or plowboy."

"All knowledge, religious or worldly, is sacred."

"Between the ages of 20 and 80 lie a person's best educational opportunities."

---

5 The quotations most closely reflect the goals of what movement?

   A The Chautauqua movement

   B The settlement house movement

   C The kindergarten movement

   D The Social Gospel movement

Use the table <u>and</u> your knowledge of social studies to answer the following question.

United States Patents, 1861–1900

Five-Year Periods	Number of Patents
1861–1865	20,725
1866–1870	58,734
1871–1875	60,976
1876–1880	64,462
1881–1885	97,156
1886–1890	110,358
1891–1895	108,420
1896–1900	112,188

Source: *Historical Statistics of the United States*

6 Which statement is best supported by the table?

   A The number of patents issued increased steadily from the Civil War to 1900.

   B More patents were issued in 1880 than in 1870.

   C More patents were issued between 1886 and 1895 than between 1876 and 1885.

   D The average number of patents issued every year between 1891 and 1895 was 10,842.

7 Which of the following would be an example of vertical integration?

   A The owner of an oil refinery buys up oil-drilling operations.

   B The owner of a railroad buys up other railroads.

   C A banker loans capital to two different copper-mining companies.

   D Three different steel companies are run by the same board of directors.

8 In which of the following pairs was the first event a direct cause of the second?

   A Spread of the Ghost Dance; Chivington Massacre

   B Destruction of the buffalo; Battle of Little Bighorn

   C Fort Laramie treaty; end of warfare between whites and Indians

   D Discovery of gold in Black Hills; Sioux War

9 "The large mass of illiterate immigrants . . . is a menace, socially, industrially, and politically." Who would have been most likely to agree with this statement?

   A Jane Addams

   B A member of the American Protective Association

   C An immigration official at Ellis Island

   D Joseph Pulitzer

Writing Practice

10 "On balance, the rapid growth of industry in the late 1800s was beneficial to the nation." List two facts that support this statement. Then, explain whether you agree or disagree and why.

11 How were the reasons that settlers moved to the western frontier in the late 1800s similar to or different from the reasons that immigrants came to the United States?

A New Role for the Nation

The Spirit of Patriotism
The Fourth of July, by Childe Hassam,
reflects Americans' growing spirit of
patriotism as the nation becomes a
world power.

> *"Whether they will or no, Americans must begin to look outward. The growing production of the country demands it."*
>
> —Alfred Thayer Mahan, naval officer (1897)

CHAPTER **22**

The Progressive Era

1876–1920

1 **Reform in the Gilded Age**
2 **The Progressives**
3 **Progressives in the White House**
4 **Women Win Reforms**
5 **Other Americans Seek Justice**

TO THE
VICTORS
BELONG THE
SPOILS.
A. JACKSON.

SPOILS   SPOILS

16 details

Cartoon attacks on the spoils system

Jacob Riis's photo of a New York City slum apartment

1883
The Pendleton Act creates a commission to conduct exams for federal job seekers.

1890
With stark views of urban poverty, Jacob Riis's book *How the Other Half Lives* shocks middle-class readers.

1895
W.E.B. Du Bois becomes the first African American to receive a Ph.D. from Harvard University.

Grover Cleveland 1893–1897

James Garfield 1881

AMERICAN EVENTS

Rutherford B. Hayes

Chester A. Arthur | Grover Cleveland | Benjamin Harrison | William McKinley

Presidential Terms: Ulysses S. Grant 1869–1877 | 1877–1881 | 1881–1885 | 1885–1889 | 1889–1893 | 1897–1901

1870 • **1885** • **1900**

WORLD EVENTS

1893 ▲
New Zealand becomes the first nation to give women the right to vote.

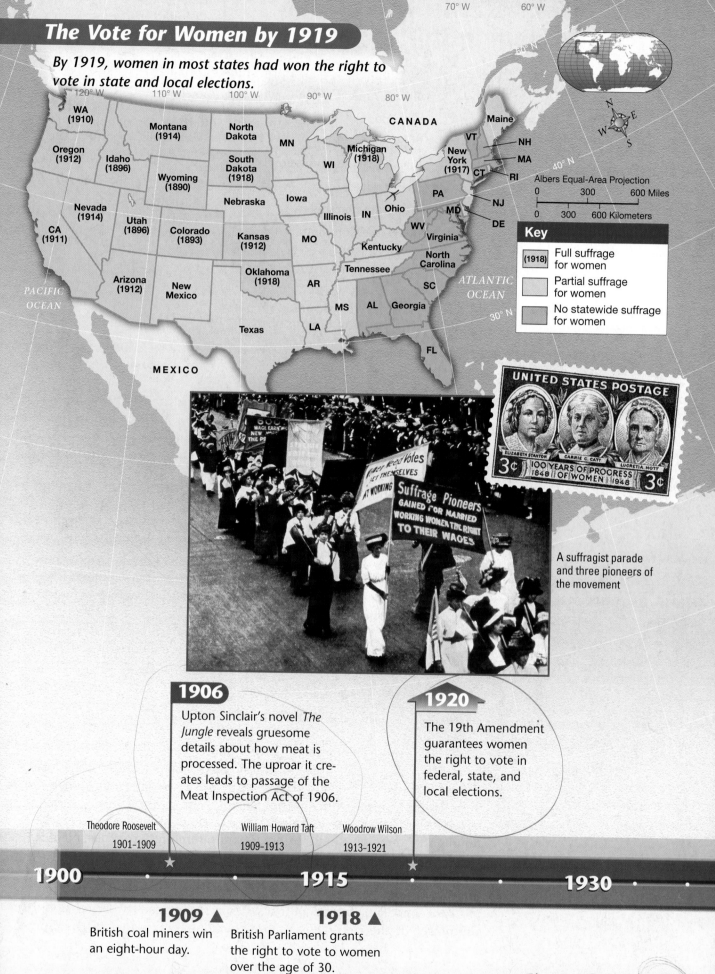

By 1919, women in most states had won the right to vote in state and local elections.

WA (1910)
Oregon (1912)
Montana (1914)
Idaho (1896)
North Dakota
MN
CANADA
Maine
Michigan (1918)
VT
NH
New York (1917)
MA
CT
RI
Nevada (1914)
Wyoming (1890)
South Dakota (1918)
WI
Iowa
PA
Utah (1896)
Nebraska
IN
Ohio
MD
NJ
DE
CA (1911)
Colorado (1893)
Kansas (1912)
MO
WV
Virginia
Kentucky
North Carolina
Arizona (1912)
New Mexico
Oklahoma (1918)
AR
Tennessee
SC
PACIFIC OCEAN
Texas
LA
MS
AL
Georgia
ATLANTIC OCEAN
MEXICO
FL

Albers Equal-Area Projection

0   300   600 Miles
0   300   600 Kilometers

Key

(1918) Full suffrage for women

Partial suffrage for women

No statewide suffrage for women

UNITED STATES POSTAGE
ELIZABETH STANTON CARRIE C. CATT LUCRETIA MOTT
3¢ 100 YEARS OF PROGRESS 1848 · 1948 OF WOMEN 3¢

A suffragist parade and three pioneers of the movement

1906

Upton Sinclair's novel *The Jungle* reveals gruesome details about how meat is processed. The uproar it creates leads to passage of the Meat Inspection Act of 1906.

1920

The 19th Amendment guarantees women the right to vote in federal, state, and local elections.

Theodore Roosevelt
1901–1909

William Howard Taft
1909–1913

Woodrow Wilson
1913–1921

1900

1915

1930

1909 ▲
British coal miners win an eight-hour day.

1918 ▲
British Parliament grants the right to vote to women over the age of 30.

1 Reform in the Gilded Age

BEFORE YOU READ

Reading Focus
- What concerns shaped politics during the Gilded Age?
- How did reformers try to change the spoils system?
- What laws were passed to regulate big business?

Key Terms

Gilded Age

patronage

merit

Civil Service Commission

civil service

interstate commerce

Interstate Commerce Commission

Sherman Antitrust Act

Taking Notes

Copy the concept web below. As you read, fill in each blank oval with important facts about reforms accomplished during the Gilded Age. Add as many ovals as you need.

Main Idea During the Gilded Age, reformers worked to end political corruption and limit the power of big business.

AS YOU READ
An American palace
Find Main Ideas How do this Newport, Rhode Island, dining room and the Martin family party symbolize the Gilded Age?

Setting the Scene The newly rich Martin family threw a huge and expensive party. They rented a fancy New York City hotel and transformed it to look like the palace of France's King Louis XIV. Critics condemned such extravagance. They pointed out that at the time, two in five Americans were out of work.

Wild spending by the wealthy was typical of the Gilded Age of the late 1800s. This era got its name from an 1873 novel by Mark Twain and Charles Dudley Warner titled *The Gilded Age*. ("Gilded" means coated with a thin layer of gold paint. It implies falseness beneath surface glitter.) For many Americans, the novel, which poked fun at the era's greed and political corruption, captured the spirit of the time. In the words of one observer, it was government "of, by, and for the rich."

The Gilded Age lasted from the 1870s through the 1890s. During this time, reformers struggled to clean up political corruption.

Politics in the Gilded Age

During the Gilded Age, political power was split between the two major parties. Usually, the North and West voted Republican, and the South voted Democrat. Neither party controlled Congress for more than a term or two, although Republicans held the White House for nearly 25 years. However, Presidents generally had less power than Congress during the period.

For Americans of the Gilded Age, elections provided great entertainment. Campaigns featured brass bands, torchlight parades, picnics, and long speeches. Americans marched, ate, drank, and listened. The turnout of voters was never again as high—almost 80 percent of eligible voters.

Two concerns shaped politics. Many Americans worried about the power of the rich. They feared that bankers, industrialists, and other wealthy men were controlling politics at the expense of the public good. The other worry was corruption, especially bribery and voter fraud. Reformers blamed much of the problem on the spoils system, the practice of rewarding political supporters with government jobs.

Reforming the Spoils System

The spoils system had grown since the days of Andrew Jackson. When a new President took office, job seekers swarmed into Washington. They demanded government jobs as rewards for their political support. Giving jobs to followers is called **patronage.**

Patronage often led to corruption. Some jobholders simply stole public money. Others had no skills for the jobs they were given. In New York, for example, one man was made court reporter even though he could neither read nor write.

Early Reform Efforts Calls for reform slowly brought change. In 1877, President Rutherford B. Hayes took steps toward ending the spoils system. He ordered an investigation of the New York customhouse. There, investigators found hundreds of appointed officials receiving high salaries but doing no work. Despite the protests of local Republican leaders, Hayes dismissed two customhouse officials. (See American Profile at right.)

In 1881, James Garfield entered the White House and was soon swamped with office seekers. He thought that government jobs should be awarded on the basis of **merit,** or ability, not politics.

That July, however, a disappointed office seeker, Charles Guiteau (gee TOH), shot the President. Garfield died two months later. The assassination sparked new efforts to end the spoils system.

Civil Service Exams Vice President Chester A. Arthur succeeded Garfield. Arthur was a product of the spoils system. In fact, he was one of the New York customhouse officials dismissed by Hayes a few years earlier! Yet, as President, Arthur worked with Congress to reform the spoils system.

In 1883, Congress passed the Pendleton Act. It created the **Civil Service Commission** to conduct exams for federal jobs. The **civil service** includes all federal jobs except elected offices and the military. The aim of the Civil Service Commission was to fill jobs on the basis of merit. People who scored highest on the civil service exams earned the posts.

At first, the Civil Service Commission controlled only a few federal jobs. However, under pressure from reformers, later Presidents placed more jobs under the Civil Service Commission. By 1900, the commission controlled about 40 percent of all federal jobs.

Regulating Big Business

In 1877, Collis Huntington, builder of the Central Pacific Railroad, tried to bribe members of Congress to kill a railroad bill that would be unfavorable to his interests. He gave large amounts of money to members of Congress. "It costs money to fix things," Huntington explained.

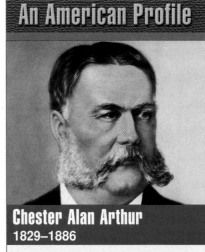

An American Profile

Chester Alan Arthur
1829–1886

Although Chester A. Arthur was an honorable man, he believed firmly in the spoils system. While running the New York customhouse, he employed far more people than the customhouse needed. These employees were loyal party workers.

In 1878, President Hayes fired Arthur. New York City bosses then turned on Hayes. To win them back, Republican leaders offered Arthur the vice presidential nomination.

To the horror of reformers, Arthur became President when President Garfield was assassinated in 1881. They were amazed when President Arthur went on to become a champion of civil service reform.

Why do you think President Arthur worked so hard to end the spoils system?

AS YOU READ **Find Main Ideas** As you read this subsection, look for ways in which the government tried to regulate big business.

Interstate Commerce Act The behavior of men like Huntington convinced many Americans that big businesses controlled the government. They demanded that something be done to limit the power of big business.

In response, the government began to regulate railroads and other large businesses. Under the Constitution, the federal government had the power to regulate interstate commerce, or business that crossed state lines. In 1887, President Grover Cleveland signed the Interstate Commerce Act. It forbade practices such as pools and rebates. (See Chapter 20.) It also set up the Interstate Commerce Commission, or ICC, to oversee the railroads.

At first, the ICC was weak. In court challenges, most judges ruled in favor of the railroads. Still, Congress had shown that it was ready to regulate big business. Later, Congress passed laws that made the ICC more effective.

Sherman Antitrust Act In 1888, President Cleveland lost his bid for reelection. Benjamin Harrison became President. In 1890, Harrison signed the Sherman Antitrust Act. The act prohibited businesses from trying to limit or destroy competition.

The Sherman Antitrust Act sounded strong, but enforcing it proved difficult. At first, judges ruled in favor of trusts. They held that the law was an illegal attempt by the government to control private property.

Instead of regulating trusts, the Sherman Antitrust Act was often used against labor unions. The courts said union strikes blocked free trade and thus threatened competition. Later on, as the reform spirit spread, the courts began to use the Sherman Act against monopolies.

Section 1 Assessment

Recall

1. **Identify** Explain the significance of **(a)** Gilded Age, **(b)** Chester A. Arthur, **(c)** Civil Service Commission, **(d)** Interstate Commerce Commission, **(e)** Sherman Antitrust Act.
2. **Define (a)** patronage, **(b)** merit, **(c)** civil service, **(d)** interstate commerce.

Comprehension

3. What two political concerns shaped politics during the Gilded Age?
4. What reforms were made to end the spoils system?

5. Describe two new laws that tried to limit the power of big business.

Critical Thinking and Writing

6. **Exploring the Main Idea** Review the Main Idea statement at the beginning of this chapter. Then, suppose that you have a government job as a result of patronage. Write two entries in your diary: one about how you got your job, and a second one telling what you think of replacing patronage with a civil service system.
7. **Drawing Conclusions** Why do you think early efforts to regulate big business had little success?

2 The Progressives

Reading Focus

- How did corruption affect city governments?
- Why were the muckrakers an important force for reform?
- What goals did the Progressives pursue?
- What political reforms did the Progressives achieve?

Key Terms

political boss
muckraker
Progressive
public interest
Wisconsin Idea
primary
initiative
referendum
recall
graduated income tax

Taking Notes

As you read, complete the following chart to show how Progressive reforms shaped the era in three areas.

AREAS OF PROGRESSIVE REFORM

City governments	Empowering voters	Two amendments
•	•	•
•	•	•

Main Idea Progressive reformers worked to end political corruption and give voters greater power.

Setting the Scene The Reverend Charles Parkhurst was furious about corruption in New York City. In one sermon, he called the city's politicians a "pack of administrative bloodhounds" who feed on the "flesh and blood of our citizenship."

A grand jury looked into these charges. They were outraged. However, their outrage was directed not against the wrongdoers but against Parkhurst. The grand jury condemned Parkhurst for encouraging the public to distrust government. Yet, Charles Parkhurst was only saying what most New Yorkers already knew. The city was riddled with corruption.

By the 1890s, more and more Americans were speaking out against corrupt politics. Soon, a new generation of reformers would fight to oust dishonest politicians and to give voters greater power.

Reforming City Governments

How did city governments become so corrupt? As cities grew, they needed to expand services such as sewers, garbage collection, and roads. Often, politicians accepted money to give away these jobs. As a result, bribes and corruption became a way of life.

Political Bosses Powerful politicians, called political bosses, gained power in many cities. Political bosses also ruled county and state governments. Bosses controlled work done locally and demanded payoffs from businesses. City bosses were popular with the poor, especially with immigrants. They provided jobs and made loans to the needy. They handed out extra coal in winter and turkeys at Thanksgiving. In exchange, the poor voted for the boss or his chosen candidate.

Boss Tweed In New York City, Boss William Tweed carried corruption to new extremes. During the 1860s and 1870s, he cheated the city out of more than $100 million.

AS YOU READ **Cartoonist Thomas Nast attacks political corruption**

Draw Inferences Which approach do you think would be a more effective weapon against corruption, Parkhurst's sermon or the above cartoon?

Journalists exposed Boss Tweed's wrongdoing. For example, cartoonist Thomas Nast pictured Tweed as a vulture feeding on the city. Nast's cartoons especially angered Tweed. His supporters might not be able to read, he said, but they could understand Nast's cartoons.

Faced with prison, Tweed fled to Spain. There, local police arrested him when they recognized him from Nast's cartoons. When Tweed died in jail in 1878, thousands of poor New Yorkers mourned for him.

Good-Government Leagues In many cities, reformers set up good-government leagues. Their goal was to replace corrupt officials with honest leaders.

The leagues had some successes. In Minneapolis, a corrupt mayor was indicted. Cleveland reformers helped elect Tom Johnson mayor. Johnson gave out contracts honestly, improved garbage and sewage systems, and set up services for the poor.

The Muckrakers

Reformers used the press to turn public opinion against corruption. Newspaper reporters described how corruption led to inadequate fire and police protection and poor sanitation services. Jacob Riis (REES), a photographer and writer, provided shocking images of slum life.

Crusading journalists like Riis became known as **muckrakers.** People said they raked the dirt, or muck, and exposed it to public view. One muckraker, Ida Tarbell, targeted the unfair practices of big business. Her articles about the Standard Oil Company led to demands for more controls on trusts.

In 1906, Upton Sinclair's novel *The Jungle* shocked the nation. Although the book was fiction it was based on facts. It revealed grisly details about the meatpacking industry. Sinclair told how the packers used meat from sick animals. He described how rats often got ground up in the meat, which was then dyed to make it seem healthy.

Muckrakers helped change public opinion. For years, middle-class Americans had ignored the need for reform. When they saw how dishonest politicians and businesses corrupted the nation—and even the food they ate—they, too, demanded change.

The Progressives

By 1900, reformers were calling themselves **Progressives.** By that, they meant that they were forward-thinking people who wanted to improve American life. Progressives won many changes during the period from 1898 to 1917. As a result, this period is called the Progressive Era.

Progressives were never a single group with a single goal. Instead, they came from many backgrounds and backed different causes. They were united by a belief that the ills of society could be solved. Progressives wanted the government to act in the **public interest,** for the good of the people.

Both religion and science inspired Progressives. The Social Gospel movement of the late 1800s stressed the duty of Christians to

---

An American Profile

Ida Tarbell 1857–1944

Ida Tarbell was not afraid of challenges. At Allegheny College, she was the only woman in her graduating class. After college, she became editor of a literary journal.

Seeking new experiences, Tarbell took her entire savings and moved to Paris to study and write. She supported herself by writing for *McClure's Magazine.* In 1902, *McClure's* began publishing her most famous work, *The History of the Standard Oil Company.*

Tarbell became one of the best-known crusading journalists of her time. She also wrote biographies, including her own life story, when she was eighty.

Do you think Tarbell would have supported an organization working for greater rights for women? Why or why not?

Progressive Political Reforms

Before		After
Party leaders pick candidates for state and local offices	**PRIMARY**	Voters select their party's candidates
Only members of state legislature can introduce bills	**INITIATIVE**	Voters can propose bills to the legislature
Only legislators pass laws	**REFERENDUM**	Voters can vote on bills directly
Only courts or legislature can remove corrupt officials	**RECALL**	Voters can remove elected officials from office

GRAPHIC ORGANIZER
Skills

In many states, Progressive reforms put more political power in voters' hands.

1. **Comprehension**
   (a) Who chooses political candidates in states with no primary? **(b)** How does the recall give more power to voters?

2. **Critical Thinking**
   Drawing Conclusions What responsibilities does a citizen have when voting on a referendum?

Civics 🏛

improve society. At the same time, Progressives used scientific studies and statistics to find ways to solve society's problems.

Progressives valued education. John Dewey, a Progressive educator, wanted schools to promote reform. Schools must teach democratic values by example, he argued. He therefore urged students to ask questions and to work together to solve problems.

Political Reforms

Among the leading Progressives was Robert La Follette of Wisconsin. "The will of the people shall be the law of the land," was his motto. His fighting spirit won him the nickname "Battling Bob."

The Wisconsin Idea As governor of Wisconsin, La Follette introduced various Progressive reforms that became known as the Wisconsin Idea. For example, he lowered railroad rates. The result was increased rail traffic, which helped both railroad owners and customers.

Empowering Voters Progressives like La Follette wanted voters to participate more directly in government. Since Andrew Jackson's time, party leaders had picked candidates for local and state offices. Progressives called, instead, for primaries. In a primary, voters choose their party's candidate for the general election. In 1903, Wisconsin was the first state to adopt a primary run by state government officials. By 1917, all but four states had done so.

AS YOU READ **Use Prior Knowledge** As you read, think about which groups or organizations today would probably have been supported by the Progressives.

Other reforms gave voters more power. They included the initiative, which gave voters the right to put a bill before a state legislature. A certain number of qualified voters must sign initiative petitions to propose a law. The referendum allowed voters to put a bill on the ballot and vote it into law. The recall allowed voters to remove an elected official from office. That reform let voters get rid of corrupt officials.

Progressives from other states visited Wisconsin to study La Follette's reforms. A number of states elected Progressive governors eager for reforms.

Two Amendments Progressives fought for other changes, too. They favored lowering tariffs on imported goods. If American industry had to compete against foreign imports, they argued, consumers would benefit from lower prices.

Some reforms led to changes in the United States Constitution. Many reformers backed a graduated income tax, which taxes people at different rates. The wealthy pay taxes at a higher rate than the poor or the middle class.

Because the Supreme Court had held that a federal income tax was unconstitutional, Progressives campaigned for a Sixteenth Amendment. It gave Congress the power to pass an income tax. By 1913, the states had ratified the amendment.

The states approved another amendment in 1913. Since 1789, state legislatures had elected senators. Powerful interest groups had sometimes bribed lawmakers to vote for certain candidates. Progressives wanted to end such abuses by having voters elect senators directly. In 1912, Congress approved the Seventeenth Amendment, which allowed for the direct election of senators. It was ratified a year later.

Section 2 Assessment

Recall

1. **Identify** Explain the significance of (a) William Tweed, (b) Ida Tarbell, (c) Progressive, (d) Robert La Follette, (e) Wisconsin Idea.

2. **Define** (a) political boss, (b) muckraker, (c) public interest, (d) primary, (e) initiative, (f) referendum, (g) recall, (h) graduated income tax.

Comprehension

3. How did political bosses corrupt city governments?

4. How did the muckrakers help change public opinion?

5. Explain three major goals of Progressive reformers.

6. Describe two Progressive reforms that increased the political power of voters.

Critical Thinking and Writing

7. **Exploring the Main Idea** Review the Main Idea statement at the beginning of this section. Then, write at least four questions to ask muckrakers about their goals and achievements.

8. **Supporting a Point of View** La Follette and other Progressives believed that people would make the right decisions about their government if given the chance. Do you agree with that view? Explain.

ACTIVITY

Drawing a Political Cartoon You are Thomas Nast. Boss Tweed and his pals are stealing millions from the city you love. Draw a political cartoon to rouse public opinion against Tweed's corruption.

The Muckrakers

A number of best-selling books allowed reformers to get their message to the general public. The messages in these books shocked Americans and led to many important reforms.

UPTON SINCLAIR
THE JUNGLE

THE SHAME OF THE CITIES

LINCOLN STEFFENS

66 The [political bosses] control the whole process of voting, and practice fraud at every stage. The assessor's list is the voting list, and the assessor is the [boss's] man. . . . The assessor pads the list with the names of dead dogs, children, and non-existent persons. 99
—Lincoln Steffens, *The Shame of the Cities*, 1904

Upton Sinclair
(1878–1968)

66 There was never the least attention paid to what was cut up for sausage; there would come all the way back from Europe old sausage that had been rejected, and that was moldy and white—it would be dosed with borax and glycerin, and . . . made over again for home consumption. 99
—Upton Sinclair, *The Jungle*, 1906

Lincoln Steffens
(1866–1936)

66 The farmer's profits were the object of attack from a score of different quarters. It was a flock of vultures descending upon a common prey—the commission merchant, the elevator combine, the mixing-house ring, the banks, the warehouse men, the laboring man, and, above all, the railroad. 99
—Frank Norris, *The Octopus*, 1901

Frank Norris
(1870–1902)

FRANK NORRIS
The Octopus

ACTIVITY

Think of yourself as a present-day muckraker. Make a list of up to five reforms you would like to see accomplished in the United States. Then, select one reform, and create a poster to encourage support for it.

3 Progressives in the White House

BEFORE YOU READ

Reading Focus

- What policies toward big business, conservation, and consumers did Theodore Roosevelt's Square Deal follow?
- Why did Progressives first support and then oppose William Howard Taft?
- What major issues affected the election of 1912?
- What policies did Woodrow Wilson follow as President?

Key Terms

trustbuster
Square Deal
Pure Food and Drug Act
conservation
national park
Bull Moose party
New Freedom
Federal Reserve Act
Federal Trade Commission

Taking Notes

Copy the table below. As you read, complete the table by listing the achievements of the three "Progressive" Presidents.

ROOSEVELT	TAFT	WILSON
• Attacks bad trusts	• Sets up child labor office	• Backs Federal Trade Commission
•	•	•
•	•	•

Main Idea During the early 1900s, three Presidents worked for Progressive goals: Theodore Roosevelt, William H. Taft, and Woodrow Wilson.

San Francisco Chronicle.

PRESIDENT M'KINLEY SHOT BY AN ANARCHIST AT BUFFALO FAIR.

Two Bullets Fired by the Assassin, but Only One Penetrates the Body— Surgeons Hopeful of Recovery—An Attempt Made to Lynch the Cowardly Murderer.

WOUNDED AT A PUBLIC RECEPTION.

A RECENT PORTRAIT OF PRESIDENT M'KINLEY.

DOCTORS DECLARE INJURIES SEVERE.

AS YOU READ **President shot!**
Use Prior Knowledge
Which previous Presidents had been assassinated while in office?

Setting the Scene An unemployed man stood nervously in line at the world's fair in Buffalo, New York. An anarchist, the man had a score to settle—with the President of the United States, William McKinley. When McKinley extended his hand, Leon Czolgosz (CHOHL goz) brushed it aside and fired two shots into the President. "Be easy with him, boys," gasped the wounded McKinley.

Doctors could not find the bullets lodged in the President's chest. They did not think to use the new X-ray machine on display at the fair.

On September 14, 1901, McKinley died. Vice President Theodore Roosevelt became President. At age 42, he was the youngest President to take office. He was also a strong supporter of Progressive goals.

Theodore Roosevelt

Teddy Roosevelt—or "TR," as he was called—came from a wealthy New York family. As a child, he suffered from asthma and was often sick. To build his strength, he lifted weights, ran, and boxed.

Political Ambitions TR could have enjoyed a life of ease. Instead, he decided to enter politics. He was determined to end corruption and work for the public interest.

TR's friends mocked his decision to devote his life to public service. They told him "that the men I met would be rough and brutal and unpleasant to deal with," he later recalled. He replied that he would not quit until he "found out whether I was really too weak to hold my own in the rough and tumble."

By age 26, Roosevelt was serving in the New York state legislature. Then, tragedy struck. In 1884, his mother and his young wife died on the same day. Overcome by grief, Roosevelt quit the legislature. He went west to work on a cattle ranch.

After two years, Roosevelt returned to the East and to politics. He served on the Civil Service Commission. He then headed New York City's police department and later became assistant secretary of the navy.

In 1898, the United States went to war against Spain. Roosevelt led a unit of troops in some daring exploits. He returned home to a hero's welcome and was elected governor of New York.

A Progressive Governor Since his days in the legislature, Roosevelt had pushed for reform. As governor, he continued to work for Progressive reforms. Other lawmakers called him a "goo goo," a mocking name for someone who wanted good government.

New York Republican bosses were relieved when Roosevelt resigned from the office of governor to become Vice President. Then, after President McKinley was shot in September 1901, Roosevelt became President. He was committed, he later wrote, to "making an old party Progressive."

TR and Big Business

Roosevelt promised to continue McKinley's probusiness policies. He was not against big business. In fact, he believed business was a positive force and that giant corporations were here to stay.

Roosevelt saw a difference, however, between good trusts and bad trusts. Good trusts, he said, were efficient and fair and should be let alone. Bad ones took advantage of workers and cheated the public. The government must either control them or break them up.

TR, the "Trustbuster" Roosevelt wanted to test the power of the government to break up bad trusts. In 1902, he asked the Attorney General, the government's chief lawyer, to bring a lawsuit against the Northern Securities Company. Northern Securities was a trust that had been formed to control competition among railroads. TR argued that the company used unfair business practices in violation of the Sherman Act.

At news of the lawsuit, stock prices fell on Wall Street, New York's center of business and finance. "Wall Street is paralyzed at the thought that a President of the United States would sink so low as to try to enforce the law," one newspaper joked. While business leaders worried, many ordinary Americans cheered the President.

In 1904, the Supreme Court ruled that Northern Securities had violated the Sherman Antitrust Act. It ordered the trust to be broken up. The decision was a victory for Progressives. For the first time, the Sherman Act had been used to break up trusts, not unions.

Next, Roosevelt had the Attorney General file suit against other trusts, including Standard Oil and the American Tobacco Company.

Viewing History

TR on the Campaign Trail

Theodore Roosevelt put tremendous energy into his speeches, shaking his fists in the air as he spoke. Here, Roosevelt is shown campaigning in Wyoming in 1903. Roosevelt's activities as an outdoorsman also helped his public image. After he refused to shoot a small captured bear, a toy company named a new product after the President: the Teddy bear. **Applying Information** *How did Roosevelt's actions as President support his image as an energetic fighter?*

▲ Past

▲ Present

Viewing History

Protecting the Consumer

United States

Before the Progressive Era, no law controlled the ads of drug manufacturers. Advertisers often made wild claims for medicines that actually did nothing. Today, every medicine label must include a list of ingredients, exact directions for use, and warnings about possible side effects.

Analyzing Information *How is the advertisement at left different from an ad for medicine that you might see in a magazine today?*

AS YOU READ **Draw Inferences** As you read, think of businesses that might have supported Theodore Roosevelt and businesses that might have opposed him.

In time, the courts ordered the breakup of both trusts because they blocked free trade.

Some business leaders called Roosevelt a trustbuster, a person who wanted to destroy all trusts. "Certainly not," replied Roosevelt, only those that "have done something we regard as wrong." He preferred to control or regulate trusts, not "bust" them.

Support for Labor Roosevelt also clashed with mine owners. In 1902, Pennsylvania coal miners went on strike for better pay and a shorter workday. Mine owners refused to negotiate with the miners' union.

As winter approached, schools and hospitals ran out of coal. Furious at the mine owners, Roosevelt threatened to send in troops to run the mines. Finally, owners sat down with the union and reached an agreement. Roosevelt was the first President to side with labor.

The Square Deal

Roosevelt ran for President in his own right in 1904. During the campaign, he promised Americans a Square Deal. By this, he meant that everyone from farmers and consumers to workers and owners should have the same opportunity to succeed. That promise helped Roosevelt win a huge victory.

Railroads were a main target of the Square Deal. The Interstate Commerce Act of 1887 had done little to end rebates and other abuses. Roosevelt therefore urged Congress to outlaw rebates. In 1906, Congress gave the ICC the power to set railroad rates.

Consumers Roosevelt wanted reforms to protect consumers. He had been shocked by Upton Sinclair's novel *The Jungle*. In response, he sent more government inspectors to meatpacking houses. The owners refused to let them in.

Roosevelt then gave the newspapers copies of a government report that exposed conditions in meatpacking plants. The public was outraged. This forced Congress to pass a law in 1906 allowing more inspectors to enter meatpacking houses.

Muckrakers had exposed drug companies for making false claims about medicines. They also showed how food companies added harmful chemicals to canned foods. In 1906, Congress passed the Pure Food and Drug Act, which required food and drug makers to list ingredients on packages. It also tried to end false advertising and the use of impure ingredients.

Conserving Resources Roosevelt also took action to protect the nation's wilderness areas. To fuel industrial growth, lumber companies were cutting up whole forests. Miners were taking iron and coal from the earth at a frantic pace and leaving gaping holes.

Roosevelt loved the outdoors and worried about the destruction of the wilderness. He pressed for conservation, the protection of natural resources. "The rights of the public to natural resources outweigh private rights," he said.

Roosevelt wanted some forest areas left as wilderness. Others could supply needed resources. He wanted lumber companies to plant new trees in the forests they were clearing. Mining, too, should be controlled.

Under Roosevelt, the government set aside about 194,000 acres for national parks. A national park is an area set aside for people to visit. It is run by the federal government.

Taft and the Progressives

Roosevelt did not want to run for reelection in 1908. Instead, he backed William Howard Taft, his Secretary of War. Taft won easily. A confident Roosevelt said:

> ❝[Taft's] policies, principles, purposes, and ideals are the same as mine. The Roosevelt policies will not go out with Roosevelt.❞
> —Theodore Roosevelt in a letter to George Trevelyan, November 6, 1908

Roosevelt then left to hunt big game in Africa. He left behind an impressive record as a reformer. He also left the presidency more powerful than it had been at any time since the Civil War.

Taft's approach to the presidency was far different from Roosevelt's. Unlike the hard-driving, energetic Roosevelt, Taft was quiet and careful. Roosevelt loved power. Taft feared it.

Nevertheless, Taft supported many Progressive causes. He broke up even more trusts than TR had. He favored the graduated income tax, approved new safety rules for mines, and signed laws giving

---

Geography and History

The National Park System

The National Park System was established to protect land, wildlife, historic sites, and recreation areas. The government manages the parks so that visitors can enjoy the scenery without disturbing the land and wildlife.

Today, the National Park System protects about 350 separate areas. These include seashores, historic battlefields, and scenic trails. Dry Tortugas Park in Florida, for example, preserves marine wildlife and has an underwater nature trail. Death Valley National Park contains spectacular desert scenery and the lowest point in the Western Hemisphere. More than 200 million people visit national parks annually.

What benefit does the National Park System provide us?

government workers an eight-hour day. Under Taft, the Commerce Department set up an office to deal with the problems of child labor.

Despite such successes, Taft lost Progressive support. In 1909, he signed a bill that raised most tariffs. Progressives opposed the new law, arguing that tariffs raised prices for consumers. Also, Taft fired a high-level Forest Service official during a dispute over the sale of wilderness lands in Alaska. Progressives then accused the President of blocking conservation efforts.

1912: A Three-Way Election

When Roosevelt returned from Africa, he found Taft under attack by reformers. In 1912, TR decided to run against Taft for the Republican nomination. Although Roosevelt had much public support, Taft controlled the Republican party leadership. At its convention, the party nominated Taft.

The Bull Moose Party Progressive Republicans stormed out of the convention. They set up a new party and chose Roosevelt as their candidate. He accepted, saying "I feel as strong as a bull moose." Roosevelt's supporters became known as the Bull Moose party.

Woodrow Wilson Democrats chose Woodrow Wilson, a Progressive, as their candidate. Born in Virginia, Wilson was the son of a Presbyterian minister. As a boy, he made up his mind always to fight for what he thought was right. Wilson served as president of Princeton University and as governor of New Jersey. He was known as a brilliant scholar and a cautious reformer.

Together, Taft and Roosevelt won more votes than Wilson. However, they split the Republican vote. Their quarrel helped Wilson win the election of 1912.

Wilson in the White House

Woodrow Wilson's inaugural address reflected his strong sense of good and evil:

> 66 The nation has been deeply stirred, stirred by a solemn passion, stirred by the knowledge of wrong, of ideals lost, of government too often . . . made an instrument of evil. The feelings with which we face this new age of right and opportunity sweep across our heart-strings like some air out of God's own presence. 99
> —Woodrow Wilson, Inaugural Address, March 1913

Wilson asked honest, forward-looking Americans to stand at his side. "I will not fail them," he said.

The New Freedom At first, Wilson tried to break up trusts into smaller companies. By doing so, he hoped to restore the competition that had once existed in the American economy. "If America is not to have free enterprise, then she can have freedom of no sort whatever," he said. Wilson called his program the New Freedom.

To spur competition, Wilson asked Congress to lower the tariff. A lower tariff would favor imports and bring in foreign competition After a struggle, Congress did lower the tariff. To make up for lost revenues, it then passed a graduated income tax.

To regulate banking, Congress passed the Federal Reserve Act in 1913. It set up a system of federal banks. The system also gave the government the power to raise or lower interest rates and control the money supply.

Regulating Competition To ensure fair competition, President Wilson also persuaded Congress to create the Federal Trade Commission (FTC) in 1914. The FTC had the power to investigate companies and order them to stop using unfair practices to destroy competitors.

Wilson signed the Clayton Antitrust Act in 1914. He had wanted a much stronger law, but the new law did ban some business practices that limited free enterprise. In addition, it stopped antitrust laws from being used against unions, a major victory for labor.

Despite Wilson's successes, the Progressive movement slowed after 1914. By then, Progressives had achieved many of their goals. Also, the outbreak of war in Europe in 1914 occupied Americans. They worried that the war might soon affect them.

Section 3 Assessment

Recall

1. **Identify** Explain the significance of (a) Theodore Roosevelt, (b) Square Deal, (c) Pure Food and Drug Act, (d) William Howard Taft, (e) Bull Moose party, (f) Woodrow Wilson, (g) New Freedom, (h) Federal Reserve Act, (i) Federal Trade Commission.
2. **Define** (a) trustbuster, (b) conservation, (c) national park.

Comprehension

3. Describe three accomplishments of Theodore Roosevelt's Square Deal.
4. Why did opposition to Taft grow among reformers?

5. Why did the Republican party split in the 1912 election?
6. Name two accomplishments of Woodrow Wilson as President.

Critical Thinking and Writing

7. **Exploring the Main Idea** Review the Main Idea statement at the beginning of this section. Then, write a one-paragraph evaluation of the Progressive Presidents: Roosevelt, Taft, and Wilson.
8. **Drawing Inferences** "I'm glad to be going," said Taft as he left the White House in 1913. Why do you think he felt this way?

ACTIVITY

Take It to the NET

Expressing an Opinion Use the Internet to find out what William Howard Taft did after he left the White House. Write a brief summary of Taft's later life. Then, write a paragraph describing what Presidents should do after their terms of office have expired. Visit *The American Nation* section of **www.phschool.com** for help in completing the activity.

One way people respond to the issues of their time is to use humor. Political cartoons use humor and exaggeration to comment on issues and to persuade others to see a particular point of view.

The cartoon shown here makes a statement about President Theodore Roosevelt's handling of the meatpacking industry after he read Upton Sinclair's muckraking novel, *The Jungle*.

"A nauseating job, but it must be done."

Learn the Skill *To analyze a political cartoon, use the following steps:*

1. **Identify the symbols.** A political cartoon often uses symbols to help convey its message. Some symbols are well known, such as Uncle Sam. Others are used specifically for a particular cartoon.

2. **Study the words and images.** Political cartoons use few words, but those that do appear—as either labels or as a comment at the bottom—are significant.

3. **Analyze the meaning.** What is the point of view of the cartoonist?

4. **Interpret the cartoon.** Draw conclusions about the point of view the cartoon presents. How does the cartoonist feel about this issue?

Practice the Skill *Answer the following questions about the cartoon above:*

1. **(a)** What is the building behind Roosevelt? What does it stand for? **(b)** What is Roosevelt holding? What is it usually used for?

2. **(a)** What label is on the object Roosevelt is holding? **(b)** What is Roosevelt investigating? **(c)** Why is Roosevelt holding his nose?

3. What is the cartoonist saying in this cartoon?

4. **(a)** How do you think the cartoonist sees Roosevelt? **(b)** How do you think the cartoonist feels about the President and the meatpacking industry?

Apply the Skill *See the Chapter Review and Assessment.*

4 Women Win Reforms

Reading Focus

- How did the women's suffrage movement help bring about the Nineteenth Amendment?
- What new opportunities did women gain in education and employment?
- Why did many women support the crusade against alcohol?

Key Terms

National Woman Suffrage Association

suffragist

Nineteenth Amendment

WCTU

Eighteenth Amendment

Taking Notes

Copy this flowchart. As you read, fill in the boxes with some of the major events in women's struggle to win the right to vote. Add as many boxes as you need.

```
• Seneca Falls Convention of 1848
            │
            ▼
• National Woman Suffrage
  Association set up in 1869
            │
            ▼
┌──────────────────────────┐
│                          │
└──────────────────────────┘
            │
            ▼
┌──────────────────────────┐
│                          │
└──────────────────────────┘
```

Main Idea During the Progressive Era, many women fought for reforms and campaigned to win the right to vote.

Setting the Scene

"Never was there such a sentence for such an offense as ours," wrote Rose Winslow from her jail cell. Winslow and other women were in jail for picketing the White House in 1917. Their cause was women's suffrage.

The women were held in solitary confinement. They then tried a new tactic: the hunger strike. In response, jailers fed them through tubes forced down their throats.

From the prison hospital, Winslow had notes smuggled out to tell people what was happening. Their hunger strike, she wrote, was meant to show "that women fighting for liberty may be considered political prisoners." She hoped it would save other women from suffering arrest and forced feedings.

During the Progressive Era, women continued their long battle for the right to vote. They also worked for other reforms, including pure food laws, an end to child labor, and a ban on the sale of alcohol.

AS YOU READ Arrested outside the White House

Find Main Ideas Do you think hunger strikes like Rose Winslow's helped win support for women's suffrage?

Working for Women's Suffrage

The struggle of women for suffrage, or the right to vote, went back many years. As you have read, the Seneca Falls Convention in 1848 was the start of the organized women's rights movement. It called for many reforms, including women's suffrage.

After the Civil War, Elizabeth Cady Stanton and Susan B. Anthony renewed calls for suffrage. They had opposed the Fifteenth Amendment because it gave the vote to African American men but not to women. In 1869, Stanton and Anthony set up the National Woman Suffrage Association, a group that worked for a constitutional amendment to give women the right to vote.

Women Vote in the West In most states, leading politicians opposed women's suffrage. Still, in the late 1800s, women won the right to vote in four western states: Wyoming, Utah, Colorado, and

Idaho. Pioneer women had worked alongside men to build farms and cities. By giving women the vote, these states recognized the women's contributions.

When Wyoming applied for statehood in 1890, many members of Congress wanted it to change its law giving women the vote. Wyoming lawmakers replied: "We may stay out of the Union for 100 years, but we will come in with our women." Wyoming barely won admission.

Growing Support for Suffrage In the early 1900s, the women's suffrage movement gained strength. More than 5 million women were earning wages outside the home. Although women were paid less than men, wages gave them some power. Many demanded a say in making the laws that affected them.

After Stanton and Anthony died, a new generation of leaders took up the cause. Among the most outspoken was Carrie Chapman Catt. She had worked as a school principal and a reporter before she became a leader of the National Woman Suffrage Association.

Catt was a brilliant organizer. She created a detailed plan to fight for suffrage, state by state. Across the nation, suffragists, or people who worked for women's right to vote, followed her strategy.

Slowly, their efforts succeeded. One by one, states in the West and Midwest gave women the vote. Generally, women in these states could vote only in state elections. At the same time, more and more women were demanding a constitutional amendment to give them the right to vote in all elections.

The Nineteenth Amendment

As the struggle dragged on, some suffragists, like Alice Paul, took more radical steps to win the vote. Paul had marched with British suffragists in London. She had been jailed and gone on hunger strikes to help British women win the vote. When Paul returned home, she fought for suffrage for American women.

Picketing the White House Soon after Wilson became President, he met with Paul and other suffragists. Wilson did not oppose women's suffrage, but he also did not back a constitutional amendment.

Paul told the President that suffragists wanted such an amendment. "And then," she recalled, "we sent him another delegation and another and another and another and another and another and another."

Early in 1917, Paul, Rose Winslow, and other women began to picket the White House. Within a few months, police started to arrest the silent protesters. Winslow and Paul were jailed for obstructing the sidewalk. A public outcry soon won their release. The women then resumed their picketing.

Victory at Last By early 1918, the tide had finally turned in favor of suffrage. President Wilson agreed to support the suffrage amendment. In 1919, Congress passed the Nineteenth Amendment. It guaranteed women the right to vote. By August 1920, three fourths of the states had ratified the amendment, which doubled the number of eligible voters.

Viewing History

Suffrage Symbol This 1915 banner hung from the windows of supporters of a constitutional amendment for women's suffrage. **Identifying Alternatives** *Why do you think the designer used this bird as a symbol? What other symbols might the designer have used?*

Women Win New Opportunities

Besides working for the vote, women struggled to gain access to jobs and education. Most states refused to grant women licenses to practice law or medicine. Myra Bradwell taught herself law, just as Abraham Lincoln had done. Still, Illinois denied her a license in 1869 because she was a woman. In 1890, Illinois finally allowed her to practice law.

Higher Education Despite obstacles, a few women managed to get the higher education needed to enter the professions. In 1877, Boston University granted the first Ph.D. to a woman. Slowly, more women entered graduate schools and earned advanced degrees. By 1900, the nation had about 1,000 women lawyers and 7,000 women doctors.

Women's Clubs During the late 1800s, middle-class women joined women's clubs. At first, most clubwomen read books and sought other ways to improve their minds. In time, many became eager reformers. They raised money for libraries, schools, and parks. They pressed for laws to protect women and children, to ensure pure food and drugs, and to win the vote.

Faced with racial barriers, African American women formed their own clubs, such as the National Association of Colored Women. They battled to end lynching and racial separation and worked for suffrage and other reforms.

Women Reformers During the Progressive Era, many women became committed to reforming society. Some women entered the new profession of social work. Others campaigned to end social evils, such as child labor. Florence Kelley investigated conditions in sweatshops. In time, she was made the chief factory inspector for the state of Illinois. Kelley's main concern, though, was child labor. She organized a boycott of goods produced by child labor. She helped publish a list of manufacturers whose factories met basic standards.

Viewing History

Women Vote for President

New York City

In the presidential election of 1920, lines outside polling places for the first time contained both men and women. This scene took place in New York City. **Applying Information** *Which constitutional amendment made this scene possible?*

The Crusade Against Alcohol

The temperance movement to end the sale of alcoholic beverages began in the early 1800s. By 1900, the movement was gaining strength.

Women often led the temperance drive. Many wives and mothers recognized alcohol as a threat to their families. Drinking often caused violence and economic hardship at home.

For political reasons, women also opposed saloons, where alcohol was served. In saloons, male political bosses made political decisions out of the reach of women. Most saloons refused entry to women.

Visualize As you read, form a mental picture of the reactions of many saloon keepers to members of the WCTU.

The WCTU In 1874, a group of women organized the Women's Christian Temperance Union, or **WCTU**. Frances Willard became its president in 1880. Willard recalled an incident at a Pittsburgh saloon:

❝ The tall, stately lady who led us placed her Bible on the bar and read a psalm. . . . Then we sang "Rock of Ages" as I thought I had never sung it before. . . . This was my Crusade baptism. ❞

—Frances E. Willard, *Glimpses of Fifty Years, the Autobiography of an American Woman,* 1889

Willard spoke tirelessly about the evils of alcohol. She called for state laws to ban the sale of liquor. She also worked to close saloons. In time, Willard joined the suffrage movement, bringing many WCTU members along with her.

Carrie Nation was a more radical temperance crusader. She dedicated her life to fighting "demon rum." After her husband died from heavy drinking, Nation often stormed into saloons. Swinging a hatchet, she smashed beer kegs and liquor bottles. Nation won publicity, but her actions embarrassed the WCTU.

The Eighteenth Amendment Temperance crusaders wanted a constitutional amendment banning the sale of liquor. Support for such an amendment grew after 1917, when the United States entered World War I. Temperance supporters argued that grain used to make liquor should be used instead to feed American soldiers.

Temperance leaders finally persuaded Congress to pass the Eighteenth Amendment in 1917. By 1919, three fourths of the states had ratified it. The amendment made it illegal to sell alcoholic drinks anywhere in the United States.

 Section 4 Assessment

Recall

1. **Identify** Explain the significance of (a) National Woman Suffrage Association, (b) Carrie Chapman Catt, (c) Alice Paul, (d) Nineteenth Amendment, (e) WCTU, (f) Frances Willard, (g) Carrie Nation, (h) Eighteenth Amendment.
2. **Define** suffragist.

Comprehension

3. Describe three highlights in the campaign to win women's suffrage through a constitutional amendment.
4. What new opportunities in jobs and education did women win during this period?

5. Why were women active in the crusade against alcohol?

Critical Thinking and Writing

6. **Exploring the Main Idea** Review the Main Idea statement at the beginning of this section. Then, create at least three slogans for banners and leaflets supporting the right of women to vote.
7. **Linking Past and Present** Frances Willard considered alcohol a threat to society. What threats does alcohol abuse pose today?

ACTIVITY

Writing a Song You have worked for passage of the Nineteenth Amendment, and it has finally become law. Using a tune you know, write the lyrics of a song celebrating this success.

5 Other Americans Seek Justice

FORE OU EAD

Reading Focus

- What struggles did African Americans face during the Progressive Era?
- How did Mexican Americans carve out a place in society?
- How did prejudice affect Asian Americans?
- What losses did Native Americans suffer during this era?

Key Terms

lynch

NAACP

barrio

mutualista

"Gentlemen's Agreement"

Society of American Indians

Taking Notes

As you read, prepare an outline of this section. Use roman numerals to indicate the major headings, capital letters for the subheadings, and numbers for the supporting details. The sample below will help you get started.

> I. African Americans
>   A. Booker T. Washington
>   1.
>   2.
>   B. W.E.B. Du Bois
>   1.
>   2.
>   C. Setbacks and successes
> II. Mexican Americans

 Main Idea African Americans and other Americans created their own communities and struggled for equality during the Progressive Era.

Setting the Scene

San Angelo, Texas, built new schools for its white children in 1910. Parents of the town's 200 Mexican children protested. Their children were forced to go to separate "Mexican" schools. The buildings were old, and the children got little education.

When seven Mexican children tried to attend one of the new schools, officials barred their way. "To admit the Mexicans to white schools," said officials, "would be to demoralize the entire system."

During the Progressive era, reformers did little to prevent such injustice. Instead, a number of minority groups struggled alone to gain basic rights.

African Americans

After Reconstruction, African Americans in the South lost many hard-won rights. Jim Crow laws led to segregation in schools, trains, and other public places. (See Chapter 18.) In the North, too, African Americans faced prejudice and discrimination. Landlords refused to rent homes in white areas to African Americans. Across the nation, African Americans were hired only for low-paying jobs.

The depression of 1893 made life even harder. In the South and elsewhere, jobless whites took out their anger on blacks. In the 1890s, more than 1,000 African Americans were lynched—murdered by mobs.

The murders outraged Ida B. Wells, an African American journalist. In her newspaper, *Free Speech*, Wells urged African Americans to protest the lynchings. She called for a boycott of streetcars and white-owned stores. Wells spoke out despite threats to her life.

Booker T. Washington

During this period, Booker T. Washington spoke for many African Americans. He called on blacks and whites to live in harmony.

AS YOU READ A segregated school in Arizona, 1913

Find Main Ideas What were the issues that led San Angelo parents to protest?

Tuskegee, Alabama

Tuskegee Institute

Two men are closely associated with the Tuskegee Institute in Tuskegee, Alabama. Booker T. Washington built Tuskegee into the nation's leading black industrial educational school. George Washington Carver revolutionized agricultural development in the South. The legacy of these two men, including Carver's work desk, has been preserved in Tuskegee today.

Take It to the NET

Virtual Field Trip For an interactive look at Tuskegee Institute, visit *The American Nation* section of **www.phschool.com**.

In *Up From Slavery*, his autobiography, Washington told his own success story. Although born into slavery, he had taught himself to read. As a youth, he worked in coal mines, attending schools whenever he could. In 1872, he graduated from the newly founded Hampton Institute. Nine years later, he helped found the Tuskegee Institute in Alabama to offer higher education to blacks.

African Americans, said Washington, must work patiently to move up in society. First, he urged them to learn trades and earn money. Then, they would have the power to demand equality.

Business tycoons like Andrew Carnegie and John D. Rockefeller backed Washington. They helped him build trade schools for African Americans. Presidents also sought his advice on racial issues.

W.E.B. Du Bois Other African Americans, like W.E.B. Du Bois (doo BOYS), took a different approach. Du Bois agreed with Booker T. Washington's view on the need for "thrift, patience, and industrial training." However, he added, "So far as Mr. Washington apologizes for injustice, . . . we must firmly oppose him." Instead of patiently accepting discrimination, Du Bois urged blacks to fight it actively.

In 1909, Du Bois, along with Jane Addams, Lincoln Steffens, and other reformers organized the National Association for the Advancement of Colored People, or **NAACP.** Blacks and whites in the NAACP worked for equal rights for African Americans.

Setbacks and Successes Most Progressives, though, gave little thought to the problems faced by African Americans. When black soldiers were accused of rioting in Brownsville, Texas, Teddy

Roosevelt had their whole regiment dishonorably discharged. Later, President Wilson ordered the segregation of black and white government workers. When blacks protested, Wilson replied that "segregation is not humiliating, but a benefit."

Despite many obstacles, some African Americans succeeded. George Washington Carver discovered hundreds of new uses for peanuts and other crops grown in the South. His writings about crop rotation changed southern farming practices. Sarah Walker, better known as Madame C. J. Walker, created a line of hair care products for African American women. She became the first American woman to earn more than $1 million.

Black-owned insurance companies, banks, and other businesses served the needs of African Americans. Other businesses provided personal services that whites refused to offer African Americans. Among these were restaurants, beauty parlors and barber shops, and funeral parlors. Black colleges trained young people for the professions. Churches like the African Methodist Episcopal Church were training grounds for African American leaders.

Mexican Americans

Thousands of Mexican Americans lived in the United States, especially in the Southwest and West. They lived in areas acquired by the United States under the Treaty of Guadalupe-Hidalgo and the Gadsden Purchase. In the early 1900s, however, large numbers of immigrants began arriving from Mexico.

In 1910, revolution and famine swept Mexico. Thousands of *Mexicanos*, or native-born Mexicans, fled their homeland into the United States. To them, it was *el norte*, "the north." The immigrants came from all levels of Mexican society. Many were poor farmers, but some came from middle-class and upper-class families. Although many Mexicanos later returned home, some remained.

Daily Life Mexican immigrants worked as field hands, built roads, and dug irrigation ditches. Some lived near the railroads they helped build. Still others worked in city factories, where they faced harsh conditions. They were paid less than white workers and were denied skilled jobs.

Like other immigrants, Mexicans created their own neighborhoods, or barrios. There, they preserved their language and culture, celebrated traditional festivals, and shared memories of Mexico. Los Angeles was home to the nation's largest barrio. Its population almost tripled between 1910 and 1920. Meanwhile, the migration was spreading to new parts of the United States. People who could not find work in the Southwest began moving to the Midwest and the Rocky Mountain region.

Mutual Aid Within the barrio, Mexican immigrants and Mexican Americans took many steps to help each other. Some formed *mutualistas,* or mutual aid groups. These groups worked like other immigrant aid societies. Members of mutualistas pooled money to buy insurance and pay for legal advice. They also collected money for the sick and needy.

Primary Source

Teaching His Culture to Others

Mexican American author Victor Villasenor (VEE-yah-sen-yor) remembers an incident from his California youth. Victor heard a Latino elder telling Victor's mother about celebrating the Mexican holiday, Cinco de Mayo:

"This year, for the first time, we want to have a big celebration with a parade and extend it past the barrio into the Americano part of town so we can include the gringos in our celebration. You see, many of our people who came here during the Revolution, . . . are beginning to think that maybe this country is going to be our permanent home. So that's why we want to include the gringos and teach them of our Mexican traditions so we don't lose our culture."

—Victor Villasenor,
Rain of Gold, 1991

Analyzing Primary Sources
Why did the elder want to teach his culture to Americans?

Asian Americans

In the 1870s, whites on the West Coast pressed Congress to pass the Chinese Exclusion Act. The Act, passed in 1882, kept Chinese from settling in the United States. With no new immigration, the Chinese population declined.

Newcomers From Japan Still, the demand for cheap labor remained high. White employers on the West Coast and in Hawaii therefore got around the Chinese Exclusion Act by hiring workers from other Asian countries, mainly the Philippines and Japan. More than 100,000 Japanese entered the United States in the early 1900s. Most had migrated to Hawaii to work on sugar plantations. When the United States annexed Hawaii in 1898, a number of Japanese saw the opportunity for a better life on the United States mainland.

Many newcomers from Japan were farmers. They settled on dry, barren land that Americans thought was useless. Through hard work and careful management of resources, the Japanese made their farms profitable. Soon, they were producing a large percentage of southern California's fruits and vegetables. Other newcomers worked in canneries, lumber mills, and mines.

Hawaiian planters brought workers from Japan, Korea, and the Philippines. They deliberately hired workers from diverse groups. They hoped this would keep workers from uniting to demand better wages or improved working conditions. Like Mexican immigrants, Asian workers were paid less than whites and were denied promotion to skilled jobs.

A "Gentlemen's Agreement" Prejudice against immigrants from Asia remained high. Many white farmers and factory workers resented the success of the Japanese. In California, the Japanese were barred from owning land and from many economic pursuits. In 1906, San Francisco forced all Asian students, including Japanese children, to attend separate schools. Japan protested the insult, and the issue threatened to cause an international crisis.

Unions and other groups also put pressure on President Roosevelt to limit immigration from Japan. Because Japan was a growing naval power in the Pacific, Roosevelt tried to soothe Japanese feelings. He condemned the segregated schools and offered his own solution. If San Francisco ended its segregation order, he would restrict further Japanese immigration.

In 1907, Roosevelt reached a "Gentlemen's Agreement" with Japan. Japan would stop any more workers from going to the United

Viewing History

Turning Swampland Into Farmland

California

Chinese and Japanese farmers took land that no one else wanted and made it productive. These Chinese farmers are harvesting a vineyard in northern California.
Formulating Questions
Create an analytical question based on this picture.

AS YOU READ **Summarize** As you read this section, think about how you would summarize in two sentences the experience of Asian Americans during the Progressive era.

States. The United States, in exchange, would allow Japanese women to join their husbands who were already in this country. Anti-Japanese feeling did not decrease with the Gentlemen's Agreement. In 1913, California passed a law which banned Asians who were not American citizens from owning land. Before long, the United States would take more drastic steps to stop immigration from Asia.

Native Americans

During the Progressive Era, Native Americans felt the effects of the Dawes Act of 1887. The act had divided reservation lands into family plots. With these lands, Indians were supposed to become farmers and enter mainstream American life.

What actually happened was quite different. Much of the land the families received was unsuited to farming. Also, many Indians had no farming tradition. They believed that the plains were an open place to ride and hunt—not something to divide into small parcels. Thus, many Native Americans simply sold their lands to speculators at very low prices. Within a short time after the Dawes Act became effective, speculators had swindled Native Americans out of millions of acres of reservation land.

In the early 1900s, a new generation of Native American leaders emerged. One group set up the Society of American Indians. It included artists, writers, Christian ministers, lawyers, and doctors from many Native American groups. The Society worked for social justice and tried to educate white Americans about Indian life. However, it supported policies to force Indians into the American mainstream by abolishing reservations. This created so much opposition among Native Americans that the Society went out of existence in 1925.

Section 5 Assessment

Recall

1. **Identify** Explain the significance of **(a)** Ida B. Wells, **(b)** Booker T. Washington, **(c)** W.E.B. Du Bois, **(d)** NAACP, **(e)** "Gentlemen's Agreement," **(f)** Society of American Indians.
2. **Define (a)** lynch, **(b)** barrio, **(c)** *mutualista*.

Comprehension

3. What problems did African Americans face during this era?
4. How did Mexican Americans protect their welfare in the United States?
5. What problems did Asian Americans face during the Progressive Era?
6. Why did Native Americans lose millions of acres of land during this period?

Critical Thinking and Writing

7. **Exploring the Main Idea** Review the Main Idea statement at the beginning of this section. Then, compare the experience of different minority groups during the Progressive Era.
8. **Identifying Points of View** "The way for people to gain their reasonable rights is not by voluntarily throwing them away." Do you think this statement was made by Washington or Du Bois? Explain.

ACTIVITY

Writing a Letter The year is 1912. You have fled famine and war in Mexico and have made a life in the United States. Write a letter to relatives back home about what they should expect if they decide to move to "el norte."

CREATING A CHAPTER SUMMARY

On a sheet of paper, draw a concept web like this one. Fill in each of the blank ovals with a key goal or reform of the Progressive Era.

For additional review and enrichment activities, see the interactive version of *The American Nation*, available on the Web and on CD-ROM.

Take It to the NET

Chapter Self-Test For practice test questions for Chapter 22, see *The American Nation* section of **www.phschool.com**.

Building Vocabulary

Use the chapter vocabulary words listed below to create a crossword puzzle. Exchange puzzles with a classmate and complete the puzzles.

1. patronage
2. civil service
3. muckraker
4. primary
5. referendum
6. graduated income tax
7. trustbuster
8. conservation
9. suffragist
10. barrio

Reviewing Key Facts

11. Why did reformers want to end the spoils system? (Section 1)
12. Explain three reforms of the Progressives that gave voters greater power. (Section 2)
13. Give two examples each of ways in which Roosevelt, Taft, and Wilson worked to achieve Progressive goals. (Section 3)
14. Explain the role played by women in the reforms of the Progressive Era. (Section 4)
15. How did Booker T. Washington and W.E.B. Du Bois disagree? (Section 5)

Critical Thinking and Writing

16. **Identifying Causes and Effects** List one event that resulted from each of the following: Nast publishes cartoons attacking Boss Tweed, Sinclair publishes *The Jungle*, Tarbell reveals business practices of Standard Oil.
17. **Comparing** **(a)** How did the role of President change during the administration of Theodore Roosevelt? **(b)** Suggest one reason for the change.
18. **Evaluating Information** Four amendments were added to the Constitution during the Gilded Age and the Progressive Era. Look up these amendments in the Constitution, which appears after Chapter 7. Choose one of these amendments, and explain how it made the United States more democratic.
19. **Connecting to Geography: Movement** The migration of people is linked to both "push factors," which drive people to leave home, and "pull factors," which attract them to a new place. Explain the push and pull factors affecting the migration of Mexicans to "el norte" in the early 1900s.

Analyzing Primary Sources

A 1905 book explained the work of a "district leader" in New York City:

   ❝Nearly everybody goes to him for assistance of one sort or another, especially the poor of the tenements. . . . He will go to the police courts to put in a good word for the 'drunks and disorderlies' or pay their fines, if a good word is not effective. He will attend christenings, weddings, and funerals. He will feed the hungry and help bury the dead. A philanthropist? Not at all. He is playing politics all the time.❞

   —William L. Riordon, *Plunkitt of Tammany Hall,* 1905

20. What were some of the tasks that the district leader performed?

21. What sort of person would make a good district leader?

22. Do you think people were more likely to go to an official charity or to the district leader if they had problems? Explain.

23. A philanthropist is someone who helps others out of kindness. Why does the writer insist that the district leader is not a philanthropist?

Analyzing Political Cartoons

E PLURIBUS UNUM (EXCEPT THE CHINESE)

This Thomas Nast cartoon comments on immigration policy. Study the cartoon and answer the following questions:

24. The castle and the man in uniform on the moat stand for
  A China and the Chinese emperor
  B the United States and American laws
  C churches and a religious leader
  D Britain's monarch and King George V

25. What point is Thomas Nast trying to make in this cartoon?

ACTIVITIES

Connecting With . . . Government and Citizenship

Creating a Timeline With a classmate or in a small group, create an illustrated timeline of key events in women's efforts to win the vote from 1789 to passage of the Nineteenth Amendment. Next to each event, note why it was important to the women's suffrage movement. Choose one event from your timeline that you think was a key turning point in the movement. Explain why you chose that event.

 ## Take It to the NET

Connecting to Today

Creating a Database Since Theodore Roosevelt's days, the United States has greatly expanded its national parks. Use the Internet to create a database about the National Park Service. Include a brief history of the national park system, a list of at least 10 national parks, and some of the issues involved in protecting wildlife and wilderness areas. For help in starting this activity, visit *The American Nation* section of **www.phschool.com**.

Preparing a Report

Finding Resources on State Reforms Choose one of the Progressive political reforms discussed on pages 635–636: the initiative, the referendum, or the recall. Use the Internet to find at least three sites that contain information about the reform you have chosen. Then, write a report on that reform. Describe whether or not that reform is law in your state. For help in starting this activity, visit *The American Nation* section of **www.phschool.com**.

Paul Laurence Dunbar

Paul Laurence Dunbar was the first African American to support himself entirely by writing. Before he died at the age of 33, Dunbar published hundreds of poems, as well as novels, short stories, and song lyrics. Much of his work dealt with the efforts of African Americans to win equality.

Vocabulary Before you read the selections, find the meanings of these words in a dictionary: **unwavering, didst, Ethiope, swarthy, consecrating, writ, blazoned, chrism, wert, bards, salient, devious, dispraise, dissension.**

Paul Laurence Dunbar
(1872–1906)

ODE TO ETHIOPIA

O Mother Race! to thee I bring
This pledge of faith unwavering,
   This tribute to thy glory.
I know the pangs which thou didst feel,
When Slavery crushed thee with its heel,
   With thy dear blood all gory.

Sad days were those—ah, sad indeed!
But through the land the fruitful seed
   Of better times was growing.
The plant of freedom upward sprung,
And spread its leaves so fresh and young—
   Its blossoms now are blowing.

On every hand in this fair land,
Proud Ethiope's swarthy children stand
   Beside their fairer neighbour;
The forests flee before their stroke,
Their hammers ring, their forges smoke,
   They stir in honest labour.

They tread the fields where honour calls;
Their voices sound through senate halls
   In majesty and power.
To right they cling; the hymns they sing
Up to the skies in beauty ring,
   And bolder grow each hour.

Be proud, my race, in mind and soul;
Thy name is writ on Glory's scroll
   In characters of fire.
High 'mid the clouds of Fame's bright sky
Thy banner's blazoned folds now fly,
   And truth shall lift them higher.

Thou hast the right to noble pride,
Whose spotless robes were purified
   By blood's severe baptism.
Upon thy brow the cross was laid,
And labour's painful sweat-beads made
   A consecrating chrism.

No other race, or white or black,
When bound as thou wert, to the rack,
   So seldom stooped to grieving;
No other race, when free again,
Forgot the past and proved them men
   So noble in forgiving.

Go on and up! Our souls and eyes
Shall follow thy continuous rise;
   Our ears shall list thy story
From bards who from thy root shall spring,
And proudly tune their lyres to sing
   Of Ethiopia's glory.

With Sweat and Toil and Ignorance He Consumes His Life by Jacob Lawrence

DOUGLASS

Ah, Douglass we have fall'n on evil days,
    Such days as thou, not even thou didst know,
    When thee, the eyes of that harsh long ago
Saw, salient, at the cross of devious ways,
And all the country heard thee with amaze.
    Not ended then, the passionate ebb and flow,
    The awful tide that battled to and fro;
We ride amid a tempest of dispraise.

Now, when the waves of swift dissension swarm,
    And Honor, the strong pilot, lieth stark,
Oh, for thy voice high-sounding o'er the storm,
    For thy strong arm to guide the shivering bark,
The blast-defying power of thy form,
    To give us comfort through the lonely dark.

Analyzing Literature

1. How does Dunbar describe the period after Emancipation?
  A "Sad days were those—ah, sad indeed!"
  B "When Slavery crushed thee with its heel, . . . "
  C "The plant of freedom upward sprung, . . . "
  D "We have fall'n on evil days, . . ."

2. According to Dunbar, when was Frederick Douglass's voice heard by the whole nation?
  A When "we have fall'n on evil days, . . ."
  B In "Such days as thou, not even thou didst know, . . ."
  C "Long ago" in a harsher time
  D "Now, when the waves of swift dissension swarm, . . ."

3. **Critical Thinking and Writing** **Comparing and Contrasting** In both poems, Dunbar is addressing the struggles of African Americans. Yet, the moods of the two poems are different. How would you describe the difference?

CHAPTER 23

Becoming a World Power

1865–1916

1 **A Pacific Empire**
2 **War With Spain**
3 **The United States in Latin America**

Captain Alfred Mahan

1867

Secretary of State William Seward purchases Alaska from Russia. Many Americans laugh at "Seward's Folly."

Check (above) used to buy Alaska (upper left)

1870s

The value of American foreign trade passes $1 billion a year.

1890

Captain Alfred Mahan publishes *The Influence of Sea Power Upon History*. He urges the United States to build up its navy.

AMERICAN EVENTS

Presidential Terms:

	Andrew Johnson	Ulysses S. Grant 1869–1877	Rutherford B. Hayes	James A. Garfield 1881 Chester A. Arthur	Grover Cleveland
	1865–1869		1877–1881	1881–1885	1885–1889

1860 · **1875** · **1890**

WORLD EVENTS

▲ **1868**
Japan begins rapid program to modernize.

1884 ▲
European powers agree to divide up most of Africa.

World Imperialism

During the Age of Imperialism, industrialized nations gained political and economic control over much of the world.

Theodore Roosevelt leading a charge in Cuba

Key

Home countries and their colonies:

- American
- Belgian
- British
- Dutch
- French
- German
- Italian
- Japanese
- Portuguese
- Russian
- Spanish

1898

The Spanish-American War breaks out. American troops win quick victories in the Philippines and Cuba.

1904

President Theodore Roosevelt declares that the United States has the right to intervene in Latin America to preserve order.

1914

The Panama Canal opens.

Benjamin Harrison	Grover Cleveland	William McKinley	Theodore Roosevelt	William H. Taft	Woodrow Wilson 1913-1921
1889-1893	1893-1897	1897-1901	1901-1909	1909-1913	

1890 — **1905** — **1920**

1895 ▲
Cubans rebel against Spanish rule.

▲ 1900
The Boxer Rebellion breaks out in China.

▲ 1910
The Mexican Revolution begins.

1 A Pacific Empire

BEFORE YOU READ

Reading Focus

- What early steps did the United States take toward expansion in the Pacific?
- What were the causes of imperialism?
- How did the United States take over Samoa and Hawaii?
- How did Americans protect their trade with China?

Key Terms

isolationism
expansionism
Treaty of Kanagawa
annex
imperialism
racism
Great White Fleet
sphere of influence
Open Door Policy
Boxer Rebellion

Taking Notes

Copy the concept web below. As you read, fill in the blank ovals with information about United States involvement in the Pacific. Add as many ovals as you need.

Perry visits Japan. — **Alaska** — **Japan** — **EXPANSION IN THE PACIFIC** — **American planters gain power.** — **Hawaii**

Main Idea At the end of the 1800s, the United States became a world power, acquiring new territories in the Pacific and the Caribbean.

Setting the Scene A tiny fleet of American ships sailed slowly out of Key West, Florida. Most of the ships had been built years before. Some were made of wood. "Two modern vessels of war," said a future admiral, "would have [destroyed us] in thirty minutes."

In the mid-1870s, the United States Navy ranked twelfth in the world, behind Denmark and Chile. Then, the nation began to build up its navy. By 1896, there were more than 10,000 American sailors in uniform and the navy ranked fifth in the world, with steel-plated battleships powered by steam. The expansion of the navy was but one sign that the United States was becoming a world power.

Isolation and Expansion

In his Farewell Address, George Washington had advised the nation to have little to do with the political affairs of other nations. Later Presidents continued this policy of isolationism. Americans had no wish to be dragged into Europe's frequent wars.

Early Expansion Yet, from its earliest existence, the American republic had also followed a policy of expansionism, or extending its national boundaries. Americans were constantly pressing westward across the continent.

At the same time, Americans conducted a lively foreign trade. Merchant ships carried American goods to Europe, as well as to Asian nations such as China. The island nation of Japan, however, refused to open its doors to American trade.

The Opening of Japan Fearing outsiders, Japanese rulers had cut themselves off from the world in the 1600s. They expelled all westerners. Only a few Dutch merchants were permitted to trade once a year at the port of Nagasaki. Any foreign sailors who were wrecked on the shores of Japan were not allowed to leave.

AS YOU READ
The USS *Iowa*
Use Prior Knowledge
How would technology and industrial growth make it easier for the United States to modernize its navy?

Americans wanted Japan to open its ports to trade, as well as to help shipwrecked sailors. To achieve these goals, President Millard Fillmore sent Commodore Matthew Perry to Japan. Perry entered Tokyo Bay with four warships in July 1853. The Japanese had never seen steam-powered ships.

Japanese rulers ordered the Americans to leave. Before departing, though, Perry presented Japanese officials with a letter from President Fillmore. It asked the Japanese to open trading relations with the United States. Perry said he would return the following year for an answer.

Perry returned in February 1854, this time with seven warships. Impressed by this show of strength, the Japanese emperor signed the **Treaty of Kanagawa.** In the treaty, Japan accepted demands to help shipwrecked sailors. It also opened two ports to American trade.

Perry's visit launched trade between Japan and the West. It also made the Japanese aware of the power of the western industrial nations. Japan soon set out to become a modern industrial nation itself, with the United States as one of its models.

Seward Looks to the Pacific

American interest in Asia and the Pacific continued. In the 1860s, Secretary of State William Seward wanted the United States to dominate trade in the Pacific. In 1867, he persuaded Congress to annex, or take over, Midway Island, in the middle of the Pacific Ocean. The island became part of the United States. Seward also made a bold deal to buy the vast territory of Alaska from Russia.

The Land Deal of the Century Seward saw Alaska as an important stepping stone for increasing United States trade in Asia and the Pacific. For their part, the Russians were eager to get rid of the territory, which was too far away to govern effectively.

One night in 1867, Seward was playing cards. Suddenly, he was interrupted by a message from the Russian ambassador. The czar, or emperor, of Russia was willing to sell Alaska to the United States for $7.2 million. Seward agreed to buy the land then and there.

"But your Department is closed," said the ambassador.

"Never mind that," Seward replied. "Before midnight you will find me at the Department, which will be open and ready for business."

Next morning, Seward completed the deal. The cost came to 2 cents an acre. The purchase of Alaska increased the area of the United States by almost one fifth.

"Seward's Folly" At the time, the purchase seemed foolish. Most Americans thought of Alaska as a barren land of icy mountains and

Viewing History

American Ship in Japan

This woodcut shows an American steamship in Japan in 1861. By this time, the Japanese were no longer shocked by the sight of the ships they had called "floating volcanoes." **Applying Information** *Could this picture have been created 10 years earlier? Explain.*

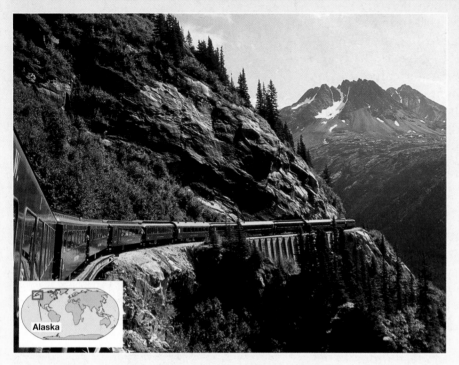

White Pass and Yukon Railroad

When the Alaska gold rush began, fortune seekers had to travel on foot. The journey became easier when the White Pass and Yukon Railroad opened. Construction began at Skagway, Alaska, in 1898. Today, you can ride a train along the same narrow trail that once carried gold seekers and supplies.

Take It to the NET

Virtual Field Trip For an interactive look at the White Pass and Yukon Railroad, visit *The American Nation* section of **www.phschool.com**.

frozen fish. They mockingly called the new territory "Seward's Ice Box" and referred to the purchase as "Seward's Folly."

Minds changed in the 1890s, after prospectors found gold in Alaska. Miners rushed to the new territory as they had once rushed to California. Since then, Seward's vision of Alaska as a valuable territory has proved correct. The lowlands of southern Alaska are well suited to farming. The land is also rich in timber, copper, petroleum, and natural gas. In 1959, Alaska became the forty-ninth state.

Imperialism

The period between 1870 and 1914 has often been called the Age of Imperialism. Imperialism is the policy of powerful countries seeking to control the economic and political affairs of weaker countries or regions. Between 1870 and 1914, European nations, such as Britain, Germany, and France, seized control of almost the entire continent of Africa and much of southern Asia. During this period, the United States and Japan also became imperial powers.

AS YOU READ **Find Main Ideas** As you read, look for three reasons for the growth of imperialism.

Why Imperialism? There were several reasons for the growth of imperialism. First, the industrial nations of Europe needed raw materials and new markets. European factories used raw materials from Africa and Asia to manufacture goods. Some of these goods would then be sold in Africa and Asia.

A second factor that shaped imperialism was **racism,** or the belief that one race is superior to another. Many Europeans felt that they had a duty to spread their religion and culture to people whom they considered to be less civilized. British writer Rudyard Kipling called this responsibility "the white man's burden." Such thinking ignored the fact that Africans and Asians already had rich cultures of their own.

A third cause was competition. When a European country colonized an area, it often closed the markets of that area to other countries. A European nation might take over an area just to keep rival nations out.

Americans Seek Empire Americans could not ignore Europe's race for colonies. By the 1890s, the United States was a world leader in both industry and agriculture. American factories turned out huge amounts of steel and other goods. American farms grew bumper crops of corn, wheat, and cotton. The nation was growing rapidly, and arguments in favor of expansion held great appeal.

Many people believed that the American economy would collapse unless the United States gained new foreign markets. Albert Beveridge of Indiana summed up the arguments for such commercial expansion:

66 Today we are raising more than we can consume. Today we are making more than we can use. Today our industrial society is congested; there are more workers than there is work. . . . Therefore we must find new markets for our produce, new occupations for our capital, new work for our labor. 99

—Albert Beveridge, quoted in *Beveridge and the Progressive Era* (Bowers)

Expansionists also argued that Americans had a right and a duty to spread western culture. Josiah Strong, a Congregational minister, declared that Americans were "divinely commissioned" to bring democracy and Christianity "down upon Mexico, down upon Central and South America, out upon the islands of the sea."

Other expansionists stressed the need to make up for the vanishing frontier. For 100 years, the economy had boomed, as Americans settled the West. The 1890 census said, however, that the frontier was gone. People in crowded eastern cities had no new land to settle. The solution, said some, was to take new land overseas.

A New Navy One leading supporter of American imperialism was naval captain Alfred Mahan. In an influential 1890 book, *The Influence of Sea Power Upon History*, Mahan argued that the prosperity of the United States depended on foreign trade. Furthermore, he said, a bigger navy was needed to protect American merchant ships. "When a question arises of control over distant regions," Mahan wrote, "it must ultimately be decided by naval power."

In Mahan's view, the United States could not expand its navy unless it controlled naval bases throughout the world. Mahan was especially interested in acquiring harbors in the Caribbean and the Pacific as links to Latin America and Asia.

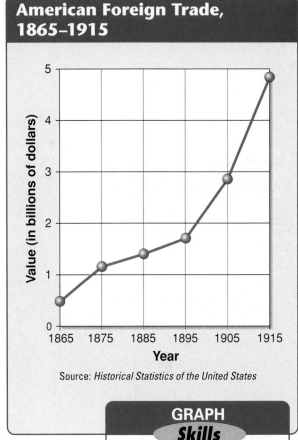

American Foreign Trade, 1865–1915

Value (in billions of dollars) vs *Year*

Source: *Historical Statistics of the United States*

GRAPH Skills

As American industry grew, so did trade between the United States and foreign countries.

1. **Comprehension** How much did the value of American imports and exports increase from 1885 to 1915?

2. **Critical Thinking Drawing Inferences** How is the information on this graph related to the growth of the United States Navy?

Economics 💲

Even before Mahan's appeal, Congress had begun to enlarge and modernize the navy. By 1900, a powerful American navy was ready for action. Its steam-powered ships were called the Great White Fleet because their steel hulls were all painted white.

Rivalry Over Samoa

As naval power grew, the United States showed increasing interest in Samoa, a chain of islands in the South Pacific. Samoa had a fine harbor that could serve as a naval base and commercial port.

Germany and Great Britain also realized the value of the harbor. As the three nations competed for control, a military clash seemed likely. In 1889, German ships fired upon Samoan villages that were friendly to the Americans. For months, German and American sailors eyed each other nervously from their warships. Then, with tensions at their highest, a powerful storm sank ships of both countries. The disaster helped ease the crisis.

Later, the three nations arranged a peaceful settlement. The United States and Germany divided Samoa, while Britain received territories elsewhere in the Pacific. The United States had demonstrated that it would assert its power in the Pacific Ocean.

Taking Over Hawaii

Another Pacific territory that had long interested the United States was Hawaii. Hawaii is a chain of eight large islands and more than 100 smaller islands. Hawaii's rich soil, warm climate, and plentiful rainfall allow farmers to grow crops all year round.

GEOGRAPHY Skills

In the 1800s, the United States gained control of a number of territories in and around the Pacific Ocean.

1. **Location** On the map, locate **(a)** Alaska, **(b)** Hawaii, **(c)** Midway Island, **(d)** American Samoa, **(e)** Japan.

2. **Region** Based on longitude and latitude, which Pacific islands acquired by the United States were in the Western Hemisphere? The Southern Hemisphere?

3. **Critical Thinking**
   Drawing Conclusions
   Why would possession of the islands shown here be important to American trade with China and Japan?

The United States Expands in the Pacific

Westerners first learned about Hawaii in 1778. A British sea captain, James Cook, dropped anchor in the islands on his way to China. In the early 1800s, American ships bound for China began stopping in Hawaii, and a few American sailors and traders settled there.

Missionaries and Planters In 1820, American missionaries began arriving in Hawaii. They were eager to convert the Hawaiians to Christianity. The missionaries and other Americans became valued advisers to the rulers of Hawaii. Americans helped write Hawaii's first constitution in 1840.

By the mid-1800s, Americans had set up large sugar plantations in Hawaii. Needing cheap labor, the planters imported thousands of workers from China, Korea, the Philippines, and Japan. By 1900, one fourth of Hawaii's population had been born in Japan.

As the sugar industry grew, so did the wealth and political power of American planters. In 1887, they forced the Hawaiian king, Kalakaua, to accept a new constitution. It reduced royal power and increased the planters' influence.

Planters Rebel Kalakaua died in 1891. The new queen, Liliuokalani (lih lee oo oh kah LAH nee), cherished Hawaiian independence. Rejecting the new constitution, she sought to reduce the influence and privileges of planters and foreign merchants.

In 1893, the American planters rebelled against the queen's attempt to limit their power. The American ambassador called for United States marines to land on Hawaii and protect American lives. In fact, the marines helped topple the queen. Faced with American guns, Liliuokalani gave up her throne:

> 66 I yield to the superior force of the United States of America. . . . To avoid any collision of armed forces and perhaps the loss of life, I do this under protest, and impelled by said force, yield my authority. 99
>
> —Liliuokalani, letter to the United States government, 1893

Annexing Hawaii With Liliuokalani gone, the planters quickly set up a republic and asked the United States to annex Hawaii. A debate raged in Congress for months. President Grover Cleveland blocked moves to take over the islands. "Our interference in the Hawaiian Revolution of 1893 was disgraceful," he later said.

Congress finally annexed Hawaii in 1898, after Cleveland left office. Two years later, Hawaii became a United States territory. In 1959, Hawaii became the fiftieth state.

Protecting Trade With China

Despite its new footholds in the Pacific, the United States was a latecomer to the race for Pacific and Asian territory. Britain, Germany, Japan, and other industrial nations were already competing for colonies in Asia. The rivalry was especially fierce in China.

Once the most advanced empire in the world, China had been weakened by years of civil war. In addition, China had refused to industrialize in the 1800s. It was unable to fight off industrial nations seeking profits from its vast resources and markets.

An American Profile

Liliuokalani 1838–1917

Liliuokalani did not reject all things foreign. As a child, she was educated by American missionaries. She later met Queen Victoria of England. She even married a non-Hawaiian, who died soon after she became queen. But as queen, she fought to reduce foreign influence.

Hawaii's last queen was also a talented songwriter. After Hawaii became a United States territory, she composed the famous "Aloha Oe," or "Farewell to Thee." Even after giving up her throne, she continued to fight, unsuccessfully suing the government for loss of property.

Why do you think Liliuokalani chose to take the actions she did?

The Open Door In the late 1800s, Britain, France, Germany, Russia, and Japan carved spheres of influence in China. A **sphere of influence** was an area, usually around a seaport, where a nation had special trading privileges. Each nation made laws for its own citizens in its own sphere.

Use Prior Knowledge Why was the United States at a disadvantage competing with the other powers?

The United States was eager to gain a share of the China trade. However, Secretary of State John Hay feared that the imperial powers would cut China off to American merchants. To prevent this, Hay sent a letter in 1899 to all the nations that had spheres of influence in China. He urged them to keep an "open door" in China permitting any nation to trade in the spheres of others. Reluctantly, the imperialist powers accepted the Open Door Policy.

The Boxers Rebel Many Chinese resented foreign influence. Some formed a secret society called the Righteous Fists of Harmony, or Boxers. In 1900, the Boxers attacked westerners, whom they called "foreign devils," all over China. More than 200 foreigners were killed. Hundreds of others were trapped in Beijing, the Chinese capital.

Foreign governments quickly organized an international army that included 2,500 Americans. Armed with modern weapons, they fought their way into Beijing. They freed the trapped foreigners and crushed the uprising.

Several nations saw the Boxer Rebellion as an excuse to seize more land in China. Secretary of State Hay sent another Open Door letter, urging all nations to respect China's independence. Britain, France, and Germany officially accepted Hay's letter. Fearing war, Japan and Russia quietly observed Hay's policy. Hay's Open Door letters showed that, to defend its interests, the United States was ready to take a larger role in world affairs.

Section 1 Assessment

Recall

1. **Identify** Explain the significance of **(a)** Matthew Perry, **(b)** Treaty of Kanagawa, **(c)** William Seward, **(d)** Alfred Mahan, **(e)** Great White Fleet, **(f)** Liliuokalani, **(g)** John Hay, **(h)** Open Door Policy, **(i)** Boxer Rebellion.
2. **Define (a)** isolationism, **(b)** expansionism, **(c)** annex, **(d)** imperialism, **(e)** racism, **(f)** sphere of influence.

Comprehension

3. How did the United States expand in the Pacific before 1870?
4. Why did the Age of Imperialism begin?

5. Why did American planters lead a rebellion in Hawaii?
6. **(a)** What was the goal of the Open Door Policy in China? **(b)** Did it succeed?

Critical Thinking and Writing

7. **Exploring the Main Idea** Review the Main Idea statement at the beginning of this section. Then, write two brief statements about American expansion from the viewpoints of William Seward and of Liliuokalani.
8. **Linking Past and Present** Do you think the United States could return to a policy of isolationism today? Write a paragraph giving reasons.

ACTIVITY

 Take It to the NET
Connecting to Today Use the Internet to find out about the role that is played by Alaska or Hawaii in the United States today. Prepare a page for an illustrated brochure focusing on the state's geography, people, resources, or culture. Visit *The American Nation* section of **www.phschool.com** for help in completing the activity.

Identifying Historical Trends

As you know, historical events are not isolated occurrences but are linked to events that preceded and that followed them. By examining different forms of evidence, you can determine how past events fit into the larger picture. This can help you identify historical trends.

In this excerpt, Albert Beveridge speaks in favor of building an American empire:

> **❝** Distance and oceans are no arguments. The fact that all the territory our fathers bought and seized is [connected by land], is no argument. In 1819 Florida was farther from New York than Puerto Rico is from Chicago today; Texas, farther from Washington in 1845 than Hawaii is from Boston in 1898; California, more inaccessible in 1847 than the Philippines are now. The ocean does not separate us from lands of our duty and desire. **❞**
> —Albert Beveridge, "The March of the Flag"

1853	Perry visits Japan
1867	United States acquires Alaska, Midway Island
1870s	Value of United States foreign trade passes $1 billion
1887	New Hawaiian constitution increases power of American planters
1890s	Great White Fleet sails
1898	Congress annexes Hawaii
1899	Hay sends Open Door letters
1900	United States forces help put down Boxer Rebellion

Growth of the United States Navy

Source: *Historical Statistics of the United States*

Learn the Skill *To learn to identify historical trends, use the following steps:*

1. **Examine the evidence.** Study the materials and identify the key facts and issues.

2. **Look for connections among the different pieces of evidence.** What similarities can you find? How are they related?

3. **Identify historical trends.** What is the direction that these events are taking? What shifts in policy do they show?

Practice the Skill *Use the excerpt, the table, and the graph above to answer the following questions:*

1. **(a)** What kinds of events does the table show? **(b)** What is the main point Beveridge makes about overseas lands? **(c)** What change in the United States Navy does the graph show?

2. **(a)** Which events on the table are related to the subject of the graph? Explain. **(b)** How would Beveridge have reacted to the events on the table and the changes shown on the graph?

3. **(a)** What trend can you identify from these three pieces of evidence? **(b)** What other kinds of information might also reflect this trend?

Apply the Skill *See the Chapter Review and Assessment.*

2 War With Spain

BEFORE YOU READ

Reading Focus

- Why did tensions in Cuba lead Americans to call for war with Spain?
- How did Americans win a quick victory in the Spanish-American War?
- How did the United States gain and rule its new empire?

Key Terms

reconcentration
atrocity
yellow journalism
Spanish-American War
Rough Riders
Buffalo Soldiers
Platt Amendment
protectorate
Foraker Act

Taking Notes

Copy this flowchart. As you read, fill in the boxes with events relating to the growth of an American empire. The first and last boxes should help you get started. Add as many boxes as you need.

Cubans revolt against Spain

↓

↓

↓

↓

United States sets up government in Philippines

Main Idea In 1898, the Spanish-American War launched an age of American imperialism in the Caribbean and the Pacific.

AS YOU READ
William McKinley
Ask Questions Based on this story, write three questions about the war between the United States and Spain. Look for the answers to these questions as you read the section.

Setting the Scene President William McKinley could not sleep. Night after night, he lay awake in his bedroom in the White House. He even had to seek the help of a doctor.

The President was worried about a looming war over Cuba, a Spanish-ruled island just 90 miles off the coast of Florida. Cuban patriots were in revolt against Spanish rule. Many Americans demanded that the President take action to help the Cubans. Almost every day, American newspapers reported stories of the cruelty and brutality of Spanish rule. The reports were often exaggerated, sometimes even made up. Nonetheless, they stirred American anger.

At first, the President resisted calls for war. But at 4 A.M. on April 25, 1898, a weary McKinley, still in his dressing gown, signed a declaration of war against Spain. The brief war that followed would launch the United States on its own age of imperialism in the Caribbean and the Pacific.

Tension in Cuba

For many years, Americans had looked longingly at Cuba. As early as 1823, Secretary of State John Quincy Adams had compared Cuba to a ripe apple. A storm, he said, might tear that apple "from its native tree"—the Spanish empire—and drop it into the hands of the United States.

By the 1890s, Spain's once-vast empire in the Western Hemisphere had shrunk to two islands in the Caribbean, Cuba and Puerto Rico. Then, Cuban rebels created the storm that Adams had hoped for.

"Cuba Libre!" In 1868, the Cuban people had rebelled against Spanish rule. The revolution was finally crushed after 10 years of fighting. Some of the revolutionaries fled to New York where they kept up the battle for freedom. Puerto Rican–born Lola Rodríguez de Tió wrote patriotic poems in support of Cuban independence. José Martí worked day and night raising funds and giving speeches

in support of Cuban independence. He told sympathetic Americans of the Cuban struggle for freedom in his newspaper, *Patria*.

In 1895, Martí returned to Cuba. With cries of *Cuba Libre!*—"Free Cuba!"—rebels launched a new fight against Spain. Martí was killed early in the fighting, but the rebels battled on. Before long, they won control of much of the island.

The rebels burned sugar cane fields and sugar mills all over Cuba. They hoped that this would make the island unprofitable for Spain and persuade the Spanish to leave. The rebels killed workers who opposed them. They even blew up some passenger trains.

In response, Spain sent a new governor to Cuba, General Valeriano Weyler (WAY ee lair). Weyler used brutal tactics to crush the revolt. In a policy known as reconcentration, his men moved about half a million Cubans into detention camps so that they could not aid the rebels. At least 100,000 Cubans in reconcentration camps died from starvation and disease.

American Opinion Splits In the United States, people watched the revolt in nearby Cuba with growing concern. The United States had vital economic links to the island. Americans had invested about $50 million in Cuban sugar and rice plantations, railroads, tobacco, and iron mines. American trade with Cuba was worth about $100 million a year.

Opinion split over whether the United States should intervene in Cuba. Many business leaders opposed American involvement. They thought that it might hurt foreign trade. Other Americans, however, sympathized with Cuban desires for freedom. They called on the government to take action. Senator Henry Cabot Lodge of Massachusetts compared the Cuban rebels to the Patriots in the American Revolution:

> 66 They have risen against oppression, compared to which the oppression which led us to rebel against England is as dust in the balance; and they feel that for this reason, if no other, they should have the sympathy of the people of the United States. 99
> —Henry Cabot Lodge, Record of the 54th Congress, 1896

Viewing History

Rebels in Cuba
This print appeared in a United States newspaper in 1896. It shows Cuban rebels leading a charge against Spanish troops.
Identifying Points of View
Do you think this artist wanted Americans to support Cuban independence from Spain? Explain.

Americans Call for War

The press whipped up American sympathies for the people of Cuba. Two New York newspapers—Joseph Pulitzer's *World* and William Randolph Hearst's *Journal*—competed to print the most grisly stories

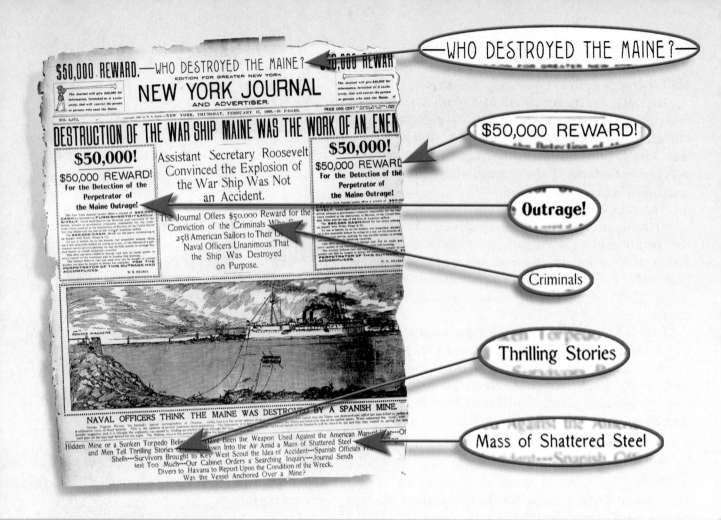

WHO DESTROYED THE MAINE?

$50,000 REWARD!

Outrage!

Criminals

Thrilling Stories

Mass of Shattered Steel

$50,000 REWARD.—WHO DESTROYED THE MAINE?

NEW YORK JOURNAL
AND ADVERTISER.

DESTRUCTION OF THE WAR SHIP MAINE WAS THE WORK OF AN ENEM

$50,000!
$50,000 REWARD!
For the Detection of the
Perpetrator of
the Maine Outrage!

Assistant Secretary Roosevelt
Convinced the Explosion of
the War Ship Was Not
an Accident.

$50,000!
$50,000 REWARD
For the Detection of the
Perpetrator of
the Maine Outrage!

The Journal Offers $50,000 Reward for the
Conviction of the Criminals Who
258 American Sailors to Their D
Naval Officers Unanimous That
the Ship Was Destroyed
on Purpose.

NAVAL OFFICERS THINK THE MAINE WAS DESTROYED BY A SPANISH MINE.

Hidden Mine or a Sunken Torpedo Belie... ...ave Been the Weapon Used Against the American Man-of-War—Of...
and Men Tell Thrilling Stories o... ...own Into the Air Amid a Mass of Shattered Steel
Shells—Survivors Brought to Key West Scout the Idea of Accident—Spanish Officials Pr...
...test Too Much—Our Cabinet Orders a Searching Inquiry—Journal Sends
Divers to Havana to Report Upon the Condition of the Wreck.
Was the Vessel Anchored Over a Mine?

WHO DESTROYED THE MAINE?

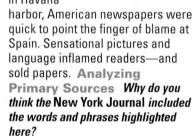

Viewing History

Yellow Journalism
When the *Maine* blew up in Havana harbor, American newspapers were quick to point the finger of blame at Spain. Sensational pictures and language inflamed readers—and sold papers. **Analyzing Primary Sources** *Why do you think the* **New York Journal** *included the words and phrases highlighted here?*

about Spanish atrocities, or wartime acts of cruelty and brutality. The publishers knew that war with Spain would boost sales of their newspapers.

Sensational Newspaper Stories To attract readers, Hearst and Pulitzer used yellow journalism, or reporting that relied on sensational stories and headlines. Often, these reports were biased or untrue. According to one story, a photographer bound for Cuba told Hearst that there was no war. "You supply the pictures," Hearst supposedly replied. "I'll supply the war." News stories described events in Cuba in graphic and horrifying detail.

Despite growing pressure, President Cleveland wanted to avoid war with Spain. He called the war fever in the United States an "epidemic of insanity." Stories in the press, he grumbled, were nonsense. When William McKinley became President in 1897, he also tried to keep the country neutral.

"Remember the *Maine!*" In 1898, fighting broke out in Havana, the Cuban capital. Acting promptly, President McKinley sent the battleship *Maine* to Havana to protect American citizens and property there.

On the night of February 15, the *Maine* lay at anchor in Havana harbor. Just after the bugler played taps, a huge explosion ripped through the ship. The explosion killed at least 260 of the 350 American sailors and officers on board.

The yellow press pounced on the tragedy. "DESTRUCTION OF THE WARSHIP *MAINE* WAS THE WORK OF AN ENEMY," screamed one New York newspaper. "THE WARSHIP *MAINE* SPLIT IN TWO BY AN ENEMY'S SECRET INFERNAL MACHINE?" blared the front page of another.

The real cause of the explosion remains a mystery. Most historians believe that a boiler blew up or there was an accident in the ship's own ammunition hold. But Americans, urged on by Pulitzer and Hearst, clamored for war. "Remember the *Maine!*" they cried.

Still hoping to avoid war, McKinley tried to get Spain to talk with the Cuban rebels. In the end, however, he gave in to war fever. On April 25, 1898, Congress declared war on Spain.

The Spanish-American War

The Spanish-American War lasted only four months. The battle-front stretched from the nearby Caribbean to the distant Philippine Islands off the coast of Southeast Asia.

Victory in the Philippines Two months earlier, Assistant Secretary of the Navy Theodore Roosevelt had begun making preparations for a possible war with Spain. Roosevelt quickly realized that a conflict with Spain would be fought not only in the Caribbean but wherever Spanish sea power lay. The Philippine Islands, a Spanish colony and Spain's main naval base in the Pacific, would be a major military objective.

Roosevelt believed it was important to attack the Spanish in the Philippines as soon as war began. He wired secret orders to Commodore George Dewey, commander of the Pacific fleet:

> **❝**Secret and confidential. Order the squadron . . . to Hong Kong. Keep full of coal. In the event of declaration of war Spain, your duty will be to see that the Spanish squadron does not leave the Asiatic coast, and then offensive operations in Philippine Islands.**❞**
>
> —Theodore Roosevelt, Telegram, February 25, 1898

Dewey followed Roosevelt's instructions. Immediately after war was declared, the Commodore sailed his fleet swiftly to Manila, the main city of the Philippines. On April 30, 1898, Dewey's ships slipped into Manila harbor under cover of darkness. There, the Spanish fleet lay at anchor.

At dawn, Dewey told his flagship commander, Charles Gridley, "You may fire when you are ready, Gridley." Taking their cue, the Americans bombarded the surprised Spanish ships. By noon, the Spanish fleet had been destroyed.

By July, American ground troops had landed in the Philippines. As in Cuba, local people there had been fighting for independence from Spain for years. With the help of these Filipino rebels, led by Emilio Aguinaldo (ah gwee NAHL doh), the American forces quickly captured Manila.

AS YOU READ **Summarize** As you read, look for information to help you write a summary explaining why the Spanish-American War covered such a vast area.

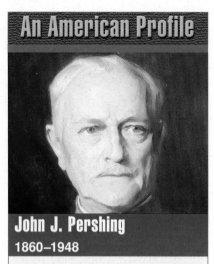
War in Cuba Meanwhile, American troops had also landed in Cuba. The expedition was badly organized. Soldiers wore heavy woolen uniforms in the tropical heat, and they often had to eat spoiled food. Yet, most were eager for battle.

None was more eager than Theodore Roosevelt. When the war broke out, Roosevelt resigned his position as Assistant Secretary of the Navy. He then organized the First Volunteer Cavalry Regiment, later called the **Rough Riders.** The Rough Riders were a mixed crew, ranging from cowboys to college students and adventurers.

The Rough Riders joined regular troops in the most notable land battle of the war. During the fight for the key Cuban city of Santiago, Americans had to gain control of the San Juan Heights overlooking the city. Under withering fire, charging American forces took two strategic hills. African American members of the 9th and 10th Cavalries, nicknamed **Buffalo Soldiers,** played a major role in the bloody victory. John J. Pershing, commander of the 10th Cavalry, later described how the troops united in what came to be called the Battle of San Juan Hill:

> 66 White regiments, black regiments, regulars and Rough Riders, representing the young manhood of the North and South, fought shoulder to shoulder, unmindful of race or color, . . . mindful of their common duty as Americans. 99
>
> —John J. Pershing, quoted in *The Life of General Pershing* (MacAdam)

Two days later, the Americans destroyed the Spanish fleet in Santiago Bay. The Spanish army in Cuba surrendered. American troops then landed on Puerto Rico and claimed the island.

A Quick End Spain was defeated. On August 12, Spain and the United States agreed to end the fighting. American losses in battle were fairly light—379 killed. However, more than 5,000 Americans died of other causes, such as yellow fever, typhoid, and malaria.

John Hay, who was soon to become Secretary of State, summed up American enthusiasm for the war. "It's been a splendid little war," he wrote. A malaria-ridden veteran of the war had a different view: "I was lucky—I survived."

The Debate Over Empire

In a peace treaty signed in Paris in December 1898, Spain agreed to grant Cuba its freedom. Spain also gave the United States two islands: Puerto Rico in the Caribbean and Guam in the Pacific. Finally, in return for $20 million, Spain handed over the Philippines to the United States.

Before the Senate approved the treaty, a great debate occurred. Many Americans objected to the treaty. They said it violated American principles of democracy by turning the United States into a colonial power.

Expansionists favored the treaty. They said that the navy needed bases in the Caribbean and the Pacific. They pointed out that the Philippines and Puerto Rico offered new territory for American businesses. Also, many Americans agreed with President McKinley, who said that the United States would "uplift and civilize and

The Spanish-American War

Polyconic Projection

0   150   300 Miles

0   150   300 Kilometers

Azimuthal Projection

0   150   300 Miles

0   150   300 Kilometers

Key

- - -→ United States Navy

——→ United States Army

——→ Spanish fleet

✦ United States victories

▨ Spanish colonies

Christianize [the Filipinos]." In fact, most Filipinos already were Christians.

Urged on by McKinley, the Senate narrowly approved the peace treaty in February 1899. At last, the United States had acquired a true overseas empire.

Ruling an Empire

Americans had to decide how to rule their new territories. When the war with Spain began, the United States pledged to "leave the government and control of [Cuba] to its people." That promise, however, was not kept.

Cuba After the war, American soldiers remained in Cuba while the United States debated. Many in Congress believed that Cuba was not ready for independence. American business leaders feared that an independent Cuba might threaten their investments there.

In the end, the United States let the Cuban people write their own constitution. However, Cuba had to accept the Platt Amendment. The amendment allowed the United States to intervene in Cuba and gave the United States control of the naval base at Guantanamo Bay.

In effect, the amendment made Cuba an American protectorate, a nation whose independence is limited by the control of a more powerful country. The United States pulled its army out of Cuba in 1902. However, American soldiers would return to Cuba in 1906 and again in 1917.

GEOGRAPHY Skills

The Spanish-American War was fought on two fronts that were half a world apart.

1. **Location** On the map, locate **(a)** Philippine Islands, **(b)** Manila Bay, **(c)** Cuba, **(d)** Santiago, **(e)** Havana.

2. **Movement** Describe the route that the United States Navy took to reach the Philippines.

3. **Critical Thinking Drawing Conclusions** Why do you think Dewey was able to trap the Spanish fleet in Manila Bay?

Puerto Rico In Puerto Rico, the United States set up a new government under the Foraker Act of 1900. The act gave Puerto Ricans only a limited say in their own affairs. In 1917, Puerto Ricans were made citizens of the United States. Americans set up schools, improved health care, and built roads on the island. Even so, many Puerto Ricans wanted to be free of foreign rule.

Revolt in the Philippines Filipino nationalists had begun fighting for independence long before the Spanish-American War. When the United States took over their land after the war, Filipinos felt betrayed. Led by Emilio Aguinaldo, they now fought for freedom against a new imperial power: the United States.

Aguinaldo, who had fought beside the Americans against Spain, accused the United States of forgetting its beginnings. The United States, he said, was using military force to keep the Filipinos from attaining "the same rights that the American people proclaimed more than a century ago."

The war in the Philippines was the first all-out Asian war in which the United States fought. It dragged on for years. At one point, about 60,000 American troops were fighting there. Finally, Aguinaldo was captured in 1901, and the war came to an end.

The war against Aguinaldo's nationalists was longer and more costly than the Spanish-American War. More than 4,000 Americans died in the Philippines. Nearly 20,000 Filipino soldiers were killed. Another 200,000 civilians died from shelling, famine, and disease.

In 1902, the United States set up a government in the Philippines similar to the one in Puerto Rico. Filipinos, however, were not made American citizens because the United States planned to give them independence in the future. It was not until 1946, however, that the United States allowed Filipinos to govern themselves.

 AFTER YOU READ **Section 2 Assessment**

Recall

1. **Identify** Explain the significance of **(a)** Lola Rodríguez de Tió, **(b)** José Martí, **(c)** Valeriano Weyler, **(d)** Spanish-American War, **(e)** George Dewey, **(f)** Emilio Aguinaldo, **(g)** Rough Riders, **(h)** Buffalo Soldiers, **(i)** Platt Amendment, **(j)** Foraker Act.
2. **Define** **(a)** reconcentration, **(b)** atrocity, **(c)** yellow journalism, **(d)** protectorate.

Comprehension

3. Why did many Americans want to intervene in Cuba?
4. Describe the American victories in the Philippines and Cuba.

5. **(a)** Why did Americans disagree about the issue of empire? **(b)** How did the United States get involved in a war in the Philippines?

Critical Thinking and Writing

6. **Exploring the Main Idea** Review the Main Idea statement at the beginning of this section. Then, create a cause-and-effect chart for the Spanish-American War.
7. **Identifying Points of View** As John Hay, write a note to President McKinley giving reasons why you called the conflict with Spain "a splendid little war."

ACTIVITY

Drawing a Political Cartoon Draw a political cartoon about the debate over acquiring an empire. Take the viewpoint of either an expansionist or an opponent of imperialism.

3 The United States in Latin America

Reading Focus

- Why did the United States want to build a canal across Panama?
- How did Theodore Roosevelt use his "big stick" in Latin America?
- Why did a crisis erupt between the United States and Mexico?

Key Terms

isthmus

corollary

Roosevelt Corollary

dollar diplomacy

moral diplomacy

Taking Notes

As you read, prepare an outline of this section. Use roman numerals to indicate the major headings, capital letters for the subheadings, and numbers for the supporting details. The sample at right will help you get started.

```
I. A Canal Across Panama
   A. Roosevelt's plan
      1. Reduce shipping costs
      2.
   B. Taking the Canal Zone
      1. Colombia refuses offer
      2.
II. Building the Canal
   A.
   B.
```

Main Idea Increasing economic ties led the United States to intervene in Latin American affairs.

Setting the Scene William Seward had dreamed of an American empire stretching southward. Under his plan, the United States would hold islands of the Caribbean as bases to protect a new water route across Central America. Mexico would be a state and Mexico City the capital of the new empire.

Seward's vision never came to pass. But as a new century dawned, the United States did stretch its power and influence across Latin America.

A Canal Across Panama

When Theodore Roosevelt became President in 1901, he was determined to build a canal through the Isthmus of Panama. An isthmus is a narrow strip of land connecting two larger bodies of land. Panama was an ideal location for a canal. Only 50 miles of land separated the Caribbean Sea and the Pacific Ocean.

Roosevelt's Plan Roosevelt knew that a canal through the isthmus would greatly benefit American commerce and military capability. By avoiding the long trip around South America, ships could shorten the journey from New York City to San Francisco by nearly 8,000 miles. Thus, a canal would reduce the cost of shipping goods. In addition, in the event of a war, the navy could quickly move ships back and forth between the Pacific Ocean and the Atlantic Ocean.

To build the canal, Roosevelt had to deal with Colombia, which owned the isthmus. Roosevelt asked Secretary of State John Hay to approach Colombia. Hay offered $10 million cash plus $250,000 a year to rent a strip of land across Panama.

Taking the Canal Zone When Columbia refused Roosevelt's offer, he was furious. "I do not think the [Colombian] lot of jack rabbits should be allowed permanently to bar one of the future highways of civilization," he exclaimed.

AS YOU READ 1901 cartoon

Draw Inferences How does the cartoon above reflect a view of the United States similar to that of William Seward?

The Panama Canal

80°W

Caribbean Sea

Key
- Canal Zone
-)(Locks
- •••• The canal

PANAMA

Colón

Gatún Lake

PANAMA

Gaillard Cut

Panama City

9°N

Balboa

PANAMA

Conformal Conic Projection

0   5   10 Miles

0   5   10 Kilometers

PACIFIC OCEAN

Cutting a path through the mountains

GEOGRAPHY *Skills*

The Panama Canal took almost 10 years to finish. The picture at right shows the digging of the Gaillard Cut.

1. **Location** On the map, locate (a) Caribbean Sea, (b) Pacific Ocean, (c) Canal Zone, (d) Gaillard Cut.

2. **Movement** In what direction did ships travel to get from the Caribbean Sea to the Pacific Ocean?

3. **Critical Thinking Synthesizing Information** Based on the map and picture, what were some of the difficulties that geography presented to canal builders?

At times like this, Roosevelt was fond of quoting an African proverb: "Speak softly and carry a big stick, and you will go far." He meant that words should be supported by strong action.

Roosevelt knew that some Panamanians wanted to break away from Colombia. He made it known that he would not help Colombia suppress the rebels. In fact, he might even support the rebellion.

On November 2, 1903, the American warship *Nashville* dropped anchor in the port of Colón, Panama. The next day, Panamanians rebelled against Colombia. American forces stopped Colombian troops from crushing the revolt. Panama then declared itself an independent republic. The United States recognized the new nation at once. Panama in turn agreed to let the United States build a canal on terms similar to those it had offered to Colombia.

Roosevelt's action in Panama angered many Latin Americans. It also upset some members of Congress. The President, however, proudly stated, "I took the Canal Zone and let Congress debate."

Building the Canal

Roosevelt now had the right to build his canal. However, before work could begin, Americans had to conquer a deadly enemy: disease.

Conquering Tropical Diseases With its tropical heat, heavy rainfall, and plentiful swamps, Panama was a "mosquito paradise." This presented serious difficulties for the canal builders. Mosquitoes carry two of the deadliest tropical diseases: malaria and yellow fever.

Dr. William Gorgas, an army physician, arrived in Panama in 1905 to help control the mosquitoes and the spread of disease. He ordered workers to locate all pools of water, where mosquitoes laid their eggs. Day after day, the workers drained swamps, sprayed tons of insecticide, and spread oil on stagnant water to kill mosquito eggs.

By 1906, Gorgas had won his battle. Yellow fever disappeared from Panama. Malaria cases dropped dramatically. Work on the Panama Canal could proceed.

The Big Dig Under the supervision of army engineer Colonel George Goethals, more than 40,000 workers struggled to dig the canal. Most were blacks from the West Indies. They blasted a path through mountains and carved out the largest artificial lake in the world up to that time. In all, they removed more than 200 million cubic yards of earth. Then, they built gigantic locks to raise and lower ships as they passed through the canal. Finally, in 1914, the first ocean-going steamship traveled through the Panama Canal.

The new waterway helped the trade of many nations. American merchants and manufacturers benefited most. They could now ship goods cheaply to South America and Asia. However, many Latin American nations remained bitter about the way in which the United States had gained control of the canal.

The "Big Stick" in Latin America

The Panama Canal involved the United States more than ever in Latin America. Gradually, President Roosevelt and succeeding Presidents established a policy of intervening in Latin America. The United States was especially concerned when disturbances threatened American lives, property, and interests.

Roosevelt Extends the Monroe Doctrine In 1902, several European countries sent warships to force Venezuela to repay its debts. The United States did not want Europeans to interfere in Latin America. President Roosevelt decided that the United States must step in to keep Europeans out. He declared:

> 66 If we intend to say 'Hands off' to the powers of Europe, then sooner or later we must keep order ourselves. 99
>
> —Theodore Roosevelt, quoted in *T. R.: The Last Romantic* (Brands)

Cause *and* Effect

Causes

- Western frontier closes
- Businesses seek raw materials and new markets
- European nations compete for resources and markets

OVERSEAS EXPANSION

Effects

- United States develops strong navy
- Open Door Policy protects trade with China
- United States governs lands in Caribbean and Pacific
- United States builds Panama Canal
- United States sends troops to Latin American nations to protect its interests

Effects Today

- United States is global superpower
- Alaska and Hawaii are 49th and 50th states
- Puerto Rico, American Samoa, Guam, and U.S. Virgin Islands remain United States territories
- United States has close economic ties with Latin America and nations along the Pacific Ocean.

GRAPHIC ORGANIZER
Skills

In the late 1800s, the United States gradually became more involved in foreign affairs.

1. **Comprehension** List three effects of United States involvement in Latin America.

2. **Critical Thinking Linking Past and Present** Which of the Effects Today listed here do you think is the most important? Explain.

THE BIG STICK IN THE CARIBBEAN SEA

In 1904, Roosevelt announced an important corollary, or addition, to the Monroe Doctrine. He claimed that the United States had a right to intervene in Latin America to preserve law and order. By using what he called "international police power," the United States could force Latin Americans to pay their debts to foreign nations. It would also keep those nations from meddling in Latin American affairs. For the next 20 years, Presidents used the Roosevelt Corollary to intervene in Latin America.

Dollar Diplomacy Roosevelt's successor, William Howard Taft, also favored a strong role in Latin America. However, he wanted to "substitute dollars for bullets." He urged American bankers to invest in Latin America. Taft's policy of building strong economic ties to Latin America became known as dollar diplomacy.

American investors responded eagerly. They helped build roads, railroads, and harbors in Latin America. These improvements increased trade, benefiting both the United States and local governments. The new railroads, for example, brought minerals and other resources to Latin American ports. From there, they were shipped all over the world.

Dollar diplomacy created problems, too. American businesses, such as the United Fruit Company, often meddled in the political affairs of host countries. Sometimes, the United States used military force to keep order. In 1912, when a revolution erupted in Nicaragua, the United States sent in marines to protect American investments.

Moral Diplomacy The next President, Woodrow Wilson, condemned the heavy-handed foreign policy of his predecessors. "The force of America," he said, "is the force of moral principle." The goals of Wilson's **moral diplomacy** were to condemn imperialism, spread democracy, and promote peace.

Nevertheless, Wilson ordered military intervention in Latin America more than any prior President. He sent marines to quell disturbances in Haiti in 1915 and in the Dominican Republic in 1916. American troops remained in Haiti until 1934.

The United States declared that its troops were restoring order and guarding American lives and property. Still, many Latin Americans denounced the United States for invading their countries and interfering in their internal affairs.

The United States and Mexico

Moral diplomacy faced its greatest test in Mexico. Porfirio Díaz, Mexico's president from 1884 to 1911, welcomed American investment. By 1912, Americans had invested about $1 billion to develop mines, oil wells, railroads, and ranches. Yet, most Mexicans remained poor. They worked the land of a few wealthy families, receiving very little for their labor.

Revolution in Mexico Mexicans rebelled against Díaz in 1910. The new leader, Francisco Madero, promised democratic reform. Then, in 1913, Madero was himself overthrown and killed by General Victoriano Huerta (WEHR tuh). As civil war raged, Wilson refused to recognize what he called Huerta's "government of butchers."

Wilson tried to stay neutral. He hoped that Mexico would develop a democratic government without American interference. As Huerta's

GEOGRAPHY *Skills*

In the early 1900s, the United States gained influence all around the Caribbean Sea.

1. **Location** On the map, locate **(a)** Colombia, **(b)** Panama, **(c)** Dominican Republic, **(d)** Haiti, **(e)** Honduras, **(f)** Puerto Rico.

2. **Region** Which of the areas shown on the map was governed directly by the United States?

3. **Critical Thinking Applying Information** Identify three places where Roosevelt's successors applied the Roosevelt Corollary.

The United States in the Caribbean

Key
- United States and possessions
- Areas of United States activity

UNITED STATES

Gulf of Mexico

MEXICO

BAHAMAS (Br.)

ATLANTIC OCEAN

PUERTO RICO (Won from Spain, 1898)

CUBA (Occupied, 1898)

VIRGIN ISLANDS (Purchased from Denmark, 1917)

ANTIGUA (Br.)

HAITI (Occupied, 1915)

GUADELOUPE (Fr.)

DOMINICAN REPUBLIC (Marines sent, 1916)

DOMINICA (Br.)

MARTINIQUE (Fr.)

BRITISH HONDURAS

JAMAICA (Br.)

HONDURAS (Marines sent, 1911)

Caribbean Sea

ST. LUCIA (Br.)

BARBADOS (Br.)

GUATEMALA

EL SALVADOR

NICARAGUA (Marines sent, 1912)

Canal Zone (Granted to U.S., 1903)

TRINIDAD (Br.)

COSTA RICA

Azimuthal Projection

0   300   600 Miles

0   300   600 Kilometers

PANAMA (Supported revolutionary government, 1903)

VENEZUELA

BRITISH GUIANA

DUTCH GUIANA

FRENCH GUIANA

COLOMBIA

dictatorship grew more brutal, Wilson authorized the sale of arms to Huerta's rival, Venustiano Carranza.

Finally, a minor incident led to American intervention. In 1914, Huerta's troops arrested several American sailors. The sailors were quickly released and an apology issued. Still, Wilson ordered the United States Navy to occupy the Mexican port of Veracruz. Rallied by the American show of strength, Carranza's forces drove Huerta from power. The United States troops withdrew.

Invading Mexico Still, civil war continued in Mexico. Now, General Francisco "Pancho" Villa hoped to overthrow Carranza. The United States supported Carranza.

In January 1916, Villa's soldiers removed 17 American citizens from a train in Mexico and shot them. In March, Villa raided the town of Columbus, New Mexico, killing 18 Americans. He hoped that his actions would weaken relations between the United States and the Carranza government. But the plan backfired.

Wilson sent General John J. Pershing with an army of several thousand soldiers into Mexico to capture Villa. When Mexico demanded that the troops be withdrawn, Wilson refused. Still, both Wilson and Carranza resisted calls for war. After 11 months, Wilson ordered Pershing to withdraw without capturing Villa. The United States had again shown its willingness to use force to protect its interests. The incident strained relations with Mexico.

As United States troops headed home from Mexico, many Americans realized that their nation's role in world affairs had dramatically changed over the years. Now, the United States stationed troops and ships in both Asia and Latin America. American business interests spanned the globe. It would be difficult for the United States to ignore the war that had been raging in Europe since 1914.

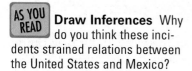 **Draw Inferences** Why do you think these incidents strained relations between the United States and Mexico?

Section 3 Assessment

Recall

1. Identify Explain the significance of **(a)** William Gorgas, **(b)** George Goethals, **(c)** Roosevelt Corollary, **(d)** Francisco "Pancho" Villa.

2. Define **(a)** isthmus, **(b)** corollary, **(c)** dollar diplomacy, **(d)** moral diplomacy.

Comprehension

3. (a) How did President Roosevelt acquire the right to build the Panama Canal? **(b)** What problems did the builders face?

4. How did Roosevelt justify increased involvement in Latin America?

5. Why did President Wilson send troops into Mexico?

Critical Thinking and Writing

6. Exploring the Main Idea Review the Main Idea statement at the beginning of this section. Then, list two arguments for and two arguments against increasing United States intervention in Latin America in the early 1900s.

7. Identifying Alternatives Instead of supporting the Panamanian rebels against Colombia, what other actions might Roosevelt have taken to get a canal built? Describe at least two alternatives.

ACTIVITY

 Take It to the NET

Creating a Timeline Use the Internet to find out more about the building of the Panama Canal. Then, use this information to create a timeline of the building and opening of the canal. Include illustrations if you like. Visit *The American Nation* section of **www.phschool.com** for help in completing the activity.

Fighting the *Deadly* Mosquito

The French were the first to try building a canal across Panama. They began construction in 1881 but were defeated by disease. Mysterious illnesses were blamed on "swamp gas." In all, 22,000 workers died before the French abandoned their work in 1889.

When American crews arrived in 1905, disease began its deadly work again. But this time, scientists knew who the enemy was: a tiny, deadly mosquito that carried yellow fever.

When President Roosevelt announced plans to build a canal, many people predicted disaster. This 1904 cartoon shows the common view of Panama.

Dr. William Gorgas declared all-out war on mosquitoes. He installed screens on windows and doors and enforced a ban on uncovered water. An army of workers, like this one, sprayed insecticide on mosquito breeding grounds.

ACTIVITY

To win his war on the mosquito, Gorgas needed an army of workers. Create a newspaper advertisement asking workers to come to Panama. Explain what they will be doing and why it is worth the risk.

Incidences of Yellow Fever in the Canal Zone, 1903–1914

Source: Ian Cameron, *The Impossible Dream: The Building of the Panama Canal*

How successful was Gorgas? This graph shows the number of cases of yellow fever during the years the canal was being built.

CREATING A CHAPTER SUMMARY

Copy the concept web below. Fill in the blank ovals with important facts and developments relating to the United States becoming a world power. Add as many ovals as you need to complete the web.

For additional review and enrichment activities, see the interactive version of *The American Nation,* available on the Web and on CD-ROM.

Take It to the NET

Chapter Self-Test For practice test questions for Chapter 23, visit *The American Nation* section of **www.phschool.com**.

Building Vocabulary

Review the meaning of the chapter vocabulary words listed below. Then, write a sentence for each word in which you define the word and describe its relation to the growing involvement of the United States in world affairs.

1. **isolationism**
2. **expansionism**
3. **annex**
4. **imperialism**
5. **racism**
6. **sphere of influence**
7. **yellow journalism**
8. **protectorate**
9. **dollar diplomacy**
10. **moral diplomacy**

Reviewing Key Facts

11. Why was the United States interested in Samoa and Hawaii? (Section 1)
12. Identify two results of the Spanish-American War. (Section 2)
13. What was the main idea of the Roosevelt Corollary? (Section 3)
14. How did Latin American nations react to United States intervention? (Section 3)

Critical Thinking and Writing

15. **Linking Past and Present** Captain Mahan insisted that the navy was the key to controlling events in distant regions. **(a)** List two supporting facts to show that his view was correct in 1890. **(b)** Do you think naval power is just as important today? Write a paragraph explaining your reasons.
16. **Making Decisions** If you had been President McKinley, would you have signed the declaration of war against Spain? List at least two reasons for and two reasons against. Then, write two or three sentences explaining your final decision.
17. **Connecting to Geography: Movement** Look at a map of the world. Write a description of the route that a merchant ship might take from New York to China in 1900. Then, write a description of the route the same ship could take in 1920.
18. **Comparing** Write a paragraph comparing the Latin American policies of Roosevelt, Taft, and Wilson. Describe how their goals and actions were similar or different.

Examine this cartoon and answer the questions that follow:

19. **(a)** What does the large figure in the center represent? **(b)** What do the seven figures in front represent?
20. Describe what is taking place in this cartoon.
21. What policy does this cartoon illustrate?
22. Do you think the cartoonist approved of American policy in China? Explain.

Exports to Latin America, 1895–1915

Source: *Statistical Abstract of the United States*

Use this graph and the cartoon on p. 678 to answer the following questions:

23. From this graph, you can conclude that
    A exports to Latin America increased as a result of the Spanish-American War
    B the Panama Canal made it easier to ship goods to Latin America
    C imports from Latin America increased
    D United States involvement in Latin America increased
24. How are the graph and the cartoon related to the same historical trend?

ACTIVITIES

Connecting With . . . Geography

Creating a Master Map With the class, create a master map titled "Becoming a World Power." Use the information found on the various maps in this chapter. Draw a large base map showing the world from Asia to North America. Use one color to show the United States as it existed in 1865. Use a second color to show territories acquired after the Civil War and a third color to show areas in which the United States became involved. Draw a line around the entire area that might be called an "American empire."

Take It to the NET

Connecting to Today

Writing Headlines To understand the techniques of yellow journalism, select a recent news story. Use the Internet to find at least two different accounts relating to that story. Note facts and opinions. Then, write two headlines about that story, one factual and the other using the style of yellow journalism. For help in starting this activity, visit *The American Nation* section of **www.phschool.com**.

Finding Visual Evidence

Writing Captions Use the Internet to find photographs of the Spanish-American War. Write captions for two of them. Use the captions in this book as a model. For help in starting this activity, visit *The American Nation* section of **www.phschool.com**.

World War I

1914–1919

1 War in Europe
2 From Neutrality to War
3 Americans in Battle
4 The Failed Peace

The assassination of Archduke Ferdinand and his wife

Sinking of the *Lusitania*

1914

The assassination of Archduke Francis Ferdinand of Austria-Hungary and his wife leads to World War I. The United States remains neutral.

1915

Nearly 1,200 people, including 128 American citizens, die when a German submarine sinks the *Lusitania*.

1916

Avoiding war helps President Wilson win reelection.

AMERICAN EVENTS

Presidential Terms: Woodrow Wilson 1913–1921

1913   **1915**   **1917**

WORLD EVENTS

1914 ▲
World War I begins in Europe

1916 ▲
An estimated one million soldiers are killed and wounded in the Battle of Verdun.

Europe at War, 1914

By 1914, the European nations were divided into different alliances. When World War I began, the Allies joined against the Central Powers.

Key
- Allies
- Central Powers
- Neutral nations
- Neutral nations that later joined the Central Powers
- Neutral nations that later joined the Allies

Azimuthal Projection

0   200   400 Miles

0   200   400 Kilometers

ATLANTIC OCEAN

NORWAY
SWEDEN
Petrograd
Moscow
North Sea
DENMARK
Baltic Sea
UNITED KINGDOM
London
NETH.
Berlin
RUSSIA
BELGIUM
GERMANY
LUX.
Paris
ALSACE-LORRAINE
FRANCE
SWITZ.
Vienna
Budapest
AUSTRIA-HUNGARY
Caspian Sea
Sarajevo
ROMANIA
Black Sea
ITALY
SERBIA
BULGARIA
Rome
MONTENEGRO
ALBANIA
Constantinople
PORTUGAL
Madrid
SPAIN
GREECE
OTTOMAN EMPIRE
Mediterranean Sea
CYPRUS (Br.)
AFRICA

World War I recruitment poster

I WANT YOU FOR U.S. ARMY
NEAREST RECRUITING STATION

ENROLL HERE!
71ST N.Y. INFANTRY
ENLISTMENT CONTRACT IS FOR THE PERIOD OF THE EMERGENCY
"GOODBYE BROADWAY - HELLO FRANCE"
THE NEW AMERICAN TIPPERARY

GARFORD
25-378

Campaign urging men to enlist

1917
The United States enters the war.

1918
An armistice ends the war on November 11.

1919
The Senate rejects the Treaty of Versailles.

1921
The United States signs a peace treaty with Germany.

1917

1919

1921

▲ **1917**
The Russian Revolution begins.

▲ **1918**
An influenza epidemic kills millions worldwide.

1 War in Europe

BEFORE YOU READ

Reading Focus

- What were the causes of World War I?
- How was war fought in the trenches?
- How did Germany's use of submarine warfare affect American neutrality?

Key Terms

nationalism
militarism
terrorist
kaiser
Central Powers
Allied Powers
stalemate
Battle of Verdun
propaganda
U-boat
Lusitania

Taking Notes

Copy the chart below. As you read, fill in the chart to show some of the causes of World War I. One cause has been filled in to help you get started. Add as many boxes as you need.

Nationalism creates mistrust among nations → ↓ ↓ ↓ ↓ → **WORLD WAR I**

Main Idea When World War I erupted in 1914, the United States remained neutral.

HEIR TO AUSTRIA'S THRONE IS SLAIN WITH HIS WIFE BY A BOSNIAN YOUTH TO AVENGE SEIZURE OF HIS COUNTRY

Francis Ferdinand Shot During State Visit to Sarajevo.

TWO ATTACKS IN A DAY

Slain by Assassin's Bullets.

AS YOU READ **Headline of assassination of Archduke Ferdinand and his wife**

Draw Inferences Why were Americans surprised by events in Europe?

Setting the Scene In August 1914, Americans opened their papers to shocking news. War had erupted in Europe! A man in North Carolina wrote:

> 66 This dreadful conflict of the nations came to most of us as lightning out of a clear sky. The horror of it kept me awake for weeks, nor has the awfulness of it all deserted me. 99
>
> —Robert N. Page, Letter, November 12, 1914

Most Americans believed that the war would not touch them. For a while, they were right. But soon, the war that had started in Europe spread across the globe.

Causes of the War

What caused the war in Europe? Tensions had been building there for years. When they erupted and war began in 1914, few Europeans were surprised.

Nationalism Extreme feelings of nationalism, or pride in one's nation, fueled the tension. In the 1870s, European nationalists demanded freedom and self-government. They believed that people with a common language and culture should throw off foreign rule and form their own countries.

While nationalism encouraged unity, it also created mistrust and bitter rivalry between nations. For example, France and Germany had gone to war in 1870. When France lost the war, it had to give Germany the iron-rich territory of Alsace-Lorraine. The French never forgot this blow to their national pride. They hoped for an opportunity to regain their lost territory.

In Eastern Europe, nationalism deepened hostility between Austria-Hungary and Russia. Russia encouraged Serbs and other minorities in Austria-Hungary to rise up against their rulers.

Imperialism and Militarism Imperialism also fueled rivalries among powerful nations. Between 1870 and 1914, Britain, France, Germany, Italy, and Russia scrambled for colonies in Africa, Asia, and the Pacific. Often, several nations competed for power in the same region. This competition sometimes led to wars in places far from Europe.

Militarism was a third source of tension. Militarism is the policy of building up strong armed forces to prepare for war. European nations expanded their armies and navies, creating new stresses. For example, Germany built up its navy. Britain responded by adding more ships to its fleet. This race for naval dominance strained relations between the two nations.

A Network of Alliances To protect themselves, European powers formed rival alliances. Germany organized the Triple Alliance with Austria-Hungary and Italy. France responded by linking itself to Russia and Britain in the Triple Entente (ahn TAHNT).

The alliance system posed a new danger. Allies agreed to support one another in case of an attack. Thus, a crisis involving one member of an alliance also affected that nation's allies. This meant that a minor incident could spark a major war. On June 28, 1914, that incident took place.

War Breaks Out

For years, nationalism had caused turmoil in the Balkan peninsula in southeastern Europe. There, the rival nations of Albania, Bulgaria,

Viewing History

European Alliances By 1914, the major European powers were involved in alliances. All were formed to produce powerful groups to protect one another in the event of an attack. Both the Allies and the Central Powers had millions of standing troops ready for war. **Applying Information** *What effect did alliances have on European armies?*

Standing Armies of Europe

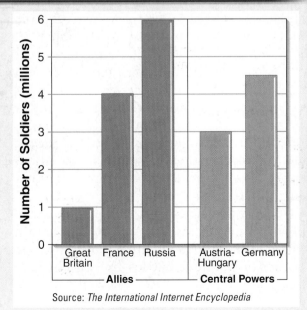

Number of Soldiers (millions) — Allies: Great Britain, France, Russia; Central Powers: Austria-Hungary, Germany

Source: *The International Internet Encyclopedia*

Greece, Montenegro, Romania, and Serbia battled for territory. At the same time, Balkan nationalists called on related ethnic groups in Austria-Hungary to throw off Austrian rule.

Assassination Sparks a Crisis In June 1914, a new crisis struck the region. Archduke Francis Ferdinand, heir to the throne of Austria-Hungary, was visiting Sarajevo, the capital of Bosnia. At the time, Bosnia was part of the Eastern European empire ruled by Austria-Hungary. Francis Ferdinand's visit angered members of the Black Hand, a Serbian terrorist group. A terrorist uses threats and violence to promote a cause. The Black Hand wanted Bosnia to break away from Austria-Hungary and join Serbia.

On June 28, the archduke and his wife, Sophie, rode through Sarajevo in an open car. Suddenly, a young terrorist named Gavrilo Princip stepped from the curb, waving a pistol. Taking aim, he fatally shot Francis Ferdinand and Sophie.

Alliance Against Alliance In the days that followed, Austria-Hungary accused the Serbian government of organizing the archduke's assassination. When Austria-Hungary threatened war, Russia moved to protect Serbia. Diplomats rushed to ease tensions, but they could not stop the system of alliances from running its fateful course.

On July 28, Austria-Hungary declared war on Serbia. The very next day, Russia ordered its forces to mobilize, or prepare for war. Austria-Hungary's ally, Germany, called on Russia to cancel the mobilization order. When it received no reply, Germany declared war on Russia on August 1.

On August 3, Germany declared war on Russia's ally France. The next day when German armies sliced through neutral Belgium on their march to France, Britain declared war on Germany. Long before, Britain had promised to defend Belgium if it were attacked.

In this way, what began as a local crisis in Bosnia exploded into a major war.

Trench Warfare

"You will be home before the leaves have fallen from the trees," the kaiser, or German emperor, promised his troops as they marched off to war. Europeans on both sides of the conflict thought the war would end soon. They were mistaken. The war dragged on for four blood-soaked years, from 1914 to 1918. At the time, the conflict was called the Great War. Later, it became known as the First World War or World War I.

The war pitted the Central Powers—Germany, Austria-Hungary, Bulgaria and the Ottoman, or Turkish, Empire—against the Allied Powers, which were France, Britain, and Russia. In time, 21 other nations, including Italy, joined the Allies.

By November 1914, a German advance and an Allied counterattack had produced nothing but a deadly stalemate. A stalemate is a deadlock in which neither side is strong enough to defeat the other. For three years, the two armies fought huge battles, but with little to show for them.

Viewing History

Trench Warfare

Europe

During World War I, soldiers on both sides fought from trenches that were usually 6 to 8 feet deep and 5 feet wide. Soldiers spent weeks in the muddy, rat-infested holes in the ground. **Analyzing Information** *How did the trenches protect soldiers?*

Both sides dug in, creating a maze of trenches protected by barbed wire. Some trenches were shallow ditches. Others were elaborate tunnels that served as headquarters and first-aid stations. Between the front-line trenches of each side lay a "no man's land" of barbed wire.

In trench warfare, soldiers spent day after day shelling the enemy trenches. An attack would begin with hours of heavy artillery fire. Then, on orders from an officer, the troops charged "over the top" of the trenches. Armed with their rifles, soldiers raced across "no man's land" to attack the enemy. With luck, they might overrun a few trenches. Before long, the enemy would launch a counterattack, with similar results. In this way, the struggle went on, back and forth, over a few hundred yards of territory.

A new weapon used on both sides was gas—chlorine and mustard were two types. The clouds of gas floated into the trenches, choking and blinding the soldiers.

Because of the nature of trench warfare, most offensives were long and deadly. The Battle of Verdun lasted for 10 months in 1916. The Germans lost some 400,000 men trying to overrun French lines. The French lost even more lives defending their positions.

Meanwhile, in the East, the vast armies of Germany and Austria-Hungary faced off against those of Russia and Serbia. Stalemate and trench warfare brought mounting tolls there as well. By mid-1916, the Russians had lost more than one million soldiers. Yet, neither side could win a decisive victory.

American Neutrality

When war broke out in Europe, the United States was determined to avoid being dragged into the conflict. The government adopted an official position of neutrality.

Public opinion, however, was divided, often along ethnic lines. Most Americans favored the Allies because of long-standing ties of language, history, and culture through Britain. Also, the United States and France had been allies in the American Revolution.

On the other hand, many of the 8 million Americans of German or Austrian descent favored the Central Powers. Millions of Irish Americans also sympathized with the Central Powers. They hated Britain, which had ruled Ireland for centuries. Many American Jews favored Germany against Russia. Some of them had fled persecution in Russia only a few years earlier.

Effects of the War The war had several immediate effects on the United States. First, the economy boomed as American farmers and manufacturers rushed to fill orders for war goods. By 1917, trade with the Allies had greatly increased. Trade with the Central Powers also increased but by a much smaller amount. This trade imbalance meant that the United States was not strictly neutral.

Both sides waged a propaganda war in the United States. Propaganda is the spreading of ideas that help a cause or hurt an opposing cause. Each side pictured the other as savage beasts who killed innocent civilians.

AS YOU READ **Summarize** As you read, list the difficulties soldiers faced while fighting in the trenches.

Viewing History

Gas Masks Gas was one of the most feared weapons of World War I. Different kinds of gas caused choking, blindness, or severe skin blisters. Soldiers wore gas masks for protection against the fumes. **Applying Information** *Why do you think nations later agreed to ban the use of poison gas?*

Submarine Warfare As a neutral nation, the United States claimed the right to trade with either side in the conflict. Early in the war, however, Britain blockaded German ports, hoping to starve Germany into surrender. In response, Germany set up a blockade around Britain. To enforce the blockade, Germany used a powerful new weapon—a fleet of submarines known as **U-boats.** German U-boats attacked any ship that entered or left British ports. This meant that neutral ships would also be attacked.

U-boat attacks on neutral shipping raised a storm of protest. Under international law, a country at war could stop and search a neutral ship suspected of carrying war goods. However, German submarines were not equipped to conduct a search. After surfacing, they simply torpedoed enemy and neutral ships, often killing scores of civilians.

Germany warned the United States and other neutral nations to keep their ships out of the blockade zone. President Wilson vowed to hold Germany responsible if its U-boats caused any loss of American life or property.

"Murder on the High Seas" Germany ignored Wilson's warning. On May 7, 1915, a German submarine torpedoed the *Lusitania,* a British passenger ship, off the coast of Ireland. Nearly 1,200 people died, including 128 Americans. An outraged Wilson threatened to break off diplomatic relations, or official ties, if Germany did not stop sinking passenger ships. Germany was not ready to strengthen the Allies by drawing the United States into the war. It agreed to restrict its submarine campaign. Before attacking any ship, U-boats would surface and give warning. This agreement, called the Sussex Pledge, kept the United States out of the war a little longer.

 AFTER YOU READ

Section 1 Assessment

Recall

1. **Identify** Explain the significance of (a) Francis Ferdinand, (b) Central Powers, (c) Allied Powers, (d) Battle of Verdun, (e) *Lusitania*.
2. **Define** (a) nationalism, (b) militarism, (c) terrorist, (d) kaiser, (e) stalemate, (f) propaganda, (g) U-boat.

Comprehension

3. List three causes of tension in Europe in 1914.
4. How did trench warfare make offensives long and deadly?

5. How did President Wilson react to Germany's use of submarine warfare?

Critical Thinking and Writing

6. **Exploring the Main Idea** Review the Main Idea statement at the beginning of this section. Then, write a paragraph explaining why it would be difficult for the United States to remain neutral in World War I.
7. **Analyzing Information** How did the alliance system help bring about war?

2 From Neutrality to War

ORE
OU
EAD

Reading Focus

- How did President Wilson try to bring about peace?
- Why did the United States move toward war?
- How did the government prepare for and manage the war effort?
- How did Americans on the home front respond to the war?

Key Terms

warmonger
Zimmermann telegram
czar
Selective Service Act
draft
illiterate
bureaucracy
Liberty Bonds
pacifist
Socialist

Taking Notes

Copy the flowchart. As you read, fill in the boxes with the major events that led to the United States entry into World War I. The first and last boxes have been filled in for you. Add as many boxes as you need.

- Wilson issues a final plea for peace

↓

↓

↓

- United States enters the war

Main Idea The United States tried to remain neutral, but the German campaign of submarine warfare finally brought the country into the war.

Setting the Scene In February 1916, Representative Jeff McLemore introduced a resolution in Congress. It warned Americans against traveling on armed ships of countries at war. If he could end American deaths by German torpedoes, McLemore hoped, the United States could remain at peace.

President Wilson did not like McLemore's idea. He was unwilling to accept any restrictions on the right of Americans to travel or work on armed vessels. Wilson pressured Congress to reject the McLemore resolution. Some members of his party were furious. "You have no right to ask me to follow this course," said one senator. "It may mean war for my country."

The senator's fears proved correct. A little more than a year later, German torpedoes brought more American deaths on the high seas, and President Wilson asked Congress for a declaration of war.

Wilson's Peace Efforts

President Wilson tried to bring both sides to peace talks. He believed that the United States, as a neutral nation, could lead warring nations to a fair peace, a "peace without victory." But Wilson's peace efforts failed.

Even as he was trying to make peace, Wilson knew that the United States might be drawn into the war. Thus, the President began to lobby for a stronger army and navy.

In 1916, Wilson ran for reelection against Republican Charles Evans Hughes. Although Hughes also favored neutrality, Democrats were able to portray him as a **warmonger,** or person who tries to stir up war. At the same time, they boosted Wilson's image with the slogan "He kept us out of war!"

The race was close. On election night, Hughes went to bed believing he had won. Just after midnight, his telephone rang. "The

A German submarine

Summarize Why was it dangerous for Americans to travel overseas?

Should the United States Declare War on Germany?

YES
BECAUSE:

- Many Americans are outraged by German submarine warfare.
- Many Americans favor Britain and France.
- The Zimmermann telegram angered many Americans.
- American trade with the Allies is growing.

NO
BECAUSE:

- The United States has a tradition of neutrality.
- Some Americans sympathize with the Central Powers.
- Wilson opposes the alliance with the Russian czar.
- Pacifists are opposed to joining the war.

GRAPHIC ORGANIZER
Skills

As World War I progressed, the United States found it harder and harder to maintain neutrality.

1. **Comprehension** (a) List two factors that led the United States to try to remain neutral. (b) List two factors that pushed the nation toward war.

2. **Critical Thinking Supporting a Point of View** Should the United States have entered the war? Explain your reasons.

President cannot be disturbed," a friend told the caller. "Well, when he wakes up," the caller replied, "just tell him he isn't President." Late returns from California had given Wilson the election.

Moving Toward War

In January 1917, Wilson issued what proved to be his final plea for peace. It was too late. In a desperate effort to break the Allied blockade, Germany had already decided to renew submarine warfare. Germany warned neutral nations that after February 1, 1917, its U-boats would have orders to sink any ship nearing Britain. German leaders knew that renewed U-boat attacks would probably bring the United States into the war. They gambled that they would defeat the Allies before American troops could reach Europe.

To protest Germany's action, Wilson broke off diplomatic relations with Germany.

The Zimmermann Plot A few weeks later, a startling discovery moved the United States closer to war. In February, Wilson learned that Arthur Zimmermann, Germany's foreign secretary, had sent a secret note to the German minister in Mexico. The Zimmermann telegram instructed the minister to urge Mexico to attack the United States if the United States declared war on Germany. In return, Germany would help Mexico win back its "lost provinces" in the American Southwest, which would include all of Texas, Arizona, and New Mexico. When Americans heard about the Zimmermann telegram, anti-German feeling soared.

Revolution in Russia Two other events in early 1917 pushed the United States still closer to war. First, German submarines sank several American merchant ships. Second, a revolution in Russia drove Czar Nicholas II from power.

For hundreds of years, czars, or Russian emperors, had ruled with absolute power. Several times in the 1800s and early 1900s, Russians revolted against czarist rule. Their efforts ended in failure.

When the war in Europe began in 1914, Russians united behind the czar. However, as the war brought heavy losses at the front and economic hardship at home, discontent resurfaced. In March 1917, riots protesting the shortage of food turned into a revolution. The czar was forced to step down. Revolutionaries then set up the Provisional Government and called for democratic reforms.

President Wilson welcomed the Russian Revolution. He was a firm believer in democracy, and it was against his principles to be an ally of an absolute ruler. Without the czar, it would be easier for Wilson to support the Allied cause.

War Comes Finally, President Wilson went before Congress on April 2, 1917, to ask for a declaration of war. "The world must be made safe for democracy," he declared. His war message assured the American people that entering the war was not only just; it was noble.

Congress voted for war 455 to 56. Among those who voted against the declaration was Jeannette Rankin of Montana, the first woman elected to Congress. She hated war as much as she loved her country. "I want to stand by my country, but I cannot vote for war. I vote no!" she said.

On April 6, the President signed the declaration of war. It thrust Americans into the deadliest war the world had yet seen.

Preparing to Fight

The day after Congress declared war, George M. Cohan wrote a new song. The patriotic tune swept the nation. Its opening lines expressed the confidence that Americans felt:

> **66** Over there, over there,
> Send the word, send the word, over there,
> That the Yanks are coming . . . **99**
> —George M. Cohan, "Over There," 1917

Its closing message promised, "We'll be over, we're coming over, And we won't come back till it's over over there."

Americans had to do more than sing patriotic tunes, however. They had to prepare to fight—and quickly. The Allies needed everything from food to arms. Britain and France were on the verge of collapse. In Russia, soldiers were deserting to join the revolution.

Raising an Army Before it could fight, the United States needed to enlarge its armed forces. On May 18, 1917, Congress passed the Selective Service Act. It required all men from ages 21 to 30 to register for the military draft. A draft is a law requiring people of a certain age to serve in the military.

In the next 18 months, 4 million men and women joined the armed forces. People from every ethnic group enlisted. About 20,000 Puerto Ricans served in the armed forces, as did many Filipinos. Scores of soldiers were immigrants who had recently arrived in the United States.

Many Native Americans were not citizens, so they could not be drafted. Large numbers of Native Americans enlisted anyway. One family of Winnebago Indians provided 35 volunteers! They served together in the same unit.

At first, the armed forces did not allow African Americans in combat. When the government abandoned this policy, more than 2 million African Americans registered for the draft. Nearly 400,000 were accepted for duty. They were formed into segregated "black only" units that were commanded mostly by white officers. Still, African Americans rallied to the war effort.

Educating the Troops For many recruits, the Army offered several firsts. It was their first exposure to military authority and discipline.

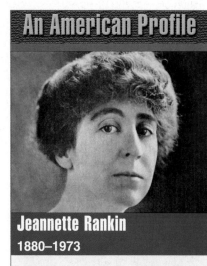

An American Profile

Jeannette Rankin
1880–1973

Jeannette Rankin championed the causes of women's rights and world peace.

Rankin worked to help women win the right to vote. In 1914, her home state of Montana granted that right. Two years later, she won election to the House of Representatives. Four days after she was sworn in, the House faced a vote on whether to enter World War I. Rankin voted no. Only 49 other members agreed.

For the next 20 years, she continued to work for peace. Serving again in Congress, she faced another war vote in December 1941. This time, she was the only member of the House to vote against entering World War II.

How did Rankin work for the causes she believed in?

It was the first time most had ventured outside their farms and villages, let alone outside their country. Some had never taken regular baths or eaten regular meals before. Others had never used indoor plumbing. About 25 percent were illiterate, that is, unable to read or write.

The army became a great educator. It taught millions of young Americans not only how to fight but also how to read, how to eat nutritious meals, and how to care for their daily health needs.

Shocking rates of illiteracy and other low test scores among recruits fueled a drive to reform public education. State and local school boards lengthened the school day and required students to spend more years in school. They raised teacher-training standards. More truancy officers patrolled the streets. By 1920, nearly 75 percent of all school-age children were enrolled in school.

Managing the War Effort

The United States reorganized its economy to produce food, arms, and other goods needed to fight the war. President Wilson set up government agencies to oversee the effort. A huge bureaucracy (byoo ROK ruh see) emerged to manage the war effort. A bureaucracy is a system of managing government through departments run by appointed officials.

Food Administration Wilson chose Herbert Hoover to be head of the Food Administration. Hoover's job was to boost food production. The nation had to feed its troops and send food to the Allies.

In keeping with the nation's democratic traditions, Hoover relied on cooperation rather than force. He tried to win support for his programs with publicity campaigns that encouraged Americans to act voluntarily. "Food Will Win the War," proclaimed one Food Administration poster.

Encouraged by rising food prices, farmers grew more crops. Citizens planted "victory gardens" to raise their own vegetables. People went without wheat on "wheatless Mondays," and without meat on "meatless Tuesdays." The food they saved helped the men in the trenches.

Managing Industry War caught the nation short of supplies. The military had on hand only around 600,000 rifles, 2,000 machine guns, and fewer than 1,000 pieces of artillery. Disorder threatened as the military competed with private industry to buy scarce materials.

To meet this crisis, President Wilson set up a new government agency, the War Industries Board. It told factories what they had to produce. It also provided for the sharing of limited resources and decided what prices should be set.

Without the support of workers, industry could not mobilize. In 1918, Wilson created the War Labor Board. It settled disputes over working hours and wages and tried to prevent strikes. With workers in short supply, unions were able to win better pay and working conditions. Railroad workers, for example, gained a large wage increase and an 8-hour workday. With the President supporting workers, union membership rose sharply and labor unrest declined.

FOOD WILL WIN THE WAR
You came here seeking Freedom
You must now help to preserve it
WHEAT is needed for the allies
Waste nothing

Viewing History

The Food Drive

United States

Civilians were asked to support the war effort in many ways. This poster urged families to eat less in order to save food for the soldiers. **Drawing Inferences** *What group does this poster appeal to?*

The Home Front

Americans on the home front united behind the war effort. Movie stars, such as Charlie Chaplin and Mary Pickford, helped sell **Liberty Bonds.** By buying bonds, American citizens were lending money to the government to pay for the war. The sale of Liberty Bonds raised $21 billion, just over half of what the United States spent on the war.

To rally public support for the war, the government sent out 75,000 speakers known as "Four-Minute Men." Their name reminded people of the heroic minutemen of 1776. It also referred to the four-minute speeches the men gave at public events, movies, and theatrical productions. The speakers urged Americans to make sacrifices for the goals of freedom and democracy.

Women Workers As men joined the armed forces, women stepped into their jobs. Women received better pay in war industries than they had in peacetime. Still, they earned less than the men they replaced.

In factories, women assembled weapons and airplane parts. Some women drove trolley cars and delivered the mail. Others served as police officers, railroad engineers, or electric-lift truck drivers. By performing well in jobs once reserved for men, women helped change the view that they were fit only for "women's work." Unfortunately, most of the gains made by women later disappeared when the men returned to the work force at the end of the war. Thousands of women lost jobs as army defense workers.

Anti-German Prejudice German Americans endured suspicion and intolerance during the war. Newspapers questioned their loyalty. Mobs attacked them on the streets. In 1918, a mob lynched Robert Prager, whose only crime was that he had been born in Germany. A jury later refused to convict the mob leaders.

Anti-German prejudice led some families to change their names. Schools stopped teaching the German language. Americans began referring to German measles as "liberty measles" and sauerkraut as "liberty cabbage."

Great Migrations The war spurred migration within the nation. Immigration from abroad had stopped. The draft drained cities and factories of needed workers. Cities soon swelled with newcomers.

During the war, almost a half million African Americans and thousands of Mexican Americans embarked on a great migration from the South and Southwest to cities in the North.

In northern cities, many blacks found better-paying jobs in war industries. As a result, black migration continued after the war ended. At the same time, however, they ran into prejudice and even violence. Competition for housing and jobs sometimes led to race riots. Thirty-nine African Americans were killed during a 1917 riot in East St. Louis, Illinois. A New York parade protested the deaths. Marchers carried signs demanding, "Mr. President, Why Not Make AMERICA Safe for Democracy?"

In the Southwest, ranchers pressed the government to let more Mexicans cross the border. Almost 100,000 Mexicans entered the

Viewing History

New Opportunities for Women Women workers became an essential part of the nation's war effort, taking jobs in war industries and defense plants. This woman worked in an ammunition factory. **Making Predictions** *How do you think wartime work helped women win the right to vote?*

AS YOU READ **Find Main Ideas** As you read, look for reasons for the migration of African Americans and Mexican Americans to northern cities.

United States to work on farms, mostly in California and Texas. By 1920, Mexicans were the leading foreign-born group in California. Some Mexicans moved on to northern cities to work in factories.

Throughout the war, Mexicans worked in cotton and beet fields, in copper mines, and in steel mills. All these jobs were important to the war effort. Yet after the war, when veterans returned and unemployment grew, the United States tried to force Mexican workers to return to Mexico.

Opposition to the War Some Americans opposed the war. Among them were Progressives such as Jane Addams. Many of these critics were pacifists, people who refuse to fight in any war because they believe that war is evil.

Antiwar feeling also ran high among Socialists and radical labor groups. A Socialist believes that the people as a whole rather than private individuals should own all property and share the profits from all businesses. Socialists argued that the war benefited factory owners but not workers.

To encourage unity, Congress passed laws making it a crime to criticize the government or to interfere with the war effort. Nearly 1,600 men and women were arrested for breaking these laws. Eugene V. Debs, socialist candidate for President five times, was jailed for protesting the draft. The government also jailed "Big Bill" Haywood, head of the Industrial Workers of the World (IWW), a radical union. Using special powers granted under the wartime laws, government authorities ransacked the IWW's offices.

A few people questioned these laws. They argued that silencing critics violated the Constitution's guarantee of freedom of speech. Most Americans, however, felt that the laws were necessary in wartime.

Section 2 Assessment

Recall

1. **Identify** Explain the significance of (a) Zimmermann telegram, (b) Jeannette Rankin, (c) Selective Service Act, (d) Herbert Hoover, (e) Liberty Bonds.
2. **Define** (a) warmonger, (b) czar, (c) draft, (d) illiterate, (e) bureaucracy, (f) pacifist, (g) Socialist.

Comprehension

3. Describe Wilson's efforts to achieve peace.
4. Identify three events that moved the United States toward war.

5. How did the United States prepare for war?
6. How did the war ignite prejudice against some groups at home?

Critical Thinking and Writing

7. **Exploring the Main Idea** Review the Main Idea statement at the beginning of this section. Then, write a newspaper editorial about the United States entry into the war.
8. **Supporting a Point of View** Do you think that the government should have the right to silence critics during wartime? Give reasons to support your point of view.

ACTIVITY

Preparing a Speech
You are one of Wilson's Four-Minute Men. Prepare a short speech urging Americans to make sacrifices for the war effort. Arrange to present your speech to the class.

On April 2, 1917, President Wilson stated that "the world must be made safe for democracy." A few days later, Congress declared war on Germany. At that time, many Americans still held strong antiwar feelings. To persuade Americans to support the decision and to mobilize for action, the government used propaganda. Propaganda is an effort to spread certain ideas and shape public opinion.

The poster shown here was used by the United States government to promote support for World War I. The term "Hun" was a negative name used for the Germans.

A propaganda poster

Learn the Skill *To recognize propaganda, use the following steps:*

1. **Identify the source.** If you know who is behind the propaganda, you can better evaluate the message.

2. **Note the frame of reference.** The place, time, and circumstances under which something is published can make a difference.

3. **Recognize the propaganda techniques.** Analyze the material to decide what approach it uses to persuade. One way is the use of negative images.

4. **Interpret the message.** What is the propaganda about? What point of view does it reflect?

Practice the Skill *Answer the following questions about the poster:*

1. Who is the publisher of the poster?

2. When was the poster published?

3. What propaganda technique is used in this poster?

4. What message do the words on the poster give?

Apply the Skill *See the Chapter Review and Assessment.*

3 Americans in Battle

BEFORE YOU READ

Reading Focus

- What setbacks did the Allies suffer in 1917 and early 1918?
- How did the American Expeditionary Force help the Allies win the war?
- What were the costs of the war?

Key Terms

Treaty of Brest-Litovsk

Harlem Hell Fighters

Battle of Belleau Wood

Battle of the Argonne Forest

armistice

abdicate

epidemic

Taking Notes

As you read, prepare an outline. Use roman numerals to indicate the major headings of this section, capital letters for the sub-headings, and numbers for the supporting details. The sample below will help you get started.

> I. Setbacks for the Allies
>   A. Russia makes a separate peace
>   1. The Bolsheviks seize power
>   2.
>   3.
>   B. The German "Peace Offensive"
>   1.
>   2.
> II. The American Expeditionary Force in France

Main Idea The United States did not enter the First World War until 1917, but its fresh troops and supplies helped the Allies to victory.

Allied soldier

Ask Questions What questions would you ask this soldier about his war experiences?

Setting the Scene

On the eve of battle in May 1918, Adrian Edwards, a young American soldier, wrote his mother from "somewhere in France." The letter was to be delivered in the event of his death. "Do not grieve," he wrote her,

> 66 . . . rather rejoice that you have given a son . . . to save civilization, to prevent future wars, to punish the Germans, . . . and to make the world safe for democracy. 99
>
> —Adrian Edwards, Letter, May 1918

Two days later, Adrian Edwards was killed, and his letter was sent home.

Two million American soldiers eventually served in France. Only a small number of them actually fought in battle. Still, they gave the war-weary Allies a much-needed boost to win the war.

Setbacks for the Allies

The first American troops reached France in June 1917. They quickly saw the desperate situation of the Allies. The Allies had lost millions of soldiers. Troops in the trenches were exhausted and ill. Civilians in Britain and France were near starvation.

Russia Makes a Separate Peace The outlook for the Allies grew even more bleak when Russia decided to withdraw from the war. In November 1917, a group known as the Bolsheviks seized power from Russia's Provisional Government. Led by Vladimir I. Lenin, the Bolsheviks wanted to stage a communist revolution in Russia.

Lenin embraced the ideas of Karl Marx, a German thinker of the 1800s. Marx had predicted that workers around the world would unite to overthrow the ruling class. After the workers revolted, they would do away with private property and set up a classless society. Lenin was determined to lead such a revolution in Russia.

Lenin opposed the war, arguing that it benefited only the ruling class. Once in power, he opened peace talks with Germany. In March 1918, Russia and Germany signed the Treaty of Brest-Litovsk, ending Russia's participation in the war. The treaty was harsh, requiring Russia to give up large amounts of land to Germany. Still, Lenin welcomed peace. With war ended, he could focus on the communist revolution.

The Allies saw the treaty as a betrayal. It gave Germany coal mines and other valuable resources in Russia. More important, with Russia out of the struggle, Germany now moved its armies away from the Russian, or eastern, front to support its armies on the western front in France.

The German "Peace Offensive" In early 1918, Germany mobilized its troops for an all-out attack on the Allies. By March 21, German forces had massed near the French town of Amiens. (See the map on this page.) The Germans were preparing what they called a "peace offensive." They hoped that a final push would end the war.

The offensive opened with dozens of German divisions lined up against a small British force. Late at night, 6,000 German cannons began pounding the British troops camped at Amiens. Despite the heavy fire, the British held on. The battle lasted for two weeks. At last, on April 4, the Germans gave up their attack.

The Germans continued their offensive elsewhere. By late May, they had smashed through Allied lines along the Aisne (EHN) River. On May 30, they reached the Marne River, just east of Château-Thierry (SHA toh tee ER ee). Paris lay only 50 miles away. At this point, American troops entered the war in force.

The American Expeditionary Force in France

By June 1918, American troops were reaching France in record numbers. More than one million American troops would arrive. Commanding the American Expeditionary Force (AEF) was General John J. Pershing. Pershing was already well known at home. He had led American troops into Mexico in 1916 to hunt for Mexican rebel leader Francisco "Pancho" Villa.

The Western Front

Key

- ——— Farthest German advance, 1914
- ——→ Allied offensive, 1918
- ····· Armistice line, 1918
- ✷ Major battles
- ▢ Allies
- ▢ Central Powers
- ▢ Neutral Nations

GEOGRAPHY Skills

Opposing armies battled back and forth across the Western Front. In 1918, the arrival of American troops gave fresh strength to the Allies.

1. **Location** On the map, locate **(a)** Paris, **(b)** Belleau Wood, **(c)** Aisne River, **(d)** Argonne Forest.

2. **Movement** **(a)** In what country did most of the fighting take place? **(b)** How close did German troops get to the French capital?

3. **Critical Thinking** According to this map, what effect did the arrival of American troops have in 1918?

Allied generals wanted the fresh troops to reinforce their own war-weary soldiers. Pershing refused. He insisted that American troops operate as separate units. The United States wanted to have an independent role in shaping the peace. Only by playing "a definite and distinct part" in the war would it win power at the peace table.

In the end, Pershing agreed to let some Americans fight with the British and French. At the same time, he set up an American operation to fight on its own.

Harlem Hell Fighters Among the first American units attached to the French Army was the 369th United States Infantry. This African American unit became known as the Harlem Hell Fighters. Although the United States allowed few African Americans to train for combat, the French respected the bravery of African American soldiers and were glad to fight side by side with them.

The Harlem Hell Fighters spent more time under fire than any other American unit. For their bravery, the French awarded them the *Croix de Guerre*, their highest military honor, and numerous other decorations.

After the war, New Yorkers greeted the returning Hell Fighters with a huge parade. "God bless you, boys!" they cheered. The unit commander felt a rush of joy. "They did not welcome us [as] a regiment of colored soldiers," he said, but as "a regiment of men who had done the work of men."

Marines Hold at Belleau Wood Meanwhile, the Germans were continuing their "peace offensive." As Germans rolled across the Aisne River, the French prepared to evacuate Paris.

In June 1918, American troops plunged into their first major battle in Belleau (BEH loh) Wood, outside Paris. A French general sent General James Harbord of the United States a message: "Have your men prepare entrenchments some hundreds of yards to the rear in case of need." Harbord sent back a firm reply: "We dig no trenches to fall back on. The marines will hold where they stand."

The Battle of Belleau Wood raged for three weeks. During a series of attacks and counterattacks, the inexperienced but combat-ready Americans performed bravely. Expert marksmen hit their targets from hundreds of yards away. Individual soldiers charged German machine gun nests. When one man fell, another stepped in promptly to take his place. The Americans suffered great casualties. But at last, on June 25, they emerged victorious from the woods. General Harbord passed along the good news: "Wood now exclusively U.S. Marine Corps."

Viewing History

The 369th Regiment
Nearly 2000 African American soldiers served in the 369th Regiment. Calling themselves the Harlem Hell Fighters, they served with distinction in the French Army. They were the first Americans to be awarded the *Croix de Guerre* (right), the French medal of honor.
Drawing Inferences *How do you think African American soldiers felt upon their return to the United States?*

Western Europe

Allies Win the War

In mid-July, the Germans launched another drive to take Paris. They pushed the Allies back until they came up against American troops. Within three days, the Allies, with American help, had forced the Germans to retreat.

The Allies now took the offensive. French Marshal Ferdinand Foch (FOHSH), commander of the Allied forces, ordered attacks along a line from Verdun to the North Sea. American forces stormed the area between the Meuse (MYOOZ) River and the Argonne Forest.

Battle of the Argonne Forest On September 26, 1918, in response to Foch's cry, "Everyone to battle!" more than one million American soldiers pushed into the Argonne Forest. This would be the final Allied offensive. Years of fierce fighting had left the land scarred with trenches and shell holes. The air still smelled of poison gas that had been used with deadly results against the men in the trenches in earlier battles.

At first, the Americans advanced despite heavy German fire. Then, rains and the thick woods slowed their movement. Small units drove forward to capture deadly German positions. Armed with a single rifle, Sergeant Alvin York of Tennessee wiped out a nest of German machine gunners. His brave act helped clear the way for advancing American troops. York became the most decorated American soldier of the war.

Finally, after 47 days, the Americans broke through the German defense. They had won the Battle of the Argonne Forest. However, the cost was high. Americans had suffered more than 100,000 casualties in the battle.

British, French, and Belgian forces also smashed through the German lines in their areas. By November, German forces were in retreat. After more than four years of fighting, the Great War was finally nearing its end.

Armistice Ends the War In September, German generals told the kaiser that the war could not be won. On October 4, Prince Max of Baden, head of the German cabinet, secretly cabled President Wilson:

66 To avoid further bloodshed, the German government requests the President to arrange the immediate conclusion of an armistice on land, by sea, and in the air. 99

—Max, Prince of Baden, Cable, October 4, 1918

An armistice is an agreement to stop fighting. President Wilson set two conditions for an armistice. First, Germany must accept his plan for peace. Second, the German emperor must abdicate, or give up power.

While German leaders debated a response, rebellion simmered in the ranks. Daily, the German army lost ground. Morale plunged among the troops. German sailors mutinied. Several German cities threatened to revolt.

On November 9, the German emperor was forced to resign. He and his son fled to Holland, and Germany became a republic. The new German leaders agreed to the armistice terms. At 11 A.M. on November 11, 1918—the eleventh hour of the eleventh day of the eleventh month—World War I ended at last.

The Costs of the War

The costs of the war were staggering. A generation of young Europeans lost their lives. Between 8 million and 9 million people died in battle—more than had died in all the wars fought during the previous 100 years. Almost 4 million Russian, French, and British soldiers were killed. Germany alone lost close to 2 million men. The United States lost over 100,000 men. Many more died of diseases. More than 20 million soldiers on both sides were wounded.

No one knows how many civilians died of disease, starvation, and other war-related causes. Some historians believe as many civilians died as soldiers.

Much of northern France lay in ruins. Millions of Germans were near starvation. In France and other nations, many children were left orphaned and homeless.

In 1918, as the world was reeling from the war, a new disaster struck. A terrible influenza epidemic spread around the globe. An epidemic is the rapid spread of a contagious disease among large numbers of people. Between 1918 and 1919, more than half a million Americans died in the flu epidemic. The death toll in other countries was even higher. All told, the epidemic killed more than 30 million people worldwide.

  Section 3 Assessment

Recall
1. **Identify** Explain the significance of **(a)** Treaty of Brest-Litovsk, **(b)** Harlem Hell Fighters, **(c)** Battle of Belleau Wood, **(d)** Battle of the Argonne Forest.
2. **Define** **(a)** armistice, **(b)** abdicate, **(c)** epidemic.

Comprehension
3. Describe the situation of the Allies when the Americans arrived in 1917.
4. What role did American troops play in the Allied victory?
5. What conditions did Europeans face after the war?

Critical Thinking and Writing
6. **Exploring the Main Idea** Review the Main Idea statement at the beginning of this section. Then, write four or five newspaper headlines highlighting the role of American forces in bringing about the end of the war.
7. **Drawing Inferences** How do you think the Treaty of Brest-Litovsk affected future relations between the Allies and Russia?

ACTIVITY

Writing a Description Choose one of the following events: the arrival of American troops in France or the Battle of Belleau Wood. Describe the event from the point of view of an American soldier, a French soldier, and a German soldier.

Honoring Our Veterans

World War I ended on November 11, 1918. Today, we celebrate that date as Veterans Day, a holiday to honor all of those who have served in the armed forces in war or peace.

> *Veterans deserve to know that we as a people honor their service. Please honor their sacrifice. Pay tribute each day to their irreplaceable gift to our nation. And take a moment to thank tomorrow's veterans. It's never too early to let them know how deeply we recognize their passionate commitment to keep America safe.*
> —2000 Veterans Day Speech, Army Public Affairs Division

The first "unknown soldier" was one of four American dead taken from the French battlefields of World War I. He was honored at Arlington National Cemetery in 1921. Since then, unknowns from World War II, the Korean War, and the Vietnam War have been buried in the "Tomb of the Unknowns." Here, a soldier solemnly stands guard at the tomb.

The Veterans of Foreign Wars (VFW) was started in 1899 by veterans of the Spanish-American War. Its membership now numbers more than 2 million. This nonprofit organization offers support to veterans. It also sponsors community projects, such as an annual essay contest for seventh, eighth, and ninth graders. Here, VFW members salute a passing parade.

ACTIVITY

With a group of classmates, plan a Veterans Day ceremony. Prepare the opening paragraph of a speech. (If you like, you may choose to focus on a specific veteran you know.) Design a banner or poster, and suggest a list of special activities for your community.

703

4 The Failed Peace

BEFORE YOU READ

Reading Focus

- What was Wilson's fourteen-point peace plan?
- What did Wilson achieve at the Paris Peace Conference?
- Why did the Versailles Treaty fail to win support in the United States?

Key Terms

Fourteen Points

self-determination

League of Nations

Big Four

reparations

Treaty of Versailles

isolationist

Taking Notes

Copy the concept web below. As you read, fill in the blank ovals with important facts about the Paris Peace Conference. Add as many ovals as you need.

Main Idea President Woodrow Wilson went to the Paris Peace Conference with high hopes but failed to achieve his goal of a just and lasting peace.

AS YOU READ
Woodrow Wilson
Find Main Ideas What were Wilson's hopes for the peace conference?

Setting the Scene The USS *George Washington* slipped out of New York harbor and headed across the Atlantic. Thousands of people cheered at dockside. Planes in formation roared overhead.

On board the *George Washington* were President Woodrow Wilson and his advisers. They were sailing to France in late 1918 to help the Allies set the terms of peace. As the ship passed the Statue of Liberty, a hopeful Wilson waved his hat to the crowd. At last, he would have a chance to keep his promise of making the world "safe for democracy."

Woodrow Wilson was the first American President to meet foreign leaders on foreign soil. He was determined to do whatever was needed to achieve his vision of a just and lasting peace. In the end, however, Wilson failed. The other Allied leaders, it turned out, did not share his vision or his hopes.

Wilson's Fourteen-Point Peace Plan

In Europe, Wilson visited Paris, London, Milan, and Rome. Everywhere, cheering crowds welcomed him. He thought that the crowds shared his goal of peace without victory. In fact, he was wrong. The Europeans who greeted Wilson so warmly scoffed at his high-minded proposals for peace. They and their leaders were determined to punish the Germans for the war.

In January 1918, even before the war ended, Wilson outlined his peace plan. Known as the Fourteen Points, it was meant to prevent international problems from causing another war.

The first point in Wilson's plan called for an end to secret agreements. Secrecy, Wilson felt, had encouraged the web of rival alliances that had helped lead to war. Next, he called for freedom of the seas, free trade, and a limit on arms. He urged peaceful settlement of

Versailles, France

The Hall of Mirrors

On June 28, 1919, Germany signed the Treaty of Versailles. This critical event took place in the Hall of Mirrors, which is part of the palace of Versailles.

Built to honor Louis XIV in the 1600s, the hall is decorated with seventeen large, richly decorated mirrors. At the time it was built, nearly all the materials available in the world to make mirrors were used in this lavish display.

 Take It to the NET

Virtual Field Trip For an interactive look at the Hall of Mirrors, visit *The American Nation* section of **www.phschool.com**.

disputes over colonies. He also supported the principle of national **self-determination,** that is, the right of national groups to have their own territory and forms of government.

For Wilson, however, the fourteenth point was the most important. It called for a "general association of nations," or **League of Nations.** Its job would be to protect the independence of all countries—large or small. His goals were clear. He stated:

> 66 An evident principle runs through the whole program that I have outlined. It is the principle of justice to all peoples and nationalities, and their right to live on equal terms of liberty and safety with one another, whether weak or strong. 99
>
> —Woodrow Wilson, Speech, January 8, 1918

Wilson persuaded the Allies to accept the Fourteen Points as the basis for making peace. However, the plan soon ran into trouble. Some goals were too vague. Others conflicted with reality. In Paris, Wilson faced a constant battle to save his Fourteen Points. He discovered that the Allies were more concerned with protecting their own interests than with forging a lasting peace.

The Paris Peace Conference

Diplomats from more than 30 nations met in Paris and Versailles (vuhr SI) to negotiate five separate peace treaties known as the Peace of Paris. Key issues were decided by the leaders of the Allied nations known as the Big Four: Woodrow Wilson of the United States, David Lloyd George of Britain, Georges Clemenceau (kleh mahn SOH) of France, and Vittorio Orlando of Italy.

Disagreement Among the Allies Each leader had his own aims. Wilson had called for "peace without victory." He opposed punishing the defeated powers.

The other Allies, however, ached for revenge. Germany must pay, they said. They insisted on large reparations, or cash payments, for the losses they had suffered during the war. Further, they wanted to include a "war guilt clause" that would force Germany to accept responsibility for the war.

The Allies were also determined to prevent Germany from rebuilding its military strength. In particular, Clemenceau wanted to weaken Germany so that it could never again threaten France. "Mr. Wilson bores me with his Fourteen Points," he complained. "Why, God Almighty has only ten!"

The haggling continued for months. In the end, Wilson had to compromise on his Fourteen Points in order to save his key goals, especially the League of Nations. He would not budge on the League. With the League in place, he believed, any mistakes made in Paris could later be corrected.

Harsh Terms for Germany By June 1919, the Treaty of Versailles, the most important treaty of the Peace of Paris, was ready. None of the Allies was satisfied with it. Germany, which had not even been allowed to send delegates to the peace talks, was shocked by the terms of the treaty. Still, its representative had no choice but to sign.

Under the treaty, Germany had to take full blame for the war.

> ❝ The Allied and Associated Governments affirm, and Germany accepts, the responsibility of Germany and her allies for causing all the loss and damage to which the Allied and Associated Governments and their nationals have been subjected as a consequence of the war imposed on them by the aggression of Germany and her allies. ❞
>
> —The Versailles Treaty, June 28, 1919, Article 231

Germany also had to pay the Allies huge reparations, including the cost of pensions for Allied soldiers or their widows and children. The total cost of German reparations would come to over $300 billion.

Other provisions of the Treaty of Versailles were aimed at weakening Germany. The treaty severely limited the size of the German military. It returned Alsace-Lorraine to France. In addition, the treaty

Europe After World War I

ICELAND (Denmark)

NORWAY

FINLAND

SWEDEN

ESTONIA

Moscow

LATVIA

ATLANTIC OCEAN

North Sea

DENMARK

Baltic Sea

LITHUANIA

GREAT BRITAIN

RUSSIA

NETH.

Berlin

GER.

Warsaw

London

BELG.

GERMANY

POLAND

LUX.

Versailles • Paris

CZECHOSLOVAKIA

Vienna

FRANCE

SWITZ.

AUSTRIA

HUNGARY

ROMANIA

ITALY

YUGOSLAVIA

Sarajevo

Black Sea

PORTUGAL

SPAIN

Madrid

BULGARIA

Rome

ALBANIA

Constantinople

TURKEY

SP. MOROCCO

GREECE

MOROCCO

ALGERIA

TUNISIA

Mediterranean Sea

Azimuthal Projection

0   200   400 Miles

0   200   400 Kilometers

Key

New nations

What Germany owed the Allies:

Compensation to civilian populations

Coal, livestock, ships, and timber

Cost for damage to Allied property

stripped Germany of its overseas colonies, which were put under the control of Britain or France. The Germans, wrote one reporter, "suffered a horrible humiliation."

A Few Victories for Wilson Wilson gained a few of his Fourteen Points, however. In Eastern Europe, the Allies provided for several new nations to be formed on the principle of self-determination, including Czechoslovakia and Yugoslavia. They were created out of lands once ruled by Germany, Russia, and Austria-Hungary. In addition, Poland regained its independence as a nation.

Some people were dissatisfied with the new boundaries. Many Germans, for example, had settled in Poland and Czechoslovakia. Before long, Germany would seek to regain control of German-speaking peoples in Eastern Europe.

To Wilson, however, his greatest achievement was persuading the Allies to include the League of Nations in the treaty. Wilson was certain that the League would prevent future wars by allowing nations

GEOGRAPHY Skills

A series of treaties ended World War I. The treaties created several new nations in Eastern Europe and restored independence in Poland.

1. **Location** On the map, locate (a) Poland, (b) Czechoslovakia, (c) Yugoslavia.

2. **Region** Which new nations bordered Russia?

3. **Critical Thinking Applying Information** Compare this map with the map of Europe at the beginning of the war on page 685. (a) How did Russia change? (b) What happened to Austria-Hungary?

to talk over their problems. If talk failed, members would join together to fight aggressors. "A living thing is born," he declared. The League "is definitely a guarantee of peace."

The Fight for the Versailles Treaty

When President Wilson returned home, he faced a new battle. He had to persuade the Senate to approve the Versailles Treaty and to approve American participation in the League of Nations.

Critics of the Treaty Most Americans favored the treaty. A vocal minority opposed it, however. Some said that it was too soft on the defeated powers. Many German Americans felt that it was too harsh. Some Republicans hoped to embarrass President Wilson, a Democrat, by rewriting or defeating the treaty. Isolationists, people who wanted the United States to stay out of world affairs, opposed the League of Nations. They were convinced that the League would lead to an "entangling alliance." Other people who were against the League felt that it did not have enough authority to solve any pressing economic problems. They thought that could lead to another war.

Critics of the treaty found a leader in Henry Cabot Lodge of Massachusetts. Lodge, a Republican, was chairman of the powerful Senate Foreign Relations Committee. Lodge accepted the idea of the League of Nations. However, he wanted changes in some provisions relating to the League. He believed that Americans were being asked to "subject our own will to the will of others."

Specifically, Lodge objected to Article 10 of the treaty. It called for the League to protect any member whose independence or territory was threatened. Lodge argued that Article 10 could involve the United States in future European wars. He wanted changes in the treaty that would ensure that the United States remained independent of the League. He also wanted Congress to have the power to decide on a case-by-case basis whether the United States would follow League policy.

Wilson believed that Lodge's changes would weaken the League. Advisers urged the President to compromise, to give up some of his demands in order to save the League. Wilson replied, "Let Lodge compromise." He refused to make any changes.

The Defeated Treaty As the battle grew hotter, the President took his case to the people. In early September 1919, Wilson set out across the country. He traveled nearly 8,000 miles and made 37 speeches in 29 cities. He urged Americans to let their senators know that they supported the treaty.

Wilson kept up a relentless pace. On September 25, the exhausted President complained of a headache. His doctors canceled the rest of the trip. Wilson returned to Washington. A week later, his wife found him unconscious. He had suffered a stroke that left him bedridden for weeks.

In November 1919, the Senate rejected the Versailles Treaty. "It is dead," Wilson mourned, "[and] every morning I put flowers on its grave." Gone, too, was Wilson's cherished goal—American membership in the League of Nations.

The United States did not sign a peace treaty with Germany until 1921. Many nations had already joined the League of Nations. Without the United States, though, the League failed to live up to its goal of protecting members against aggression. Wilson's dream of a world "safe for democracy" would have to wait.

 Ask Questions If you could have interviewed two senators, one who voted for and another who voted against the Versailles Treaty, what would you have asked them? How might they have responded?

Section 4 Assessment

Recall

1. **Identify** Explain the significance of **(a)** Fourteen Points, **(b)** League of Nations, **(c)** Big Four, **(d)** Treaty of Versailles, **(e)** Henry Cabot Lodge.
2. **Define (a)** self-determination, **(b)** reparations, **(c)** isolationist.

Comprehension

3. Describe the major points of Wilson's peace plan.
4. Why did Wilson's plan run into trouble at Versailles?
5. Why did the Senate reject the Versailles Treaty?

Critical Thinking and Writing

6. **Exploring the Main Idea** Review the Main Idea statement at the beginning of this section. Then, write a paragraph explaining why you think Wilson failed in his efforts to win "peace without victory."
7. **Making Predictions (a)** List three ways that the Treaty of Versailles punished Germany. **(b)** What do you think the effects of this harsh treatment might be?

ACTIVITY

 Take It to the NET
Connecting to Today
The United States did not join the League of Nations. However, after World War II it helped to form the United Nations (UN). Use the Internet to find out more about American participation in the UN today. Write a brief report. Visit *The American Nation* section of **www.phschool.com** for help in completing the activity.

CREATING A CHAPTER SUMMARY

Copy the flowchart below. As you read, fill the boxes with information about World War I. Add as many boxes as you need. The first two boxes have been completed to help you get started.

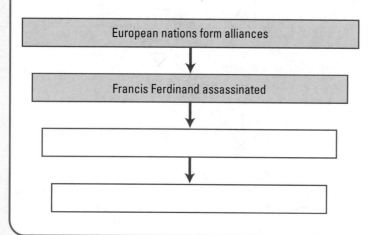

European nations form alliances

Francis Ferdinand assassinated

i TEXT

For additional review and enrich- ment activities, see the interactive version of *The American Nation*, available on the Web and on CD-ROM.

Take It to the NET

Chapter Self-Test For prac- tice test questions for Chapter 24, see *The American Nation* section of **www.phschool.com**.

Building Vocabulary

Review the meaning of the chapter vocabulary words listed below. Then, write a sentence for each word in which you define the word and describe its relation to World War I.

1. **nationalism**
2. **stalemate**
3. **draft**
4. **illiterate**
5. **pacifist**
6. **armistice**
7. **epidemic**
8. **self-determination**
9. **reparations**
10. **isolationist**

Reviewing Key Facts

11. What was the immediate cause of World War I? (Section 1)
12. What policy did the United States adopt at the outbreak of World War I? (Section 1)
13. Why did the United States declare war on Germany? (Section 2)
14. How did Russia's withdrawal from the war affect the Allied war effort? (Section 3)
15. **(a)** What were Wilson's goals for the peace? **(b)** Did he achieve them? Explain. (Section 4)

Critical Thinking and Writing

16. **Connecting to Geography: Interaction** How do you think trench warfare affected the land and resources of the battlefront area?
17. **Analyzing Information** **(a)** How did the United States regulate the economy during the war? **(b)** Why do you think Americans accepted gov- ernment controls on the economy during World War I?
18. **Organizing Information** Review the subsection titled "The Home Front" on page 695. Make a concept web for the information presented in the subsection.
19. **Supporting a Point of View** Do you think the way in which American society viewed women changed after World War I? Explain.
20. **Drawing Inferences** Many historians blame Wilson for the defeat of the Versailles Treaty in Congress. What reasons do you think they might give to support that position?

Analyzing Primary Sources

President Wilson made the following statement to journalist Frank I. Cobb in 1917. Read the statement, and answer the questions that follow:

> ❝[If you] lead this people into war, . . . they'll forget there ever was such a thing as tolerance. To fight you must be brutal and ruthless, and the spirit of ruthless brutality will enter into the very fiber of our national life, infecting Congress, the courts, the policeman on the beat, the man in the street. . . . Conformity would be the only virtue . . . and every man who refused to conform would have to pay the penalty.❞
>
> —President Wilson in conversation with Frank I. Cobb, 1917

21. According to Wilson, how would war affect United States citizens?

22. Why would conforming be necessary?

23. What was the penalty for not conforming?

24. **(a)** What was Wilson's view of war? **(b)** How do you think this view affected his plan for the League of Nations?

Recognizing Propaganda

IN BELGIUM

HELP

THE NATIONAL COMMITTEE FOR RELIEF IN BELGIUM. TRAFALGAR BUILDINGS. TRAFALGAR SQUARE. LONDON.

This 1916 poster is the work of a Dutch artist. Study the poster. Answer the questions.

25. What organization distributed this poster?
   A U.S. citizens in Belgium
   B A relief group in Germany
   C An English citizens' group in Belgium
   D A Belgium relief committee in London

26. What propaganda techniques are used?

ACTIVITIES

Connecting With . . . Culture

Writing a Poem Read the following poem written by British poet Siegfried Sassoon during the third year of the war.

> ❝ You smug-faced crowds with kindling eye
> Who cheer when soldier lads march by,
> Sneak home and pray you'll never know
> The [place] where youth and laughter go.❞
>
> —Siegfried Sassoon, "Suicide in the Trenches," 1917

Then, review the lyrics of "Over There," the patriotic song by George M. Cohan, on page 693, that swept the United States as it went off to war in 1918.

Why do you think the mood of these two works is so different? Express your answer in a short poem of your own.

Take It to the NET

Connecting to Today

A Television Documentary The Treaty of Versailles set up the nation of Yugoslavia. Use the Internet to find out about Yugoslavia today. Then, prepare a TV documentary showing Yugoslavia's development up to the present. *Hint:* In the late 1900s, civil war broke Yugoslavia into several independent states. For help in starting this activity, visit *The American Nation* section of **www.phschool.com**.

Writing an Essay

Analyzing Information Use the Internet to find sites dealing with the causes of World War I. Then, write a short essay on whether the war could have been avoided. For help in starting this activity, visit *The American Nation* section of **www.phschool.com**.

TEST PREPARATION

Use the table <u>and</u> your knowledge of social studies to answer the following question.

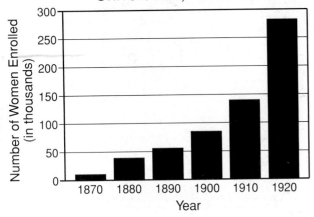

Women Enrolled in Colleges and Universities, 1870–1920

Source: Mabel Newcomer, *A Century of Higher Education for American Women*

1 Which decade saw the largest percentage increase in the number of women who attended colleges and universities?

   A 1870s

   B 1880s

   C 1890s

   D 1910s

2 Which of the following actions would be classified as an application of the Roosevelt Corollary?

   A Roosevelt orders the navy to capture Manila Bay.

   B Americans invest in railroads in South America.

   C Taft sends United States marines to Nicaragua.

   D Wilson refuses to recognize Huerta's government in Mexico.

3 W.E.B. Du Bois disagreed most strongly with Booker T. Washington on which issue?

   A The importance of education for African Americans

   B The need for African Americans to better their economic status

   C How to fight discrimination against African Americans

   D Whether black and white Americans should work together

Use the quotation <u>and</u> your knowledge of social studies to answer the following question.

Senator Robert M. La Follette, speech in the United States Senate, April 1917 (adapted)

"Countless millions are suffering from want and privation; countless other millions are dead and rotting on foreign battlefields. We are pledged by the President to make this fair, free, and happy land of ours the same shambles and bottomless pit of horror that we see in Europe today."

---

4 How would you summarize La Follette's position in the speech?

   A The United States should not enter World War I.

   B The United States should declare war on Spain.

   C The United States should protest German submarine attacks.

   D The United States should not join the League of Nations.

5 During World War I, which of the following did some Americans view as a violation of the First Amendment?

 A Military draft law

 B Laws to silence antiwar critics

 C Segregation in the military

 D Attacks on German Americans

6 Which of the following does not belong with the other three?

 A Foraker Act

 B Platt Amendment

 C Battle of San Juan Hill

 D Revolt in the Philippines

7 "A free, open-minded and absolutely impartial adjustment of all colonial claims based upon [the principle of self-determination]." Which of the following causes of World War I is addressed in this part of Woodrow Wilson's Fourteen Points?

 A Militarism

 B Imperialism

 C The alliance system

 D Extreme nationalism

8 The relationship of Thomas Nast to the downfall of Boss Tweed is most like which of the following?

 A The relationship of Ida Tarbell to civil service reform

 B The relationship of Theodore Roosevelt to conservation of natural resources

 C The relationship of Carrie Chapman Catt to the Nineteenth Amendment

 D The relationship of Upton Sinclair to the Pure Food and Drug Act

Use the map and your knowledge of social studies to answer the following question.

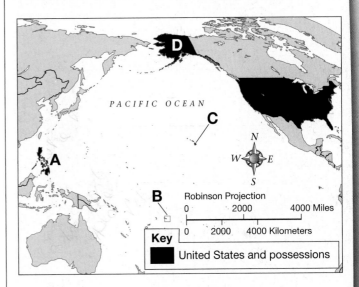

9 Which of the territories shown on the map is correctly matched with the method by which the United States acquired it?

 A A—war

 B B—purchase

 C C—purchase

 D D—annexation

Writing Practice

10 Compare and contrast the reasons that the government took steps to regulate the economy during the Progressive Era and during World War I. Include examples.

11 Historians consider Theodore Roosevelt one of the most important Presidents. Give reasons to support this viewpoint, using at least one example of domestic policy and one example of foreign policy. Then, make two generalizations about Roosevelt.

Unit 8

Prosperity, Depression, and War

Hard Times
Drought Stricken Area, by Alexandre Hogue, mirrors the economic hardships that struck both rural and urban Americans in the 1930s.

"I see one-third of a nation ill-housed, ill-clad, ill-nourished."

—President Franklin Delano Roosevelt (1937)

The Roaring Twenties

1919–1929

1 Politics and Prosperity
2 New Ways of Life
3 The Roaring Twenties
4 A Nation Divided

A poster supporting Prohibition

A stock certificate

Telegraphic ticker from the 1920s

AMERICAN EVENTS

1919
The Eighteenth Amendment bans the making or selling of alcoholic beverages.

1920s
The economic boom of the 1920s boosts the stock market.

1921
The Emergency Quota Act limits immigration to the United States.

1923
The Senate Public Lands Committee begins investigating the Teapot Dome Scandal.

Presidential Terms: Woodrow Wilson   1913–1921   Warren G. Harding 1921–1923

• **1918** ★   ★   ★   ★   **1921**   ★   **1924** •

WORLD EVENTS

▲ **1919**
The Treaty of Versailles is signed.

▲ **1922**
The Union of Soviet Socialist Republics is formed.

The Roaring Twenties

In the decade after World War I, a new energy swept the country. New dances, music, and fashions appeared, and the economy boomed.

Key

🎷 Jazz
🎥 Movies
📖 Literature
📰 Newspapers
💡 Harlem Renaissance
📻 Radio broadcasts

Albers Equal-Area Projection

Lindbergh, standing by the *Spirit of St. Louis*

1925
John Scopes is arrested for teaching the theory of evolution.

1927
Charles Lindbergh flies alone across the Atlantic Ocean.

1929
The Great Depression begins.

Calvin Coolidge 1923–1929

1924 · · **1927** · · **1930** ·

1926 ▲
The United States intervenes in Nicaragua.

1928 ▲
The Kellogg-Briand Pact outlaws war.

1 Politics and Prosperity

Reading Focus

- What scandals hurt Republicans in the 1920s?
- How did Coolidge's policies increase prosperity?
- What role did the United States play in world affairs?

Key Terms

recession
Teapot Dome Scandal
installment buying
stock
bull market
communism
disarmament
Kellogg-Briand Pact

Taking Notes

Copy the chart below. As you read, complete the chart to show the effects of Republican leadership on the United States during the 1920s. Add as many boxes as you need.

REPUBLICAN LEADERSHIP → Strong support of business

Main Idea As the Republican party returned to power in the 1920s, the economy boomed.

Warren G. Harding

Predict How do you think the country will change with Harding as President?

Setting the Scene

"The change is amazing," wrote a reporter just after the inauguration of President Warren G. Harding on March 4, 1921. Woodrow Wilson and the Democrats were out; Harding and the Republicans were in. Wilson had been ill, remote, and increasingly sour. Harding was warm, friendly, and open.

During the campaign, Harding's slogan had been "Back to Normalcy." By "normalcy," he meant "a regular steady order of things . . . normal procedure. . . ."

The 1920s turned out to be anything but normal. As one official said, the decade ushered in a "new era," of Republican leadership, booming prosperity, and changes in everyday life.

Republicans in Office

World War I had helped the economy. Europeans ordered vast amounts of supplies from American factories. After the United States entered the war in 1917, American factories expanded rapidly to meet the demand for military supplies.

When the war ended, more than 2 million soldiers came home and began to look for jobs. At the same time, factories stopped turning out war materials. The result was a sharp **recession,** or economic slump.

Harding Takes Office The recession fed voter discontent with the Democrats, who had held power for eight years. In the 1920 election, Warren Harding swamped his Democratic opponent.

For the top Cabinet posts, Harding chose able men who strongly followed pro-business policies. Andrew Mellon, a wealthy financier, became secretary of the treasury. Mellon balanced the budget and lowered taxes.

Herbert Hoover became the new secretary of commerce. During World War I, Hoover had earned the world's admiration by organizing efforts to supply food to millions of starving Belgians. As

POLITICAL CARTOON
Skills

The Teapot Dome Scandal
This cartoon, published in 1924, comments on the Teapot Dome Scandal.

1. **Comprehension**
   (a) Why are the officials running? (b) How do you think the White House will be affected?

2. **Understanding Main Ideas** What is the significance of the rolling oil tank?

3. **Identifying Points of View** According to the cartoon, how will this scandal affect the government?

Civics

secretary of commerce, he worked to help American businesses expand overseas.

Corruption and Scandals To fill most other Cabinet posts, however, Harding brought in his old friends. They became known as the "Ohio Gang." Harding himself was honest and hard-working, but the Ohio Gang saw government service as a way to enrich themselves. A series of scandals resulted. For example, Harding made Charles Forbes head of the Veterans Bureau. Forbes was later convicted of stealing millions of dollars from the bureau.

Harding looked upon Forbes's crime as a betrayal. When rumors of new scandals surfaced, he grew even more distressed. In August 1923, Harding died of a heart attack. Many believed that the scandals contributed to his sudden death.

After Harding died, new scandals came to light. The most serious involved Secretary of the Interior Albert Fall. Two oil executives had bribed Fall. In return, he secretly leased them government land in California and at Teapot Dome, Wyoming. As a result of the Teapot Dome Scandal, Fall became the first Cabinet official ever sent to prison.

Coolidge Takes Office On the day Harding died, Vice President Calvin Coolidge was visiting his father's farm in Vermont. Coolidge recalled, "I was awakened by my father. . . . I noticed that his voice trembled." Coolidge's father, a justice of the peace, used the family Bible to swear his son in as President.

"Silent Cal" Coolidge was very different from Harding. Harding loved throwing parties and making long speeches. Coolidge was tight with both money and words. A woman reportedly told Coolidge she had bet that she could get him to say more than two words. "You lose," Coolidge replied.

Coolidge set out to repair the damage caused by the scandals. He forced the officials involved in scandals to resign. In 1924, Coolidge ran against Democrat John Davis and Progressive Robert La Follette. Voters chose to "Keep Cool With Coolidge" and returned the cautious New Englander to office.

Coolidge Prosperity

Like Harding, Coolidge believed that prosperity for all Americans depended on business prosperity. Coolidge cut regulations on business. He also named business leaders to head government agencies.

Industry Booms Coolidge's pro-business policies contributed to a period of rapid economic growth. People referred to this boom as "Coolidge prosperity." As factories switched to consumer goods, the postwar recession ended. From 1923 to 1929, the quantity of goods made by industry almost doubled.

For most Americans, incomes rose. As a result, they were able to buy a flood of new consumer products. Electric refrigerators, radios, phonographs, vacuum cleaners, and many other appliances took their places in American homes.

Businesses used advertising to boost sales of consumer goods. Advertisements encouraged people to think that their happiness depended on owning a wealth of shiny, new products.

Faced with so many goods, people often wanted to buy things they could not afford. In response, businesses allowed installment buying, or buying on credit. For example, buyers could take home a new refrigerator by putting down just a few dollars. Each month, they paid an installment until they had paid the full price, plus interest.

The new policy of "buy now, pay later" increased the demand for goods. At the same time, however, consumer debt jumped. By the end of the decade, consumers owed more than the amount of the federal budget.

A Soaring Stock Market The economic boom of the 1920s gave the stock market a giant boost. As you read in Chapter 20, corporations sold stocks, or shares of ownership, to investors. Investors made or lost money depending upon whether the price of the shares went up or down.

By the later 1920s, more people were investing in the stock market than ever before. Stock prices rose so fast that some people made fortunes almost overnight. Stories of ordinary people becoming rich drew others into the stock market. Such a period of increased stock trading and rising stock prices is known as a bull market.

Many people bought stocks on margin. Under this system, an investor bought a stock for as little as a 10 percent down payment. The buyer held the stock until the price rose, and then sold it at a profit. Margin buying worked as long as stock prices kept going up.

In 1928 and 1929, however, the prices of many stocks rose faster than the value of the companies themselves. A few experts warned

Connecting to Today

The Stock Market

Maybe you have heard a business reporter announce, "The Dow Jones is up." The reporter is referring to the Dow Jones Industrial Average, sometimes called "the Dow." The Dow is calculated by averaging the stock value of 30 large corporations.

Average prices of stocks are quoted in points rather than dollars. On a day when more people buy than sell shares in the Dow stocks, the Dow average might rise by, say, 30 points. On a very good day, the Dow may rise 100 or more points. Of course, on a bad day, it might go down by an equal amount.

Investors use many different sources of information to decide whether to buy or sell. They consider national and world events, corporate reports, and the opinions of financial experts. In the end, however, no one can really predict how the Dow will do in any given day, month, or even year.

Why is it hard to predict whether the Dow will go up or down?

that the bull market could not last forever. Still, most investors ignored the warnings.

A Limited Role in World Affairs

After World War I, the United States was the world's leading economic power. Europeans expected the United States to take a major role in world affairs. Presidents Harding and Coolidge wanted to keep the hard-won peace in Europe. However, they did not want to commit the United States to the job of keeping world peace. The United States sent observers to the League of Nations but refused to join. Most Americans supported this return to prewar isolationism.

Latin America During the war, Latin American nations had been cut off from Europe. As a result, United States trade and investment in Latin America increased. This trend continued after the war. However, the United States limited its role abroad for fear that more involvement might push the country into another war.

At times, the United States intervened to protect its economic interests in Latin America. In 1926, for example, a revolution broke out in Nicaragua, where Americans owned plantations and railroads. Coolidge sent marines to oversee new elections.

In 1927, Mexico announced plans to take over foreign-owned oil and mining companies. American investors called on President Coolidge to send in troops. Instead, Coolidge sent a diplomat, Dwight Morrow, to Mexico. After much hard bargaining, Morrow was able to work out a compromise with the Mexican government.

Viewing History

Consumer Credit

United States

With install-ment plans and the appearance of mail-order catalogs, people bought radios, vacuum cleaners, and other new products on credit. Some stores showed attractive window displays of furniture available for purchase on credit. **Analyzing Information** *How did Americans' ideas about owing money change in the 1920s?*

AS YOU READ **Draw Inferences** Why do you think Coolidge chose to send a diplomat, instead of troops, to Mexico?

The Soviet Union Meanwhile, in the Soviet Union, V. I. Lenin created the world's first communist state.* **Communism** is an economic system in which all wealth and property are owned by the community as a whole.

The United States refused to recognize Lenin's government. Most Americans disliked communism. It shocked them when the Soviet government did away with private property and attacked religion. Yet, despite disapproval of the Soviet government, Congress voted $20 million in aid when famine threatened Russia in 1921. American aid may have saved as many as 10 million Russians from starvation.

Pursuing Peace An arms race in Europe had helped cause World War I. For this reason, many people in the 1920s favored the reduction of armed forces and weapons of war, or **disarmament.** Pacifist groups such as the Women's International League for Peace and Freedom, founded by Jane Addams, led the call for disarmament in the United States and Europe.

Presidents Harding and Coolidge also backed peace efforts. At the Washington Conference of 1921, the United States, Britain, and Japan agreed to limit the size of their navies. Seven years later, the United States and 61 other nations signed the **Kellogg-Briand Pact.** This treaty outlawed war.

The treaty, however, had a fatal flaw. It did not set up any means for keeping the peace. One nation could still use force against another without fear of punishment. Still, many hailed the Kellogg-Briand Pact as the beginning of a new age of peace.

---

* In 1922, Russia became the most powerful state in the newly created Union of Soviet Socialist Republics, or Soviet Union.

Section 1 Assessment

Recall

1. Identify Explain the significance of **(a)** Warren G. Harding, **(b)** Teapot Dome Scandal, **(c)** Calvin Coolidge, **(d)** Kellogg- Briand Pact.
2. Define (a) recession, **(b)** installment buying, **(c)** stock, **(d)** bull market, **(e)** communism, **(f)** disarmament.

Comprehension

3. How did corruption hurt the Republicans during the 1920s?
4. How did Americans benefit from "Coolidge prosperity"?
5. What role did most Americans in the 1920s think that the United States should take in world affairs? Explain.

Critical Thinking and Writing

6. Exploring the Main Idea Review the Main Idea statement at the beginning of this section. Then, explain why Calvin Coolidge made this statement: "The business of America is business."
7. Making Predictions During the 1920s, many Americans bought consumer goods on credit and stocks on margin. How would this make economic conditions worse after the economy began to slow down?

 Take It to the NET
Connecting to Today
The shared economic interests of Mexico and the United States still exist. Use the Internet to find out about the North American Free Trade Agreement (NAFTA). Summarize the purpose of NAFTA. Then, discuss the effects of the agreement today. Visit *The American Nation* section of **www.phschool.com** for help in completing the activity.

Determining Relevance

As you have read, many Americans enjoyed a new prosperity in the years following World War I. Numerous causes contributed to this economic growth in the 1920s. In examining these causes, it is important to determine how pertinent, or relevant, your information is to the topic. What logical connection exists between your topic and a piece of information?

Not only were radios a source of family entertainment and news, they also provided an effective means of selling consumer goods.

An advertisement for a radio

In 1922, Emily Post published a book on manners called *Etiquette*. This excerpt tells how a considerate guest should behave:

"Courtesy demands that you, when you are a guest, shall show neither annoyance nor disappointment—no matter what happens. . . . If you neither understand nor care for dogs or children, and both insist on climbing all over you, you must seemingly like it."

"You must pretend that six is a perfect dinner hour though you never dine before eight or . . . you must wait until eight-thirty or nine . . . though your dinner hour is six. . . ."

—Emily Post, *Etiquette*, 1922

Learn the Skill *To determine if information is relevant, use the following steps:*

1. **Clarify the topic.** Be clear about the topic you are studying. Often, it is helpful to restate it in your own words.

2. **Examine the evidence.** Look carefully at the information you have. What does it represent?

3. **Determine the relevance.** How does the information relate to the topic? Ask yourself questions, for example, How would consumer spending contribute to economic growth?

Practice the Skill *Answer the following questions based on the chapter and the information on this page:*

1. Restate the topic in your own words.

2. **(a)** Which piece of information represents economic issues? **(b)** Which information is about another topic?

3. **(a)** How did the radio affect economic growth during the 1920s? **(b)** How is etiquette related to economic growth?

Apply the Skill *See the Chapter Review and Assessment.*

2 New Ways of Life

BEFORE YOU READ

Reading Focus

- What was Prohibition?
- What new rights did women gain?
- How did the automobile and a new popular culture change American life?

Key Terms

Prohibition
bootleggers
repeal
League of Women Voters
Equal Rights Amendment
suburb

Taking Notes

Copy the concept web below. As you read, fill in the blank ovals with the new ways of life that occurred during the 1920s. Add as many ovals as you need.

Main Idea A surge of new ideas and products and a new popular culture changed the values and customs of Americans during the 1920s.

AS YOU READ Federal agents destroy barrels of illegal liquor

Summarize What was the goal of the "noble experiment"?

Setting the Scene At the stroke of midnight on the morning of January 16, 1920, church bells rang all across the United States. What some people called the "noble experiment" had begun. The experiment was **Prohibition,** a ban on the manufacture, sale, and transportation of liquor anywhere in the United States.

Supporters of Prohibition were overjoyed. Popular preacher Billy Sunday predicted that the ban on alcohol would cure a wide variety of social ills: "The slums will soon be only a memory. We will turn our prisons into factories and our jails into storehouses and corncribs. Men will walk upright now. Women will smile and children will laugh."

Only time would tell if the "noble experiment" would succeed or fail.

Prohibition was one of many developments that had a dramatic impact on society in the 1920s. New ideas, new products, and new forms of entertainment were rapidly changing the American way of life.

Prohibition

For nearly a century, reformers like the Woman's Christian Temperance Union had worked to ban alcoholic beverages. They finally achieved this when the states ratified the Eighteenth Amendment in January 1919. One year later, Prohibition went into effect.

In 1920, as today, alcohol abuse was a serious problem. Many Americans hoped the ban on liquor would improve American life. In fact, the ban did have some positive effects. Alcoholism declined during Prohibition. However, in the end, the ban did not work.

Evading the Law One reason that Prohibition failed was that many Americans found ways to get around the law. Some people manufactured their own alcohol in homemade stills. Others smuggled in liquor from Canada and the Caribbean. Because these smugglers sometimes hid bottles of liquor in their boots, they became known as **bootleggers.**

Illegal bars, called speak-easies, opened in nearly every city and town. In some ways, speak-easies made drinking liquor more popular than ever. To enforce the ban, the government sent out federal Prohibition agents. These "g-men" traveled across the United States, shutting down speak-easies, breaking up illegal stills, and stopping smugglers.

Rise of Organized Crime Prohibition gave a huge boost to organized crime. Every speak-easy needed a steady supply of liquor. Professional criminals, or gangsters, took over the job of meeting this need. As bootleggers earned big profits, crime became a big business. Gangsters divided up cities and forced speak-easy owners in their "territories" to buy liquor from them. Sometimes, gangsters used some of their profits to bribe police officers, public officials, and judges.

Repeal of Prohibition Gradually, more Americans began to think that Prohibition was a mistake. The ban reduced drinking but never stopped it. Even worse, argued critics, Prohibition was undermining respect for the law. Every day, millions of Americans were buying liquor in speak-easies. By the mid-1920s, almost half of all federal arrests were for Prohibition crimes.

By the end of the decade, many Americans were calling for the **repeal,** or cancellation, of Prohibition. In 1933, the states ratified the Twenty-first Amendment, which repealed the Eighteenth Amendment.* The noble experiment was over.

New Rights for Women

Another constitutional amendment, the Nineteenth Amendment, also changed American life, but in a very different way. Ratified in 1920, it gave women the right to vote.

Women Voters Women went to the polls nationwide for the first time in November 1920. Their votes helped elect Warren Harding President. Women did not vote as a group, however, as some people had predicted. Like men, some women voted for Republicans, and some for Democrats, and many did not vote at all.

In 1920, Carrie Chapman Catt, head of the National Woman Suffrage Association, set up the League of Women Voters. The organization worked to educate voters, as it does today. It also worked to guarantee other rights, such as the right of women to serve on juries.

Women served as delegates in the 1924 Republican and Democratic conventions. That year, the first two women governors were elected—Nellie Tayloe Ross of Wyoming and Miriam A. Ferguson of Texas.

As women in the United States voted for the first time, women in Puerto Rico asked if the new law applied to them. They were told

An American Profile

Nellie Tayloe Ross
1876–1977

Nellie Tayloe Ross, the nation's first female governor, took office in Wyoming on January 5, 1925. Governor Ross had not sought a political career. She taught kindergarten for two years before her health failed. After she married, she was a homemaker and mother. Then, in 1922, her husband was elected governor of Wyoming. When he died in office, his supporters urged his widow to run for his vacant seat. Nellie Ross was elected governor. Later she became a popular speaker for the Democratic National Committee, and in 1933 she became the first female Director of the U.S. Mint.

Why do you think people urged Nellie Tayloe Ross to run for governor? Explain.

---

* To date, the Eighteenth Amendment is the only constitutional amendment that has ever been repealed.

that it did not. Led by Ana Roqué de Duprey, an educator and writer, Puerto Rican women crusaded for the vote. In 1929, their crusade finally succeeded.

An Equal Rights Amendment Leaders in the suffrage movement also worked for other goals. Alice Paul, who had been a leading suffragist, pointed out that women still lacked many legal rights. For example, many professional schools still barred women, and many states gave husbands legal control over their wives' earnings. Paul called for a new constitutional amendment in 1923. Paul's proposed Equal Rights Amendment (ERA) stated that "equality of rights under the law shall not be denied or abridged by the United States or by any State on account of sex."

Many people feared that the ERA went too far. Some even argued that women would lose some legal safeguards, such as laws that protected them in factories. Paul worked vigorously for the ERA until her death in 1977. The amendment passed but was never ratified.

Changes for Working Women Women's lives changed in other ways in the 1920s. During World War I, thousands of women had worked outside the home for the first time. They filled the jobs of men who had gone off to war. When the troops came home, many women were forced to give up their jobs. Still, some remained in the work force.

For some women, working outside the home was nothing new. Poor women and working-class women had been cooks, servants, and seamstresses for many years. In the 1920s, they were joined by middle-class women who worked as teachers, typists, secretaries, and store clerks. A few women even managed to become doctors and lawyers despite discrimination.

Life at home also changed for women. More of them bought ready-made clothes than sewed for the whole family as they had done in the past. Electric appliances such as refrigerators, washers, irons, and vacuum cleaners made housework easier. On the other hand, such conveniences also encouraged some women to spend even more time on housework. Women who worked outside the home found that they had to work a second shift when they came home. Most husbands expected their wives to cook, clean, and care for children even if they held full-time jobs.

AS YOU READ **Predict** Read the subheadings of this section. Then, predict how the automobile affected American life in the 1920s. Read to check your predictions.

Impact of the Automobile

"Why on earth do you need to study what's changing this country?" one man asked the experts. "I can tell you what's happening in just four letters: A-U-T-O." In the 1920s, Americans traveled to more places and moved more quickly than ever before—all because of the automobile.

The auto industry played a central role in the business boom of the 1920s. Car sales grew rapidly during the decade. The auto boom spurred growth in related industries such as steel and rubber.

Affordable Cars Lower prices sparked the auto boom. By 1924, the cost of a Model T had dropped from $850 to $290. As a result, an American did not have to be rich to buy a car.

Rise in Auto Sales, 1920–1929

Graph: Number of Cars (in thousands) vs. Year, 1920–1929

Car prices fell because factories became more efficient. As you have read, Henry Ford introduced the assembly line in his automobile factory in 1913. Before the assembly line, it took 14 hours to put together a Model T. In Ford's new factory, workers could assemble a Model T in 93 minutes.

Other companies copied Ford's methods. In 1927, General Motors passed Ford as the top automaker. Unlike Ford, General Motors sold cars in a variety of models and colors. Henry Ford had once boasted that people could have his cars in "any color so long as it's black." When General Motors introduced a low-priced car available in different colors, Ford lost many customers. Faced with the success of General Motors, he changed his mind. His next car, the Model A, came in different colors. Before long, car companies were offering new makes and models every year.

Economic Effects Car sales spurred growth in other parts of the economy. By 1929, some four million Americans owed their jobs to the automobile, directly or indirectly. Tens of thousands of people worked in steel mills, producing metal parts for cars. Others made tires, paint, and glass for cars. Some drilled for oil in the Southwest or worked in the oil refineries where crude petroleum was converted into usable gasoline.

The car boom had other effects. States and towns paved more roads and built new highways. In 1925, the Bronx River Parkway in New York was the first of many highways in parklike settings.

Gas stations, garages, car dealers, motels, and roadside restaurants sprang up across the country to serve the millions who traveled by car. In 1920, there were only about 1,500 filling stations in the entire United States. By 1929, there were more than 120,000. Mechanic shops, or places to repair automobiles, also became a necessity.

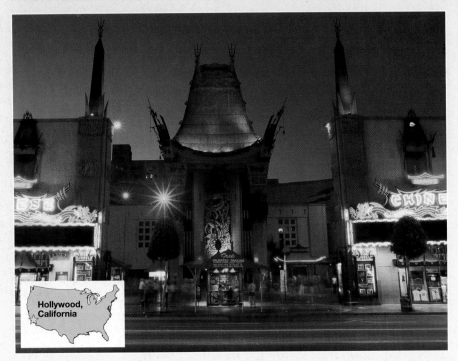

Hollywood, California

Hollywood Boulevard

As the movie industry grew during the 1920s, so did the fame of Hollywood in California. It was the home of movie stars and the glittering world of the entertainment industry. In addition to the many places you can visit along historic Hollywood Boulevard, you can also see 2,000 bronze stars, each with a celebrity's name, embedded in the sidewalk.

 Take It to the NET

Virtual Field Trip For an interactive look at Hollywood Boulevard, visit *The American Nation* section of **www.phschool.com**.

Social Effects Cars shaped life in the city and in the country. Many city dwellers wanted to escape crowded conditions. They moved to nearby towns in the country, which soon grew into suburbs. A suburb is a community located outside a city. With cars, suburban families could drive to the city even though it was many miles away. They could also drive to stores, schools, or work. No longer did people have to live where they could walk or take a trolley to work.

Another major shift came when suburban housewives refused to be confined to the passenger seat. Instead, they took their place behind the wheels of their own automobiles. As they did, they broke down still another barrier that separated the worlds of men and women.

In the country, cars brought people closer to towns, shops, and the movies. Such trips had taken several hours by horse and buggy. One farm woman bought a car before she got indoor plumbing. "You can't go to town in a bathtub," she explained.

Creating a Mass Culture

By making travel easier, cars helped Americans from different parts of the country learn more about one another. They played a role in creating a new national culture that crossed state lines.

New forms of entertainment also contributed to the rise of a mass culture. In the 1920s, rising wages and labor-saving appliances gave families more money to spend and more leisure time in which to spend it.

Radio Radio became very popular in the 1920s. The country's first radio station, KDKA, started broadcasting in Pittsburgh in 1920. By 1929, more than 10 million American families owned radios.

A new lifestyle emerged. Each night after dinner, families gathered around the radio to tune in to shows such as "Roxy and His Gang" or "Jack Frost's Melody Moments." Radio listeners enjoyed comedies and westerns, classical music and jazz, news reports and play-by-play sports broadcasts.

The Movies In the 1920s, the movie industry came of age. Southern California's warm, sunny climate allowed filming all year round. Soon, Hollywood became the movie capital of the world.

Movies contributed to the new mass culture. Millions of Americans went to the movies at least once a week. They thrilled to westerns, romances, adventures, and comedies. In small towns, theaters were bare rooms with hard chairs. In cities, they were huge palaces with red velvet seats.

The first movies had no sound. Audiences followed the plot by reading "title cards" that appeared on the screen. A pianist played music that went with the action.

Fans adored Hollywood movie stars. Cowboy stars like Tom Mix thrilled audiences with their heroic adventures. Clara Bow won fame playing restless, fun-seeking young women. The most popular star of all was comedian Charlie Chaplin, nicknamed "The Little Tramp." In his tiny derby hat and baggy pants, Chaplin presented a comical figure. His attempts to triumph over the problems of everyday life moved audiences to both laughter and tears.

In 1927, Hollywood caused a sensation when it produced *The Jazz Singer*. The film was a "talkie"—a movie with a soundtrack. Soon, all new movies were talkies.

Section 2 Assessment

Recall

1. **Identify** Explain the significance of **(a)** Prohibition, **(b)** Carrie Chapman Catt, **(c)** League of Women Voters, **(d)** Ana Roqué de Duprey, **(e)** Alice Paul, **(f)** Equal Rights Amendment, **(g)** Henry Ford, **(h)** Charlie Chaplin.
2. **Define (a)** bootleggers, **(b)** repeal, **(c)** suburb.

Comprehension

3. Why did Prohibition fail?
4. How did the Nineteenth Amendment change women's lives?
5. **(a)** How did the automobile affect the economy? **(b)** Discuss the effect of radio and the movies on the culture during the 1920s.

Critical Thinking and Writing

6. **Exploring the Main Idea** Review the Main Idea statement at the beginning of this section. Then, discuss two ideas that changed the way Americans lived during the 1920s.
7. **Analyzing Information** How did changes in technology contribute to new ways of life during the 1920s?

ACTIVITY

Writing Title Cards
You are a moviemaker producing a silent film about the Roaring Twenties. Write ten title cards for scenes that show what the decade was like.

3 The Roaring Twenties

Reading Focus

- What fads and fashions became popular during the 1920s?
- How did a new group of writers and the new jazz music affect American culture?
- What was the Harlem Renaissance?
- What heroes were celebrated during the 1920s?

Key Terms

fad

flapper

jazz

expatriate

Taking Notes

As you read, prepare an outline of this section. Use roman numerals to indicate the major headings of this section, capital letters for subheadings, and numbers for the supporting details. The sample below will help you get started.

> I. New Fads and Fashions
>   A. Following the latest fads
>   1.
>   2.
>   B. Flappers set the style
>   1.
>   2.
> II. The Jazz Age

Main Idea While new lifestyles and new ideas affected fashion and music, a new generation of writers rebelled by criticizing American life.

A dancing couple from the 1920s

Find Main Ideas What forms of entertainment were popular during the 1920s?

Setting the Scene When asked about her favorite pastime, one young woman of the 1920s promptly replied, "I adore dancing. Who doesn't?" New dance crazes such as the Charleston, the Lindy Hop, and the Shimmy forever marked the decade as the "Jazz Age" and the "Roaring Twenties."

During the 1920s, new dances, new music, new games, and other new ways to have fun swept the country. For all the serious business of the 1920s, the decade also roared with laughter. At the same time, a new generation of writers were taking a critical look at American society.

New Fads and Fashions

"Ev'ry morning, ev'ry evening, ain't we got fun?" went a hit song of 1921. During the "Era of Wonderful Nonsense"—yet another nickname for the 1920s—fun came in many forms.

Following the Latest Fads Fads caught on, then quickly disappeared. A fad is an activity or a fashion that is taken up with great passion for a short time. Flagpole sitting was one fad of the 1920s. Young people would perch on top of flagpoles for hours, or even days. Another fad was the dance marathon, where couples danced for hundreds of hours at a time to see who could last the longest. Crossword puzzles and mah-jongg, a Chinese game, were other popular fads of the 1920s.

Dance crazes came and went rapidly. The most popular new dance was probably the Charleston. First performed by African Americans in southern cities like Charleston, South Carolina, the dance became a national craze after 1923. Moving to a quick beat, dancers pivoted their feet while kicking out first one leg, then the other, backward and forward.

Flappers Set the Style Perhaps no one pursued the latest fads more intensely than the flappers. These young women rebelled against traditional ways of thinking and acting. Flappers wore their hair bobbed, or cut short. They wore their dresses short, too—shorter than Americans had ever seen. Flappers shocked their parents by wearing bright red lipstick.

To many older Americans, the way flappers behaved was even more shocking than the way they looked. Flappers smoked cigarettes in public, drank bootleg alcohol in speak-easies, and drove fast cars. "Is 'the old-fashioned girl,' with all that she stands for in sweetness, modesty, and innocence, in danger of becoming extinct?" wondered one magazine in 1921.

Only a few young women were flappers. Still, they set a style for others. Slowly, older women began to cut their hair and wear make-up and shorter skirts. For many Americans, the bold fashions pioneered by the flappers symbolized a new sense of freedom.

The Jazz Age

Another innovation of the 1920s was jazz. Born in New Orleans, jazz combined West African rhythms, African American work songs and spirituals, and European harmonies. Jazz also had roots in the ragtime rhythms of composers like Scott Joplin.

Louis Armstrong was one of the brilliant young African American musicians who helped create jazz. Armstrong learned to play the trumpet in the New Orleans orphanage where he grew up. Armstrong had the ability to take a simple melody and experiment with the notes and the rhythm. This allowed his listeners to hear many different versions of the basic tune. Other great early jazz musicians included "Jelly Roll" Morton and singer Bessie Smith.

Jazz quickly spread from New Orleans to Chicago, Kansas City, and the African American section of New York known as Harlem. White musicians, such as trumpeter Bix Beiderbecke, also began to adopt the new style. Before long, the popularity of jazz spread to Europe as well.

Many older Americans worried that jazz and the new dances were a bad influence on the nation's young people. Despite their complaints, jazz continued to grow more popular. Today, jazz is recognized as an original art form developed by African Americans. It is considered one of the most important cultural contributions of the United States.

New Writers

A new generation of American writers earned worldwide fame in the 1920s. Many of them were horrified by their experiences in World War I. They criticized Americans for caring too much about money and fun. Some became so unhappy with life in the United States that they moved to Paris, France. There, they lived as expatriates, people who leave their own country to live in a foreign land.

Hemingway and Fitzgerald Ernest Hemingway was one of the writers who lived for a time in Paris. Still a teenager at the outbreak

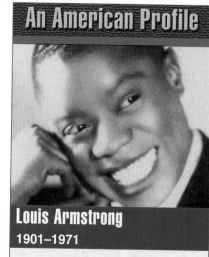

An American Profile

Louis Armstrong
1901–1971

Eleven-year-old Louis Armstrong often played a little tin horn on a rag wagon. He hoped people would throw rags and bottles into the wagon. Then, he could sell them for a penny. When he spotted a five-dollar cornet in a pawnshop window, he wondered what kind of music he could make with a real horn. He saved fifty cents a week and bought the horn. At 17, he was playing the cornet in New Orleans street parades. At 18, he joined a band on a riverboat. A listener later wrote, "That cornet [filled] the night with the hottest, the sweetest and purest jazz I'd ever heard."

Discuss Louis Armstrong's statement that at age 11, he was convinced he had music in his soul.

of World War I, he traveled to Europe to drive an ambulance on the Italian front. Hemingway drew on his war experiences in *A Farewell to Arms*, a novel about a young man's growing disgust with war. In *The Sun Also Rises*, he examined the lives of American expatriates in Europe.

Hemingway became one of the most popular writers of the 1920s. His simple but powerful style influenced many other writers.

The young writer who best captured the mood of the Roaring Twenties was Hemingway's friend F. Scott Fitzgerald. In *The Great Gatsby* and other novels, Fitzgerald examined the lives of wealthy young people who attended endless parties but could not find happiness. His characters included flappers, bootleggers, and moviemakers. Fitzgerald became a hero to college students and flappers, among others.

Other Writers Sinclair Lewis grew up in a small town in Minnesota and later moved to New York City. In novels such as *Babbitt* and *Main Street*, he presented small-town Americans as dull and narrowminded. Lewis's attitude reflected that of many city dwellers toward rural Americans. In fact, the word *babbitt* became a popular nickname for a smug businessman uninterested in literature or the arts. In 1930, Lewis was the first American to win the Nobel Prize for literature.

Poet Edna St. Vincent Millay was enormously popular. She expressed the frantic pace of the 1920s in her verse, such as her short poem "First Fig":

> 66 My candle burns at both ends;
> / It will not last the night; / But ah,
> my foes, and oh, my friends— / It
> gives a lovely light. 99
> —Edna St. Vincent Millay, "First Fig," 1920

Another writer, Eugene O'Neill, revolutionized the American theater. Most earlier playwrights had presented romantic, unrealistic stories. O'Neill shocked audiences with powerful, realistic dramas based on his years at sea. In other plays, he used experimental methods to expose the inner thoughts of tortured young people.

Harlem Renaissance

In the 1920s, large numbers of African American musicians, artists, and writers settled in Harlem, in New York City. "Harlem was like a great magnet for the Negro intellectual," said one black writer. This gathering of black artists and musicians led to the Harlem Renaissance, a rebirth of African American culture.

During the Harlem Renaissance, young black writers celebrated their African and

MAIN STREET

RESEBUD MOVIE

SINCLAIR LEWIS

A Changing American Culture

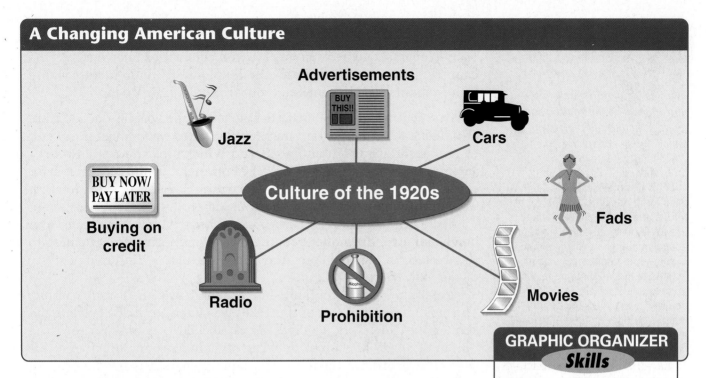

Advertisements

Jazz

Cars

BUY NOW/ PAY LATER

Buying on credit

Culture of the 1920s

Fads

Radio

Prohibition

Movies

GRAPHIC ORGANIZER
Skills

The 1920s were a time of change in the United States. A number of new inventions, ideas, and practices contributed to this change.

1. **Comprehension** Identify two items on this graphic organizer that were linked to the economic boom of the 1920s.

2. **Critical Thinking Applying Information** (a) Which items shown here affected American leisure activities? (b) Of these, which are still popular?

American heritages. They also protested prejudice and racism. For the first time, too, a large number of white Americans took notice of the achievements of black artists and writers.

Langston Hughes Probably the best-known poet of the Harlem Renaissance was Langston Hughes. He published his first poem, "The Negro Speaks of Rivers," soon after graduating from high school. The poem connected the experiences of black Americans living along the Mississippi River with those of ancient Africans living along the Nile and Niger rivers. Like other writers of the Harlem Renaissance, Hughes encouraged African Americans to be proud of their heritage.

In other poems, Hughes protested racism and acts of violence against African Americans. In addition to his poems, Hughes wrote plays, short stories, and essays about the black experience.

Other Writers Other poets such as Countee Cullen and Claude McKay also wrote of the experiences of African Americans. A graduate of New York University and Harvard, Cullen taught in a Harlem high school. In the 1920s, he won prizes for his books of poetry.

McKay came to the United States from Jamaica. In his poem "If We Must Die," he condemned the lynchings and other mob violence that black Americans suffered after World War I. The poem concludes with the lines "Like men we'll face the murderous, cowardly pack, / Pressed to the wall, dying but fighting back!"

Zora Neale Hurston, who grew up in Florida, wrote novels, essays, and short stories. Hurston grew concerned that African American folklore "was disappearing without the world realizing it had ever been." In 1928, she set out alone to travel through the South in a battered car. For two years, she collected the folk tales, songs, and prayers of black southerners. She later published these in her book *Mules and Men.*

An Age of Heroes

Radio, movies, and newspapers created celebrities known across the country. Americans followed the exploits of individuals whose achievements made them stand out from the crowd.

Sports Figures Some of the best-loved heroes of the decade were athletes. Each sport had its stars. Bobby Jones won almost every golf championship. Bill Tilden and Helen Wills ruled the tennis courts. Jack Dempsey reigned as world heavyweight boxing champion for seven years. At the age of 19, Gertrude Ederle became the first woman to swim across the English Channel.

College football also drew huge crowds. Many Americans who had never attended college rooted for college teams. They thrilled to the exploits of football stars like Red Grange, the "Galloping Ghost" of the University of Illinois.

Americans loved football, but baseball was their real passion. The most popular player of the 1920s was Babe Ruth. He became the star of the New York Yankees. Fans flocked to games to see "the Sultan of Swat" hit home runs. The 60 home runs he hit in one season set a record that lasted more than 30 years. His lifetime record of 714 home runs was not broken until 1974.

"Lucky Lindy" The greatest hero was Charles A. Lindbergh. On a gray morning in May 1927, he took off from an airport in New York to fly nonstop across the Atlantic Ocean—alone.

For more than 33 hours, Lindbergh piloted his tiny single-engine plane, the *Spirit of St. Louis,* over the stormy Atlantic. He carried no map, no parachute, and no radio. At last, he landed in Paris, France. The cheering crowd carried him across the airfield. "Lucky Lindy" returned to the United States as the hero of the decade.

AFTER YOU READ ★ ★ Section 3 Assessment ★ ★ ★

Recall

1. **Identify** Explain the significance of **(a)** Louis Armstrong, **(b)** Ernest Hemingway, **(c)** F. Scott Fitzgerald, **(d)** Sinclair Lewis, **(e)** Eugene O'Neill, **(f)** Langston Hughes, **(g)** Countee Cullen, **(h)** Claude McKay, **(i)** Zora Neale Hurston, **(j)** Babe Ruth, **(k)** Charles Lindbergh.
2. **Define** **(a)** fad, **(b)** flapper, **(c)** jazz, **(d)** expatriate.

Comprehension

3. How did flappers reflect changes in American fashion?
4. What aspects of American life did writers criticize?

5. What themes did the writers of the Harlem Renaissance address in their works?
6. Why was Charles A. Lindbergh a hero?

Critical Thinking and Writing

7. **Exploring the Main Idea** Review the Main Idea statement at the beginning of this section. Then, describe three cultural achievements of the 1920s.
8. **Analyzing Ideas** Review Edna St. Vincent Millay's poem on page 732. How does it reflect the spirit of the 1920s?

ACTIVITY

Take It to the NET

The Winter Olympics
Before 1924, the Olympic games featured only summer sports. As sports became popular in the 1920s, people wanted competition in winter sports. Use the Internet to research the 1924 Winter Olympics. Write a brief article for a sports magazine. Visit *The American Nation* section of **www.phschool.com** for help in completing the activity.

THE HARLEM RENAISSANCE

During the 1920s, the New York district of Harlem was the center of a surge of creative activity with lasting effects on American culture. Originally known as the Negro Movement, the Harlem Renaissance produced writers, artists, and jazz and blues musicians.

The best-known poet of the movement was Langston Hughes. Much of his poetry captures the rhythms of blues and jazz. Hughes also wove themes of the African American experience, history, and folklore into his work. Recognized as the Poet Laureate of Harlem, Hughes wrote more than 50 books.

The type of music known as the blues originated in the South in the late 1800s but reached a high point of development with the blues artists of the Harlem Renaissance. Their music contributed to the development of jazz and has influenced rock, folk, and country music. One of the most influential blues singers of the period was Bessie Smith, who became known as "Empress of the Blues." Her recordings were popular with black and white audiences alike.

Harlem was home to many popular nightclubs, where people came to dance, listen to jazz and blues musicians, and watch floor-shows. The Cotton Club was one of the most well-known. Duke Ellington's band was the regular club band, later alternating with the band of Cab Calloway. Both of these musicians became legendary figures in jazz.

Duke Ellington

ACTIVITY

How would you celebrate the culture of your neighborhood? Write a poem or lyrics for a song that describes your pride in your neighborhood.

4 A Nation Divided

BEFORE YOU READ

Reading Focus

- Which Americans did not share in the prosperity of the 1920s?
- Why did the Red Scare lead Americans to demand limits on immigration?
- What did the Scopes trial and the revival of the Klan reveal about society in the 1920s?
- What happened during the election of 1928?

Key Terms

company union

sabotage

anarchist

deport

nativism

quota system

Taking Notes

Copy this flowchart. As you read, fill in the boxes with some of the major events described in this section that led to limits on immigration. The first and last boxes have been completed to help you get started. Add as many boxes as you need.

- Many Americans fear communism

↓

↓

↓

- Limits on immigration

Main Idea In spite of the prosperity of the 1920s, the nation was divided between rich and poor, native-born and immigrant, and black and white.

AS YOU READ **Three farmers**
Drawing Inferences
How do you think farmers felt about "Coolidge prosperity"?

Setting the Scene In the 1920s, John J. Raskob was convinced that everyone should be rich. Raskob had been an executive with General Motors. Now he listed his job simply as "capitalist." By investing wisely, he wrote, "anyone not only can be rich but ought to be rich."

Yet, most Americans in the 1920s were not rich. In 1929, at the height of "Coolidge prosperity," more than half of American families earned less than $2,000 a year. Farmers and factory workers were experiencing hardships. Most Americans could not afford the bare necessities, let alone the investments to make them rich.

Beneath the glittering prosperity of the 1920s, the economy was already in trouble.

The Perils of Prosperity

Many Americans did not share in the boom of the 1920s. Workers in the clothing industry, for example, were hurt by changes in women's fashions. Shorter skirts meant that less cloth was needed to make dresses. Coal miners also faced hard times as oil replaced coal as the major source of energy. Railroads slashed jobs because trains were losing business to cars and trucks.

Trouble on the Farm Farmers were hit the hardest. During World War I, Europeans had bought American farm products, sending prices up. Farmers borrowed money to buy more land and tractors. They planned to pay off these loans with profits from increased production.

When the war ended, however, European farmers were again able to produce enough for their own needs. As a result, prices for American farm products dropped sharply throughout the 1920s. Farmers were unable to pay their debts. By the end of the decade, the farmers' share of national income had shrunk by almost half.

Setbacks for Labor For labor unions, too, the 1920s were a disaster. During the war, unions had worked with the government to keep production high. Labor's cooperation contributed to victory. In return, union leaders expected the government to support labor.

During the war, wages had not kept up with prices. Now, with the war over, workers demanded higher pay. When employers refused, unions launched a wave of strikes. Management moved quickly to crush the strikes. Because the government did not step in to help them, workers felt betrayed and management gained power.

The strikes turned the public against labor. One strike in particular angered Americans. In 1919, the city of Boston fired 19 police officers who had tried to join the American Federation of Labor (AFL). Boston police struck in protest. The sight of police leaving their posts shocked the country.

The later 1920s saw even more setbacks for labor. In one court case after another, judges limited the rights of unions. At the same time, employers created company unions, labor organizations that were actually controlled by management. As a result, union membership dropped from 5 million in 1920 to 3.4 million by 1929. Without strong unions, labor had little power to win higher wages.

The Red Scare

During the war, Americans had been on the alert for enemy spies and sabotage, or the secret destruction of property or interference with work in factories. These wartime worries led to a growing fear of foreigners.

The rise of communism in the Soviet Union fanned that fear. Lenin, the communist leader, called on workers everywhere to overthrow their governments. Many Americans saw the strikes that swept the nation as the start of a communist revolution.

Hunting Up Radicals The actions of anarchists, or people who oppose organized government, added to the sense of danger. One group of anarchists plotted to kill well-known Americans, including John D. Rockefeller, the head of Standard Oil. Because many anarchists were foreign-born, their attacks led to an outcry against all foreigners.

The government took harsh actions against both anarchists and Communists, or "Reds." During the Red Scare, thousands of radicals were arrested and jailed. Many foreigners were deported, or expelled from the country.

Sacco and Vanzetti The trial of two Italian immigrants in Massachusetts came to symbolize the antiforeign feeling of the 1920s. Nicola Sacco and Bartolomeo Vanzetti were arrested for robbery and murder in 1920. The two men admitted being anarchists but insisted they had committed no crime. A jury convicted them, however. Sacco and Vanzetti were then sentenced to death.

Viewing History

Seeking Justice for Sacco and Vanzetti

Did Sacco and Vanzetti get a fair trial? Many Americans did not think so. One artist created this poster calling for a new trial. Writers such as Edna St. Vincent Millay and Countee Cullen also supported the two Italian-born anarchists. In spite of protests, Sacco and Vanzetti were executed in 1927.

Analyzing Information *Why did some people question the verdict in the Sacco and Vanzetti trial?*

The Scopes Trial

Dayton, Tennessee

During the Scopes trial, the famous Chicago lawyer Clarence Darrow defended John Scopes. William Jennings Bryan, who attacked Darwin's theory of evolution, opposed Darrow. **Drawing Inferences** *How did this trial reflect some Americans' concerns about modern ideas?*

AS YOU READ **Summarize** As you read, look for important information about how nativism affected the United States in the 1920s.

The Sacco and Vanzetti trial created a furor across the nation. The evidence against the two men was limited. The judge was openly prejudiced against the two immigrants. Many Americans thought that Sacco and Vanzetti were convicted, not because they were guilty, but because they were immigrants and radicals. The two men waited in jail during a six-year fight to overturn their convictions. Their appeals were turned down. In 1927, they were executed.

The issue of whether Sacco and Vanzetti received a fair trial has been debated ever since. In the meantime, many Americans felt the case proved that the United States had to keep out dangerous radicals.

Limiting Immigration

In the end, the Red Scare died down. Yet, anger against foreigners led to a new move to limit immigration. As you recall, this kind of anti-foreign feeling is known as **nativism.**

The Quota System After years of war, millions of Europeans hoped to find a better life in the United States. American workers feared that a flood of newcomers would force wages down. Others worried that communists and anarchists would invade the United States.

Congress responded by passing the Emergency Quota Act in 1921. The act set up a quota system that allowed only a certain number of people from each country to enter the United States. Only 3 percent of the people in any national group already living in the United States in 1910 could be admitted.

The quota system favored immigrants from Northern Europe, especially Britain. In 1924, Congress passed new laws that further cut immigration, especially from Eastern Europe, which was seen as a center of anarchism and communism. In addition, Japanese were added to the list of Asians denied entry to the country.

Newcomers From Latin America Latin Americans and Canadians were not included in the quota system. As a result, Mexican immigrants continued to move to the United States. Farms and factories in the Southwest depended on Mexican workers. The pay was low, and the housing was poor. Still, the chance to earn more money was a very powerful lure. By 1930, a million or more Mexicans had crossed the border.

The Jones Act of 1917 granted American citizenship to Puerto Ricans. Poverty on the island led to a great migration to the north. In 1910, about 1,500 Puerto Ricans lived on the mainland. By 1930, there were about 53,000.

The Scopes Trial

In the 1920s, cities drew thousands of people from farms and small towns. Those who stayed in rural areas often feared that new ways of life in the city were a threat to traditional values.

The clash between old and new values erupted in the small town of Dayton, Tennessee. At the center of the controversy was Charles Darwin's theory of evolution. Darwin, a British scientist, had claimed that all life had evolved, or developed, from simpler forms over a long period of time.

Some churches condemned Darwin's theory, saying it denied the teachings of the Bible. Tennessee, Mississippi, and Arkansas passed laws that banned the teaching of Darwin's theory. In 1925, John Scopes, a biology teacher in Dayton, taught evolution to his class. Scopes was arrested and tried.

Two of the nation's best-known figures opposed each other in the Scopes trial. William Jennings Bryan, who had run for President three times, argued the state's case against Scopes. Clarence Darrow, a Chicago lawyer who had helped unions and radicals, defended Scopes.

As the trial began, the nation's attention was riveted on Dayton. Reporters recorded every word of the battle between Darrow and Bryan. "Scopes isn't on trial," Darrow thundered at one point, "civilization is on trial." In the end, Scopes was convicted and fined. The laws against teaching evolution remain on the books, although they are rarely enforced.

The New Klan

Fear of change gave new life to an old organization. In 1915, a group of white men in Georgia declared the rebirth of the Ku Klux Klan. The original Klan had used terror to keep African Americans from voting after the Civil War. The new Klan had a broader aim: to preserve the United States for white, native-born Protestants.

The new Klan waged a campaign not only against African Americans, but also against immigrants, especially Catholics and Jews. Klan members burned crosses outside people's homes. They used whippings and lynchings to terrorize immigrants and African Americans. The Klan strongly supported efforts to limit immigration.

Primary Source

The Ku Klux Klan

Journalist and author William Allen White strongly opposed the Ku Klux Klan. He states his view in a letter to Herbert Swope, editor of the New York World:
"To make a case against a birthplace, a religion, or a race is wickedly un-American and cowardly. The whole trouble with the Ku Klux Klan is that it is based upon such deep foolishness that it is bound to be a menace to good government in any community."
—William Allen White, *Selected Letters of William Allen White,* 1899–1943

Analyzing Primary Sources
Why does White feel that prejudice is cowardly?

Viewing History

Marcus Garvey

New York City

Known as "The Black Moses," Jamaican-born Marcus Garvey (at right in car) offered urban African Americans hope of relief from their difficult lives. The certificate at left is for a share of the *Black Star Line.* The ship was provided by Garvey's organization to take African Americans to Africa. **Drawing Conclusions** *Why do you think African Americans were drawn to Garvey's message?*

Because of its large membership, the Klan gained political influence. In the mid-1920s, however, many Americans became alarmed at the Klan's growing power. At the same time, scandals surfaced that showed Klan leaders had stolen money from members. Klan membership dropped sharply.

Racial Tensions in the North African Americans had hoped that their service during World War I would weaken racism at home. However, returning black soldiers found that the South was still a segregated society. In the North, too, racial prejudice was widespread.

Many African Americans moved north during and after the war. They took factory jobs in Chicago, Detroit, New York, Philadelphia, and other large cities. The newcomers often found that the only jobs open to them were low-paying ones. Also, in many neighborhoods, whites refused to rent apartments to blacks.

At the same time, many blacks newly arrived from the South wanted to live near one another. As a result, areas with large black populations grew up in many northern cities.

Many northern white workers felt threatened by the arrival of so many African Americans. Racial tension grew. In 1919, less than eight months after the end of World War I, race riots broke out in several cities. The worst took place in Chicago, leaving 38 dead.

Marcus Garvey Shocked by the racism they found, African Americans looked for new ways to cope. Marcus Garvey became one of the most popular black leaders. He started the first widespread black nationalist movement in the United States. Garvey organized the Universal Negro Improvement Association. He hoped to promote unity and pride among African Americans. He believed that African Americans needed to rely on themselves rather than white people to get ahead. "I am the equal of any white man," Garvey said.

Garvey urged African Americans to seek their roots in Africa. Although few black Americans actually went to Africa, Garvey's "Back to Africa" movement built racial pride.

Election of 1928

By 1928, Republicans had led the nation for eight years. They pointed to prosperity as their outstanding achievement. Still, when asked about the upcoming election, President Coolidge said tersely, "I do not choose to run." Instead, Secretary of Commerce Herbert Hoover easily won the Republican nomination. The Democrats chose as their candidate Alfred E. Smith, a former governor of New York.

The contrast between the candidates revealed the tensions lurking below the surface of American life. Smith, the son of Irish immigrants, was the first Catholic to run for President. City dwellers, including many immigrants and Catholics, rallied around Smith. Hoover was a self-made millionaire from the Midwest. He won votes from rural Americans and big business. Supporters of Prohibition also supported Hoover because Smith favored repeal.

In the election, Smith won the country's 12 largest cities. Rural and small-town voters supported Hoover. He won by a landslide.

Americans hoped Hoover would keep the country prosperous. Less than a year after he took office, however, the economy would come crashing down.

Section 4 Assessment

Recall
1. **Identify** Explain the significance of (a) Red Scare, (b) Sacco and Vanzetti, (c) Emergency Quota Act, (d) Jones Act, (e) Scopes trial, (f) Ku Klux Klan, (g) Marcus Garvey, (h) Herbert Hoover, (i) Alfred E. Smith.
2. **Define** (a) company union, (b) sabotage, (c) anarchist, (d) deport, (e) nativism, (f) quota system.

Comprehension
3. Describe the problems farmers and labor unions faced.
4. What limits were placed on immigration?

5. (a) What was the Scopes trial? (b) Why was the Ku Klux Klan revived?
6. How did African Americans fight racism during the 1920s?
7. What did Americans hope Hoover could achieve?

Critical Thinking
8. **Exploring the Main Idea** Review the Main Idea statement at the beginning of this section. Then, describe the conditions that divided the nation during the 1920s.
9. **Supporting a Point of View** Do you think most veterans returning from World War I were pleased with conditions at home? Explain.

ACTIVITY
Writing a Speech It is 1928, and Herbert Hoover and Alfred E. Smith are running for President. You are a speechwriter. Write a brief speech that Hoover might use to win votes. Then, write a speech that Smith might use.

CREATING A CHAPTER SUMMARY

Copy the chart below. As you read, fill in the boxes with information about the many factors that shaped the decade of the 1920s. Add as many entries as you need.

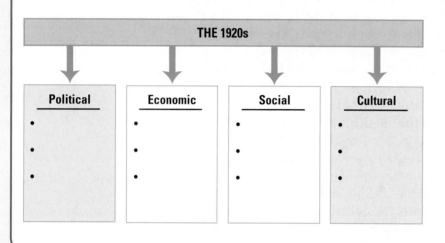

THE 1920s

Political	Economic	Social	Cultural
•	•	•	•
•	•	•	•
•	•	•	•

i TEXT

For additional review and enrichment activities, see the interactive version of *The American Nation*, available on the Web and on CD-ROM.

Take It to the NET

Chapter Self-Test For practice test questions for Chapter 25, visit *The American Nation* section of **www.phschool.com**.

Building Vocabulary

Use the chapter vocabulary words listed below to create a crossword puzzle. Exchange puzzles with a classmate. Complete the puzzles, and then check each other's answers.

1. recession
2. bull market
3. Prohibition
4. repeal
5. suburb
6. flapper
7. expatriate
8. company union
9. anarchist
10. deport

Reviewing Key Facts

11. How did Harding and Coolidge support big business? (Section 1)
12. Describe the impact of Henry Ford on American business and society. (Section 2)
13. What trends in society did the new generation of writers in the 1920s find troubling? (Section 3)
14. What contributed to the spread of anti-immigrant feelings during the 1920s? (Section 4)

Critical Thinking and Writing

15. **Connecting to Geography: Interaction** Why did so many African Americans leave the rural South during and after World War I?
16. **Sequencing (a)** Which came first, the rise of communism in Russia or the Red Scare in the United States? **(b)** How did one event follow from the other? **(c)** Were those feelings justified? Explain.
17. **Analyzing Information** How might the general atmosphere of the 1920s have contributed to the failure of Prohibition?
18. **Linking Past and Present** Movie stars and sports figures were among the people considered heroes in the 1920s. Write a brief essay about people who are viewed as heroes today.

Analyzing Primary Sources

College football was a favorite sport in the 1920s. In the following excerpt, John R. Tunis writes about the national pastime. After reading the excerpt, answer the questions that follow:

66 Attempt to question the sacredness of football and any athletic director will immediately overwhelm you with a flood of unanswerable statistics. He will show that football is the godfather of games within and without the walls of the university, that with its gate receipts are built swimming pools and squash courts, that from its profits spring crews fully armed and golf and tennis teams fully clothed. **99**

—John R. Tunis, "The Great God Football," *Harper's Monthly*, November 1928

19. **(a)** What terms are used to describe football? **(b)** What does this tell you about how people regard the sport?
20. How does football benefit the college?
21. How did the prosperity of the 1920s help football become a big business?

Determining Relevance

Value of Farmland, 1920–1925

Source: *Agricultural Statistics*

22. What happened to the value of farmland between 1920 and 1925?
   - **A** The value doubled.
   - **B** The value declined for two years and then increased.
   - **C** The value fell steadily.
   - **D** There was no significant change.
23. Is this information relevant to the economy of the 1920s? Explain.

ACTIVITIES

Connecting With . . . Government and Citizenship

Understanding Freedom of Speech The First Amendment of the Constitution allows freedom of expression, even if the ideas expressed are not popular. Choose an incident from this chapter such as the Red Scare or the Scopes trial. Write an essay analyzing whether free speech was limited or violated. Be sure to discuss relevant issues of the time that may have contributed to the incident you chose.

Take It to the NET

Connecting to Today

Exploring Economics A few experts predicted that the United States economy was headed for trouble in the 1920s. Use the Internet to find out what economists are predicting about today's economy. Write a report explaining the predictions. For help in starting this activity, visit *The American Nation* section of **www.phschool.com**.

Researching

Researching Modern Art Use the Internet to find information about an American artist of the 1920s such as Georgia O'Keeffe, Grant Wood, or Edward Hopper. Choose one artist and prepare a classroom presentation on his or her work. For help in starting this activity, visit *The American Nation* section of **www.phschool.com**.

CHAPTER 26
The Great Depression

1929–1941

1 **The Great Crash**
2 **FDR and the New Deal**
3 **Response to the New Deal**
4 **The Nation in Hard Times**

The depression spares no one: a 1932 cartoon

One-time millionaire selling apples on a street

1929
The stock market crash in October marks the beginning of the Great Depression.

1932
Jobless Bonus Army marchers protest for two months outside the Capitol building in Washington, D.C.

1933
Promising "a new deal" for the American people, Franklin D. Roosevelt becomes President.

AMERICAN EVENTS

Presidential Terms: Herbert Hoover 1929–1933   Franklin D. Roosevelt 1933–1945

1929   **1932**   **1935**

WORLD EVENTS

▲ **1929**
The depression spreads to Europe and then throughout the world.

1933 ▲
Adolf Hitler comes to power in Germany.

Drought and Dust Bowl During the Great Depression

Devastating drought and wind erosion ruined farmlands across much of the Great Plains in the 1930s.

Key
- Drought and erosion
- Dust Bowl

Albers Equal-Area Projection

0   200   400 Miles
0   200   400 Kilometers

Franklin Delano Roosevelt on the campaign trail

Gone With the Wind poster

1936

Roosevelt easily wins reelection as President.

1930s

Huge dust storms turn portions of the Great Plains into a Dust Bowl.

1939

Millions of Americans escape from their worries by watching the movie *Gone With the Wind*.

1935 —— • —— 1938 —— • —— 1941 —— •

1938 ▲
Mexico seizes foreign oil holdings.

1 The Great Crash

Reading Focus

- What were the signs of economic trouble that led to the crash of 1929 and the Great Depression?
- How did the hard times affect American families?
- How did President Hoover's response to the depression lead to the actions of the Bonus Army?

Key Terms

on margin
Black Tuesday
Great Depression
bankrupt
relief program
soup kitchen
public works
Hooverville
bonus
Bonus Army·

Taking Notes

Copy the concept web below. Include three or four blank ovals. As you read, fill in each blank oval with information on the causes of the Great Depression. Some ovals have been filled in to help get you started.

Wages do not keep up with prices

CAUSES OF THE DEPRESSION

Overproduction

Main Idea The prosperity of the 1920s hid weaknesses in the economy that led to the Great Depression of the 1930s.

Before the crash

Predict Based on what you have read in the Setting the Scene at right, what do you think will happen to President Hoover's popularity within a few months of his taking office?

Setting the Scene Most Americans had great confidence in their new President, Herbert Hoover, when he was inaugurated in March 1929. For most of the 1920s, Hoover had served in the Cabinet as secretary of commerce. In that role, he had helped to create the greatest prosperity the country had ever seen. During the 1928 campaign, he assured voters, "we in America are nearer the final triumph over poverty than ever before in the history of any land."

Then, only seven months after Hoover's inauguration, the stock market crashed. The United States began a plunge into the worst economic depression in its history. Everywhere, stunned people asked, How could this have happened?

Signs of Economic Trouble

When Hoover took office in 1929, he saw a growing economy. Along with most of the nation's leaders, he did not recognize the signs of trouble.

Hoover did realize that some Americans had not shared in the prosperity of the 1920s. Some industries, such as textiles and soft-coal mining, had been depressed throughout the 1920s. For workers in those industries, a booming economy was something they only read about in the newspapers. The words on a Pennsylvania mining town tombstone reflected their feelings of frustration. "For forty years beneath the sod / With pick and spade I did my task / The coal king's slave, but now, thank God / I'm free at last."

Farmers also faced hard times. Throughout the 1920s, farm expenses had risen much faster than the prices that farmers received for their products. Farmers did not reduce production. As a result, prices for farm products stayed low and farmers' income fell. With it went much of their power to buy goods and pay off loans.

In the mid-1920s, the economy began to slow down. No one noticed the slowdown because at that time the government did not keep detailed statistics.

The Crash

By August 1929, some investors worried that the boom might soon end. They began selling their stocks. In September, more people decided to sell. The rash of selling caused stock prices to fall. Hoover reassured investors that the "business of the country . . . is on a sound and prosperous basis." Despite the President's calming words, the selling continued and stock prices tumbled.

Many investors had bought stocks on margin. Buyers of stocks on margin pay only part of the cost of the stock when they make the purchase. They borrow the rest from their stockbrokers. With prices falling, brokers asked investors to pay back what they owed. Investors who could not repay their loans had to sell their stock.

A panic quickly set in. Between October 24 and October 29, desperate people tried to unload millions of shares. As a result, stock prices dropped even further.

When the stock market opened on Tuesday, October 29, a wild stampede of selling hit the New York Stock Exchange. Prices plunged because there were no buyers. People who thought they owned valuable stocks were left with worthless paper.

After Black Tuesday, as it came to be called, business leaders tried to restore confidence in the economy. John D. Rockefeller told reporters, "My son and I have for some days been purchasing some common stocks." Replied comedian Eddie Cantor, "Sure, who else has any money left?"

The Great Depression Begins

The period of economic hard times that followed the crash is known as the Great Depression. It lasted from 1929 to 1941.

The stock market crash did not cause the Great Depression, but it did shake people's confidence in the economy. As the depression worsened, people tried to understand how the prosperity of the 1920s had vanished.

Causes of the Great Depression Among the chief causes of the Great Depression was overproduction. American factories and farms produced vast amounts of goods in the 1920s. Yet, because wages did not keep up with prices, workers could not afford to buy many goods. Farmers also had little money for cars and other items. Soon, factories

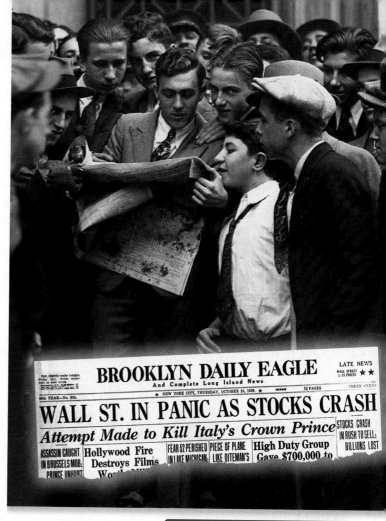

Viewing History

Panic on Wall Street!

Wall Street, New York City

Screaming headlines announced the stock market crash of October 1929. Here, people gather on the street to read the alarming news. **Applying Information** *What impact might headlines such as the one above have had on public confidence in the economy?*

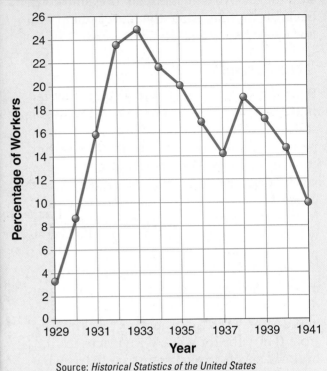

Unemployment 1929–1941

Source: *Historical Statistics of the United States*

Viewing History

Out of Work and Out of Luck

New York City

People were desperate for jobs during the depression. Painter Isaac Soyer captured the despair of unemployment in this painting. **Linking Past and Present** *If an artist today painted a scene of job seekers, do you think the mood would be any different than it is in this Isaac Soyer painting?*

and farms were producing more goods than people were buying. As orders slowed, factories closed or laid off workers.

Another cause of the depression was weakness in the banking system. During the 1920s, banks made unwise loans. For example, banks lent money to people who invested in the stock market. When the stock market crashed, borrowers could not repay their loans. Without the money from the loans, the banks could not give depositors their money when they asked for it. As a result, many banks were forced to close.

More than 5,000 banks closed between 1929 and 1932. When a bank closed, depositors lost the money that they had deposited in the bank. Often, a family's lifetime savings disappeared overnight.

The Downward Spiral After the stock market crash, the economy slid downhill at a fast pace. One disaster triggered another. The stock market crash, for example, ruined many investors. Without capital, or money, from investors, businesses could no longer grow and expand. Businesses could not turn to banks for capital because the banks were also in trouble.

As factories cut back on production, they cut wages and laid off workers. Unemployed workers, in turn, had little money to spend, so demand for goods fell further. In the end, many businesses went **bankrupt**—they were unable to pay their debts. As bankrupt businesses closed, even more people were thrown out of work.

The Great Depression led to a worldwide economic crisis. In the 1920s, the United States had loaned large sums to European nations so that they could repay their debts from World War I. When

American banks stopped making loans or demanded repayment of existing loans, European banks began to fail. The depression spread from nation to nation. By 1930, it had led to a worldwide economic collapse.

Hard Times

The United States had suffered earlier economic depressions. None, however, was as severe or lasted as long as the Great Depression. In earlier times, most Americans lived on farms and grew their own food. In the 1930s, millions of Americans lived in cities and worked in factories. When factories closed, the jobless had no money for food and no land on which to grow it.

Rising Unemployment As the depression spread, the unemployment rate soared. By the early 1930s, one in every four workers was jobless. Millions more worked shortened hours or took pay cuts. Many of the jobless lost their homes. On city streets, people sold apples and pencils, begged for money, and picked through garbage dumps for scraps of food.

The chance of finding work was small. On an average day, one New York job agency had 5,000 people looking for work. Only about 300 found jobs. In another city, police had to keep order as 15,000 women pushed and shoved to apply for six jobs cleaning offices. Some of the jobless shined shoes on street corners. Others set up sidewalk stands and sold apples.

The Human Cost During the depression, families suffered. Marriage and birth rates dropped. Hungry parents and children searched through city dumps and restaurant garbage cans. In one school, a teacher ordered a thin girl to go home to eat. "I can't," replied the girl. "This is my sister's day to eat."

The pressure of hard times led some families to split up. Fathers and even children as young as 13 or 14 years old left home to hunt for work. Their leaving meant the family had fewer people to feed.

Jobless men and women drifted from town to town looking for work. Some "rode the rails," living in railroad cars and hitching rides on freight trains. Louis Banks, a young African American, later described what it was like to ride the rails:

66 Twenty-five or thirty would be out on the side of the rail, white and colored. They didn't have no mothers or sisters, they didn't have no home, they were dirty, they had overalls on, they didn't have no food, they didn't have anything. 99

— Louis Banks, Interview, 1970

Americans did their best to cope. Neighbors shared what little they had. Some families doubled up, taking in aunts, uncles, and cousins. Some families began to grow vegetables and can foods instead of shopping in stores.

The Great Depression shook Americans' belief in themselves. "No matter that others suffered the same fate, the inner voice whispered, 'I'm a failure,'" one unemployed man wrote.

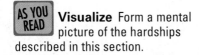

AS YOU READ **Visualize** Form a mental picture of the hardships described in this section.

Hoover Responds

President Hoover was deeply concerned about the suffering. However, Hoover did not believe that government should become directly involved in helping to end the business crisis. He feared that government might become too powerful. It was up to businesses, he felt, to work together to end the downslide.

Government Aid At first, Hoover also opposed government **relief programs**—programs to help the needy. Instead, the President urged business leaders to keep workers employed and to maintain wages.

Hoover also called on private charities to help the needy. Churches set up **soup kitchens,** places where the hungry could get a free meal. Ethnic communities organized their own relief efforts. In San Francisco's Chinatown, fraternal societies gave out food and clothing. Father Divine, an African American religious leader in New York's Harlem, fed 3,000 hungry people a day. Mexican Americans and Puerto Ricans turned to aid societies. Still, the numbers of the needy soon overwhelmed private charities.

As conditions grew worse, Hoover realized that he had to take other steps. He set up public works programs. **Public works** are projects built by the government for public use. The government hired workers to build schools, construct dams, and pave highways. By providing jobs, these programs enabled people to earn money.

Hoover also asked Congress to approve the Reconstruction Finance Corporation, or RFC, in 1932. The RFC loaned money to banks, railroads, and insurance companies to help them stay in business. Saving these businesses, Hoover hoped, would save thousands of jobs.

The Depression Deepens Hoover did more to reverse hard times than any previous President. However, his efforts were too little and came too late. In 1931, as the third winter of the depression approached, more and more people joined the ranks of the hungry and homeless. "Men are sitting in the parks all day long and all night long," wrote one man in Detroit.

Many people blamed the President for doing too little. They gave the name **Hoovervilles** to the shacks where the homeless lived. People spoke of "Hoover blankets," the newspapers used by the homeless to keep warm when they slept outside. A cardboard patch that covered a hole in a shoe was called "Hoover leather." Men, women, and children lined up for "Hoover stew," the name they gave to the thin soup they received in soup kitchens.

Viewing History

On the Soup Kitchen Line

New York City

Long lines of hungry people were a common sight in towns and cities during the depression. These New Yorkers wait for a soup kitchen to open. **Drawing Inferences** *What impact do you think eating at soup kitchens had on the self-esteem of these men?*

The Bonus Army

While people waited for the government to help, one group of Americans took action. After World War I, Congress had voted to give veterans a **bonus,** or additional sum of money, to be paid in 1945. In 1932, more than 20,000 jobless veterans marched to Washington to demand the bonus right away. For two months, the **Bonus Army,** as the veterans were called, camped in a tent city along the Potomac River.

The House of Representatives voted to give the veterans the bonus at once, but the Senate rejected the bill. Senators thought that the cost would prevent government action to aid the country's recovery. Many discouraged veterans then went home. However, thousands of others remained, vowing to stay until 1945 if necessary.

Local police tried to force the veterans to leave. Battles with police left four people dead. Hoover then ordered General Douglas MacArthur to clear out the veterans. Using cavalry, tanks, machine guns, and tear gas, MacArthur moved into the camp and burned it to the ground. An editorial in the *Washington News* years later expressed the shock many Americans felt at the time:

> 66 What a pitiful spectacle is that of the great American Government, mightiest in the world, chasing unarmed men, women, and children with Army tanks. . . . If the Army must be called out to make war on unarmed citizens, this is no longer America. 99
> —*Washington News,* "The Summer of the BEF," November 23, 1946

After the attack on the Bonus Army, the President lost what little support he still had. Convinced that the country needed a change, Americans turned to a new leader.

 AFTER YOU READ

Section 1 Assessment

Recall

1. **Identify** Explain the significance of **(a)** Herbert Hoover, **(b)** Black Tuesday, **(c)** Great Depression, **(d)** Hooverville, **(e)** Bonus Army.
2. **Define (a)** on margin, **(b)** bankrupt, **(c)** relief program, **(d)** soup kitchen, **(e)** public works, **(f)** bonus.

Comprehension

3. List two signs of economic trouble in the 1920s.
4. What impact did the Depression have on American families?
5. What was Hoover's response to the depression and to the Bonus Army?

Critical Thinking and Writing

6. **Exploring the Main Idea** Review the Main Idea statement at the beginning of this section. Then, write at least three questions that you would ask an economist in order to determine the causes of the Great Depression.
7. **Finding the Main Idea** Review the subsection "Hoover Responds" on page 750. **(a)** What is the main idea of the subsection? **(b)** State two facts that support the main idea.

ACTIVITY

 Take It to the NET

Writing a News Report Use the Internet to find information on the Bonus Army. Then, prepare the outline of a script for a TV news program reporting on the grievances of the Bonus Army veterans. Visit *The American Nation* section of **www.phschool.com** for help in starting the activity.

2 FDR and the New Deal

BEFORE YOU READ

Reading Focus

- Why did voters elect Franklin D. Roosevelt President in 1932?
- What was the Hundred Days, and what were its accomplishments?
- How did the New Deal provide relief and promote recovery?
- What economic reforms were aimed at preventing another depression?

Key Terms

polio
bank holiday
fireside chat
Hundred Days
New Deal
Civilian Conservation Corps
National Recovery Administration
Tennessee Valley Authority

Taking Notes

As you read, fill in the table with New Deal programs aimed at relief, recovery, or preventing another depression.

RELIEF FOR THE JOBLESS	PLANS FOR ECONOMIC RECOVERY	PREVENTING ANOTHER DEPRESSION
•	•	•
•	•	•

Main Idea The New Deal restored hope by providing programs that aimed at relief, recovery, and economic reform.

As You Read

Looking for new leadership

Use Prior Knowledge Based on what you have read in Section 1, summarize what you think Roosevelt's top priorities were when he became President in March 1933.

Setting the Scene

In Albany, New York, Governor Franklin Roosevelt read about the Bonus Army tragedy in the morning papers. Roosevelt was angry at the way Hoover had handled the marchers.

Roosevelt said he would have handled things differently. He understood the despair of the American people. He had told a friend, "I have looked into the faces of thousands of Americans. They have the frightened look of lost children. . . . They are saying: 'We're caught in something we don't understand.'"

Roosevelt knew that the government seemed helpless to most people. He saw that Americans looked for new leadership. In 1932, the Democrats chose him to run for President.

The election results gave Roosevelt his chance. His New Deal program began a new relationship between government and the economy. From then on, the federal government took an active role in managing the American economy.

Franklin D. Roosevelt

Franklin Delano Roosevelt, known as FDR, came from a wealthy, influential family. He attended Harvard University and Columbia Law School. In 1905, he married a distant cousin, Anna Eleanor Roosevelt.

During World War I, FDR served as assistant secretary of the navy. In 1920, he was the Democratic candidate for Vice President but lost in the Harding landslide.

A Devastating Disease Then, in the summer of 1921, Roosevelt was stricken with a severe case of polio. A disease caused by a virus, polio has been almost totally wiped out in the United States today. However, before the development of a vaccine in the 1950s, polio was a devastating disease. FDR's legs were totally paralyzed. He struggled for years to rebuild his strength.

In time, Roosevelt returned to public life. In 1928, he was elected governor of New York. Then, in 1932, the Democrats made him their presidential candidate. The Republicans again nominated Herbert Hoover, even though they knew he had little chance of winning.

A Call to Action Roosevelt set a new tone right from the start. He broke with tradition by flying to the Democratic convention to accept the nomination in person. Standing before the delegates, he declared: "I pledge myself to a new deal for the American people."

Roosevelt did not spell out what he meant by "a new deal." Still, he sounded a hopeful note. In campaign speeches, he promised to help the jobless, poor farmers, and the elderly.

Voters responded to FDR's confident manner and personal charm. On election day, he won a landslide victory. Democrats also gained many seats in Congress. On inauguration day, the new President addressed the American people with optimism:

> 66 This great nation will endure as it has endured, will revive and will prosper. So, first of all, let me assert my firm belief that the only thing we have to fear is fear itself— nameless, unreasoning, unjustified terror which paralyzes needed efforts to convert retreat into advance. 99
> —Franklin D. Roosevelt, Inaugural Address, March 4, 1933

President Roosevelt then issued a call to action. "This nation asks for action and action now," he said. Many Americans welcomed this energetic new President, especially since Hoover's more cautious approach had failed to end the nation's economic crisis.

The Hundred Days

During his campaign for the presidency, FDR had sought advice on how to fight the depression. He turned to a number of college professors who were experts on economic issues. These experts, nicknamed the Brain Trust, helped Roosevelt to plan bold new programs.

Once in office, President Roosevelt chose able advisers. Harold Ickes (IH keez), a Republican reformer from Chicago, became secretary of the interior. The President named social worker Frances Perkins the secretary of labor. Perkins was the first woman to hold a Cabinet post.

The new President moved forward on many fronts. He urged his staff to "take a method and try it. If it fails, admit it and try another. But above all try something."

Saving the Banks Roosevelt's first challenge was the nation's crumbling banking system. Many banks had closed. Fearful depositors had withdrawn their savings from other banks. People hid their money under mattresses or buried it in their yards.

The President knew that without sound banks, the economy could not recover. On his second day in office, he declared a **bank holiday.** He closed every bank in the country for four days. He then asked Congress to pass the Emergency Banking Relief Act. Under

American Profiles

Franklin Roosevelt 1882–1945
Eleanor Roosevelt 1884–1962

Both Franklin and Eleanor Roosevelt came from wealthy and well-known families. Both believed that the wealthy had a responsibility to help those less fortunate. As President, FDR put this belief into action with his New Deal. As First Lady, Eleanor spoke out on issues ranging from conditions in coal mines to justice for African Americans. She also acted as the President's "eyes and ears," traveling about the country and reporting back to him.

After FDR's death in 1945, Eleanor won fame in her own right. From 1945 to 1953, she represented the United States at the United Nations.

Do wealthy people have a duty to aid those who are less fortunate? Explain.

this act, only those banks with enough funds to meet depositors' demands could reopen. Others had to stay closed.

A week after taking office, President Roosevelt spoke to Americans by radio. Under the new law, the President told the people, "it is safer to keep your money in a reopened bank than under your mattress."

The radio broadcast worked. FDR explained things so clearly, said humorist Will Rogers, that even the bankers understood the situation. Reassured by the President, depositors returned their money to banks, and the banking system grew stronger.

FDR gave 30 radio speeches while in office. He called them fireside chats because he spoke from a chair near a fireplace in the White House. All across the nation, families gathered around their radios to listen to Roosevelt. Many felt the President understood their problems.

A Flood of New Laws The bank bill was the first of many bills that FDR sent to Congress during his first three months in office. Between March 9 and June 16, 1933, Congress passed a record 15 major new laws. Even the President admitted he was "a bit shell-shocked" by the Hundred Days, as this period was called.

The bills covered programs from job relief to planning for economic recovery. Together, they made up Roosevelt's New Deal. The New Deal laid out three main goals: relief for the jobless, plans for economic recovery, and reforms to prevent another depression.

AS YOU READ **Find Main Ideas** As you read the information under the next three blue headings, jot down the main accomplishments of the New Deal.

Relief for the Jobless

In 1933, when Roosevelt took office, 13 million Americans were out of work. The President asked Congress for a variety of programs to help the jobless.

CCC and FERA Among the earliest New Deal programs was the Civilian Conservation Corps (CCC). The CCC hired unemployed single men between the ages of 18 and 25. For $1 a day, they planted trees, built bridges, worked on flood-control projects, and developed new parks. The CCC served a double purpose. It conserved natural resources, and it gave jobs to young people. The Federal Emergency Relief Administration (FERA) gave federal money to state and local agencies. These agencies then distributed the money to the unemployed.

WPA The Works Progress Administration (WPA) came into existence in 1935. The WPA put the jobless to work making clothes and building hospitals, schools, parks, playgrounds, and airports.

The WPA also hired artists, photographers, actors, writers, and composers. Artists painted murals on public buildings. The Federal Theatre put on new plays for adults and children, as well as classics by such writers as Shakespeare.

WPA writers collected information about American life, folklore, and traditions. Some WPA writers interviewed African Americans who had lived under slavery. Today, scholars still use these interviews to learn firsthand about slave life.

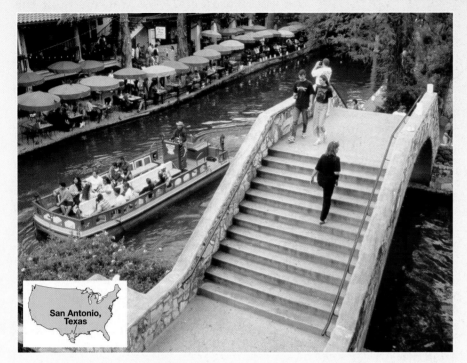

San Antonio, Texas

San Antonio River Walk

The Works Progress Administration built hundreds of buildings, bridges, and highways during the depression. On the San Antonio River in Texas, WPA workers constructed a network of concrete walkways, bridges, and stairs. Today, tourists from around the world enjoy the hotels, shops, and restaurants along the San Antonio River Walk, or Paseo del Rio.

 Take It to the NET

Virtual Field Trip For an interactive look at the River Walk, visit *The American Nation* section of **www.phschool.com**.

Critics accused the WPA of creating make-work projects that did little to benefit the nation in the long run. "People don't eat in the long run," replied a New Dealer. "They eat every day."

Promoting Recovery

To bring about recovery, the President had to boost both industry and farming. He developed programs that greatly expanded the government's role in the economy.

Helping Industry Overproduction and declining prices had been a major cause of the depression. Low prices during the depression had caused business to fail and created widespread unemployment. To help industry, New Dealers drew up plans to control production, stabilize prices, and keep workers on the job.

A key new law was the National Industrial Recovery Act (NIRA). Under this law, each industry wrote a code, or set of rules and standards, for production, wages, prices, and working conditions. The NIRA tried to end price cutting and worker layoffs.

To enforce the new codes, Congress set up the National Recovery Administration (NRA). Companies that followed the NRA codes stamped a blue eagle on their products. The government encouraged people to do business only with companies displaying the NRA eagle. The NRA soon ran into trouble, however. Many companies ignored the codes. Also, small businesses felt that the codes favored the biggest firms.

The NIRA also set up the Public Works Administration (PWA). It promoted recovery by hiring workers for thousands of public works projects. PWA workers built the Grand Coulee Dam in Washington, public schools in Los Angeles, two aircraft carriers for the navy, and a deep-water port in Brownsville, Texas. Despite these efforts, the PWA did little to bring about recovery.

Helping Farmers On farms, overproduction remained the main problem. Surpluses kept prices and farmers' incomes low. A surplus occurs when farmers produce more than they can sell.

To help farmers, the President asked Congress to pass the Agricultural Adjustment Act (AAA). Under the AAA, the government paid farmers not to grow certain crops. Roosevelt hoped that with smaller harvests, the laws of supply and demand would force prices to rise.

The government also paid farmers to plow surplus crops under the soil and to destroy surplus cows and pigs. Many Americans were outraged that crops and livestock were being destroyed when people in the cities were going hungry. Yet, the plan seemed necessary to help farmers recover and keep them growing food.

The Rural Electrification Administration (REA) was created to help people in rural areas get the same electrical service as people in urban areas. The REA provided money to extend electric lines to rural areas. The number of farms with electricity rose from 10 percent to 25 percent. Electricity helped save many farms from ruin. For example, with refrigeration, dairy farmers did not have to worry about milk going sour before it could be sent to market.

Tennessee Valley Authority Perhaps the boldest program of the Hundred Days was the Tennessee Valley Authority (TVA). It set out to remake the Tennessee River Valley. This vast region often suffered from terrible floods. Because the farmland was so poor, more than half the region's families were on relief.

The TVA was a daring experiment in regional planning. To control flooding, TVA engineers built 49 dams in seven states. (See the map on page 758.) The dams also produced cheap electric power. In addition to building dams, the TVA deepened river channels for shipping. It planted new forests to conserve soil and developed new fertilizers to improve farmland. The agency also set up schools and health centers.

The TVA sparked a furious debate. Critics argued that the government had no right to take business away from private companies in the region. Power companies in the Tennessee River Valley were especially outraged. They pointed out that the government, which did not have to make a profit for shareholders, could supply electrical power more cheaply than a private company could. Having to compete with the government, they said, might force them out of business.

Supporters replied that the TVA showed how the government could use its resources to help private enterprise. In the end, the program transformed a region of desperate poverty into a prosperous and productive area.

Preventing Another Depression

The third New Deal goal was to prevent another depression by reforming the economic system. During the Hundred Days, Congress passed laws regulating the stock market and the banking system. The Truth-in-Securities Act was designed to end the risky buying and selling of stocks in the hope of making a quick profit. Experts agreed that uncontrolled buying and selling was a leading cause of the 1929 crash.

Another law set up the Federal Deposit Insurance Corporation (FDIC). It insured savings accounts in banks approved by the government. If a bank insured by the FDIC failed, the government would make sure depositors received their money.

Later New Deal laws brought about other kinds of reforms. Laws regulated gas and electric companies. In 1938, a new law extended the Pure Food and Drug Act of 1906. It protected consumers by requiring manufacturers to list the ingredients in certain products. It also made sure that new medicines passed strict tests before they were put on the market.

AFTER YOU READ

Section 2 Assessment

Recall

1. **Identify** Explain the significance of **(a)** Franklin Roosevelt, **(b)** Hundred Days, **(c)** New Deal, **(d)** Civilian Conservation Corps, **(e)** National Recovery Administration, **(f)** Tennessee Valley Authority.
2. **Define (a)** polio, **(b)** bank holiday, **(c)** fireside chat.

Comprehension

3. What issues were responsible for FDR's victory in 1932?
4. What measures did the government take during the Hundred Days to end the depression?

5. What New Deal measures provided relief for the jobless and promoted recovery from the depression?
6. What laws were passed to prevent another depression?

Critical Thinking and Writing

7. **Exploring the Main Idea** Review the Main Idea statement at the beginning of this section. Then, write an outline for a speech that FDR might give to explain the goals of his New Deal programs.
8. **Drawing Inferences** What evidence in this section suggests the reasons why poor Americans were so drawn to the wealthy FDR?

ACTIVITY

Asking Questions
Write five questions that you might ask if you were conducting an interview with FDR. Include questions about his illness, his family, and the goals of the New Deal.

The TVA Today

The Tennessee Valley Authority has more than met the goals it set when it began in 1933. The TVA has helped people who live in the Tennessee Valley by generating electric power, promoting business growth, and supporting a healthy river system.

Americans can enjoy the clean waters of the TVA's lakes and rivers.

The TVA works with local communities to protect wildlife and clean up rivers and streams.

Tennessee Valley Authority

Illinois 90°W · Indiana 85°W · Kentucky
Ohio R.
Missouri
Virginia
Cumberland R.
80°W
Nashville · Knoxville · North Carolina
Arkansas · Tennessee · Asheville
35°N · Memphis · Chattanooga
Huntsville · South Carolina
Georgia
Mississippi · Birmingham · Atlanta · Albers Equal-Area Projection
0   50   100 Miles
Alabama
0 50 100 Kilometers
Jackson

Key
↘ Major dam   ☐ Area served by TVA electric power

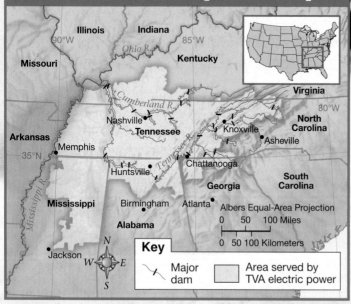

Dams built by the TVA provide electricity, control flooding, increase the region's water supply, and provide lakes for recreation.

Since 1933, the TVA has built 49 giant dams and many smaller ones. The largest dams are shown on this map. The TVA is now the largest publicly owned power company in the United States. It provides electricity to eight million people who live in seven different states.

ACTIVITY

Your family has lived in the Tennessee Valley since the 1920s. Your grandfather has told you what life was like before the TVA. Pick any song you know, and write lyrics to celebrate the accomplishments of the TVA.

3 Response to the New Deal

Reading Focus

- How did critics of the New Deal propose to end the depression?
- Why did FDR try to expand the Supreme Court?
- What New Deal measures were meant to provide labor reform and social security?
- On balance, did the New Deal benefit or hurt the country?

Key Terms

pension
National Labor Relations Act
collective bargaining
Congress of Industrial Organizations
sit-down strike
Social Security Act
deficit spending
national debt

Taking Notes

As you read, complete the following chart to show some of the effects of the New Deal. One box has been filled in to help get you started. Add as many boxes as you need.

THE NEW DEAL

Increased protection for unions

Main Idea As the New Deal came under criticism, Roosevelt launched a series of far-reaching reforms.

Setting the Scene

By 1934, New Deal programs had restored hope, but they had not brought back prosperity. Although FDR was very popular, not all Americans supported him. Some people believed that government was doing too much—that it was interfering too much in people's lives. Others believed that it was doing too little—that it should take more drastic steps to aid the American people. One of the latter was Upton Sinclair, the novelist and muckraker who had written *The Jungle*.

In 1934, Sinclair ran for governor of California. Under the slogan "End Poverty in California," Sinclair proposed that the state rent or purchase unused factories and give them to workers. The workers could then keep what they manufactured.

Sinclair lost the election, but his good showing was a warning to Roosevelt. Voices of protest could be heard across the land. They reminded FDR that more needed to be done to end the depression.

Critics of the New Deal

Some of Roosevelt's most severe critics were people who had supported him in 1932. Among the most outspoken of these was Senator Huey Long of Louisiana. Long believed that the New Deal had not gone far enough to help the poor. Adopting the motto "Share Our Wealth," Long called for heavy taxes on the rich. He promised to use the tax money to provide every American family with a house, a car, and a decent annual income. Millions of people, especially the poor, cheered Long's idea. They overlooked the fact that he had used bribery and threats of violence to win political power.

A California doctor, Francis Townsend, also had a plan. The government, he said, had turned its back on older citizens. Townsend

AS YOU READ A Roosevelt critic campaigns

Use Prior Knowledge Based on what you read about Upton Sinclair in Chapter 22, do you think that the writer was pushing FDR to create a more active or less active role for government?

ALL I SAID WAS "GIMME SIX MORE JUSTICES!"

"Packing" the Supreme Court

This 1937 cartoon comments on the reaction of the Congress to the plan to expand the Supreme Court.

1. **Comprehension** **(a)** Who is the man leaning on the fence? **(b)** What does the donkey represent?

2. **Finding the Main Idea** How does the cartoonist show that the court-packing plan caused a huge uproar?

3. **Critical Thinking** **Interpreting a Political Cartoon** According to the cartoonist, what was the impact of Roosevelt's Supreme Court plan on party loyalty?

Civics

wanted everyone over age 60 to get a pension of $200 a month. A **pension** is a sum of money paid to people on a regular basis after they retire. People receiving the pension would have to retire, thus freeing up a job for someone else. They would also agree to spend the pension money at once to boost the economy.

On the other hand, many conservatives feared the new government programs. They formed the Liberty League to combat FDR's actions. The League complained that the New Deal interfered too much with business and with people's lives. The government, they warned, was taking away basic American freedoms.

FDR and the Supreme Court

In 1935, members of the Supreme Court began to attack the New Deal. In that year, the Supreme Court ruled that the National Industrial Recovery Act was unconstitutional. The NIRA, said the Court, gave too much power to the President and to the federal government. A year later, the Court struck down the Agricultural Adjustment Act. Then, it overturned eight other New Deal laws. To Roosevelt, the Supreme Court rulings threatened not only the New Deal but also his ability to lead the nation.

A Plan to Expand the Court Roosevelt waited until after the 1936 election to take action. In that election, he easily beat his Republican opponent, Alf Landon of Kansas.

Soon after his inauguration in January 1937, Roosevelt put forward a plan to enlarge the federal courts. He called for raising the number of Justices on the Supreme Court from 9 to 15. The change

New Deal Programs

PROGRAM	INITIALS	BEGUN	PURPOSE
Civilian Conservation Corps	CCC	1933	Provided jobs for young men to plant trees, build bridges and parks, and set up flood-control projects
Tennessee Valley Authority	TVA	1933	Built dams to provide cheap electric power to seven southern states; set up schools and health centers
Federal Emergency Relief Act	FERA	1933	Gave relief to unemployed and needy
Agricultural Adjustment Act	AAA	1933	Paid farmers not to grow certain crops
National Recovery Administration	NRA	1933	Enforced codes that regulated wages, prices, and working conditions
Public Works Administration	PWA	1933	Built ports, schools, and aircraft carriers
Federal Deposit Insurance Corporation	FDIC	1933	Insured savings accounts in banks approved by the government
Rural Electrification Administration	REA	1935	Loaned money to extend electricity to rural areas
Works Progress Administration	WPA	1935	Employed men and women to build hospitals, schools, parks, and airports; employed artists, writers, and musicians
Social Security Act	SSA	1935	Set up a system of pensions for the elderly, the unemployed, dependent children, and people with disabilities

would make it possible for him to appoint six new Justices who supported his programs.

Mixed Results The President's move raised a loud outcry. Both supporters and critics of the New Deal accused him of trying to "pack" the Court with Justices who supported his views. They saw his move as a threat to the principle of separation of powers.

For six months, the President fought for his plan. Even his allies in Congress deserted him. Finally, he withdrew his proposal.

Still, in the end, Roosevelt got the Supreme Court majority he wanted without a battle. One Justice who had voted against many New Deal laws changed his views. Another retired. Roosevelt filled his place with a new Justice who was favorable to his programs.

Labor Reforms

During the years of the New Deal, FDR supported programs to help workers. In 1935, Congress passed the National Labor Relations Act, or Wagner Act. Senator Robert Wagner of New York, the act's sponsor, was a strong supporter of labor.

Unions Grow Stronger The Wagner Act protected American workers from unfair management practices, such as firing a worker for joining a union. It also guaranteed workers the right to collective bargaining. Collective bargaining is the process by which a union representing a group of workers negotiates with management for a contract. Workers had fought for this right since the late 1800s.

CHART Skills

Congress passed dozens of laws as part of the New Deal. This chart describes 10 major New Deal programs created to fight the depression.

1. **Comprehension** (a) Which programs provided work for the unemployed? (b) Which provided financial aid?

2. **Critical Thinking Making Generalizations** Based on the "Begun" column in the chart, what generalization can you make about when most New Deal laws were passed?

Civics

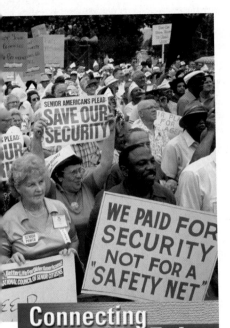

The Wagner Act helped union membership grow from 3 million to 9 million during the 1930s. Union membership got a further boost when John L. Lewis set up the Congress of Industrial Organizations (CIO). The CIO represented workers in whole industries, such as steel, automobiles, and textiles.

With more members, unions increased their bargaining power. They also became a powerful force in politics.

Struggles and Victories Despite the Wagner Act, employers tried to stop workers from joining unions. Violent confrontations often resulted.

Workers then tried a new strategy. At the Goodyear Tire Factory in Akron, Ohio, workers staged a sit-down strike. They stopped all machines and refused to leave the factory until Goodyear recognized their union. The tactic worked. Workers at other factories made use of sit-down strikes until the Supreme Court outlawed them in 1939.

Social Security

On another front, the President sought to help the elderly. In the 1930s, the United States was the only major industrial nation that did not have a formal pension program. Roosevelt and Secretary of Labor Perkins pushed to enact an old-age pension program.

In September 1935, Congress passed the Social Security Act. The new law had three parts. First, it set up a system of pensions for older people. Payments from employers and employees supported this system.

Second, the new act set up the nation's first system of unemployment insurance. People who lost their jobs received small payments until they found work again. Third, the act gave states money to support dependent children and people with disabilities.

Critics condemned the Social Security law. Some liberals pointed out that it did not include farm workers, domestic servants, or the self-employed—many of whom were women or members of minority groups. Conservatives, on the other hand, saw Social Security as another way for the government to take money away from people who had jobs.

Despite these attacks, the Social Security system survived and expanded over the years. Today, it provides medical benefits and pensions to older Americans as well as unemployment insurance to workers.

The New Deal Balance Sheet

The New Deal changed American government forever. Ever since, Americans have debated whether the change was good or bad for the country.

Arguments Against the New Deal Before the 1930s, most Americans had little contact with the federal government. New Deal programs, however, touched almost every citizen. The federal government grew in size and power.

Many people worried about the increased power of government. They complained that the government was intruding in people's

Connecting to Today

Social Security

Americans rely on the Social Security system today as much as they did in the 1930s. Yet, population trends suggest that problems may lie ahead for the system. For one, a large number of people will be retiring between now and 2020. Also, people tend to live longer today than they did in the past. These two trends mean that the system will have to pay out more money. In fact, the system may soon be paying more out in benefits than it is bringing in from worker taxes.

The government is looking at ways to solve the problem. Many solutions have been proposed. They include making benefits smaller, raising taxes, and having people work more years before they retire.

What problem may affect the Social Security system?

AS YOU READ **Draw Inferences** In what ways do you think the New Deal "changed American government forever"?

lives, threatening both individual freedoms and private property. These critics called for a return to the traditional policy of laissez faire—the idea that government should play as small a role as possible in the economy.

Critics also expressed alarm because the government was spending more than it took in. This practice of **deficit spending** was creating a huge increase in the **national debt,** or the total sum of money the government owes.

Finally, despite its vast spending, the New Deal had not achieved its major goal—ending the depression. In fact, full economic recovery did not come until 1941. By then, the United States was producing goods for nations fighting in World War II.

Arguments for the New Deal Supporters of the New Deal noted that FDR had steered the nation through the worst days of the depression. New Deal legislation had ended the banking crisis, protected farmers, and found work for millions of unemployed.

Supporters also argued that the government had a responsibility to use its power to help all its citizens, not just business and the wealthy. Programs like Social Security, New Dealers said, were necessary for national survival.

Most important of all, supporters argued, the New Deal had saved the nation's democratic system. Elsewhere in the world, people were turning to dictators to lead them out of hard times. President Roosevelt, on the other hand, restored the nation to economic health while preserving its liberties.

Over the years, Americans have continued to discuss the expanded role of government that began during the New Deal. The issue of whether government management of the economy helps or harms the free enterprise system remains a lively one today.

Section 3 Assessment

Recall
1. **Identify** Explain the significance of **(a)** National Labor Relations Act, **(b)** Congress of Industrial Organizations, **(c)** Social Security Act.
2. **Define** **(a)** pension, **(b)** collective bargaining, **(c)** sitdown strike, **(d)** deficit spending, **(e)** national debt.

Comprehension
3. How did New Deal critics propose to end the depression?
4. Why did many people oppose FDR's court-packing plan?
5. What New Deal laws dealt with labor reform and social security?

6. Was the New Deal good or bad for the country?

Critical Thinking and Writing
7. **Exploring the Main Idea** Review the Main Idea statement at the beginning of this section. Then, write a series of headlines that might have appeared in a newspaper of the times dealing with critics of the New Deal, FDR's plan to pack the Supreme Court, and New Deal measures after 1935.
8. **Analyzing Information** Using the chart on page 761, explain why labor unions strongly supported FDR.

ACTIVITY

Take It to the NET
Connecting to Today
Use the Internet to find out more about the impact of the New Deal on the way we live today. Then, organize a debate on the following topic: "The New Deal saved the free enterprise system." Visit *The American Nation* section of **www.phschool.com** for help in completing the activity.

Evaluating Long-Term Effects

Historical events may have both short-term and long-term effects. Short-term effects take place soon after an event, but long-term effects build up over time. Evaluating long-term effects is often helpful in understanding the present and anticipating the future.

Look at the chart of short-term and long-term effects of New Deal laws. Note that some of the long-term effects are totally different from the immediate effects of the New Deal.

Short-Term and Long-Term Effects

THE NEW DEAL

Short-Term Effects

- Social Security payments enable people to retire with pensions
- Union membership and power grow
- Farmers benefit from agricultural price supports
- The FDIC insures bank deposits
- The Securities and Exchange Commission oversees the stock market

Long-Term Effects

- Social Security protects millions of Americans but may not be able to pay full benefits in the future
- High-wage and low-wage earners continue to have different kinds of protection and benefits
- Americans have economic safeguards provided by the government
- A split between liberals and conservatives still affects public life

Learn the Skill *To evaluate long-term effects, use the following steps:*

1. **Identify the short-term effects.** Determine the immediate effects of an event.

2. **Identify the long-term effects.** Determine the consequences over time.

3. **Evaluate the long-term effects.** How do the lasting effects continue to influence people?

Practice the Skill *Study the chart and then answer the following questions:*

1. What was one short-term effect of the New Deal?

2. What is one long-term effect of the New Deal?

3. **(a)** How does the New Deal continue to affect Americans? **(b)** Why are some Americans worried about the future of Social Security? **(c)** Select one current political or social issue and describe how liberals and conservatives differ on that issue.

Apply the Skill *See the Chapter Review and Assessment.*

4 The Nation in Hard Times

Reading Focus

- What caused the Dust Bowl?
- How did the depression affect women?
- How did the New Deal reach out to help African Americans and other groups of Americans?
- How did the creative arts reflect the needs of Americans during the depression?

Key Terms

Dust Bowl

migrant worker

Black Cabinet

civil rights

Indian New Deal

Taking Notes

As you read, prepare an outline of this section. Use roman numerals to indicate the major headings, capital letters for the subheadings, and numbers for the supporting details. The sample below will help you get started.

> I. The Dust Bowl
>   A.
>   B.
> II. Women Face the Depression
>   A.
>   B. An active first lady
> III. African Americans

Main Idea Many Americans found relief from the hard times of the Great Depression in the work of creative artists.

Setting the Scene In 1933, a reporter named Lorena Hickok set out from Washington on a government assignment. She was to report firsthand on conditions in rural areas. What she saw shocked even this veteran newswoman:

> ❝ I visited one group of . . . miners and their families, who had been living in tents for two years. . . . It [was] fairly common to see children entirely naked. . . . And some had nothing at all, actually hadn't eaten for a couple of days. ❞
>
> —Lorena Hickok, "Report From West Virginia," August 13–26, 1933

Few Americans suffered as much as the miners of West Virginia during the depression. Most people were able to eat adequately. Most still had some work. Some were helped by the New Deal; others were left out. Yet, almost all learned to live much more cheaply as they struggled to make ends meet.

The Dust Bowl

During much of the 1930s, states from Texas to the Dakotas suffered a severe drought. One region in the central Great Plains was especially hard hit. The topsoil dried out. High winds carried the soil away in blinding dust storms. As a result, this area became known as the Dust Bowl.

Buried Under Dust Dust storms buried farmhouses, fences, and even trees over large areas of the plains. People put shutters over doors and windows, but the dust blew in anyway. Even food crunched when it was chewed. One storm blew dust from Oklahoma to Albany, New York. A Kansas farmer sadly reported that he sat by his window counting the farms going by.

AS YOU READ Struggling to survive

Find Main Ideas How did scenes such as this affect Lorena Hickok?

What caused the disaster? Years of over-grazing by cattle and plowing by farmers destroyed the grasses that once held the soil in place. The drought of the 1930s and high winds did the rest.

Migrant Workers Hardest hit by the drought and dust storms were poor farmers in Oklahoma and other Great Plains states. Hundreds of these "Okies" packed their belongings into cars and trucks and headed west. They became migrant workers—people who move from one region to another in search of work. They hoped to find jobs in the orchards and farms of California, Oregon, or Washington.

Once they reached the West Coast, the migrants faced a new hardship—they were not wanted. Local citizens feared that the newcomers would take away their jobs. Sometimes, angry crowds blocked the highways and sent the migrants away. Those migrants who did find work were paid little.

Women Face the Depression

Traditional roles took on added importance during the depression. Homemakers had to stretch family budgets to make ends meet. Some women took in laundry to earn extra money. Others took in boarders to help pay the rent. Wives also found that unemployed husbands needed more nurturing to feel worthwhile.

Working women faced special problems during the depression. If jobs were available, employers hired men before they would hire women. In order to spread jobs around, the federal government refused to hire a woman if her husband had a job.

Women in the Workplace Despite such obstacles, millions of women earned wages in order to support themselves and their families. During the 1930s, the number of married women in the work force increased by 52 percent. Educated women took jobs as secretaries, schoolteachers, and social workers. Other women earned livings as maids, factory workers, and seamstresses.

Some women workers struck for better pay. In San Antonio, Texas, at least 80 percent of the pecan shellers were Mexican American women. When employers lowered their pay, a young worker, Emma Tenayuca, organized the shellers and led them off the job. Tenayuca said later, "I had a basic faith in the American idea of freedom and fairness. I felt something had to be done."

An Active First Lady Eleanor Roosevelt created a new role for the First Lady. Acting as the President's "eyes and ears," she toured the nation. She visited farms and Indian reservations and traveled deep into a coal mine. She talked to homemakers, studying the condition of their clothing on the washline to measure how well they were doing.

Viewing History

Scarce Jobs

New York City

When the depression hit, opportunities for women faded. Programs like WPA provided some work, but not enough for all who needed employment. Here, women sew clothes in a WPA factory. **Identifying Causes and Effects** *How did the depression affect the role of women in the family?*

AS YOU READ **Ask Questions** What questions would you like to have asked Eleanor Roosevelt?

The First Lady did more than just aid the President. She used her position to speak out for women's rights, as well as other issues. In her newspaper column, "My Day," she called on Americans to live up to the goal of equal justice for all. By speaking out on social issues, Eleanor Roosevelt angered some people. However, many other Americans admired her strong stands.

African Americans

When the Great Depression hit, African American workers were often the first to lose their jobs. By 1934, black workers were suffering a 50 percent unemployment rate, more than twice the national average. Often, they were denied public works jobs. Some charities even refused to serve blacks at centers giving out food to the needy.

Eleanor Roosevelt and others close to the President urged him to improve the situation of African Americans. The President responded to their needs. For example, thousands of young black men learned a trade through the CCC.

In aiding African Americans, FDR won their support for the Democratic party. The President invited black leaders to the White House to advise him. These unofficial advisers became known as the Black Cabinet. They included Robert C. Weaver, a Harvard-educated economist, and Mary McLeod Bethune, a well-known Florida educator. Roosevelt appointed Bethune to head the National Youth Administration's Division of Negro Affairs. She was the first African American to head a government agency.

Often, Roosevelt followed the advice of the Black Cabinet. However, when African American leaders pressed the President to support an antilynching law, he refused. He feared that by doing so he would lose the support of southerners in Congress for his New Deal programs.

Many black leaders called on African Americans to unite to obtain their civil rights—the rights due to all citizens. African Americans used their votes, won higher-level government jobs, and kept up pressure for equal treatment. Slowly, they made a few gains. However, the struggle for civil rights would take many more years.

Other Americans Face the Depression

The hard times of the Great Depression created fear and insecurity among many Americans. These feelings sometimes erupted in violence and discrimination against groups of Americans who were outside of the mainstream.

Mexican Americans By the 1930s, Mexican Americans worked in many cities around the country. A large number, however, were farmworkers in the West and Southwest. There, they faced discrimination in education and jobs and at the polls.

In good times, employers had encouraged Mexicans to move north and take jobs in factories or on farms. When hard times struck, however, many Americans wanted Mexicans to be sent back to their original country. More than 400,000 people were rounded up and sent to Mexico. Some of them were American citizens.

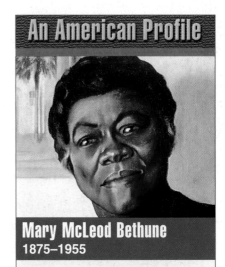

An American Profile

Mary McLeod Bethune
1875–1955

Mary McLeod Bethune was the 15th of 17 children born to a poor farm couple in South Carolina. As a child, Mary decided that she needed an education to fight her way out of poverty.

She was such a good student that she won numerous scholarships. After graduation, she taught and then founded a school in Florida. At first, she had only six students but after years of struggle, was able to raise the number to more than 300. For 40 years, Bethune served as president of what is today called Bethune-Cookman College. During this time, she founded and became the first president of the National Council of Negro Women.

Why do you think Bethune emphasized education so much?

Asian Americans Some Americans resented Chinese, Japanese, and Filipino workers who competed with them for scarce jobs. Sometimes, violence against Asians erupted. Responding to pressure, the government sought to reduce the number of Asians in the United States. In 1935, FDR signed a law that provided free transportation for Filipinos who agreed to return to the Philippines and not come back.

Native Americans In 1924, Congress had granted all Native Americans citizenship. Still, most Indians continued to live in deep poverty. President Roosevelt encouraged new policies toward Native Americans.

In the 1930s, Congress passed a series of laws that have been called the Indian New Deal. The laws gave Native American nations greater control over their own affairs.

The President chose John Collier, a longtime defender of Indian rights, to head the Bureau of Indian Affairs. Collier ended the government policy of breaking up Indian landholdings. In 1934, Congress passed the Indian Reorganization Act (IRA). It protected and even expanded landholdings of Native American reservations. The Roosevelt administration also strengthened Native American governments by letting reservations organize corporations and develop their own business projects.

To provide jobs during the depression, the government set up the Indian Emergency Conservation Work Group. It employed Native Americans in programs of soil-erosion control, irrigation, and land development.

The Arts of the Depression

Creative artists powerfully portrayed the hardships of depression life. Many writers depicted the hard times Americans faced across the country. In his 1939 novel *The Grapes of Wrath*, John Steinbeck told the heartbreaking story of the Okies streaming over the mountains trying to find new homes in California. (See Primary Source feature at left.)

Painting and Photography During the Depression Many painters turned to familiar themes. The huge murals of Thomas Hart Benton brought the history of the frontier to life. In *American Gothic*, Grant Wood painted an Iowa farmer and his daughter who look determined enough to survive any hardship.

The government sent out photographers to create a lasting record of American life during the Great Depression. The vivid photographs of Dorothea Lange (see page 756) showed the suffering of Dust Bowl farm families. Margaret Bourke-White photographed poor tenant farmers in the South.

Radio During the Depression Americans found ways to escape the hard times of the 1930s. Listening to the radio and going to the movies were among their favorite pastimes.

Every night, millions of Americans tuned in to their favorite radio programs. Comedians such as the husband-and-wife team,

Primary Source

The Grapes of Wrath

In the novel The Grapes of Wrath, *John Steinbeck told how suffering farmers headed west, hoping to find a better life in California:*

"Carloads, caravans, homeless and hungry: . . . They streamed over the mountains, hungry and restless, . . . restless as ants, scurrying to find work to do—to lift, to push, to pull, to pick, to cut—anything, any burden to bear, for food. The kids are hungry. We got no place to live. Like ants scurrying for work, for food, and most of all for land.

We ain't foreign. Seven generations back Americans, and beyond that Irish, Scotch, English, German. One of our folks in the Revolution, an' they was lots of our folks in the Civil War—both sides. Americans."

—John Steinbeck,
The Grapes of Wrath (1939)

Analyzing Primary Sources
Why were the migrants attracted to California?

George Burns and Gracie Allen, made people forget their troubles for a time. With so many people out of work, daytime radio shows became popular. People listened to dramas like "Ma Perkins" that told the story of families weathering the depression. Because soap companies sponsored many of these serials, the programs became known as soap operas.

Perhaps the most famous broadcast took place in 1938. On Halloween night, actor Orson Welles presented a "newscast" based on a science fiction novel, *The War of the Worlds*. Welles grimly reported the landing of invaders from the planet Mars. People who tuned in late mistook the program for a real newscast. Thousands of terrified people ran into the streets, seeking ways to escape the Martian invasion.

Movies During the Depression In the 1930s, moviemakers tried to restore Americans' faith in the future. Movies told optimistic stories about happy families or people finding love and success. Shirley Temple became a hugely popular star at the age of five. When Temple sang "On the Good Ship Lollipop," her upbeat spirit cheered up audiences.

One of the most popular movies was Walt Disney's *Snow White and the Seven Dwarfs*. It was the first full-length animated film. In 1939, Judy Garland won American hearts in *The Wizard of Oz*. The movie told of a young girl's escape from a bleak life in depression-era Kansas to the magical land of Oz.

The most expensively made and most popular movie of the 1930s was *Gone With the Wind*. It showed the Civil War in a romantic light. For more than three hours, many Americans forgot their worries as they watched the story of love and loss in the Old South. The movie also encouraged many Americans. They had survived hard times before. They would do so again.

Section 4 Assessment

Recall

1. **Identify** Explain the significance of **(a)** Dust Bowl, **(b)** Black Cabinet, **(c)** Mary McLeod Bethune, **(d)** Indian New Deal, **(e)** John Collier.
2. **Define** **(a)** migrant worker, **(b)** civil rights.

Comprehension

3. What was the Dust Bowl, and what problems did it create for American farmers?
4. What special hardships did women face during the Great Depression?
5. How did the depression affect African Americans, Mexican Americans, Asian Americans, and Native Americans?
6. How did the depression affect the creative arts?

Critical Thinking and Writing

7. **Exploring the Main Idea** Review the Main Idea statement at the beginning of this section. Then, make a list of the ways in which the arts filled needs during the depression.
8. **Analyzing Primary Sources** In *The Grapes of Wrath*, why does John Steinbeck compare the migrating farmers to ants?

CREATING A CHAPTER SUMMARY

On a sheet of paper, draw a timeline like this one. Include six to eight boxes. Fill in each box with a key event or development of the Great Depression. For each event, include its date.

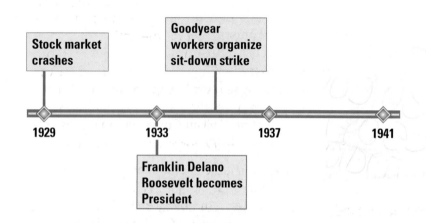

| Stock market crashes | | Goodyear workers organize sit-down strike | | |

1929   1933   1937   1941

Franklin Delano Roosevelt becomes President

For additional review and enrichment activities, see the interactive version of *The American Nation*, available on the Web and on CD-ROM.

Take It to the NET

Chapter Self-Test For practice test questions for Chapter 26, see *The American Nation* section of **www.phschool.com**.

Building Vocabulary

Write sentences using the chapter vocabulary words listed below, leaving blanks where the vocabulary words would go. Exchange your sentences with another student, and fill in the blanks in each other's sentences.

1. **on margin**
2. **bankrupt**
3. **soup kitchen**
4. **public works**
5. **bonus**
6. **pension**
7. **sit-down strike**
8. **national debt**
9. **migrant worker**
10. **civil rights**

Reviewing Key Facts

11. Why did Herbert Hoover not act more forcefully to end the depression? (Section 1)
12. What was the TVA, and why was it controversial? (Section 2)
13. How did the New Deal help farmers? (Section 2)
14. Why did Roosevelt try to enlarge the Supreme Court? (Section 3)

15. How did the depression affect women? (Section 4)

Critical Thinking and Writing

16. **Sequencing (a)** What problem did FDR tackle first upon taking office? **(b)** Why did he make this his first priority?
17. **Connecting to Geography: Interaction (a)** Name one major environmental problem in the world today. **(b)** How is it similar to, and how is it different from, the Dust Bowl problems of the 1930s?
18. **Analyzing Information** Why do you think African Americans suffered greater discrimination during the depression than during good times?
19. **Identifying Points of View** President Roosevelt urged his staff to "take a method and try it. If it fails, admit it and try another. But above all try something." How did this point of view reflect the nation's experience with Herbert Hoover?

Analyzing Primary Sources

During the depression, photographers captured the sufferings of the rural poor in powerful pictures. Study this photo, and then answer the questions that follow:

20. What evidence is there in the picture that the men are making a long trip?
21. What is the sign at the right of the photograph advertising?
22. What message is the photographer trying to convey?
23. Why do you think photographs such as this one are such a powerful record of the depression?

Evaluating Long-Term Effects

Read this summary of the long-term impact of the New Deal and answer the questions that follow:

> 66 The great public works of the depression era—the bridges, dams, tunnels, public buildings, sewage systems, port facilities, and hospitals—remind us of this extraordinary period of government support for the national welfare. . . . In national and state parks and on mountain trails and oceanfront walks, Americans still reap advantages from the restoration and conservation work of the Civilian Conservation Corps. 99
>
> —Cayton et al., *America: Pathways to the Present*

24. Which title best reflects the viewpoint of the author of the quotation?
    A Our Crumbling Public Works
    B Conserving Our Natural Heritage
    C Failure of the New Deal
    D The Heritage of the New Deal
25. (a) List three other long-term effects of FDR's presidency besides those mentioned in the quotation. (b) Select one long-term effect, and tell how it affects you today.

ACTIVITIES

Connecting With . . . Civics

Understanding the Role of Charities
Working with a classmate, locate an organization in your community that helps people in need. Interview the leaders of the organization about what they do and where they get funds. Report to the class what you have learned.

Take It to the NET

Connecting to Today

Understanding Economic Systems The Great Depression brought into question the future of free enterprise. Use the Internet to research the economic systems of free enterprise and communism. Then, make a graphic organizer that compares and contrasts the different economic systems. For help in starting this activity, visit *The American Nation* section of **www.phschool.com**.

Writing a Brief Biography

Depression-Era Leaders Use the Internet to research a person who was important during the Depression. Then, write a brief biography of that person. Focus on how he or she affected the course of history. Be sure to list the sources you used in writing your biography. For help in starting this activity, visit *The American Nation* section of **www.phschool.com**.

27 The World War II Era

1935–1945

1 **The Gathering Storm**
2 **World War II Begins**
3 **Americans in Wartime**
4 **The Allies Turn the Tide**
5 **The End of the War**

Neutrality poster

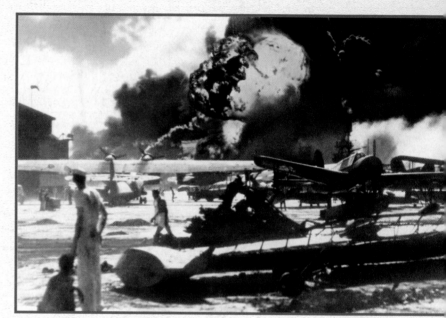

Bombing of Pearl Harbor

1935

Congress passes the first Neutrality Act. The law is intended to keep the United States out of foreign conflicts.

1939

World War II begins as Germany invades Poland. Although the United States remains neutral, President Roosevelt seeks to aid the Allies, such as Britain and France.

1941

Japanese planes bomb the United States fleet at Pearl Harbor, Hawaii. The next day, the United States enters World War II on the Allied side.

AMERICAN EVENTS

Presidential Terms: Franklin D. Roosevelt 1933–1945

1935   **1938**   **1941**

WORLD EVENTS

▲ **1935**
Italy invades Ethiopia.

▲ **1937**
Japan launches an all-out war against China.

1940 ▲
France surrenders to Germany.

Aggression in Europe

Under Adolf Hitler, Germany expanded across Europe, sparking the largest war in world history.

Key
- Areas taken over by Germany by September 1, 1939
- Areas taken over by Italy by September 1, 1939

Azimuthal Projection

FINLAND
ESTONIA
SWEDEN
LATVIA
IRELAND
DENMARK
LITHUANIA
GREAT BRITAIN
North Sea
Baltic Sea
GER.
SOVIET UNION
NETH.
GERMANY
POLAND
BELG.
Rhineland
To Hungary (1939)
LUX.
CZECHOSLOVAKIA (1939)
Saar Basin
Sudetenland (1938)
FRANCE
SWITZ.
AUSTRIA (1938)
To Hungary (1938)
HUNGARY
ROMANIA
ATLANTIC OCEAN
PORTUGAL
SPAIN
Corsica
YUGOSLAVIA
BULGARIA
Black Sea
ITALY
Sardinia
ALBANIA (1939)
GREECE
TURKEY
Mediterranean Sea
Sicily
To Ethiopia (1935)
Dodecanese Is. (It.)
AFRICA

0 200 400 Miles
0 200 400 Kilometers

American troops come ashore at Normandy

1944

1942
The United States Navy defeats Japan at the Battle of Midway.

On D-Day, June 6, Allied troops land at Normandy in France. Within a few months, France is liberated from the Nazis.

1945
World War II ends with the surrender of Germany in May and Japan in September.

Harry S Truman 1945-1953

1941 • 1944 • 1947

▲ **1942**
Britain defeats German forces in Egypt.

▲ **1944**
German troops are driven out of the Soviet Union.

1 The Gathering Storm

Reading Focus

- What kind of dictatorship did Stalin set up in the Soviet Union?
- How did authoritarian governments come to power in Italy, Germany, and Japan?
- Why did the United States adopt a policy of isolationism?

Key Terms

totalitarian state
Fascism
aggression
Nazis
scapegoat
concentration camp
Neutrality Acts
Good Neighbor Policy

Taking Notes

Copy the table below. As you read, complete the table with information about the world in the 1930s.

COUNTRY	LEADER	GOVERNMENT/ POLICIES
Soviet Union		
Italy		
Germany		
Japan		
United States		

> **Main Idea** In the 1930s, as dictators elsewhere embarked on a path of aggression, the United States tried to stay out of the conflict.

Benito Mussolini

Use Prior Knowledge
List five words or ideas that come to mind when you hear the word *dictator.*

Setting the Scene A man strutted onto a balcony in Rome. A sea of people cheered in the plaza below. He thrust his jaw forward, puffed out his chest, raised his arm, and began a fiery speech. *"Duce! Duce!"* the crowd cried. "Leader! Leader!"

In the 1920s, Benito Mussolini set the style for a new breed of dictators, men with absolute power and visions of conquest. Some Americans worried about the war clouds gathering in Europe and Asia. But most hoped to isolate themselves from the conflict.

Stalin's Totalitarian State

As you have read, Lenin had set up a communist government in the Soviet Union. After Lenin's death in 1924, Joseph Stalin gained power. Stalin ruled as a totalitarian dictator. In a **totalitarian state,** a single party controls the government and every aspect of people's lives. Citizens must obey the government without question. Criticism of the government is severely punished.

Stalin took brutal measures to modernize Soviet industry and agriculture. He ordered peasants to hand over land and animals to government-run farms. Millions who resisted were executed or sent to labor camps. Stalin also staged trials and executions of his political enemies. Many confessed to false charges under torture.

Fascist Italy

Totalitarian leaders also came to power in Italy and Germany. Unlike Stalin, these dictators were Fascists (FAH shists): **Fascism** was rooted in militarism, extreme nationalism, and blind loyalty to the state. Fascist dictators vowed to create new empires. While Communists drew much of their support from the working classes, Fascists found allies among business leaders and landowners.

Mussolini In 1922, Benito Mussolini and his Fascist party seized power in Italy. He played on anger about the Versailles Treaty ending World War I. Many Italians felt cheated because the treaty did not grant Italy the territory it wanted. Mussolini also used economic unrest and fears of a communist revolution to win support.

Once in power, Mussolini outlawed all political parties except his own. He controlled the press and banned criticism of the government. Critics were jailed or simply murdered. In schools, children recited the motto "Mussolini Is Always Right!"

Conquering Ethiopia In the 1930s, Mussolini used foreign conquest to distract Italians from economic problems. Promising to restore the greatness of ancient Rome, he embarked on a program of military aggression. Aggression is a warlike act by one country against another without just cause.

Mussolini invaded the African nation of Ethiopia in 1935. The Ethiopians fought bravely. However, their cavalry and outdated rifles were no match for Italy's modern tanks and airplanes.

Ethiopian emperor Haile Selassie (HI lee suh LAS ee) asked the League of Nations for aid. The League responded weakly. Britain and France were caught up in their own economic problems and unwilling to risk another war. Without help, Ethiopia fell to the invaders.

Nazi Germany

In Germany, Adolf Hitler brought the National Socialist German Workers' Party, or Nazis, to power. Like Mussolini, Hitler played on anger about the Versailles Treaty. Germans bitterly resented the treaty because it blamed their country for World War I and made them pay heavy war costs.

Hitler Becomes Dictator Hitler assured Germans that they had not lost the war. Rather, he said, Jews and other traitors had "stabbed Germany in the back." The argument was false, but in troubled times people were eager to find a scapegoat—a person or group on whom to blame their problems.

Hitler was a powerful speaker and skillful politician. By the time depression struck, many Germans looked to him as a strong leader with answers to their problems.

In 1933, Hitler became chancellor, or head of the German government. Within two years, he ended democratic rule and created a militaristic totalitarian state. In Nazi Germany, the government controlled the press, the schools, and religion.

The following year, Hitler organized a week-long rally in Nuremberg. Crowds chanted slogans praising Hitler. Uniformed soldiers

Viewing History

Soviet Propaganda Poster The Soviet totalitarian state was built on the glorification of Stalin (left). This poster celebrated the adoption of a new Soviet constitution in 1937.
Evaluating Information
What emotions did this propaganda poster try to stir in the Soviet people?

CONSTITUTION
De L'U.R.S.S.
Article 1.—L'Union des républiques soviétiques socialistes est un État socialiste des ouvriers et des paysans.

Viewing History

Nazi Germany

Adolf Hitler (left) was determined to build a mighty military machine. Here, lines of German troops march at the 1934 Nuremberg rally. Their banners display the swastika, symbol of the Nazi party. **Drawing Conclusions** *What impact do you think pictures like these had on Germans? On people in neighboring countries?*

AS YOU READ **Predict** Make a prediction about what might happen if German aggression continues.

marched in endless parades and engaged in mock battles. American reporter William Shirer described the Nuremberg rally:

> 66 It is difficult to exaggerate the frenzy of the three hundred thousand German spectators when they saw their soldiers go into action, heard the thunder of the guns, and smelt the powder. 99

—William L. Shirer, *Berlin Diary*

Attacks on Jews Hitler preached that Germans belonged to a race that was biologically superior to Jews, Gypsies, and other peoples. The Nazi government singled out the Jews for special persecution. Jews were deprived of their citizenship, forbidden to use public facilities, and driven out of almost every type of work. Later, Jews were rounded up and sent to concentration camps, prison camps for civilians who are considered enemies of the state. In time, as you will read, Hitler would unleash a plan to kill all the Jews in Europe.

The Nazi War Machine Hitler claimed that Germany had a right to expand to the east. In defiance of the Versailles treaty, he began to build up Germany's armed forces. Although the League of Nations condemned his actions, Hitler predicted that the rest of Europe would "never act. They'll just protest. And they will always be too late."

In 1936, German troops moved into the Rhineland, near the border with France and Belgium. France and Britain protested, but they took no action.

Military Rule in Japan

Japan's economy suffered severely in the Great Depression. As many Japanese grew impatient with their democratic government, military leaders took power. Like Hitler, these leaders preached racial superiority. They believed that the Japanese were purer than, and superior to, other Asians as well as non-Asians.

The military rulers set out to expand into Asia. In 1931, Japanese forces seized Manchuria in northeastern China. Manchuria was rich in coal and iron, two resources scarce in Japan. The Japanese set up a state in Manchuria called Manchukuo.

China called on the League of Nations for help. The League condemned Japanese aggression but did little else. The United States refused to recognize Manchukuo but took no action.

American Isolationism

In the United States, the strong isolationist mood of the 1920s continued. (See page 721.) As war clouds gathered overseas, Americans were determined to keep from becoming involved.

Neutrality Acts In 1935, Congress passed the first of a series of Neutrality Acts, which banned arms sales or loans to countries at war. Congress also warned Americans not to travel on ships of countries at war. By limiting economic ties with warring nations, isolationists hoped to stay out of any foreign conflict.

Good Neighbor Policy Closer to home, the United States tried to improve relations with Latin American nations. In 1930, President Hoover rejected the Roosevelt Corollary. (See Chapter 23.) The United States, he declared, no longer claimed the right to intervene in Latin American affairs.

Franklin Roosevelt also worked to build friendlier relations with Latin America. Under his Good Neighbor Policy, FDR withdrew American troops from Nicaragua and Haiti. He also canceled the Platt Amendment, which had limited the independence of Cuba.

As world tensions increased, the need to strengthen ties in the Americas became more pressing. On a visit to Argentina, Roosevelt warned that any foreign aggressor "will find a hemisphere wholly prepared to consult together for our mutual safety."

Primary Source

The Good Neighbor Policy

In this speech, President Roosevelt describes the results of his policy toward Latin America:
"The whole world now knows that the United States cherishes no predatory ambitions. We are strong; but less powerful nations know that they need not fear our strength. We seek no conquest: we stand for peace. . . . The twenty-one American republics are not only living together in friendship and in peace—they are united in the determination to so remain."
—Franklin D. Roosevelt,
Speech at Chautauqua, New York,
August 14, 1936

Analyzing Primary Sources
According to FDR, was the Good Neighbor Policy a success? Explain.

Section 1 Assessment

Recall
1. **Identify** Explain the significance of **(a)** Joseph Stalin, **(b)** Fascism, **(c)** Benito Mussolini, **(d)** Adolf Hitler, **(e)** Nazi, **(f)** Neutrality Acts, **(g)** Good Neighbor Policy.
2. **Define (a)** totalitarian state, **(b)** aggression, **(c)** scapegoat, **(d)** concentration camp.

Comprehension
3. Describe Stalin's totalitarian rule in the Soviet Union.
4. What factors helped dictators come to power in **(a)** Italy, **(b)** Germany, **(c)** Japan?

5. What were the goals of American isolationists?

Critical Thinking and Writing
6. **Exploring the Main Idea** Review the Main Idea statement at the beginning of this section. Then, make a list of at least two arguments for and two arguments against American isolationism in the 1930s.
7. **Drawing Inferences** Write a paragraph explaining why you think so many people were willing to reject democracy and turn to dictators in the 1930s.

ACTIVITY

Drawing a Political Cartoon Draw a political cartoon about the nature of totalitarian dictatorships. You might focus on how the government of a totalitarian state differs from the American system of government.

2 World War II Begins

Reading Focus
- How did aggression lead to war in Asia and Europe?
- How did the United States respond to the outbreak of World War II?
- Why did the United States finally enter the war?

Key Terms

Munich Conference

appeasement

Nazi-Soviet Pact

blitzkrieg

Axis

Allies

Battle of Britain

Lend-Lease Act

Atlantic Charter

Taking Notes

Copy the causes chart below. As you read, fill in some of the events and developments that led to United States entry into World War II.

World War II begins in Europe → UNITED STATES ENTERS WAR

Main Idea Japanese and German aggression plunged the world into a war that eventually involved the United States.

Franklin Roosevelt
Find Main Ideas
Restate the main idea of FDR's speech in your own words.

Setting the Scene

On October 5, 1937, President Roosevelt addressed a large crowd in Chicago. He was there to see whether Americans were ready to abandon isolationism. Claiming that the "epidemic of world lawlessness" was spreading, he said:

> 66 There is no escape through mere isolation or neutrality. Those who cherish their freedom . . . must work together for the triumph of law and moral principles in order that peace, justice, and confidence may prevail in the world. 99
> —Franklin D. Roosevelt, "Quarantine Speech" October 5, 1937

Roosevelt's speech produced no change in the isolationist mood of Americans. "It is a terrible thing," he commented, "to look over your shoulder when you are trying to lead—and find no one there."

During the 1930s, neither the United States nor European nations were prepared to halt aggression in Europe or Asia. As the armies of Germany, Italy, and Japan conquered more territory, the democracies still hoped to avoid another world war.

Japan Sparks War in Asia

In 1937, Japan began an all-out war against China. Japanese planes bombed China's major cities. Thousands of people were killed. In the city of Nanjing alone, some 300,000 civilians and prisoners of war were murdered in a six-week massacre. Japanese troops defeated Chinese armies and occupied northern and central China.

The Japanese advance into China alarmed American leaders. They felt it undermined the Open Door Policy, which promised equal access to trade in China. It also threatened the Philippines, which the United States controlled. Nevertheless, isolationist feelings remained strong among the American people and kept the United States from taking a firm stand against the Japanese.

Germany Brings War to Europe

In Europe, Hitler continued his plans for German expansion. In 1938, just two years after occupying the Rhineland, Hitler annexed Austria. This action again violated the Treaty of Versailles. Once again, Britain and France took no action against Germany.

Later that year, Hitler claimed the Sudetenland, the western part of Czechoslovakia. He justified his demand by claiming that the Sudetenland contained many people of German heritage.

Appeasement Britain and France had signed treaties to protect Czechoslovakia but were reluctant to go to war. The two nations sought a peaceful solution. In September 1938, the leaders of Britain, France, Italy, and Germany met in Munich, Germany.

At the **Munich Conference,** Hitler promised that Germany would seek no further territory once it had acquired the Sudetenland. To preserve the peace, Britain and France agreed that Germany should have the Sudetenland. This practice of giving in to aggression in order to avoid war is known as **appeasement.**

The policy of appeasement failed. Nazi Germany seized the rest of Czechoslovakia the very next year. At last, Britain and France realized that they had to take a firm stand against Nazi aggression.

Invasion of Poland Hitler next eyed Poland. In August 1939, he signed the **Nazi-Soviet Pact** with Stalin. The two rival dictators agreed not to attack each other. Secretly, they also agreed to divide Poland and other parts of Eastern Europe.

In September 1939, Hitler launched a **blitzkrieg,** or lightning war, against Poland. Unable to withstand up-to-date German planes and tanks, the Poles soon surrendered.

Meanwhile, the Soviet Union seized eastern Poland. Stalin's forces also invaded Finland and later annexed Estonia, Lithuania, and Latvia. Stalin claimed that these steps were needed to build Soviet defenses.

A Second World War

Two days after Hitler's invasion of Poland, Britain and France declared war on Germany. A new world war had begun.

World War II was truly a global conflict. Military forces fought all over the world. Italy, Japan, and six other nations joined Germany to form the **Axis** powers. Opposing the Axis powers were the **Allies.** Before the war was over, the Allies would include Britain, France, the Soviet Union, the United States, China, and 45 other countries.

Viewing History

Japan Attacks China
The baby shown here miraculously survived the Japanese bombing of a train station in Shanghai, China. This famous photograph was widely circulated in the United States. **Drawing Conclusions** *Why do you think this photograph became so well known? What effect do you think it had?*

Miracle at Dunkirk

The situation at Dunkirk looked hopeless. French and British troops had their backs to the North Sea. Advancing German troops pinned down the army, cutting off a possible retreat through ports on the English Channel. British Navy ships were too few to carry so many troops to safety in time.

In a massive effort, the British put to use nearly everything that could float. Civilians piloted fishing boats, private yachts, tugboats, motorboats, and ferries across the rough waters. Luckily, an approaching storm in the Atlantic had turned north before hitting the English Channel. By June 4, 1940, some 338,000 troops had been miraculously rescued from the beaches of Dunkirk.

 Why do you think that so many civilians helped with the evacuation effort?

AS YOU READ **Summarize** As you read this subsection and the next one, list the information that you would include in a summary of the steps by which the United States became involved in World War II.

Fall of France In the spring of 1940, Hitler's armies marched north and west. In April, they smashed through Denmark and Norway. In May, they overran Holland and Belgium and pushed into France. Hitler's ally, Italy, also attacked France.

Britain sent troops to help France resist the assault. The British and French, however, were quickly overpowered. By May, the Germans had forced them to retreat to Dunkirk, a French port on the English Channel. In a bold action, the British sent every available ship across the channel to rescue the trapped soldiers.

Unhindered, German armies entered France and marched on to Paris, the French capital. On June 22, 1940, barely six weeks later, France surrendered. The fall of France shocked the world.

Battle of Britain Britain now stood alone. Even so, the new prime minister, Winston Churchill, was confident. He vowed:

66 We shall fight on the beaches, we shall fight on the landing grounds, we shall fight in the fields and in the streets . . . we shall never surrender. 99
—Winston Churchill, Speech to House of Commons, June 4, 1940

German planes dropped bombs on London and other British cities during the Battle of Britain. British fighter pilots fought back, gunning down nearly 2,000 German planes. By late 1940, after months of bombing, Hitler gave up his planned invasion of Britain.

In the United States, people listened to radio reports from London. Hearing of Britain's brave stand against Hitler, Americans wondered how much longer they could stay out of the war.

The United States Moves Toward War

After the invasion of Poland, President Roosevelt announced that the United States would remain neutral. He knew that most Americans favored the Allies but did not want to go to war.

Aid to the Allies Roosevelt sought ways to help the Allies. He asked Congress to repeal the neutrality law that banned the sale of arms to warring nations. Isolationists blocked the move, but FDR won a compromise. The United States could sell arms to the Allies under a "cash-and-carry" plan. The Allies had to pay cash for the goods and carry them away in their own ships.

By 1940, German submarines had sunk many British ships. Roosevelt agreed to give Britain 50 old American destroyers. In exchange, Britain gave the United States 99-year leases on military bases in Newfoundland and the Caribbean.

Prepared for War The United States also took several steps to prepare for war. Congress approved greater spending for the army and navy and set up a military draft. It was the first time young men were required to serve in the army during peace.

Isolationists opposed these moves, especially aid for Britain. "I have been forced to the conclusion that we cannot win this war for England, regardless of how much assistance we extend," warned Charles Lindbergh, the hero pilot of the 1920s. Many other

"Ho hum! When he's finished pecking down that last tree he'll quite likely be tired."

Americans, however, felt that the United States had no choice. If Britain fell, Hitler might control the Atlantic Ocean.

A Third Term for FDR The threat of war persuaded FDR to run for a third term in 1940. His decision broke the precedent set by George Washington of serving only two terms as President.

Republicans nominated Wendell Willkie, an Ohio businessman. Willkie was a strong critic of FDR's New Deal. Still, he agreed with Roosevelt on many issues, such as sending aid to Britain. Both candidates also pledged not to send Americans into any foreign wars.

Republicans—and some Democrats—criticized Roosevelt for breaking the two-term tradition. Still, the voters gave FDR a clear victory. After his defeat, Willkie worked to win Republican support for Roosevelt's war aims.

Lend-Lease By late 1940, Britain was running out of cash. Roosevelt boldly suggested lending supplies to Britain. He proclaimed that Britain was defending democracy against totalitarian forces.

Despite opposition from isolationists, Congress passed the Lend-Lease Act in March 1941. It allowed sales or loans of war materials to "any country whose defense the President deems vital to the defense of the United States." Under Lend-Lease, the United States sent airplanes, tanks, guns, and ammunition to Britain. British merchant ships transported the goods, with escorts of American warships providing protection as far as Iceland.

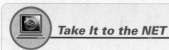

Pearl Harbor, Hawaii

USS *Arizona* Memorial

On the morning of December 7, 1941, Japanese fighter planes bombed the United States fleet anchored at Pearl Harbor, Hawaii. The battleship Arizona *sank with 1,102 sailors inside. Today, you can take a navy shuttle to view the sunken hull of the* Arizona. *At the "remembrance exhibit," you can pay tribute to the first Americans to give their lives in World War II.*

Take It to the NET

Virtual Field Trip For an interactive look at the USS *Arizona* Memorial, visit *The American Nation* section of **www.phschool.com**.

In June 1941, Hitler launched a surprise invasion of the Soviet Union. The Soviets were now fighting on the Allied side. Although Roosevelt condemned Stalin's totalitarian rule, he extended Lend-Lease aid to the Soviet Union.

War Goals In August 1941, Roosevelt and Churchill issued the Atlantic Charter, which set goals for the postwar world. The two leaders agreed to seek no territory from the war. They pledged to support "the right of all peoples to choose the form of government under which they will live." The charter also called for a "permanent system of general security" similar to the League of Nations.

War Comes to the United States

To Roosevelt, Japanese aggressions in Asia were as alarming as Germany's advance through Europe. The Japanese had seized much of China. After Germany defeated France in 1940, Japan took control of French colonies in Southeast Asia. In September 1940, the Japanese signed an alliance with Germany and Italy.

An Embargo The United States tried to stop Japanese aggression by refusing to sell oil and scrap metal to Japan. This embargo angered the Japanese because they badly needed these resources. "Sparks will fly before long," predicted an American diplomat.

Japanese and American officials met in November 1941. Japan asked the United States to lift its trade embargo. The United States called on Japan to withdraw its armies from China and Southeast

Asia. Neither side would compromise. As the talks limped along, Japan completed plans for a secret attack on the United States.

Japan Attacks Pearl Harbor On Sunday morning, December 7, 1941, the American Pacific fleet was peacefully anchored at Pearl Harbor, Hawaii. Suddenly, Japanese planes swept through the sky. In less than two hours, they sank or seriously damaged 19 American ships, destroyed almost 200 planes, and killed about 2,400 people.

The attack was a desperate gamble by Japanese leaders. They knew they lacked the resources to win a long war with the United States. They believed, however, that Americans were weak and had no stomach for fighting. The Japanese thought the sneak attack would force the United States to beg for peace immediately. Instead, Pearl Harbor united Americans in their determination to fight.

The Japanese made two other mistakes. First, they failed to sink the aircraft carriers stationed at Pearl Harbor. The carriers were at sea at the time of the attack. Second, the Japanese did not bomb the fuel oil tanks in Hawaii. Oil and aircraft carriers would become two keys to American victory in the war that followed.

The next day, a grave President Roosevelt addressed Congress. "Yesterday, December 7, 1941—a date which will live in infamy—" he began. He told Congress and the nation:

> 66 No matter how long it may take us to overcome this premeditated invasion, the American people, in their righteous might, will win through to absolute victory. 99
>
> —Franklin D. Roosevelt, War Message to Congress, December 8, 1941

Congress declared war on Japan. In response, Germany and Italy declared war on the United States. Americans were now united in the cause of freedom. Even isolationists backed the war effort.

AFTER YOU READ

Section 2 Assessment

Recall

1. **Identify** Explain the significance of **(a)** Munich Conference, **(b)** Nazi-Soviet Pact, **(c)** Axis, **(d)** Allies, **(e)** Winston Churchill, **(f)** Battle of Britain, **(g)** Wendell Willkie, **(h)** Lend-Lease Act, **(i)** Atlantic Charter.
2. **Define** **(a)** appeasement, **(b)** blitzkrieg.

Comprehension

3. **(a)** How did Britain and France respond to German aggression at first? **(b)** Why did they finally declare war on Germany?
4. Describe two actions the United States took to support the Allies.

5. What were the results of the attack on Pearl Harbor?

Critical Thinking and Writing

6. **Exploring the Main Idea** Review the Main Idea statement at the beginning of this section. Then, write a letter telling British and French leaders at the Munich Conference how you think they should respond to Nazi aggression.
7. **Drawing Conclusions** "Until December 7, 1941, the United States followed a neutral course." Do you agree or disagree? Write a paragraph explaining your reasoning.

ACTIVITY

Presenting a Scene With two or three classmates, present a scene in which an American family listens to FDR's war message on the radio on December 8, 1941. Have the family discuss what they think the war will mean to them.

3 Americans in Wartime

BEFORE YOU READ

Reading Focus

- How did Americans mobilize the economy in World War II?
- What impact did the war have on African Americans?
- Why did Japanese Americans and other groups face special problems during the war?

Key Terms

War Production Board

rationing

victory garden

Rosie the Riveter

"Double V" campaign

Tuskegee Airmen

compensation

bracero program

Taking Notes

Copy the concept web below. As you read, fill in the blank ovals with information about Americans during World War II. Add as many ovals as you need.

Main Idea Despite economic sacrifices, as well as discrimination faced by certain groups, Americans pulled together as never before to help defeat the enemy.

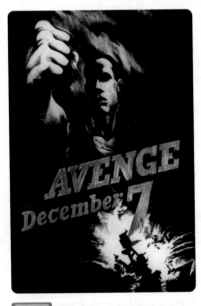

AS YOU READ

1942 American poster

Visualize Picture the scene in the airplane described in Setting the Scene. How do you think an American passenger would react to seeing the words "Remember Pearl Harbor" on a pat of butter?

Setting the Scene An English visitor was flying over the United States in 1943. Fresh from war-torn Europe, he was impressed by the calm below. There were no bombs falling or armies fighting. It was even hard to tell that the country was at war. Then, a flight attendant put his lunch tray in front of him. He recalled:

> 66 As I reached . . . to attack my butter pat, there, neatly inscribed on it, was the [command to] REMEMBER PEARL HARBOR. It needed the butter to remind one of the guns. 99
>
> —H. G. Nicholas, quoted in *V Was for Victory* (Blum)

The Japanese attack on Pearl Harbor plunged the United States into World War II. Americans united as never before. The cry "Remember Pearl Harbor" became a reminder that the efforts of Americans on the home front were vital to victory.

Mobilizing the Home Front

During World War II, more than 15 million Americans served in the military. Many millions more spent the war years at home, far from the battlefields. Winning the war depended on mobilizing the home front to support and supply the armed forces.

Combat Training In 1941, the military's first task was to train forces for combat. Army, navy, and air bases were built all over the country. Recruits were trained to fight in the jungles of the Pacific, the deserts of North Africa, and the towns and farmlands of Europe.

Women joined all the armed services. Women pilots logged 60 million air miles ferrying bombers from base to base, towing targets, and teaching men to fly. Although women were not allowed in combat, many served close to the front lines.

A Miracle of Production Even more than in World War I, the government controlled the economy during World War II. Government agencies set the prices of goods, negotiated with labor unions, and decided what should be produced.

The War Production Board helped factories shift from making consumer goods to making guns, ships, aircraft, and other war materials. Automobile makers, for example, switched to producing tanks and trucks.

A Nazi leader once scoffed that "Americans can't build planes, only electric iceboxes and razor blades." He was wrong. Americans performed a miracle of production. In 1942 alone, American workers produced more than 48,000 planes and shipped more than 8 million tons of goods.

As production of war materials grew, consumer goods became scarcer. The government imposed rationing, or limitations on the amounts of certain goods that people could buy. Americans used ration coupons to purchase coffee, sugar, meat, gasoline, and many other goods. When people ran out of coupons, they could not buy the items until new coupons were issued.

To combat food shortages, many Americans planted victory gardens. At the height of the war, more than 20 million victory gardens produced 40 percent of all vegetables grown in the country.

To pay for the war, the government raised taxes. It also borrowed money from millions of American citizens by selling war bonds. Movie stars took part in drives to sell bonds and boost patriotic spirit.

The war quickly ended the Great Depression. Unemployment fell as millions of jobs opened up in factories. Minority workers found jobs where they had been rejected in the past.

Women in the Wartime Economy

"If you can drive a car, you can run a machine." Newspapers and magazines echoed this call to American women to work for victory. "Why do we need women workers?" asked a radio announcer. "You can't build ships, planes, and guns without them."

Women responded to the urgent demand for their labor. Almost five million women entered the work force. They replaced the men who joined the armed services. Many women worked in offices. Millions more kept the nation's factories operating around the clock. Some welded, ran huge cranes, and tended blast furnaces. Others became bus drivers, police officers, and gas station attendants. The image of Rosie the Riveter, a fictional factory worker, became a symbol of American women's contribution to the war effort.

Viewing History

Rosie the Riveter

United States

Rosie the Riveter became one of the most familiar images of World War II. In this magazine cover by popular artist Norman Rockwell, Rosie treads on a book written by Adolf Hitler. **Applying Information** *How does this image reflect what you have read about women's contributions to the war effort?*

Because women were badly needed in industry, they were able to win better pay and working conditions. The government agreed that women and men should get the same pay for the same job. Many employers, however, found ways to avoid equal pay.

The war changed fashions for women. Instead of wearing skirts on the job, many women dressed in trousers. They wore overalls and tied scarves around their hair. More important, war work gave many women a new sense of confidence. One former welder recalled:

> 66 I will never regret my two years or more in the ship-yards. It gave me a good start in life. . . . I decided that if I could learn to weld like a man, I could do anything it took to make a living. 99
> —Nova Lee McGhee Holbrook, quoted in *A Mouthful of Rivets* (Wise)

African Americans at War

When the war began, African Americans rallied to their nation's cause, as they had during World War I. This time, however, African Americans decided to pursue a "Double V" campaign—victory over the enemy abroad and victory over discrimination at home.

Fighting Discrimination at Home As industry geared up for war, factories replaced "No Help Wanted" signs with "Help Wanted, White" signs. Such discrimination angered African Americans.

In 1941, A. Philip Randolph, head of the Brotherhood of Sleeping Car Porters, called for a protest march on Washington. The government, he said, "will never give the Negro justice until they see masses—ten, twenty, fifty thousand Negroes on the White House lawn."

Government officials worried that such a march would feed Hitler's propaganda machine. After meeting with Randolph, FDR ordered employers that did business with the government to end

Viewing History

Relocation of Japanese Americans

California

Here, American troops oversee the movement of Japanese American families on the West Coast to relocation camps. "Herd 'em up, pack 'em off" was the reaction of one newspaper columnist.

Identifying Points of View
How do you think the families shown in this picture felt about what was happening?

discrimination in hiring. As a result, the employment of skilled black workers doubled during the war.

However, as black employment increased, so did racial tension. Thousands of Americans—black and white—moved to cities to work in industry. Competition for scarce housing led to angry incidents. In 1943, race riots broke out in Detroit, New York, and other cities.

Courage Under Fire While FDR acted against discrimination in hiring, he refused to end segregation of the races in the military. Nearly a million African Americans enlisted or were drafted. They had to serve in all-black units commanded by white officers.

African Americans served heroically in all branches of the armed forces. One of the earliest heroes of the war was Dorie Miller, an African American sailor serving on the battleship *West Virginia.* During the attack on Pearl Harbor, Miller dragged his wounded captain to safety. Then, though he had no training as a gunner, Miller manned a machine gun to defend his ship against enemy planes. For heroism in action, Miller was awarded the Navy Cross.

In the army, African American soldiers formed artillery and tank units. African Americans in the navy served as gunners' mates and helped build bases in the Pacific. African American marines helped defend American posts against Japanese attacks. The Tuskegee Airmen were African American fighter pilots who trained at Tuskegee, Alabama. By the end of the war, the Tuskegee airmen had destroyed or damaged about 400 enemy aircraft.

The contributions of African Americans to the war effort increased their determination to win justice at home. After the war, black veterans would be at the forefront of a renewed campaign for civil rights.

A Calamity for Japanese Americans

The war brought suffering to many Japanese Americans. Most lived on the West Coast or in Hawaii. Many of those on the West Coast were successful farmers and business people. For years, they had faced prejudice, in part because of their success.

Forced Relocation After the attack on Pearl Harbor, many people on the West Coast questioned the loyalty of Japanese Americans. Japanese Americans, they said, might act as spies and help Japan invade the United States. No evidence of disloyalty existed. Yet, President Roosevelt signed an order allowing the army to move Japanese Americans from their homes to "relocation camps." Many were American citizens by birth.

About 110,000 Japanese Americans were forced to sell their homes, farms, or businesses at great loss. "We didn't know where we were going," recalled Peter Ota, who was 15 at the time. "We didn't know what to take. A toothbrush, toilet supplies, some clothes. Only what you could carry." In the camps, Japanese Americans lived in crowded barracks behind barbed wire.

In the Service Despite unfair treatment, thousands of Japanese American men served in the armed forces. Most were put in segregated units and sent to fight in Europe. There, they won many honors

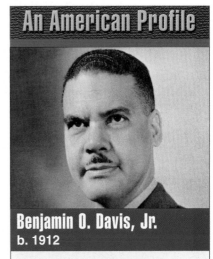

An American Profile

Benjamin O. Davis, Jr.
b. 1912

Benjamin O. Davis, Jr., had a history-making career. During World War II, he organized and took command of the Tuskegee Airmen. Davis flew 60 combat missions but rarely took credit for any victory. "The mission was always the dominating factor," he said. "It was a life and death operation, and it was important to our nation."

After the war, Davis helped end segregation in the Air Force. He flew combat again in the Korean War, and in 1959 he became the first African American to be awarded the rank of Major General.

What attitude did Davis have toward duty?

for bravery. The 442nd Nisei Regimental Combat Team became the most highly decorated military unit in United States history.

Years later, in 1988, Congress apologized to Japanese Americans who had been driven from their homes in World War II. Congress also approved **compensation,** or repayment for losses, in the amount of $20,000 to every survivor of the camps.

Other Groups Face Problems

Japanese Americans were not the only group to face wartime restrictions. About 11,000 German Americans and several hundred Italian Americans were also held in government camps as "enemy aliens." Other German Americans and Italian Americans faced curfews or travel restrictions.

A growing Mexican American population also faced problems. Because of the need for workers, the United States signed a treaty with Mexico in 1942. It allowed the recruitment of Mexican laborers to work in the United States. Under this **bracero program,** many Mexicans moved north to work on farms and railroads.

In June 1943, a group of sailors on leave attacked some young Mexican Americans, beating them on the streets. The incident led to several days of rioting in Los Angeles. Newspapers blamed the violence on the Mexican Americans. But in her newspaper column, Eleanor Roosevelt argued that the riots were the result of "longstanding discrimination against the Mexicans in the Southwest."

Still, like other groups, Mexican Americans served bravely in the military during World War II. Despite lingering problems at home, Americans were united in their resolve to push on to victory in Europe and the Pacific.

Section 3 Assessment

Recall
1. **Identify** Explain the significance of **(a)** War Production Board, **(b)** Rosie the Riveter, **(c)** "Double V" campaign, **(d)** A. Philip Randolph, **(e)** Tuskegee Airmen.
2. **Define** **(a)** rationing, **(b)** victory garden, **(c)** compensation, **(d)** bracero program.

Comprehension
3. Describe two economic policies that helped the American war effort.
4. What gains did African Americans make at home as a result of the war?

5. How did the war affect Japanese Americans on the West Coast?

Critical Thinking and Writing
6. **Exploring the Main Idea** Review the Main Idea statement at the beginning of this section. Then, write a letter from an American to a relative fighting overseas explaining why you are willing to make sacrifices for the war effort.
7. **Supporting a Point of View** Do you think the government is ever justified in suspending citizens' rights during wartime? Write a paragraph explaining your reasons.

ACTIVITY
Designing a Poster
With a partner, design a poster to encourage young Americans to serve in World War II. Your poster may focus on either military or nonmilitary service.

A WARTIME Economy

With the outbreak of World War II, the nation geared its economy to one goal: victory. The home front was alive with patriotic enthusiasm. Everyone, young and old, was expected to do his or her part.

During the war, the government rationed essential items such as sugar, gasoline, coffee, meat, and even ketchup. Citizens were given ration books to keep track of the "points" allotted to each family.

SALVAGE IN WORLD WAR II

SAVE ...	CAN BE MADE INTO ...
30,000 razor blades	50 machine guns (.30 caliber)
30 lipstick tubes	20 ammunition cartridges
2,300 pairs of nylons	1 parachute
1 pound of fat	$\frac{1}{3}$ pound of gunpowder
2,500 tons of tin and 190,000 tons of steel	5,000 tanks

Source: The National D-Day Museum

Children went to the streets to collect scrap metal, paper, rubber—anything that could be recycled to help win the war. At left, members of New York's Tin Can Club Number One wash their day's haul. The chart (above) shows how some everyday products were turned into needed war materials.

ACTIVITY

You are a young person during World War II. Working in a small group, make a list of things that you and your friends could do at home and in the community to help win the war.

4 The Allies Turn the Tide

BEFORE YOU READ

Reading Focus

- What defeats did the Allies suffer during the bleak days of 1942?
- How did D-Day and the opening of the "Second Front" help to turn the tide of battle in Europe?
- How did the war in Europe come to an end?

Key Terms

Battle of Midway

Operation Overlord

D-Day

Battle of the Bulge

Taking Notes

Copy this flowchart. As you read, fill in the boxes with events that led to the Allied victory in Europe. Add as many boxes as you need.

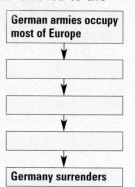

German armies occupy most of Europe

↓

↓

↓

↓

Germany surrenders

Main Idea Despite some early defeats, a series of Allied military successes helped to turn the tide of battle in Europe.

AS YOU READ

American World War II medal

Draw Inferences How do you think an American soldier would have reacted to Hitler's words?

Setting the Scene When Adolf Hitler learned of the Japanese attack on Pearl Harbor, he was delighted. "Now it is impossible for us to lose the war," he predicted. "We now have an ally who has never been vanquished in 3,000 years." Although Germany's alliance with Japan did not require it, Hitler promptly declared war on the United States.

At first, Hitler's prediction looked as if it might come true. In 1942, German armies occupied most of Europe and much of North Africa. Japan was sweeping across Asia and the Pacific. By 1944, however, the tide of battle had turned.

Bleak Days for the Allies

In early 1942, the situation looked bleak for the Allies. The German war machine seemed unbeatable. German submarines were sinking ships faster than the Allies could replace them. Most of Europe was in Axis hands.

Soviets Under Siege In the Soviet Union, German armies were closing in on Moscow, Leningrad, and Stalingrad. The Soviets resisted heroically. They burned crops and destroyed farm equipment so that the Germans could not use them.

Still, the German attack caused terrible hardships. During the 900-day siege of Leningrad, more than one million Russian men, women, and children died, mostly of starvation.

Japanese Advances Meanwhile, Japanese forces were on the move in the Pacific. After the bombing of Pearl Harbor, they seized Guam, Wake Island, Hong Kong, and Singapore. (See the map on page 797.)

General Douglas MacArthur commanded United States forces in the Pacific. With few troops, MacArthur had to defend a huge area. He directed American and Filipino troops in the defense of the

Philippines and the island of Bataan. They fought bravely against enormous odds. A reporter described the final defeat at Bataan:

> 66 Besieged on land and blockaded by sea, cut off from all sources of help in the Philippines and in America, these intrepid fighters have done all that human endurance could bear. . . . Bataan has fallen, but the spirit that made it stand—a beacon to all liberty-loving peoples of the world—cannot fall! 99
>
> —Norman Reyes, "Voice of Freedom" broadcast, 1942

In the end, MacArthur was forced to withdraw. "I shall return," he vowed.

The Japanese pressed on. They captured Malaya, Burma, and the Dutch East Indies. They threatened India to the west and Australia and New Zealand to the south.

The Tide Turns

To succeed against the Axis powers, the Allies had to agree on a strategy. Even before Pearl Harbor, American and British leaders had decided that the Allies must defeat Germany and Italy first. Then, they would send their combined forces to fight Japan.

Japanese Defeats Adopting a "beat Hitler first" strategy did not mean abandoning the war in the Pacific. With the aircraft carriers that had survived the attack on Pearl Harbor, a naval task force met a Japanese fleet in the Coral Sea near Java in May 1942. After a three-day battle, the Japanese fleet turned back. It was the first

GEOGRAPHY *Skills*

Early in the war, the Axis powers gained control of much of Western Europe and North Africa. The tide later began to turn in favor of the Allies.

1. **Location** On the map, locate **(a)** El Alamein, **(b)** Stalingrad, **(c)** Sicily, **(d)** Normandy, **(e)** Berlin.

2. **Movement** In what year did Allied troops first enter Italy? Germany?

3. **Critical Thinking Drawing Conclusions** Why do you think the Allies did not attack France by way of the Spanish-French border?

World War II in Europe and Africa

Key
- Main Axis powers, 1942
- Greatest extent of Axis control, 1942
- Neutral nations, 1942
- Allied territory, 1942
- → Allied advances
- ✷ Major battles

Azimuthal Projection
0   250   500 Miles
0   250   500 Kilometers

naval battle in history in which the ships never engaged one other directly. All the damage was done by airplanes from the carriers.

One month later, the United States Navy won a stunning victory at the Battle of Midway. American planes sank four Japanese aircraft carriers. The battle severely hampered the Japanese offensive. It also kept Japan from attacking Hawaii again.

Victories in North Africa Allied forces began to push back the Germans in North Africa. In October 1942, the British won an important victory at El Alamein in Egypt. German forces under General Erwin Rommel were driven west into Tunisia.

Meanwhile, American troops under the command of Generals Dwight D. Eisenhower, Omar Bradley, and George S. Patton landed in Morocco and Algeria. They then pushed east. Allied armies trapped Rommel's forces in Tunisia. In May 1943, his army had to surrender.

Success in Europe From bases in North Africa, the Allies organized the invasion of Italy. They used paratroopers and soldiers brought by sea to capture Sicily. In early September 1943, the Allies crossed from Sicily to the mainland of Italy.

By then, Mussolini had been overthrown. The Germans, however, still occupied much of Italy. In a series of bloody battles, the Allies slowly fought their way up the peninsula. On June 4, 1944, Allied troops marched into Rome. It was the first European capital to be freed from Nazi control.

The Soviet army repelled the Germans from Leningrad in 1943. At Stalingrad, after months of fierce house-to-house fighting, Soviet soldiers forced the German army to surrender. Slowly, the Soviet army pushed the Germans westward through Eastern Europe.

Opening a Second Front

Fighting in Russia and Eastern Europe was fierce. The Soviet Union would eventually lose some 9 million soldiers, more than any other country.

For years, Stalin had urged Britain and the United States to send armies across the English Channel into France. Such an attack would create a second front in Western Europe and ease pressure in the East. However, not until 1944 were Churchill and Roosevelt prepared to attempt an invasion of Western Europe.

Years of planning went into Operation Overlord, the code name for the invasion of Europe. General Eisenhower was appointed commander of Allied forces in Europe. He faced an enormous task. He had to organize a huge army, ferry it across the English Channel, and provide it with ammunition, food, and other supplies. By June 1944, almost 3 million troops were ready for the invasion.

The Germans knew that an attack was coming, but not when or where. To guard against the Allied invasion, they had mined beaches and strung barbed wire. Machine guns and concrete antitank walls stood ready to stop an advance.

D-Day Invasion On June 6, 1944—D-Day, as it was known—a fleet of 4,000 Allied ships carried the invasion force to France. Allied

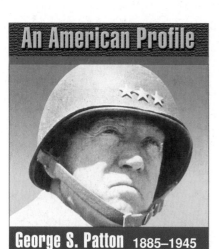

An American Profile

George S. Patton 1885–1945

A brilliant general, George Patton was known as "Old Blood and Guts" for his toughness and drive. "We'll win this war," he predicted, "by showing the Germans we've got more guts than they have." He led American tanks to victory after victory in North Africa.

Patton pushed his troops hard, but he was always ready to get down in the mud and blood with them. Once, marching alongside his men, he saw a soldier with a horribly wounded leg. Patton gave the soldier a dose of painkiller and stayed with the dying man until an ambulance arrived.

Why do you think Patton was willing to walk alongside his troops?

The Allies Advance

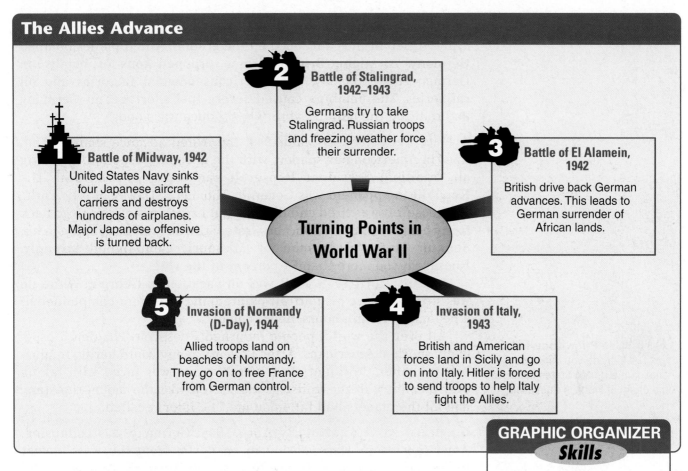

Turning Points in World War II

1 Battle of Midway, 1942
United States Navy sinks four Japanese aircraft carriers and destroys hundreds of airplanes. Major Japanese offensive is turned back.

2 Battle of Stalingrad, 1942–1943
Germans try to take Stalingrad. Russian troops and freezing weather force their surrender.

3 Battle of El Alamein, 1942
British drive back German advances. This leads to German surrender of African lands.

4 Invasion of Italy, 1943
British and American forces land in Sicily and go on into Italy. Hitler is forced to send troops to help Italy fight the Allies.

5 Invasion of Normandy (D-Day), 1944
Allied troops land on beaches of Normandy. They go on to free France from German control.

GRAPHIC ORGANIZER
Skills

Several key victories helped the Allies turn the tide against the Axis powers.

1. **Comprehension** Which of the military actions described above was a turning point in the Pacific war?

2. **Critical Thinking Sequencing** Describe how one of the victories was a necessary first step to another.

troops scrambled ashore at Normandy. One American soldier who landed in the first wave recalled:

> ❝ It all seemed unreal, a sort of dreaming while awake, men were screaming and dying all around me. . . . I honestly could have walked the full length of the beach without touching the ground, they were that thickly strewn about. ❞
>
> —Melvin B. Farrell, *War Memories*

Despite intense German gunfire and heavy losses, Allied forces pushed on. Every day, more soldiers landed to reinforce the advance.

On August 25, 1944, the Allies entered Paris. After four years under Nazi rule, the Parisians greeted their liberators with joy. Within a month, all of France was free.

Victory in Europe

By September, the Allies were moving east toward Germany. However, a shortage of truck fuel slowed the advance.

Advancing Toward Germany On December 16, 1944, German forces began a fierce counterattack. They pushed the Allies back, creating a bulge in the front lines. During the Battle of the Bulge, as it was later called, Audie Murphy emerged as the most honored American hero of the war. At one point, Murphy climbed aboard a burning tank. Alone and wounded, he used the tank's machine gun to hold off enemy troops on three sides.

The Battle of the Bulge slowed the Allies but did not stop them. While Allied armies advanced on the ground, Allied planes bombed Germany. At night, British airmen dropped tons of bombs on German cities. By day, the Americans bombed factories and oil refineries. The bombing caused severe fuel shortages in Germany and reduced the nation's ability to produce war goods.

A New President By mid-1944, the Allied advance shared head-lines in American newspapers with the upcoming election. Breaking all tradition, President Roosevelt ran for a fourth term. His Republican opponent was Governor Thomas E. Dewey of New York.

Roosevelt was tired and ill. "All that is within me cries to go back to my home on the Hudson," he wrote. Still, he and his running mate, Senator Harry S Truman of Missouri, campaigned strongly. Roosevelt won more than 54 percent of the vote.

In early April 1945, FDR was on vacation in Georgia. While he was sitting to have his portrait painted, the President complained of a headache. Within hours, he was dead.

All over the world, people mourned Roosevelt. His death espe-cially shocked Americans. After 12 years, many could hardly remem-ber any other President. As for Truman, he was faced with taking over a country in the midst of war. "I felt like the moon, the stars, and all the planets had fallen on me," he later recalled.

Germany Is Defeated By April 1945, Germany was collapsing. American troops were closing in on Berlin from the west. Soviet troops were advancing from the east. On April 25, American and Soviet troops met at Torgau, 60 miles south of Berlin.

As Allied air raids pounded Berlin, Hitler hid in his underground bunker. Unwilling to accept defeat, he committed suicide. One week later, on May 7, 1945, Germany surrendered to the Allies. On May 8, the Allies celebrated the long-awaited V-E Day—Victory in Europe.

AS YOU READ **Use Prior Knowledge** Why do you think people outside the United States mourned the death of Franklin Roosevelt?

AFTER YOU READ

Section 4 Assessment

Recall

1. **Identify** Explain the signifi-cance of **(a)** Douglas MacArthur, **(b)** Battle of Midway, **(c)** Dwight D. Eisenhower, **(d)** Operation Overlord, **(e)** D-Day, **(f)** Battle of the Bulge, **(g)** Audie Murphy, **(h)** Harry S Truman.

Comprehension

2. Why did the war look bleak for the Allies in 1942?
3. How did the Allies open a sec-ond front in Europe?
4. Describe the final stage of the war in Europe.

Critical Thinking and Writing

5. **Exploring the Main Idea** Review the Main Idea state-ment at the beginning of this section. Then, choose two events described in this sec-tion. For each, write a headline and opening paragraph that might have appeared in an American newspaper.

6. **Making Decisions** If you had been an adviser to Franklin Roosevelt in 1944, would you have encouraged him to run for a fourth term in spite of ill health? Write a note to FDR explaining your reasons.

ACTIVITY

Take It to the NET **Connecting to Today** Use the Internet to read other first-person accounts of the invasion of France. Then, write an essay about why you think Americans are still fascinated by D-Day. Visit *The American Nation* section of **www.phschool.com** for help in completing the activity.

Evaluating the Validity of Internet Sources

Today, there are dozens of Internet sites devoted to World War II, as well as to other historical topics. As a student of history, it is important to evaluate the different Web sites to determine how valid the information is. The page below is from a Web site devoted to the D-Day invasion of France.

Source: The National D-Day Museum, 945 Magazine Street, New Orleans, LA

Learn the Skill *To learn how to evaluate Internet sources, use the following steps:*

1. **Determine the Web site's purpose.** Does the Web site provide information? Is it trying to sell something or to promote a particular point of view?

2. **Examine the information.** Does the site include visuals? Does it include firsthand accounts and other primary source materials?

3. **Compare the information to what you already know.** Does the information agree with what you have read in a textbook or other reliable print source? What other information is provided?

4. **Evaluate the source.** Is the source an established organization? Can you tell who provided the information?

Practice the Skill *Use the information given above to answer the following questions:*

1. What seems to be the purpose of this Web site?

2. **(a)** What kinds of information can you access from this page? **(b)** What other features and links does it include?

3. What additional information does this Web site provide to the facts given in your textbook?

4. **(a)** Who is the provider for this site? **(b)** If you were writing a paper about D-Day, do you think you could use the information provided on this Web site? Why or why not?

Apply the Skill *See the Chapter Review and Assessment.*

5 The End of the War

BEFORE YOU READ

Reading Focus

- How did American forces advance in the Pacific?
- Why did Japan finally surrender?
- What made World War II the deadliest war in history?

Key Terms

island hopping

Navajo code-talkers

kamikaze

Potsdam Declaration

Bataan Death March

Holocaust

Nuremberg Trials

Taking Notes

As you read, prepare an outline of this section. Use roman numerals to indicate the major headings, capital letters for the subheadings, and numbers for the supporting details. The sample at right will help you get started.

> I. War in the Pacific
>   A. U.S. goals
>   1.
>   2.
>   B. Island hopping
>   1.
>   2.
>   C.
> II. The Surrender of Japan
>   A.
>   B.

Main Idea In the Pacific, the Japanese continued to resist American advances until two atomic bombs were dropped on their home islands.

AS YOU READ

American troops at Saipan

Predict What might happen if other islands in the Pacific prove as hard to capture as Saipan?

Setting the Scene As Allied armies swept into Europe, a battle raged on the Pacific island of Saipan (si PAN). An American force of nearly 100,000 pounded a Japanese garrison of 32,000 troops. By the end, the Americans would suffer some 14,000 casualties. The Japanese would lose almost every soldier on Saipan.

Although greatly outnumbered, the Japanese fought to the bitter end. Many charged to their deaths shouting *"banzai"* ("ten thousand years") and carrying nothing but spears. Others jumped from cliffs to avoid capture. One reporter wondered, "Do the suicides . . . mean that the whole Japanese race will choose death before surrender?"

The surrender of Germany left only Japan to defeat. Still, as the battle of Saipan showed, the price of final victory could be immense.

War in the Pacific

While the war raged in Europe, the Allies kept up pressure on Japan. The United States had two main goals in the Pacific war: to regain the Philippines and to invade Japan.

Island Hopping To gain control of the Pacific Ocean, American forces used a strategy of capturing some Japanese-held islands and going around others. In this island-hopping campaign, each island that was won became another steppingstone to Japan.

A deadly routine developed. First, American ships shelled an island. Next, troops waded ashore under heavy gunfire. Then, in hand-to-hand fighting, Americans overcame fierce Japanese resistance.

Navajo soldiers made a key contribution to American strategy in the Pacific. Using their own language, they radioed vital messages from island to island. The Japanese intercepted the messages but were unable to understand these Navajo code-talkers.

In October 1944, American forces under General MacArthur finally returned to the Philippines. In hard-fought battles, the Americans then captured the islands of Iwo Jima (EE woh JEE muh) and Okinawa (oh kuh NAH wuh) from the Japanese.

Japanese leaders stressed an ancient code known as *Bushido,* or the Way of the Warrior. It emphasized loyalty, honor, and sacrifice. To surrender was to "lose face" or be dishonored. In suicide missions, kamikaze (kah muh KAH zee) pilots loaded old planes with bombs and then deliberately crashed them into Allied ships.

Attacking the Home Islands By April 1945, American forces were close enough to launch attacks against the Japanese home islands. American bombers pounded factories and cities. American warships bombarded the coast and sank ships. The Japanese people suffered terribly. Yet, their leaders promised a glorious victory.

United States military leaders made plans to invade Japan in the autumn. They warned that the invasion might cost between 150,000 and 250,000 American casualties.

The Surrender of Japan

Truman, Churchill, and Stalin met at Potsdam, Germany, in July 1945. While there, Truman received word that American scientists had successfully tested a secret new weapon, the atomic bomb. A single bomb was powerful enough to destroy an entire city. Some scientists believed that it was too dangerous to use.

From Potsdam, the Allied leaders sent a message warning Japan to surrender or face "prompt and utter destruction." Japanese

GEOGRAPHY
Skills

After the Battle of Midway, the United States took the offensive against the Japanese Empire.

1. **Location** On the map, locate **(a)** Pearl Harbor, **(b)** Midway Island, **(c)** Philippine Islands, **(d)** Iwo Jima, **(e)** Okinawa, **(f)** Hiroshima.

2. **Movement** Which battle did the United States have to win before moving against Iwo Jima and Okinawa?

3. **Critical Thinking Drawing Conclusions** Based on this map, why do you think aircraft carriers were vital to American strategy in the Pacific?

World War II in the Pacific

▲ **Past**

▲ **Present**

Viewing History

Americans Remember the Holocaust

In 1945, American troops were shocked by the sight of Jewish prisoners in Nazi concentration camps (left). Today, many cities in the United States and other countries have Holocaust museums. At right, a visitor looks at pictures of some of the victims. The remembrance banner was created by an American student. **Linking Past and Present** *Why is it important for us to remember the Holocaust?*

leaders did not know about the destructive power of the atomic bomb. They ignored the Potsdam Declaration.

On August 6, 1945, the American bomber *Enola Gay* dropped an atomic bomb on Hiroshima, Japan. The blast destroyed most of the city, killing at least 70,000 people and injuring an equal number. On August 9, a second atomic bomb was dropped, on Nagasaki. About 40,000 residents died instantly. In both Nagasaki and Hiroshima, many more people later died from the effects of atomic radiation.

On August 14, 1945, the emperor of Japan announced that his nation would surrender. The formal surrender took place on September 2 aboard the USS *Missouri* in Tokyo Bay. The warship flew the same American flag that had waved over Washington, D.C., on the day that Japan bombed Pearl Harbor.

V-J ("Victory in Japan") Day sparked wild celebrations across the United States. People honked their car horns. Soldiers and sailors danced in victory parades.

The Deadliest War in History

World War II was the deadliest war in history. The exact number of casualties will probably never be known. However, historians estimate that between 30 million and 60 million people were killed.

World War I had been fought mainly in trenches. During World War II, bombers destroyed houses, factories, and farms. By 1945, millions were homeless and had no way to earn a living.

After the war, Americans heard horrifying stories of the brutal mistreatment of prisoners of war. When the Japanese captured the Philippines in 1942, they forced about 75,000 American and Filipino prisoners to march 65 miles with little food or water. About 10,000 prisoners died or were killed during the Bataan Death March.

 Visualize Form a mental picture of the Bataan Death March. Describe what you see and how you think the people involved felt.

The Holocaust In the last months of the European war, Allied forces uncovered other horrors. The Allies had heard about Nazi death camps. As they advanced into Germany and Eastern Europe, they discovered the full extent of the Holocaust, the slaughter of Europe's Jews by the Nazis. During the war, the Nazis imprisoned Jews from Germany and the nations they conquered. More than 6 million Jews were tortured and murdered.

When Allied troops reached the death camps, they saw the gas chambers the Nazis had used to murder hundreds of thousands. The battle-hardened veterans wept at the sight of the dead and dying. After touring one death camp, General Omar Bradley wrote:

> 66 The smell of death overwhelmed us even before we passed through. . . . More than 3,200 naked, emaciated bodies had been flung into shallow graves. 99
> —Omar N. Bradley, *A General's Life*

Nearly 6 million Poles, Slavs, and Gypsies were also victims of the death camps. Nazis killed many prisoners of war, as well as people they considered unfit because of physical or mental disabilities.

War Crimes Trials As the full truth of the Holocaust was revealed, the Allies decided to put Nazi leaders on trial. In 1945 and 1946, they conducted war crimes trials in Nuremberg, Germany. As a result of the Nuremberg Trials, 12 Nazi leaders were sentenced to death. Thousands of other Nazis were imprisoned. The Allies also tried and executed Japanese leaders accused of war crimes.

Section 5 Assessment

Recall
1. **Identify** Explain the significance of **(a)** Navajo code-talkers, **(b)** Potsdam Declaration, **(c)** Bataan Death March, **(d)** Holocaust, **(e)** Nuremberg Trials.
2. **Define** **(a)** island hopping, **(b)** kamikaze.

Comprehension
3. What strategy did the United States follow in the Pacific?
4. How did the United States force Japan to surrender?
5. Why was World War II more deadly than World War I?

Critical Thinking and Writing
6. **Exploring the Main Idea** Review the Main Idea statement at the beginning of this section. Then, write the opening words of a speech President Truman might have given to explain why he decided to use the atomic bomb.
7. **Drawing Inferences** The Allies did not try enemy leaders as war criminals after World War I. Write a paragraph explaining why you think they conducted such trials after World War II and whether you agree with this decision.

ACTIVITY

 Take It to the NET

Preparing a Report Use the Internet to find out about the Manhattan Project, the secret government project to develop the atomic bomb. Write a summary of its goals and progress. Visit *The American Nation* section of **www.phschool.com** for help in completing the activity.

CREATING A CHAPTER SUMMARY

Copy the timeline below. Fill in each date with key events of each year of the World War II era. One entry has been included to help you get started.

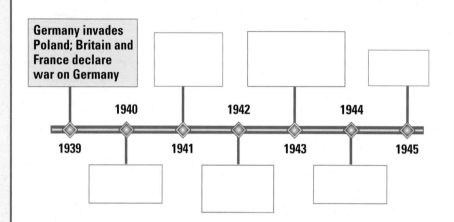

Germany invades Poland; Britain and France declare war on Germany

1939   1940   1941   1942   1943   1944   1945

TEXT

For additional review and enrichment activities, see the interactive version of *The American Nation,* available on the Web and on CD-ROM.

Take It to the NET

Chapter Self-Test For practice test questions for Chapter 27, visit *The American Nation* section of **www.phschool.com**.

Building Vocabulary

Review the chapter vocabulary words listed below. Then, use the words and their definitions to create a matching quiz. Exchange quizzes with another student. Check each other's answers when you are finished.

1. totalitarian state
2. aggression
3. concentration camp
4. appeasement
5. blitzkrieg
6. rationing
7. victory garden
8. compensation
9. island hopping
10. kamikaze

Reviewing Key Facts

11. What are the main features of Fascism? (Section 1)
12. What were the goals of the Atlantic Charter? (Section 2)
13. What role did women play in the American war effort? (Section 3)
14. Why was D-Day important? (Section 4)
15. Describe the terrible costs of World War II. (Section 5)

Critical Thinking and Writing

16. **Identifying Alternatives** What actions do you think the United States and the European democracies might have taken to discourage aggression? List at least two alternatives.

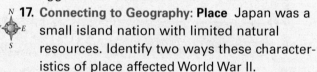

17. **Connecting to Geography: Place** Japan was a small island nation with limited natural resources. Identify two ways these characteristics of place affected World War II.
18. **Making Decisions** Why do you think many young Japanese Americans were eager to volunteer for military service during World War II? Write a letter as though you were a member of the 442nd Nisei Regimental Combat Team explaining your reasons to a friend.
19. **Evaluating Information** What qualities do you think Dwight D. Eisenhower needed to succeed as commander of the Allied forces in Europe?
20. **Linking Past and Present** List three ways in which the world today might be different if the Allies had not defeated the Axis powers in World War II.

Analyzing Primary Sources

A reporter filed this account after flying with the team that dropped the atomic bomb on Nagasaki:

> 66 Observers in the tail of our ship saw a giant ball of fire rise as though from the bowels of the earth, belching forth enormous white smoke rings. Next they saw a giant pillar of purple fire, ten thousand feet high, shooting skyward with enormous speed. . . . It was a living thing, a new species of being, born right before our incredulous eyes. 99

—William L. Laurence, *New York Times,*
September 9, 1945

21. What words does Laurence use to create a strong visual image?
22. To what does he compare the bombing?
23. What emotions does this report convey?
24. The bombing took place on August 9. Why do you think this report was not published until a month later?

Evaluating the Validity of Internet Sources

The source information below might be found on an Internet site. Read the words and answer the questions that follow.

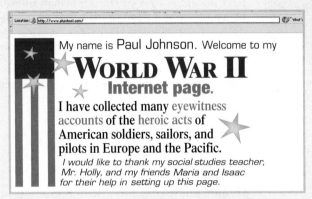

My name is Paul Johnson. Welcome to my
WORLD WAR II
Internet page.
I have collected many eyewitness accounts of the heroic acts of American soldiers, sailors, and pilots in Europe and the Pacific.
I would like to thank my social studies teacher, Mr. Holly, and my friends Maria and Isaac for their help in setting up this page.

25. Based on the above statements alone, would you consider this Web site a valid source of information?
    A Yes, because it is on the Internet.
    B No, because it is not a government Web site.
    C No, because it was created by a student.
    D No, because Johnson does not identify where he found the stories.
26. What information would you need before using in a report any of the eyewitness stories found on this Web site?

ACTIVITIES

Connecting With . . . Culture

Interviewing Find somebody in your family or community who grew up during World War II. Prepare a series of 5–10 questions, and interview that person about memories of life on the home front, people whom they knew in the service, or the victory celebrations. Record the interview in writing or on tape, and present it to the class. (If you cannot find an appropriate person, use your questions to prepare a mock interview with a partner.)

Take It to the NET

Connecting to Today

Writing a Report Use the Internet to find out about the planning and building of the National World War II Memorial in the early 2000s. Write a report describing how the campaign started and how it proceeded. For help in starting this activity, visit *The American Nation* section of **www.phschool.com**.

Researching

Making a Map Use the Internet to find out more about one land or sea battle during World War II. Then, use this information to prepare a battle map that shows the locations and movements of opposing forces. For help in starting this activity, visit *The American Nation* section of **www.phschool.com**.

The Human Comedy

William Saroyan

William Saroyan

Introduction Published in 1943, *The Human Comedy* was one of the first novels to look at the American home front during World War II. The hero is 14-year-old Homer Macauley, who works after school delivering telegrams. Here, for the first time, he must bring a message telling a mother that her son has been killed in battle.

Vocabulary Before you read the selection, find the meaning of these words in a dictionary: **awkwardly, disgrace.**

Homer knew that Mrs. Rosa Sandoval was shocked to see him. Her first word was the first word of surprise. She said "Oh," as if instead of a messenger she had thought of opening the door to someone she had known a long time and would be pleased to sit down with. Before she spoke again she studied Homer's eyes and Homer knew that she knew the message was not a welcome one.

"You have a telegram?" she said.

It wasn't Homer's fault. His work was to deliver telegrams. Even so, it seemed to him that he was part of the whole mistake. He felt awkward and almost as if he *alone* were responsible for what had happened. At the same time he wanted to come right out and say, "I'm only a messenger, Mrs. Sandoval. I'm very sorry I must bring you a telegram like this, but it is only because it is my work to do so."

"Who is it for?" the Mexican woman said.

"Mrs. Rosa Sandoval, 1129 G Street," Homer said. He extended the telegram to the Mexican woman, but she would not touch it.

"Are you Mrs. Sandoval?" Homer said.

"Please," the woman said. "Please come in. I cannot read English. I am Mexican. I read only *La Prensa* which comes from Mexico City." She paused a moment and looked at the boy standing awkwardly as near the door as he could be and still be inside the house.

"Please," she said, "what does the telegram say?"

"Mrs. Sandoval," the messenger said, "the telegram says—"

But now the woman interrupted him. "But you must open the telegram and *read* it to me," she said. "You have not opened it."

"Yes ma'am," Homer said as if he were speaking to a school teacher who had just corrected him.

He opened the telegram with nervous fingers. The Mexican woman stooped to pick up the torn envelope, and tried to smooth it out. As she did so she said, "Who sent the telegram—my son Juan Domingo?

"No ma'am," Homer said. "The telegram is from the War Department."

"War Department?" the Mexican woman said.

"Mrs. Sandoval," Homer said swiftly, "your son is dead. Maybe it's a mistake. Everybody makes a mistake, Mrs. Sandoval. Maybe it wasn't your son. Maybe it was somebody else. The telegram *says* it was Juan Domingo. But maybe the telegram is wrong."

The Mexican woman pretended not to hear.

"Oh, do not be afraid, " she said. "Come inside. Come inside. I will bring you candy." She took the boy's arm and brought him to the table at the center of the room and there she made him sit.

"All boys like candy," she said. "I will bring you candy." She went into another room and soon returned with an old chocolate candy box. She opened the box at the table and in it Homer saw a strange kind of candy.

"Here," she said. "Eat this candy. All boys like candy."

Homer took a piece of the candy from the box, put it into his mouth, and tried to chew.

"You would not bring me a bad telegram," she said. "You are a good boy—like my little Juanito when he was a little boy. Eat another piece." And she made the messenger take another piece of the candy.

Homer sat chewing the dry candy while the Mexican woman talked. "It is our own candy," she said "from cactus. I make it for my Juanito when he come home, but *you* eat it. You are my boy too."

Now suddenly she began to sob, holding herself in as if weeping were a disgrace. Homer wanted to get up and run but he knew he would stay. He even thought he might stay the rest of his life. He just didn't know what else to do to try to make the woman less unhappy, and if she had *asked* him to take the place of her son, he would not have been able to refuse, because he would not have known how.

Mother and child of an American soldier

Analyzing Literature

1. What is Mrs. Sandoval's first reaction to finding out that she has received a telegram?
   A Anger
   B Relief
   C Fear
   D Sorrow

2. Why does Homer tell Mrs. Sandoval the telegram may be a mistake?
   A He knows Juan Domingo is still alive.
   B He wants to make Mrs. Sandoval feel better.
   C He hopes to get a piece of candy.
   D He does not care about Mrs. Sandoval's feelings.

3. **Critical Thinking and Writing** **Drawing Inferences** Write a paragraph explaining how you would have felt about working as a telegraph messenger during World War II.

TEST PREPARATION

1 Which of the following New Deal programs is correctly matched with one of its main goals?

   A TVA: prevent another depression

   B WPA: reduce unemployment

   C CCC: provide relief for farmers

   D FDIC: promote industrial recovery

Use the quotation <u>and</u> your knowledge of social studies to answer the following question.

> **Ernie Pyle, *Brave Men* (adapted)**
>
> "On the beach lay, expended, sufficient men and mechanism for a small war. They were gone forever now. And yet we could afford it . . . because we were on, we had our toehold, and behind us there were enormous replacements for this wreckage on the beach."

2 In the above passage, Pyle is describing the aftermath of what event?

   A Bombing of Pearl Harbor

   B Battle of Midway

   C D-Day

   D Bombing of Hiroshima

3 What was a chief goal of the quota system introduced in the 1920s?

   A To end immigration

   B To control sources of immigration

   C To prevent labor unions from going on strike

   D To limit union membership

4 Which of the following was not an economic effect of World War II?

   A Increased production of consumer goods

   B Rationing of gasoline and rubber

   C Increase in taxes

   D End of the Great Depression

Use the map <u>and</u> your knowledge of social studies to answer the following question.

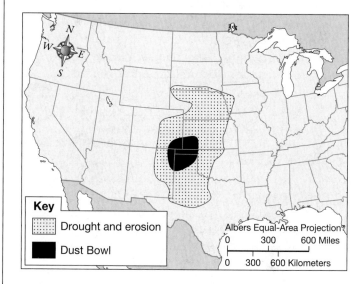

5 Which statement is best supported by this map?

   A The most severe dust storms hit the state of Oklahoma.

   B Drought and dust storms had no impact on California.

   C Soil erosion was a severe problem in Kansas and Nebraska.

   D Ten states were hit by drought and erosion during the depression.

6 Which of the following was not an effect of mass production of automobiles?

A It made automobiles less expensive to buy.

B It helped create a new mass culture.

C It stimulated the growth of other industries.

D It contributed to a decline in the rural population.

Use the graph <u>and</u> your knowledge of social studies to answer the following question.

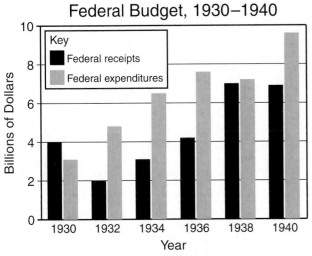

Federal Budget, 1930–1940

Key
■ Federal receipts
▨ Federal expenditures

Billions of Dollars / Year

Source: *Historical Statistics of the United States*

7 What development is best illustrated by this graph?

A Deficit spending as a result of the New Deal

B Economic impact of the stock market crash

C Government regulation of the economy under the New Deal

D Effects of World War II on the federal budget

8 "Writers of the 1920s were often critical of traditional American values." Which of the following facts best supports this generalization?

A Sinclair Lewis poked fun at small-town life.

B Langston Hughes expressed pride in his African heritage.

C F. Scott Fitzgerald included flappers as characters in many of his novels.

D Ernest Hemingway's simple, powerful writing style influenced a new generation of writers.

9 In which of the following pairs was the first event a direct cause of the second?

A Japan bombs Pearl Harbor; World War II begins

B France and Britain declare war on Germany; Hitler invades Poland

C Atlantic Charter is signed; United States sends aid to Britain

D Holocaust is revealed; Nuremberg Trials are held

Writing Practice

10 Compare and contrast the economic views and policies of Calvin Coolidge, Herbert Hoover, and Franklin Roosevelt.

11 "During World War II, Americans put aside their differences to work together for a common goal." Do you agree with this statement, disagree with this statement, or partly agree with this statement? Give reasons to support your answer.

Unit 9

The Bold Experiment Continues

A World Drawn Closer
In *The World,* Diana Ong shows the many people of the United States as part of a world that has grown increasingly closer together.

"We have a place, all of us, in a long story. . . . It is the American story; a story of flawed and fallible people, united across the generations by grand and enduring ideals."

—President George W. Bush (2001)

The Cold War Era

1945–1991

Cheering the Berlin Airlift

Rocketing into orbit

1948

United States planes break a Soviet blockade by bringing desperately needed food, fuel, and supplies to the people of Berlin.

1950

The Korean War begins.

1962

Friendship 7, with astronaut John Glenn aboard, blasts off for orbit around Earth.

AMERICAN EVENTS

Presidential Terms | John F. Kennedy 1961–1963 | | Lyndon B. Johnson

Harry S Truman 1945–1953 | Dwight D. Eisenhower 1953–1961 | 1963–1969

1944 ★ ★ **1956** ★ **1968**

WORLD EVENTS

▲ **1946**
The Philippines gains its independence from the United States.

▲ **1959**
Fidel Castro comes to power in Cuba.

The Global Cold War

For more than 40 years, a bitterly contested Cold War divided the world into opposing camps.

East Germany
Poland
Czechoslovakia
SOVIET UNION
Hungary
Greece
Turkey
Korea
UNITED STATES
Lebanon
Iraq
Iran
Afghanistan
CHINA
Israel
Cuba
PACIFIC OCEAN
El Salvador
Grenada
Nicaragua
ATLANTIC OCEAN
Cambodia
Vietnam
PACIFIC OCEAN
Ethiopia
Somalia
Malaysia
Congo
INDIAN OCEAN
Angola
Chile

60°N
30°N
0°
30°S

150°W 120°W 90°W 60°W 30°W 0° 30°E 60°E 90°E 120°E 150°E

Robinson Projection
0   1000   2000 Miles
0 1000 2000 Kilometers

Key

Communist countries

★ Cold War hot spots

On patrol in Vietnam's Mekong Delta

Russian children and a toppled statue of one-time communist leader Vladimir Lenin

1968
More than a half million American troops are fighting in Vietnam.

1974
The United States removes the last of its combat troops from South Vietnam.

1991
Statues of former communist leaders are toppled as communism falls and the Soviet Union breaks up.

| Richard M. Nixon | Gerald R. Ford | Jimmy Carter | Ronald Reagan 1981–1989 | George | H. W. Bush |
| 1969–1974 | 1974–1977 | 1977–1981 | | 1989– | 1993 |

1968 · · **1980** · · · **1992** ·

1975 ▲
Communists win control over all of South Vietnam, ending the Vietnam War.

1989 ▲
The Berlin Wall is torn down by the people of Berlin.

1 The Cold War Begins

Reading Focus

- How did the Cold War begin?
- How did the United States respond to Soviet expansion?
- How did the crisis over Berlin lead to new Cold War alliances?
- What happened in 1949 to increase Cold War tensions?

Key Terms

Cold War
satellite nation
containment
Truman Doctrine
Marshall Plan
Berlin Airlift
Berlin Wall
North Atlantic Treaty Organization
Warsaw Pact
United Nations

Taking Notes

Copy this flowchart. As you read, fill in the boxes with some of the major events described in this section that raised Cold War tensions between the United States and the Soviet Union. The first box has been completed to help you get started.

- Soviet Union occupies Eastern Europe

Main Idea After World War II, distrust between the United States and the Soviet Union led to the Cold War.

AS YOU READ **The Red Army marches**

Draw Inferences Why might the Soviet Union want to expand its power into Eastern Europe?

Setting the Scene

An important telegram arrived at the State Department in Washington, D.C., in February 1946. It was from George Kennan, a top American diplomat in Moscow. Kennan was worried by the activities of the Soviet Union. At the time, communist forces were attempting to take over nations in Asia, Eastern Europe, and Southern Europe. As he later wrote, the Soviet Union was like a toy car "wound up and headed in a given direction, stopping only when it meets some unanswerable force."

Kennan especially worried about Soviet actions in Eastern Europe. There, Soviet dictator Joseph Stalin was using brutal methods to put communist governments in power. Kennan urged the United States to oppose these Soviet policies.

After World War II, the United States and the Soviet Union plunged into a new kind of war. They did not clash directly in battle. Instead, they competed for power around the world.

This intense rivalry became known as the Cold War. It lasted for nearly 50 years. The Cold War pitted the West (the United States and its allies) against the East (the Soviet Union and its allies).

Origins of the Cold War

During World War II, the United States, Britain, and the Soviet Union had worked together. Yet, even before the war ended, tensions surfaced among the Allies.

Growing Distrust The United States and Britain distrusted the Soviet Union. They disliked the communist rejection of religion and private property. They were angered by Soviet efforts to overthrow noncommunist governments. In fact, Soviet leaders boasted that communism would soon destroy free enterprise systems around the world.

The Soviets, in turn, distrusted the Western powers. They feared that the United States, now the world's most powerful nation, would use its military power to attack the Soviet Union. They feared that the United States would try to rebuild Germany in order to challenge the Soviet Union.

Broken Promises Before World War II ended, Soviet armies drove German forces out of the Soviet Union and Eastern Europe and back into Germany. As a result, Soviet troops occupied much of Eastern Europe.

Stalin promised to hold free elections "as soon as possible" in these Eastern European nations. He soon broke that promise. "A freely elected government in any of the Eastern European countries would be anti-Soviet," he said, "and that we cannot allow."

By 1948, Communists controlled the government of every Eastern European country. Except for Yugoslavia, these countries became satellite nations of the Soviet Union. A satellite nation is one that is dominated politically and economically by a more powerful nation. In each satellite nation, the Soviets backed harsh dictators. Citizens who protested were imprisoned or killed.

The "Iron Curtain" As early as 1946 the British statesman Winston Churchill had warned against Soviet expansion into Eastern Europe. Naming two cities that were located in the north and south of Europe, he said: "From Stettin in the Baltic to Trieste in the Adriatic, an iron curtain has descended across the Continent." The "iron curtain" cut off Soviet-run Eastern Europe from the democratic governments of the West.

Western fears of communism deepened as communist parties, backed by Stalin, achieved success in other parts of Europe. Italian Communists won many seats in the Italian parliament. In Greece, communist rebels waged a civil war to topple the Greek government. Communist-led unions conducted strikes that paralyzed the weak economies.

The United States Responds

President Harry S Truman was determined to keep Soviet influence contained within existing boundaries. Thus, his Cold War policy was known as containment.

The Truman Doctrine In March 1947, President Truman asked Congress for $400 million in military and economic aid for Greece and Turkey. Eventually, with American aid, both countries held off communist threats.

This program to encourage nations to resist communist expansion became known as the Truman Doctrine. Truman explained the need for this policy:

> 66 The free peoples of the world look to us for support in maintaining their freedoms. If we falter in our leadership, we may endanger the peace of the world—and we shall surely endanger the welfare of our own nation. 99

—Harry Truman, Speech, March 12, 1947

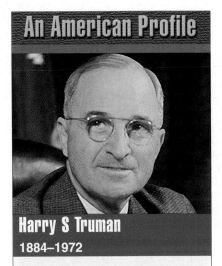

An American Profile

Harry S Truman
1884–1972

When the United States entered World War I, Harry Truman was 32 and barely able to see without glasses. He could easily have escaped the draft. But, Harry wanted to serve his country. So, he memorized the eye chart and was accepted.

Truman was sent to France as an artillery captain. During a night skirmish, he was on horseback when his unit came under fire from German positions. Abandoning their weapons, the soldiers began to run. In the panic, Truman was thrown from his horse. He remounted and, with shells exploding all around, shamed his men into returning to their guns. For the rest of the war, the unit fought bravely and well.

What leadership qualities did Truman show in combat?

The Marshall Plan Other European nations needed aid, too. The war had left Europe's homes, roads, and factories in ruins. When Secretary of State George Marshall toured Europe, he saw millions of homeless, hungry refugees.

Marshall feared that these conditions might encourage communist revolutions. So in June 1947, he proposed an ambitious plan to help Europe rebuild. The President and Congress accepted the Marshall Plan.

Between 1948 and 1952, the Marshall Plan provided more than $12 billion in aid to Western European countries. By helping these nations rebuild their economies, the Marshall Plan reduced the threat of communist revolutions in Western Europe.

Crisis Over Berlin

In 1948, a crisis developed in Berlin, Germany's largest city. After the war, the Allies had divided Germany into four zones. American, British, French, and Soviet troops each occupied a zone. Berlin, too, was divided among the four Allies, even though it lay inside the Soviet zone.

By 1948, the United States, Britain, and France wanted to reunite their zones. Stalin opposed that plan. A reunited Germany, he felt, would again be a threat to the Soviet Union. To show his determination to prevent a united Western Germany, Stalin closed all roads, railway lines, and river routes connecting Berlin with West Germany. The blockade cut off West Berlin from the rest of the world.

Berlin Airlift President Truman would not let West Berlin fall into Soviet hands. At the same time, he did not want to order American troops to open a path to West Berlin through the Soviet-occupied zone. That move could trigger war.

Instead, Truman approved a huge airlift. During the Berlin Airlift, hundreds of American and British planes carried tons of food, fuel, and other supplies to the two million West Berliners every day.

The airlift lasted for almost a year. Stalin finally saw that the West would not abandon West Berlin. In May 1949, he lifted the blockade. After the blockade, the United States, Great Britain, and France merged their zones into the Federal Republic of Germany, or West Germany.

Berlin Wall Both Germany and Berlin remained divided throughout the 1950s. With American aid, West Germany rebuilt its economy and became a prosperous nation. In time, the Soviet zone became the German Democratic Republic, or East Germany.

East Germany was much poorer than West Germany, and it had a government that was undemocratic. For years, East Germans fled communism by crossing into West Berlin. The flight of so many people embarrassed the communists.

Viewing History

Devastated Europe

Europe

Like this German city, much of Europe lay in ruins after World War II. Homes, factories, roads, and farms had been destroyed. **Identifying Alternatives** *What sort of aid do you think was most helpful to the people of Europe?*

Cold War in Europe

Key
- NATO nations, 1955
- Warsaw Pact, 1955
- Neutral nations
- Areas added to the Soviet Union after World War II

Albers Equal-Area Projection

In 1961, the East German government built a huge concrete wall topped with barbed wire. It sealed off East Berlin from West Berlin. East Berliners who tried to scale the wall were shot by East German border guards. The Berlin Wall cut off contact between families and friends. It became a bitter symbol of the Cold War that divided Europe and the world.

New Alliances

New military alliances emerged during the Cold War. A world peace-keeping organization was also set up.

Cold War Alliances To contain Soviet influences, the United States set up alliances with friendly nations. In 1949, it joined with many Western European countries to form the North Atlantic Treaty Organization, or NATO. A key NATO goal was to defend Western Europe against any Soviet threat.

In 1955, the Soviet Union formed its own military alliance, the Warsaw Pact. The Soviet Union dominated its Warsaw Pact neighbors, forcing them to follow its policies.

United Nations Many disputes were brought before a new world organization, the United Nations (UN). Fifty-one nations ratified the UN charter in October 1945. Over time, membership in the United Nations expanded as new nations were admitted.

Under the UN charter, member nations agree to bring disputes

GEOGRAPHY
Skills

By 1955, the United States and 14 other nations belonged to NATO. That same year, the Soviet Union and seven Eastern European nations formed the Warsaw Pact.

1. **Location** On the map, locate **(a)** the Soviet Union, **(b)** Poland, **(c)** East Germany, **(d)** West Germany, **(e)** Yugoslavia.

2. **Region** Which NATO nations bordered Warsaw Pact nations?

3. **Critical Thinking Drawing Conclusions** Why do you think most of the nations of Western Europe joined NATO?

before the body for peaceful settlement. Every member has a seat in the General Assembly, where problems can be discussed. A smaller Security Council also discusses conflicts that threaten peace.

Over the years, the UN has succeeded best in fighting hunger and disease and in improving education. UN relief programs have provided food, medicine, and supplies to victims of famine, war, and other disasters. Preserving peace has proved more difficult. Some nations have rejected United Nations resolutions. Still, UN negotiators and peacekeeping forces have sometimes eased dangerous crises.

1949: Year of Shocks

Until 1949, most Americans felt that they had the upper hand in the Cold War. After all, the United States was the only country with the atomic bomb. Then in September 1949, the United States learned that the Soviet Union had tested an atomic bomb.

A second shock followed. Communist forces, led by Mao Zedong (mow dzuh DOONG), gained power in China. The United States had long backed the Nationalists, led by Jiang Jieshi (jyawng jeh SHEE).* After a long civil war, Mao's forces triumphed. In October 1949, Mao set up the People's Republic of China. Jiang and his forces retreated to Taiwan, an island off the coast of China.

Communist leaders in China and the Soviet Union often disagreed with each other. Yet together, the two nations controlled almost a quarter of the globe. Many Americans feared that communism would spread still farther.

AS YOU READ **Predict** How might American foreign policy change as a result of the shocks of 1949?

---

* In earlier textbooks, this name is spelled Chiang Kai-shek.

Section 1 Assessment

Recall

1. **Identify** Explain the significance of **(a)** Cold War, **(b)** Truman Doctrine, **(c)** Marshall Plan, **(d)** Berlin Airlift, **(e)** Berlin Wall, **(f)** North Atlantic Treaty Organization, **(g)** Warsaw Pact, **(h)** United Nations.
2. **Define** **(a)** satellite nation, **(b)** containment.

Comprehension

3. Describe two reasons for the tensions that led to the Cold War.
4. How did the United States try to stop the spread of communism in Europe?

5. What military alliances emerged during the Cold War?
6. What two 1949 crises raised Cold War tensions?

Critical Thinking and Writing

7. **Exploring the Main Idea** Review the Main Idea statement at the beginning of this section. Then, write a dialog between a Soviet and an American diplomat on the causes of the Cold War.
8. **Drawing Inferences** After World War I, the United States refused to join the League of Nations. Why do you think it joined the United Nations after World War II?

ACTIVITY

 Take It to the NET **Connecting to Today** Since World War II, the United States has played a leading role in international organizations such as NATO. Using the Internet, find out more about NATO's history. Then, describe some of NATO's activities today. Visit *The American Nation* section of **www.phschool.com** for help in completing the activity.

Predicting Consequences

Historical events often have effects that reach far into the future. To predict these consequences, it is necessary to weigh current evidence carefully. By drawing conclusions from a variety of sources, it is possible to make informed predictions about future developments.

This excerpt from a conversation with Joseph Stalin in 1945 addresses the growing split between the Soviet Union and the Western powers:

“In Poland, in the Balkans, and in China, everywhere agents [of the United States and Great Britain] spread the information that the war with us will break out any day now. . . . [They want] to push us away from our allies—Poland, Romania, Yugoslavia and Bulgaria. I asked them directly when they were starting the war against us. And they said ‘What are you saying?’ Whether in thirty years or so they want to have another war. . . . This would bring them great profit, particularly in the case of America, which is beyond the oceans and couldn't care less about the effects of the war. Their policy of sparing Germany testifies to that. He who spares the aggressor wants another war.”

—Joseph Stalin, November 14, 1945

Learn the Skill *To predict consequences, use the following steps:*

1. **Identify the developments.** What events or developments have taken place? Are conflicts evident?

2. **Analyze information.** What facts are available? What opinions are given? What conclusions can be drawn?

3. **Predict possible future consequences.** How might present events affect the future? What trends are developing?

Practice the Skill *Answer the following questions based on Stalin's conversation and the cartoon above.*

1. **(a)** What prompted Stalin's angry comments? **(b)** What development prompted the cartoon from an American newspaper?

2. **(a)** What does Stalin expect future relations between the Western powers and the Soviet Union to be like? **(b)** What symbols does the cartoonist use to show the Soviet Union, France, Britain, and the United States?

3. Based on the speech and the cartoon, what consequences might you predict for future relations between the United States and the Soviet Union?

Apply the Skill *See the Chapter Review and Assessment.*

2 The Korean War Period

BEFORE YOU READ

Reading Focus

- Why did the United States become involved in the conflict in Korea?
- How did the fighting in Korea end?
- What were the results of the hunt for Communists at home?

Key Terms

38th parallel

demilitarized zone

perjury

censure

Taking Notes

On a sheet of paper, draw a concept web like the one shown here. As you read this section, fill in each blank oval with important facts about how the Cold War affected the United States in the 1950s.

EFFECTS OF THE COLD WAR

North Korea attacks South Korea

Main Idea During the Korean War, the United States and the United Nations defended South Korea against attack from North Korea and China.

AS YOU READ

Wounded in Korea

Use Prior Knowledge

Freewrite a list of three to five things that you know about Korea.

Setting the Scene The sound of exploding shells woke Joseph Darrigo early on June 25, 1950. Darrigo was an American military adviser to the South Korean army. He was stationed at the **38th parallel,** the dividing line between South Korea and communist North Korea.

Darrigo knew at once what was happening. The North Koreans were attacking across the 38th parallel. He hurried to alert a nearby military base but arrived too late. North Korean soldiers were already there. He later recalled:

> 66 Once they fired four or five bullets and I still hadn't been shot, I figured God was steering them away from me. 99
>
> —Joseph Darrigo, Interview, 1995

Darrigo survived the attack, but many others did not.

The fighting that erupted that day in Korea was directly linked to the Cold War. It soon involved not only Koreans, but also the United Nations, the United States, China, and other powers.

The Korean Conflict

Korea is a peninsula in East Asia. Russia and China border it to the north and the west. Japan lies across the Sea of Japan to the east. In the past, these powerful neighbors often competed to control Korea. From 1910 to 1945, Japan ruled Korea as a colony.

Korea Divided As World War II ended, the United States and the Soviet Union agreed to a temporary division of Korea at the 38th parallel of latitude. Both nations agreed that Korea would soon be reunited.

As the Cold War deepened, however, Korea remained divided. The United States backed a noncommunist government in South Korea. The Soviet Union supported the communist government of

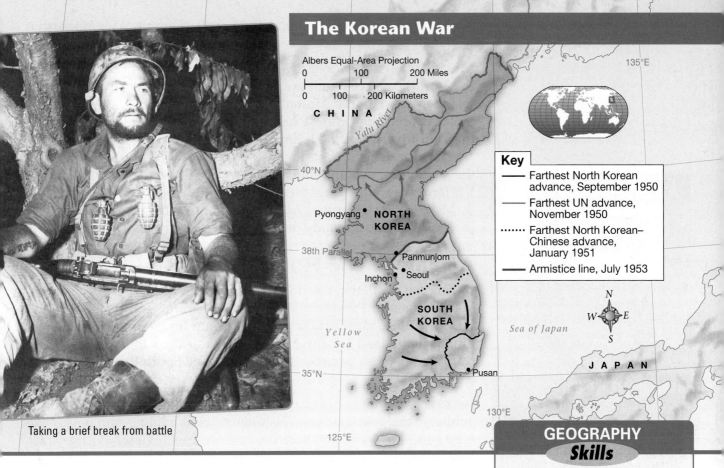

The Korean War

Albers Equal-Area Projection

CHINA

NORTH KOREA

Pyongyang

38th Parallel

Panmunjom

Inchon • Seoul

SOUTH KOREA

Yellow Sea

Sea of Japan

JAPAN

Pusan

Key
— Farthest North Korean advance, September 1950
— Farthest UN advance, November 1950
······ Farthest North Korean–Chinese advance, January 1951
— Armistice line, July 1953

Taking a brief break from battle

North Korea. There was no agreement on when, or how, to reunite Korea.

Invasion In June 1950, North Korean troops swept across the 38th parallel into South Korea. The South Korean army was quickly overwhelmed. Within days, North Korean forces occupied Seoul (SOLE), capital of South Korea.

President Truman responded forcefully to the attack. He asked the United Nations to send a military force to Korea. The UN Security Council voted to set up a force, to be commanded by a general chosen by Truman. The President chose General Douglas MacArthur, who had commanded Allied forces in the Pacific during World War II. Although 16 nations joined the UN action in Korea, about 80 percent of the troops were American.

Landing at Inchon At first, UN forces were outnumbered and poorly supplied. Armed with new Soviet tanks, the North Koreans pushed steadily southward. They soon occupied almost all of South Korea.

MacArthur then launched a daring counterattack by sea. He landed United Nations forces at Inchon behind North Korean lines. Caught by surprise, the North Koreans were forced back across the 38th parallel.

MacArthur's original orders called for him only to drive the invaders out of South Korea. Truman and his advisers, however, wanted to punish North Korea for its aggression. They also wanted to unite

GEOGRAPHY
Skills

When North Korean forces drove deep into South Korea, a United Nations force came to the aid of the South.

1. **Location** On the map, locate **(a)** North Korea, **(b)** South Korea, **(c)** 38th parallel, **(d)** Inchon, **(e)** Seoul, **(f)** Yalu River.

2. **Movement** Which side controlled Seoul **(a)** in September 1950, **(b)** in November 1950, **(c)** at the end of the war?

3. **Critical Thinking**
Making Predictions Based on this map, do you think communist forces would have won control over all of Korea if the UN had not sent in troops?

Korea. With these goals in mind, they won UN approval for MacArthur to cross into North Korea.

China Enters the War While MacArthur advanced northward, the Chinese government warned that it would not "sit back with folded hands" if the United States invaded North Korea. As UN forces neared the Chinese border, masses of Chinese troops crossed the Yalu River into North Korea.

Once again, the fighting seesawed. The Chinese overwhelmed the UN forces, pushing them back deep into South Korea. Then, the UN forces regrouped and pushed the Chinese back into North Korea. By March 1951, UN troops had regained control of the south. The war then turned into a bloody deadlock.

An End to the Fighting

During the deadlock, a serious disagreement arose between General MacArthur and President Truman. MacArthur felt that to win the war, UN forces must attack China. Truman feared that an attack on China might lead to a world war. He hoped to limit the war and restore the border between North Korea and South Korea at the 38th parallel.

Truman Fires MacArthur A frustrated MacArthur complained publicly that politicians in Washington were holding him back. "We must win," he insisted. "There is no substitute for victory." Angry that MacArthur was defying orders, Truman fired the popular general.

Truman's action outraged many Americans. They gave MacArthur a hero's welcome when he returned home. Truman, however, defended his decision. Under the Constitution, he pointed out, the President is commander in chief, responsible for key decisions about war and peace. MacArthur's statements, said Truman, undermined attempts to reach a peace settlement.

Armistice Peace talks began in mid-1951. At first there was little progress. Meanwhile, the deadly fighting continued.

Republicans nominated Dwight Eisenhower, the popular World War II general, as their presidential candidate in 1952. During the campaign, Eisenhower pledged that if he were elected, he would personally go to Korea. At the same time, he would work to get the stalled peace talks going again.

Eisenhower won the election and visited Korea within a few weeks of his victory. By then, both sides were eager for a cease-fire. The only remaining problem was the return of prisoners of war. After long negotiations, the two sides finally agreed to turn this issue over to an international commission.

Finally, in July 1953, the two sides signed an armistice to end the fighting. It redrew the border between North Korea and South Korea near the 38th parallel, where it had been before the war. Along the border, it also set up a demilitarized zone (DMZ), an area with no military forces. On either side of the DMZ, however, heavily armed troops dug in. They remain there today.

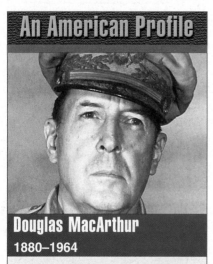

An American Profile

Douglas MacArthur
1880–1964

Douglas MacArthur was raised on army posts and attended the U.S. Military Academy at West Point. There, he achieved one of the highest records in Academy history. During World War I, he fought in France, winning numerous decorations for bravery and leadership.

In World War II, MacArthur commanded Allied forces fighting Japan in the Southwest Pacific. After the war, he led the Allied occupation of Japan. Under MacArthur, the power of the Japanese military was broken, land was distributed to poor farmers, and new rights were given to Japanese women.

What do you think was MacArthur's greatest accomplishment?

In a sense, the Korean War changed nothing. Korea remained divided. On the other hand, UN forces did push back North Korean forces. Through this action, the United States and its allies showed that they were ready to fight to prevent communist expansion.

Costs The human costs of the Korean War were staggering. About 54,000 Americans lost their lives in the war. Nearly 2 million Koreans and Chinese were also killed. Yet, the Korean war changed little in terms of borders. The cease-fire set the border between North and South Korea near the 38th parallel. This was close to where it had been before the war.

Hunting Communists at Home

For many Americans, the Korean War increased worries about Communists at home. Communist sympathizers and spies, they feared, might be secretly working to overthrow the government. These concerns helped spark a hunt for Communists within American society.

During the Great Depression, some Americans had turned against democracy and free enterprise. They had rejected the efforts of the New Deal as ineffective. To them, communism offered the only solution to the nation's deep economic troubles. In time, however, many American Communists recognized that Soviet leader Joseph Stalin was a brutal dictator, and they left the party.

Search for Spies Still, some remained avid Communists. Between 1946 and 1950, several people in the United States, Canada, and Britain were arrested as Soviet spies. In the United States, Ethel and Julius Rosenberg were sentenced to death for passing atomic secrets to the Soviets. Despite protests, both were executed in 1953. The Rosenberg case made many Americans wonder if other Soviet spies were living among them as ordinary citizens.

Viewing History

Peace Talks

The Korean peace talks dragged on for two long years. Only in mid-1953, was an armistice finally signed. **Drawing Conclusions** *Why do you think the United States accepted an armistice in Korea without a total victory?*

Americans also worried that there were Communists in high government positions. In 1950, Alger Hiss, a State Department official, was imprisoned for **perjury,** or lying under oath. Hiss had denied that he was part of a Soviet spy ring. Later evidence would suggest that Hiss and several other high government officials were passing secrets to the Soviet Union. It would also make it clear that Julius Rosenberg had indeed passed atomic secrets to the Soviets.

In 1947, President Truman ordered investigations of government workers to determine if they were loyal to the United States. Thousands of government employees were questioned. Some people were forced to resign. Many of those had done nothing disloyal to the United States.

AS YOU READ

Ask Questions If you were able to interview Senator McCarthy after the "McCarthy era," what questions would you have asked him? How do you think he might have responded?

The McCarthy Era In 1950, Senator Joseph McCarthy of Wisconsin made a shocking announcement. He claimed to have a list of 205 State Department employees who were Communist party members. McCarthy was never able to prove his claims. Yet, McCarthy's dramatic charges won him national attention.

During the next four years, McCarthy's campaign spread suspicion across the nation. Businesses and colleges questioned employees. Many people were fired.

In 1954, the Senate held televised hearings to investigate a new McCarthy charge. He insisted that there were Communists in the United States Army. This time, McCarthy had gone too far. On national television, he came across as a bully, not a hero. His popularity plunged.

In December 1954, the Senate passed a resolution to **censure,** or officially condemn, McCarthy for "conduct unbecoming a member." As a result, McCarthy lost much of his support. By the time he died three years later, the Communist scare was mostly over.

AFTER YOU READ ★ ★ ★ **Section 2 Assessment** ★ ★ ★ ★

Recall

1. **Identify** Explain the significance of **(a)** 38th parallel, **(b)** Douglas MacArthur, **(c)** Ethel and Julius Rosenberg, **(d)** Joseph McCarthy.
2. **Define (a)** demilitarized zone, **(b)** perjury, **(c)** censure.

Comprehension

3. Describe how the United States became involved in the conflict in Korea.
4. What was the outcome of the Korean War?
5. How did the McCarthy era grow out of the hunt for Communists at home?

Critical Thinking and Writing

6. **Exploring the Main Idea** Review the Main Idea statement at the beginning of this section. Then, write five headlines that trace the course of the Korean War from beginning to end.
7. **Linking Past and Present** Television played a key role in the downfall of Senator Joseph McCarthy. Give at least three examples of how television influences public opinion today.

ACTIVITY

Take It to the NET

Charting Military Spending Use the Internet to research the military budgets of the United States from 1945 to 2000. Then, draw a line graph showing how spending increased during this period. Visit *The American Nation* section of **www.phschool.com** for help in completing the activity.

3 Regional Conflicts

Reading Focus

- Why did the Cold War spread to Africa and Asia?
- Why did Cuba become a crisis spot during the Cold War?
- Why did the United States intervene in Latin America during the Cold War?
- How did the Cold War lead to an arms race?

Key Terms

superpower

exile

Bay of Pigs invasion

Cuban missile crisis

Alliance for Progress

Peace Corps

Organization of American States

National Aeronautics and Space Administration

Taking Notes

As you read, complete this table listing Cold War conflicts and the actions taken by the superpowers. Add as many rows as you need to finish the table.

REGION OR COUNTRY	ISSUE OR CONFLICT	SUPERPOWER ACTIONS
Africa and Asia		
Cuba	Castro set up communist government	
Other Parts of Latin America		

Main Idea Superpower rivalries heightened conflicts in many parts of the world during the Cold War.

Setting the Scene In September 1959, the Soviet leader, Nikita Khrushchev (KROOSH chawf), arrived in New York to address the United Nations. Khrushchev, who had gained power a few years after Stalin died in 1953, spoke calmly at first. He expressed hopes that the Cold War between the United States and the Soviet Union would end. Then, gradually his manner changed. Twice, he became so angry that he took off his shoe and pounded it on the table.

Khrushchev's trip to the UN symbolized the fact that the Cold War had become global. Although the Cold War had started in Europe, the United States and the Soviet Union now competed for allies and influence among the members of the United Nations.

The Cold War in Africa and Asia

For years, many of the nations of Africa and Asia had been governed as colonies of European and other foreign powers. After World War II, many colonial people demanded and won independence. Some achieved independence peacefully. Others had to fight for it.

In the colonies, Communists often joined other groups to fight foreign control. Khrushchev called these struggles "wars of national liberation." Both openly and secretly, the Soviets gave economic and military aid to rebel forces.

The West tried to prevent the Soviets from expanding their influence. In their efforts, American leaders faced difficult choices. Should the United States provide aid to a colonial power? Should Americans use secret aid to counter the Soviets? Should they send troops into another nation to influence its internal affairs? In the end, the United States used all these tactics at one time or another to contain communism.

UNION OF SOVIET SOCIALIST REPUBLICS

AS YOU READ **Khrushchev at the United Nations**

Use Prior Knowledge Why might the Soviet leader be angry with the United States?

POLITICAL CARTOON
Skills

American Comic Strips and Communism

This comic-strip panel appeared in an American comic book during the 1950s.

1. **Comprehension (a)** Who is the man standing by the globe? **(b)** Who are the other men seated at the table?

2. **Finding the Main Idea** What are the men discussing?

3. **Critical Thinking Identifying Points of View** What is the cartoonist's opinion of the communist world?

The Philippines The United States also had to deal with its own colony. In 1946, it withdrew from the Philippines, which it had acquired during the Spanish-American War. Crowds in Manila cheered as the American flag was lowered and the Filipino flag was hoisted high.

Since then, the Philippines has struggled to preserve a democratic government. It has suffered from poverty, local uprisings, and dictatorships. Under the rule of Ferdinand Marcos, who was in power from 1965 to 1986, opposition parties were repressed. In the years that followed, the Philippines struggled to find stable and honest government.

Cold War Rivalries in Africa During the 1950s and 1960s, more than 30 African nations won freedom from European rule. Both the United States and the Soviet Union sought allies among these new nations.

After independence, some new nations faced civil wars among rival ethnic or tribal groups. Some fought border wars with their neighbors. The superpowers backed opposing sides in these struggles. As a result, the Cold War turned local conflicts into international crises.

In East Africa, the United States and the Soviet Union took sides in a long war between Somalia and Ethiopia. The United States backed Somalia, while the Soviet Union supported Ethiopia. In southern Africa, the Cold War intensified a civil war in Angola.

India, Pakistan, and Indochina In 1947, India won independence from Britain. The Indian subcontinent was divided into two nations: India and Pakistan. Both the United States and the Soviet Union tried to win the support of these new nations.

Feeling threatened by the Soviet Union to its north, Pakistan became an ally of the United States. India accepted both American and Soviet aid but remained neutral in the Cold War.

French-ruled Indochina included present-day Laos, Cambodia, and Vietnam. In each country, separate nationalist groups fought for independence. The wars lasted for almost 30 years and eventually drew in the United States, as you will read in Section Four.

Crisis Over Cuba

By the 1960s, the United States and the Soviet Union had emerged as superpowers—nations with enough military, political, and economic strength to influence events worldwide. The rivalry between the superpowers led to clashes in many places, including Cuba, an island in the Caribbean.

In 1959, Fidel Castro led a revolution that set up a communist state in Cuba. Castro's government took over private companies, including many owned by American businesses. Thousands of Cubans, especially those from the upper and middle classes, fled to the United States.

Bay of Pigs Invasion The Soviet Union began supplying Cuba with large amounts of aid. The growing ties between the Soviet Union and Castro's Cuba worried American officials. Cuba lies just 90 miles off the coast of Florida.

In 1961, President John F. Kennedy approved a plan for Cuban exiles to overthrow Castro. Exiles are people who have been forced to leave their own country.

A force of about 1,200 Cuban exiles landed at the Bay of Pigs on Cuba's south coast. The invasion was badly planned. Castro's forces quickly rounded up and jailed the invaders. The Bay of Pigs invasion strengthened Castro in Cuba and embarrassed the United States.

Cuban Missile Crisis After the Bay of Pigs invasion, the Soviet Union gave Cuba more weapons. In October 1962, President Kennedy learned that the Soviets were secretly building missile bases on the island. If the bases were completed, atomic missiles could reach American cities within minutes.

Kennedy announced that American warships would stop any Soviet ship carrying missiles. The world waited tensely as Soviet ships steamed toward Cuba. At the last minute, the Soviet ships turned back. "We're eyeball to eyeball," said Secretary of State Dean Rusk, "and I think the other fellow just blinked."

Kennedy's strong stand led the Soviets to compromise. Khrushchev agreed to remove Soviet missiles from Cuba. In turn, the United States promised not to invade the island. Still the Cuban missile crisis had shaken both American and Soviet officials. In all the years of the Cold War, the world never came closer to a full-scale nuclear war.

Intervening in Latin America

In the early 1900s, the United States had frequently intervened in the internal affairs of Latin American nations. Now,

Viewing History

Caribbean Conflict
A United States plane flies low over a Soviet freighter during the Cuban missile crisis. Americans were checking the boat for any evidence of Soviet missiles aboard. **Identifying Alternatives** *Were there other policies that President Kennedy could have followed to end the missile crisis? Explain.*

The Peace Corps

Peace Corps volunteers work hard during their two-year tour of duty. A volunteer might set up a health clinic, build an irrigation system, or start a new school. Many volunteers live in remote villages. All are expected to use the local language and live as the local people do.

Peace Corps members feel that they do much more than building, doctoring, and teaching. Said one:

"By communications on a person-to-person level the people of the world may some day eliminate the word [stranger]. Communication, after all, can breed understanding. And understanding can breed peace. I like to think that is what the Peace Corps is all about."

 What are some jobs that Peace Corps volunteers do?

Cold War tensions led the United States to resume its active role. A number of Presidents tried to contain communism in other Latin American nations.

Social and Economic Problems Latin America had long faced severe social and economic problems. A huge gap existed between the wealthy few and the majority of people. In most countries, rural people lived in desperate poverty. When the poor migrated to cities seeking work, they were often forced to live in shacks, without heat, light, or water.

Many poor Latin Americans saw communism as a solution to their problems. Communists called for land to be distributed to the poor and for governments to take over foreign corporations. Some non-Communists also supported this view.

Aid Programs Many American leaders agreed with the need for reform. They hoped that American aid would help make Latin American nations more democratic, ease the lives of the people, and lessen communist influence.

In 1961, President Kennedy created an ambitious aid program called the Alliance for Progress. He urged Latin American countries to make reforms to improve the lives of their people. In return, the United States contributed aid to build schools and hospitals and improve farming and sanitation services. The Alliance brought a few improvements, but it did not end the causes of poverty.

Kennedy also set up the Peace Corps. Under this program, American volunteers worked in developing countries as teachers, engineers, and technical advisers. Volunteers lived with local people for two years, teaching or giving technical advice.

The United States was also a leading member of the Organization of American States, or OAS. Through the OAS, the United States promoted economic progress in the Americas by investing in transportation and industry.

To battle communism, the United States also gave military aid to train and arm Latin American military forces. The United States spoke up for democracy and pressed governments to make reforms. Often, though, the United States ended up supporting military dictators because they opposed communism.

Intervention During the Cold War, the United States returned to a policy of intervention in Latin American affairs. Between 1950 and 1990, it intervened in Guatemala, the Dominican Republic, Panama, and Grenada.

During the 1970s and 1980s, civil wars raged in several Central American countries. Rebels in El Salvador and Guatemala fought to overthrow harsh governments. The United States backed the governments because they were strongly anticommunist.

The wars cost tens of thousands of lives. To escape the fighting, thousands of refugees fled to the United States.

In Nicaragua, a rebel group known as the Sandinistas overthrew a longtime dictator in 1979 and set up a socialist government. President Reagan, afraid that Nicaragua would become another

Cuba, aided a group opposed to the Sandinistas. They were known as "Contras," from the Spanish word for "against."

Many members of Congress disagreed with President Reagan's policy in Nicaragua. They passed laws banning military aid to the Contras. Even so, some people on the President's staff arranged for military aid secretly. When details of the arrangement became public, many Americans were outraged. Two Reagan officials were tried and convicted of lying to Congress, though the convictions were later successfully appealed

Finally, in 1990, Nicaragua held new elections. Nicaraguans rejected the Sandinistas and voted in new leaders.

AS YOU READ **Draw Inferences** Why do you think many members of Congress disagreed with President Reagan's policy in Nicaragua?

The Arms Race

By the 1950s, both the Soviet Union and the United States had developed large stocks of nuclear bombs and missiles. Then, in 1957, the Soviet Union launched *Sputnik*, the world's first artificial satellite. Americans were stunned. If the Soviets had a rocket powerful enough to launch a satellite, could their rockets armed with atomic weapons reach the United States?

Sputnik sparked a new round of spending on weapons systems by both the Soviet Union and the United States. The United States soon launched its own satellites. Both superpowers now raced to send larger satellites farther into space. The United States also set up the National Aeronautics and Space Administration, or NASA. Its mission was to direct an American space program to compete with that of the Soviets.

By 1970, the two superpowers had stockpiles of weapons large enough to destroy each other many times over. With Soviet-American relations tense, it seemed possible that these weapons would someday be used.

AFTER YOU READ

Section 3 Assessment

Recall

1. **Identify** Explain the significance of **(a)** Bay of Pigs invasion, **(b)** Cuban missile crisis, **(c)** Alliance for Progress, **(d)** Peace Corps, **(e)** Organization of American States, **(f)** National Aeronautics and Space Administration.
2. **Define** **(a)** superpower, **(b)** exile.

Comprehension

3. How did superpower rivalries spread to Africa and Asia?
4. How did the superpowers come to the brink of war over Cuba?

5. What form did United States intervention in Latin America take during the Cold War?
6. Why did the Cold War superpowers become involved in an arms race?

Critical Thinking and Writing

7. **Exploring the Main Idea** Review the Main Idea statement at the beginning of the section. Then, list at least four examples of the global impact of the Cold War.
8. **Identifying Points of View** Why do you think that relations between the United States and Latin America were often strained during the Cold War?

> **ACTIVITY**
>
> **Writing a Position Statement** You are an adviser to the President of the United States during the Cold War. The President is trying to decide whether the United States should support an anticommunist dictator in an Asian nation. Write a brief statement explaining your position.

NASA and the Space Age

NASA grew out of the race between the United States and the Soviet Union to create a rocket that could reach outer space. Its greatest achievement was to land astronauts on the moon. This occurred on July 20, 1969, when *Apollo 11* astronaut Neil Armstrong set foot on the moon. His words were heard by millions of viewers worldwide: "One small step for a man, one giant leap for mankind."

In July 1969, American astronauts became the first humans to walk on the moon.

NASA's space station Skylab was launched in 1973. It enabled astronauts to work and live in space for months.

NASA's first astronaut team, 1959—(left to right) Walter Schirra, Alan Shepard, Virgil Grissom, Donald Slayton, John Glenn, Scott Carpenter, and Gordon Cooper—became instant American heroes.

This rock, collected by *Apollo* astronauts on the lunar surface, is billions of years old.

ACTIVITY

If you could make a time capsule to be placed by American astronauts on the moon, what objects would you put in it? List ten objects that would fit in a capsule about the size of a refrigerator that would give a good picture of life in the United States today.

4 The War in Vietnam

ORE
OU
EAD

Reading Focus

- How did the United States get involved in the Vietnam War?
- How did the Vietnam War affect Americans at home?
- How did the Tet Offensive help lead to the war's end?
- What impact did the Vietnam War have on the United States and Southeast Asia?

Key Terms

Vietcong
guerrilla
domino theory
Gulf of Tonkin Resolution
escalate
draft
Tet Offensive
Khmer Rouge
boat people

Taking Notes

Copy this flowchart. As you read, fill in the boxes with events that led to the communist takeover of Vietnam. Two boxes have been completed to help you get started. Add as many boxes as you need.

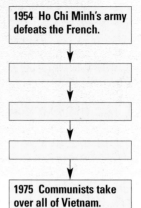

1954 Ho Chi Minh's army defeats the French.

↓

↓

↓

↓

1975 Communists take over all of Vietnam.

Main Idea In an effort to stop the spread of communism in Southeast Asia, the United States became involved in the long and unpopular Vietnam War.

Setting the Scene

President Lyndon B. Johnson faced a difficult decision in May 1964. The United States was helping the government of South Vietnam battle communist rebels. Johnson had to decide whether to commit more forces to the struggle.

The President had doubts. "I don't think it's worth fighting for," he told a close adviser, "and I don't think we can get out. I don't see that we can ever hope to get out of there once we are committed."

The President never expressed those doubts publicly. In fact, he sent a growing number of Americans to fight in South Vietnam. Like many other Americans, he believed that the Vietnam War was justified because its goal was to stop the spread of communism.

While Lyndon Johnson was President, the fighting in Vietnam increased. It grew into the longest, most unpopular war in American history.

AS YOU READ President Johnson and his generals

Use Prior Knowledge What other wars in Asia had involved American forces?

Early Involvement in Vietnam

Vietnam is a narrow country that stretches about 1,000 miles along the South China Sea. Since the late 1800s, it had been ruled by France as a colony.

The United States became involved in Vietnam slowly, step by step. During the 1940s, Ho Chi Minh (HO CHEE MIHN), a Vietnamese nationalist and a Communist, had led the fight for independence. Ho's army finally defeated the French in 1954.

An international peace conference divided Vietnam into two countries. Ho Chi Minh led communist North Vietnam. Ngo Dinh Diem (NOH DIN dee EHM) was the noncommunist leader of South Vietnam. In the Cold War world, the Soviet Union supported North Vietnam. The United States backed Diem in the south.

War in Southeast Asia

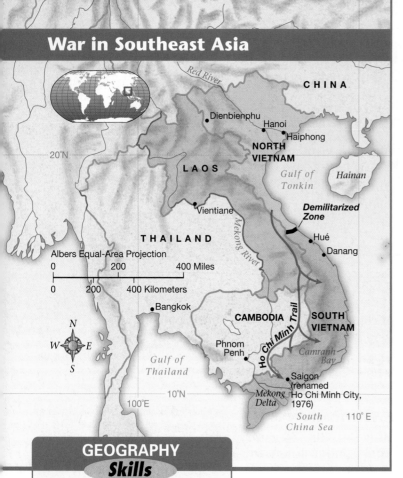

GEOGRAPHY Skills

During the Vietnam War, North Vietnam supplied arms to communist guerrillas in South Vietnam. The system of supply routes from the North was known as the Ho Chi Minh Trail.

1. **Location** On the map, locate (a) North Vietnam, (b) South Vietnam, (c) Gulf of Tonkin, (d) Hanoi, (e) Cambodia.

2. **Movement** Through which countries did the Ho Chi Minh Trail run?

3. **Critical Thinking**
Applying Information According to the domino theory, what nations would be threatened if the Communists won control of South Vietnam?

Discontent Diem lost popular support during the 1950s. Many South Vietnamese thought that he favored wealthy landlords and was corrupt. He failed to help the nation's peasant majority and ruled with a heavy hand.

As discontent grew, many peasants joined the Vietcong—guerrillas who opposed Diem. Guerrillas (guh RIHL uhz) are fighters who make hit-and-run attacks on the enemy. They do not wear uniforms or fight in large battles. In time, the Vietcong became communist and were supported by North Vietnam. Vietcong influence quickly spread, especially in the villages.

American Aid Vietcong successes worried American leaders. If South Vietnam fell to communism, they believed, other countries in the region would follow—like a row of falling dominoes. This idea became known as the domino theory. The United States decided that it must keep South Vietnam from becoming the first domino.

During the 1950s and 1960s, Presidents Eisenhower and Kennedy sent financial aid and military advisers to South Vietnam. The advisers went to help train the South Vietnamese army, not to fight the Vietcong. Diem, however, continued to lose support. In November 1963, Diem was assassinated. A few weeks later, President John F. Kennedy was assassinated. Vice President Lyndon Baines Johnson became President.

The Fighting in Vietnam Expands

Lyndon Johnson was also determined to keep South Vietnam from falling to the communists. He increased aid to South Vietnam, sending more arms and advisers. Still, the Vietcong continued to make gains.

Gulf of Tonkin Resolution In August 1964, President Johnson announced that North Vietnamese torpedo boats had attacked an American ship patrolling the Gulf of Tonkin off the coast of North Vietnam. At Johnson's urging, Congress passed the Gulf of Tonkin Resolution. It allowed the President "to take all necessary measures to repel any armed attack or to prevent further aggression." Johnson used the resolution to order the bombing of North Vietnam and Vietcong-held areas in the south.

With the Gulf of Tonkin Resolution, the role of Americans in Vietnam changed from military advisers to active fighters. The war in Vietnam escalated, or expanded. By 1968, President Johnson had sent more than 500,000 troops to fight in Vietnam.

Jungle Warfare The Vietnam War differed from other wars that Americans had fought. Rather than trying to gain ground,

Americans attempted to destroy enemy positions. However, the Vietcong were hard to pin down. When Americans found an enemy stronghold, the guerrillas disappeared into the jungle. When the Americans left, the Vietcong returned. As a result, Americans found themselves going back again and again to fight in the same areas.

Worse still, American soldiers often could not tell which villagers were Vietcong. The enemy might be the old woman cooking rice outside her hut or the man walking down a village path. "The farmer you waved to from your jeep in the day," explained an American soldier, "would be the guy with the gun out looking for you at night."

The War at Home

As American casualties mounted, public support for the war faded. For the first time, Americans watched a war on television. They saw villages burned, children and old people caught in battle, and soldiers wounded and killed.

To raise troops, the United States expanded the draft, or system of mandatory enlistment. The draft affected American youth unequally. Many young middle-class men found ways to avoid the draft, such as attending college. As a result, many of the draftees sent to Vietnam were poor. A large number were African American and Latino.

By the mid-1960s, a growing number of Americans were protesting the war. The country split between "hawks" and "doves." Hawks supported the Vietnam War as a battle against communism. Doves opposed it. They saw it as a civil war involving the Vietnamese only.

The protests spread. On some college campuses, students staged marches and sit-ins, burned draft cards, and discussed how to avoid the draft.

Protesters charged that American lives and money were being wasted on an unjust war. The South Vietnamese government, they said, was corrupt and brutal, and the United States should not support it. They wanted the huge sums being spent on the war to be spent on social programs at home.

The antiwar protests fed a spirit of rebellion among young people. During the 1960s and early 1970s, many young people rejected traditional American values. They adopted new fashions in clothing and music. Their rebellious way of life often shocked their elders. Sadly, many experimented with illegal drugs. The use of these drugs took a tragic toll on the young and has remained a problem ever since.

The Tet Offensive: A Turning Point

In January 1968, the Vietcong launched surprise attacks on cities throughout South Vietnam. Guerrillas even stormed the American embassy in Saigon, the capital of South Vietnam. The attack became known as the Tet Offensive because it took place during Tet, the Vietnamese New Year's holiday.

In the end, American and South Vietnamese forces pushed back the enemy. Still, the Vietcong had won a major political victory. The

AS YOU READ **Summarize** In your own words, summarize the differences between fighting World War II and the war in Vietnam.

Primary Source

Memories of Vietnam

One steamy day in 1969, a young Marine named Paul O'Connell was in a foxhole when American jets providing air cover swooped low over his position:
"I took cover in a cave. . . . The jets came screaming in; and, just after you heard their jet roar, the earth shook; and the concussions left our ears ringing. One screaming jet after another. . . . I wondered if it was ever going to stop. I even wondered if the jets were on target; and if they were, it meant the enemy was very close to our positions. Finally, the bombing stopped; and the word was passed that it was okay to come out from our cover. . . . I decided I wasn't coming out from the cave. Never."

—Paul O'Connell, *Letters Home,*
Vietnam Veterans Home Page

Analyzing Primary Sources
The bombing frightened O'Connell. Did this make him a poor soldier? Explain.

Washington, D.C.

Vietnam Veterans Memorial

Since 1982, millions of Americans have visited the Vietnam Veterans Memorial in Washington, DC. The memorial is composed of two black granite walls inscribed with the names of more than 58,000 Americans killed in Vietnam. Says designer Maya Lin: "This memorial is for those who have died, and for us to remember."

 Take It to the NET

Virtual Field Trip For an interactive look at the Vietnam Veterans Memorial, visit *The American Nation* section of **www.phschool.com**.

Tet Offensive showed that even with half a million American troops, no part of South Vietnam was safe from Vietcong attack. Many more Americans began to protest the war.

Hoping to restore calm to a nation rocked by protests, a weary President Johnson decided not to seek reelection in 1968. That year, Richard Nixon, a Republican, was elected President on a pledge to end the war.

The War Ends

President Nixon at first widened the war, hoping to weaken the enemy. For years, North Vietnamese soldiers had used trails in nearby Cambodia to supply their soldiers in South Vietnam. They also escaped to Cambodia when American and South Vietnamese units attacked.

In 1969, Nixon ordered the bombing of communist bases in Cambodia. Then, American and South Vietnamese forces invaded by land. These moves helped plunge Cambodia into its own civil war between communist and noncommunist forces.

United States Withdrawal Under pressure at home, President Nixon began to turn the war over to South Vietnam and withdraw American troops. Meanwhile, peace talks were held in Paris. In January 1973, the two sides reached a cease-fire agreement. The next year, the last American combat troops left Vietnam.

The United States continued to send large amounts of aid to South Vietnam. Even so, the South Vietnamese were unable to stop the North Vietnamese advance. In April 1975, communist forces captured Saigon. They renamed it Ho Chi Minh City. Soon after, Vietnam was united under a communist government.

Tragedy in Cambodia That year, the communist Khmer Rouge (kuh MER ROOJ) won the civil war in Cambodia. The Khmer Rouge imposed a brutal reign of terror on their own people. More than a million Cambodians starved to death or were killed.

In 1979, Vietnam invaded Cambodia and set up a new communist government. It was less harsh than the Khmer Rouge, but it could not end the fighting. Not until the 1990s would a shaky peace be restored in Cambodia.

Impact of the Vietnam War

The Vietnam War was a costly conflict. More than 58,000 American soldiers lost their lives. More than a million Vietnamese soldiers and perhaps half a million civilians died. The war shattered the Vietnamese economy.

After 1975, hundreds of thousands of people fled Vietnam and Cambodia. Refugees from Vietnam escaped in small boats. Many of these boat people drowned or died of hunger and thirst. Others made it to safety. Eventually, many were allowed to settle in the United States.

The Vietnam War was a painful episode in American history. Besides its huge cost, the war produced no victory and divided the nation. It left Americans wondering about how far the nation should go to fight communism.

AFTER YOU READ

Section 4 Assessment

Recall

1. **Identify** Explain the significance of **(a)** Ho Chi Minh, **(b)** Ngo Dinh Diem, **(c)** Vietcong, **(d)** Gulf of Tonkin Resolution, **(e)** Tet Offensive, **(f)** Khmer Rouge.
2. **Define** **(a)** guerrilla, **(b)** domino theory, **(c)** escalate, **(d)** draft, **(e)** boat people.

Comprehension

3. Describe the events that led the United States to play a major role in the Vietnam War.
4. List three ways that the Vietnam War affected Americans at home.

5. What was the relationship between the Tet Offensive and the war's end?
6. Describe the impact of the Vietnam War on the United States and Southeast Asia.

Critical Thinking and Writing

7. **Exploring the Main Idea** Review the Main Idea statement at the beginning of this section. Then, suppose you are an American soldier in Vietnam in 1968. Write a letter to your child explaining why you are there.
8. **Analyzing Information** How did the Cold War affect American policy in Vietnam?

ACTIVITY

Summarizing Write a series of newspaper headlines that summarize the history of the Vietnam War. Include headlines that describe events in Vietnam, Southeast Asia as a whole, and the United States. Be sure to write headlines that would have caught your attention if you had been an American teenager at the time.

5 The Cold War Ends

BEFORE YOU READ

Reading Focus

- How did President Richard Nixon change the course of American foreign policy?
- Why did new Cold War tensions emerge after 1979?
- What conditions led to the fall of communism in the Soviet Union and Eastern Europe?
- How did the Cold War affect American society?

Key Terms

détente

SALT Agreement

Star Wars

Solidarity

martial law

glasnost

summit meeting

Taking Notes

As you read, prepare an outline of this section. Use roman numerals to indicate the major headings of this section, capital letters for the subheadings, and numbers for supporting details. The sample below will help you get started.

> I. Changes in American Foreign Policy
>   A. The United States and China
>   B.
> II. New Tensions
>   A. Soviet defeat
>   B.

Main Idea The Cold War dominated relations between the superpowers until the breakup of the Soviet Union in 1991 ended the Cold War.

AS YOU READ **The Berlin Wall comes down**

Summarize Why was Berlin a focus of superpower tensions throughout the Cold War?

Setting the Scene On a November night in 1989, television news programs carried a startling sight. There were Germans, young and old, swinging pickaxes and sledgehammers. Bit by bit, they were knocking down the huge concrete wall that had divided East Berlin from West Berlin for nearly 30 years.

Berliners from both sides of the wall danced, hugged, and kissed. East Berliners eagerly snatched up maps of West Berlin. For the first time, many East Berliners would be able to reunite with family and friends who were on the other side of the wall.

As you have read, communist East Germany had built the Berlin Wall to prevent its citizens from fleeing to the West. The wall had become a symbol of Cold War divisions. By the late 1980s, however, the Cold War was ending. All over Eastern Europe, nations were throwing off their communist rulers. The end of the Berlin Wall became the symbol of revolutionary changes throughout the communist world.

Changes in American Foreign Policy

In 1971, while Americans were still fighting in Vietnam, the Cold War showed signs of a thaw. President Nixon moved to ease world tensions. His first move was to seek improved relations with the People's Republic of China.

The United States and China Since 1949, the United States had refused to recognize Mao Zedong's communist government in China. Instead, it recognized the Chinese Nationalists, now confined to the island of Taiwan. The United States gave arms and aid to the Nationalists and supported their claim to being the legitimate government of all China.

Richard Nixon had long been one of the most outspoken opponents of recognizing the communist government in China. As President, though, Nixon allowed secret talks with Chinese officials that led to new openings for the two countries. To show its goodwill, China invited the American Ping-Pong team to a competition in Beijing.

To the surprise of many Americans, Nixon then visited the People's Republic of China in 1972. Television cameras captured the President walking along the Great Wall of China and attending state dinners with Chinese leaders. The visit was a triumph for Nixon and the start of a new era in relations with China. As tensions eased, the United States and China established formal diplomatic relations in 1979.

A Policy of Détente President Nixon followed his visit to China with another historic trip. In May 1972, he became the first American President to visit the Soviet Union since the beginning of the Cold War. The trip was part of Nixon's effort to reduce tensions between the superpowers. This policy was known as détente (day TAHNT).

Détente eased the Cold War by establishing more trade and other contacts between the superpowers. It also led them to sign a treaty to limit the number of nuclear warheads and missiles. The treaty was known as the SALT Agreement. (SALT stands for Strategic Arms Limitation Talks.)

The next two Presidents, Gerald Ford and Jimmy Carter, continued the policy of détente. Trade between the United States and the Soviet Union increased. Under President Ford, Soviet and American astronauts conducted a joint space mission. In 1979, President Carter met with Soviet leader Leonid Brezhnev (BREHZH nehf). They worked out the details of a SALT II Treaty.

New Tensions

Détente ended suddenly in 1979. In December, Soviet troops swept into Afghanistan, a mountainous nation on the Soviet Union's southern border. Soviet troops were sent there to help a pro-Soviet government that had just seized power.

A Soviet Defeat The United States condemned the Soviet invasion of Afghanistan. President Carter withdrew the SALT II Treaty from Senate approval hearings. The United States also refused to let

Cause *and* Effect

Causes

- Soviet Union takes control of Eastern European nations
- Communism gains influence in Western Europe, the Middle East, and Asia
- Western powers fear Soviet expansion

THE COLD WAR

Effects

- Arms race between United States and Soviet Union results in heavy military spending
- Western powers and Soviet Union create separate military alliances
- Armed conflicts erupt in Korea and Vietnam
- United States and Soviet Union compete for influence in developing nations

Effects Today

- United States is world's greatest military power
- Eastern Europe and Russia are struggling to create democratic governments
- Southeast Asian countries are still recovering from wars

GRAPHIC ORGANIZER
Skills

For 45 years, the Cold War pitted the United States against the Soviet Union.

1. **Comprehension**
   (a) What events in Europe helped spark the Cold War? **(b)** Which effects of the Cold War involved Americans in actual fighting?

2. **Critical Thinking**
   Analyzing Information How did the Cold War help the United States become the world's greatest military power?

its athletes compete in the 1980 summer Olympic Games in Moscow.

Despite worldwide criticism, Soviet troops remained in Afghanistan for ten years. They suffered heavy losses as Afghan rebels, supplied by the United States, battled the communist government. The war in Afghanistan became so costly for the Soviets that it eventually contributed to the downfall of the Soviet Union. In 1989, the Soviets were forced to pull all troops out of Afghanistan.

Reagan's Strong Stand Ronald Reagan took office in 1981 firmly believing that the Soviet Union was "the focus of evil in the modern world." He called on Americans to "oppose it with all our might." Reagan also took a tough anticommunist stand in Latin America, as you have read.

Reagan wanted to deal with the Soviets from a position of strength. To achieve this, he persuaded Congress to increase military spending by more than $100 billion during his first five years in office. He also called for the development of a new weapons system that he hoped could destroy Soviet missiles from space. The system was nicknamed Star Wars after a popular movie of the time. Only the early stages of research were completed.

During Reagan's first term in office, the two superpowers continued to view each other with deep mistrust. In December 1981, Poland's communist government cracked down on Solidarity, an independent labor union. Solidarity members had gone on strike at Polish shipyards to demand labor reforms. Under Soviet pressure, the Polish government imposed martial law, or emergency military rule, on the country.

President Reagan condemned the move. He urged the Soviets to allow Poland to restore basic human rights. The United States also put economic pressure on Poland to end martial law.

Decline of the Soviet Union

Cracks began to appear in the Soviet empire in the mid-1980s. Economic problems grew in part because of the huge sums the Soviets were spending on their military. There was little money left for producing consumer goods. Soviet citizens stood in line for hours waiting for poorly made products. They complained that the communist system was breaking down. The time was ripe for reform.

Gorbachev's Reforms In 1985, a new Soviet leader, Mikhail Gorbachev (mee kah EEL GOR buh chawf), rose to power. He believed that only major reforms would allow the Soviet system to survive.

Viewing History

Improved Relations Soviet premier Mikhail Gorbachev and President Ronald Reagan held three summit meetings. At this one, in 1987, they signed an arms control pact known as the INF Treaty. **Linking Past and Present** *How have relations between Americans and Russians changed since 1987?*

Find Main Ideas As you read, look for sentences that describe the main reasons for the decline of the Soviet Union.

Gorbachev backed **glasnost,** the Russian term for speaking out openly. Glasnost, Gorbachev hoped, would lead citizens to find solutions to pressing economic and social problems. This new openness was a break with the past, when any criticism of government policies had been quickly silenced.

Summit Meetings Gorbachev realized that he could not solve the Soviet Union's economic problems without cutting military spending sharply. To do so, he had to have better relations with the United States.

President Reagan and Gorbachev met at several summit meetings. A **summit meeting** is a conference between the highest-ranking officials of different nations. Reagan agreed to these meetings because he approved of Gorbachev's new policy of openness.

In 1987, the two leaders signed an arms control pact called the Intermediate Nuclear Force (INF) Treaty. In it, both nations agreed to get rid of their stockpiles of short- and medium-range missiles. To prevent cheating, each side would have the right to inspect the other's missile sites. Two years later, Gorbachev withdrew Soviet troops from Afghanistan. This action removed another barrier to cooperation between the superpowers.

Communism Falls in Eastern Europe

For more than 50 years, the communist governments of Eastern Europe had banned any open discussion of political issues. As in the Soviet Union, only one political party, the Communist party, was allowed to win elections. People were denied many basic rights, such as freedom of speech.

At times, the Soviet Union had used force to maintain its control over the satellite nations. In 1956, Hungary had tried to follow its own independent course. The Soviet Union had sent in the Red Army, which brutally crushed the revolution. In 1968, Soviet troops marched into Czechoslovakia when a Czech leader tried to introduce some reforms.

Now, in the late 1980s, Eastern European governments could no longer control the rising demands of the people for democratic and economic reforms. With opposition so widespread, most of those governments did not dare to use military force to oppose change. Furthermore, the Soviet Union did not have the power to suppress these protests. It was too busy trying to solve its own problems.

In 1989, Poland held its first free elections in 50 years. Polish voters rejected communist candidates in favor of those put up by the trade union, Solidarity. Solidarity

Viewing History

Soviet Crackdown Lined up on a street in Prague, Czechoslovakia in August 1968, Soviet tanks are ready to put down any resistance by the Czech people. **Summarizing** *In two sentences, summarize the ways by which the Soviet Union maintained control over Eastern Europe during the Cold War.*

Celebrating Communism's Fall

Russians carry the banner of their country through Moscow. The breakup of the Soviet Union marked the end of 45 years of bitter Cold War tensions. **Identifying Points of View** *How do you think most Americans reacted to scenes such as this coming from Russia?*

leader, Lech Walesa (vah LEHN sah), had once been jailed by the Communists for almost a year. After the elections, he became head of a new Polish government.

One by one, Communist governments fell in Czechoslovakia, Hungary, Bulgaria, and Albania. In Romania, a violent revolt toppled the country's longtime communist dictator.

In East Germany, protests forced the Communists from power. As you have read, Berliners smashed through the wall that had divided their city for so long. By 1990, Germany was reunited under a democratic government.

The Soviet Union Collapses

The Soviet Union was made up of 15 different republics held together by a strong central government in Moscow. Under Soviet rule, the republics had few freedoms. All important policy decisions were made in Moscow.

By 1990, resentment of Moscow was high. Some Soviet people, including Lithuanians, Latvians, and Estonians, demanded self-rule. Attempting to quiet the unrest, Gorbachev allowed political parties to form. For nearly 70 years, the Soviet Union had been a one-party state.

Some of the new parties openly opposed the Communists. Hard-line communist officials were outraged. A group of them tried to oust Gorbachev. Their revolt did not last long. A Moscow politician, Boris Yeltsin, led thousands of Russians in protest. They surrounded the Parliament building and forced Soviet troops to pull back.

The attempted revolt weakened Gorbachev. In the months that followed, republic after republic declared its independence from the Soviet Union. In late 1991, Gorbachev resigned. By then, the Soviet Union had collapsed.

Fifteen new nations emerged from the old Soviet Union. Of these, Russia was the largest and most powerful. Under President Yeltsin, it began the difficult task of building a new economy based on a free-market system. In a free market, individuals decide what and how much to produce and sell. Under communism, the government had made such economic decisions.

The United States and Western European nations provided economic aid to Russia and the other republics. American experts offered advice to Russia's political and business leaders on the free-market system.

The United States was eager to see stable, democratic governments emerge in the old communist world. It also hoped that the new nations would become profitable trading partners.

Shifting to a free-market economy, however, brought terrible disruptions. Many people lost their jobs, their savings, and their sense of security. Crime and corruption grew. Many Russians began to wonder whether democracy could solve their country's many problems.

The Cold War: A Look Back

For almost 50 years, the Cold War deeply affected American life. Students in the 1950s practiced crouching under their desks in case of atomic attack. Hundreds of thousands of Americans went off to fight in the Korean and Vietnam wars. About 112,000 of them did not return.

Americans cheered the end of the Cold War and the emergence of democratic governments in Eastern Europe. Victory was costly, though. From 1946 to 1990, the United States spent over $6 trillion on national defense. The development of nuclear weapons and the arms race had created new dangers for the world. During and after the Cold War, other nations besides the superpowers tried to develop their own nuclear weapons.

The Cold War had divided Americans at times. The search for Communists in the 1950s had created an atmosphere of fear and suspicion. The Vietnam War had split the American public in an often-bitter debate.

Americans had strongly disagreed about foreign policy during the Cold War. Despite these disagreements, Americans valued their freedom, especially the right to free speech and open debate. Although some argued over how the Cold War was fought, Americans could agree that freedom was worth fighting for.

Section 5 Assessment

Recall

1. **Identify** Explain the significance of **(a)** SALT Agreement, **(b)** Ronald Reagan, **(c)** Star Wars, **(d)** Solidarity, **(e)** Mikhail Gorbachev, **(f)** glasnost, **(g)** Boris Yeltsin.
2. **Define (a)** détente, **(b)** martial law, **(c)** summit meeting.

Comprehension

3. What foreign policy changes did President Nixon make?
4. How did the Soviet invasion of Afghanistan cause tensions between the superpowers?
5. Give two reasons why communism collapsed in the Soviet Union and Eastern Europe.

6. Describe two results of the Cold War.

Critical Thinking and Writing

7. **Exploring the Main Idea** Review the Main Idea statement at the beginning of this section. Then, make a list of the ten most important events of the Cold War. Rank the events in order of importance. Explain your ranking.
8. **Solving Problems** **(a)** Describe two ways in which the United States could help former communist nations make the shift to democracy. **(b)** Do you think that the United States should provide such help? Why or why not?

Review and Assessment

CREATING A CHAPTER SUMMARY

On a sheet of paper, draw a concept web like the one shown here. In the blank ovals, write key events in the Cold War in different parts of the world. Add more ovals as needed.

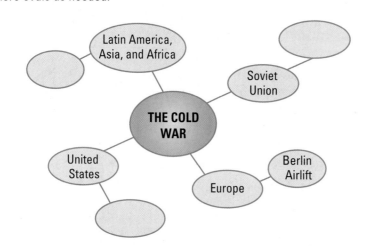

Latin America, Asia, and Africa

Soviet Union

THE COLD WAR

United States

Europe

Berlin Airlift

i TEXT

For additional review and enrichment activities, see the interactive version of *The American Nation,* available on the Web and on CD-ROM.

Take It to the NET

Chapter Self-Test For practice test questions for Chapter 28, see *The American Nation* section of **www.phschool.com**.

Building Vocabulary

Use the chapter vocabulary words listed below to create a crossword puzzle. Exchange puzzles with a classmate. Complete the puzzles, and then check each other's answers.

1. **containment**
2. **demilitarized zone**
3. **perjury**
4. **superpower**
5. **exile**
6. **guerrilla**
7. **escalate**
8. **détente**
9. **martial law**
10. **summit meeting**

Reviewing Key Facts

11. Describe two actions President Truman took to combat the spread of communism in Europe after World War II. (Section 1)
12. What impact did the Korean War have on events in the United States? (Section 2)
13. Give one example of how superpower rivalries affected nations around the world. (Section 3)
14. Describe three results of the Vietnam War. (Section 4)

15. Describe President Reagan's policies toward the Soviet Union. (Section 5)

Critical Thinking and Writing

16. **Connecting to Geography: Location** (a) Where is Cuba located relative to the United States? (b) How did Cuba's location play a role in the Cold War crises over the island nation?
17. **Linking Past and Present** Do you think people today worry as much about nuclear war as people did during the Cold War? Explain.
18. **Comparing** Compare and contrast the Korean War and the Vietnam War in terms of (a) results, (b) popular support.
19. **Sequencing** (a) Which began first: glasnost or the breakup of the Soviet Union? (b) Explain why these two events occurred in the order in which they did, rather than the other way around.

Analyzing Primary Sources

American cartoonists expressed the fears of Americans about the Cold War's rising tensions. This cartoon is from a 1947 newspaper.

20. What does the basketball symbolize?
21. **(a)** Who is the man in the cartoon? **(b)** How does the cartoonist show that the man represents the Soviet Union?
22. Why is the man blocking the basketball?
23. What comment is the cartoonist making about the relationship between the Soviet Union and the United States after World War II?

Predicting Consequences

This 1946 telegram would later prove valuable to those who tried to predict the consequences of Soviet propaganda on the Russian people:

> ❝ [Communist propaganda] does not represent natural outlook of Russian people. Latter are, by and large, friendly to outside world, . . . eager above all to live in peace and enjoy fruits of their own labor. Party line only represents [ideas] which official propaganda machine puts forward with great skill. . . . ❞
>
> —George Kennan, telegram to the State Department, February 22, 1946

24. A government official could conclude that Kennan thought that the Soviet people
    A were ready to rebel against their government
    B would never challenge their government
    C would eventually turn against their government's policies
    D were especially warlike and anti-American
25. **(a)** In what ways did Soviet policies prevent the Soviet people from enjoying the "fruits of their own labor"? **(b)** What challenges lie ahead for Russia's rulers today based on Kennan's 1946 statements?

ACTIVITIES

Connecting With . . . Culture

Writing Slogans Write three slogans that might have appeared on posters during the Cold War period. Topics might include the search for communists in the United States during the 1950s, Truman versus MacArthur, the Berlin Wall, the Vietnam War, the fall of communism in the Soviet Union, the Cuban missile crisis.

Take It to the NET

Connecting to Today

Creating a Brochure Use the Internet to find out about the Korean War Veterans Memorial. Make a tourist brochure describing the memorial, its design, its meaning for veterans and others, and its place in American history. For help in starting this activity, visit *The American Nation* section of **www.phschool.com**.

Creating a Timeline

Central America and the United States Use the Internet to find sites with information about relations between the United States and Central America during the Cold War. Then, draw a timeline that lists at least five important events that shaped relations between the two regions. For help in starting this activity, visit *The American Nation* section of **www.phschool.com**.

Prosperity, Rebellion, and Reform

1945–1980

1 **Postwar Policies and Prosperity**
2 **The Civil Rights Movement**
3 **Protest, Reform, and Doubt**
4 **The Crusade for Equal Rights**

Jackie Robinson

President Johnson signs the 1964 Civil Rights Act

AMERICAN EVENTS

1947
Jackie Robinson breaks the color barrier in baseball.

1950s
The baby boom increases the United States population.

1963
Civil rights supporters protesting discrimination march on Washington, D.C.

1964
The Civil Rights Act of 1964 is passed.

John F. Kennedy

Presidential Terms: Harry S. Truman 1945-1953   Dwight D. Eisenhower 1953-1961   1961-1963

1945 · · · · ★ · · · · **1955** · · · · · · · **1965** ★ ★

WORLD EVENTS

▲ **1950**
The Korean War begins.

▲ **1957**
Ghana becomes the first West African colony to win its independence.

Centers of the Human Rights Movement

During the protests of the 1960s and 1970s African Americans, women, and other minorities demanded that their civil rights be recognized and respected.

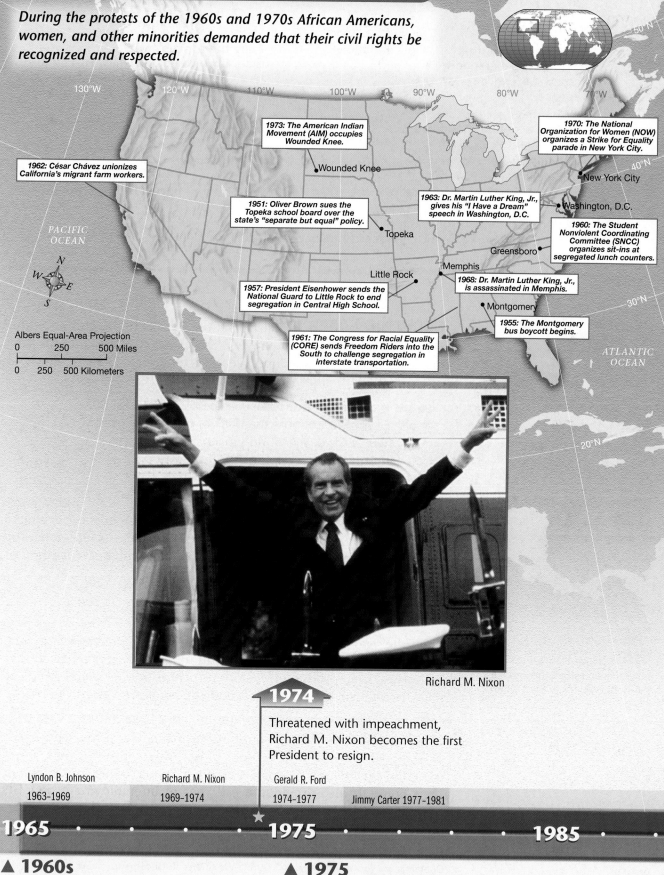

1973: The American Indian Movement (AIM) occupies Wounded Knee.

• Wounded Knee

1962: César Chávez unionizes California's migrant farm workers.

1951: Oliver Brown sues the Topeka school board over the state's "separate but equal" policy.

• Topeka

1963: Dr. Martin Luther King, Jr., gives his "I Have a Dream" speech in Washington, D.C.

1970: The National Organization for Women (NOW) organizes a Strike for Equality parade in New York City.

New York City

Washington, D.C.

Greensboro •

1960: The Student Nonviolent Coordinating Committee (SNCC) organizes sit-ins at segregated lunch counters.

Memphis

Little Rock •

1968: Dr. Martin Luther King, Jr., is assassinated in Memphis.

1957: President Eisenhower sends the National Guard to Little Rock to end segregation in Central High School.

• Montgomery

1955: The Montgomery bus boycott begins.

1961: The Congress for Racial Equality (CORE) sends Freedom Riders into the South to challenge segregation in interstate transportation.

PACIFIC OCEAN

ATLANTIC OCEAN

Albers Equal-Area Projection

0   250   500 Miles

0   250   500 Kilometers

Richard M. Nixon

1974

Threatened with impeachment, Richard M. Nixon becomes the first President to resign.

Lyndon B. Johnson
1963–1969

Richard M. Nixon
1969–1974

Gerald R. Ford
1974–1977

Jimmy Carter 1977–1981

1965 · · · · **1975** · · · · **1985** ·

▲ **1960s**
The United States involvement in Vietnam grows.

▲ **1975**
The Helsinki Agreement defines basic human rights.

1 Postwar Policies and Prosperity

Reading Focus

- What problems did Americans experience as they shifted from war to peace?
- What factors contributed to the economic and baby booms of the 1950s?
- How did American lifestyles change in the 1950s?

Key Terms

inflation

baby boom

productivity

standard of living

suburb

beatnik

Taking Notes

Copy the concept web below. As you read, fill in the blank ovals with important facts about the way life changed in the United States in the 1950s. Add as many ovals as you need.

The economy

LIFE IN THE 1950s

Main Idea After World War II, the American economy boomed, bringing dramatic changes in the way Americans worked and lived.

A 1950 car ad
Draw Inferences How does this ad reflect the economy of the United States in the 1950s?

Setting the Scene

A British visitor coming to the United States in 1948 was amazed. "There never was a country more fabulous than America," he observed. Three years after World War II, much of Europe still lay in ruins. But America, he wrote,

> sits bestride the world like a Colossus. . . . Half of the wealth of the world, more than half of the productivity, nearly two-thirds of the world's machines are concentrated in American hands; the rest of the world lies in the shadow of American industry. **99**
>
> —Robert Payne, 1949

In the decades after World War II, the United States experienced a boom like no other in its history. The population mushroomed, the economy prospered, and Americans enjoyed the highest standard of living any people had ever known.

From War to Peace

When the war ended in 1945, two thirds of all American men between the ages of 18 and 34 were in uniform. Experts feared that without wartime production, many returning soldiers might find no jobs. Unemployment would rise, and the economy would tumble.

Economic Difficulties Even before the war ended, Congress passed the GI Bill of Rights* to help returning veterans. Under this law, the government spent billions of dollars to help veterans set up farms and businesses. Many GIs received loans to pay for college or a new home. It also provided a full year of unemployment benefits for veterans who could not find work.

---

*GI stands for "government issue." During World War II, GI came to mean any member of the United States armed forces.

Inflation, or rising prices, was a major postwar problem. During the war, the government had controlled prices and wages. After the war, the controls ended. The price of goods rose.

Workers demanded higher wages to pay for the price increases. When employers refused, labor unions called strikes.

President Harry Truman was sympathetic to workers but feared that higher wages would only add to inflation. He urged strikers to return to work.

Truman's Surprise Victory As the election of 1948 approached, President Truman and his Democratic party seemed doomed to defeat. Labor strikes and soaring prices had already helped Republicans win a majority in both the House and the Senate for the first time since the 1920s. Among Democrats, unhappy liberals and conservatives deserted Truman to form parties of their own. The Republicans confidently nominated Governor Thomas Dewey of New York for President.

Truman fought back. During his campaign, Truman traveled thousands of miles across the country by train. At every stop, he attacked the Republicans as "do-nothings" and "gluttons of privilege." When all the votes were counted, Truman won a surprise victory over Dewey.

A New Round of Reform During his presidency, Truman proposed a new round of reform called the Fair Deal. He wanted to extend the liberal policies of his predecessor, Franklin D. Roosevelt.

In Congress the Fair Deal faced heavy opposition from conservative Democrats and Republicans. Only a few of the proposals passed: a higher minimum wage, expanded Social Security benefits, and loans for buying low-cost houses. Congress rejected most of Truman's reforms, including a bold plan to provide government-financed health insurance.

The Eisenhower Years In 1952, President Truman chose not to run for reelection. Democrats nominated Adlai Stevenson of Illinois. Republicans chose General Dwight D. Eisenhower, a hero of World War II. Eisenhower, known as "Ike," promised to end the conflict in Korea and lead Americans through the Cold War.

For the first time, television played a major role in a presidential campaign. Instead of long speeches, Republicans used 20-second TV "spots" of Ike responding to questions from hand-picked citizens. Complained one critic: "It was selling the President like toothpaste." Still, enough voters were impressed with Ike's military experience and foreign policy skills to give him a landslide victory.

Like most Republicans, President Eisenhower believed in limiting federal spending and reducing federal regulation of the economy. He called his political course the "straight road down the middle."

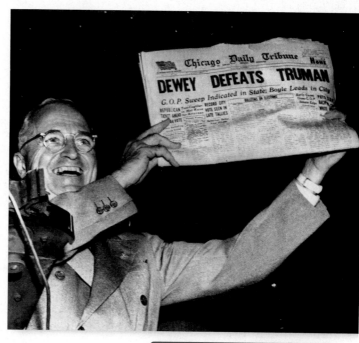

Viewing History

A Truman Victory
Based on early results, the *Chicago Daily Tribune* declared Truman the loser in the 1948 election. Here, Truman proudly displays the newspaper headline. **Draw Inferences** *What does this headline suggest about the election?*

Increase in Homeownership 1940–1960

*Estimated
†The first year for which Hawaii and Alaska are included

Source: *Historical Statistics of the United States*

He favored cutting the federal budget but expanding Social Security benefits and some other New Deal programs.

Most Americans supported Eisenhower's middle-of-the-road approach. In the 1956 presidential election, voters reelected Ike to a second term of office.

An Economic and Baby Boom

During the Great Depression and World War II, many Americans had put off having families. When the war ended and prosperity returned, the number of births soared.

Population experts called the phenomenon a baby boom. In the 1930s, the population of the United States had grown by only 9 million. In the 1940s it grew by 19 million and in the 1950s by an astounding 29 million! Most couples married young, had an average of three children, and completed their families by their late twenties.

Improvements in health care and nutrition contributed to the baby boom. Better care for pregnant women and newborn infants meant that more babies survived. Fewer children died from childhood diseases than had died in the past.

Economic Boom In addition to the baby boom, there was an economic boom. The economy rapidly expanded in the postwar years. When an economy expands, more goods are produced and sold and more jobs are created.

Federal projects also increased factory production. The government spent more money to build new roads, houses, and schools. In the middle of the Cold War, government spending on military goods spurred the economy, too.

New technology added to the boom by promoting steady rises in productivity, or the average output per worker. Corporations began using computers to perform calculations and keep records.

High productivity allowed the United States to manufacture and consume, or use, more goods than any other country. Increased productivity also led to a workweek that averaged 40 hours. Americans now had more leisure time.

AS YOU READ **Summarize** Write one or two sentences summarizing the two "booms" in the United States after World War II.

Lifestyles of the 1950s

The economic boom raised Americans' standard of living, an index based on the amount of goods, services, and leisure time people have. Americans bought washing machines, vacuum cleaners, televisions, automobiles, and many other consumer goods.

Because so many of their purchases revolved around home and family, few Americans worried that they were saving little. Instead, most Americans enjoyed a life in which they had more money to spend. This consumer spending reshaped the country.

Suburban Living With their newfound wealth, many people bought homes in the suburbs, or communities outside the cities. The GI Bill encouraged home building in the suburbs by offering low-interest loans to veterans. During the 1950s, suburbs grew 40 times faster than cities.

Builder William Levitt pioneered a new way of building suburban houses. He bought large tracts of land and then divided them into small lots. On each lot, he built a house identical to every other house in the tract. Because these houses were mass-produced, they cost much less to build than custom-made houses. They could also be constructed rapidly. Using preassembled materials, teams of carpenters, plumbers, and electricians could put up a Levitt house in 16 minutes.

Levitt began his first big project in 1947, on Long Island, where he put up 17,000 new homes. It was the largest housing development ever built by an American. Levitt called the project Levittown. African Americans were barred from owning or renting in Levittown. Levitt feared that if he sold to blacks, whites would not buy.

Shopping centers with modern department stores sprang up near the suburban housing developments. There were eight shopping centers in 1946. By the end of the 1950s, there were 4,000. No longer did consumers have to travel to the city to buy what they wanted. Shiny new shopping centers were only a short drive away.

As millions flocked to the suburbs, central cities began a slow decline. Suburbs and shopping centers drained cities of businesses and taxes. Since most of those who moved were white, some critics complained that the United States was turning into a nation of "chocolate cities and vanilla suburbs."

Sunbelt Living Americans also flocked to the Sunbelt, a region stretching across the southern rim of the country. States from Florida to Texas and California began to experience dramatic growth.

▲ Past

▲ Present

Viewing History

United States

The Cinema

Drive-in theaters became popular during the 1940s and peaked in the 1950s. Customers could buy snacks and enjoy a movie while sitting in their cars. Today, movie fans can watch their favorite movies at home. Most movies are available on video cassettes or DVD (digital video disc) which can be bought or rented from a local video store.

Evaluating Information
What does the popularity of the drive-in movie tell you about the 1950s?

For Americans on the move, the Sunbelt, both then and now, had many lures: a warm climate; good jobs; a prosperous economy based on agriculture, oil, and electronics; and national defense industries. Businesses still move to the region for its low taxes and growing work force. The work force included recent immigrants from Latin America and Asia. Like many ambitious newcomers, they were willing to work hard for low pay.

Car Crazy During the 1950s, cars became more important to daily life. People living in the suburbs or the Sunbelt usually needed a car to drive to work. By 1960, 9 out of 10 families living in the suburbs owned a car. Since few people bought foreign cars, the American automobile companies, such as General Motors, profited greatly.

To accommodate the increase in automobiles, the federal government built thousands of miles of highways. In 1956, Congress passed the Federal-Aid Highway Act. This act called for a network of high-speed roads linking the nation. It set aside $41 billion to build 40,000 miles of highway.

The new highway system boosted the economy, especially the automobile and trucking industries. Americans could travel more easily for business or pleasure. As a result, a new roadside culture of motels and fast-food restaurants emerged.

Television Television caught on slowly. However, as TV sets shrank in price and grew in size, almost everybody wanted one. Nine out of 10 households had at least one television by 1960.

Television brought news and entertainment into people's homes. Commercials encouraged spending and buying. Television also helped to make the 1950s a time when people wanted to look and act the same as everyone else. Many programs presented the same single view of the ideal middle-class family. Fathers knew best, mothers were loving and supportive, and children were always obedient.

Rock Music In the mid-1950s, a new type of music appeared. Rock-and-roll combined the sounds of rhythm, blues, country, and gospel with a hard-driving beat. Adults worried that the music was too wild. However, many teenagers liked rock-and-roll because it provided an opportunity for them to show their independence. *Teenager* was a word first used in the 1950s to describe someone between 13 and 19 years old.

African American singers Chuck Berry and Little Richard gained national fame. From Texas came Buddy Holly, and from California, Latino singer Richie Valens. No one attracted more attention than Memphis's Elvis Presley. His slick hair, sideburns, and steamy dancing alarmed parents but made Elvis a hit with teenagers. They dressed like him, bought his records, and nicknamed him "the King."

Signs of Discontent Not all Americans in the 1950s were happy about the emphasis on getting and spending. A small group of writers and artists criticized what they saw as the growing materialism of American society and its lack of individuality. Novelist Jack Kerouac coined the term *beat*, meaning "weariness with all forms of the modern industrial state." Middle-class observers called Kerouac and others like him beatniks. Still, Kerouac's best-selling novel, *On the Road*, influenced many young Americans.

Most Americans paid little attention to these signs of discontent. Soon, however, a growing outcry could not be ignored.

Section 1 Assessment

Recall

1. **Identify** Explain the significance of (a) GI Bill of Rights, (b) Fair Deal, (c) Dwight D. Eisenhower, (d) Levittown, (e) Sunbelt, (f) Federal-Aid Highway Act, (g) Elvis Presley, (h) Jack Kerouac.
2. **Define** (a) inflation, (b) baby boom, (c) productivity, (d) standard of living, (e) suburb, (f) beatnik.

Comprehension

3. What economic difficulties did Americans face immediately after World War II?

4. Discuss the significance of the baby boom of the late 1940s.
5. Describe the effect of television on American life in the 1950s.

Critical Thinking and Writing

6. **Exploring the Main Idea** Review the Main Idea statement at the beginning of this section. Then, write two generalizations about the way most Americans lived in the 1950s.
7. **Identifying Points of View** Why did some people dislike the cultural changes that were occurring in the 1950s?

ACTIVITY

Writing Interview Questions As a news reporter, you are assigned to write an article on how the United States changed during the 1950s. Write five questions that you would ask someone who had lived during those years. Each question should be based on one of the headings in this section.

The Early Days of Television

After coast-to-coast broadcasting began in 1951, the number of TV sets soared from 6 million to 60 million within a decade. Americans were fascinated with the broad range of visual entertainment available at home, and television quickly became a part of the American culture.

Television News Edward R. Murrow, pioneer of television journalism, hosted *See It Now,* the model of quality TV documentaries. On *Person to Person,* Murrow spoke from his TV studio to celebrities in their homes. Walter Cronkite, another well-known journalist, hosted *You Are There,* newsreels of historic events.

I Love Lucy became an overnight sensation in 1951 and went on to become the most popular situation comedy in the history of television. More than 70 percent of the nation's TV sets were tuned in to the show when characters Lucy and Ricky Ricardo became parents to "Little Ricky."

TV families of the 1950s were warmly portrayed in such shows as *Father Knows Best* (shown here), *Lassie, Leave It to Beaver,* and *The Adventures of Ozzie and Harriet.*

The Howdy Doody Show was the most popular children's show of the 1950s.

ACTIVITY

Use the Internet to find out about the quiz show scandal of 1959. Why do you think TV networks replaced high-stakes quiz shows with Westerns and detective shows in the aftermath of the scandal?

2 The Civil Rights Movement

Reading Focus

- How did discrimination affect the lives of minorities in the United States?
- What role did the courts play in helping African Americans and Mexican Americans gain civil rights?
- What was the role of Martin Luther King in the Montgomery bus boycott?

Key Terms

segregation

integration

civil rights movement

boycott

civil disobedience

Taking Notes

Copy this flowchart. As you read, describe the events that began to end segregation during the late 1940s and 1950s. The first and last boxes have been completed to help you get started. Add as many boxes as you need.

The NAACP becomes more active in working against segregation

↓

↓

↓

Groups against segregation

Main Idea After World War II, African Americans and other minorities began to demand their full civil rights and an end to discrimination.

Setting the Scene

Driving north from the South every summer, young George knew that the trip must be carefully planned. The family had to take food and water. But, they also had to map out which roads to take and where to stop. In the racially divided South, blacks were not always welcome. Going to the restroom was a difficult problem during the trip. At stop after stop, George saw signs that read "Whites only" or "No coloreds allowed."

George later became a college president but only after decades of struggle had broken down barriers of discrimination. Across the United States, African Americans and other racial minorities faced discrimination not just on the road but also in jobs, housing, and education. After World War II, their struggles for equality and civil rights intensified.

AS YOU READ A segregated water fountain

Find Main Ideas How did segregation laws affect African Americans in the South?

Discrimination Creates Barriers

Throughout the nation, discrimination limited the lives of millions of Americans. Qualified African Americans found themselves barred from good jobs and decent housing in the North. In the South, laws enforced strict separation, or segregation, of the races in schools, theaters, restaurants, and other public places. Facilities for blacks were inferior to those for whites.

Discrimination also limited Mexican Americans and other Latinos. They were not subject to strict segregation laws. However, other laws—as well as traditions—worked against them. In the Southwest, all-white schools closed their doors to Mexican American children. Instead, poorly equipped "Mexican schools" served them. Custom kept Mexican Americans from living in certain neighborhoods or using certain hotels or restaurants. Often, better-paying jobs were not open to them.

Breaking Down the Barriers For African Americans, the NAACP (National Association for the Advancement of Colored People) led the drive against discrimination. During World War II, NAACP membership rocketed from 50,000 to 500,000. Under Thurgood Marshall, its Legal Defense Fund mounted several court battles against segregation. It also helped blacks register to vote and fought for equal opportunity in housing and employment.

Historic Firsts There were two significant events in the 1940s in the fight against segregation. Jackie Robinson broke the color barrier in Major League Baseball in 1947 when he joined the Brooklyn Dodgers. He was even named rookie of the year. Not since Moses Fleetwood Walker had a black player joined the major leagues. Walker was the first African American player to join a major league team in 1884.

Under pressure from civil rights groups, President Truman ordered integration, or the mixing of different racial groups, in the armed forces in 1948. During the Korean War, black and white soldiers fought side by side.

After risking their lives abroad, veterans were unwilling to accept discrimination at home. Often they became leaders in the struggle for equal rights. "Veterans," explained an observer, "have acquired a new courage, and have become more vocal in protesting inequalities."

The Court Fight for Civil Rights

During the 1950s, African Americans and Mexican Americans stepped up the struggle for equality. They took their cases to court but also protested in the streets. Their efforts became known as the civil rights movement.

In Schools The U.S. Supreme Court had decided in 1896 in *Plessy* v. *Ferguson* that "separate but equal" facilities for blacks and whites were constitutional. During the 1940s, the NAACP did not attack this idea head on. Instead, its lawyers argued that an individual facility like a state college or law school was not equal to the local white school.

Such a legal strategy might improve black schools and other segregated facilities case by case, but those cases did little to end segregation. By the early 1950s, laws in 21 states and the District of Columbia still enforced separate black and white public schools. Virtually all of the black schools were inferior to the white ones.

Oliver Brown of Topeka, Kansas, decided to challenge the Kansas law. He asked the local school board to let his daughter, Linda, attend a nearby white school rather than the distant black school to which she had been assigned. When board members refused, Brown filed a suit against the school board with the help of the NAACP. The case of *Brown* v. *Board of Education of Topeka* reached the Supreme Court.

To present the case in court, Brown hired lawyer Thurgood Marshall, who specialized in civil rights cases. Marshall had served as legal director of the NAACP for more than ten years. He decided to challenge the whole idea of "separate but equal." Segregated

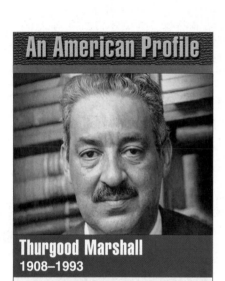

An American Profile

Thurgood Marshall
1908–1993

Thurgood Marshall made history at the United States Supreme Court. In 1954, he argued before the Court the case that ended the practice of separate schools for white and black students—*Brown* v. *Board of Education of Topeka*. Later, he became the first African American to become a justice of the Supreme Court.

After Marshall had graduated from law school, he joined a team of lawyers working for the NAACP. Marshall's plan was to chip away at the laws that treated African Americans unfairly. He argued 32 cases before the Supreme Court and won 29 times.

How did Marshall work to gain racial equality for African Americans?

schools, he argued, could never provide equal education. By their very nature, said Marshall, segregated schools violated the Fourteenth Amendment, which gave "equal protection" to all citizens.

The Supreme Court ruled in Brown's favor in 1954. Chief Justice Earl Warren noted that segregation affected the "hearts and minds" of black students "in a way unlikely ever to be undone." The unanimous decision declared:

> 66 We conclude that in the field of public education, the doctrine of 'separate but equal' has no place. Separate educational facilities are always unequal. 99

Desegregating Public Schools A year later, the Court ordered the schools to be desegregated "with all deliberate speed." In a few places, schools were integrated without much trouble. In many others, officials resisted. White politicians in these places decided that the phrase "with all deliberate speed" could mean they could take years to integrate their schools. Or, perhaps they would never obey the decision.

Arkansas Governor Orval Faubus called out the National Guard in 1957 in order to keep African American students from attending all-white Central High School in Little Rock. President Eisenhower finally sent in federal troops because the Arkansas governor was defying a federal law. Under their protection, black students entered Central High.

Eisenhower was the first President since Reconstruction to use armed federal troops in support of African American rights. The action showed that the federal government could play a key role in protecting civil rights.

On Juries Mexican Americans organized their own fight for civil rights. Mexican American veterans founded the American GI Forum of the United States (AGIF) in 1948 in order to campaign for equal rights. Similar to the NAACP, the AGIF supported legal challenges to discrimination.

In 1954, the same year as *Brown* v. *Board of Education*, Mexican Americans won an important legal battle when the Supreme Court ruled on the case of *Hernández* v. *Texas.*

Pete Hernández, a Mexican American, had been convicted of murder by an all-white jury in Texas. Among the lawyers who appealed his conviction was Gus Garcia, one of the leaders of the AGIF. Attorney James DeAnda, another Mexican American, also helped. He had previously worked to desegregate areas of Corpus Christi, Texas, where Mexican Americans were not allowed to buy houses.

Hernández's lawyers argued that Mexican Americans in Texas were denied equality under the law because they were excluded from juries. The Supreme Court agreed. It overturned the conviction and ended the exclusion of Mexican Americans from Texas juries. In the future, other minority groups would use this decision to help win their civil rights.

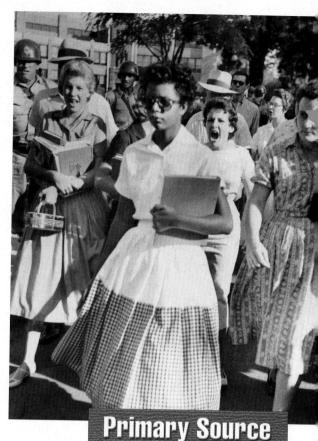

Primary Source

The Little Rock Nine

Elizabeth Eckford was one of the original nine African American students to attend Central High School in Little Rock. Years later, she described her experience:
"I tried to find a friendly face somewhere in the mob. I looked at [a white girl] again and she spat on me. . . . Then I saw a bench at the bus stop. When I got there, I don't think I could have gone another step. I sat down and the mob crowded up and began shouting all over again. Just then a white man sat down beside me, put his arm around me and patted my shoulder. He raised my chin and said, 'Don't let them see you cry.'"

—Elizabeth Eckford, in an interview

Analyzing Primary Sources
Why did the man tell Eckford not to let the other students see her cry?

Rosa Parks

Walking to work

The Montgomery Bus Boycott

Court cases were not enough to end discrimination, as Rosa Parks discovered in December 1955. She was riding home from work on a crowded bus in Montgomery, Alabama. The driver ordered her to move to the back of the bus so that a white man could have her seat, as Alabama's segregation laws required. Parks, a well-known activist and a former secretary of the local chapter of the NAACP, refused to leave her seat. She was arrested and put in jail.

Rosa Parks's arrest angered African Americans in Montgomery. That night, several women from the NAACP composed a letter asking all African Americans to boycott, or refuse to use, the buses. The boycott, they hoped, would hurt the city financially and force an end to segregation on the buses. The women distributed thousands of copies of the letter to the African Americans of Montgomery.

To support the protest, Montgomery's black leaders formed a new organization, the Montgomery Improvement Association (MIA). They chose Dr. Martin Luther King, Jr., a Baptist minister, as its head.

Dr. King spoke at a meeting in the Holt Street Baptist Church. Hundreds packed the church. Thousands more stood outside. "We are here this evening . . . for serious business," King began. "Yes, yes!" the crowd shouted. As the crowd cheered him on, King continued:

❝ You know, my friends, there comes a time when people get tired of being trampled over by the iron feet of oppression. . . . We are determined here in Montgomery . . . to work and fight until justice runs down like water, and righteousness like a mighty stream! ❞

—Martin Luther King, Jr., Speech, December 2, 1955

On December 5, 1955, most African Americans in Montgomery refused to travel by bus.

King is arrested   A successful end

The Boycott Continues The boycott lasted from December 5 to December 20 of the next year. MIA carpools took some 20,000 African Americans to and from work each day. Many people simply walked. One elderly woman coined a phrase that became a motto of the boycott: "My feets is tired, but my soul is rested."

Angry whites fought back. Employers threatened to arrest African Americans if they did not abandon the boycott. Police handed out traffic tickets to harass boycotters and they frequently stopped African American drivers and demanded to see their licenses. They arrested King for speeding and kept him in jail for several days. King's house was bombed. Still, the boycott continued.

King insisted that his followers limit their actions to civil disobedience, or nonviolent protests against unjust laws. He said, "We must use the weapon of love. We must have compassion and understanding for those who hate us."

Throughout the bus boycott, African American churches were vital to its success. Churches played a central role in the lives of African Americans across the country. In Montgomery, mass meetings were held in black churches. There, boycotters sang together, prayed together, and listened to stories of sacrifice. The churches kept morale high, provided leadership, and helped boycotters give each other courage and inspiration.

Finally, the MIA filed a federal lawsuit to end bus segregation in Montgomery. In 1956, almost a year after Rosa Parks had refused to move to the back of the bus, the Supreme Court ruled that segregation on Alabama buses was unconstitutional. The Montgomery bus company agreed to integrate the buses and to hire black bus drivers.

Wide-reaching Effects The effects of the bus boycott reached far beyond Montgomery. The boycott brought the civil rights movement to national attention. It launched nonviolent protest as a key tactic in the struggle for equality. Finally, the boycott introduced the nation to a new generation of African American leaders. Many were ministers from African American churches.

Martin Luther King, Jr.

One of the most important of these new national figures was boycott leader Martin Luther King, Jr. He was the son of a prominent Baptist minister. King had graduated from Morehouse College, a leading black college. Later, he had earned a Ph.D. in religion and served as pastor of an African American church in Montgomery.

King had studied a wide range of philosophers and political thinkers. He had come to admire especially Mohandas Gandhi, a lawyer who had pioneered the use of nonviolence to end British rule in India.

Following the Montgomery victory, King and other African American leaders founded the Southern Christian Leadership Conference (SCLC) to carry on the crusade for civil rights. The group, consisting of nearly 100 black ministers, elected King president and the Reverend Ralph Abernathy treasurer. The SCLC urged African Americans to fight injustice by using civil disobedience:

 Draw Inferences How do you think nonviolent resistance can "transform weakness into strength"?

66 Understand that nonviolence is not a symbol of weakness or cowardice, but as . . . demonstrated, nonviolent resistance transforms weakness into strength and breeds courage in the face of danger. 99
— SCLC statement, January 10–11, 1957

Still, discrimination and segregation remained widespread. The civil rights movement of the 1950s would soon grow into a howling wind of protest that would sweep across the country.

AFTER YOU READ ★ ★ ★ **Section 2 Assessment** ★ ★ ★

Recall

1. **Identify** Explain the significance of (a) NAACP, (b) Jackie Robinson, (c) *Brown* v. *Board of Education of Topeka,* (d) Thurgood Marshall, (e) AGIF, (f) *Hernández* v. *Texas,* (g) Rosa Parks, (h) Martin Luther King, Jr.
2. **Define** (a) segregation, (b) integration, (c) civil rights movement, (d) boycott, (e) civil disobedience.

Comprehension

3. Describe how discrimination limited the lives of minorities.

4. Discuss the impact of the *Brown* v. *Board of Education of Topeka* decision.
5. Discuss the methods that Dr. Martin Luther King, Jr., used to help end segregation on Montgomery's buses.

Critical Thinking and Writing

6. **Exploring the Main Idea** Review the Main Idea statement at the beginning of this section. Then, make a concept web with facts about the early civil rights movement.
7. **Supporting a Point of View** Do you think that civil disobedience is an effective method of protest? Explain.

 ACTIVITY

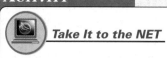 **Take It to the NET**

Researching Civil Rights Cases Use the Internet to find out about court cases that challenged segregation in education before *Brown* v. *Board of Education of Topeka.* With a partner, prepare a chart with interesting facts about each case. Visit *The American Nation* section of **www.phschool.com** for help in completing the activity.

Interpreting Oral History

As time passes, events of the present quickly become events of the past—a part of history. Often, you can learn about recent historical events by interpreting the recollections of people who were present. These memories can help you understand what people thought and how they felt. Many recollections come to us as oral history that is later written down.

A black activist, John Lewis was one of the leaders in the 1965 march through Selma, Alabama. He describes events as he leads a group of demonstrators through the streets.

66 Down Water Street we went, turning right and walking along the river until we reached the base of the bridge, the Edmund Pettus Bridge. . . .

When we reached the crest of the bridge, I stopped dead still. . . .

There, facing us at the bottom of the other side, stood a sea of blue-helmeted, blue-uniformed Alabama state troopers, line after line of them, dozens of battle-ready lawmen stretched from one side of U.S. highway 80 to the other. . . . the officer in charge . . . stepped forward, holding a small bull-horn up to his mouth.

'This is an unlawful assembly. . . . Your march is not conducive to the public safety. You are ordered to disperse and go back to your church or to your homes.'

I wasn't about to turn around. We were there. We couldn't turn and go back even if we wanted to. . . . There was only one option left that I could see.

'We should kneel and pray.' . . . We turned and passed the word back to begin bowing down in a prayerful manner. But that word didn't get far. It didn't have time. One minute after he issued his warning . . . Major Cloud issued an order . . . 'Troopers. Advance!' 99

Learn the Skill *To interpret oral history, use the following steps:*

1. **Examine the evidence.** What information does it give? What period or event is being discussed?

2. **Identify the point of view.** How does the speaker "see" the event?

3. **Determine the reliability.** What was the person's role in the event? How might that role affect his or her recollections?

4. **Interpret the recollection.** What can you learn from this oral history? What conclusions can you draw?

Practice the Skill *Answer the following questions based on the passages above:*

1. What event is Lewis describing?

2. What was Lewis's viewpoint on the march?

3. **(a)** What was Lewis's role in the events he recalls? **(b)** How reliable would you judge the account to be?

4. What did you learn from the account of John Lewis?

Apply the Skill *See the Chapter Review and Assessment.*

3 Protest, Reform, and Doubt

Reading Focus

- What goals did Presidents Kennedy and Johnson set for the nation?
- Why did protest movements increase in the 1960s?
- What problems did President Nixon face?
- What principles guided the Carter administration?

Key Terms

counterculture movement

silent majority

stagflation

Taking Notes

As you read, prepare an outline of this section. Use roman numerals to indicate the major headings, capital letters for the subheadings, and numbers for the supporting details. The sample will help you get started.

> I. Kennedy in the White House
> A. Election of 1960
>   1. The issue of Kennedy's religion
>   2.
> B. Kennedy's policies
>   1. Poverty program
>   2.
> C. Tragedy in Dallas

Main Idea The 1960s was a decade filled with problems: political assassinations, scandals, political crises, and protest movements.

AS YOU READ

John F. Kennedy

Summarize Write two or three sentences describing what President Kennedy felt Americans needed to do.

Setting the Scene John F. Kennedy took the presidential oath of office on January 20, 1961. At 43, he was the youngest man ever elected President and the first to be born in the twentieth century. "Let the word go forth," he said, "that the torch has been passed to a new generation of Americans."

Kennedy's youth and idealism had inspired Americans during the campaign. Now he called them to service:

> 66 The trumpet summons us again . . . to bear the burden of a long twilight struggle . . . against the common enemies of man: tyranny, poverty, disease, and war itself. . . . And so, my fellow Americans: ask not what your country can do for you—ask what you can do for your country. 99
>
> —John F. Kennedy, Inaugural Address, January 20, 1961

For all his youth and high hopes, Kennedy and the Presidents who followed him faced tough challenges. The 1960s and 1970s were years of idealism. They also turned out to be a time of uncertainty, tragedy, and turmoil for Americans of all ages.

Kennedy in the White House

The election of 1960 pitted Republican Vice President Richard Nixon against Kennedy, a Democrat and Senator from Massachusetts.

Election of 1960 The election was a close contest. Many Americans voted against Kennedy because they felt he did not have enough experience to be President. Others worried about Kennedy's religion, Catholicism. No Roman Catholic had ever been President. Many Americans feared that Kennedy might be more loyal to the Roman Catholic Church than to the country. Kennedy reassured voters that he believed in the separation of church and state.

Merritt Island, Florida

Kennedy Space Center

The history of United States space exploration is on display at the Kennedy Space Center in Florida. Visitors can view IMAX movies, walk among actual rockets, explore a simulated space station, and climb aboard a full-sized replica of a space shuttle. Exhibits honor the past achievements of American astronauts and highlight goals for the future.

Take It to the NET

Virtual Field Trip For an interactive look at the Kennedy Space Center, visit *The American Nation* section of **www.phschool.com**.

Television turned the tide for Kennedy. In the first televised debates ever held in a presidential campaign, Kennedy appeared youthful and confident. Nixon, recovering from a recent illness, looked tired and nervous. Kennedy won the election by a narrow margin.

Kennedy's Policies During the campaign, Kennedy had been shocked to find hungry families living in the United States. "Just imagine," he said, "kids who never drank milk!" As President, he urged Congress to pass laws to help the millions of Americans living in poverty.

Congress blocked the President's poverty programs. But it did fund the Peace Corps—volunteers sent to teach or provide technical help in developing nations. It also approved Kennedy's proposal to explore the "new frontier" of space. Before any other proposals could be enacted, a tragic event cut down the young President and shattered the nation.

Tragedy in Dallas On November 22, 1963, Kennedy traveled to Dallas, Texas, on a political tour. As his convertible passed cheering crowds, shots rang out. The President slumped in his seat. Later, John F. Kennedy died. That afternoon, Vice President Lyndon Johnson was sworn in as President.

A special government commission headed by Chief Justice Earl Warren later concluded that a lone gunman, Lee Harvey Oswald, had murdered the President. After his arrest, Oswald himself was killed

Viewing History

Getting a Head Start

President Johnson favored programs to help young people. Head Start programs helped children from low-income families prepare for elementary school. Here, Lady Bird Johnson joins in a special ceremony. The two boys (top right) are having fun with clay. **Analyzing Information** *How might this program benefit young children? Explain.*

United States

by another gunman. Today, most historians agree with the Warren Commission.

Johnson's Great Society

"Let us continue," said Johnson. He steered many of Kennedy's proposals through Congress. In November 1964, voters returned him to the White House in a landslide victory. Johnson had his own program. He called it the Great Society. It boldly aimed at creating a decent living standard for every American. In a first step, Johnson declared a "war on poverty."

Congress had not supported Kennedy's poverty program. However, Johnson was much more persuasive. He cornered members of Congress. Johnson successfully used his years of political experience to help get what he wanted. In just two years in office, Johnson pushed 50 new laws through Congress.

The Great Society had many programs. Under Medicare, the government helped pay hospital costs for senior citizens. Medicaid gave states money to help poor citizens with medical bills. A new Office of Economic Opportunity created job-training programs for the unemployed. It gave loans to needy farmers and to businesses in poor sections of cities.

Programs to build housing for low-income and middle-income families were also part of the Great Society. To carry out these programs, Congress established the Department of Housing and Urban Development, or HUD. Robert Weaver headed the department. He was the first African American ever appointed to the Cabinet.

The Great Society had a mixed record. It aided the poor but at great cost to taxpayers. Government grew in size and intruded on people's lives as never before. Corruption sometimes plagued antipoverty programs. Still, Medicare, Medicaid, and other reforms helped millions and became permanent parts of American life.

Protest Movements

Despite these social reforms, protest movements grew in the 1960s. The civil rights movement expanded. Opposition to the war in Vietnam grew. Some young people began to reject the values and lifestyles of their parents.

The Counterculture Movement Many young Americans joined the counterculture movement. They criticized competition and the drive for personal success. Instead of going to college, they "dropped out." Instead of traditional families, they lived together in groups or communes. Many listened to new forms of rock music. Some "turned on," or experimented with illegal drugs.

Inspired by the civil rights movement, counterculture protesters called for peace, justice, and social equality. They wore torn, faded jeans and work shirts to blur the differences between rich and poor. Men grew long hair and beards. Women refused to put on makeup. All wanted to look more natural and less like their parents.

Like the beatniks of the 1950s, members of the counterculture said American life was empty and materialistic. Some turned to eastern religions such as Buddhism in search of spiritual meaning.

AS YOU READ **Ask Questions** What questions would you ask members of the counterculture about their views of the 1960s and 1970s and their views of today?

The Antiwar Movement As more and more young men were sent to fight in the Vietnam War, an antiwar movement gained strength. Protesters staged rallies, burned draft cards, and refused to serve in the military. Many of the largest demonstrations took place on college campuses.

By 1968, the antiwar movement was peaking. As a result, President Johnson's popularity plummeted. To avoid angry protesters, Johnson stayed in the White House more and more. He decided against running for the presidency again.

The Election of 1968 Johnson's decision opened the way for other Democrats to seek their party's nomination in 1968. New York senator Robert Kennedy, brother of the late President, made a strong run. While campaigning in Los Angeles, however, Kennedy was killed by a Palestinian who opposed the senator's support for Israel. The Democrats selected Vice President Hubert Humphrey as their candidate. The Republicans again nominated former Vice President Richard Nixon. Nixon promised "peace with honor" in Vietnam and "law and order" at home. Alabama governor George Wallace entered the race as a third-party candidate. Helped by this and by divisions among Democrats over the Vietnam War, Nixon won a narrow victory.

The Nixon Years

As President, Nixon tried to reduce government involvement in people's lives. He cut funds for many Great Society programs, including job training, education, and low-income housing. He also sought to return power to the states. He called this transfer of power the "New Federalism."

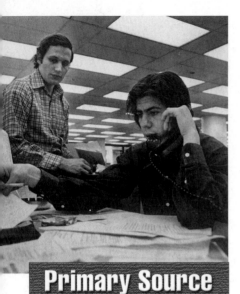

Law and Order During the campaign, Nixon said that he wanted to help what he called the silent majority. These Americans were disturbed by the unrest of the 1960s but did not protest publicly. They were, Nixon explained, the "great majority of Americans, the nonshouters, the nondemonstrators."

True to his campaign promise, Nixon began a "law-and-order" program. Federal funds were used to help local police departments. Nixon also named four conservative justices to the Supreme Court. They tended to favor dealing harshly with lawbreakers.

The Space Program Nixon inherited the space program from Kennedy and Johnson. Its greatest triumph came in 1969 just as Nixon took office. In 1969, two astronauts landed a small craft on the moon's surface. With millions of television viewers around the world watching, Neil A. Armstrong became the first person to step onto the moon. "That's one small step for a man—one giant leap for mankind," he radioed back to Earth. American astronauts visited the moon five more times.

The Economy During the Nixon years, the economy suffered from stagflation, a combination of rising prices, high unemployment, and slow economic growth. To halt inflation, Nixon froze wages and prices. To stimulate economic growth, he increased federal spending.

Still, economic problems would not go away. Increased federal spending caused federal budget deficits, that is, the government spent more than it received in revenues. Early in Nixon's second term, an oil embargo put added pressure on the economy. Higher energy prices caused the price of goods to rise even more.

Scandal Brings Down a President In Nixon's second term in office, a scandal brought the President down. It began while Nixon was campaigning for reelection. On June 17, 1972, police caught five men breaking into Democratic party headquarters in the Watergate apartment building in Washington, D.C. Evidence linked the burglars to Nixon's reelection committee. The President assured the public that no one in the White House was involved in the Watergate Affair.

Despite Nixon's denials, a Senate committee began public hearings in May 1973. The hearings revealed that Nixon had made secret tape recordings of conversations in his office. These tapes showed that the President and several close advisers had tried to cover up the truth about the Watergate break-in.

In the middle of the Watergate Affair, another scandal erupted. Vice President Spiro Agnew was accused of taking bribes and was forced to resign. The President chose Representative Gerald R. Ford of Michigan to replace him. The Watergate crisis came to a head in July 1974. A House of Representatives committee passed articles of impeachment against the President. One charge was obstructing, or blocking, justice. Even the President's strongest defenders found the evidence convincing. In August 1974, before an impeachment trial could begin, Richard Nixon became the first President to resign from office.

Ford Pardons Nixon Gerald Ford, the new President, had a difficult job. He faced a troubled economy and the challenge of helping the nation emerge from a major political scandal. In response to the nation's troubled mood, President Ford granted Nixon a "full, free, and absolute pardon." He did so a month after Nixon resigned. Some felt that Nixon should have been brought to trial. Ford, however, wanted to save the country from a bitter debate over Watergate. Ford lost a great deal of public support because of that decision.

Carter in the White House

In 1976, Republicans nominated Ford for President. Democrats chose Jimmy Carter, the former governor of Georgia.

Carter had no experience in Washington but used to his advantage the fact that he was a Washington outsider. He pointed out that "the vast majority of Americans . . . are also outsiders." After years of scandal in Washington, Carter's fresh face and promises of a new approach carried him to a narrow victory.

Carter's term began with a whirlwind of activity. In his first year, the new President sent Congress almost a dozen major bills. They included reforms in the Social Security system and in the tax code. But Carter's lack of experience in Washington hurt him. Congress refused to support his legislation.

The President did not fare much better with the problem of high inflation. When the government tried to slow inflation, prices only kept rising. Many families had trouble paying for food, clothing, and rent.

In foreign affairs, Carter was a strong defender of human rights. The United States had signed the Helsinki Agreement just before he took office. Thirty-five nations pledged to respect basic rights such as religious freedom and freedom of speech. The United States, Carter said, should keep this pledge and not aid countries that violated human rights.

Section 3 Assessment

Recall

1. **Identify** Explain the significance of **(a)** Peace Corps, **(b)** Warren Commission, **(c)** Great Society, **(d)** Medicare, **(e)** Medicaid, **(f)** Neil Armstrong, **(g)** Watergate Affair, **(h)** Gerald Ford, **(i)** Jimmy Carter, **(j)** Helsinki Agreement.

2. **Define** **(a)** counterculture movement, **(b)** silent majority, **(c)** stagflation.

Comprehension

3. Describe two Great Society programs that became law.

4. How did some Americans oppose United States involvement in the Vietnam War?

5. Explain how Nixon tried to deal with **(a)** stagflation, **(b)** the Watergate Affair.

6. Did Carter achieve the goals of his domestic program? Explain.

Critical Thinking and Writing

7. **Exploring the Main Idea** Review the Main Idea statement at the beginning of this section. Then, discuss the efforts of Presidents during the 1960s and 1970s to bring about reform.

8. **Comparing** Compare Presidents Kennedy, Johnson, Nixon, and Carter in terms of their relationships with Congress.

ACTIVITY

Take It to the NET

Making Information Pamphlets Use the Internet to learn more about Medicare and Medicaid. Who is eligible? What are the benefits? How can a person apply? Use the information to make pamphlets about the programs. Visit *The American Nation* section of **www.phschool.com** for help in completing the activity.

4 The Crusade for Equal Rights

BEFORE YOU READ

Reading Focus

- How did African Americans work for equal rights during the 1960s and 1970s?
- Why did the women's movement grow stronger?
- How did the Latinos' drive for equal rights compare with the efforts of other groups?

Key Terms

sit-in

affirmative action

migrant worker

bilingual

Taking Notes

Copy the chart below. As you read, complete the chart to show some of the effects of the protests by groups demanding equal rights. Add as many entries as you need.

```
          GROUPS PROTEST
         FOR EQUAL RIGHTS
      ↓           ↓            ↓
  African      Women
  Americans
  • Civil Rights Act
    of 1964
```

Main Idea In the 1960s and 1970s, a crusade for equal rights swept across the country, producing a new era of protest and reform.

AS YOU READ **Sit-in at a lunch counter**

Draw Inferences How would you describe the reaction of the people sitting at the lunch counter?

Setting the Scene

In 1963 Anne Moody was a senior in college when she and two friends sat down at a "whites only" lunch counter in Jackson, Mississippi. The waitress told them to move to the black section. Anne and her friends, all African Americans, stayed put. "We would like to be served," Anne said politely.

A crowd of whites pulled them from their seats. They beat one of Anne's friends, who was promptly arrested. When Anne and her other friend returned to their seats, they were joined by a white woman from her school. "Now there were three of us," Anne recalled, "and we were integrated." The crowd smeared them with ketchup and mustard and dragged them from the lunch counter.

Anne and her friends were using a form of protest called sit-ins, in which people sit and refuse to leave. The first sit-in took place at a lunch counter in Greensboro, North Carolina, in 1960. During the 1960s, thousands of blacks and whites were conducting sit-ins at public places across the South. The protests signaled a new determination to end segregation and discrimination.

African Americans Crusade for Equality

Across the South, segregation laws limited the rights of black Americans not only at lunch counters but also in bus stations, restrooms, and other public facilities. In the 1960s, sit-ins and other forms of protest fanned the crusade for equality.

Nonviolent Direct Action Civil rights groups planned the protests, but it was often young people like Anne Moody who carried them out. The Congress of Racial Equality (CORE), for example, organized "Freedom Rides." Busloads of young Freedom Riders—black and white—rode from town to town to integrate bus terminals in the South.

These early civil rights groups held firmly to the tactics of what Martin Luther King, Jr., called "nonviolent direct action." Sit-ins,

---

boycotts, marches, and other peaceful methods were used to achieve their goals.

Police sometimes responded by using attack dogs or water hoses against protesters. Houses and churches of black leaders were bombed. Civil rights workers—black and white—were sometimes injured or killed. By remaining nonviolent, protesters gained a moral advantage and the sympathy of many Americans.

In 1963, more than 200,000 Americans marched on Washington, D.C. They wanted Congress to pass laws to end discrimination and to help the poor. Among the speakers that day was Martin Luther King, Jr. In a now-famous speech, he proclaimed:

> 66 When we let freedom ring . . . we will be able to speed up that day when all of God's children, black men and white men, Jews and Gentiles, Protestants and Catholics, will be able to join hands and sing in the words of the old Negro spiritual, 'Free at last! Free at last! Thank God Almighty, we are free at last!' 99
>
> —Martin Luther King, Jr., Speech, August 28, 1963

Federal Civil Rights Laws The demonstrations spurred Presidents Kennedy and Johnson to press for federal civil rights laws. Kennedy failed, but Johnson succeeded in pushing through the Civil Rights Act of 1964, which protected the right of all citizens to vote. It also outlawed discrimination in hiring and ended segregation in public places.

At the Democratic National Convention in 1964, Fannie Lou Hamer, an African American, told of her experiences while trying to register to vote in Mississippi. Her efforts, along with the help of others, were successful in gaining voting rights.

In 1965, the Voting Rights Act allowed federal officials to register voters in states practicing discrimination. It also ended literacy tests used to block African Americans from voting. As a result, tens of thousands of African Americans voted for the first time.

The new civil rights laws did not end all discrimination. In the North, no formal system of segregation existed. Informally, though, housing in certain neighborhoods and employment in many companies remained closed to African Americans.

Black Power Some African Americans believed that nonviolent protest had failed. The Black Panthers and other radical groups told African Americans to arm themselves. Blacks, they said, had to be ready to protect themselves and to fight for their rights.

Black Muslims, such as Malcolm X, argued that African Americans could succeed only if they separated from white society. Before being assassinated in 1965, Malcolm X began to change his views. He called for "a society in which there could exist honest white-black brotherhood."

Both moderates and radicals found common ground in talk of "black power." They urged African Americans to achieve economic independence by starting their own businesses and shopping in black-owned stores. Leaders also called for "black pride," encouraging African Americans to learn more about their heritage and culture.

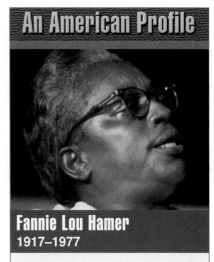

An American Profile

Fannie Lou Hamer
1917–1977

When Fanny Lou Hamer was born, African Americans had few rights. They faced discrimination that denied them chances to get ahead. For nearly 50 years, Hamer lived a quiet, hard-working life.

One day, members of civil rights groups came to Hamer's area. They wanted volunteers to help win voting rights for blacks. Hamer joined the effort—even though she suffered in several ways as a result. She lost her job. Her family had to move. She was arrested and severely beaten. Still, she continued to work for the cause. In 1964, Hamer became a leader of the Mississippi Freedom Democratic Party. In this role, she won fame.

How did Hamer show her dedication to civil rights?

Marching for Women's Rights

Harrisburg, Pennsylvania

American women became politically active during the 1960s and 1970s. Many joined the efforts of the National Organization for Women. Here, women march together to express their solidarity. **Applying Information** *What causes are important to these women?*

Protest Turns Violent In crowded city neighborhoods, many blacks were angry about discrimination, lack of jobs, and poverty. Beginning in 1965, their anger boiled over into violence. During six days in August, rioters in Watts, a black neighborhood in Los Angeles, set fire to buildings and looted stores. Some 4,000 people were arrested, 34 were killed, and 1,000 were injured. Over the next two years, Chicago, Detroit, and dozens of other cities exploded with violence, destruction, and death.

King Is Killed Martin Luther King, Jr., continued to preach nonviolence. In April 1968, he went to Memphis, Tennessee, to support a strike of black sanitation workers. When he stepped outside his motel room, a white gunman killed him.

King's life has continued to inspire Americans to work for peaceful change. To honor his memory, his birthday was declared a national holiday in 1986.

Some Results The civil rights movement began to show some results in the 1970s. African Americans won public offices in small towns and large cities. Atlanta, Cleveland, Detroit, New Orleans, and Los Angeles had all elected black mayors by 1979.

African Americans also made gains in the federal government. In 1967, Edward Brooke of Massachusetts became the first black senator since Reconstruction. A year later, President Johnson appointed Thurgood Marshall to the Supreme Court.

Many businesses and universities adopted affirmative action programs. These programs sought to hire and promote minorities, women, and others who had faced discrimination. By the 1970s, more African Americans were entering such professions as medicine and law. Yet, for all their efforts, blacks still had to contend with bias in hiring, promotions, and pay.

The Women's Rights Movement

Women had long fought inequality. Since the 1960s, their drive for equal rights has been known as the Women's Rights Movement.

In the workplace qualified women found that male employers were unwilling to hire them for certain jobs, and they were usually paid less than men, even for the same work. They were fired before men and promoted less quickly.

In 1966, writer Betty Friedan helped to set up the National Organization for Women (NOW), which worked for equal rights for women in jobs, pay, and education. It also helped women bring discrimination cases to court and campaigned for maternity leave and child-care centers. Urging women to be more politically active, NOW organized the Strike for Equality Parade down New York's Fifth Avenue in 1970. Some 50,000 women marched.

New laws helped women make some gains. The Equal Pay Act of 1963 required equal pay for equal work. The Civil Rights Act of 1964 outlawed discrimination in hiring based on gender and on race.

In the 1970s, the women's movement suffered a major defeat. In 1972, Congress passed a proposal for the Equal Rights Amendment (ERA) to the Constitution. The amendment would ban discrimination based on gender. However, Phyllis Schlafly and other conservative women led a successful campaign against ratification of the amendment. They said the ERA would lead to women being drafted into the military and would harm the traditional family. Despite this defeat, the women's movement brought women more power and equality.

The Latino Drive for Equality

By the end of the 1970s, more than 10 million Latinos lived in the United States. Like African Americans, women, and other minorities, Latinos worked for equal rights.

Mexican Americans Mexican Americans are the largest group of Latinos living in the United States. From 1960 to 1980, the greatest number of immigrants to the United States came from Mexico.

Many Mexican Americans lived and worked in cities. Many more labored as migrant workers who traveled from farm to farm looking for work. Low wages and harsh working conditions made life difficult for them. Discrimination made things worse. Mexican Americans were often barred from better-paying jobs and from better neighborhoods. Few schools offered programs for those whose first language was Spanish. Migrants moved so often that it was hard for their children to attend school regularly.

AS YOU READ **Visualize** Form a mental picture of what it would be like to be the child of migrant workers.

Puerto Rican Americans Latinos in the eastern United States often came from Puerto Rico. In the 1950s, thousands left Puerto Rico in search of work in the United States. Many took jobs in the factories of New York City, New Jersey, Connecticut, and Pennsylvania. Some went to Boston, Chicago, and San Francisco. Puerto Ricans also faced discrimination in housing and jobs wherever they settled.

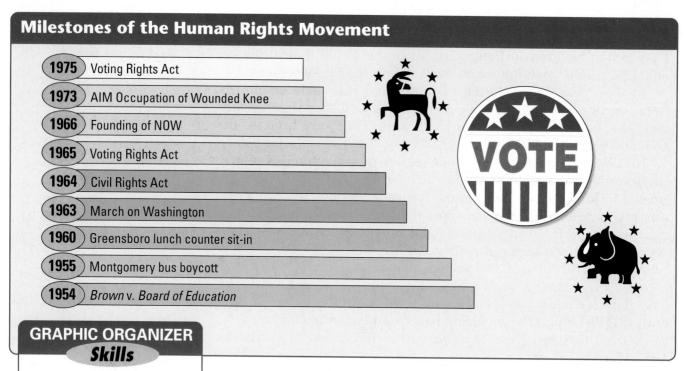

Milestones of the Human Rights Movement

Year	Event
1975	Voting Rights Act
1973	AIM Occupation of Wounded Knee
1966	Founding of NOW
1965	Voting Rights Act
1964	Civil Rights Act
1963	March on Washington
1960	Greensboro lunch counter sit-in
1955	Montgomery bus boycott
1954	*Brown* v. *Board of Education*

GRAPHIC ORGANIZER
Skills

The period from the mid-1950s to the mid-1970s was an eventful time for the human rights movement.

1. **Comprehension** In which decade was the human rights movement most active?

2. **Critical Thinking Identifying Points of View** Which milestone on this chart was part of the women's rights movement?

Civics

Cuban Americans A third group of Latinos came in two waves from Cuba. Between 1959 and 1962, some 200,000 people fled to southern Florida when Fidel Castro set up a communist government in Cuba. These immigrants were often middle class and well educated. They adapted quickly to their new home. A second wave of immigrants came in 1980 after Castro allowed thousands of people to leave the island. Most of the new refugees were unskilled. They had a hard time making a living.

As their numbers grew, Cuban Americans became a force in southern Florida. Miami took on a new look. Shop windows displayed signs in Spanish. Cuban restaurants and shops opened. Cubans published Spanish-language newspapers and operated radio and television stations. Cuban American politicians were soon elected.

Latinos Organize In the 1960s, new Latino organizations sought change. César Chávez formed a union of migrant workers, the United Farm Workers. When farm owners refused to talk to the union, Chávez called for a nationwide boycott of farm products. In the end, the owners recognized the union, and workers won higher wages.

By the mid-1960s, Latinos began to publicly take pride in their history and culture. Mexican Americans called themselves Chicanos, a name that comes from the Spanish word *Mexicano.*

Latino groups also registered voters and made sure that voting laws were enforced. These new voters helped to elect more Latino officials to represent their interests.

One result of these efforts was the Voting Rights Act of 1975. It required areas with many non-English-speaking citizens to hold bilingual elections. Bilingual means in two languages. In a bilingual election, information is provided in more than one language. With a ballot that was written in Spanish, it was easier for Latinos to vote.

The Bilingual Education Acts of 1968 and 1973 promoted bilingual programs in public schools with Spanish-speaking and Asian students.

Asian Americans Asian Americans joined the civil rights movement. In 1968, students at the University of California at Berkeley founded the Asian American Political Alliance (AAPA). Students of Chinese, Japanese, Filipino, and other Asian descent joined to promote the rights and culture of Asian Americans. As a result, between 1968 and 1973, universities across the nation created programs in Asian American studies.

Native Americans Native Americans also worked for their full rights. They claimed rights not only as individuals but also as members of tribal groups. Over the years, the federal government had recognized tribal governments by signing treaties with them.

During the late 1940s and the 1950s, the federal government tried to break up tribal governments. They also encouraged Indians to leave the reservations. By the late 1960s, more than half of all American Indians lived off the reservations, mainly in cities. Gradually, city life weakened traditional tribes and customs.

Native Americans organized against these government policies. The National Congress of American Indians regularly sent delegations to Washington to defend Indian rights.

The American Indian Movement (AIM) protested the treatment of Indians. In 1973, AIM members occupied Wounded Knee, South Dakota, for several weeks. As you have read, the United States Army had killed nearly 300 Indians at Wounded Knee in 1890. AIM wanted to remind people of the government's failure to deal fairly with American Indians. Protests and court cases have won sympathy for Indian causes and more rights for Native Americans.

Viewing History

Migrant Workers Unite

California

César Chávez organized migrant farmworkers to rally for better working conditions and higher wages. **Applying Information** *Why might it have been difficult to organize migrant farmworkers?*

AFTER YOU READ

Section 4 Assessment

Recall

1. **Identify** Explain the significance of (a) Freedom Ride, (b) Civil Rights Act of 1964, (c) Voting Rights Act, (d) Black Panthers, (e) Malcolm X, (f) National Organization for Women, (g) César Chávez, (h) Bilingual Education Acts, (i) Asian American Political Alliance, (j) American Indian Movement.

2. **Define** (a) sit-in, (b) affirmative action, (c) migrant worker, (d) bilingual.

Comprehension

3. How did African Americans fight for equal rights?

4. What was the purpose of NOW?

5. Describe the success of groups seeking equal rights.

Critical Thinking and Writing

6. **Exploring the Main Idea** Review the Main Idea statement at the beginning of this section. Then, write a paragraph about how the civil rights movement paved the way for other groups to work for equal rights.

7. **Drawing Conclusions** Why do you think the political goals of Cuban Americans differed from those of Mexican Americans? Explain.

ACTIVITY

Debating an Issue
Dr. Martin Luther King, Jr., and Malcolm X are at a meeting before Malcolm X changed his views in 1965. Write a dialogue between the two leaders debating how to end discrimination against African Americans.

CREATING A CHAPTER SUMMARY

Copy the timeline below. As you read, enter the important political, economic, and social events of the 1950s and 1960s. Add as many entries as you need.

Neil Armstrong is the first person to step on the moon

1952

1950

1969

Dwight Eisenhower is elected

For additional review and enrichment activities, see the interactive version of *The American Nation*, available on the Web and on CD-ROM.

Take It to the NET

Chapter Self-Test For practice test questions for Chapter 29, visit *The American Nation* section of **www.phschool.com**.

Building Vocabulary

Review the chapter vocabulary words listed below. Then, use the words and their definitions to create a matching quiz. Exchange quizzes with another student. Check each other's answers when you are finished.

1. inflation
2. productivity
3. beatnik
4. boycott
5. civil disobedience
6. counterculture
7. silent majority
8. stagflation
9. affirmative action
10. bilingual

Reviewing Key Facts

11. Describe two factors that helped the economy to expand after World War II. (Section 1)
12. What three victories occurred in the civil rights movement during the 1950s? (Section 2)
13. Explain Nixon's views on the role of the federal government in people's lives. (Section 3)
14. Describe one way in which each of the following groups fought against injustice: **(a)** African Americans, **(b)** Latino Americans, **(c)** Asian Americans, **(d)** Native Americans, **(e)** women. (Section 4)

Critical Thinking and Writing

15. **Applying Information** How did the federal government support the Supreme Court's decision in *Brown* v. *Board of Education of Topeka?*
16. **Connecting to Geography: Movement** What were the causes and effects of the growth of the suburbs in the 1950s?
17. **Linking Past and Present** One of the reforms of the civil rights era was the establishment of bilingual education. Today, some people question the benefits of that program. Do you agree or disagree? Explain.
18. **Synthesizing Information** Which pieces of legislation that were passed during Johnson's or Kennedy's presidency do you think have had the most lasting effect on American society? Explain.

Analyzing Primary Sources

Vice President Gerald Ford became President on August 9, 1974, after Richard Nixon resigned. Read the following excerpt from the speech Ford made to the nation that day. Answer the questions that follow:

> 66 My fellow Americans, our long national nightmare is over. Our Constitution works; our great Republic is a Government of laws and not of men. . . . As we restore the internal wounds of Watergate, more painful and more poisonous than those of foreign wars, . . . let us restore the golden rule to our political process, and let brotherly love purge our hearts of suspicion and hate. 99
>
> —Gerald Ford, speech on August 9, 1974

19. Of what national nightmare is Ford speaking?
20. (a) According to Ford, how is the country governed? (b) Why do you think he makes this statement?
21. How do you know that Ford will pardon Nixon? Explain.

Interpreting Oral History

The Apollo 11 crew landed on the moon July 20, 1969. Michael Collins was part of the team along with Neil Armstrong and Edwin Aldrin. This is Collins's account of the trip. Read the passage and answer the questions.

> 66 The moon I had known all my life, that small, flat yellow disk in the sky [was] replaced by the most awesome sphere I had ever seen.
>
> It was huge. . . . I could almost reach out and touch it. It was between us and the sun [which] created a halo around it [and made] the moon's surface dark and mysterious. . . . It didn't look like a very friendly place, but Neil summed it up: 'It's worth the price of the trip.' 99
>
> —Michael Collins, *Flying to the Moon and Other Strange Places*

22. How does Collins describe the moon?
    A It is a large, orange disk.
    B It is large, round, and mysterious.
    C It is a flat, blue disk.
    D It is huge with a bluish rim.
23. (a) What do you think Armstrong's statement means? (b) What did you learn from this account?

ACTIVITIES

Connecting With . . .
Government and Citizenship

President Lyndon B. Johnson made the following statement at a staff meeting in 1965:

> "Look, I've just been elected and right now we'll have a honeymoon with Congress. . . . I'll have a good chance to get my program through.
>
> But after I make my recommendation, I'm going to start to lose the power and authority I have . . . that's in the nature of what the President does."

Think about what you have read about Presidents in this chapter and what you know about past Presidents. Then, write a paragraph discussing whether or not Presidents lose their popularity and power while in office.

Take It to the NET

Connecting to Today

Researching Civil Rights Since the Civil Rights Act of 1964, the Supreme Court has decided various cases involving discrimination. Use the Internet to research one case. (For example, you might look at a case involving the Americans With Disabilities Act.) Prepare a chart with information about the case. For help in starting the activity, visit *The American Nation* section of **www.phschool.com**.

Protest Songs

Analyzing Song Lyrics Protest songs were popular in the 1960s and 1970s. Use the Internet to research three songs. Explain how the lyrics related to social and political issues of the era. For help in starting the activity, visit *The American Nation* section of **www.phschool.com**.

CHAPTER
30 The Nation in a New World

1970–PRESENT

1 **The Conservative Revolt**
2 **American Leadership in a New World**
3 **The Spread of Regional Conflict**
4 **A Global Economy**
5 **New Challenges for the Nation**

Rationing gas during the oil embargo

Ronald Reagan

1973

Oil-producing Arab nations cut off oil shipments to the United States. The oil embargo causes severe fuel shortages.

1980

Ronald Reagan is elected President. Reagan ushers in a new conservative era as he promises to reduce the size of government.

1990

The Americans With Disabilities Act outlaws discrimination against people with physical or mental impairments.

AMERICAN EVENTS

Presidential Terms:

Richard M. Nixon	Gerald R. Ford	Jimmy Carter	Ronald Reagan 1981–1989
1969–1974	1974–1977	1977–1981	

1970 · · · **1980** · · · **1990**

WORLD EVENTS

1979 ▲
Israel and Egypt sign a peace treaty.

1989 ▲
China crushes prodemocracy demonstrations.

North American Trade

In 1993, the North American Free Trade Agreement encouraged the growth of United States trade with Canada and Mexico.

CANADA

UNITED STATES

Canada (top chart):
1990 $82,967
1995 $127,226
2000 $176,430

Canada (right chart):
1990 $91,372
1995 $144,370
2000 $229,209

Mexico (left chart):
1990 $30,172
1995 $62,101
2000 $135,911

Mexico (right chart):
1990 $28,376
1995 $46,292
2000 $111,721

MEXICO

PACIFIC OCEAN

ATLANTIC OCEAN

Key
- Imports (in millions of dollars)
- Exports (in millions of dollars)

Albers Equal-Area Projection
0   250   500 Miles
0   250   500 Kilometers

Firefighters in the rubble of the World Trade Center

1990s
The Internet booms as more people use computers to communicate, get information, and do business.

2001
After terrorist attacks on the Pentagon and New York's World Trade Center, President Bush launches a campaign to defeat world terrorism.

George H. W. Bush
1989–1993   William J. Clinton 1993–2001   George W. Bush 2001–

1990   **2000**   **2010**

▲ 1991
The Soviet Union breaks apart.

▲ 1998
India and Pakistan test nuclear weapons.

1 The Conservative Revolt

BEFORE YOU READ

Reading Focus

- How did President Ronald Reagan forward a conservative agenda?
- What problems did Presidents Bush and Clinton face?
- Why was the election of 2000 controversial?

Key Terms

Moral Majority

Reaganomics

deregulation

balanced budget

downsizing

recession

Contract With America

surplus

Taking Notes

Copy this flow-chart. As you read, fill in the boxes with key events during the terms of President Reagan and his successors. Add as many boxes as you need.

RONALD REAGAN (1981–1989)
- Conservative agenda
- Tax cuts
-

↓

GEORGE H. W. BUSH (1989–1993)

↓

↓

Main Idea The election of Ronald Reagan in 1980 ushered in a new era of conservatism in politics and public policy.

AS YOU READ **1980 Reagan campaign button**

Use Prior Knowledge Based on what you read in the last chapter, list two reasons that Americans might have wanted a change at the end of the 1970s.

Setting the Scene

The sun beamed as Ronald Reagan began his inaugural address on January 20, 1981. The day matched the sunny optimism of the new President. Just shy of his seventieth birthday, Reagan brought new ideas to Washington. "Government," he said, "is not the solution to our problems, government is the problem."

Ronald Reagan led a conservative revolt against years of government expansion. In two terms as President, he began to move the nation in a new direction.

The Conservative Agenda

Ronald Reagan swept into office on a rising conservative tide. A growing number of Americans saw conservative ideas and values as the answer to the nation's problems. These ideas contrasted sharply with the political thinking that had prevailed in the 1960s and 1970s.

Limiting Government Since the 1930s, the federal government had grown steadily. President Franklin D. Roosevelt had begun this trend to help people through the Great Depression. Harry Truman, John Kennedy, and Lyndon Johnson continued the expansion. These liberal presidents believed that government should play a large role in managing the economy and providing social programs.

Beginning in the 1960s, a conservative movement warned against growing federal power. Arizona senator Barry Goldwater led the way. He argued for smaller government nearer the people:

> 66 Our towns and our cities, then our counties and our states, then our regional compacts—and only then the national government. That, let me remind you, is the ladder of liberty built by decentralized power. 99
>
> —Barry Goldwater, Speech at Republican National Convention, July 16, 1964

By the 1980s, conservatives dominated the Republican party. Led by Ronald Reagan, they believed that federal social programs had become too costly and that federal regulations kept businesses from growing. State and local governments, they argued, were closest to the people and should decide what regulations were needed.

Traditional Values After decades of social change, many conservatives called for a return to traditional values. These included religion, family, and patriotism.

Reflecting the renewed emphasis on traditional values, evangelical Christian churches grew rapidly during the 1970s and 1980s. Evangelicals stressed personal conversion and sought to convert others. Evangelical ministers used television to widen their audience.

Many evangelicals took an active role in conservative political causes. In 1979, the Reverend Jerry Falwell founded the Moral Majority. The group aided political candidates who favored conservative religious goals, such as a constitutional amendment to allow organized prayer in public schools. In 1980, strong support from the Moral Majority and other conservative religious organizations helped to put Ronald Reagan in the White House.

The Reagan-Bush Era

Reagan was a handsome man with a relaxed, friendly air. He had been a movie star before winning election as governor of California. His skill at presenting ideas in terms that ordinary people could understand earned him the nickname the Great Communicator.

In 1980, Reagan defeated Jimmy Carter for President. After an era of protests, scandals, and high prices, voters embraced Reagan's promise to "Make America Great Again." He was reelected in 1984 by an even wider margin.

Reaganomics The new President's first priority was his economic program, often called Reaganomics. He persuaded Congress to cut taxes. Reagan hoped that taxpayers would use the extra money to buy more and save more. Buying more would spur business growth. Saving more would allow banks to invest in new business ventures.

Reaganomics also involved cutting federal spending to reduce the size of government. The President persuaded Congress to slow down spending increases on social programs such as welfare and aid to education. Critics charged that those cuts hurt the poor, the elderly, and children. Supporters responded that Reagan was just trimming programs that did not work.

A third goal of Reaganomics was deregulation, or reduction of restrictions on businesses. Earlier Presidents had slowly begun to

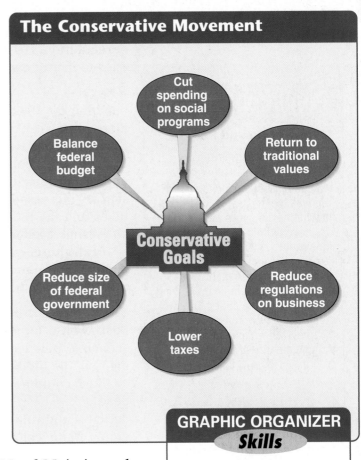

The Conservative Movement

- Cut spending on social programs
- Balance federal budget
- Return to traditional values
- **Conservative Goals**
- Reduce size of federal government
- Reduce regulations on business
- Lower taxes

GRAPHIC ORGANIZER
Skills

The conservative movement had social, political, and economic goals.

1. **Comprehension** Which of the goals shown here are primarily related to economics?

2. **Critical Thinking Applying Information** Ronald Reagan said he wanted to "get government off the back of the people." Which of the goals shown here support this statement?

 Civics

deregulate a few industries. Reagan increased the pace and scope of deregulation. He opposed all laws, for example, that required industries to install expensive antipollution devices.

Reagan's Balance Sheet After a slow start, the economy was booming by 1982. When Reagan left office, there were 16 million more jobs, while inflation had been held in check.

Another of Reagan's goals—a balanced budget—proved harder to achieve. A **balanced budget** requires the government to spend only as much as it takes in. But with Cold War tensions high, Reagan sharply increased military spending. As military spending rose and taxes fell, the budget deficit soared. For 1986, the deficit jumped to an all-time high of $240 billion.

Still, the economy continued to expand, and Reagan remained popular. For many Americans, he had succeeded in restoring faith in the presidency, which had been so badly tarnished in recent years.

Bush's Economic Troubles Reagan's Vice President, George H. W. Bush, won a big victory in 1988. Bush vowed to continue Reagan's economic policies, cutting the deficit without raising taxes. "Read my lips," he pledged during the campaign. "No new taxes."

Bush could not keep his promise. By 1990, he and Congress were deadlocked over which government programs to cut to reduce the deficit. Finally, Bush agreed to raise taxes to save some popular programs. Many conservatives felt betrayed.

As taxes rose, the economy grew weaker. To make matters worse, a banking crisis developed. Deregulation had led some banks to make risky loans. When those loans were not repaid, many banks failed. Without bank loans, the economy slowed. Many businesses cut costs by **downsizing,** or reducing their workforces. Downsizing increased business profits but also increased joblessness.

These conditions soon produced a recession. A **recession** is an economic slump that is milder than a depression. The recession continued for more than a year.

Conservatives on the Court Reagan and Bush appointed a total of five Justices to the Supreme Court. (One of Reagan's choices, Sandra Day O'Connor, was the first woman to serve on the Court.) The new Justices were more conservative than those they replaced.

The more conservative Court placed new limits on the rights of suspected criminals, as well as on the right of prisoners to appeal convictions. The Court made it harder for workers to win job discrimination cases. It also reduced busing, which some school districts had used since the 1960s to achieve racial integration in public schools.

Clinton and the Conservatives

Bush faced a stiff reelection challenge in 1992. Recession and unemployment continued. Bickering between Congress and the President left voters unhappy with Washington politics. The Democratic nominee, Arkansas governor Bill Clinton, promised more government involvement in areas ignored by Reagan and Bush.

On Election Day, voters signaled their dissatisfaction. Only 38 percent voted for Bush. Clinton received less than half the popular

---

Primary Source

A View of Ronald Reagan

A former speechwriter for President Reagan evaluates his style and his impact on the nation: "He was the master. No one could do what he did, move people that way, talk to them so that they understood. . . . He brought a whole generation of young activists into government; they never would have been there if he hadn't opened the doors; they are creating the new conservatism that may well shape our politics through the turn of the century."

— Peggy Noonan, *What I Saw at the Revolution*

Analyzing Primary Sources
Do you think Noonan's prediction about Reagan's impact came true? Explain.

Teng

CARTOONISTS & WRITERS SYNDICATE http://CartoonWeb.com

POLITICAL CARTOON
Skills

Clinton and the Congress
The 1994 elections left the nation with a Democrat as President and a Republican-controlled Congress. In this cartoon from a Singapore newspaper, the elephant is used as the traditional symbol of the Republican party.

1. **Comprehension**
   (a) Who is operating the boat? **(b)** Can Clinton move in the direction he wants without their help? Why or why not?

2. **Understanding Main Ideas** What is the cartoonist saying about the situation in Washington after the 1994 congressional elections?

3. **Critical Thinking Identifying Points of View** Can you tell whether this cartoonist favored the President or the Congress? Explain.

Civics 🏛

vote—43 percent. The remaining 19 percent went to Ross Perot, a Texas billionaire who ran as an independent candidate.

A Middle Road President Clinton followed a middle-of-the-road course. On the one hand, he moved cautiously when he persuaded Congress to increase some taxes and reduce spending. For the first time in over 40 years, the federal deficit began a steady decline.

On the other hand, Clinton pushed for bold reform of the health care system. In 1994, some 37 million Americans had no health insurance. Clinton called for a national system of health insurance for almost all Americans. After heated debate, however, Congress defeated the plan. Many Americans worried that it would be too costly and involve the government too deeply in their lives.

To many Americans, the struggle over health care showed that Washington was paralyzed. Democrats controlled both Congress and the White House, yet the President could not get his own plan enacted.

Conservatives Win Control Voter frustration helped Republicans win a resounding victory in the 1994 congressional elections. For the first time since the 1950s, Republicans held a majority in both the Senate and the House of Representatives. "It was a revolution," cheered Toby Roth, a Wisconsin Republican.

Newt Gingrich of Georgia became Speaker of the House. Under his leadership, House Republicans drew up a "Contract With America." This set of proposed laws included trimming social welfare programs, reducing environmental regulations, and slashing taxes.

The President attacked many of the proposals as unfair to poor and middle-class Americans. After a bitter fight, he compromised with Congress on a plan to balance the federal budget by the year

The Election of 2000

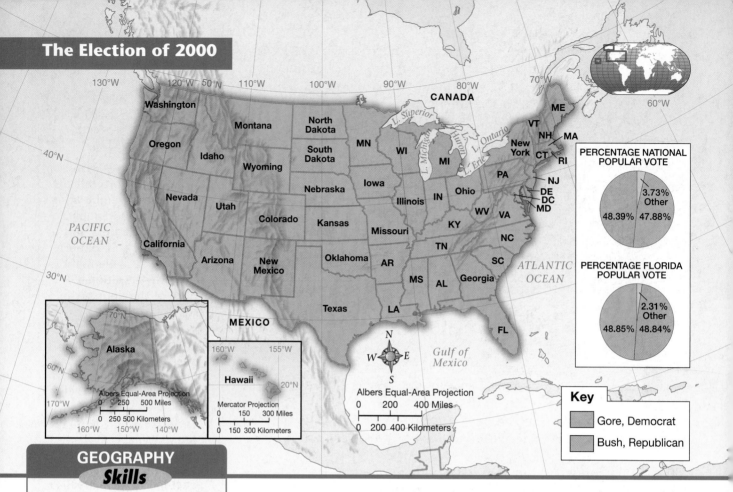

PERCENTAGE NATIONAL
POPULAR VOTE

3.73%
Other
48.39% 47.88%

PERCENTAGE FLORIDA
POPULAR VOTE

2.31%
Other
48.85% 48.84%

Key

Gore, Democrat

Bush, Republican

GEOGRAPHY *Skills*

The presidential election of 2000 was the most disputed race since 1876.

1. **Location** On the map, locate **(a)** Florida, **(b)** Tennessee, **(c)** Texas.

2. **Region** In what areas of the country did Al Gore receive his strongest support?

3. **Critical Thinking**
Drawing Conclusions
What role did candidates of other parties play in the election?

2002. In fact, the economy grew so strongly that in 1998 the government reported a budget surplus, in which income exceeded spending. Over the next two years, the surplus grew even larger.

Congress and Clinton also compromised on welfare reform. The government limited the length of time a person could receive welfare benefits. In this way, it hoped to encourage unemployed Americans to find jobs.

Impeachment and Trial In 1996, Clinton easily won reelection. Yet, controversy engulfed his second term. Federal prosecutors investigated Clinton for real estate dealings while he was governor of Arkansas. Prosecutors found no evidence of lawbreaking. However, they did accuse the President of lying under oath about an improper relationship with a White House intern.

Amid heated debate, the House voted to impeach the President. For only the second time in history, the Senate tried a President. In February 1999, Clinton was acquitted. All 45 Democratic senators supported the President. All but five Republicans voted to convict.

A Controversial Election

In the presidential election of 2000, the Republicans nominated Texas governor George W. Bush, son of former President George H. W. Bush. Along with vice presidential nominee Richard Cheney, Bush campaigned to return "honor and decency" to the White House and to end party bickering in Washington.

Vice President Al Gore ran for the Democrats. For his running mate he chose Senator Joseph Lieberman of Connecticut. Lieberman was the first Jewish candidate nominated for Vice President by a major party. The Democratic nominees asked voters to remember that the nation's economy had boomed during the Clinton years.

Dispute Over Florida Gore won the popular vote by a narrow margin. But the electoral vote remained in doubt because of disputed ballots in Florida. There, Bush clung to a slim lead.

With the Florida vote so close, Gore asked for a hand recount in several key counties. Bush opposed that request. While the votes were being counted, both sides took the dispute to court. After 46 days, the Supreme Court finally ruled that the Florida recount would have to stop. Gore conceded and Bush was declared the winner. Still, many Americans wondered if the bitter election dispute would hamper Bush's ability to be an effective President.

Bush as President Bush soon faced the added challenge of working with a divided Congress. The elections had left the House of Representatives in Republican hands and the Senate evenly split between 50 Democrats and 50 Republicans. Then, in May 2001, one Republican Senator quit the party. With the Democrats now in control of the Senate, President Bush would have a harder time pushing his proposals through Congress.

Early in his term, Bush won a major victory. Fulfilling a campaign promise, he convinced Congress to pass the largest tax cut since the Reagan era. "We must give over-charged taxpayers some of their own money back," he said. The tax cut was a clear sign that the conservative revolution was far from over.

 Draw Inferences How did President George W. Bush's tax cut reflect conservative ideas?

Section 1 Assessment

Recall

1. **Identify** Explain the significance of **(a)** Ronald Reagan, **(b)** Moral Majority, **(c)** Reaganomics, **(d)** George H. W. Bush, **(e)** Bill Clinton, **(f)** Newt Gingrich, **(g)** Contract With America, **(h)** George W. Bush, **(i)** Al Gore.
2. **Define** **(a)** deregulation, **(b)** balanced budget, **(c)** downsizing, **(d)** recession, **(e)** surplus.

Comprehension

3. Describe two conservative goals of Ronald Reagan.
4. How did Bill Clinton compromise with conservatives?

5. What were the immediate results of the 2000 presidential election?

Critical Thinking and Writing

6. **Exploring the Main Idea** Review the Main Idea statement at the beginning of this section. Then, write a paragraph explaining why Ronald Reagan's presidency has been called a "revolution."
7. **Drawing Conclusions** List three reasons that appointing Justices to the Supreme Court is one of the President's most important powers under the Constitution.

ACTIVITY

Composing Slogans
You are a campaign worker for one of the Presidents discussed in this section. Write two slogans that President could have used in an election campaign. You may want to present your slogan as part of a poster or button.

2 American Leadership in a New World

BEFORE YOU READ

Reading Focus

- What were the responsibilities of the United States as the last superpower?
- How did the United States help promote democracy?
- How did the United States ease conflicts in Eastern Europe and elsewhere?
- Why did nuclear arms remain a threat?

Key Terms

mediator

apartheid

sanctions

Dayton Accord

Strategic Arms Reduction Treaty

Comprehensive Test Ban Treaty

Taking Notes

Copy the table below. As you read, complete the table with information about the role of the United States in the post–Cold War world.

PROMOTING DEMOCRACY	RESOLVING CONFLICT
• South Africa: sanctions against apartheid	• Yugoslavia
•	•

Main Idea After the Cold War, the United States led the search for peace and stability in the world.

AS YOU READ
American flags
Find Main Ideas How does this picture relate to Scowcroft's view of the position of the United States in the world?

Setting the Scene "We were suddenly in a unique position," said Brent Scowcroft, "without experience, without precedent, and standing alone at the height of power." Scowcroft was referring to the end of the Cold War, when he was National Security Advisor to President George H. W. Bush. The superpower rivalry between the United States and the Soviet Union was gone "in a blink of an eye," he wrote. Now Americans faced a new world:

66 It was, it is, an unparalleled situation in history, one which presents us with the rarest opportunities to shape the world and the deepest responsibility to do so wisely. 99

— George H. W. Bush and Brent Scowcroft, *A World Transformed*

Despite the end of the Cold War, conflict still threatened many areas of the world. As the last superpower, the United States led the search for a new international order that would bring stability and lasting peace to the world.

The Last Superpower

As you have read, the Soviet Union split apart in 1991. The breakup brought an end to the Cold War. The United States stood alone as the last superpower.

Americans debated their function in the post–Cold War world. Some people wanted to reduce the role of the United States in world affairs. "In the post–Cold War world, we will no longer require our people to carry an unfair burden for the rest of humanity," said Representative Dana Rohrabacher.

Others argued that the nation must not retreat from the world. Like Brent Scowcroft, they thought that the United States had a responsibility to use its power wisely. "The United States must lead, period," declared Speaker of the House Newt Gingrich.

Neither President George H. W. Bush nor President Bill Clinton turned his back on the world. Both realized that fostering freedom and democracy abroad would only strengthen the United States. Even before becoming President, Clinton noted:

66 The defense of freedom and the promotion of democracy around the world aren't merely a reflection of our deepest values; they are vital to our national interests. Global democracy means nations at peace with one another, open to one another's ideas and one another's commerce. **99**

— Bill Clinton, Speech, 1991

Promoting Global Democracy

When Bill Clinton called for "global democracy," he was only describing a process that was already underway. Political freedom was spreading across the globe. With it came economic freedom, where companies and individuals could compete in free markets with less interference from the state. In the 1980s and 1990s, the United States encouraged both of these trends. American leadership met with both failures and successes.

American leadership took many forms. Sometimes the United States worked to influence foreign governments through quiet diplomacy or economic pressure. Sometimes it acted as a mediator. A mediator is an agent that helps conflicting parties iron out their differences. Occasionally the United States used military force, often in cooperation with other nations.

Asia In 1986, thousands of Filipinos protested the rule of dictator Ferdinand Marcos. They accused Marcos of fraud in a recent election. Proclaiming "people power," they refused to recognize Marcos as president. When the army supported the people, Marcos fled. The United States backed Corazon Aquino, the woman who had run against him. During the 1990s, the United States continued to provide economic aid for the young Filipino democracy.

Other nations in Asia had mixed success with political reforms. In the 1980s and 1990s, fierce protests shook corrupt, undemocratic governments in South Korea and Indonesia. The protests led to freer elections and the possibility of greater democratic reforms.

China After President Nixon's historic visit to China, many hoped that the communist nation would begin to reform. During the 1980s, China did begin to build a free market economy. However, Chinese leaders refused to accept political reforms.

In 1989, students and workers launched a bold campaign to bring democracy to China. Hundreds of thousands gathered at Tiananmen Square in the nation's capital, Beijing. However, the army crushed the demonstrations. Many people were killed or arrested.

President George H. W. Bush disapproved of the crackdown but took no strong action against the Chinese government. He hoped to influence China by keeping communication open. President Clinton

An American Profile

Chai Ling born 1966

A student at Beijing University, Chai Ling was known for her forceful leadership skills. At age 23, she became chief commander of the democracy movement in China.

After the army crushed the protests in Tiananmen Square, Chai Ling was one of the most wanted women in China. She escaped to Hong Kong, nailed inside a wooden crate in the hold of a leaky boat. In time, she came to the United States. She became a software entrepreneur while continuing to work for reform in China. Chai Ling has twice been nominated for the Nobel Peace Prize.

Why do you think Chai Ling chose to immigrate to the United States?

followed a similar policy. On a 1998 visit to China, he pledged to strengthen ties between the two nations. At the same time, he publicly debated human rights issues with China's president.

In 2001, China won its bid to host the 2008 Olympic games. Many hoped that the worldwide attention brought by the Olympics would encourage reform.

AS YOU READ **Use Prior Knowledge** What role had North Korea and Cuba played in the Cold War?

North Korea and Cuba Other communist nations refused to reform even when their people faced hard times. In the 1990s severe famine struck North Korea. To encourage reform, the United States and the UN sent famine relief, but little changed.

The fall of the Soviet Union deprived Cuba of its main source of trade and economic aid. As the Cuban economy spiraled downward, some 30,000 Cubans fled by boat to the United States. Still, after four decades, Fidel Castro remained in power. He blamed the United States for Cuba's severe poverty.

In 1994, the United States signed an agreement with Cuba to allow Cubans to emigrate more freely. At the same time, the United States continued to enforce a 40-year-old embargo aimed at toppling Castro. However, Americans began a serious debate over whether to resume trade with Cuba.

South Africa The cause of global democracy had its most dramatic success in South Africa. Since 1948, the government of South Africa had enforced a policy of apartheid (uh PAHR tayt), or strict separation of races. The nation's nonwhite majority was segregated and allowed no voice in the government.

In 1986, Congress approved economic sanctions against South Africa to force an end to apartheid. Sanctions are measures designed to make a country change its policy. American companies were no longer permitted to invest in South Africa or import South African products.

In the 1990s, South Africa moved to end minority rule. Under a new constitution, all races were permitted to vote for the first time in 1994. Nelson Mandela, a black who had spent 27 years in prison for opposing apartheid, was elected president.

Russia and Eastern Europe

After the Cold War, the former Soviet republics and the nations of Eastern Europe struggled to adapt to their new freedom. As former communist governments sold off businesses to private enterprise, inflation and unemployment rose.

Russian president Boris Yeltsin sought to build a stable democracy. His efforts faltered when he failed to put down an independence movement in the Russian province of Chechnya. After Yeltsin resigned in 2000, Vladimir Putin took over. Putin, a former communist official, seemed less interested in promoting democracy.

Civil War in Bosnia In Eastern Europe, Yugoslavia faced a civil war. Yugoslavia was made up of several republics, including Croatia, Serbia, and Bosnia-Herzegovina. In 1991, Croatia and Bosnia declared their independence. However, Serbs in Croatia and Bosnia wanted to remain part of Yugoslavia. With help from Serbia, they fought to prevent the new governments from splitting away. During four years of civil war, more than 250,000 people died, including many children and teenagers.

In November 1995, the United States hosted peace talks in Dayton, Ohio. The Dayton Accord called for Bosnia to remain a single nation, but to be governed as two separate republics. To help guarantee the peace, President Clinton sent about 20,000 American ground troops to Bosnia. There, they joined NATO and Russian forces in a peacekeeping mission. The troops helped to restore order.

Crisis in Kosovo The Dayton Accord did not end the troubles in the former Yugoslavia. Kosovo, a province within Serbia, also sought greater independence. The Albanians living there were in the majority and resented Serbian rule.

In 1998, Serbs launched a series of attacks against Albanian rebels in Kosovo. Hundreds of thousands of Albanians fled the province. Others were killed.

President Clinton condemned the attacks as "feeding the flames of ethnic and religious division." In March 1999, American forces joined NATO in bombing Serbia. The War Crimes Tribunal in the Netherlands charged the president of Serbia, Slobodan Milosevic (SLOH boh dahn mih LOH soh vitch), with "crimes against humanity."

Serbian troops left Kosovo in return for an end to the bombing. NATO peacekeeping forces then entered the province. Still, rebuilding would be a slow process.

Easing Conflict Elsewhere

The United States worked to bring stability to other war-torn regions of the world. In 1992, American forces led a UN mission to Somalia in Africa. They distributed food during a famine caused by civil war.

The United States used diplomacy to ease conflict in Northern Ireland. The many Catholics there wanted the region to be reunited with Ireland. Most Protestants wanted to remain under British rule. From 1969 to 1998, police, rival gangs, and bombings killed more than 3,000 people.

To aid with peace talks, President Clinton sent former Senator George Mitchell of Maine to Ireland. He helped to produce a peace agreement in April 1998. Although the peace process was slow and often bumpy, hopes for a lasting settlement remained high.

Eastern Europe

Key

Former territory of

- Czechoslovakia
- East Germany
- Yugoslavia

GEOGRAPHY
Skills

After the Cold War ended, Eastern Europe underwent a period of change and conflict.

1. **Location** On the map, locate **(a)** Russia, **(b)** Yugoslavia, **(c)** Bosnia-Herzegovina, **(d)** Albania.

2. **Region** Compare this map to the map on page 813. Which nations shown here had been part of the Soviet Union?

3. **Critical Thinking Drawing Inferences** Which Western nations do you think would be most concerned about people fleeing from Yugoslavia?

The Threat of Nuclear Arms

As the former Soviet Union collapsed, the world faced a menacing challenge, the spread of nuclear weapons. The United States and Russia still had thousands of nuclear missiles in their possession. Other nations were developing nuclear weapons, too.

Reducing Nuclear Arms The United States and the old Soviet Union had already agreed to several treaties reducing nuclear arms. In 1991, they signed the most important agreement yet, the Strategic Arms Reduction Treaty, or START. Even more reductions followed in 1993, when the United States and Russia negotiated START II. They agreed to destroy one third of their nuclear weapons.

A New Arms Race Despite such progress, a new arms race loomed. During the Cold War, Britain, France, and China had all developed nuclear weapons. American intelligence agencies believed that Israel, Iran, Iraq, and North Korea also possessed nuclear weapons programs.

In 1998, India announced that it had conducted five nuclear tests. Two weeks later, Pakistan, its neighbor and deadly rival, exploded five nuclear devices of its own. World leaders saw the tests as the beginning of a dangerous new arms race. President Clinton called for economic sanctions against both India and Pakistan but with little effect.

A Failed Treaty Clinton had already taken steps to contain the growing nuclear threat. In 1996, the Clinton administration helped to draft the Comprehensive Test Ban Treaty. Its goal was to end further testing of nuclear weapons.

Many nations were unwilling to give up nuclear testing. Russia and China made no move to adopt the treaty. President Clinton signed it, but the Senate finally rejected the treaty in 1999. Its provisions were "unenforceable," warned Senator Trent Lott of Mississippi.

 AS YOU READ **Use Prior Knowledge** Compare the new arms race described here to the Cold War arms race between the United States and the Soviet Union described in Chapter 28.

AFTER YOU READ

Section 2 Assessment

Recall

1. **Identify** Explain the significance of **(a)** Corazon Aquino, **(b)** Nelson Mandela, **(c)** Dayton Accord, **(d)** Strategic Arms Reduction Treaty, **(e)** Comprehensive Test Ban Treaty.
2. **Define (a)** mediator, **(b)** apartheid, **(c)** sanctions.

Comprehension

3. How did Americans differ about the role of the United States after the end of the Cold War?
4. Give two examples of how the United States encouraged democracy in other countries.
5. What role did the United States play in Bosnia?

6. Describe one success and one failure of the effort to control nuclear arms.

Critical Thinking and Writing

7. **Exploring the Main Idea** Review the Main Idea statement at the beginning of this section. Then, write a letter to the President expressing your view of the role of the United States in the post–Cold War world.
8. **Identifying Alternatives** List at least two alternative courses President Bush might have followed when China crushed the pro-democracy movement in 1989.

ACTIVITY

Take It to the NET

Making a Map Use the Internet to find out which nations of the world have nuclear weapons. On an outline map of the world, use a color code to show countries that are known or suspected to have nuclear weapons. Visit *The American Nation* section of **www.phschool.com** for help in completing the activity.

3 The Spread of Regional Conflict

Reading Focus

- What role did the United States play in the struggle between Israelis and Arabs?
- How did Americans become involved in conflicts in Iran and Iraq?
- How did Americans respond to terrorist attacks in September 2001?

Key Terms

OPEC

Camp David Accords

PLO

Persian Gulf War

terrorism

Taking Notes

Copy the effects chart below. As you read, fill in some of the events and developments that followed American involvement in regional conflicts.

UNITED STATES INVOLVED IN REGIONAL CONFLICTS → Persian Gulf War | | | |

Main Idea A series of regional conflicts in the Middle East eventually spread to the United States.

Setting the Scene

On the evening of September 11, 2001, Americans across the nation gathered in grief. Many people wept openly. Some held candles. On the steps of the Capitol Building, the leaders of Congress, Democrats and Republicans alike, stood shoulder to shoulder, united in a new resolve "to fight evil."

The candlelight vigils marked the end of a tragic day. That morning, hijackers from the Middle East had flown two airliners into the Twin Towers of the World Trade Center, the tallest buildings in New York and symbols of American financial might. The towers burned and collapsed. A third hijacked plane struck American military headquarters at the Pentagon. A fourth crashed in Pennsylvania. An estimated 3,000 to 4,000 people died. It was the deadliest day on American soil in more than a century.

As you have read, the United States was often called upon to take the lead in resolving regional conflicts. But, as grief-stricken Americans learned on September 11, world leadership could carry a high price.

The Arab-Israeli Conflict

Conflict had long troubled the Middle East, a region extending from southwestern Asia across North Africa. Over the centuries, friction among religious groups has led to discord and violence. European attempts to colonize the Middle East and, more recently, competition for large oil reserves in the region have added to tensions.

The United States has conflicting interests in the Middle East. It has strongly supported the Jewish state of Israel. Yet, it also has ties to the Islamic Arab states that dominate the region. Arab nations such as Saudi Arabia supply much of the oil used by Americans.

Israelis and Arabs In the late 1800s, European Jews arrived in Palestine along the Mediterranean coast. They hoped to create a Jewish state in their ancient homeland. Jewish settlement grew in the 1930s as European Jews fled Nazi persecution. In 1948, Arabs rejected

 Americans honor attack victims

Ask Questions What questions do you think Americans were asking after the attacks of September 11?

a plan to divide the land into one Jewish and one Palestinian state. Jews in Palestine announced the creation of the state of Israel. The United States and other nations quickly recognized the new nation.

Neighboring Arab nations refused to recognize the Jewish state. Instead, they attacked. But Israel won the 1948 war. More than 500,000 Palestinian Arabs fled to refugee camps in nearby states. Most were not permitted to return after the war and were not paid for their lands and homes. Arab nations attacked again in 1967 and 1973. In these wars, Israel won portions of Egypt, Jordan, and Syria. Arabs called these lands the "occupied territories."

The United States sent aid to Israel in the 1973 war. Arab members of OPEC, the Organization of Petroleum Exporting Countries, retaliated. They cut off oil shipments to the United States and slowed down oil production. Oil prices shot up in the face of world-wide oil shortages. OPEC finally lifted the oil embargo in 1974.

Egyptian president Anwar el-Sadat took a bold step toward peace in 1977. He became the first Arab head of state to visit Israel. When peace talks between the two nations broke down, President Jimmy Carter invited Sadat and Israeli Prime Minister Menachem Begin (muh NAHK uhm BAY gihn) to Camp David, the President's retreat in Maryland. In the Camp David Accords of 1978, Israel agreed to return the Sinai Peninsula to Egypt and Egypt agreed to recognize Israel. The two nations signed a peace treaty in 1979.

The Palestinian Issue Palestinian Arabs waged guerrilla war against Israel. Under Israeli rule, Palestinians in the occupied territories had limited rights. Those living outside Israel wanted to return to their homeland under a Palestinian government. Many supported the Palestine Liberation Organization, or PLO. Its leader, Yasir Arafat, stated that the goal of the PLO was to destroy Israel.

In 1987, Palestinians in the occupied territories took to the streets to protest Israeli rule. The unrest, called the *Intifada,* focused attention on the need to end the Israeli-Palestinian conflict.

AS YOU READ **Monitor Your Reading** As you read about the difficult peace process, check that you understand the roots of the conflict between Israelis and Palestinian Arabs.

After years of effort, the United States persuaded Israel and the PLO to come to the bargaining table. In 1993, the longtime enemies signed a pact in Washington, D.C. The PLO agreed to recognize Israel's right to exist and promised to give up violence. Israel agreed to limited self-rule for Palestinians in the Gaza Strip and in Jericho. Two years later, Israel recognized the right of Palestinians to govern some areas of the West Bank under Arafat's leadership.

By 2002, prospects for peace looked grim. Palestinian groups launched a series of deadly suicide bombings in Israeli cities. In response, Israel bombed Palestinian targets and placed Arafat under house arrest. Still, the United States continued to encourage peace efforts.

Conflict With Iran and Iraq

The United States was deeply involved in other Middle East conflicts. In 1953, the United States helped to overthrow the elected government of Iran and to return the dethroned Shah Muhammad Reza Pahlavi to power. Then, in 1979, a revolution forced the unpopular shah to flee. A religious leader, the Ayatollah Khomeini (i yuh TOH luh koh MAYN ee), took control of Iran.

Iran Hostage Crisis The shah had been a firm ally of the United States. The Ayatollah was strongly anti-American. Where the shah had favored westernizing Iran, the new ruler wanted to return to the strict traditions of Islam. Neither, however, favored democracy.

In November 1979, President Carter let the shah enter the United States for medical treatment. In response, Iranian revolutionaries seized the American embassy and took 53 Americans hostage. The hostages were not freed until January 1981. The hostage crisis poisoned American relations with Iran for decades.

War With Iraq In August 1990, Saddam Hussein, the dictator of Iraq, sent 100,000 troops to invade oil-rich Kuwait. President George H. W. Bush feared that the invasion was the start of a larger plan to gain control of Middle East oil.

To prevent further Iraqi aggression, Bush sent American forces to Saudi Arabia. He also persuaded the UN to impose a trade boycott on Iraq. Hussein ignored UN demands to withdraw from Kuwait by January 15, 1991. The United States and its UN allies then launched an air attack on Iraq. Troops from 28 nations—including some Arab countries—joined the effort. Bombers besieged the Iraqi capital of Baghdad. The Persian Gulf War lasted six weeks. By the end of February, UN troops drove the Iraqis out of Kuwait.

Although the war was over, the UN boycott against Iraq continued. The goal was to force Saddam Hussein to stop his chemical and biological weapons programs. Hussein refused to cooperate with UN arms inspectors, even after American and British planes launched a four-day air strike against Iraq in 1998. Meanwhile, the sanctions took their toll on the Iraqi people.

GEOGRAPHY *Skills*

Oil wealth and religious conflict have helped shape events in the Middle East.

1. **Location** On the map, locate **(a)** Israel, **(b)** Egypt, **(c)** Iran, **(d)** Iraq, **(e)** Kuwait, **(f)** Afghanistan.

2. **Region** In what area are the most oil fields located?

3. **Critical Thinking Applying Information (a)** If this were a map printed in 1978, what color would the Sinai Peninsula be? **(b)** Why did this situation change?

The Middle East

Terrorism and the United States

After the 1960s, terrorist bombings, kidnappings, and hijackings became more common in Europe, the Middle East, and elsewhere. Terrorism is the deliberate use of violence to spread fear and to achieve political goals. Often, the victims are civilians and the targets symbolic, such as embassies or centers of economic power.

In troubled areas such as Northern Ireland and Israel, acts of terror played a key role in conflict. They were usually carried out by extremists who wanted dramatic change but felt powerless to achieve it through nonviolent means. As regional conflicts deepened, they occasionally spread through terrorism.

Americans and Terrorism In the Middle East, some radical Muslim groups sponsored terrorism. They were angered by the Persian Gulf War, by United States support for Israel, and by other American policies. Extremists also saw American culture as immoral, and offensive to their own very strict brand of Islam, normally a peaceful religion.

As a result, fanatical groups targeted American sites overseas for terrorist acts. In 1988, an explosion killed 270 people on an American passenger airliner over Scotland. Between 1998 and 2000, bombs hit two United States embassies in Africa and a navy ship off the coast of Yemen in the Middle East.

Attacks on the United States Terrorism from abroad spread to the United States itself. In 1993, a bomb damaged the World Trade Center in New York. Six Arab men were later convicted of the crime.

On September 11, 2001, as you have read, terrorists slammed three airliners into the World Trade Center and the Pentagon. On a fourth hijacked airliner, courageous passengers fought back. The plane crashed in a field in Pennsylvania. All on board were killed, but the plane was prevented from hitting any target on the ground.

The Human Cost The terrorist attacks of September 11 took more lives than the Japanese sneak-attack on Pearl Harbor in 1941. In New York, the victims included hundreds of firefighters and police officers rushing to the rescue. In addition to Americans, citizens from more than 80 countries died in the tragedy.

Children lost parents. Parents lost children. Wives and husbands who had gone happily off to work that morning never returned. Some, like those on the hijacked airliners, phoned loved ones to tell them what was happening or to say goodbye. Those who escaped sometimes carried co-workers and strangers to safety.

All Americans lost something that day. If not their lives or their loved ones, they lost their sense of security.

A Spirit of Unity Americans were quick to respond to the attacks. Millions lined up to give blood, aided in rescue efforts, or donated money and supplies to help victims and rescuers. Across the nation, people displayed American flags to show their unity and patriotism.

Sadly, a few people vented their anger on Arab Americans and American Muslims, as well as Sikhs mistaken for Muslims. Still, such acts were the exception. Unlike World War II, when Japanese Americans were interned, a spirit of tolerance prevailed. President George W. Bush and other leaders cautioned against taking revenge on

Primary Source

The Nation Is Attacked

Nine days after the September 11 attacks, President Bush addressed Congress and the nation:
"We have seen the state of our union in the endurance of rescuers working past exhaustion. We've seen the unfurling of flags, the lighting of candles, the giving of blood, the saying of prayers in English, Hebrew, and Arabic. . . . The entire world has seen for itself the state of our union, and it is strong.

Tonight we are a country awakened to danger and called to defend freedom. Our grief has turned to anger and our anger to resolution. Whether we bring our enemies to justice or bring justice to our enemies, justice will be done."

—George W. Bush, Address to Congress, September 20, 2001

Analyzing Primary Sources
Restate in your own words the main point of the last sentence above.

innocent people. Religious leaders of all faiths, including Islam, stood side by side at a national memorial service in Washington, D.C.

The spirit of unity extended overseas. Nation after nation pledged its support in tracking down those responsible, although all did not agree on the method. The headline of one French newspaper captured the feeling of many in the world: "WE ARE ALL AMERICANS."

A Campaign Against Terrorism President Bush voiced the nation's outrage. The attacks, he said, "were acts of war." He committed the country to an all-out campaign against terrorists. He also created a new cabinet-level post, the Office of Homeland Security, to defend against terrorism. Meanwhile, Congress set aside $40 billion in emergency aid to help victims of the attacks.

Early on, Bush blamed al-Qaida (KI duh), a terrorist network led by a wealthy Saudi, Osama bin Laden. Bin Laden was hiding in Afghanistan, protected by a brutal dictatorship, the Taliban. Vowing to bring bin Laden to Justice, Bush told Americans not to "expect one battle but a lengthy campaign unlike any we have ever seen."

The campaign against terrorism moved along three fronts: diplomatic, economic, and military. First, the President asked other nations to stand with the United States against terrorism. Second, Bush sought to find and block the money supplies of terrorist organizations. Third, American forces attacked military sites and terrorist training camps in Afghanistan. At the same time, the United States provided humanitarian aid to Afghan victims of the Taliban.

With the aid of Afghan rebels, American forces soon toppled the Taliban. Still, the search for Osama bin Laden continued. President Bush announced that the next target of the antiterrorism campaign might be Saddam Hussein in Iraq.

As the campaign unfolded, the President's popularity soared. Meanwhile, Americans went on with their lives with a new spirit of determination and patriotism.

Section 3 Assessment

Recall
1. **Identify** Explain the significance of **(a)** OPEC, **(b)** Camp David Accords, **(c)** PLO, **(d)** Ayatollah Khomeini, **(e)** Saddam Hussein, **(f)** Persian Gulf War, **(g)** Osama bin Laden.
2. **Define** terrorism.

Comprehension
3. How did the United States try to promote peace between Israel and its Arab neighbors?
4. Identify the causes of the Persian Gulf War.

5. Describe the aftermath of the terrorist attacks in 2001.

Critical Thinking and Writing
6. **Exploring the Main Idea** Review the Main Idea statement at the beginning of this section. Then, list reasons for and against getting involved in regional conflicts.
7. **Identifying Causes and Effects** Write a paragraph explaining how oil has shaped how Americans respond to events in the Middle East.

ACTIVITY

Writing a Dialogue
Write and stage a television panel discussion about the events of September 11, 2001, and their aftermath. Your dialogue should focus on what a hero is and how the heroes of that event should be honored.

4 A Global Economy

BEFORE YOU READ

Reading Focus

- How did competition and cooperation in international trade affect the United States?
- What problems did the environment pose for the global economy?
- How did the new networked world of information change the global economy?

Key Terms

trade deficit

North American Free Trade Agreement

environmentalist

Environmental Protection Agency

renewable resource

Earth Summit

global warming

Internet

e-commerce

Taking Notes

Copy the concept web below. As you read, fill in the blank ovals with information about the new global economy. Add as many ovals as you need.

Main Idea Global economic links, the global environment, and a global information network tie the modern world together.

Setting the Scene

The trouble began in Asia. First, the booming economy of Japan turned sharply downward in the mid-1990s. Then, in 1997, banks in Thailand began to fail. From there, the financial crisis spread to other Asian powerhouses—South Korea, Indonesia, and Hong Kong.

The crisis threatened to engulf the world. Asian nations bought fewer raw materials and manufactured goods. Soon, nations in Latin America, the Middle East, and Europe were feeling the crunch. Led by the United States, international organizations pumped over $200 billion into these shaky economies. Such actions averted a global financial collapse.

By the 1990s, the world was so tightly connected that financial trouble in far-off Asia could ripple quickly across the globe. Issues of the global economy were also affected by the global environment and the new global network of information. These would challenge the United States to cooperate with other nations more than ever.

AS YOU READ

Japanese currency
Predict What do you think might have happened if other nations had not taken steps to reverse the crisis?

Competition and Cooperation

As the Asian financial crisis shows, American businesses operate in a global economy. In recent decades, trade with other nations has grown dramatically. In 1970, foreign trade made up about 10 percent of the American economy. By 1997, foreign trade amounted to nearly 25 percent.

Tough Competition In this growing world economy, the United States faces tough competition from industrialized countries in Europe and Asia. In general, American companies pay their workers higher wages than companies in most other nations. As a result, foreign products are often cheaper to manufacture and less expensive to buy than American ones.

Foreign competition has led to trade deficits for the United States. A trade deficit occurs when a nation buys more goods and services from foreign countries than it sells to them. To reduce this deficit, many American firms have built more efficient factories in order to lower costs. They have also tried to increase sales abroad by producing better products than foreign rivals.

Some people have called upon the government to protect American industries by raising tariffs on foreign goods. Others oppose high tariffs. They warn that other nations might raise their own tariffs in response, leading to costly "trade wars."

Removing Trade Barriers Opponents of tariffs won a victory in 1993. After bitter debate, Congress ratified the North American Free Trade Agreement (NAFTA). In this treaty, the United States and its neighbors, Canada and Mexico, agreed to cooperate in removing tariffs and other trade barriers among them.

Most economists agreed that NAFTA encouraged new trade and created jobs. However, critics pointed out that NAFTA hurt some industries and the environment. Auto parts makers moved factories to Mexico, where wages were lower. Also, foreign countries did not have the same strict antipollution laws as the United States.

In 1997, Congress refused to give President Clinton extra powers to negotiate more free-trade agreements. The debate over foreign trade continued into the new century.

The Environment and the Global Economy

No issue has more global impact than the environment. Environmental problems do not stop at national borders. But not all nations agree on what needs to be done or on the price to be paid to protect the environment.

The Environmental Movement In the United States, marine biologist Rachel Carson sounded the alarm on environmental dangers. In 1962, she charged that chemical pesticides were poisoning the planet. Her book *Silent Spring* described a bleak future:

> 66 It was a spring without voices. On the mornings that had once throbbed with the dawn chorus of robins, catbirds, doves, jays, wrens . . . there was now no sound; only silence lay over the fields and woods and marsh. 99
> —Rachel Carson, *Silent Spring*

Reformers known as environmentalists called attention to environmental dangers. Chemical wastes turned rivers into sewers.

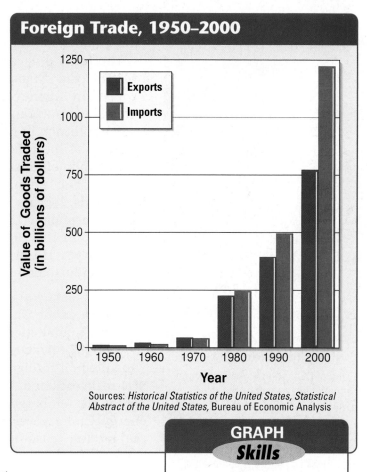

Foreign Trade, 1950–2000

Value of Goods Traded (in billions of dollars)

- Exports
- Imports

Year: 1950, 1960, 1970, 1980, 1990, 2000

Sources: *Historical Statistics of the United States, Statistical Abstract of the United States,* Bureau of Economic Analysis

GRAPH Skills

Many Americans worry because the United States imports more goods than it exports. This situation is called a trade deficit.

1. **Comprehension** According to this graph, during what decade did the United States develop a trade deficit?

2. **Critical Thinking Analyzing Information** During the 1990s, which grew more—imports or exports? Explain.

Economics $

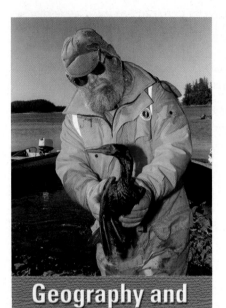

Geography and History

Oil in the Sound

One of the nation's worst environmental disasters took place on March 24, 1989. The oil tanker *Exxon Valdez* struck a submerged reef, spilling 11 million gallons of crude oil into Prince William Sound on Alaska's southern coast. For hours, oil poured into the waters of one of the most environmentally sensitive regions of the world. The fragile ecosystem contains whales, sea lions, seals, bears, deer, sea otters, salmon, and the tiny plankton upon which larger creatures feed.

Within a week, thousands of dead birds and animals littered the shoreline. Workers from around the world rushed to Alaska to capture and clean oil-soaked survivors.

 Why do you think people far from Alaska were concerned about the effects of an oil spill on animals in a remote sound?

Factory smokestacks belched foul-smelling fumes. Massive tankers ran aground, spilling oil into the sea.

The federal government responded to environmental concerns. In 1970, the Nixon administration created the **Environmental Protection Agency** (EPA). The Clean Air Act of 1970 required automakers to clean up car exhausts. The Clean Water Act of 1972 fought pollution in rivers and lakes. The Waste Cleanup Act of 1980 created a "superfund" to clean up chemical dumps.

Environmentalists have faced opposition, often on economic grounds. For example, while environmentalists try to preserve forestlands, loggers point out that forest products are vital to the nation's economy. They also warn that restrictions on logging may cost jobs. In the 1980s, President Reagan sought to ease environmental laws. He argued that strict regulation was too costly for American businesses.

Energy Conservation Environmentalists also directed attention to energy use in the United States. Americans make up only 5 percent of the world's population but consume over a quarter of its energy supply.

The 1973 Arab oil embargo showed Americans how much they depended on foreign energy sources. When oil shipments resumed, prices skyrocketed. Within 10 years, fuel cost four times as much as before the embargo. In response, Americans worked to conserve energy. Under government pressure, carmakers produced autos that ran on less gasoline. Homeowners added insulation to cut the amount of fuel used in homes.

Americans have also sought to develop other sources of energy. Many factories have switched from oil to coal. The United States has about one quarter of the world's usable coal reserves. Coal, however, is a dirtier fuel than oil. Coal-burning plants must use expensive devices to reduce the smoke and acids they emit into the air. Such devices add to the cost of using coal.

Today, nuclear plants generate about one fifth of the nation's electric power. Still, nuclear power is costly, and it produces long-lasting radioactive wastes that are difficult to dispose of. Even worse, an accident at a nuclear power plant could release harmful radioactive gases into the air.

Other scientists are working to harness renewable resources such as sun or wind power. A **renewable resource** is one that can be quickly replaced by nature. However, solar energy, or sun power, is expensive for many uses.

In 2001, a series of blackouts hit homes and businesses in California. Utility companies failed to provide enough electricity to meet consumer demand. The California blackouts highlighted the continuing problem of energy use.

Global Cooperation Environmental problems across the globe led nations to cooperate. In 1992, President George H. W. Bush joined other world leaders at the **Earth Summit** in Brazil. The goal of the conference was to discuss key environmental issues.

One issue involved rising global temperatures. A prolonged period of warmer-than-usual weather led some scientists to believe that the Earth's atmosphere was warming up. Human activities, such as

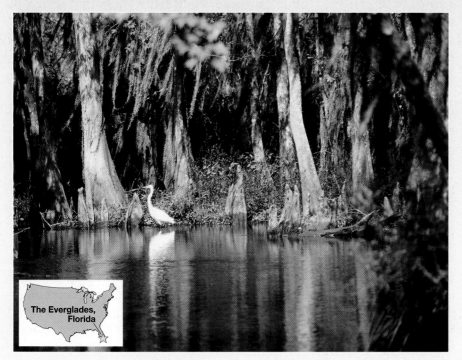

The Everglades, Florida

Everglades National Park

The Everglades is the largest sub-tropical wilderness in the United States. Starting in the 1960s, Florida resident Marjorie Stoneman Douglas began a historic battle to protect the area's vital water supplies and its rare plant and animal life. Today, you can camp, hike, or canoe in the area that Douglas called "one of the unique regions of the Earth."

Take It to the NET

Virtual Field Trip For an interactive look at the Everglades, visit *The American Nation* section of **www.phschool.com**.

driving cars and operating factories, were adding carbon dioxide to the atmosphere. Carbon dioxide holds in heat that would otherwise escape into space. The scientists predicted a slow but steady rise in the world's average temperature. This **global warming,** they warned, might one day turn green fields into deserts! Leaders at the Earth Summit pledged to reduce the amounts of carbon dioxide their countries released into the atmosphere.

Some scientists disagreed with the global warming theory. They pointed out that the Earth had gone through many cold and warm cycles in the past. In 2001, President George W. Bush announced that the United States would slow efforts to control carbon dioxide emissions. He believed there was not enough evidence of environmental damage to warrant the cost to American businesses.

A second problem raised at the Earth Summit involved the layer of ozone gas that surrounds the earth miles above its surface. This layer blocks out damaging ultraviolet rays from the sun. In the 1980s, scientists warned that gases used in homes and industries were creating holes in the ozone layer. Especially dangerous were gases used in aerosol cans, refrigerators, and air conditioners. Nations all over the world agreed to phase out their use.

A Networked World

Today, technology ties the world together as never before. Cellular phones and pagers have changed the way people live and do business. No device has had greater impact than the computer.

A Computer Revolution In the 1950s, most people had barely heard of computers. Computing was done on mainframes, large and expensive machines found only in big businesses, universities, or government offices. One mainframe could fill a room and weigh 30 tons or more.

AS YOU READ **Monitor Your Reading** As you read, identify the chief turning points in the computer revolution.

Slowly scientists began to make computers smaller and smaller. But even small computers required complex programs to run them. Then, in the 1970s, a Harvard dropout named Bill Gates developed a new program that allowed ordinary people to operate computers. By the 1980s, powerful personal computers could be found in homes, small businesses, and schools.

The Internet During the 1960s, a scientist at the Massachusetts Institute of Technology dreamed of connecting computers all over the world into a single "Galactic Network." Eventually this idea evolved into the Internet, a series of interconnected computers that gave users access to computerized information. Through the Internet, computer users could exchange information.

Personal computers and the Internet have produced an information revolution. A world of facts and figures is now available at an instant to anyone with access to a computer. E-mail has become more popular than the postal mail. In 1998, the post office handled about 630 million letters a day. Meanwhile, more than 2 billion e-mails were being sent daily.

Computers and the Internet revolutionized business. They increased efficiency and productivity and allowed more people to work at home and still be in touch with their offices. E-commerce, or business and trade over the Internet, boomed. In 1999 alone, more than 200 million consumers internationally and 100 million Americans made over $300 billion in purchases online.

AFTER YOU READ **Section 4 Assessment**

Recall

1. **Identify** Explain the significance of **(a)** North American Free Trade Agreement, **(b)** Rachel Carson, **(c)** Environmental Protection Agency, **(d)** Earth Summit, **(e)** Bill Gates, **(f)** Internet.
2. **Define** **(a)** trade deficit, **(b)** environmentalist, **(c)** renewable resource, **(d)** global warming, **(e)** e-commerce.

Comprehension

3. How did the United States develop a trade deficit?
4. Describe two environmental problems the United States and the world faced.

5. How did the development of the Internet affect business?

Critical Thinking and Writing

6. **Exploring the Main Idea** Review the Main Idea statement at the beginning of this section. Then, write a paragraph explaining whether you think the new world of global links is good or bad for the nation.
7. **Making Decisions** Would you be willing to give up or pay a higher price for many products in order to protect the environment? State your decision and list the reasons.

ACTIVITY

Writing an Advertisement It is 1980, and the Internet is a new idea. Write and design an advertisement encouraging schools, businesses, or private citizens to sign up for the Internet. Explain the benefits of the service.

Oil: A Valuable Resource

Throughout history, natural resources—from water to spices—have shaped politics, caused wars, and led to the rise and fall of nations. Today, oil plays such a role in the global economy. Oil shortages and rising oil prices touch everybody.

Giant derricks remove crude oil from the ground or the bottom of the sea. What happens if the companies or nations that sell the crude oil cut back on production or raise the price? People have to pay more for gasoline, heating oil, and a wide variety of other products.

What do sneakers, candles, and lipsticks have in common? They are all manufactured using petroleum—along with ink, bubble gum, transparent tape, telephones, crayons, dolls, and skate wheels. If oil prices go up, so will the prices of these products that we all use.

World Energy Use, 1998

- .65% — Geothermal/solar/wind
- 6.5% — Nuclear power
- 7.1% — Hydroelectric
- 23.3% — Coal
- 23.2% — Natural gas
- 39.8% — Oil

Source: CNN.com [online]

Oil is not the only source of energy in the world. But, as this pie chart shows, it is still the most vital to the world's economy.

ACTIVITY

Oil is a basic ingredient in plastics. Make a list of plastic products that you use every day. Then, see if you can identify alternatives for each that are not made of plastic. Make a poster that shows three plastic products and your ideas for substitutes.

5 New Challenges for the Nation

BEFORE YOU READ

Reading Focus

- Who were the new immigrants?
- What groups added their voices to the call for equal rights?
- What challenges does the United States face in the twenty-first century?

Key Terms

refugee

illegal alien

Immigration Reform and Control Act

American Indian Religious Freedom Act

mainstreaming

Americans With Disabilities Act

American Association of Retired Persons

Taking Notes

As you read, prepare an outline of this section. Use roman numerals to indicate the major headings, capital letters for the subheadings, and numbers for the supporting details. The sample at right will help you get started.

> I. The New Immigrants
>   A. Changing patterns
>   1. Asian immigration
>   2.
>   B. New policies
>   1.
>   2.
> II. The Struggle for Equal Rights Continues
>   A.
>   B.

Main Idea New immigrants and continuing struggles for equal rights brought a new look to the American dream of liberty and freedom.

AS YOU READ
Immigrants take citizenship oath

Draw Inferences What do you think the phrase "the American dream" means to new citizens like these?

Setting the Scene

In an auditorium in Austin, Texas, a woman from India stood clutching a small American flag. Nearby stood another woman from Jordan. Karolyn Mora, who had come from Costa Rica five years earlier, was also there. She confessed:

> 66 When I first came, I felt like a stranger, but now I feel like I am part of America. That's all I wanted—the American dream. 99
>
> —Karolyn Mora, Interview, April 6, 2001

These women were among 473 immigrants from 73 countries who had just become American citizens. Officials at the ceremony in the spring of 2001 had never seen so many nations represented before.

Immigrants from every corner of the globe flock to the United States, pursuing their dreams and adding to the nation's diversity. Increasing diversity has brought new challenges as groups have struggled to protect their rights. But diversity has added strengths, among them an uncommon ability to cope with difference in a shrinking world.

The New Immigrants

In 1965, Congress ended the old quota system that favored Europeans. New laws made it easier for non-Europeans to enter the country. Since then, immigrants have been arriving at a rate faster than at any time since the early 1900s. Most recent immigrants have come from Latin America, the Caribbean, and Asia.

Changing Patterns Asian Americans are the nation's fastest-growing ethnic group. Wars and famines pushed many Asians into other parts of the world. After the Vietnam War, "boat people" from Southeast Asia sought refuge in the United States. Many immigrants from the Philippines, India, and Korea sought economic opportunity.

Many Latin American immigrants were refugees from civil wars in Nicaragua, El Salvador, and Guatemala during the 1980s. Refugees are people who flee their homelands to seek safety elsewhere. Others fled harsh governments in Cuba and Chile or poverty in Mexico and other nations. By 2001, Latin Americans and their descendants were the largest ethnic group in the country.

Hundreds of thousands of immigrants have also come from islands of the Caribbean. These people bring a rich mixture of African, European, Native American, and other backgrounds.

New immigration patterns have fueled a debate over what it means to be American. Many new citizens are eager to adopt American ways. At the same time, they do not want to abandon their old traditions.

New Policies New immigrants must apply for admission. Those with relatives in the United States or with valuable job skills are most likely to be accepted. Thousands of others are turned down. Those entering without permission are illegal aliens.

To reduce illegal immigration, Congress passed the Immigration Reform and Control Act in 1986. It allowed people who arrived illegally before 1982 to stay and apply for citizenship. But the act tried to discourage future illegal immigration by imposing fines on employers who hired undocumented, or illegal, workers.

Rising costs of medical care, education, and other services for illegal immigrants strained the resources of several states. In 1994, California adopted a controversial law that banned schooling and most health services for illegal aliens. Two years later, Congress passed a new law allowing local police to arrest illegal immigrants.

The Struggle for Equal Rights Continues

As you read, in the 1960s, the struggle for equal rights expanded from African Americans to other groups. While these Americans achieved significant successes, challenges remained.

African Americans African Americans made notable advances in government. In 1989, Douglas Wilder of Virginia became the first black elected governor of a state. That same year, General Colin Powell was named chairman of the Joint Chiefs of Staff. Later, as Secretary of State, Powell was a key figure in the campaign against terrorism.

The civil rights movement had opened new jobs and educational opportunities. By 1998, 92 percent of African Americans seeking jobs found employment, compared with 87 percent in 1980. The black middle class grew steadily. More African Americans were attending college than ever before, and fewer lived below the poverty level.

Despite such successes, many African Americans continued to battle economic hardship. The wages of African Americans lagged behind those of whites. Unemployment for blacks was over twice that for whites. Poverty and lack of education trapped many African Americans in urban slums. In 2000, African Americans still remained less well educated and owned less property than whites.

Native Americans After shrinking for centuries, the American Indian population is growing. By 2000, it had reached about 2.4 million. Over half live in urban areas. Another third live on reservations.

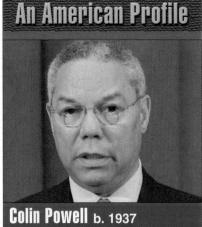

An American Profile

Colin Powell b. 1937

In Colin Powell's family, every child was expected to work for a college education. After earning degrees in geology and business administration, he joined the army. He won a Purple Heart in Vietnam.

Powell helped found America's Promise to encourage Americans to volunteer for public service. A reporter wrote, "Spend an hour talking with General Colin Powell about his crusade to save America's kids and, despite the many problems that confront today's youngsters, you come away enthused and optimistic about the next generation."

Why do you think Colin Powell has been named one of the most admired Americans?

Women Working Outside the Home, 1960–2000

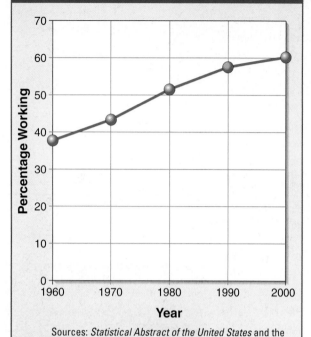

Percentage Working

Year

Sources: *Statistical Abstract of the United States* and the Women's Bureau of the U.S. Department of Labor

GRAPH Skills

For most of the nation's history, most women did not work outside the home. That situation changed after the 1960s.

1. **Comprehension** During what decade did the majority of women work outside the home for the first time?

2. **Critical Thinking Making Predictions** Do you think the trend shown on this graph will continue? Why or why not?

Economics

By 1970, the federal government had ended its policy of encouraging Indians to leave their reservations. Native American tribes and organizations won greater power to govern themselves. The American Indian Religious Freedom Act of 1978 directed federal agencies not to interfere with Native American religious practices.

Native American groups have worked to develop economic independence. Many reservations set up banks, factories, and other businesses. Several tribes opened their own colleges and universities.

Women The women's rights movement continued to press for equal treatment of women. Progress came but not as quickly or completely as many women hoped.

In government, women have taken more prominent roles, especially on the local and state levels. On the national level, women won more seats in Congress. By the late 1990s, two of the nine Supreme Court Justices were women. In 1997, Madeleine Albright became the first female secretary of state, the highest-ranking cabinet position.

About 60 percent of American women worked outside the home by 2000. Women held jobs once closed to them, from firefighters to professional basketball players. As more women were promoted to higher positions in business, their incomes rose. The gap between women's and men's wages narrowed but did not disappear. On average, women earned less than 75 percent of what men earned.

An increasing number of single women were heads of households. More than half the children in these households lived in poverty. Working mothers also had the problem of finding affordable, adequate day care.

New Voices for Change

Other groups of Americans organized to promote change. These groups cut across racial, ethnic, and gender lines.

Americans With Disabilities Americans with disabilities joined the battle for equal rights. Veterans of Vietnam and other wars took a leading role. Many had lost limbs or become paralyzed serving their country. They insisted on their right to gain entrance to public buildings and transportation and to make a living.

People in wheelchairs often had limited access to public transportation and buildings. Disabled rights organizations pressed for laws requiring reserved parking spaces, ramped curbs, and wheelchair lifts on buses.

A 1975 law ensured access to public schools for children with disabilities. Some schools began mainstreaming, or placing children with special needs in regular classes. Others schools offered small classes with specialized help.

In 1990, Congress passed the Americans With Disabilities Act. The new law outlawed discrimination in hiring people with physical or mental impairments. It also required employers to provide "reasonable accommodations," such as ramps for workers in wheelchairs.

Older Americans The American population is aging rapidly. Birth rates have declined, and medical care is improving. As "baby boomers" born in the 1940s and 1950s age, the number of senior citizens will jump dramatically. By 2000, one American in eight was over the age of 65. That number may reach one in five by 2030.

The aging population presents challenges to both older and younger Americans. Who will care for these seniors? How will they pay their medical bills? What role will the government play?

Organizations such as the American Association of Retired Persons (AARP) pay special attention to issues of concern to older Americans. These include Social Security and Medicare, which provide pensions and medical assistance to the elderly. As their membership grows, such groups gain political power. Older citizens also gain influence by exercising their power to vote in great numbers.

Challenges for a New Century

At the dawn of the twenty-first century, Americans face both opportunities and challenges. The nation is changing and so is the rest of the world. As Americans adjust, they find themselves tested anew.

Terrorism The attacks on the World Trade Center and Pentagon in 2001 were part of a global campaign of terror. But terrorism could be homegrown as well. In 1995, a blast at a federal building in Oklahoma City killed 168 people. Two Americans who resented the government were convicted for the Oklahoma City bombing.

In the wake of the 2001 attacks, a new form of terrorism emerged. Pieces of mail were infected with the disease anthrax. Most of the people exposed were treated in time, but a number died.

In October 2001, Congress voted to give law enforcement agencies broad new powers to fight terrorism. Americans had to face the challenge of safeguarding the nation without sacrificing the basic rights and freedoms guaranteed by the Constitution.

Violence and Drug Abuse In 1999, two students at a Colorado high school opened fire on fellow students, killing 15 people. The shocking incident was one of several school shootings that led Americans to debate how such violence could be prevented.

Another serious problem is drug abuse. Schools are in the front lines here, too, as they try to protect students from dangerous and illegal substances such as cocaine and heroin.

Viewing History

Accommodating Americans With Disabilities

United States

Today, many laws require businesses and public buildings to provide access and services for people with disabilities. These accommodations include wheelchair lifts on buses (above). **Drawing Conclusions** *How can accommodations like this help Americans with disabilities to achieve economic independence?*

Americans are torn between two approaches to fighting illegal drugs. Some see drug abuse as a social problem. They favor using treatment centers to help drug users. To others, drug abuse is a criminal problem. They want stiffer penalties for drug dealers and users. The United States has spent billions of dollars pursuing drug smugglers and dealers. Yet, drug abuse remains widespread.

Meeting Challenges Anew The United States faces complex issues and great dangers in the new century. Yet, Americans have met such challenges before. In 1776, the problems were so great that many believed the new nation would not survive. Instead, it grew into a superpower and a model for democracies everywhere.

From the beginning, the motto of the United States has been *E pluribus unum*—"Out of many, one." The motto reflects the unity of the nation's many regions and people. Together with democracy, diversity lies at the source of the nation's strength.

President John F. Kennedy struck those themes as he took the oath of office in 1961. He called on his "fellow Americans" to serve their democratic republic: "Ask not what your country can do for you—ask what you can do for your country." Less remembered is the challenge he issued to a divided world in his next breath:

66 My fellow citizens of the world, ask not what America will do for you, but what together we can do for the freedom of man. 99

—John F. Kennedy, Inaugural Address, January 20, 1961

AS YOU READ **Visualize** Form a mental picture of the dreams you have for the nation's future. What opportunities do you see for new beginnings?

At the dawn of the twenty-first century, America again beckons the world to join the common cause of freedom. Only by overcoming our differences and relying on one another's strengths can Americans and their "fellow citizens of the world" succeed.

Section 5 Assessment

AFTER YOU READ

Recall

1. **Identify** Explain the significance of **(a)** Immigration Reform and Control Act, **(b)** Colin Powell, **(c)** American Indian Religious Freedom Act, **(d)** Americans With Disabilities Act, **(e)** American Association of Retired Persons.
2. **Define** **(a)** refugee, **(b)** illegal alien, **(c)** mainstreaming.

Comprehension

3. How did immigration patterns change in the late 1900s?
4. Describe one issue concerning each of the following: **(a)** African Americans, **(b)** women, **(c)** Americans with disabilities.

5. What two approaches have Americans taken to meet the challenge of drug abuse?

Critical Thinking and Writing

6. **Exploring the Main Idea** Review the Main Idea statement at the beginning of this section. Then, write a letter to new immigrants to the United States. Describe what will be expected of them and what they can expect in return.
7. **Drawing Conclusions** Write a paragraph explaining why younger Americans should be concerned about issues affecting older people.

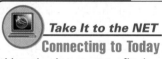

ACTIVITY

Take It to the NET
Connecting to Today
Use the Internet to find out about recent programs designed to prevent violence in schools. Then, write up an action plan explaining how you might deal with the problem in your own school. Visit *The American Nation* section of **www.phschool.com** for help in completing the activity.

Transferring Information

Historical information comes in many forms. Sometimes, it is helpful to organize information so that you can compare it with other data.

The data below relate to sources of immigration in 1900. These data have been used to create the pie chart below.

Asia	4 percent
Americas	1.2 percent
Europe	94.7 percent
Africa	less than 1 percent
Other	less than 1 percent

The paragraph below describes modern immigration trends.

Immigration patterns have changed. In 1998, the largest percentage—45.2—came from the Americas. Another sizable percentage—33.2—were people from Asia. Africans now made up 6.2 percent, while Europeans accounted for 13.7 percent. About 1.7 percent of immigrants came from other places.

Immigrants, 1900

Where They Came From

1900

94.7%

4%

1.2%

less than .1%

- Europe
- Asia
- Americas
- Africa and others

Source: *Historical Statistics of the United States*

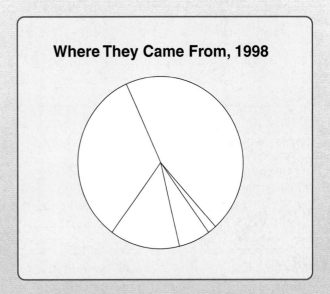

Where They Came From, 1998

Learn the Skill *To learn how to transfer information, use the following steps:*

1. **Identify the raw data.** As you read a selection, note the facts given. If many statistics are included, think about how you might organize them so that they are easier to see and use.

2. **List the data.** Compile a list of the facts. Organize the percentages from greatest to least.

3. **Transfer the data.** To make a pie chart, divide a circle into parts that add up to 100. Color a portion of the circle to represent each percentage you want to include. Label the chart.

4. **Draw conclusions based on the data.** What can you learn by looking at the data in this form?

Practice the Skill *Use the information above to answer the following questions:*

1. What percentage of immigrants to the United States in 1998 were from Europe? From Asia?

2. **(a)** List the data in the paragraph in order of percentage. **(b)** Where did the largest group of immigrants come from in 1998?

3. Copy the blank pie chart, and fit the data from the paragraph into it. Use the same color code as in the completed pie chart.

4. Describe how immigration patterns changed between 1900 and 1998.

Apply the Skill *See the Chapter Review and Assessment.*

CREATING A CHAPTER SUMMARY

Copy the chart below. Fill in each box with events or developments affecting the United States from the 1970s to the present.

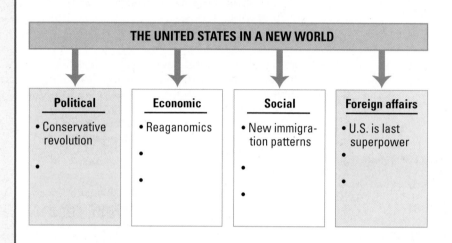

THE UNITED STATES IN A NEW WORLD

Political
- Conservative revolution
-

Economic
- Reaganomics
-
-

Social
- New immigration patterns
-
-

Foreign affairs
- U.S. is last superpower
-
-

For additional review and enrichment activities, see the interactive version of *The American Nation,* available on the Web and on CD-ROM.

Take It to the NET

Chapter Self-Test For practice test questions for Chapter 30, visit *The American Nation* section of **www.phschool.com**.

Building Vocabulary

Write sentences using the words listed below, leaving blanks where the words would go. Exchange your sentences with another student, and fill in the blanks in each other's sentences.

1. **deregulation**
2. **downsizing**
3. **recession**
4. **sanctions**
5. **terrorism**
6. **trade deficit**
7. **environmentalist**
8. **renewable resource**
9. **e-commerce**
10. **mainstreaming**

Reviewing Key Facts

11. How did conservatives view the role of the federal government? (Section 1)
12. What policy did the United States follow toward Cuba? (Section 2)
13. What were the results of the Persian Gulf War? (Section 3)
14. Why was the development of smaller computers important? (Section 4)
15. How did the economic status of women change? (Section 5)

Critical Thinking and Writing

16. **Contrasting** Review what you learned about President Franklin Roosevelt in Chapters 26 and 27. Then, write three sentences comparing and contrasting Roosevelt and Ronald Reagan.
17. **Supporting a Point of View** President Bill Clinton said that Americans must "overcome a dangerous and growing temptation . . . to focus solely on the problems we face here in America." Write a paragraph explaining whether you agree and why.
18. **Comparing** Review what you read in Chapter 27 about American reaction to the bombing of Pearl Harbor. How was reaction to the terrorist attacks of 2001 similar?

19. **Connecting to Geography: Interaction** How do environmentalists and their opponents reflect differing views of human-environment interaction?
20. **Ranking** What do you think are the two greatest challenges facing Americans today? Give reasons for your ranking.

Analyzing Primary Sources

Journalist Tom Brokaw spoke to a college graduating class about the future:

> **"** No piece of software, no server or search engine will offer you the irreplaceable rewards of a loving personal relationship, the strength and comfort of a real community of shared values and common dreams, the moral underpinning of a life lived well, whatever the financial scorecard. Nor will this new technology make you more racially tolerant . . . more courageous to take a firm stand for what you know is right. **"**
> —Tom Brokaw, Speech at Santa Fe College, May 15, 1999

21. How does this excerpt reflect the technological revolution that took place in the late 1900s?

22. Summarize Brokaw's main idea in your own words.

23. What personal and civic values does Brokaw support?

24. Do you agree or disagree with this viewpoint? Explain.

Transferring Information

The chart below gives raw data about United States exports in 1999. Examine the data, and answer the questions that follow.

U.S. Exports by Region

REGION	PERCENTAGE OF U.S. EXPORTS
Europe	24.7
NAFTA (Canada and Mexico)	36.4
Other Latin American Countries	8.0
Asia	27.4
Australia and Oceania	2.1
Africa	1.4

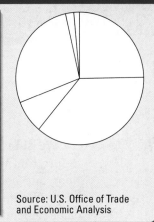

Source: U.S. Office of Trade and Economic Analysis

25. What percentage of United States exports went to Canada and Latin America in 1999?
  A 36.4 percent
  B 8 percent
  C 44.4 percent
  D cannot tell from the data given

26. Copy the blank pie chart shown here. Use the data given in the table to complete the pie chart.

ACTIVITIES

Connecting With . . .
Culture

Creating a Banner Think about the motto of the United States, *E pluribus unum*—"Out of many, one." Then, with a partner, design and create a banner around this theme. Use words and symbols to express what this motto means to you.

Take It to the NET

Connecting to Today

Use the Internet to find out about changes in the population of the United States over the last 50 years. You may focus on ethnic makeup, immigration, age, family income, or another topic. Use the information you discover to create a graph. For help in starting this activity, visit *The American Nation* section of **www.phschool.com**.

Evaluating Internet Sites

Reviewing News Sites Use the Internet to find Web sites for a national or local news agency, newspaper, or television station. Report on what kinds of news you can get from that site and how you can use it to stay informed about current and future issues. If possible, include two sample pages. For help in starting this activity, visit *The American Nation* section of **www.phschool.com**.

The House on Mango Street

Sandra Cisneros

Sandra Cisneros

Introduction Born in Chicago, Sandra Cisneros was one of the first Mexican American novelists to achieve widespread success. Her best-known book is *The House on Mango Street,* published in 1984. In a series of short episodes, the book paints a vivid picture of life in a Latino neighborhood in a large American city. The fictional narrator is Esperanza Cordero, the young daughter of Mexican immigrants. In the opening episode of the book, below, Esperanza describes her feelings when her family moves from one part of Chicago to another.

We didn't always live on Mango Street. Before that we lived on Loomis on the third floor, and before that we lived on Keeler. Before Keeler it was Paulina, and before that I can't remember. But what I remember most is moving a lot. Each time it seemed there'd be one more of us. By the time we got to Mango Street we were six—Mama, Papa, Carlos, Kiki, my sister Nenny and me.

The house on Mango Street is ours, and we don't have to pay rent to anybody, or share the yard with the people downstairs, or be careful not to make too much noise, and there isn't a landlord banging on the ceiling with a broom. But even so, it's not the house we'd thought we'd get.

We had to leave the flat on Loomis quick. The water pipes broke and the landlord wouldn't fix them because the house was too old. We had to leave fast. We were using the washroom next door and carrying water over in empty milk gallons. That's why Mama and Papa looked for a house, and that's why we moved into the house on Mango Street, far away, on the other side of town.

They always told us that one day we would move into a house, a real house that would be ours for always so we wouldn't have to move each year. And our house would have running water and pipes that worked. And inside it would have real stairs, not hallway stairs, but stairs inside like the houses on T.V. And we'd have a basement and at least three washrooms so when we took a bath we wouldn't have to tell everybody. Our house would be white with trees around it, a great big yard and grass growing without a fence. This was the house Papa talked about when he held a lottery ticket and this was the house Mama dreamed up in the stories she told us before we went to bed.

But the house on Mango Street is not the way they told it at all. It's small and red with tight steps in front and windows so small you'd think they were holding their breath. Bricks are crumbling in place, and the front door is so swollen you have to push hard to get in. There is no front yard, only four little elms the city planted by the curb. Out back is a small garage for the car we don't own yet and a small yard that looks smaller between the two buildings on either side. There are stairs in our house, but they're ordinary hallway stairs, and the house has only one washroom. Everybody has to share a bedroom—Mama and Papa, Carlos and Kiki, me and Nenny.

Once when we were living on Loomis, a nun from my school passed by and saw me playing out front. The laundromat downstairs had been boarded up because it had been robbed two days before and the owner had painted on the wood YES WE'RE OPEN so as not to lose business.

Where do you live? she asked.

There, I said pointing up to the third floor.

You live *there?*

Latino family in a mural in San Francisco, California

There. I had to look where she pointed—the third floor, the paint peeling, wooden bars Papa had nailed on the windows so we wouldn't fall out. You live *there?* The way she said it made me feel like nothing. *There.* I lived there. I nodded.

I knew then I had to have a house. A real house. One I could point to. But this isn't it. The house on Mango Street isn't it. For the time being, Mama says. Temporary, says Papa. But I know how those things go.

Analyzing Literature

1. What is one reason Esperanza is disappointed in the family's new home on Mango Street?

   A The new house has broken water pipes.

   B The new house is located above a laundromat.

   C The new house does not have its own front yard.

   D The new house is located on the poor side of town.

2. How does Esperanza feel when she is talking to the nun?

   A She is ashamed of the place where she lives.

   B She is proud that the nun spoke to her.

   C She is angry with her parents.

   D She is hopeful about the new house on Mango Street.

3. **Critical Thinking and Writing** **Comparing** How are the hopes, feelings, and experiences of Esperanza and her parents similar to those of earlier immigrants and their families?

TEST PREPARATION

Use the map <u>and</u> your knowledge of social studies to answer the following question.

1 During the Cold War, the relation of nation A to nation D was the same as which of the following?

  A Nation B to nation C

  B Nation E to nation F

  C Nation A to nation E

  D Nation C to nation D

2 Which of the following does not belong with the other three?

  A Fair Deal

  B William Levitt

  C GI Bill of Rights

  D Decline of inner cities

3 Which of the following was not an effect of the oil embargo of the 1970s?

  A Increased inflation

  B Call for energy conservation

  C Persian Gulf War

  D Fuel shortages

4 Which of the following statements is true of both the Korean War and the war in Vietnam?

  A The war bitterly divided Americans at home.

  B American involvement in the fighting escalated gradually over several years.

  C After fighting ended, tensions remained high between the North and the South.

  D The Soviet Union backed the communist North, but did not face the United States directly.

Use the quotation <u>and</u> your knowledge of social studies to answer the following question.

> "We conclude that . . . the doctrine of 'separate but equal' has no place. Separate . . . facilities are inherently unequal."

5 The above passage is an excerpt from what document?

  A Supreme Court decision in *Plessy* v. *Ferguson*

  B Supreme Court decision in *Brown* v. *Board of Education*

  C Martin Luther King's "I Have a Dream" speech

  D Civil Rights Act of 1964

6 Which of the following events was an effect of the other three?

A Military spending strains Soviet economy.

B Soviet republics declare independence.

C Cold War ends.

D Gorbachev and Reagan meet.

Use the graph <u>and</u> your knowledge of social studies to answer the following question.

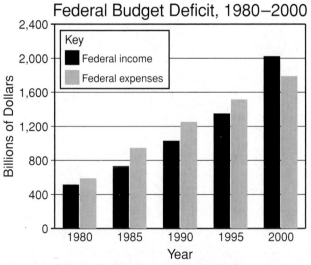

Federal Budget Deficit, 1980–2000

Key
■ Federal income
□ Federal expenses

Billions of Dollars (y-axis: 0, 400, 800, 1,200, 1,600, 2,000, 2,400)

Year (x-axis: 1980, 1985, 1990, 1995, 2000)

Sources: *Statistical Abstract of the United States* and the Office of Management and Budget Web site

7 Which is a valid conclusion that can be drawn from this graph?

A The budget deficit increased during President Reagan's term.

B President Clinton reduced federal spending.

C In 1992, the budget deficit was about $500 billion.

D The budget deficit decreased steadily throughout the 1990s.

8 The relationship of Barry Goldwater to the conservative revolution is most like which of the following?

A The relationship of Ronald Reagan to the Cold War

B The relationship of Rachel Carson to the environmental movement

C The relationship of Malcolm X to the civil rights movement

D The relationship of George Bush to the Persian Gulf War

9 The Watergate affair best illustrates which principle of the Constitution?

A Judicial review

B Federalism

C Popular sovereignty

D Checks and balances

Writing Practice

10 "Both the Cold War and the civil rights movement were related to a belief in American democracy." Explain the meaning of this statement and whether or not you agree with it. Include supporting details from your reading.

11 Describe the immediate effects of the 2001 terrorist attacks on New York and Washington, D.C. Explain why you think such crises often unite Americans.

Reference Section

Washington Crossing the Delaware
by Emanuel Gottlieb Leutze

The Declaration of Independence

On June 7, 1776, the Continental Congress approved the resolution that "these United Colonies are, and of right ought to be, free and independent States." Congress then appointed a committee to write a declaration of independence. The committee members were John Adams, Benjamin Franklin, Robert Livingston, Roger Sherman, and Thomas Jefferson.

Jefferson actually wrote the Declaration, but he got advice from the others. On July 2, Congress discussed the Declaration and made some changes. On July 4, 1776, it adopted the Declaration of Independence in its final form.

The Declaration is printed in black. The headings have been added to show the parts of the Declaration. They are not part of the original text. Annotations, or explanations, are on the white side of the page. Difficult words are defined.

When in the course of human events it becomes necessary for one people to dissolve the political bands which have connected them with another and to assume, among the powers of the earth, the separate and equal station to which the laws of nature and of nature's God entitle them, a decent respect to the opinions of mankind requires that they should declare the causes which impel them to the separation.

dissolve: break ***powers of the earth:*** other nations ***station:*** place ***impel:*** force

The colonists feel that they must explain to the world the reasons why they are breaking away from England.

The Purpose of Government Is to Protect Basic Rights

We hold these truths to be self-evident, that all men are created equal; that they are endowed by their Creator with certain unalienable rights; that among these are life, liberty, and the pursuit of happiness. That, to secure these rights, governments are instituted among men, deriving their just powers from the consent of the governed; that, whenever any form of government becomes destructive of these ends, it is the right of the people to alter or to abolish it, and to institute a new government, laying its foundation on such principles and organizing its powers in such form, as to them shall seem most likely to effect their safety and happiness. Prudence, indeed, will dictate that governments long established should not be changed for light and transient causes; and, accordingly, all experience hath shown that mankind are more disposed to suffer, while evils are sufferable, than to right themselves by abolishing the forms to which they are accustomed. But when a long train of abuses and usurpations, pursuing invariably the same object, evinces a design to reduce them under absolute despotism, it is their right, it is their duty, to throw off such government and to provide new guards for their future security. Such has been the patient sufferance of these colonies, and such is now the necessity which constrains them to alter their former systems of government. The history of the present King of Great Britain is a history of repeated injuries and usurpations, all having, in direct object, the establishment of an absolute tyranny over these States. To prove this, let facts be submitted to a candid world:

endowed: given ***unalienable rights:*** so basic that they cannot be taken away ***secure:*** protect ***instituted:*** set up ***deriving:*** getting ***alter:*** change ***effect:*** bring about

People set up governments to protect their basic rights. Governments get their power from the consent of the governed. If a government takes away the basic rights of the people, the people have the right to change the government.

prudence: wisdom ***transient:*** temporary, passing ***disposed:*** likely

usurpations: taking and using powers that do not belong to a person ***invariably:*** always ***evinces a design to reduce them under absolute despotism:*** makes a clear plan to put them under complete and unjust control ***sufferance:*** endurance

constrains: forces ***absolute tyranny:*** harsh and unjust government ***candid:*** free from prejudice

People do not readily change governments. But they are forced to do so when a government becomes tyrannical. King George III has a long record of abusing his power.

Wrongs Done by the King

assent: approval **relinquish:** give up **inestimable:** too great a value to be measured **formidable:** causing fear

This part of the Declaration spells out three sets of wrongs that led the colonists to break with Britain.

The first set of wrongs is the king's unjust use of power. The king refused to approve laws that are needed. He has tried to control the colonial legislatures.

depository: storehouse **fatiguing:** tiring out **compliance:** giving in **dissolved:** broken up **annihilation:** total destruction **convulsions:** disturbances

The king has tried to force colonial legislatures into doing his will by wearing them out. He has dissolved legislatures (such as those of Massachusetts).

endeavored: tried **obstructing:** blocking **naturalization:** process of becoming a citizen **migration:** moving **hither:** here **appropriations:** grants **obstructed the administration of justice:** prevented justice from being done **judiciary powers:** system of law courts **tenure:** term (of office) **erected:** set up **multitude:** large number **swarms:** huge crowds **harass:** cause trouble **render:** make

Among other wrongs, he has refused to let settlers move west to take up new land. He has prevented justice from being done. Also, he has sent large numbers of customs officials to cause problems for the colonists.

jurisdiction: authority **quartering:** housing **mock:** false

The king has joined with others, meaning Parliament, to make laws for the colonies. The Declaration then lists the second set of wrongs—unjust acts of Parliament.

He has refused his assent to laws the most wholesome and necessary for the public good.

He has forbidden his governors to pass laws of immediate and pressing importance, unless suspended in their operation till his assent should be obtained; and, when so suspended, he has utterly neglected to attend to them.

He has refused to pass other laws for the accommodation of the large districts of people, unless those people would relinquish the right of representation in the legislature; a right inestimable to them and formidable to tyrants only.

He has called together legislative bodies at places unusual, uncomfortable, and distant from the depository of their public records, for the sole purpose of fatiguing them into compliance with his measures.

He has dissolved representative houses, repeatedly for opposing, with manly firmness, his invasions on the rights of the people.

He has refused, for a long time after such dissolutions, to cause others to be elected: whereby the legislative powers, incapable of annihilation, have returned to the people at large for their exercise; the state remaining, in the meantime, exposed to all the danger of invasion from without and convulsions within.

He has endeavored to prevent the population of these States; for that purpose, obstructing the laws for naturalization of foreigners, refusing to pass others to encourage their migration hither, and raising the conditions of new appropriations of lands.

He has obstructed the administration of justice by refusing his assent to laws for establishing judiciary powers.

He has made judges dependent on his will alone for the tenure of their offices and the amount and payment of their salaries.

He has erected a multitude of new offices and sent hither swarms of officers to harass our people and eat out their substance.

He has kept among us, in time of peace, standing armies, without the consent of our legislatures.

He has affected to render the military independent of, and superior to, the civil power.

He has combined with others to subject us to a jurisdiction foreign to our Constitution and unacknowledged by our laws, giving his assent to their acts of pretended legislation:

For quartering large bodies of armed troops among us;

For protecting them by a mock trial from punishment for any murders which they should commit on the inhabitants of these States;

For cutting off our trade with all parts of the world;

For imposing taxes on us without our consent;

For depriving us, in many cases, of the benefit of trial by jury;

For transporting us beyond seas to be tried for pretended offences;

For abolishing the free system of English laws in a neighboring province, establishing therein an arbitrary government, and enlarging its boundaries, so as to render it at once an example and fit instrument for introducing the same absolute rule into these colonies;

For taking away our charters, abolishing our most valuable laws, and altering, fundamentally, the powers of our governments;

For suspending our own legislatures and declaring themselves invested with power to legislate for us in all cases whatsoever.

He has abdicated government here by declaring us out of his protection and waging war against us.

He has plundered our seas, ravaged our coasts, burnt our towns, and destroyed the lives of our people.

He is, at this time, transporting large armies of foreign mercenaries to complete the works of death, desolation, and tyranny already begun with circumstances of cruelty and perfidy scarcely paralleled in the most barbarous ages, and totally unworthy the head of a civilized nation.

He has constrained our fellow citizens, taken captive on the high seas, to bear arms against their country, to become the executioners of their friends and brethren, or to fall themselves by their hands.

He has excited domestic insurrections amongst us and has endeavored to bring on the inhabitants of our frontiers, the merciless Indian savages, whose known rule of warfare is an undistinguished destruction of all ages, sexes, and conditions.

In every state of these oppressions, we have petitioned for redress in the most humble terms; our repeated petitions have been answered only by repeated injury. A prince whose character is thus marked by every act which may define a tyrant is unfit to be the ruler of a free people.

Nor have we been wanting in attention to our British brethren. We have warned them, from time to time, of attempts made by their legislature to extend an unwarrantable jurisdiction over us. We have reminded them of the circumstances of our emigration and settlement here. We have appealed to their native justice and magnanimity, and we have conjured them, by the ties of our common kindred, to disavow these usurpations, which would inevitably interrupt our connections and correspondence. They, too, have been deaf to the voice of justice and consanguinity. We must, therefore, acquiesce in the necessity which denounces our separation, and hold them, as we hold the rest of mankind, enemies in war, in peace, friends.

imposing: forcing **depriving:** taking away **transporting us beyond seas:** sending colonists to England for trial **neighboring province:** Quebec **arbitrary government:** unjust rule **fit instrument:** suitable tool **invested with power:** having the power

During the years leading up to 1776, the colonists claimed that Parliament had no right to make laws for them because they were not represented in Parliament. Here, the colonists object to recent laws of Parliament, such as the Quartering Act and the blockade of colonial ports, which cut off their trade. They also object to Parliament's claim that it had the right to tax them without their consent.

abdicated: given up **plundered:** robbed **ravaged:** attacked **mercenaries:** hired soldiers **desolation:** misery **perfidy:** falseness **barbarous:** uncivilized **constrained:** forced **brethren:** brothers **domestic insurrections:** internal revolts

Here, the Declaration lists the third set of wrongs—warlike acts of the king. Instead of listening to the colonists, the king has made war on them. He has hired soldiers to fight in America.

oppressions: harsh rule **petitioned:** asked **redress:** relief **unwarrantable jurisdiction over:** unfair authority **magnanimity:** generosity **conjured:** called upon **common kindred:** relatives **disavow:** turn away from **consanguinity:** blood relationships, kinship **acquiesce:** agree **denounces:** speaks out against

During this time, colonists have repeatedly asked for relief. But their requests have brought only more suffering. They have appealed to the British people but received no help. So they are forced to separate.

Colonies Declare Independence

We, therefore, the representatives of the United States of America, in general Congress assembled, appealing to the Supreme Judge of the world for the rectitude of our intentions, do, in the name and by the authority of the good people of these colonies, solemnly publish and declare, that these united colonies are, and of right ought to be, free and independent states: that they are absolved from all allegiance to the British Crown, and that all political connection between them and the state of Great Britain is, and ought to be, totally dissolved; and that, as free and independent states, they have full power to levy war, conclude peace, contract alliances, establish commerce, and to do all other acts and things which independent states may of right do. And, for the support of this declaration, with a firm reliance on the protection of Divine Providence, we mutually pledge to each other our lives, our fortunes, and our sacred honor.

Signers of the Declaration of Independence

John Hancock, President

Charles Thomson, Secretary

New Hampshire
Josiah Bartlett
William Whipple
Matthew Thornton

Massachusetts
Samuel Adams
John Adams
Robert Treat Paine
Elbridge Gerry

Rhode Island
Stephen Hopkins
William Ellery

Connecticut
Roger Sherman
Samuel Huntington
William Williams
Oliver Wolcott

Delaware
Caesar Rodney
George Read
Thomas McKean

New York
William Floyd
Philip Livingston
Francis Lewis
Lewis Morris

New Jersey
Richard Stockton
John Witherspoon
Francis Hopkinson
John Hart
Abraham Clark

Georgia
Button Gwinnett
Lyman Hall
George Walton

Maryland
Samuel Chase
William Paca
Thomas Stone
Charles Carroll

North Carolina
William Hooper
Joseph Hewes
John Penn

Virginia
George Wythe
Richard Henry Lee
Thomas Jefferson
Benjamin Harrison
Thomas Nelson, Jr.
Francis Lightfoot Lee
Carter Braxton

South Carolina
Edward Rutledge
Thomas Heyward, Jr.
Thomas Lynch, Jr.
Arthur Middleton

Pennsylvania
Robert Morris
Benjamin Rush
Benjamin Franklin
John Morton
George Clymer
James Smith
George Taylor
James Wilson
George Ross

The Constitution of the United States of America

The Constitution is printed in black. The titles of articles, sections, and clauses are not part of the original document. They have been added here to help you find information in the Constitution. Some words or lines are crossed out because they have been changed by amendments or no longer apply. Annotations, or explanations, are on the tan side of the page. Difficult words are defined.

Preamble

We the people of the United States, in order to form a more perfect Union, establish justice, insure domestic tranquillity, provide for the common defense, promote the general welfare, and secure the blessings of liberty to ourselves and our posterity, do ordain and establish this Constitution for the United States of America.

The Preamble describes the purpose of the government set up by the Constitution. Americans expect their government to defend justice and liberty and provide peace and safety from foreign enemies.

Article 1. The Legislative Branch

Section 1. A Two-House Legislature

All legislative powers herein granted shall be vested in a Congress of the United States, which shall consist of a Senate and House of Representatives.

The Constitution gives Congress the power to make laws. Congress is divided into the Senate and the House of Representatives.

Section 2. House of Representatives

1. **Election of Members**   The House of Representatives shall be composed of members chosen every second year by the people of the several states, and the electors in each state shall have the qualifications requisite for electors of the most numerous branch of the state legislature.

2. **Qualifications**   No person shall be a Representative who shall not have attained to the age of twenty-five years, and been seven years a citizen of the United States, and who shall not, when elected, be an inhabitant of that state in which he shall be chosen.

3. **Determining Representation**   Representatives and direct taxes shall be apportioned among the several states which may be included within this Union, according to their respective numbers which shall be determined by adding to the whole number of free persons, including those bound to service for a term of years, and excluding Indians not taxed, three fifths of all other persons. The actual enumeration shall be made within three years after the first meeting of the Congress of the United States, and within every subsequent term of ten years, in such manner as they shall by law direct. The number of Representatives shall not exceed one for every 30,000, but each state shall have at least one Representative; and until such enumeration shall be made, the state of New Hampshire shall be entitled to choose three; Massachusetts, eight; Rhode Island and Providence Plantations, one; Connecticut, five; New York, six; New Jersey, four; Pennsylvania, eight; Delaware, one; Maryland, six; Virginia, ten; North Carolina, five; South Carolina, five; and Georgia, three.

Clause 1   *Electors* refers to voters. Members of the House of Representatives are elected every two years. Any citizen allowed to vote for members of the larger house of the state legislature can also vote for members of the House.

Clause 2   A member of the House of Representatives must be at least 25 years old, an American citizen for 7 years, and a resident of the state he or she represents.

Clause 3   The number of representatives each state elects is based on its population. An *enumeration,* or census, must be taken every 10 years to determine population. Today, the number of representatives in the House is fixed at 435.
 This is the famous Three-Fifths Compromise worked out at the Constitutional Convention. *Persons bound to service* meant indentured servants. *All other persons* meant slaves. All free people in a state were counted. However, only three fifths of the slaves were included in the population count. This three-fifths clause became meaningless when slaves were freed in 1865 by the Thirteenth Amendment.

Clause 4 *Executive authority* means the governor of a state. If a member of the House leaves office before his or her term ends, the governor must call a special election to fill the seat.

Clause 5 The House elects a speaker. Today, the speaker is usually chosen by the party that has a majority in the House. Also, only the House has the power to *impeach,* or accuse, a federal official of wrongdoing.

Clause 1 Each state has two senators, who serve for six-year terms. The Seventeenth Amendment changed the way senators were elected.

Clause 2 Every two years, one third of the senators run for reelection. Thus, the makeup of the Senate is never totally changed by any one election. The Seventeenth Amendment changed the way that *vacancies,* or empty seats, are filled. Today, the governor of a state must choose a senator to fill a vacancy that occurs between elections.

Clause 3 A senator must be at least 30 years old, an American citizen for 9 years, and a resident of the state he or she represents.

Clause 4 The Vice President presides over Senate meetings, but he or she can vote only to break a tie.

Clause 5 *Pro tempore* means "temporary." The Senate chooses a member to serve as president *pro tempore* when the Vice President is absent.

Clause 6 The Senate acts as a jury if the House impeaches a federal official. The Chief Justice of the Supreme Court presides if the President is on trial. Two thirds of all senators present must vote for *conviction,* or a finding of guilty. No President has ever been convicted, though the House impeached President Andrew Johnson in 1868 and President Bill Clinton in 1998. In 1974, President Richard Nixon resigned before he could be impeached.

Clause 7 If an official is found guilty by the Senate, he or she can be removed from office and barred from holding federal office in the future. These are the only punishments the Senate can impose. However, the convicted official can still be tried in a criminal court.

4. **Filling Vacancies** When vacancies happen in the representation from any state, the executive authority thereof shall issue writs of election to fill such vacancies.

5. **Selection of Officers; Power of Impeachment** The House of Representatives shall choose their Speaker and other officers; and shall have the sole power of impeachment.

Section 3. The Senate

1. **Selection of Members** The Senate of the United States shall be composed of two Senators from each state ~~chosen by the legislature thereof~~, for six years, and each Senator shall have one vote.

2. **Alternating Terms; Filling Vacancies** Immediately after they shall be assembled in consequence of the first election, they shall be divided as equally as may be into three classes. ~~The seats of the Senators of the first class shall be vacated at the expiration of the second year, of the second class at the expiration of the fourth year, and of the third class at the expiration of the sixth year,~~ so that one-third may be chosen every second year; ~~and if vacancies happen by resignation, or otherwise, during the recess of the legislature of any state, the executive thereof may make temporary appointments until the next meeting of the legislature, which shall then fill such vacancies.~~

3. **Qualifications** No person shall be a Senator who shall not have attained to the age of thirty years, and been nine years a citizen of the United States, and who shall not, when elected, be an inhabitant of that state for which he shall be chosen.

4. **President of the Senate** The Vice-President of the United States shall be president of the Senate, but shall have no vote, unless they be equally divided.

5. **Election of Senate Officers** The Senate shall choose their other officers, and also a president *pro tempore,* in the absence of the Vice-President, or when he shall exercise the office of the President of the United States.

6. **Impeachment Trials** The Senate shall have the sole power to try all impeachments. When sitting for that purpose, they shall be on oath or affirmation. When the President of the United States is tried, the Chief Justice shall preside; and no person shall be convicted without the concurrence of two-thirds of the members present.

7. **Penalties Upon Conviction** Judgment in cases of impeachment shall not extend further than to removal from office, and disqualification to hold and enjoy any office of honor, trust, or profit under the United States; but the party convicted shall nevertheless be liable and subject to indictment, trial, judgment, and punishment, according to law.

Section 4. Elections and Meetings

1. **Election of Congress**   The times, places, and manner of holding elections for Senators and Representatives shall be prescribed in each state by the legislature thereof; but the Congress may at any time by law make or alter such regulations, except as to the places of choosing Senators.

2. **Annual Sessions**   The Congress shall assemble at least once in every year, ~~and such meeting shall be on the first Monday in December, unless they shall by law appoint a different day.~~

Section 5. Rules for the Conduct of Business

1. **Organization**   Each house shall be the judge of the elections, returns, and qualifications of its own members, and a majority of each shall constitute a quorum to do business; but a smaller number may adjourn from day to day, and may be authorized to compel the attendance of absent members, in such manner, and under such penalties, as each house may provide.

2. **Procedures**   Each house may determine the rules of its proceedings, punish its members for disorderly behavior, and with the concurrence of two-thirds, expel a member.

3. **A Written Record**   Each house shall keep a journal of its proceedings, and from time to time publish the same, excepting such parts as may in their judgment require secrecy; and the yeas and nays of the members of either house on any question shall, at the desire of one-fifth of those present, be entered on the journal.

4. **Rules for Adjournment**   Neither house, during the session of Congress, shall, without the consent of the other, adjourn for more than three days, nor to any other place than that in which the two houses shall be sitting.

Section 6. Privileges and Restrictions

1. **Salaries and Immunities**   The Senators and Representatives shall receive a compensation for their services, to be ascertained by law and paid out of the Treasury of the United States. They shall in all cases, except treason, felony, and breach of the peace, be privileged from arrest during their attendance at the session of their respective houses, and in going to and returning from the same; and for any speech or debate in either house, they shall not be questioned in any other place.

2. **Restrictions on Other Employment**   No Senator or Representative shall, during the time for which he was elected, be appointed to any civil office under the authority of the United States, which shall have been created, or the emoluments whereof shall have been increased, during such time; and no person holding any office under the United States shall be a member of either house during his continuance in office.

Clause 1 Each state legislature can decide when and how congressional elections take place, but Congress can overrule these decisions. In 1842, Congress required each state to set up congressional districts with one representative elected from each district. In 1872, Congress decided that congressional elections must be held in every state on the same date in even-numbered years.

Clause 2 Congress must meet at least once a year. The Twentieth Amendment moved the opening date of Congress to January 3.

Clause 1 Each house decides whether a member has the qualifications for office set by the Constitution. A *quorum* is the smallest number of members who must be present for business to be conducted. Each house can set its own rules about absent members.

Clause 2 Each house can make rules for the conduct of members. It can only expel a member by a two-thirds vote.

Clause 3 Each house keeps a record of its meetings. *The Congressional Record* is published every day with excerpts from speeches made in each house. It also records the votes of each member.

Clause 4 Neither house can **adjourn**, or stop meeting, for more than three days unless the other house approves. Both houses of Congress must meet in the same city.

Clause 1 *Compensation* means "salary." Congress decides the salary for its members. While Congress is in session, a member is free from arrest in civil cases and cannot be sued for anything he or she says on the floor of Congress. This allows for freedom of debate. However, a member can be arrested for a criminal offense.

Clause 2 *Emolument* also means "salary." A member of Congress cannot hold another federal office during his or her term. A former member of Congress cannot hold an office created while he or she was in Congress. An official in another branch of government cannot serve at the same time in Congress. This strengthens the separation of powers.

Section 7. Law-Making Process

1. **Tax Bills**   All bills for raising revenue shall originate in the House of Representatives; but the Senate may propose or concur with amendments as on other bills.

2. **How a Bill Becomes a Law**   Every bill which shall have passed the House of Representatives and the Senate shall, before it become a law, be presented to the President of the United States; if he approve, he shall sign it, but if not, he shall return it, with his objections, to that house in which it shall have originated, who shall enter the objections at large on their journal, and proceed to reconsider it. If after such reconsideration two-thirds of that house shall agree to pass the bill, it shall be sent, together with the objections, to the other house, by which it shall likewise be reconsidered, and, if approved by two-thirds of that house, it shall become a law. But in all such cases the votes of both houses shall be determined by yeas and nays, and the names of the persons voting for and against the bill shall be entered on the journal of each house respectively. If any bill shall not be returned by the President within ten days (Sundays excepted) after it shall have been presented to him, the same bill shall be a law, in like manner as if he had signed it, unless the Congress by their adjournment prevent its return, in which case it shall not be a law.

How a Bill Becomes a Law

GRAPHIC ORGANIZER
Skills

The House of Representatives, the Senate, and the President all play a role in the law-making process.

1. **Comprehension**
   (a) Where can a bill be introduced? (b) At what point do members of the House and Senate come together? (c) What can the President do?

2. **Critical Thinking**
   Drawing Inferences
   Every year thousands of bills are introduced. Why do you think committees hold hearings on bills?

Civics

Introduction	Committee Action	Floor Action		Enactment Into Law	
Introduced in House	Referred to House committee	House debates and passes its form of bill	House and Senate members confer, reach compromise on single form of bill	President signs bill into law	The bill becomes law
Introduced in Senate	Referred to Senate committee	Senate debates and passes its form of bill			With a two-thirds majority vote of Congress, the bill is passed over the President's veto
		House and Senate approve compromise		President vetoes bill	
Most bills begin as similar proposals in House and Senate	Committee holds hearings, makes changes, recommends passage				Congress does not override the President's veto
		All bills must go through both House and Senate before reaching President			The bill fails to become law

3. Resolutions Passed by Congress   Every order, resolution, or vote to which the concurrence of the Senate and House of Representatives may be necessary (except on a question of adjournment) shall be presented to the President of the United States; and before the same shall take effect, shall be approved by him, or being disapproved by him, shall be repassed by two-thirds of the Senate and House of Representatives, according to the rules and limitations prescribed in the case of a bill.

Section 8. Powers Delegated to Congress

The Congress shall have the power

1. **Taxes**   To lay and collect taxes, duties, imposts, and excises, to pay the debts and provide for the common defense and general welfare of the United States; but all duties, imposts, and excises shall be uniform throughout the United States;

2. **Borrowing**   To borrow money on the credit of the United States;

3. **Commerce**   To regulate commerce with foreign nations, and among the several states, and with the Indian tribes;

4. **Naturalization; Bankruptcy**   To establish a uniform rule of naturalization, and uniform laws on the subject of bankruptcies throughout the United States;

5. **Coins; Weights; Measures**   To coin money, regulate the value thereof, and of foreign coin, and fix the standard of weights and measures;

6. **Counterfeiting**   To provide for the punishment of counterfeiting the securities and current coin of the United States;

7. **Post Offices**   To establish post offices and post roads;

8. **Copyrights; Patents**   To promote the progress of science and useful arts by securing for limited times to authors and inventors the exclusive right to their respective writings and discoveries;

9. **Federal Courts**   To constitute tribunals inferior to the Supreme Court;

10. **Piracy**   To define and punish piracies and felonies committed on the high seas and offenses against the law of nations;

Clause 3   Congress can pass resolutions or orders that have the same force as laws. Any such resolution or order must be signed by the President (except on questions of adjournment). This clause prevents Congress from bypassing the President simply by calling a bill by another name.

Clause 1   *Duties* are tariffs. *Imposts* are taxes in general. *Excises* are taxes on the production or sale of certain goods. Congress has the power to tax and spend tax money. Taxes must be the same in all parts of the country.

Clause 2   Congress can borrow money for the United States. The government often borrows money by selling *bonds,* or certificates that promise to pay the holder a certain sum of money on a certain date.

Clause 3   Only Congress has the power to regulate foreign and *interstate trade,* or trade between states. Disagreement over interstate trade was a major problem with the Articles of Confederation.

Clause 4   *Naturalization* is the process whereby a foreigner becomes a citizen. *Bankruptcy* is the condition in which a person or business cannot pay its debts. Congress has the power to pass laws on these two issues. The laws must be the same in all parts of the country.

Clause 5   Congress has the power to coin money and set its value. Congress has set up the National Bureau of Standards to regulate weights and measures.

Clause 6   *Counterfeiting* is the making of imitation money. *Securities* are bonds. Congress can make laws to punish counterfeiters.

Clause 7   Congress has the power to set up and control the delivery of mail.

Clause 8   Congress may pass copyright and patent laws. A *copyright* protects an author. A *patent* makes an inventor the sole owner of his or her work for a limited time.

Clause 9   Congress has the power to set up *inferior,* or lower, federal courts under the Supreme Court.

Clause 10   Congress can punish *piracy,* or the robbing of ships at sea.

Clause 11 Only Congress can declare war. Declarations of war are granted at the request of the President. *Letters of marque and reprisal* were documents allowing merchant ships to arm themselves. They are no longer issued.

Clauses 12, 13, 14 These clauses place the army and navy under the control of Congress. Congress decides on the size of, and the amount of money to spend on, the armed forces. It also has the power to write rules governing the armed forces.

Clauses 15, 16 The *militia* is a body of citizen soldiers. Congress can call up the militia to put down rebellions or fight foreign invaders. Each state has its own militia, today called the National Guard. Normally, the militia is under the command of a state's governor. However, it can be placed under the command of the President.

Clause 17 Congress controls the district around the national capital. In 1790, Congress made Washington, D.C., the nation's capital. In 1973, it gave residents of the District the right to elect local officials.

Clause 18 Clauses 1–17 list the powers delegated to Congress. The framers added Clause 18 so that Congress could make laws as needed to carry out the first 17 clauses. Clause 18 is sometimes called the elastic clause because it lets Congress stretch the meaning of its power.

Clause 1 *Such persons* refers to slaves. This clause resulted from a compromise between the supporters and the opponents of the slave trade. In 1808, as soon as Congress was permitted to abolish the slave trade, it did so. The import tax was never imposed.

Clause 2 A *writ of habeas corpus* is a court order requiring government officials to bring a prisoner to court and explain why he or she is being held. A writ of habeas corpus protects people from unlawful imprisonment. This right cannot be suspended except in times of rebellion or invasion.

11. **Declarations of War** To declare war, ~~grant letters of marque and reprisal,~~ and make rules concerning captures on land and water;

12. **Army** To raise and support armies, but no appropriation of money to that use shall be for a longer term than two years;

13. **Navy** To provide and maintain a navy;

14. **Rules for the Military** To make rules for the government and regulation of the land and naval forces;

15. **Militia** To provide for calling forth the militia to execute the laws of the Union, suppress insurrections, and repel invasions;

16. **Rules for the Militia** To provide for organizing, arming, and disciplining the militia, and for governing such part of them as may be employed in the service of the United States, reserving to the states, respectively, the appointment of the officers, and the authority of training the militia according to the discipline prescribed by Congress;

17. **National Capital** To exercise exclusive legislation in all cases whatsoever, over such district (not exceeding ten miles square) as may, by cession of particular states, and the acceptance of Congress, become the seat of government of the United States, and to exercise like authority over all places purchased by the consent of the legislature of the state in which the same shall be, for the erection of forts, magazines, arsenals, dock-yards, and other needful buildings;—and

18. **Necessary Laws** To make all laws which shall be necessary and proper for carrying into execution the foregoing powers, and all other powers vested by this Constitution in the government of the United States, or in any department or officer thereof.

Section 9. Powers Denied to the Federal Government

1. **The Slave Trade** ~~The migration or importation of such persons as any of the states now existing shall think proper to admit shall not be prohibited by the Congress prior to the year 1808; but a tax or duty may be imposed on such importation, not exceeding $10 for each person.~~

2. **Writ of Habeas Corpus** The privilege of the writ of habeas corpus shall not be suspended, unless when in cases of rebellion or invasion the public safety may require it.

3. **Bills of Attainder and *Ex Post Facto* Laws**   No bill of attainder or *ex post facto* law shall be passed.

4. **Apportionment of Direct Taxes**   ~~No capitation or other direct tax shall be laid, unless in proportion to the census or enumeration herein before directed to be taken.~~

5. **Taxes on Exports**   No tax or duty shall be laid on articles exported from any state.

6. **Special Preference for Trade**   No preference shall be given any regulation of commerce or revenue to the ports of one state over those of another; nor shall vessels bound to, or from, one state, be obliged to enter, clear, or pay duties in another.

7. **Spending**   No money shall be drawn from the Treasury, but in consequence of appropriations made by law; and a regular statement and account of the receipts and expenditures of all public money shall be published from time to time.

8. **Creation of Titles of Nobility**   No title of nobility shall be granted by the United States; and no person holding any office of profit or trust under them, shall, without the consent of the Congress, accept of any present, emolument, office, or title, of any kind whatever, from any king, prince, or foreign state.

Section 10. Powers Denied to the States

1. **Unconditional Prohibitions**   No state shall enter into any treaty, alliance, or confederation; grant letters of marque and reprisal; coin money; emit bills of credit; make anything but gold and silver coin a tender in payment of debts; pass any bill of attainder, *ex post facto* law, or law impairing the obligation of contracts, or grant any title of nobility.

2. **Powers Conditionally Denied**   No state shall, without the consent of the Congress, lay any imposts or duties on imports or exports, except what may be absolutely necessary for executing its inspection laws; and the net produce of all duties and imposts, laid by any state on imports or exports, shall be for the use of the Treasury of the United States; and all such laws shall be subject to the revision and control of the Congress.

3. **Other Denied Powers**   No state shall, without the consent of Congress, lay any duty of tonnage, keep troops, or ships of war in time of peace, enter into any agreement or compact with another state, or with a foreign power, or engage in war, unless actually invaded, or in such imminent danger as will not admit of delay.

Clause 3 A ***bill of attainder*** is a law declaring that a person is guilty of a particular crime. An ***ex post facto law*** punishes an act which was not illegal when it was committed. Congress cannot pass such laws.

Clause 4 A ***capitation tax*** is a tax placed directly on each person. ***Direct taxes*** are taxes on people or on land. They can be passed only if they are divided among the states according to population. The Sixteenth Amendment allowed Congress to tax income without regard to the population of the states.

Clause 5 This clause forbids Congress to tax exports. Southerners insisted on this clause because their economy depended on exports.

Clause 6 Congress cannot make laws that favor one state over another in commerce. Also, states cannot place tariffs on interstate trade.

Clause 7 The federal government cannot spend money unless Congress ***appropriates*** it, or passes a law allowing it. The government must publish a statement showing how it spends public funds.

Clause 8 The government cannot award titles of nobility, such as Duke or Duchess. Americans cannot accept titles of nobility from foreign governments without the consent of Congress.

Clause 1 The writers of the Constitution did not want the states to act like separate nations. So, they prohibited states from making treaties or coining money. Some powers denied to the federal government are also denied to the states. For example, states cannot pass *ex post facto laws*.

Clauses 2, 3 Powers listed here are forbidden to the states, but Congress can lift these prohibitions by passing laws that give these powers to the states.
 Clause 2 forbids states from taxing imports and exports without the consent of Congress. States may charge inspection fees on goods entering the states. Any profit from these fees must be turned over to the United States Treasury.
 Clause 3 forbids states from keeping an army or navy without the consent of Congress. States cannot make treaties or declare war unless an enemy invades or is about to invade.

Article 2. The Executive Branch

Section 1. President and Vice-President

1. **Chief Executive**   The executive power shall be vested in a President of the United States of America. He shall hold his office during the term of four years, and together with the Vice-President, chosen for the same term, be elected as follows:

2. **Selection of Electors**   Each state shall appoint, in such manner as the legislature thereof may direct, a number of electors, equal to the whole number of Senators and Representatives to which the state may be entitled in the Congress; but no Senator or Representative, or person holding an office or trust or profit under the United States, shall be appointed an elector.

3. **Electoral College Procedures**   The electors shall meet in their respective states, and vote by ballot for two persons, of whom one at least shall not be an inhabitant of the same state with themselves. And they shall make a list of all the persons voted for, and of the number of votes for each; which list they shall sign and certify, and transmit sealed to the seat of the government of the United States, directed to the president of the Senate. The president of the Senate shall, in the presence of the Senate and House of Representatives, open all the certificates, and the votes shall then be counted. The person having the greatest number of votes shall be President, if such number be a majority of the whole number of electors appointed; and if there be more than one who have such majority, and have an equal number of votes, then the House of Representatives shall immediately choose by ballot one of them for President; and if no person have a majority, then from the five highest on the list the said House shall in like manner choose the President. But in choosing the President the votes shall be taken by states, the representation from each state having one vote. A quorum for this purpose shall consist of a member or members from two thirds of the states, and a majority of all the states shall be necessary to a choice. In every case, after the choice of the President, the person having the greatest number of votes of the electors shall be the Vice President. But if there should remain two or more who have equal votes, the Senate shall choose from them by ballot the Vice President.

4. **Time of Elections**   The Congress may determine the time of choosing the electors, and the day on which they shall give their votes; which day shall be the same throughout the United States.

Clause 1 The President is responsible for *executing*, or carrying out, laws passed by Congress.

Clauses 2, 3 Some writers of the Constitution were afraid to allow the people to elect the President directly. Therefore, the Constitutional Convention set up the electoral college. Clause 2 directs each state to choose electors, or delegates to the electoral college, to vote for President. A state's electoral vote is equal to the combined number of senators and representatives. Each state may decide how to choose its electors. Members of Congress and federal officeholders may not serve as electors. This much of the original electoral college system is still in effect.

Clause 3 called upon each elector to vote for two candidates. The candidate who received a majority of the electoral votes would become President. The runner-up would become Vice President. If no candidate won a majority, the House would choose the President. The Senate would choose the Vice President.

The election of 1800 showed a problem with the original electoral college system. Thomas Jefferson was the Republican candidate for President, and Aaron Burr was the Republican candidate for Vice President. In the electoral college, the vote ended in a tie. The election was finally decided in the House, where Jefferson was chosen President. The Twelfth Amendment changed the electoral college system so that this could not happen again.

Clause 4 By a law passed in 1792, electors are chosen on the Tuesday after the first Monday of November every four years. Electors from each state meet to vote in December.

Today, voters in each state choose *slates*, or groups, of electors who are pledged to a candidate for President. The candidate for President who wins the popular vote in each state wins that state's electoral vote.

5. Qualifications for President No person except a natural-born citizen ~~or a citizen of the United States, at the time of the adoption of this Constitution,~~ shall be eligible to the office of the President; neither shall any person be eligible to that office who shall not have attained to the age of thirty-five years, and been fourteen years a resident within the United States.

6. Presidential Succession In case of the removal of the President from office, or of his death, resignation, or inability to discharge the powers and duties of the said office, the same shall devolve on the Vice-President, and the Congress may by law provide for the case of removal, death, resignation, or inability, both of the President and Vice-President, declaring what officer shall then act as President, and such officer shall act accordingly, until the disability be removed, or a President shall be elected.

7. Salary The President shall, at stated times, receive for his services, a compensation, which shall neither be increased nor diminished during the period for which he shall have been elected, and he shall not receive within that period any other emolument from the United States, or any of them.

8. Oath of Office Before he enter on the execution of his office, he shall take the following oath or affirmation:—"I do solemnly swear (or affirm) that I will faithfully execute the office of President of the United States, and will to the best of my ability, preserve, protect, and defend the Constitution of the United States."

Section 2. Powers of the President

1. Commander in Chief of the Armed Forces The President shall be Commander in Chief of the Army and Navy of the United States, and of the militia of the several states, when called into the actual service of the United States; he may require the opinion, in writing, of the principal officer in each of the executive departments, upon any subject relating to the duties of their respective offices, and he shall have power to grant reprieves and pardons for offenses against the United States, except in cases of impeachment.

Clause 5 The President must be a citizen of the United States from birth, at least 35 years old, and a resident of the country for 14 years. The first seven Presidents of the United States were born under British rule, but they were allowed to hold office because they were citizens at the time the Constitution was adopted.

Clause 6 The powers of the President pass to the Vice President if the President leaves office or cannot discharge his or her duties. The wording of this clause caused confusion the first time a President died in office. When President William Henry Harrison died, it was uncertain whether Vice President John Tyler should remain Vice President and act as President or whether he should be sworn in as President. Tyler persuaded a federal judge to swear him in. So he set the precedent that the Vice President assumes the office of President when it becomes vacant. The Twenty-fifth Amendment replaced this clause.

Clause 7 The President is paid a salary. It cannot be raised or lowered during his or her term of office. The President is not allowed to hold any other federal or state position while in office. Today, the President's salary is $200,000 a year.

Clause 8 Before taking office, the President must promise to protect and defend the Constitution. Usually, the Chief Justice of the Supreme Court gives the oath of office to the President.

Clause 1 The President is head of the armed forces and the state militias when they are called into national service. So, the military is under *civilian*, or nonmilitary, control.

The President can get advice from the heads of executive departments. In most cases, the President has the power to grant a reprieve or pardon. A *reprieve* suspends punishment ordered by law. A *pardon* prevents prosecution for a crime or overrides the judgment of a court.

2 The President has the [power to] make treaties with other [nations]. Under the system of checks and balances, all treaties must be approved by two thirds of the Senate. Today, the President also makes agreements with foreign governments. These executive agreements do not need Senate approval.

The President has the power to appoint ambassadors to foreign countries and to appoint other high officials. The Senate must **confirm**, or approve, these appointments.

Clause 3 If the Senate is in **recess**, or not meeting, the President may fill vacant government posts by making temporary appointments.

The President must give Congress a report on the condition of the nation every year. This report is now called the State of the Union Address. Since 1913, the President has given this speech in person each January.

The President can call a special session of Congress and can adjourn Congress if necessary. The President has the power to receive, or recognize, foreign ambassadors.

The President must carry out the laws. Today, many government agencies oversee the execution of laws.

Civil officers include federal judges and members of the Cabinet. **High crimes** are major crimes. **Misdemeanors** are lesser crimes. The President, Vice President, and others can be forced out of office if impeached and found guilty of certain crimes.

Judicial power is the right of the courts to decide legal cases. The Constitution creates the Supreme Court but lets Congress decide the size of the Supreme Court. Congress has the power to set up inferior, or lower, courts. The Judiciary Act of 1789 set up district and circuit courts, or courts of appeal. Today, there are 94 district courts and 13 courts of appeal. All federal judges serve for life.

2. **Making Treaties and Nominations** He shall have power, by and with the advice and consent of the Senate, to make treaties, provided two-thirds of the Senators present concur; and he shall nominate, and by and with the advice and consent of the Senate, shall appoint ambassadors, other public ministers and consuls, judges of the Supreme Court, and all other officers of the United States, whose appointments are not herein otherwise provided for, and which shall be established by law; but the Congress may by law vest the appointment of such inferior officers, as they think proper, in the President alone, in the courts of law, or in the heads of departments.

3. **Temporary Appointments** The President shall have power to fill up all vacancies that may happen during the recess of the Senate, by granting commissions which shall expire at the end of their next session.

Section 3. Duties

He shall from time to time give to the Congress information of the state of the Union, and recommend to their consideration such measures as he shall judge necessary and expedient; he may, on extraordinary occasions, convene both houses, or either of them, and in case of disagreement between them, with respect to the time of adjournment, he may adjourn them to such time as he shall think proper; he shall receive ambassadors and other public ministers; he shall take care that the laws be faithfully executed, and shall commission all the officers of the United States.

Section 4. Impeachment and Removal From Office

The President, Vice-President, and all civil officers of the United States, shall be removed from office on impeachment for, and conviction of, treason, bribery, or other high crimes or misdemeanors.

Article 3. The Judicial Branch

Section 1. Federal Courts

The judicial power of the United States shall be vested in one Supreme Court, and in such inferior courts as the Congress may from time to time ordain and establish. The judges, both of the Supreme and inferior courts, shall hold their offices during good behavior, and shall, at stated times, receive for their services a compensation, which shall not be diminished during their continuance in office.

Separation of Powers

Legislative Branch (Congress)	Executive Branch (President)	Judicial Branch (Supreme Court and Other Federal Courts)
Passes Laws	**Carries Out Laws**	**Interprets Laws**
• Can override President's veto • Approves treaties and presidential appointments • Can impeach and remove President and other high officials • Creates lower federal courts • Appropriates money • Prints and coins money • Raises and supports the armed forces • Can declare war • Regulates foreign and interstate trade	• Proposes laws • Can veto laws • Negotiates foreign treaties • Serves as commander in chief of the armed forces • Appoints federal judges, ambassadors, and other high officials • Can grant pardons to federal offenders	• Can declare laws unconstitutional • Can declare executive actions unconstitutional

GRAPHIC ORGANIZER
Skills

The Constitution set up three branches of government. Each branch has its own powers.

1. **Comprehension**
   (a) Who heads the executive branch? **(b)** What is the role of the legislative branch?

2. **Critical Thinking**
   Analyzing Information
   Based on this chart, what is the relationship between the judicial branch and the legislative branch?

Civics

Section 2. Jurisdiction of Federal Courts

1. **Scope of Judicial Power** The judicial power shall extend to all cases, in law and equity, arising under this Constitution, the laws of the United States, and treaties made or which shall be made, under their authority; to all cases affecting ambassadors, other public ministers and consuls; to all cases of admiralty and maritime jurisdiction; to controversies to which the United States shall be a party; to controversies between two or more states; ~~between a state and citizens of another state;~~ between citizens of the same state claiming lands under grants of different states, and between a state or the citizens thereof, and foreign states, citizens, or subjects.

2. **The Supreme Court** In all cases affecting ambassadors, other public ministers and consuls, and those in which a state shall be a party, the Supreme Court shall have original jurisdiction. In all the other cases before mentioned, the Supreme Court shall have appellate jurisdiction, both as to law and fact, with such exceptions, and under such regulations as the Congress shall make.

Clause 1 *Jurisdiction* refers to the right of a court to hear a case. Federal courts have jurisdiction over cases that involve the Constitution, federal laws, treaties, foreign ambassadors and diplomats, naval and maritime laws, disagreements between states or between citizens from different states, and disputes between a state or citizen and a foreign state or citizen.

In *Marbury* v. *Madison,* the Supreme Court established the right to judge whether or not a law is constitutional.

Clause 2 *Original jurisdiction* means the power of a court to hear a case where it first arises. The Supreme Court has original jurisdiction over only a few cases, such as those involving foreign diplomats. More often, the Supreme Court acts as an appellate court. An *appellate court* does not decide guilt. It decides whether the lower court trial was properly conducted and reviews the lower court's decision.

3. Trial by Jury   The trial of all crimes, except in cases of impeachment, shall be by jury; and such trial shall be held in the state where the said crimes shall have been committed; but when not committed within any state, the trial shall be at such place or places as the Congress may by law have directed.

Section 3. Treason

1. Definition   Treason against the United States shall consist only in levying war against them, or in adhering to their enemies, giving them aid and comfort. No person shall be convicted of treason unless on the testimony of two witnesses to the same overt act, or on confession in open court.

2. Punishment   The Congress shall have power to declare the punishment of treason, but no attainder of treason shall work corruption of blood or forfeiture except during the life of the person attainted.

Article 4. Relations Among the States

Section 1. Official Records and Acts

Full faith and credit shall be given in each state to the public acts, records, and judicial proceedings of every other state. And the Congress may by general laws prescribe the manner in which such acts, records, and proceedings shall be proved, and the effect thereof.

Section 2. Privileges of Citizens

1. Privileges   The citizens of each state shall be entitled to all privileges and immunities of citizens in the several states.

2. Extradition   A person charged in any state with treason, felony, or other crime, who shall flee from justice, and be found in another state, shall on demand of the executive authority of the state from which he fled, be delivered up, to be removed to the state having jurisdiction of the crime.

3. Return of Fugitive Slaves   ~~No person held to service or labor in one state, under the laws thereof, escaping into another, shall in consequence of any law or regulation therein, be discharged from such service or labor, but shall be delivered up on claim of the party to whom such service or labor may be due.~~

Section 3. New States and Territories

1. New States   New states may be admitted by the Congress into this Union; but no new state shall be formed or erected within the jurisdiction of any other state; nor any state be formed by the junction of two of more states, or parts of states, without the consent of the legislatures of the states concerned as well as of the Congress.

2. Federal Lands   The Congress shall have power to dispose of and make all needful rules and regulations respecting the territory or other property belonging to the United States; and nothing in this Constitution shall be so construed as to prejudice any claims of the United States, or of any particular state.

---

3 This clause guarantees ... a jury trial for anyone ...sed of a federal crime. The only exceptions are impeachment cases. The trial must be held in the state where the crime was committed.

Clause 1 Treason is clearly defined. An *overt act* is an actual action. A person cannot be convicted of treason for what he or she thinks. A person can be convicted of treason only if he or she confesses or two witnesses testify to it.

Clause 2 Congress has the power to set the punishment for traitors. Congress may not punish the children of convicted traitors by taking away their civil rights or property.

Each state must recognize the official acts and records of any other state. For example, each state must recognize marriage certificates issued by another state. Congress can pass laws to ensure this.

Clause 1   All states must treat citizens of another state in the same way it treats its own citizens. However, the courts have allowed states to give residents certain privileges, such as lower tuition rates.

Clause 2 *Extradition* means the act of returning a suspected criminal or escaped prisoner to a state where he or she is wanted. State governors must return a suspect. However, the Supreme Court has ruled that governors cannot be forced to do so if they feel that justice will not be done.

Clause 3 *Persons held to service or labor* refers to slaves or indentured servants. This clause required states to return runaway slaves to their owners. The Thirteenth Amendment replaces this clause.

Clause 1 Congress has the power to admit new states to the Union. Existing states cannot be split up or joined together to form new states unless both Congress and the state legislatures approve. New states are equal to all other states.

Clause 2 Congress can make rules for managing and governing land owned by the United States. This includes territories not organized into states, such as Puerto Rico, and federal lands within a state.

The Federal System

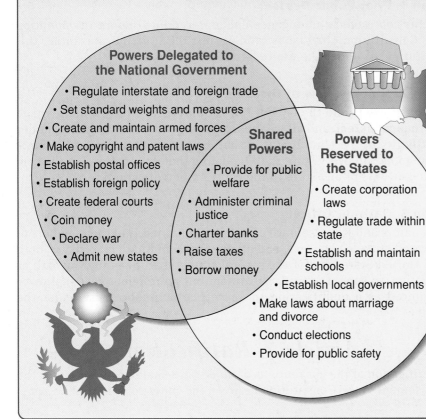

Powers Delegated to the National Government
- Regulate interstate and foreign trade
- Set standard weights and measures
- Create and maintain armed forces
- Make copyright and patent laws
- Establish postal offices
- Establish foreign policy
- Create federal courts
- Coin money
- Declare war
- Admit new states

Shared Powers
- Provide for public welfare
- Administer criminal justice
- Charter banks
- Raise taxes
- Borrow money

Powers Reserved to the States
- Create corporation laws
- Regulate trade within state
- Establish and maintain schools
- Establish local governments
- Make laws about marriage and divorce
- Conduct elections
- Provide for public safety

GRAPHIC ORGANIZER
Skills

Federalism is the distribution of power between the national government and the state governments.

1. **Comprehension**
   (a) Name two powers reserved to the states.
   (b) Name two powers shared by the national and state governments.

2. **Critical Thinking**
   Applying Information
   Why do you think the power to create and maintain the armed forces was delegated to the national government?

Civics

Section 4. Guarantees to the States

The United States shall guarantee to every state in this Union a republican form of government, and shall protect each of them against invasion; and on application of the legislature, or of the executive (when the legislature cannot be convened) against domestic violence.

In a *republic*, voters choose representatives to govern them. The federal government must protect the states from foreign invasion and from *domestic*, or internal, disorder if asked to do so by a state.

Article 5. Amending the Constitution

The Congress, whenever two-thirds of both houses shall deem it necessary, shall propose amendments to this Constitution, or, on the application of the legislatures of two-thirds of the several states, shall call a convention for proposing amendments, which, in either case, shall be valid to all intents and purposes, as part of this Constitution, when ratified by the legislatures of three-fourths of the several states, or by conventions in three-fourths thereof, as the one or the other mode of ratification may be proposed by the Congress; provided that ~~no amendments which may be made prior to the year 1808 shall in any manner affect the first and fourth clauses in the Ninth Section of the First Article; and that~~ no state, without its consent, shall be deprived of its equal suffrage in the Senate.

The Constitution can be *amended*, or changed, if necessary. An amendment can be proposed by (1) a two-thirds vote of both houses of Congress or (2) a national convention called by Congress at the request of two thirds of the state legislatures. (This second method has never been used.) An amendment must be *ratified*, or approved, by (1) three fourths of the state legislatures or (2) special conventions in three fourths of the states. Congress decides which method will be used.

Article 6. National Supremacy

Section 1. Prior Public Debts

The United States government promised to pay all debts and honor all agreements made under the Articles of Confederation.

All debts contracted and engagements entered into, before the adoption of this Constitution, shall be as valid against the United States under this Constitution, as under the Confederation.

Section 2. Supreme Law of the Land

The Constitution, federal laws, and treaties that the Senate has ratified are the supreme, or highest, law of the land. Thus, they outweigh state laws. A state judge must overturn a state law that conflicts with the Constitution or with a federal law.

This Constitution, and the laws of the United States which shall be made in pursuance thereof, and all treaties made, or which shall be made, under the authority of the United States, shall be the supreme law of the land; and the judges in every state shall be bound thereby, anything in the constitution or laws of any state to the contrary notwithstanding.

Section 3. Oaths of Office

State and federal officeholders take an oath, or solemn promise, to support the Constitution. However, this clause forbids the use of religious tests for officeholders. During the colonial period, every colony except Rhode Island required a religious test for officeholders.

The Senators and Representatives before mentioned, and the members of the several state legislatures, and all executive and judicial officers, both of the United States and of the several states, shall be bound by oath or affirmation, to support this Constitution; but no religious test shall ever be required as a qualification to any office or public trust under the United States.

Article 7. Ratification

During 1787 and 1788, states held special conventions. By October 1788, the required nine states had ratified the Constitution.

The ratification of the conventions of nine states shall be sufficient for the establishment of the Constitution between the states so ratifying the same.

Done in convention, by the unanimous consent of the states present, the seventeenth day of September, in the year of our Lord one thousand seven hundred and eighty-seven, and of the independence of the United States of America the twelfth. In Witness *whereof, we have hereunto subscribed our names.*

Attest: William Jackson
Secretary

George Washington
President and deputy from Virginia

New Hampshire
John Langdon
Nicholas Gilman

Massachussetts
Nathaniel Gorham
Rufus King

Connecticut
William Samuel
 Johnson
Roger Sherman

New York
Alexander Hamilton

New Jersey
William Livingston
David Brearley
William Paterson
Jonathan Dayton

Pennsylvania
Benjamin Franklin
Thomas Mifflin
Robert Morris
George Clymer
Thomas FitzSimons
Jared Ingersoll
James Wilson
Gouverneur Morris

Delaware
George Read
Gunning Bedford, Jr.
John Dickinson
Richard Bassett
Jacob Broom

Maryland
James McHenry
Dan of St. Thomas
 Jennifer
Daniel Carroll

Virginia
John Blair
James Madison, Jr.

North Carolina
William Blount
Richard Dobbs Spaight
Hugh Williamson

South Carolina
John Rutledge
Charles Cotesworth
 Pinckney
Charles Pinckney
Pierce Butler

Georgia
William Few
Abraham Baldwin

Amendments to the Constitution

Amendment 1

Freedoms of Religion, Speech, Press, Assembly, and Petition

Congress shall make no law respecting an establishment of religion, or prohibiting the free exercise thereof; or abridging the freedom of speech, or of the press; or the right of the people peaceably to assemble, and to petition the government for a redress of grievances.

Congress cannot set up an established, or official, church or religion for the nation. During the colonial period, most colonies had established churches. However, the authors of the First Amendment wanted to keep government and religion separate.

Congress may not *abridge*, or limit, the freedom to speak and write freely. The government may not censor, or review, books and newspapers before they are printed. This amendment also protects the right to assemble, or hold public meetings. *Petition* means "ask." *Redress* means "to correct." *Grievances* are wrongs. The people have the right to ask the government for wrongs to be corrected.

Amendment 2

Right to Bear Arms

A well-regulated militia, being necessary to the security of a free state, the right of the people to keep and bear arms shall not be infringed.

Each state has the right to maintain a *militia,* an armed force for its own protection. Today, the militia is the National Guard. The national government and the states can and do regulate the private ownership and use of firearms.

Amendment 3

Lodging Troops in Private Homes

No soldier shall, in time of peace, be quartered in any house, without the consent of the owner; nor in time of war, but in a manner to be prescribed by law.

During the colonial period, the British quartered, or housed, soldiers in private homes without the permission of the owners. This amendment limits the government's right to use private homes to house soldiers.

Amendment 4

Search and Seizure

The right of the people to be secure in their persons, houses, papers, and effects, against unreasonable searches and seizures, shall not be violated; and no warrants shall issue but upon probable cause, supported by oath or affirmation, and particularly describing the place to be searched, and the persons or things to be seized.

This amendment protects Americans from unreasonable searches and seizures. Search and seizure are permitted only if a judge has issued a *warrant,* or written court order. A warrant is issued only if there is probable cause. This means an officer must show that it is probable, or likely, that the search will produce evidence of a crime. A search warrant must name the exact place to be searched and the things to be seized. In some cases, courts have ruled that searches can take place without a warrant. For example, police may search a person who is under arrest. However, evidence found during an unlawful search cannot be used in a trial.

This amendment protects the rights of the accused. **Capital crimes** are those that can be punished with death. **Infamous crimes** are those that can be punished with prison or loss of rights. The federal government must obtain an **indictment,** or formal accusation, from a **grand jury** to prosecute anyone for such crimes. A grand jury is a panel of between 12 and 23 citizens who decide if the government has enough evidence to justify a trial. This procedure prevents prosecution with little or no evidence of guilt. (Soldiers and the militia in wartime are not covered by this rule.)

Double jeopardy is forbidden. This means that a person cannot be tried twice for the same crime—unless a court sets aside a conviction because of a legal error. A person on trial cannot be forced to testify, or give evidence, against himself or herself. A person accused of a crime is entitled to **due process of law,** or a fair hearing or trial. Finally, the government cannot seize private property for public use without paying the owner a fair price for it.

In criminal cases, the jury must be **impartial,** or not favor either side. The accused is guaranteed the right to a trial by jury. The trial must be speedy. If the government purposely postpones the trial so that it becomes hard for the person to get a fair hearing, the charge may be dismissed. The accused must be told the charges against him or her and be allowed to question prosecution witnesses. Witnesses who can help the accused can be ordered to appear in court.

The accused must be allowed a lawyer. Since 1942, the federal government has been required to provide a lawyer if the accused cannot afford one. In 1963, the Supreme Court decided that states must also provide lawyers for a defendant too poor to pay for one.

Common law refers to rules of law established by judges in past cases. This amendment guarantees the right to a jury trial in lawsuits where the sum of money at stake is more than $20. An appeals court cannot change a verdict because it disagrees with the decision of the jury. It can set aside a verdict only if legal errors made the trial unfair.

Bail is money the accused leaves with the court as a pledge to appear for trial. If the accused does not appear for trial, the court keeps the money. **Excessive** means too high. This amendment forbids courts to set unreasonably high bail. The amount of bail usually depends on the seriousness of the charge and whether the accused is likely to appear for the trial. The amendment also forbids cruel and unusual punishments such as mental and physical abuse.

Amendment 5

Rights of the Accused

No person shall be held to answer for a capital, or otherwise infamous, crime, unless on a presentment or indictment of a grand jury, except in cases arising in the land or naval forces, or in the militia, when in actual service in time of war or public danger; nor shall any person be subject for the same offense to be twice put in jeopardy of life and limb; nor shall be compelled, in any criminal case, to be a witness against himself; nor be deprived of life, liberty, or property, without due process of law; nor shall private property be taken for public use, without just compensation.

Amendment 6

Right to Speedy Trial by Jury

In all criminal prosecutions, the accused shall enjoy the right to a speedy and public trial, by an impartial jury of the state and district wherein the crime shall have been committed, which district shall have been previously ascertained by law, and to be informed of the nature and cause of the accusation; to be confronted with the witnesses against him; to have compulsory process for obtaining witnesses in his favor, and to have the assistance of counsel for his defense.

Amendment 7

Jury Trial in Civil Cases

In suits at common law, where the value in controversy shall exceed $20, the right of trial by jury shall be preserved, and no fact tried by a jury shall be otherwise re-examined in any court of the United States than according to the rules of the common law.

Amendment 8

Bail and Punishment

Excessive bail shall not be required, nor excessive fines imposed, nor cruel and unusual punishments inflicted.

Amendment 9

Powers Reserved to the People

The enumeration in the Constitution, of certain rights, shall not be construed to deny or disparage others retained by the people.

People have rights not listed in the Constitution. This amendment was added because some people feared that the Bill of Rights would be used to limit rights to those actually listed.

Amendment 10

Powers Reserved to the States

The powers not delegated to the United States by the Constitution, nor prohibited by it to the states, are reserved to the states respectively, or to the people.

This amendment limits the power of the federal government. Powers that are not given to the federal government belong to the states. The powers reserved to the states are not listed in the Constitution.

Amendment 11

Suits Against States

Passed by Congress on March 4, 1794. Ratified on January 23, 1795.

The judicial power of the United States shall not be construed to extend to any suit in law or equity, commenced or prosecuted against one of the United States, by citizens of another state, or by citizens or subjects of any foreign state.

This amendment changed part of Article 3, Section 2, Clause 1. As a result, a private citizen from one state cannot sue the government of another state in federal court. However, a citizen can sue a state government in a state court.

Amendment 12

Election of President and Vice-President

Passed by Congress on December 9, 1803. Ratified on June 15, 1804.

The electors shall meet in their respective states, and vote by ballot for President and Vice-President, one of whom, at least, shall not be an inhabitant of the same state with themselves; they shall name in their ballots the person voted for as President, and in distinct ballots the person voted for as Vice-President, and they shall make distinct lists of all persons voted for as President, and of all persons voted for as Vice-President, and of the number of votes for each, which lists they shall sign and certify, and transmit, sealed, to the seat of government of the United States, directed to the President of the Senate; the President of the Senate shall, in the presence of the Senate and House of Representatives, open all the certificates and the votes shall then be counted; the person having the greatest number of votes for President shall be the President, if such number be a majority of the whole number of electors appointed; and if no person have such majority, then from the persons having the highest numbers not exceeding three on the list of those voted for as President, the House of Representatives shall choose immediately, by ballot, the President. But in choosing the President, the votes shall be taken by the states, the representation from each state having one vote; a quorum for this purpose shall consist of a member or members from two-thirds of the states, and a majority of all the states shall be necessary to a choice. And if the House of Representatives shall not choose a President whenever the right of choice shall devolve upon them, before the fourth day of March next following, then the Vice-President shall act as President, as in the case of the death or other constitutional disability of the President. The person having the greatest number of votes as Vice-President, shall be the Vice-President, if such number be a majority of the whole

This amendment changed the way the electoral college voted. Before the amendment was adopted, each elector simply voted for two people. The candidate with the most votes became President. The runner-up became Vice President. In the election of 1800, however, a tie vote resulted between Thomas Jefferson and Aaron Burr.

In such a case, the Constitution required the House of Representatives to elect the President. Federalists had a majority in the House. They tried to keep Jefferson out of office by voting for Burr. It took 35 ballots in the House before Jefferson was elected President.

To keep this from happening again, the Twelfth Amendment was passed and ratified in time for the election of 1804.

This amendment provides that each elector choose one candidate for President and one candidate for Vice President. If no candidate for President receives a majority of electoral votes, the House of Representatives chooses the President. If no candidate for Vice President receives a majority, the Senate elects the Vice President. The Vice President must be a person who is eligible to be President.

This system is still in use today. However, it is possible for a candidate to win the popular vote and lose in the electoral college. This happened in 1876 and again in 2000.

number of electors appointed, and if no person have a majority, then, from the two highest numbers on the list, the Senate shall choose the Vice-President; a quorum for the purpose shall consist of two-thirds of the whole number of Senators, and a majority of the whole number shall be necessary to a choice. But no person constitutionally ineligible to the office of President shall be eligible to that of Vice-President of the United States.

Amendment 13

Abolition of Slavery

Passed by Congress on January 31, 1865. Ratified on December 6, 1865.

Section 1. Neither slavery nor involuntary servitude, except as a punishment for crime whereof the party shall have been duly convicted, shall exist within the United States, or any place subject to their jurisdiction.

Section 2. Congress shall have power to enforce this article by appropriate legislation.

Amendment 14

Rights of Citizens

Passed by Congress on June 13, 1866. Ratified on July 9, 1868.

Section 1. Citizenship All persons born or naturalized in the United States and subject to the jurisdiction thereof, are citizens of the United States and of the state wherein they reside. No state shall make or enforce any law which shall abridge the privileges or immunities of citizens of the United States; nor shall any state deprive any person of life, liberty, or property, without due process of law; nor deny to any person within its jurisdiction the equal protection of the laws.

The Emancipation Proclamation (1863) freed slaves only in areas controlled by the Confederacy. This amendment freed all slaves. It also forbids *involuntary servitude,* or labor done against one's will. However, it does not prevent prison wardens from making prisoners work.
 Section 2 says that Congress can pass laws to carry out this amendment.

Section 1 defines citizenship for the first time in the Constitution, and it extends citizenship to blacks. It also prohibits states from denying the rights and privileges of citizenship to any citizen. This section also forbids states to deny due process of law.
 Section 1 guarantees all citizens "equal protection under the law." For a long time, however, the Fourteenth Amendment did not protect blacks from discrimination. After Reconstruction, separate facilities for blacks and whites sprang up. In 1954, the Supreme Court ruled that separate facilities for blacks and whites were by their nature unequal. This ruling, in the case of *Brown* v. *Board of Education,* made school segregation illegal.

 Section 2 replaced the three-fifths clause. It provides that representation in the House of Representatives is decided on the basis of the number of people in the state. It also provides that states which deny the vote to male citizens over age 21 will be punished by losing part of their representation in the House. This provision has never been enforced.
 Despite this clause, black citizens were often prevented from voting. In the 1960s, federal laws were passed to end voting discrimination.

Section 2. Apportionment of Representatives Representatives shall be apportioned among the several states according to their respective numbers, counting the whole number of persons in each state, excluding Indians not taxed. But when the right to vote at any election for the choice of electors for President and Vice-President of the United States, Representatives in Congress, the executive and judicial officers of a state, or the members of the legislature thereof, is denied to any of the male inhabitants of such state, being twenty-one years of age and citizens of the United States, or in any way abridged, except for participation in rebellion, or other crime, the basis of representation therein shall be reduced in the proportion which the number of such male citizens shall bear to the whole number of male citizens twenty-one years of age in such state.

This section prohibited people who had been federal or state officials before the Civil War and joined the Confederate cause from serving again as government officials. In 1872, Congress restored the rights of former Confederate officials.

Section 3. Former Confederate Officials No person shall be a Senator or Representative in Congress, or elector of President and Vice-President, or hold any office, civil or military, under the United States, or under any state, who, having previously taken an oath, as a member of Congress, or as an officer of the United

States, or as a member of any state legislature, or as an executive or judicial officer of any state, to support the Constitution of the United States, shall have engaged in insurrection or rebellion against the same, or given aid or comfort to the enemies thereof. But Congress may, by vote of two-thirds of each house, remove such disability.

Section 4. Government Debt The validity of the public debt of the United States, authorized by law, including debts incurred for payment of pensions and bounties for services in suppressing insurrection or rebellion, shall not be questioned. But neither the United States nor any state shall assume or pay any debt or obligation incurred in aid of insurrection or rebellion against the United States or any claim for the loss or emancipation of any slave; but all such debts, obligations, and claims shall be held illegal and void.

This section recognized that the United States must repay its debts from the Civil War. However, it forbade the repayment of debts of the Confederacy. This meant that people who had loaned money to the Confederacy would not be repaid. Also, states were not allowed to pay former slave owners for the loss of slaves.

Section 5. Enforcement The Congress shall have power to enforce, by appropriate legislation, the provisions of this article.

Congress can pass laws to carry out this amendment.

Amendment 15

Voting Rights
Passed by Congress on February 26, 1869. Ratified on February 2, 1870.

Section 1. Extending the Right to Vote The right of citizens of the United States to vote shall not be denied or abridged by the United States or any state on account of race, color, or previous condition of servitude.

Previous condition of servitude refers to slavery. This amendment gave blacks, both former slaves and free blacks, the right to vote. In the late 1800s, southern states used grandfather clauses, literacy tests, and poll taxes to keep blacks from voting.

Section 2. Enforcement The Congress shall have power to enforce this article by appropriate legislation.

Congress can pass laws to carry out this amendment. The Twenty-fourth Amendment barred the use of poll taxes in national elections. The Voting Rights Act of 1965 gave federal officials the power to register voters in places where there was voting discrimination.

Amendment 16

The Income Tax
Passed by Congress on July 12, 1909. Ratified on February 3, 1913.

The Congress shall have power to lay and collect taxes on incomes, from whatever source derived, without apportionment among the several states, and without regard to any census or enumeration.

Congress has the power to collect taxes on people's income. An income tax can be collected without regard to a state's population. This amendment changed Article 1, Section 9, Clause 4.

Amendment 17

Direct Election of Senators
Passed by Congress on May 13, 1912. Ratified on April 8, 1913.

Section 1. Method of Election The Senate of the United States shall be composed of two Senators from each state, elected by the people thereof, for six years; and each Senator shall have one vote. The electors in each state shall have the qualifications requisite for electors of the most numerous branch of the state legislatures.

This amendment replaced Article 1, Section 3, Clause 1. Before it was adopted, state legislatures chose senators. This amendment provides that senators are directly elected by the people of each state.

Section 2. Vacancies When vacancies happen in the representation of any state in the Senate, the executive authority of such state shall issue writs of election to fill such vacancies: *Provided* that the legislature of any state may empower the executive thereof to make temporary appointments until the people fill the vacancies by election as the legislature may direct.

When a Senate seat becomes vacant, the governor of the state must order an election to fill the seat. The state legislature can give the governor power to fill the seat until an election is held.

Senators who had already been elected by the state legislatures were not affected by this amendment.

This amendment, known as **Prohibition,** banned the making, selling, or transporting of alcoholic beverages in the United States. Later, the Twenty-first Amendment **repealed,** or canceled, this amendment.

Both the states and the federal government had the power to pass laws to enforce this amendment.

This amendment had to be approved within seven years. The Eighteenth Amendment was the first amendment to include a time limit for ratification.

Neither the federal government nor state governments can deny the right to vote on account of sex. Thus, women won **suffrage,** or the right to vote. Before 1920, some states had allowed women to vote in state elections.

Congress can pass laws to carry out this amendment.

The date for the President and Vice President to take office is January 20. Members of Congress begin their terms of office on January 3. Before this amendment was adopted, these terms of office began on March 4.

Congress must meet at least once a year. The new session of Congress begins on January 3. Before this amendment, members of Congress who had been defeated in November continued to hold office until the following March. Such members were known as **lame ducks.**

By Section 3, if the President-elect dies before taking office, the Vice President–elect becomes President. If no President has been chosen by January 20 or if the elected candidate fails to qualify for office, the Vice President–elect acts as President, but only until a qualified President is chosen.

Section 3. Exception   ~~This amendment shall not be so construed as to affect the election or term of any Senator chosen before it becomes valid as part of the Constitution.~~

Amendment 18

Prohibition of Alcoholic Beverages

Passed by Congress on December 18, 1917. Ratified on January 16, 1919.

Section 1. Ban on Alcohol   ~~After one year from the ratification of this article the manufacture, sale, or transportation of intoxicating liquors within, the importation thereof into, or the exportation thereof from, the United States and all territory subject to the jurisdiction thereof for beverage purposes is hereby prohibited.~~

Section 2. Enforcement   ~~The Congress and the several states shall have concurrent power to enforce this article by appropriate legislation.~~

Section 3. Method of Ratification   ~~This article shall be inoperative unless it shall have been ratified as an amendment to the Constitution by the legislatures of the several states, as provided in the Constitution, within seven years from the date of the submission hereof to the states by the Congress.~~

Amendment 19

Women's Suffrage

Passed by Congress on June 4, 1919. Ratified on August 18, 1920.

Section 1. The Right to Vote   The right of citizens of the United States to vote shall not be denied or abridged by the United States or by any state on account of sex.

Section 2. Enforcement   Congress shall have power to enforce this article by appropriate legislation.

Amendment 20

Presidential Terms; Sessions of Congress

Passed by Congress on March 2, 1932. Ratified on January 23, 1933.

Section 1. Beginning of Term   The terms of the President and Vice-President shall end at noon on the 20th day of January, and the terms of Senators and Representatives at noon on the 3rd day of January, of the years in which such terms would have ended if this article had not been ratified; and the terms of their successors shall then begin.

Section 2. Congressional Sessions   The Congress shall assemble at least once in every year, and such meeting shall begin at noon on the 3rd day of January, unless they shall by law appoint a different day.

Section 3. Presidential Succession   If at the time fixed for the beginning of the term of the President, the President-elect shall have died, the Vice-President-elect shall become President. If a President shall not have been chosen before the time fixed for the beginning of his term, or if the President-elect shall have failed to qualify, then the Vice-President-elect shall act as President until a President shall have qualified; and the Congress may by law provide for the case wherein neither a President-elect nor a Vice-President-elect shall have qualified, declaring who shall then act as President, or the manner in which one who is to act shall be selected, and such person shall act accordingly until a President or Vice-President shall have qualified.

Section 4. Elections Decided by Congress The Congress may by law provide for the case of the death of any of the persons from whom the House of Representatives may choose a President whenever the right of choice shall have devolved upon them, and for the case of the death of any of the persons from whom the Senate may choose a Vice-President whenever the right of choice shall have devolved upon them.

Section 5. Date of Effect ~~Sections 1 and 2 shall take effect on the 15th day of October following the ratification of this article.~~

Section 6. Ratification Period ~~This article shall be inoperative unless it shall have been ratified as an amendment to the Constitution by the legislatures of three fourths of the several states within seven years from the date of its submission.~~

Amendment 21

Repeal of Prohibition

Passed by Congress on February 20, 1933. Ratified on December 5, 1933.

Section 1. Repeal of National Prohibition The eighteenth article of amendment to the Constitution of the United States is hereby repealed.

Section 2. State Laws The transportation or importation into any state, territory, or possession of the United States for delivery or use therein of intoxicating liquors, in violation of the laws thereof, is hereby prohibited.

Section 3. Ratification Period ~~This article shall be inoperative unless it shall have been ratified as an amendment to the Constitution by conventions in the several states, as provided in the Constitution, within seven years from the date of the submission hereof to the states by the Congress.~~

Amendment 22

Limit on Number of President's Terms

Passed by Congress on March 12, 1947. Ratified on March 1, 1951.

Section 1. Two-Term Limit No person shall be elected to the office of the President more than twice, and no person who has held the office of President, or acted as President, for more than two years of a term to which some other person was elected President shall be elected to the office of the President more than once. ~~But this Article shall not apply to any person holding the office of President when this Article was proposed by the Congress, and shall not prevent any person who may be holding the office of President, or acting as President, during the term within which this Article becomes operative from holding the office of President or acting as President during the remainder of such term.~~

Finally, Congress can choose a person to act as President if neither the President-elect nor Vice President-elect is qualified to take office.

Congress can pass laws in cases where a presidential candidate dies while an election is being decided in the House. Congress has similar power in cases where a candidate for Vice President dies while an election is being decided in the Senate.

Section 5 sets the date for the amendment to become effective.

Section 6 sets a time limit for ratification.

The Eighteenth Amendment is repealed, making it legal to make and sell alcoholic beverages. Prohibition ended December 5, 1933.

Each state was free to ban the making and selling of alcoholic drink within its borders. This section makes bringing liquor into a "dry" state a federal offense.

Special state conventions were called to ratify this amendment. This is the only time an amendment was ratified by state conventions rather than state legislatures.

Before Franklin Roosevelt became President, no President served more than two terms in office. Roosevelt broke with this custom and was elected to four terms. This amendment provides that no President may serve more than two terms. A President who has already served more than half of someone else's term can serve only one more full term. However, the amendment did not apply to Harry Truman, who had become President after Franklin Roosevelt's death in 1945.

A seven-year time limit is set for ratification.

Amendment 23

Presidential Electors for District of Columbia

Passed by Congress on June 16, 1960. Ratified on April 3, 1961.

Section 1. Determining the Number of Electors The District constituting the seat of Government of the United States shall appoint in such manner as the Congress may direct: A number of electors of President and Vice-President equal to the whole number of Senators and Representatives in Congress to which the District would be entitled if it were a State, but in no event more than the least populous State; they shall be in addition to those appointed by the States, but they shall be considered, for the purposes of the election of President and Vice-President, to be electors appointed by a State; and they shall meet in the District and perform such duties as provided by the twelfth article of amendment.

This amendment gives residents of Washington, D.C., the right to vote in presidential elections. Until this amendment was adopted, people living in Washington, D.C., could not vote for President because the Constitution had made no provision for choosing electors from the nation's capital. Washington, D.C., has three electoral votes.

Congress can pass laws to carry out this amendment.

Section 2. Enforcement The Congress shall have power to enforce this article by appropriate legislation.

Amendment 24

Abolition of Poll Tax in National Elections

Passed by Congress on August 27, 1962. Ratified on January 23, 1964.

Section 1. Poll Tax Banned The right of citizens of the United States to vote in any primary or other election for President or Vice-President, for electors for President or Vice-President, or for Senator or Representative in Congress, shall not be denied or abridged by the United States or any state by reason of failure to pay any poll tax or other tax.

A *poll tax* is a tax on voters. This amendment bans poll taxes in national elections. Some states used poll taxes to keep blacks from voting. In 1966, the Supreme Court struck down poll taxes in state elections, also.

Congress can pass laws to carry out this amendment.

Section 2. Enforcement The Congress shall have the power to enforce this article by appropriate legislation.

Amendment 25

Presidential Succession and Disability

Passed by Congress on July 6, 1965. Ratified on February 11, 1967.

Section 1. President's Death or Resignation In case of the removal of the President from office or his death or resignation, the Vice-President shall become President.

If the President dies or resigns, the Vice President becomes President. This section clarifies Article 2, Section 1, Clause 6.

When a Vice President takes over the office of President, he or she appoints a Vice President who must be approved by a majority vote of both houses of Congress. This section was first applied after Vice President Spiro Agnew resigned in 1973. President Richard Nixon appointed Gerald Ford as Vice President.

Section 2. Vacancies in Vice-Presidency Whenever there is a vacancy in the office of the Vice-President, the President shall nominate a Vice-President who shall take the office upon confirmation by a majority vote of both houses of Congress.

Section 3. Disability of the President   Whenever the President transmits to the President *pro tempore* of the Senate and the Speaker of the House of Representatives his written declaration that he is unable to discharge the powers and duties of his office, and until he transmits to them a written declaration to the contrary, such powers and duties shall be discharged by the Vice-President as Acting President.

If the President declares in writing that he or she is unable to perform the duties of office, the Vice President serves as Acting President until the President recovers.

Section 4.   Whenever the Vice-President and a majority of either the principal officers of the executive departments or of such other body as Congress may by law provide, transmit to the President *pro tempore* of the Senate and the Speaker of the House of Representatives their written declaration that the President is unable to discharge the powers and duties of his office, the Vice-President shall immediately assume the powers and duties of the office as Acting President.

Thereafter, when the President transmits to the President *pro tempore* of the Senate and the Speaker of the House of Representatives his written declaration that no inability exists, he shall resume the powers and duties of his office unless the Vice-President and a majority of either the principal officers of the executive department or of such other body as Congress may by law provide, transmit within four days to the President *as* of the Senate and the Speaker of the House of Representatives their written declaration that the President is unable to discharge the powers and duties of his office. Thereupon Congress shall decide the issue, assembling within 48 hours for that purpose if not in session. If the Congress, within 21 days after receipt of the latter written declaration, or, if Congress is not in session, within 21 days after Congress is required to assemble, determines by two-thirds vote of both houses that the President is unable to discharge the powers and duties of his office, the Vice-President shall continue to discharge the same as Acting President; otherwise, the President shall assume the powers and duties of his office.

Two Presidents, Woodrow Wilson and Dwight Eisenhower, have fallen gravely ill while in office. The Constitution contained no provision for this kind of emergency.
 Section 3 provided that the President can inform Congress that he or she is too sick to perform the duties of office. However, if the President is unconscious or refuses to admit to a disabling illness, Section 4 provides that the Vice President and Cabinet may declare the President disabled. The Vice President becomes Acting President until the President can return to the duties of office. In case of a disagreement between the President and the Vice President and Cabinet over the President's ability to perform the duties of office, Congress must decide the issue. A two-thirds vote of both houses is needed to decide that the President is disabled or unable to fulfill the duties of office.

Amendment 26

Voting Age
Passed by Congress on March 23, 1971. Ratified on July 1, 1971.

Section 1. Lowering of Voting Age   The right of citizens of the United States, who are 18 years of age or older, to vote shall not be denied or abridged by the United States or any state on account of age.

In 1970, Congress passed a law allowing 18-year-olds to vote. However, the Supreme Court decided that Congress could not set a minimum age for state elections. So this amendment was passed and ratified.

Section 2. Enforcement   The Congress shall have the power to enforce this article by appropriate legislation.

Congress can pass laws to carry out this amendment.

Amendment 27

Congressional Pay Increases
Proposed by Congress on September 25, 1789. Ratified on May 7, 1992.

No law varying the compensation for the services of the Senators and Representatives shall take effect, until an election of Representatives shall have intervened.

If members of Congress vote themselves a pay increase, it cannot go into effect until after the next congressional election.

Presidents of the United States

1 George Washington (1732–1799)

Years in office:
1789–1797
Party:
none
Elected from:
Virginia
Vice President:
John Adams

2 John Adams (1735–1826)

Years in office:
1797–1801
Party:
Federalist
Elected from:
Massachusetts
Vice President:
Thomas
    Jefferson

3 Thomas Jefferson (1743–1826)

Years in office:
1801–1809
Party:
Democratic
    Republican
Elected from:
Virginia
Vice President:
1) Aaron Burr,
2) George Clinton

4 James Madison (1751–1836)

Years in office:
1809–1817
Party:
Democratic
    Republican
Elected from:
Virginia
Vice President:
1) George Clinton,
2) Elbridge Gerry

5 James Monroe (1758–1831)

Years in office:
1817–1825
Party:
Democratic
    Republican
Elected from:
Virginia
Vice President:
Daniel Tompkins

6 John Quincy Adams (1767–1848)

Years in office:
1825–1829
Party:
National
    Republican
Elected from:
Massachusetts
Vice President:
John Calhoun

7 Andrew Jackson (1767–1845)

Years in office:
1829–1837
Party:
Democratic
Elected from:
Tennessee
Vice President:
1) John Calhoun,
2) Martin Van
    Buren

8 Martin Van Buren (1782–1862)

Years in office:
1837–1841
Party:
Democratic
Elected from:
New York
Vice President:
Richard Johnson

9 William Henry Harrison* (1773–1841)

Years in office:
1841
Party:
Whig
Elected from:
Ohio
Vice President:
John Tyler

10 John Tyler (1790–1862)

Years in office:
1841–1845
Party:
Whig
Elected from:
Virginia
Vice President:
none

11 James K. Polk (1795–1849)

Years in office:
1845–1849
Party:
Democratic
Elected from:
Tennessee
Vice President:
George Dallas

12 Zachary Taylor* (1784–1850)

Years in office:
1849–1850
Party:
Whig
Elected from:
Louisiana
Vice President:
Millard Fillmore

*Died in office

13 Millard Fillmore (1800–1874)

Years in office:
1850–1853
Party:
Whig
Elected from:
New York
Vice President:
none

14 Franklin Pierce (1804–1869)

Years in office:
1853–1857
Party:
Democratic
Elected from:
New Hampshire
Vice President:
William King

15 James Buchanan (1791–1868)

Years in office:
1857–1861
Party:
Democratic
Elected from:
Pennsylvania
Vice President:
John Breckinridge

16 Abraham Lincoln** (1809–1865)

Years in office:
1861–1865
Party:
Republican
Elected from:
Illinois
Vice President:
1) Hannibal
   Hamlin,
2) Andrew
   Johnson

17 Andrew Johnson (1808–1875)

Years in office:
1865–1869
Party:
Republican
Elected from:
Tennessee
Vice President:
none

18 Ulysses S. Grant (1822–1885)

Years in office:
1869–1877
Party:
Republican
Elected from:
Illinois
Vice President:
1) Schuyler
   Colfax,
2) Henry Wilson

19 Rutherford B. Hayes (1822–1893)

Years in office:
1877–1881
Party:
Republican
Elected from:
Ohio
Vice President:
William Wheeler

20 James A. Garfield** (1831–1881)

Years in office:
1881
Party:
Republican
Elected from:
Ohio
Vice President:
Chester A. Arthur

21 Chester A. Arthur (1829–1886)

Years in office:
1881–1885
Party:
Republican
Elected from:
New York
Vice President:
none

22 Grover Cleveland (1837–1908)

Years in office:
1885–1889
Party:
Democratic
Elected from:
New York
Vice President:
Thomas
   Hendricks

23 Benjamin Harrison (1833–1901)

Years in office:
1889–1893
Party:
Republican
Elected from:
Indiana
Vice President:
Levi Morton

24 Grover Cleveland (1837–1908)

Years in office:
1893–1897
Party:
Democratic
Elected from:
New York
Vice President:
Adlai Stevenson

**Assassinated

25 William McKinley** (1843–1901)

Years in office:
1897–1901
Party:
Republican
Elected from:
Ohio
Vice President:
1) Garret Hobart,
2) Theodore Roosevelt

26 Theodore Roosevelt (1858–1919)

Years in office:
1901–1909
Party:
Republican
Elected from:
New York
Vice President:
Charles Fairbanks

27 William Howard Taft (1857–1930)

Years in office:
1909–1913
Party:
Republican
Elected from:
Ohio
Vice President:
James Sherman

28 Woodrow Wilson (1856–1924)

Years in office:
1913–1921
Party:
Democratic
Elected from:
New Jersey
Vice President:
Thomas Marshall

29 Warren G. Harding* (1865–1923)

Years in office:
1921–1923
Party:
Republican
Elected from:
Ohio
Vice President:
Calvin Coolidge

30 Calvin Coolidge (1872–1933)

Years in office:
1923–1929
Party:
Republican
Elected from:
Massachusetts
Vice President:
Charles Dawes

31 Herbert C. Hoover (1874–1964)

Years in office:
1929–1933
Party:
Republican
Elected from:
California
Vice President:
Charles Curtis

32 Franklin D. Roosevelt* (1882–1945)

Years in office:
1933–1945
Party:
Democratic
Elected from:
New York
Vice President:
1) John Garner,
2) Henry Wallace,
3) Harry S Truman

33 Harry S Truman (1884–1972)

Years in office:
1945–1953
Party:
Democratic
Elected from:
Missouri
Vice President:
Alben Barkley

34 Dwight D. Eisenhower (1890–1969)

Years in office:
1953–1961
Party:
Republican
Elected from:
New York
Vice President:
Richard M. Nixon

35 John F. Kennedy** (1917–1963)

Years in office:
1961–1963
Party:
Democratic
Elected from:
Massachusetts
Vice President:
Lyndon B. Johnson

36 Lyndon B. Johnson (1908–1973)

Years in office:
1963–1969
Party:
Democratic
Elected from:
Texas
Vice President:
Hubert Humphrey

*Died in office
**Assassinated

37 Richard M. Nixon*** (1913–1994)

Years in office:
1969–1974
Party:
Republican
Elected from:
New York
Vice President:
1) Spiro Agnew,
2) Gerald R. Ford

38 Gerald R. Ford (b. 1913)

Years in office:
1974–1977
Party:
Republican
Appointed from:
Michigan
Vice President:
Nelson
  Rockefeller

39 Jimmy Carter (b. 1924)

Years in office:
1977–1981
Party:
Democratic
Elected from:
Georgia
Vice President:
Walter Mondale

40 Ronald W. Reagan (b. 1911)

Years in office:
1981–1989
Party:
Republican
Elected from:
California
Vice President:
George H.W.
  Bush

41 George H.W. Bush (b. 1924)

Years in office:
1989–1993
Party:
Republican
Elected from:
Texas
Vice President:
J. Danforth
  Quayle

42 William J. Clinton (b. 1946)

Years in office:
1993–2001
Party:
Democratic
Elected from:
Arkansas
Vice President:
Albert Gore, Jr.

43 George W. Bush (b. 1946)

Years in office:
2001–
Party:
Republican
Elected from:
Texas
Vice President:
Richard Cheney

***Resigned

The Fifty States

State	Date of Entry to Union (Order of Entry)	Land Area in Square Miles	Population (In Thousands)	Number of Representatives in House*	Capital	Largest City
Alabama	1819 (22)	50,750	4,447	7	Montgomery	Birmingham
Alaska	1959 (49)	570,374	627	1	Juneau	Anchorage
Arizona	1912 (48)	113,642	5,131	8	Phoenix	Phoenix
Arkansas	1836 (25)	52,075	2,673	4	Little Rock	Little Rock
California	1850 (31)	155,973	33,872	53	Sacramento	Los Angeles
Colorado	1876 (38)	103,730	4,301	7	Denver	Denver
Connecticut	1788 (5)	4,845	3,406	5	Hartford	Bridgeport
Delaware	1787 (1)	1,955	784	1	Dover	Wilmington
Florida	1845 (27)	53,997	15,982	25	Tallahassee	Jacksonville
Georgia	1788 (4)	57,919	8,186	13	Atlanta	Atlanta
Hawaii	1959 (50)	6,423	1,212	2	Honolulu	Honolulu
Idaho	1890 (43)	82,751	1,294	2	Boise	Boise
Illinois	1818 (21)	55,593	12,419	19	Springfield	Chicago
Indiana	1816 (19)	35,870	6,080	9	Indianapolis	Indianapolis
Iowa	1846 (29)	55,875	2,926	5	Des Moines	Des Moines
Kansas	1861 (34)	81,823	2,688	4	Topeka	Wichita
Kentucky	1792 (15)	39,732	4,042	6	Frankfort	Louisville
Louisiana	1812 (18)	43,566	4,469	7	Baton Rouge	New Orleans
Maine	1820 (23)	30,865	1,275	2	Augusta	Portland
Maryland	1788 (7)	9,775	5,296	8	Annapolis	Baltimore
Massachusetts	1788 (6)	7,838	6,349	10	Boston	Boston
Michigan	1837 (26)	56,809	9,938	15	Lansing	Detroit
Minnesota	1858 (32)	79,617	4,919	8	St. Paul	Minneapolis
Mississippi	1817 (20)	46,914	2,845	4	Jackson	Jackson
Missouri	1821 (24)	68,898	5,595	9	Jefferson City	Kansas City
Montana	1889 (41)	145,556	902	1	Helena	Billings
Nebraska	1867 (37)	76,878	1,711	3	Lincoln	Omaha
Nevada	1864 (36)	109,806	1,998	3	Carson City	Las Vegas
New Hampshire	1788 (9)	8,969	1,236	2	Concord	Manchester
New Jersey	1787 (3)	7,419	8,414	13	Trenton	Newark
New Mexico	1912 (47)	121,365	1,819	3	Santa Fe	Albuquerque
New York	1788 (11)	47,224	18,976	29	Albany	New York
North Carolina	1789 (12)	48,718	8,049	13	Raleigh	Charlotte
North Dakota	1889 (39)	68,994	642	1	Bismarck	Fargo
Ohio	1803 (17)	40,953	11,353	18	Columbus	Columbus
Oklahoma	1907 (46)	68,679	3,451	5	Oklahoma City	Oklahoma City
Oregon	1859 (33)	96,003	3,421	5	Salem	Portland
Pennsylvania	1787 (2)	44,820	12,281	19	Harrisburg	Philadelphia
Rhode Island	1790 (13)	1,045	1,048	2	Providence	Providence
South Carolina	1788 (8)	30,111	4,012	6	Columbia	Columbia
South Dakota	1889 (40)	75,898	755	1	Pierre	Sioux Falls
Tennessee	1796 (16)	41,220	5,689	9	Nashville	Memphis
Texas	1845 (28)	261,914	20,852	32	Austin	Houston
Utah	1896 (45)	82,168	2,233	3	Salt Lake City	Salt Lake City
Vermont	1791 (14)	9,249	609	1	Montpelier	Burlington
Virginia	1788 (10)	39,598	7,079	11	Richmond	Virginia Beach
Washington	1889 (42)	66,582	5,894	9	Olympia	Seattle
West Virginia	1863 (35)	24,087	1,808	3	Charleston	Charleston
Wisconsin	1848 (30)	54,314	5,364	8	Madison	Milwaukee
Wyoming	1890 (44)	97,105	494	1	Cheyenne	Cheyenne
District of Columbia		61	572	1 (nonvoting)		

Self-Governing Areas, Possessions, and Dependencies	Land Area in Square Miles	Population (In Thousands)	Capital
Puerto Rico	3,515	809	San Juan
Guam	209	155	Agana
U.S. Virgin Islands	132	121	Charlotte Amalie
American Samoa	77	65	Pago Pago

Sources: Department of Commerce, Bureau of the Census   *As of 108th Congress.

State Flags

Alabama

Alaska

Arizona

Arkansas

California

Colorado

Connecticut

Delaware

Florida

Georgia

Hawaii

Idaho

Illinois

Indiana

Iowa

Kansas

Kentucky

Louisiana

Maine

Maryland

Massachusetts

Michigan

Minnesota

Mississippi

Missouri

Montana

Nebraska

Nevada

New Hampshire

New Jersey

New Mexico

New York

North Carolina

North Dakota

Ohio

Oklahoma

Oregon

Pennsylvania

Rhode Island

South Carolina

South Dakota

Tennessee

Texas

Utah

Vermont

Virginia

Washington

West Virginia

Wisconsin

Wyoming

The World: Political

Caribbean

Azimuthal Projection

0   150   300 Miles
0   150   300 Kilometers

Key

⊛ Capital

• Other city

Robinson Projection

0   1000   2000 Miles

0   1000   2000 Kilometers

Africa

Mercator Projection

0   250   500 Miles

0   250   500 Kilometers

Europe — Azimuthal Projection

0   250   500 Miles

0   250   500 Kilometers

* The United Kingdom, the official name of the country, is more often referred to as Great Britain.

United States: Political

CANADA

Pacific Time Zone
Mountain Time Zone
Central Time Zone

Seattle
Spokane •
Washington (1889)
Olympia ★

Portland •
★ Salem
Eugene •

Oregon (1859)

Great Falls •
Helena ★
Montana (1889)

Billings •

★ Boise
Idaho (1890)
Pocatello •

Minot •
Grand Forks •
North Dakota (1889)
★ Bismarck

South Dakota (1889)
★ Pierre

Rapid City •

Sioux Falls •

Wyoming (1890)
Casper •

Ogden •
Great Salt Lake
★ Salt Lake City

Reno •
★ Carson City
Nevada (1864)

San Francisco •
Oakland •
San Jose •
★ Sacramento

Utah (1896)

Cheyenne ★

★ Denver
Colorado (1876)
Colorado Springs •

Sioux City •

Nebraska (1867)
Omaha •
Lincoln •

Topeka ★

Kansas (1861)
Wichita •

California (1850)

Las Vegas •

Salton Sea
Los Angeles •
Long Beach •
San Diego •

Arizona (1912)

★ Phoenix

Tucson •

★ Santa Fe
Albuquerque •

New Mexico (1912)

Las Cruces •
El Paso •

Tulsa •

Oklahoma (1907)
Oklahoma City ★

Dallas •
Fort Worth •

Texas (1845)

★ Austin

San Antonio •

PACIFIC OCEAN

MEXICO

Hawaii–Aleutian Time Zone
Hawaii (1959)
Honolulu •

PACIFIC OCEAN

Mercator Projection
0   50   100 Miles
0 50 100 Kilometers

Hawaii–Aleutian Time Zone

PACIFIC OCEAN

RUSSIA

Alaska Time Zone
Alaska (1959)
Fairbanks •

Anchorage •

Pacific Time Zone
Mountain Time Zone

CANADA

Juneau •

Bering Sea

Gulf of Alaska

Albers Conic Equal-Area Projection
0   200   400 Miles
0 200 400 Kilometers

Geographic Atlas

90°W   85°W   80°W   75°W   70°W   65°W   60°W   55°W

45°N

Atlantic Time Zone

CANADA

Maine
(1820)
• Bangor

Minnesota
(1858)
• Duluth

L. Superior

Vermont
(1791)

Eastern Time Zone

• Burlington
Augusta ★
Lewiston •
• Montpelier
Portland •

Michigan (1837)

L. Huron

40°N

New Hampshire
(1788)

Wisconsin
(1848)

St. Paul ★
• Green Bay
•eapolis

L. Michigan

Grand
Rapids • Lansing ★
Madison • Milwaukee
•owa
846)
• Des Moines
★

Detroit •

Concord ★
Manchester •

Massachusetts

Rochester •
Albany ★
Boston ★
Providence (1788)
Rhode Island (1790)

L. Ontario

New York
(1788)
Buffalo •
Hartford ★
Connecticut
(1788)

L. Erie

Chicago •
Gary •
Fort Wayne •
Toledo •
Cleveland •

Pennsylvania
(1787)

Newark •
New York •
Jersey City •
Trenton ★
New Jersey
(1787)

Peoria •

Pittsburgh •
Philadelphia •

Illinois
(1818)
Springfield ★

Indiana
(1816)
Indianapolis ★

Ohio Akron •
(1803)

Harrisburg ★
Wilmington •
Dover ★
Delaware
(1787)

Columbus ★

Cincinnati •

Baltimore •
Washington, D.C. ✪
Annapolis ★
Maryland
(1788)

Missouri
(1821)

West
Virginia
★(1863)
Charleston •

Virginia
(1788)
Richmond ★

Louisville •

Huntington •
Frankfort ★
Lexington •

St. Louis •
•ansas
City
• Jefferson
City

Norfolk •

35°N

ATLANTIC
OCEAN

• Springfield

Kentucky
(1792)
Nashville ★

Knoxville •

Winston-
Salem •
Greensboro •
Raleigh ★

N
W   E
S

Tennessee
(1796)

Charlotte •

North Carolina
(1789)

Arkansas
(1836)

Memphis •

• Fort Smith

Atlanta ★

South Carolina
(1788)
★ Columbia

• Little Rock

Birmingham •

Charleston •

Mississippi
(1817)

Alabama
(1819)

Macon •
Columbus •

30°N

Georgia
(1788)

Savannah •

Jackson ★
Montgomery ★

• Shreveport

Louisiana
(1812)

Jacksonville •

Mobile •
Pensacola •
Tallahassee ★

Baton Rouge ★
L. Pontchartrain
• New Orleans

•ouston

Florida
(1845)
• Tampa

Gulf of Mexico

L. Okeechobee

BAHAMAS

25°N

• Miami

Tropic of Cancer

20°N

CUBA

Key

✪   National capital

★   State capital

•   Other city

(1787)   Year of admission to the Union

Boundaries of time zones

Albers Conic Equal-Area Projection
0   150   300 Miles
0   150   300 Kilometers

95°W   90°W   85°W   80°W   75°W   70°W

Geographic Atlas ★ **943**

Gazetteer of American History

This gazetteer, or geographic dictionary, lists places that are important in American history. The approximate latitude and longitude are given for cities, towns, and other specific locations. See text page 4 for information about latitude and longitude. In the Gazetteer, each listing usually includes two numbers in parentheses. The first number refers to the text page where you can find out about the place. The second appears in slanted, or *italic,* type and refers to a map (*m*) where the place is shown.

A

Abilene (39°N/97°W) (p. 554, *m548*)
Afghanistan (p. 833, *m941*)
Africa (p. 52, *m51*)
Alabama (*m943*)
Alamo (29°N/99°W) (p. 387, *m386*)
Alaska (*m942*)
Albany (43°N/74°W) (p. 143, *m142*)
Andes (p. 39)
Antarctica (*m940*)
Appalachian Mountains (p. 13, *m12*)
Appomattox Court House (37°N/79°W) (p. 509, *m509*)
Arctic Ocean (p. 11, *m12*)
Argentina (p. 349, *m349*)
Argonne Forest (49°N/6°E) (p. 703, *m701*)
Arizona (*m942*)
Arkansas (*m943*)
Armenia (p. 601, *m941*)
Asia (p. 50, *m941*)
Atlanta (34°N/84°W) (p. 508, *m470*)
Atlantic Ocean (p. 11, *m943*)
Atlantic Plain (p. 13, *m12*)
Australia (*m941*)
Austria Hungary (p. 687, *m685*)

B

Baltimore (39°N/77°W) (p. 323, *m323*)
Beijing (40°N/116°E) (p. 666, *m797*)
Belleau Wood (49°N/3°E) (p. 702, *m701*)
Bering Sea (p. 69, *m37*)
Berlin (53°N/13°E) (p. 812)
Bosnia (p. 880, *m941*)
Boston (42°N/71°W) (p. 102, *m103*)
Brazil (p. 350, *m349*)
Breed's Hill (42°N/71°W) (p. 170)
Buena Vista (26°N/101°W) (p. 396, *m395*)
Buffalo (43°N/79°W) (p. 341, *m340*)
Bunker Hill (42°N/71°W) (p. 170)

C

Cahokia (39°N/90°W) (p. 189, *m187*)
California (*m942*)
Cambodia (p. 830, *m828*)
Canada (p. 145, *m942–943*)
Canadian Shield (p. 13, *m12*)
Caribbean Sea (p. 69, *m76*)
Central America (p. 40, *m349*)
Central Plains (p. 13, *m12*)
Chancellorsville (38°N/78°W) (p. 493, *m491*)
Charleston (33°N/80°W) (p. 115, *m115*)
Chesapeake Bay (p. 114, *m115*)
Chicago (42°N/88°W) (p. 410, *m943*)
China (p. 53, *m941*)
Chisholm Trail (p. 553, *m548*)
Cincinnati (39°N/84°W) (p. 410, *m943*)
Cleveland (41°N/82°W) (*m943*)
Coastal Plains (p. 13, *m12*)
Colombia (p. 675, *m679*)
Colorado (*m942*)
Columbia River (p. 310, *m308*)
Concord (43°N/71°W) (p. 159, *m170*)
Connecticut (*m943*)
Cowpens (35°N/82°W) (p. 192, *m192*)
Cuba (22°N/79°W) (p. 668, *m673*)
Cumberland Gap (37°N/84°W) (p. 148, *m329*)
Cuzco (14°S/72°W) (p. 39, *m35*)
Czechoslovakia (p. 709, *m709*)

D

Dallas (33°N/97°W) (p. 7, *m943*)
Delaware (*m943*)
Delaware River (p. 85, *m90*)
Denver (40°N/105°W) (*m548*)
Detroit (42°N/83°W) (p. 321, *m323*)
District of Columbia (p. 281, *m943*)
Dominican Republic (p. 679, *m679*)
Dunkirk (51°N/2°E) (p. 780, *m791*)
Dust Bowl (p. 765, *m745*)

E

Egypt (p. 884, *m885*)
El Alamein (31°N/29°E) (p. 792, *m791*)
El Salvador (p. 824, *m940*)
England (p. 81, *m82*)
English Channel (p. 780)
Equator (p. 4, *m940–941*)
Erie Canal (p. 340, *m340*)
Europe (p. 68, *m941*)

F

Florida (*m943*)
Fort Donelson (37°N/88°W) (p. 494, *m507*)
Fort Henry (37°N/88°W) (p. 494, *m507*)
Fort McHenry (39°N/77°W) (p. 323)
Fort Necessity (40°N/79°W) (p. 143, *m142*)
Fort Pitt (40°N/80°W) (p. 144, *m187*)
Fort Sumter (33°N/80°W) (p. 481)
Fort Ticonderoga (44°N/74°W) (p. 144, *m142*)
France (p. 83, *m941*)
Fredericksburg (38°N/78°W) (p. 493, *m491*)

G

Gadsden Purchase (p. 397, *m379*)
Gaza Strip (31°N/34°E) (p. 884, *m885*)
Georgia (*m943*)
Germany (p. 415, *m941*)
Gettysburg (40°N/77°W) (p. 506, *m491*)
Goliad (29°N/97°W) (p. 388, *m386*)

Gazetteer

Q

Quebec (47°N/71°W) (p. 83, *m82*)

R

Rhode Island (*m943*)
Richmond (38°N/78°W) (p. 490, *m491*)
Rio Grande (p. 15, *m12*)
Roanoke Island (36°N/76°W) (p. 87, *m90*)
Rocky Mountains (p. 13, *m12*)
Russia (p. 545, *m941*)

S

Sacramento (39°N/122°W) (p. 400, *m400*)
St. Augustine (30°N/81°W) (p. 77, *m77*)
St. Lawrence River (p. 15, *m82*)
St. Louis (38°N/90°W) (p. 309, *m308*)
Salt Lake City (41°N/112°W) (p. 399, *m400*)
San Antonio (29°N/99°W) (p. 386, *m386*)
San Diego (33°N/117°W) (p. 392, *m400*)
San Francisco (38°N/122°W) (p. 393, *m400*)
Santa Fe (35°N/106°W) (p. 77, *m76*)

Santa Fe Trail (p. 392, *m400*)
Saratoga (43°N/75°W) (p. 183, *m182*)
Savannah (32°N/81°W) (p. 116, *m115*)
Serbia (p. 688, *m685*)
Sierra Nevada (p. 12, *m12*)
Songhai (p. 53, *m35*)
South Africa (p. 880, *m941*)
South America (p. 11, *m67*, *m940*)
South Carolina (*m943*)
South Dakota (*m942*)
Soviet Union (p. 774, *m773*)
Spain (p. 60, *m82*, *m941*)
Spanish Florida (p. 350, *m363*)
Stalingrad (49°N/45°E) (p. 790, *m791*)
Sudetenland (p. 779, *m773*)

T

Tennessee (*m943*)
Tenochtitlán (19°N/99°W) (p. 38, *m35*)
Texas (*m942*)
Timbuktu (17°N/3°W) (p. 53, *m51*)
Trenton (41°N/74°W) (p. 182, *m182*)

U

United Kingdom See Great Britain. (*m941*)
Utah (*m942*)

V

Valley Forge (40°N/76°W) (p. 185, *m182*)
Veracruz (19°N/96°W) (p. 396, *m395*)
Vermont (*m943*)
Vicksburg (42°N/86°W) (p. 505, *m507*)
Vietnam (p. 562, *m941*)
Vincennes (39°N/88°W) (p. 189, *m187*)
Virgin Islands (18°N/64°W) (*m940*)
Virginia (p. 616, *m620–621*)
Virginia City (39°N/120°W) (p. 548, *m548*)

W

Washington (*m942*)
Washington, D.C. (39°N/77°W) (p. 281, *m323*, *m943*)
West Indies (p. 69, *m77*)
West Virginia (*m943*)
Wisconsin (*m943*)
Wounded Knee (43°N/102°W) (p. 561, *m560*)
Wyoming (*m942*)

Y

Yalu River (p. 818, *m817*)
Yorktown (37°N/76°W) (p. 193, *m192*)
Yugoslavia (p. 880, *m881*)

Gazetteer

Glossary

This glossary defines all vocabulary words and many important historical terms and phrases. These words and terms appear in blue type the first time that they are used in the text. The page number(s) after each definition refers to the page(s) on which the word or phrase is defined in the text. For other references, see the index.

Pronunciation Key

When difficult names or terms first appear in the text, they are respelled to help you with pronunciation. A syllable printed in small capital letters receives the greatest stress. The pronunciation key below lists the letters and symbols that will help you pronounce the word. It also includes examples of words using each of the sounds and shows how each word would be pronounced.

Symbol	Example	Respelling
a	hat	(hat)
ay	pay, late	(pay), (layt)
ah	star, hot	(stahr), (haht)
ai	air, dare	(air), (dair)
aw	law, all	(law), (awl)
eh	met	(meht)
ee	bee, eat	(bee), (eet)
er	learn, sir, fur	(lern), (ser), (fer)
ih	fit	(fiht)
i	mile	(mīl)
ir	ear	(ir)
oh	no	(noh)
oi	soil, boy	(soil), (boi)
oo	root, rule	(root), (rool)
or	born, door	(born), (dor)
ow	plow, out	(plow), (owt)

Symbol	Example	Respelling
u	put, book	(put), (buk)
uh	fun	(fuhn)
yoo	few, use	(fyoo), (yooz)
ch	chill, reach	(chihl), (reech)
g	go, dig	(goh), (dihg)
j	jet, gently bridge	(jeht), (JEHNT lee), (brihj)
k	kite, cup	(kīt), (kuhp)
ks	mix	(mihks)
kw	quick	(kwihk)
ng	bring	(brihng)
s	say, cent	(say), (sehnt)
sh	she, crash	(shee), (krash)
th	three	(three)
y	yet, onion	(yeht), (UHN yuhn)
z	zip, always	(zihp), (AWL wayz)
zh	treasure	(TREH zher)

A

abdicate give up power (p. 701)

abolitionist person who wanted to end slavery (p. 440)

acculturation process of holding on to older traditions while adapting to a new culture (p. 604)

adobe sun-dried brick (p. 41)

affirmative action program to provide more job and education opportunities for people who faced discrimination in the past (p. 864)

AFL (American Federation of Labor) an organization of trade unions that represented skilled workers (p. 592)

aggression warlike act by one country without just cause (p. 775)

alliance agreement between nations to aid and protect one another (p. 85)

Alliance for Progress economic aid program for Latin America developed by President Kennedy (p. 824)

Allied Powers military alliance of France, Britain, Russia, Italy, and 20 other nations during World War I (p. 688)

Allies World War II military alliance of Britain, France, the Soviet Union, the United States, China, and 45 other countries (p. 779)

ally nation that works with another nation for a common purpose (p. 183)

altitude height above sea level (p. 15)

amend change (p. 218)

American Association of Retired Persons (AARP) organization that monitors issues of concern to older Americans (p. 897)

American Indian Religious Freedom Act a 1978 law that directed federal agencies not to interfere with Native American religious practices (p. 896)

Americans With Disabilities Act law passed in 1990 that prohibits discrimination in hiring people with physical or mental impairments (p. 897)

Glossary

amnesty government pardon (p. 517)

anarchist person who opposes organized government (pp. 592, 737)

annex to add on or take over (pp. 389, 661)

anthropology the study of how people and cultures develop (p. 30)

Antifederalists people who opposed the Constitution and a strong national government (p. 215)

apartheid strict separation of races practiced in South Africa (p. 880)

appeal to ask that a decision be reviewed by a higher court (p. 256)

appeasement practice of giving in to aggression in order to avoid war (p. 779)

apprentice person who learns a trade or craft from a master (p. 128)

archaeology the study of evidence left by early peoples in order to find out about their way of life (p. 22)

armistice an agreement to stop fighting (p. 701)

arsenal place where guns are stored (p. 476)

Articles the main body of the Constitution, which establishes the framework for the United States government (p. 249)

Articles of Confederation first American constitution, passed in 1777, which created a loose alliance of 13 independent states (p. 201)

artifact object made by humans (p. 22)

artisan skilled worker (p. 413)

assembly line method of production in which workers stay in one place as products edge along past them on a moving belt (p. 588)

astrolabe navigational instrument used to determine latitude (p. 59)

Atlantic Charter a 1941 program developed by the United States and Britain that set goals for the postwar world (p. 782)

atrocity act of cruelty and brutality (p. 670)

authenticity the quality or condition of being genuine (p. 21)

Axis World War II military alliance of Germany, Italy, Japan, and six other nations (p. 779)

Glossary

B

baby boom large increase in the birthrate from the late 1940s through the early 1960s (p. 844)

balanced budget condition that exists when the government spends only as much as it takes in (p. 874)

bank holiday closing of banks for four days during the Great Depression (p. 753)

bankrupt unable to pay debts (p. 748)

barrio Mexican neighborhood in the United States (p. 651)

Bataan Death March long trek across the Philippines that American and Filipino prisoners of war were forced to make by the Japanese in 1942 (p. 799)

Battle of Belleau Wood hard-fought American victory over the Germans in France in 1918 (p. 700)

Battle of Britain Germany's failed attempt to subdue Britain in 1940 in preparation for invasion (p. 780)

Battle of Midway a 1942 battle in the Pacific during which American planes sank four Japanese aircraft carriers (p. 792)

Battle of the Argonne Forest defeat of the Germans by French and American troops in France in October 1918 (p. 701)

Battle of the Bulge German counterattack in December 1944 that temporarily slowed the Allied invasion of Germany (p. 793)

Battle of Verdun prolonged World War I battle in which more than 1 million died or were wounded (p. 689)

Bay of Pigs invasion failed invasion of Cuba in 1961 when a force of 1,200 Cuban exiles, backed by the United States, landed at the Bay of Pigs (p. 823)

beatnik 1950s person who criticized American culture for conformity and devotion to business (p. 847)

Berlin Airlift American and British relief effort to airlift supplies to West Berliners from 1948 to 1949 (p. 812)

Berlin Wall wall built by the communist East German government in 1961 to seal off East Berlin from West Berlin (p. 813)

Bessemer process method developed in the 1850s to produce stronger steel at a lower cost (p. 578)

bias a leaning toward or against a certain person, group, or idea (p. 22)

Big Four leaders of Britain, France, the United States, and Italy after World War I (p. 706)

bilingual in two languages (p. 866)

bill proposed law (p. 253)

bill of rights written list of freedoms the government promises to protect (pp. 123, 200)

Bill of Rights first 10 amendments to the United States Constitution (p. 218)

Black Cabinet group of black leaders who unofficially advised President Franklin D. Roosevelt concerning the situation of African Americans (p. 767)

black codes Southern laws that severely limited the rights of African Americans after the Civil War (p. 521)

Black Tuesday (October 29, 1929) day the stock market crashed, signaling start of the Great Depression (p. 747)

blitzkrieg the swift attacks launched by Germany in World War II (p. 779)

blockade the shutting of a port to keep people or supplies from moving in or out (p. 171)

boat people after the Vietnam War, refugees who escaped from Vietnam in small boats (p. 831)

bond certificate that promises to repay money loaned, plus interest, on a certain date (p. 280)

bonus additional sum of money (p. 751)

Bonus Army veterans who marched to Washington in 1932 to demand immediate payment of a World War I bonus (p. 751)

bootlegger person who smuggled liquor into the United States during Prohibition (p. 725)

border state slave state that remained in the Union during the Civil War (p. 487)

Boxer Rebellion uprising in China against westerners and Western influence in 1900 (p. 666)

boycott to refuse to buy or use certain goods or services (pp. 150, 852)

bracero program recruitment of Mexican laborers to work in the United States during World War II (p. 788)

building code standards for construction and safety of buildings (p. 609)

bull market period of increased stock trading and rising stock prices (p. 720)

Bull Moose party Progressive Republicans who supported Theodore Roosevelt during the election of 1912 (p. 642)

bureaucracy system of managing government through departments run by appointed officials (p. 695)

burgess representative to the colonial Virginia government (p. 90)

C

Cabinet group of officials who head government departments and advise the President (p. 279)

Camp David Accords 1979 peace treaty between Israel and Egypt in which Israel agreed to return the Sinai Peninsula to Egypt and Egypt agreed to recognize Israel (p. 884)

capital money raised for a business venture (p. 331)

capitalist person who invests in a business to make a profit (p. 331)

caravan group of people who travel together for safety (p. 52)

carpetbagger uncomplimentary nickname for a northerner who went to the South after the Civil War (p. 527)

cartographer person who makes maps (p. 8)

cash crop crop sold for money at market (p. 111)

cash economy economy in which people exchange money for goods and services (p. 27)

cattle drive herding and moving herds of cattle, usually to railroad lines (p. 553)

caucus private meeting; often a political meeting (p. 364)

causeway raised road made of packed earth (p. 38)

cavalry troops on horseback (p. 184)

cede to give up (pp. 202, 396)

censure to officially condemn (p. 820)

Central Powers military alliance of Germany, Austria-Hungary, Bulgaria, and the Ottoman Empire during World War I (p. 688)

charter legal document giving certain rights to a person or company (p. 88)

checks and balances a principle of the United States Constitution that gives each branch of government the power to check the other branches (p. 251)

Chinese Exclusion Act 1882 law that barred Chinese laborers from entering the United States (p. 605)

chronology sequence of events over time (p. 25)

circumnavigate travel all the way around the Earth (p. 71)

citizen person who owes loyalty to a particular nation and is entitled to all its rights and protections (p. 265)

city-state large town that has its own government and controls the surrounding countryside (p. 52)

civic virtue the willingness to work for the good of the nation or community even at great sacrifice (p. 266)

civics the study of the rights and responsibilities of citizens (p. 29)

civil relating to lawsuits involving the private rights of individuals (p. 261)

civil disobedience idea that people have a right to disobey laws they consider to be unjust, if their consciences demand it (pp. 451, 853)

civil rights the rights due to all citizens (p. 767)

civil rights movement the efforts of African Americans to win equal rights (p. 850)

civil service all federal jobs except elected offices and those in the military (p. 631)

Civil Service Commission government agency created by the Pendleton Act of 1883 to fill federal jobs on the basis of merit (p. 631)

civil war war between people of the same country (p. 465)

Civil War amendments the Thirteenth, Fourteenth, and Fifteenth amendments to the United States Constitution (p. 261)

civilian nonmilitary (p. 249)

Civilian Conservation Corps New Deal program that hired unemployed men to work on natural conservation projects (p. 754)

clan group of two or more related families (p. 48)

climate average weather of a place over a period of 20 to 30 years (p. 15)

clipper ship fast-sailing ship of the mid-1800s (p. 410)

Cold War after World War II, long period of intense rivalry between the Soviet Union and the United States (p. 810)

collective bargaining process by which a union representing a group of workers negotiates with management for a contract (pp. 592, 761)

colony group of people who settle in a distant land but are still ruled by the government of their native land (p. 70)

Columbian Exchange the global exchange of goods and ideas resulting from the encounter between the peoples of the Eastern and Western hemispheres (p. 71)

committee of correspondence letter-writing campaign that became a major tool of protest in the colonies (p. 153)

communism economic system in which all wealth and property are owned by the state (p. 722)

company union labor organization that is actually controlled by management (p. 737)

compensation repayment for losses (p. 788)

Comprehensive Test Ban Treaty agreement proposed in 1996 to end all testing of nuclear weapons (p. 882)

compromise settlement in which each side gives up some of its demands in order to reach an agreement (p. 208)

compulsory education requirement that children attend school to a certain grade or age (p. 617)

concentration camp prison camp for civilians who are considered enemies of the state (p. 776)

confederation league of independent states or nations (p. 317)

Congress of Industrial Organizations (CIO) labor organization founded in the 1930s to represent workers in basic mass-production industries (p. 762)

conquistador name for the Spanish explorers who claimed lands in the Americas for Spain (p. 74)

conservation protection of natural resources (p. 641)

Conservatives during Reconstruction, white southerners who resisted change (p. 527)

consolidate combine (p. 575)

constitution document that sets out the laws, principles, organization, and processes of a government (p. 200)

Constitutional Convention gathering of state representatives on May 25, 1787, to revise the Articles of Confederation (p. 206)

consumer user of goods and services (p. 27)

containment the policy of trying to prevent the spread of Soviet influence beyond where it already existed (p. 811)

Glossary

continental divide mountain ridge that separates river systems flowing toward opposite sides of a continent (p. 309)

Contract With America legislative package drawn up by House Republicans in 1994 that included trimming social welfare programs and slashing taxes (p. 875)

cooperative group of farmers who pool their money to buy seeds and tools wholesale (p. 565)

Copperhead northerner who opposed using force to keep the southern states in the Union (p. 501)

corduroy road road made of logs (p. 339)

corollary addition to an earlier stated principle (p. 678)

corporation business that is owned by investors (p. 580)

corral enclosure for animals (p. 545)

"cottonocracy" name for the wealthy planters who made their money from cotton in the mid-1800s (p. 422)

counterculture movement protest movement in the 1960s that rejected traditional American values and culture (p. 859)

coureur de bois French colonist who lived in the woods as a fur trapper (p. 83)

cow town settlement that grew up at the end of a cattle trail (p. 554)

creole person born in Spain's American colonies to Spanish parents (pp. 78, 348)

Cuban missile crisis major Cold War confrontation in 1962 (p. 823)

culture entire way of life developed by a people (pp. 22, 40)

culture area region in which people share a similar way of life (p. 42)

currency money (p. 202)

czar Russian emperor (p. 692)

D

D-Day (June 6, 1944) day of the invasion of Western Europe by Allied forces (p. 792)

dame school school run by a woman, usually in her own home (p. 128)

Dayton Accord 1995 peace agreement negotiated among Bosnia, Croatia, and Serbia (p. 881)

debtor person who cannot pay money he or she owes (pp. 116, 436)

Declaration of Independence a 1776 document stating that the 13 English colonies were a free and independent nation (p. 175)

deficit spending government practice of spending more than is taken in from taxes (p. 763)

demilitarized zone (DMZ) area from which military forces are prohibited (p. 818)

democratic ensuring that all people have the same rights (p. 302)

department store large retail store offering a variety of goods organized in separate departments (p. 613)

deport expel from a country (p. 737)

depression period when business activity slows, prices and wages fall, and unemployment rises (pp. 204, 373)

deregulation reduction of restrictions on businesses (p. 873)

détente policy to reduce tensions between two countries (p. 833)

dictatorship government in which one person or a small group holds complete authority (pp. 212, 386)

dime novel in the late 1800s, low-priced paperbacks offering adventure stories (p. 619)

direct democracy form of government in which ordinary citizens have the power to govern (p. 57)

disarmament reduction of armed forces and weapons of war (p. 722)

discrimination policy that denies equal rights to certain groups of people (p. 417)

dividend share of a corporation's profit (p. 580)

dollar diplomacy President Taft's policy of building strong economic ties to Latin America (p. 678)

domestic tranquillity peace and order at home (p. 249)

domino theory belief that if South Vietnam fell to communism, other countries in the region would follow (p. 828)

"Double V" campaign African American civil rights campaign during World War II (p. 786)

downsizing reducing a workforce (p. 874)

draft law that requires people of a certain age to enlist in the military (pp. 502, 693, 829)

Dred Scott v. Sandford an 1857 Supreme Court case that brought into question the federal power over slavery in the territories (p. 471)

Dust Bowl region in the central Great Plains that was hit by a severe drought during the 1930s (p. 765)

E

e-commerce business and trade over the Internet (p. 892)

Earth Summit meeting of world leaders in 1992 to discuss key environmental issues (p. 890)

economics the study of how people manage limited resources to satisfy their wants and needs (p. 26)

Eighteenth Amendment a 1917 amendment to the United States Constitution that made it illegal to sell alcoholic drinks (p. 648)

electoral college group of electors from every state who meet every four years to vote for the President and Vice President of the United States (p. 255)

elevation height above sea level (p. 13)

emancipate to set free (p. 497)

Emancipation Proclamation Lincoln's 1863 declaration freeing slaves in the Confederacy (p. 497)

embargo ban on trade (p. 314)

encomienda land granted to Spanish settlers that included the right to demand labor or taxes from Native Americans (p. 78)

Environmental Protection Agency federal government agency that works to reduce pollution (p. 890)

environmentalist person who works to reduce pollution and protect the natural environment (p. 889)

epidemic rapid spread of a contagious disease (p. 702)

Equal Rights Amendment a 1923 proposed constitutional amendment intended to prohibit all discrimination based on sex; the amendment was never ratified (p. 726)

erosion gradual wearing away (p. 13)

escalate to expand (p. 828)

established church chosen religion of a state (p. 94)

execute carry out (p. 201)

executive branch branch of government that carries out laws (p. 208)

exile person who has been forced to leave his or her own country (p. 823)

expansionism policy of extending a nation's boundaries (p. 660)

Glossary

expatriate person who renounces his or her own country and takes up residence in a foreign land (p. 731)

expedition long voyage of exploration (p. 308)

export trade product sent to markets outside a country (p. 120)

extended family family group that includes grandparents, parents, children, aunts, uncles, and cousins (pp. 53, 425)

F

faction opposing group within a party (p. 287)

factory system method of producing goods that brought workers and machinery together in one place (p. 331)

fad activity or fashion that is taken up with great passion for a short time (p. 730)

famine severe food shortage (p. 415)

Fascism political system that is rooted in militarism, extreme nationalism, and blind loyalty to the state (p. 774)

Federal Reserve Act a 1913 law that set up a system of federal banks and gave government the power to control the money supply (p. 643)

Federal Trade Commission (FTC) government agency created in 1914 to ensure fair competition (p. 643)

federalism a principle of the United States Constitution that establishes the division of power between the federal government and the states (p. 251)

Federalist supporter of the Constitution who favored a strong federal government (pp. 215, 289)

Federalist Papers series of essays by Federalists James Madison, Alexander Hamilton, and John Jay in support of ratifying the Constitution (p. 216)

feudalism system of rule by lords who ruled their own lands but owed loyalty and military service to a monarch (p. 58)

Fifteenth Amendment an 1869 amendment to the United States Constitution that forbids any state to deny African Americans the right to vote because of race (p. 524)

54th Massachusetts Regiment African American unit in the Union Army (p. 499)

fireside chat radio speech given by President Franklin D. Roosevelt while in office (p. 754)

First Amendment amendment to the United States Constitution that safeguards basic individual liberties (p. 260)

first global age era at beginning of 1400s, when long-distance trade and travel increased dramatically (p. 50)

flapper young woman in the 1920s who rebelled against traditional ways of thinking and acting (p. 731)

flatboat boat with a flat bottom used for transporting heavy loads on inland waterways (p. 337)

Foraker Act law passed by Congress in 1900 under which the United States gave Puerto Ricans a limited say in government (p. 674)

foreign policy actions that a nation takes in relation to other nations (p. 285)

Fort Wagner fort in South Carolina that was the site of an attack by the African American 54th Massachusetts Regiment in 1863 (p. 499)

forty-niner one of the more than 80,000 people who joined the gold rush to California in 1849 (p. 400)

Founding Fathers leaders who laid the groundwork for the United States (p. 211)

Fourteen Points President Wilson's goals for peace after World War I (p. 706)

Fourteenth Amendment an 1868 amendment to the United States Constitution that guarantees equal protection of the laws (p. 522)

free enterprise system economic system in which businesses are owned by private citizens who decide what to produce, how much to produce, and what prices to charge (pp. 28, 581)

free market economic system in which goods and services are exchanged with little regulation (p. 303)

Free-Soil party bipartisan antislavery party founded in the United States in 1848 to keep slavery out of the western territories (p. 462)

freedmen men and women who had been slaves (p. 517)

Freedmen's Bureau government agency founded during Reconstruction to help former slaves (p. 517)

French and Indian War a war that took place from 1754 to 1763 that led to the end of French power in North America (p. 142)

frigate fast-sailing ship with many guns (p. 292)

fugitive runaway (p. 464)

Fugitive Slave Act law passed in 1850 that required all citizens to aid in the capture of runaway slaves (p. 465)

G

gauge width of a train track (p. 574)

general welfare well-being of all the citizens of a nation (p. 249)

"Gentlemen's Agreement" a 1907 agreement between the United States and Japan to limit Japanese immigration (p. 652)

gentry highest social class in the 13 English colonies (p. 126)

geography the study of people, their environments, and their resources (p. 4)

Gettysburg Address speech made by President Lincoln in 1863 after the Battle of Gettysburg (p. 507)

Gilded Age the period in American history lasting from the 1870s to the 1890s, marked by political corruption and extravagant spending (p. 630)

glacier thick sheet of ice (p. 36)

glasnost policy in the Soviet Union of speaking openly about problems (p. 835)

global warming the slow but steady rise in the world's average temperature (p. 891)

Good Neighbor Policy President Franklin Roosevelt's policy intended to strengthen friendly relations with Latin America (p. 777)

graduated income tax tax on earnings that charges different rates for different income levels (p. 636)

grandfather clause law that excused a voter from a literacy test if his father or grandfather had been eligible to vote on January 1, 1867 (p. 532)

Great Depression worst period of economic decline in United States history, beginning in 1929 (p. 747)

Great White Fleet name for the steam-powered ships of the enlarged and modernized American navy of the early 1900s (p. 664)

guerrilla fighter who uses hit-and-run attacks (pp. 192, 828)

Gulf of Tonkin Resolution Congressional resolution passed in 1964 that authorized military action in Vietnam (p. 828)

Glossary

H

habeas corpus the right not to be held in prison without first being charged with a specific crime (pp. 213, 502)

Harlem Hell Fighters the African American infantry unit that fought with the French Army in World War I (p. 700)

Haymarket Riot labor rally in Chicago in 1886 that ended in violence when a bomb exploded (p. 592)

Holocaust slaughter of Europe's Jews by the Nazis before and during World War II (p. 799)

Hooverville group of shacks in which the homeless lived during the Great Depression (p. 750)

House of Representatives the larger of the two bodies that make up the legislative branch of the United States government (p. 252)

Hull House settlement house founded by Progressive reformer Jane Addams in Chicago in 1889 (p. 610)

Hundred Days first hundred days of President Franklin D. Roosevelt's presidency (p. 754)

I

ILGWU (International Ladies' Garment Workers Union) union of garment workers formed in 1900 (p. 593)

illegal alien immigrant who enters a country without permission (p. 895)

illiterate unable to read or write (p. 694)

immigrant person who enters another country in order to settle there (p. 266)

Immigration Reform and Control Act law that allowed people who arrived illegally in the United States before 1982 to apply for citizenship (p. 895)

impeach to bring charges of serious wrongdoing against a public official (pp. 257, 523)

imperialism policy of powerful countries seeking to control the economic and political affairs of weaker countries or regions (p. 662)

import trade product brought into a country (p. 120)

impressment practice of forcing people into military service (p. 313)

inauguration ceremony in which the President officially takes the oath of office (p. 278)

income tax a tax on people's earnings (p. 502)

incriminate to give evidence against (p. 260)

indentured servant person who agreed to work without wages for a period of time in exchange for passage to the colonies (p. 126)

Indian New Deal series of laws passed in the 1930s that gave Native American nations greater control over their own affairs (p. 768)

indigo plant used to make a valuable blue dye (p. 115)

individualism concept that stresses the importance of each individual (p. 451)

Industrial Revolution gradual process by which machines replaced hand tools (p. 330)

inflation a rise in prices and a decrease in the value of money (pp. 503, 565, 848)

infrastructure system of roads, bridges, and tunnels (p. 263)

initiative process by which voters can put a bill directly before the state legislature (pp. 263, 636)

installment buying buying on credit (p. 720)

integration mixing of different racial or ethnic groups (p. 850)

interchangeable parts identical, machine-made parts for a tool or an instrument (p. 332)

internal improvements improvements to roads, bridges, and canals (p. 346)

Internet series of interconnected computers that allow users to access and exchange computerized information (p. 892)

interstate commerce business that crosses state lines (pp. 346, 632)

Interstate Commerce Commission (ICC) government agency organized to oversee railroad commerce (p. 632)

intervention direct involvement (p. 351)

Intolerable Acts series of laws passed in 1774 to punish Boston for the Tea Party (p. 157)

irrigation bringing water to dry lands (p. 6)

Islam monotheistic religion founded by the prophet Muhammad in the early 600s (p. 50)

island hopping during World War II, Allied strategy of capturing Japanese-held islands to gain control of the Pacific Ocean (p. 796)

isolationist after World War I, American who wanted the United States to stay out of world affairs (pp. 660, 708)

isthmus narrow strip of land connecting two larger bodies of land (pp. 11, 675)

J

jazz music style that developed from blues, ragtime, and other earlier styles (p. 731)

jerky dried meat (p. 545)

Jim Crow laws laws that separated people of different races in public places in the South (p. 532)

judicial branch branch of government that decides if laws are carried out fairly (p. 208)

judicial review power of the Supreme Court to decide whether the acts of a President or laws passed by Congress are constitutional (p. 305)

Judiciary Act a 1789 law that created the structure of the Supreme Court and set up a system of district courts and circuit courts for the nation (p. 279)

jury duty the responsibility of every citizen to serve on a jury when called (p. 268)

K

kachina masked dancer at religious ceremonies of the Southwest Indians (p. 47)

kaiser title of the German emperor (p. 688)

kamikaze World War II Japanese pilot trained to make a suicidal crash attack, usually upon a ship (p. 797)

Kansas-Nebraska Act an 1854 law that established the territories of Nebraska and Kansas, giving the settlers the right of popular sovereignty to decide on the issue of slavery (p. 468)

Kellogg-Briand Pact a 1928 treaty outlawing war (p. 722)

Khmer Rouge communist party in Cambodia that imposed a reign of terror on Cambodian citizens (p. 831)

kinship sharing a common ancestor (p. 53)

Knights of Labor an American labor organization founded in 1869 to protect the rights of workers (p. 591)

Ku Klux Klan secret society organized in the South after the Civil War to reassert white supremacy by means of violence (p. 527)

L

laissez faire idea that government should play as small a role as possible in economic affairs (p. 303)

latitude distance north or south from the equator (p. 4)

lawsuit legal case brought to settle a dispute between a person or group (p. 471)

League of Nations association of nations formed after World War I under Wilson's Fourteen Points plan (p. 705)

League of the Iroquois alliance of the five Iroquois nations (p. 48)

League of Women Voters organization established in 1920 to promote rights for women (p. 725)

legislative branch branch of government that passes laws (p. 208)

legislature group of people who have the power to make laws (p. 122)

Lend-Lease Act during World War II, the law that allowed the United States to sell arms and equipment to Britain (p. 781)

libel act of publishing a statement that may unjustly damage a person's reputation (p. 130)

liberty freedom (p. 249)

Liberty Bonds bonds sold by the United States government to raise money for World War I (p. 695)

limited government a principle of the United States Constitution that states that government has only the powers that the Constitution gives it (p. 250)

literacy test examination to see if a person can read and write; used in the past to restrict voting rights (p. 532)

local color speech and habits of a particular region (p. 620)

local government government on the county, parish, city, town, village, or district level (p. 263)

locomotive engine that pulls a railroad train (p. 409)

lode rich vein of gold, silver, or other valuable ore (p. 547)

longitude distance east or west from the Prime Meridian (p. 4)

Louisiana Purchase vast territory between the Mississippi River and Rocky Mountains, purchased from France in 1803 (p. 308)

Lusitania British passenger ship that was torpedoed by a German U-boat in 1915; 1,200 people died, including 128 Americans (p. 690)

lynch for a mob to illegally seize and execute someone (pp. 401, 649)

M

Magna Carta signed in 1215, a British document that contained two basic ideas: monarchs themselves have to obey the laws, and citizens have basic rights (pp. 90, 213)

mainstreaming placing children with special needs in regular classes (p. 896)

majority more than half (p. 362)

Manifest Destiny 1800s belief that Americans had the right to spread across the continent (p. 393)

manor district ruled by a lord, including the lord's castle and the lands around it (p. 58)

map projection way of drawing Earth on a flat surface (p. 8)

Marbury v. *Madison* an 1803 court case in which the Supreme Court ruled that it had the power to decide whether laws passed by Congress were constitutional (p. 305)

Marshall Plan American plan to help European nations rebuild their economies after World War II (p. 812)

martial law rule by the army instead of the elected government (pp. 487, 834)

martyr person who dies for his or her beliefs (p. 476)

mass production process of making large quantities of a product quickly and cheaply (p. 588)

Mayflower Compact a 1620 agreement for ruling the Plymouth Colony (p. 95)

mediator agent who helps conflicting parties iron out their differences (p. 879)

mercantilism theory that a nation's economic strength came from keeping a strict control over its colonial trade (p. 120)

mercenary soldier who fights merely for pay, often for a foreign country (p. 171)

merit ability (p. 631)

mestizo in Spain's American colonies, person of mixed Spanish and Indian background (p. 78)

middle class in the 13 English colonies, a class that included skilled craftworkers, farmers, and some trades-people (p. 126)

migrant worker person who moves from one region to another in search of work (pp. 766, 865)

militarism the policy of building up strong armed forces to prepare for war (p. 687)

militia army of citizens who serve as soldiers during an emergency (p. 158)

minuteman colonial militia volunteer who was prepared to fight at a minute's notice (p. 159)

mission religious settlement run by Catholic priests and friars (p. 78)

missionary person who tries to spread certain religious beliefs among a group of people (pp. 56, 84)

Missouri Compromise agreement, proposed in 1819 by Henry Clay, to keep the number of slave and free states equal (p. 460)

Monitor ironclad Union warship (p. 492)

monopoly a company or group having control of all or nearly all of the business of an industry (p. 581)

Monroe Doctrine President Monroe's foreign policy statement warning European nations not to interfere in Latin America (p. 351)

moral diplomacy President Wilson's policy of condemning imperialism, spreading democracy, and promoting peace (p. 679)

Moral Majority religious organization that backed conservative political causes in the 1980s (p. 873)

mountain man trapper who explored and hunted in Oregon Territory in the early 1800s (p. 381)

moving assembly line method of production by which workers stay in one place as products travel past on a moving belt (p. 580)

muckraker journalist who exposed corruption and other problems of the late 1800s and early 1900s (p. 634)

mudslinging the use of insults to attack an opponent's reputation (p. 374)

Munich Conference a 1938 meeting of the leaders of Britain, France, Italy, and Germany at which an agreement was signed giving part of Czechoslovakia to Hitler (p. 779)

mutualista Mexican American mutual aid group (p. 651)

Glossary

N

NAACP (National Association for the Advancement of Colored People) organization founded in 1909 to work toward equal rights for African Americans (p. 650)

National Aeronautics and Space Administration (NASA) government agency that directs the American space program (p. 825)

national debt total sum of money that a government owes to others (pp. 280, 763)

National Labor Relations Act law passed in 1935 that protects American workers from unfair management practices (p. 761)

national park area set aside by the federal government for people to visit (p. 641)

National Recovery Administration government agency set up during the Great Depression to enforce new codes designed to stabilize industry (p. 755)

National Woman Suffrage Association group set up in 1869 to work for a constitutional amendment to give women the right to vote (p. 645)

nationalism excessive pride in one's nation (pp. 318, 686)

nativism antiforeign belief opposed to immigration (p. 738)

natural resources materials that humans can take from the environment to survive and satisfy their needs (p. 5)

natural rights rights that belong to all people from birth (p. 175)

naturalize to complete the official process for becoming a citizen (p. 265)

Navajo code-talkers during World War II, Navajo soldiers who used their own language to radio vital messages during the island-hopping campaign (p. 796)

Nazi member of the National Socialist German Workers' Party (p. 775)

Nazi-Soviet Pact agreement signed between Hitler and Stalin in 1939 in which the two dictators agreed not to attack each other (p. 779)

network system of connected railroad lines (p. 575)

neutral not taking sides in a conflict (p. 285)

Neutrality Acts series of laws passed by Congress in 1935 that banned arms sales or loans to countries at war (p. 777)

New Deal program of President Franklin D. Roosevelt to end the Great Depression (p. 754)

New Freedom President Wilson's program to break up trusts and restore American economic competition (p. 643)

"New South" term to describe the South in the late 1800s when efforts were made to expand the economy by building up industry (p. 533)

Nineteenth Amendment a 1919 amendment to the United States Constitution that gives women the right to vote (pp. 261, 646)

nominating convention meeting at which a political party chooses a candidate (p. 364)

North American Free Trade Agreement (NAFTA) treaty among the United States, Canada, and Mexico to gradually remove tariffs and other trade barriers (p. 889)

North Atlantic Treaty Organization (NATO) alliance formed in 1949 by the United States and Western European nations to fight Soviet aggression (p. 813)

northwest passage a waterway through or around North America (p. 81)

nullification idea that a state has the right to nullify, or cancel, a federal law that the state leaders consider to be unconstitutional (p. 371)

Nuremberg Trials Nazi war crimes trials held in 1945 and 1946 (p. 799)

O

on margin practice that allows people to buy stock with a down payment of a portion of the full value (p. 747)

OPEC (Organization of Petroleum Exporting Countries) multinational organization that sets a common policy for the sale of petroleum (p. 884)

Open Door Policy policy issued by Secretary of State John Hay in 1899 that allowed a nation to trade in any other nation's sphere of influence in China (p. 666)

Operation Overlord code name for the Allied invasion of Europe in 1944 (p. 792)

Organization of American States (OAS) international organization that promotes peace and economic progress in the Americas (p. 824)

override to overrule, as when Congress overrules a presidential veto (p. 257)

P

pacifist person who objects to any war; believes war is evil (p. 696)

Palestine Liberation Organization (PLO) Palestinian-Arab organization founded in 1964 to destroy Israel, mainly through the use of armed force (p. 884)

Parliament representative assembly in England (p. 90)

parochial church-sponsored; often used to refer to church-sponsored schools (p. 617)

patent license for a new invention (p. 584)

patriotism feeling of love and devotion toward one's country (p. 266)

patronage the practice of awarding government jobs to political supporters (p. 631)

patroon owner of a large estate in a Dutch colony (p. 109)

Peace Corps government organization that sends American volunteers to developing countries to teach or give technical advice (p. 824)

peninsulare person from Spain who held a position of power in a Spanish colony (p. 78)

pension sum of money paid to people on a regular basis after they retire (p. 760)

perjury to lie under oath (p. 820)

persecution mistreatment or punishment of a group of people because of their beliefs (p. 94)

Persian Gulf War a 1991 war in which the United States and its UN allies drove invading Iraqi forces out of neighboring Kuwait (p. 885)

petition formal written request to someone in authority that is signed by a group of people (p. 149)

Pickett's Charge failed Confederate charge at the Battle of Gettysburg (p. 506)

pit house house in the Arctic region dug into the ground and covered with wood and skins (p. 43)

plantation large estate farmed by many workers (p. 80)

Platt Amendment amendment to the 1902 Cuban constitution that allowed the United States to intervene in Cuba (p. 673)

Glossary

Plessy v. Ferguson an 1896 court case in which the Supreme Court ruled that segregation in public facilities was legal as long as the facilities were equal (p. 532)

pogrom in Eastern Europe, an organized attack on a Jewish community (p. 600)

polio highly infectious disease that causes inflammation of the nerve cells of the brain stem and spinal cord, leading to paralysis (p. 752)

political boss powerful politician who controls work done locally and demands payoffs from businesses (p. 633)

political science the study of government (p. 29)

poll tax tax required before a person can vote (p. 532)

pool system in which several railroad companies agreed to divide up the business in an area (p. 576)

popular sovereignty in the mid-1800s, a term referring to the idea that each territory could decide for itself whether or not to allow slavery (pp. 250, 462)

potlatch ceremonial dinner held by some Native Americans of the Northwest Coast to show off their wealth (p. 44)

Potsdam Declaration message sent by the Allies in July 1945 calling for Japanese surrender (p. 798)

preamble introduction to a declaration, constitution, or other official document (pp. 175, 248)

precedent act or decision that sets an example for others to follow (pp. 96, 278)

precipitation water that falls in the form of rain, sleet, hail, or snow (p. 15)

predestination Protestant idea that God decided in advance which people would attain salvation after death (p. 435)

presidio fort where soldiers lived in the Spanish colonies (p. 77)

primary election in which voters choose their party's candidate for the general election (p. 635)

primary source firsthand information about people or events (p. 20)

productivity average output per worker (p. 845)

profiteer person who takes advantage of a crisis to make money (p. 503)

Progressive reformer in the late 1800s and early 1900s who wanted to improve American life (p. 634)

Prohibition ban on the manufacture, sale, and transportation of liquor anywhere in the United States from 1920 to 1933 (p. 724)

propaganda spreading of ideas to help a cause or hurt an opposing cause (p. 689)

proprietary colony English colony in which the king gave land to proprietors in exchange for a yearly payment (p. 109)

protectorate nation whose independence is limited by the control of a more powerful country (p. 673)

Protestant Reformation movement to reform the Roman Catholic Church in the 1500s; led to the creation of many different Christian churches (p. 83)

psychology the study of how people think and behave (p. 30)

public interest the good of the people (p. 634)

public school school supported by taxes (p. 128)

public works projects built by the government for public use (p. 750)

pueblo a town in the Spanish colonies; Anasazi village (pp. 41, 77)

pull factor condition that attracts people to move to a new area (p. 600)

Pure Food and Drug Act a 1906 law that requires food and drug makers to list ingredients on packages (p. 641)

push factor condition that drives people from their homeland (p. 600)

Q

quipu device made of cord or string with knots that stood for quantities; used by the Incas to keep accounts and records (p. 40)

quota system system that limited immigration by allowing only a certain number of people from each country to immigrate to the United States (p. 738)

R

racism belief that one race is superior to another (pp. 119, 662)

radical person who wants to make drastic changes in society (p. 173)

Radical Reconstruction period beginning in 1867, when the Republicans, who had control in both houses of Congress, took charge of Reconstruction (p. 523)

Radical Republican member of Congress during Reconstruction who wanted to ensure that freedmen received the right to vote (p. 522)

ragtime popular music of the late 1800s that had a lively, rhythmic sound (p. 615)

ratify to approve (p. 194)

rationing limitations on the amount of certain goods that people can buy (p. 785)

Reaganomics President Reagan's economic program that cut taxes, cut federal spending on social programs, and increased military spending (p. 873)

realist writer or artist who shows life as it really is (p. 620)

rebate discount (p. 576)

recall process by which voters can remove an elected official from office (p. 636)

recession economic slump that is milder than a depression (pp. 718, 874)

reconcentration policy of moving large numbers of people into camps for political or military purposes (p. 669)

Reconstruction rebuilding of the South after the Civil War (p. 517)

Reconstruction Act an 1867 law that threw out the southern state governments that had refused to ratify the Fourteenth Amendment (p. 523)

referendum process by which people vote directly on a bill (p. 636)

refuge place where one is safe from persecution (p. 399)

refugee person who flees his or her homeland to seek safety elsewhere (p. 895)

relief program government program to help the needy (p. 750)

religious tolerance willingness to let others practice their own beliefs (p. 104)

rendezvous yearly meeting where mountain men traded furs (p. 382)

renewable resource resource that can be quickly replaced by nature (p. 890)

reparations cash payments made by a defeated nation to a victorious nation to pay for losses suffered during a war (p. 706)

repeal to cancel (pp. 150, 725)

representative government political system in which voters elect representatives to make laws for them (p. 90)

Glossary

republic system of government in which citizens choose representatives to govern them (pp. 57, 211)

Republican party political party established in the United States in 1854 with the goal of keeping slavery out of the western territories (p. 473)

resident alien noncitizen living in the country (p. 266)

revival large outdoor religious meeting (p. 435)

Roosevelt Corollary statement by Theodore Roosevelt that the United States had a right to intervene in Latin America to preserve law and order (p. 678)

Rosie the Riveter fictional factory worker who became a symbol of American women's contribution to the war effort during World War II (p. 785)

Rough Riders nickname for a military unit organized by Theodore Roosevelt during the Spanish-American War (p. 672)

royal colony colony under the direct control of the English crown (p. 109)

rugged individualist person who follows his or her own independent course in life (p. 381)

S

sabotage secret destruction of property or interference with production in a factory or other workplace (p. 737)

sachem member of the tribal chief council in the League of the Iroquois (p. 48)

SALT Agreement (Strategic Arms Limitation Talks) treaty between the United States and the Soviet Union to limit the number of nuclear warheads and missiles (p. 833)

salvation everlasting life (p. 56)

Salvation Army an international charitable organization (p. 609)

sanctions measures designed to make a country change its policy (p. 880)

satellite nation nation that is dominated politically and economically by a more powerful nation (p. 811)

savanna region of grasslands (p. 52)

scalawag white southerner who supported the Republicans during Reconstruction (p. 526)

scapegoat person or group who is made to bear the blame for others (p. 775)

secede to withdraw from membership in a group (p. 463)

Second Amendment amendment to the United States Constitution related to the right to bear arms (p. 260)

secondary source account provided after the fact by people who did not directly witness or participate in the event (p. 21)

sectionalism loyalty to a state or section rather than to the whole country (p. 345)

sedition stirring up rebellion against a government (p. 293)

segregation legal separation of people based on racial, ethnic, or other differences (pp. 532, 849)

Selective Service Act law passed by Congress in 1917 that required all men from ages 21 to 30 to register for the military draft (p. 693)

self-determination right of national groups to have their own territory and forms of government (p. 705)

self-sufficient able to produce enough for one's own needs (p. 392)

Senate the smaller of the two bodies that make up the legislative branch of the United States government (p. 253)

Seneca Falls Convention an 1848 meeting at which leaders of the women's rights movement called for equal rights for women (p. 445)

separation of powers principle by which the powers of government are divided among separate branches (p. 214)

settlement house community center organized in the late 1800s to offer services to the poor (p. 609)

sharecropper person who rents a plot of land from another person and farms it in exchange for a share of the crop (p. 529)

Sherman Antitrust Act an 1890 law that banned the formation of trusts and monopolies in the United States (pp. 582, 632)

siege military blockade or bombardment of an enemy town or position in order to force it to surrender (pp. 193, 387, 506)

silent majority term for Americans who were disturbed by unrest in the 1960s but did not protest publicly (p. 860)

sit-down strike strike in which workers refuse to leave the workplace until a settlement is reached (p. 762)

sit-in form of protest in which people sit and refuse to leave (p. 862)

skyscraper tall building with many floors supported by a lightweight steel frame (p. 612)

slave code laws that controlled the lives of enslaved African Americans and denied them basic rights (pp. 119, 424)

smuggling importing or exporting goods in violation of trade laws (p. 314)

Social Gospel movement within American Protestantism in the late 1800s that attempted to apply biblical teachings to society's problems (p. 609)

social reform an organized attempt to improve what is unjust or imperfect in society (p. 434)

social sciences studies that relate to human society and social behavior (p. 29)

Social Security Act a 1935 law that set up a system of pensions for older people and set up the nation's first system of unemployment insurance (p. 762)

Socialist person who supports community ownership of property and the sharing of all profits (p. 696)

Society of American Indians group that worked for social justice and tried to push Native Americans into the American mainstream (p. 653)

sociology the study of how people behave in groups (p. 30)

sod house house built of soil held together by grass roots (p. 564)

sodbuster farmer on the Great Plains in the late 1800s (p. 564)

Solidarity independent labor union that challenged Poland's communist government (p. 834)

soup kitchen place where food is provided to the needy at little or no charge (p. 750)

Spanish-American War war between Spain and the United States in 1898 (p. 671)

speculator someone who invests in a risky venture in the hope of making a large profit (p. 280)

sphere of influence area where a nation had special trading privileges (p. 666)

spinning jenny machine developed in 1764 that could spin several threads at once (p. 331)

spoils system practice of rewarding supporters with government jobs (p. 366)

Glossary

Square Deal Theodore Roosevelt's campaign promise that all groups would have an equal opportunity to succeed (p. 640)

stagflation combination of rising prices, high unemployment, and slow economic growth (p. 860)

stalemate deadlock in which neither side is strong enough to defeat the other (p. 688)

standard of living index based on the amount of goods, services, and leisure time people have (p. 845)

Star Wars President Reagan's proposed weapons system to destroy Soviet missiles from space (p. 834)

states' rights the right of states to limit the power of the federal government (pp. 293, 370)

Statue of Liberty a large statue symbolizing hope and freedom on Liberty Island in New York Harbor (p. 602)

steerage on a ship, the cramped quarters for passengers paying the lowest fares (p. 601)

stock share of ownership in a corporation (pp. 580, 720)

Strategic Arms Reduction Treaty (START) a 1991 treaty signed by the United States and Soviet Union to reduce nuclear weapons (p. 882)

strike refusal by workers to do their jobs until their demands are met (p. 414)

strikebreaker replacement for a striking worker (p. 591)

subsidy financial aid or land grant from the government (p. 550)

suburb residential area on the outskirts of a city (pp. 613, 728, 845)

suffrage the right to vote (p. 361)

suffragist person who worked for women's right to vote (p. 646)

summit meeting conference between the highest-ranking officials of different nations (p. 835)

superpower nation with the military, political, and economic strength to influence events worldwide (p. 823)

Supreme Court highest court in the United States established by the Constitution (p. 256)

surplus extra; condition that exists when income exceeds spending (pp. 37, 876)

sweatshop workplace where people labor long hours in poor conditions for low pay (p. 591)

T

tariff tax on foreign goods brought into a country (p. 281)

Teapot Dome Scandal, political scandal during President Harding's administration (p. 719)

telegraph communications device that sends electrical signals along a wire (p. 409)

temperance movement campaign against alcohol consumption (p. 436)

Ten Percent Plan Lincoln's plan that allowed a southern state to form a new government after 10 percent of its voters swore an oath of loyalty to the United States (p. 517)

tenement small apartment in a city slum building (p. 607)

Tennessee Valley Authority New Deal program that built dams to control flooding and produce cheap electric power (p. 756)

tepee tent made by stretching buffalo skins on tall poles (p. 545)

terrace wide shelf of land cut into a hillside (p. 40)

terrorism deliberate use of violence to spread fear and achieve political goals (pp. 688, 886)

Tet Offensive North Vietnamese and Vietcong surprise attack on American forces in Vietnam on the Vietnamese New Year's holiday in 1968 (p. 829)

Thanksgiving day at the end of the harvest season set aside by the Pilgrims to give thanks to God (p. 97)

thematic map map that deals with a specific topic, such as population, natural resources, or elections (p. 9)

Thirteenth Amendment an 1865 amendment to the United States Constitution that bans slavery throughout the nation (p. 519)

38th parallel dividing line between South Korea and North Korea (p. 816)

total war all-out war that affects civilians at home as well as soldiers in combat (p. 508)

totalitarian state country where a single party controls the government and every aspect of people's lives (p. 774)

town meeting meeting in colonial New England where settlers discussed and voted on issues (p. 107)

trade deficit condition that exists when a nation buys more goods and services from foreign countries than it sells to them (p. 889)

trade union association of trade workers formed to gain higher wages and better working conditions (pp. 414, 592)

traitor person who betrays his or her country (p. 175)

transatlantic crossing or spanning the Atlantic Ocean (p. 585)

transcendentalists New England writers and thinkers who believed that the most important truths in life transcended, or went beyond, human reason (p. 450)

 transcontinental railroad railroad that stretches across a continent from coast to coast (p. 549)

travois sled pulled by a dog or horse (p. 545)

treason actions against one's country (p. 476)

Treaty of Brest-Litovsk a 1918 treaty between Russia and Germany that ended Russia's involvement in World War I (p. 699)

Treaty of Kanagawa an 1854 treaty between Japan and the United States that opened up ports to American trade in Japan (p. 661)

Treaty of Versailles treaty signed on June 28, 1919, by Germany and the Allies; formally placed the responsibility for the war on Germany and its allies (p. 706)

Triangle Fire fire in 1911 at the Triangle Shirtwaist Factory in New York City that killed nearly 150 workers (p. 593)

triangular trade colonial trade route between New England, the West Indies, and Africa (p. 121)

tribe community of people that share common customs, language, and rituals (p. 42)

tributary stream or smaller river that flows into a larger one (p. 15)

tribute bribe (p. 313)

Truman Doctrine President Truman's policy of giving American aid to nations threatened by communist expansion (p. 811)

trust group of corporations run by a single board of directors (p. 581)

trustbuster person who wanted to break up all trusts (p. 640)

turning point moment in history that marks a decisive change (p. 70)

turnpike road built by a private company that charges a toll to use it (p. 339)

Glossary ★ **957**

Tuskegee Airmen African American fighter pilots who trained in Tuskegee, Alabama, during World War II (p. 787)

tutor private teacher (p. 128)

Twenty-sixth Amendment amendment to the United States Constitution that lowered the minimum voting age from 21 to 18 (p. 261)

U

U-boat German submarine used in World War I and World War II (p. 690)

Uncle Tom's Cabin an 1852 novel by Harriet Beecher Stowe written to show the evils of slavery and the injustice of the Fugitive Slave Act (p. 466)

unconstitutional not permitted by the Constitution (pp. 257, 288)

Underground Railroad network of abolitionists who secretly helped slaves escape to freedom (p. 441)

United Nations world organization established in 1945 to provide peaceful resolutions to international conflicts (p. 813)

urbanization movement of population from farms to cities (pp. 335, 606)

V

vaquero Spanish or Mexican cowhand (pp. 392, 553)

vaudeville variety show made popular in the late 1800s that included comedians, song-and-dance routines, and acrobats (p. 615)

vertical integration practice in which a single manufacturer controls all of the steps used to change raw materials into finished products (p. 579)

veto to reject, as when the President rejects a law passed by Congress (p. 257)

victory garden during World War II, vegetable garden planted to combat food shortages in the United States (p. 785)

Vietcong Vietnamese guerrillas who opposed the noncommunist government of South Vietnam (p. 828)

vigilante self-appointed enforcer of the law (pp. 401, 549)

Virginia ironclad warship used by the Confederates to break the Union blockade (p. 492)

W

Wade-Davis Bill an 1864 plan for Reconstruction that denied the right to vote or hold office to anyone who had volunteered to fight for the Confederacy (p. 517)

War Production Board government agency created during World War II to help factories shift from making consumer goods to making war materials (p. 785)

warmonger person who tries to stir up war (p. 691)

Warsaw Pact military alliance, established in 1955, of the Soviet Union and other communist states in Europe (p. 813)

WCTU (Women's Christian Temperance Union) group organized in 1874 that worked to ban the sale of liquor in the United States (p. 648)

weather condition of the earth's atmosphere at a given time and place (p. 15)

wholesale buying or selling something in large quantities at lower prices (p. 565)

Wilmot Proviso law passed in 1846 that banned slavery in any territories won by the United States from Mexico (p. 461)

Wisconsin Idea series of Progressive reforms introduced in the early 1900s by Wisconsin governor Robert La Follette (p. 635)

women's rights movement organized campaign to win property, education, and other rights for women (p. 446)

writ of assistance legal document that allowed British customs officials to inspect a ship's cargo without giving a reason (p. 150)

Y

yellow journalism news reporting, often biased or untrue, that relies on sensational stories and headlines (pp. 619, 670)

Young Men's Hebrew Association (YMHA) organization founded in Baltimore in 1854 to provide community services to Jewish neighborhoods (p. 609)

Z

Zimmermann telegram a 1917 telegram sent from Germany's foreign secretary to the German minister in Mexico instructing the minister to urge Mexico to attack the United States if the United States declared war on Germany (p. 692)

Glossary

Spanish Glossary

A

abdicate/abdicar entregar el poder (pág. 701)

abolitionist/abolicionista persona que quería acabar la esclavitud (pág. 440)

acculturation/aculturación proceso por el cual se mantienen viejas tradiciones mientras se va adoptando otra cultura (pág. 604)

adobe/adobe ladrillo secado al sol (pág. 41)

affirmative action/acción afirmativa programa que proporciona más oportunidades de trabajo y educación a personas que sufrieron discriminación en el pasado (pág. 864)

AFL/AFL (Federación Americana de Trabajadores) organización de sindicatos que representaba a trabajadores cualificados (pág. 592)

aggression/agresión acto similar a un acto de guerra de un país contra otro sin que haya una causa justa (pág. 775)

alliance/alianza acuerdo entre naciones para ayudarse y protegerse mutuamente (pág. 85)

Alliance for Progress/Alianza para el Progreso programa que desarrolló el presidente Kennedy para promover reformas sociales en América Latina (pág. 824)

Allied Powers/potencias aliadas alianza militar entre Francia, Inglaterra, Rusia, Italia y 20 otras naciones durante la Primera Guerra Mundial (pág. 688)

Allies/aliados alianza militar entre Inglaterra, Francia, la Unión Soviética, Estados Unidos, China y otros 45 países (pág. 779)

ally/aliado nación que trabaja con otra nación hacia una meta común (pág. 183)

altitude/altura elevación sobre el nivel del mar (pág. 15)

amend/reformar cambiar (pág. 218)

American Association of Retired Persons/Asociación Americana de Personas Jubiladas (AARP) organización que lleva a cabo el seguimiento y control de los asuntos de interés para personas de edad más avanzada (pág. 897)

American Indian Religious Freedom Act/Ley de Libertad Religiosa de los Indígenas Estadounidenses ley de 1978 que obligó a las agencias federales a no obstaculizar las prácticas religiosas de los indígenas (pág. 896)

Americans With Disabilities Act/Ley de los Estadounidenses Discapacitados ley de 1990 que prohíbe la discriminación al contratar a personas con dificultades físicas o mentales (pág. 897)

amnesty/amnistía perdón del gobierno (pág. 517)

anarchist/anarquista persona que se opone a todas las formas de gobierno organizado (págs. 592, 737)

annex/anexar agregar; incorporar un territorio (págs. 389, 661)

anthropology/antropología estudio de cómo se desarrollan las personas y las culturas (pág. 30)

Antifederalists/antifederalistas personas que se oponían a la constitución y a un gobierno nacional fuerte (pág. 215)

apartheid/apartheid separación estricta de las razas practicada anteriormente en Sudáfrica (pág. 880)

appeal/apelar pedir a una corte de mayor autoridad que reconsidere una decisión (pág. 256)

appeasement/apaciguamiento aceptación de agresiones para evitar una guerra (pág. 779)

Appomattox Court House/Appomattox Court House ciudad de Virginia en donde la Confederación se rindió en 1865 (pág. 509)

apprentice/aprendiz persona que aprende un oficio o artesanía de un maestro (pág.128)

archaeology/arqueología estudio de las evidencias dejadas por culturas antiguas con el objeto de conocer su forma de vida (pág. 22)

armistice/armisticio acuerdo para detener el combate (pág. 701)

arsenal/arsenal depósito de armas (pág. 476)

Articles/artículos parte principal de la constitución que establece la estructura del gobierno de Estados Unidos (pág. 249)

Articles of Confederation/Artículos de la Confederación primera constitución de Estados Unidos; aprobada en 1777, creó una alianza tenue entre los 13 estados independientes (pág. 201)

artifact/artefacto objeto hecho por seres humanos (pág. 22)

artisan/artesano trabajador manual cualificado (pág. 413)

assembly line/cadena de montaje método de producción según el cual los trabajadores permanecen en un lugar fijo mientras los productos pasan frente a ellos sobre una cinta transportadora (pág. 588)

astrolabe/astrolabio instrumento de navegación que se usa para determinar la latitud (pág. 59)

amnesty/amnistía perdón del gobierno (pág. 517)

Atlantic Charter/Cédula del Atlántico programa creado por Estados Unidos e Inglaterra en 1941, que estableció objetivos para el mundo en la posguerra (pág. 782)

atrocity/atrocidad acto de crueldad y brutalidad (pág. 670)

authenticity/autenticidad condición de ser genuino (pág. 21)

Axis/eje alianza militar durante la Segunda Guerra Mundial entre Alemania, Italia, Japón y otras seis naciones (pág. 779)

B

baby boom/baby boom gran incremento de la tasa de natalidad en Estados Unidos desde finales de la década de1940 hasta principios de la década de 1960 (pág. 844)

balanced budget/presupuesto equilibrado condición que se da cuando el gobierno sólo gasta la cantidad que recibe (pág. 874)

bank holiday/feriado bancario cierre de los bancos por cuatro días durante la Gran Depresión (pág. 753)

bankrupt/en bancarrota sin capacidad para pagar las deudas (pág. 748)

barrio/barrio término que se refiere vecindarios de población mexicano-americana (pág. 651)

Bataan Death March/marcha de la muerte de Bataan viaje largo y difícil a través de Filipinas que los japoneses obligaron a realizar a prisioneros de guerra estadounidenses y filipinos en 1942 (pág. 799)

Battle of Antietam/batalla de Antietam sangrienta batalla librada en Maryland en 1862 durante la Guerra Civil (pág. 493)

Battle of Belleau Wood/batalla del bosque de Belleau difícil victoria de Estados Unidos sobre Alemania, en Francia en 1918 (pág. 700)

Battle of Britain/batalla de Inglaterra intento fracasado de Alemania de someter a Inglaterra en 1940, como preparación para una invasión (pág. 780)

Battle of Bull Run/batalla de Bull Run primera gran batalla de la Guerra Civil, librada en Virginia en 1861 (pág. 491)

Battle of Chancellorsville/batalla de Chancellorsville batalla librada en Virginia en 1863 durante la Guerra Civil; fue una victoria importante para la Confederación (pág. 493)

Battle of Fredericksburg/batalla de Fredericksburg batalla librada en

Virginia en 1862 durante la Guerra Civil; fue una de las peores derrotas de la Unión (pág. 493)

Battle of Gettysburg/batalla de Gettysburg batalla librada en Pennsylvania en 1863 durante la Guerra Civil; evitó que los Confederados invadieron el Norte (pág. 506)

Battle of Midway/batalla de Midway batalla de 1942 en el Pacífico en la que aviones de Estados Unidos hundieron cuatro portaviones japoneses (pág. 792)

Battle of Shiloh/batalla de Shiloh batalla librada en 1862 en Tennessee, que terminó en una victoria de la Unión (pág. 494)

Battle of the Argonne Forest/ batalla del bosque de Argonne derrota de los alemanes en Francia en octubre de 1918 por las tropas francesas y estadounidenses (pág. 701)

Battle of the Bulge/batalla de Bulge contraataque alemán en diciembre de 1944, que atrasó por un tiempo la invasión de los aliados a Alemania (pág. 793)

Battle of Verdun/batalla de Verdún batalla prolongada de la Primera Guerra Mundial en la que murieron o fueron heridas más de un millón de personas (pág. 689)

Bay of Pigs invasion/invasión de la bahía de los Cochinos intento fallido de invadir Cuba en 1961 por cubanos anticastristas (pág. 823)

beatnik/*beatnik* en la década de 1950, persona que criticaba a la cultura estadounidense por su conformidad y devoción por los negocios (pág. 847)

Berlin Airlift/puente aéreo de Berlín operación de ayuda llevada a cabo por aviones estadounidenses y británicos para transportar suministros a los habitantes de Berlín occidental durante el bloqueo soviético de 1948 a 1949 (pág. 812)

Berlin Wall/muro de Berlín muro construido por el gobierno comunista de Alemania oriental en 1961 para aislar Berlín oriental de Berlín occidental (pág. 813)

Bessemer process/sistema Bessemer método inventado en la década de 1850 para producir un acero más resistente a un menor costo (pág. 578)

bias/prejuicio inclinación a favor o en contra de cierta persona, grupo o idea (pág. 22)

Big Four/los cuatro grandes los líderes de las naciones aliadas (Gran Bretaña, Estados Unidos, Francia e Italia) después de la Primera Guerra Mundial (pág. 706)

bilingual/bilingüe en dos idiomas (pág. 866)

bill/proyecto de ley ley que se propone para su aprobación (pág. 253)

bill of rights/declaración de derechos lista escrita de las libertades que el gobierno promete proteger (págs. 123, 200)

Bill of Rights/Declaración de Derechos las primeras 10 enmiendas de la Constitución de Estados Unidos (pág. 218)

Black Cabinet/Gabinete Negro líderes afroamericanos que asesoraban extraoficialmente al presidente Franklin D. Roosevelt en asuntos importantes para los afroamericanos (pág. 767)

black codes/códigos de negros leyes aprobadas por los estados del Sur después de la Guerra Civil que limitaban con severidad los derechos de los afroamericanos (pág. 521)

Black Tuesday/Martes Negro (29 de octubre de 1929) día en que calló el mercado de valores, marcando el comienzo de la Gran Depresión (pág. 747)

blitzkrieg/*blitzkrieg* palabra alemana que significa guerra relámpago, los rápidos ataques lanzados por Alemania en la Segunda Guerra Mundial (pág. 779)

blockade/bloqueo cierre de un puerto para que ni las personas ni las provisiones entren o salgan (pág. 171)

boat people/balseros después de la guerra de Vietnam, refugiados que huyeron de Vietnam en pequeñas embarcaciones (pág. 831)

bond/bono certificado que promete el pago de dinero que se ha prestado, más el interés, en una determinada fecha (pág. 280)

bonus/bono cantidad adicional de dinero (pág. 751)

Bonus Army/ejército del bono veteranos que marcharon hacia Washington en 1932 para exigir que se aprobara un proyecto de ley que proveía el pago inmediato del bono que les correspondía por la Primera Guerra Mundial (pág. 751)

bootlegger/contrabandista persona que introducía de contrabando bebidas alcohólicas en Estados Unidos durante la época de la Ley Seca (pág. 725)

Border Ruffians/rufianes de frontera bandas proesclavistas que a menudo combatían las fuerzas anti-esclavistas en Kansas (pág. 470)

border state/estado de frontera estado esclavista que permaneció en la Unión durante la Guerra Civil (pág. 487)

Boxer Rebellion/rebelión de los Boxers revuelta contra Occidente y la influencia occidental en China en 1900 (pág. 666)

boycott/boicot rechazar la compra o el uso de ciertos bienes o servicios (págs. 150, 852)

bracero program/programa de braceros contratación de jornaleros mexicanos para trabajar en Estados Unidos durante la Segunda Guerra Mundial (pág. 788)

Buffalo Soldiers/soldados búfalos sobrenombre de los afroamericanos integrantes de los batallones de caballería noveno y décimo durante la guerra Hispano-Americana (pág. 672)

building code/código de construcción normas para la construcción y seguridad de los edificios (pág. 609)

bull market/mercado alcista período en el cual la compraventa de acciones aumenta y suben los precios de las acciones (pág. 720)

Bull Moose party/partido del alce republicanos progresistas que apoyaron a Theodore Roosevelt durante la elección de 1912 (pág. 642)

bureaucracy/burocracia sistema de administración del gobierno mediante departamentos dirigidos por funcionarios nombrados (pág. 694)

burgess/burgués representante del gobierno colonial de Virginia (pág. 90)

C

Cabinet/gabinete grupo de funcionarios que dirigen departamentos gubernamentales y aconsejan al presidente (pág. 279)

Camp David Accords/acuerdos de Camp David tratado de paz firmado en 1997 entre Israel y Egipto en el que Israel accedió a devolver a Egipto la península de Sinaí y Egipto accedió a reconocer a Israel (pág. 884)

capital/capital dinero con el que se inicia un negocio (pág. 331)

capitalist/capitalista persona que invierte en un negocio con el fin de obtener beneficios (pág. 331)

caravan/caravana grupo de personas que viajaban juntas por razones de seguridad (pág. 52)

carpetbagger/*carpetbagger* sobrenombre despreciativo dado a los norteños que se mudaron al Sur después de la Guerra Civil (pág. 527)

cartographer/cartógrafo persona que hace mapas (pág. 8)

cash crop/cosecha de contado cosecha vendida por dinero en el mercado (pág. 111)

cash economy/cultivo comercial economía en la que se intercambian dinero por mercancías y servicios (pág. 27)

cattle drive/arreo de ganado conducir y llevar ganado, normalmente hacia las vías del ferrocarril (pág. 553)

caucus/reunión encuentro privado, a menudo de carácter político (pág. 364)

causeway/paso elevado camino elevado hecho con tierra comprimida (pág. 38)

cavalry/caballería tropas a caballo (pág. 184)

cede/ceder entregar (págs. 202, 396)

censure/censurar condenar oficialmente (pág. 820)

Central Powers/potencias centrales alianza militar entre Alemania, el Imperio Austro-Húngaro, Bulgaria y el Imperio Otomano durante la Primera Guerra Mundial (pág. 688)

charter/carta legal documento que da ciertos derechos a una persona o compañía (pág. 88)

checks and balances/controlar y equilibrar principio de la Constitución de Estados Unidos que da a cada rama del gobierno el poder de vigilar las otras ramas (pág. 251)

Chinese Exclusion Act/Ley de la Exclusión China ley aprobada por el Congreso en 1882 que prohibía a los trabajadores chinos entrar a Estados Unidos (pág. 605)

chronology/cronología secuencia de sucesos a través del tiempo (pág. 25)

circumnavigate/circunnavegar viajar alrededor de la Tierra (pág. 71)

citizen/ciudadano persona que debe lealtad a una nación particular y se beneficia de la protección y de todos los derechos de dicha nación (pág. 265)

city-state/ciudad estado ciudad grande que tiene su propio gobierno y controla el campo que la rodea (pág. 52)

civic virtue/virtud cívica deseo de trabajar por el bien de una nación o comunidad aun a costa de grandes sacrificios (pág. 266)

civics/educación cívica estudio de los derechos y responsabilidades de los ciudadanos (pág. 29)

civil/civil se refiere a los juicios sobre derechos privados de los individuos (pág. 261)

civil disobedience/desobediencia civil idea de que las personas tienen derecho a desobedecer las leyes que consideren injustas, si su conciencia lo exige (págs. 451, 853)

civil rights/derechos civiles los derechos que corresponden a todos los ciudadanos (pág. 767)

civil rights movement/movimiento de los derechos civiles lucha de los afroamericanos para conseguir igualdad de derechos (pág. 850)

civil service/servicio civil todos los puestos federales excepto los que se eligen por votación y los puestos militares (pág. 631)

Civil Service Commission/Comisión de Servicio Civil agencia del gobierno creada en 1883 para asignar puestos federales basándose en el mérito de los candidatos (pág. 631)

civil war/guerra civil guerra entre personas del mismo país (pág. 465)

Civil War amendments/enmiendas de la Guerra Civil enmiendas Trece, Catorce y Quince de la Constitución de Estados Unidos (pág. 261)

civilian/civil no militar (pág. 249)

Civilian Conservation Corps/ Cuerpo de Conservación Civil programa del Nuevo Acuerdo que daba trabajo a hombres solteros y desempleados en proyectos de conservación de la naturaleza en todo el país (pág. 754)

clan/clan grupo de dos o más familias emparentadas (pág. 48)

climate/clima promedio del tiempo de un lugar en un período de 20 a 30 años (pág. 15)

clipper ship/clíper barco de mediados del siglo XIX que navegaba velozmente (pág. 410)

Cold War/Guerra Fría después de la Segunda Guerra Mundial, largo período de intensa rivalidad entre la Unión Soviética y Estados Unidos (pág. 810)

collective bargaining/negociación colectiva proceso por el cual un sindicato que representa un grupo de trabajadores negociaba un contrato con la dirección de la empresa (págs. 592, 761)

colony/colonia grupo de personas que se establece en una tierra distante pero sigue bajo la dirección del gobierno de su tierra natal (pág. 70)

Columbian Exchange/intercambio colombino intercambio global de bienes e ideas que resulta del encuentro entre los pueblos de los hemisferios occidental y oriental (pág. 71)

committee of correspondence/ comité de correspondencia campaña que consistió en escribir cartas y se convirtió en un importante instrumento de protesta en la colonia (pág. 153)

communism/comunismo sistema económico según el cual toda la propiedad y la riqueza pertenecen al Estado (pág. 722)

company union/sindicato de empresa organización de trabajadores cuyo control recae realmente en la dirección de la empresa (pág. 737)

compensation/compensación pago por pérdidas (pág. 788)

Comprehensive Test Ban Treaty/ Tratado de Prohibición de Ensayos Nucleares acuerdo propuesto en 1996 con el fin de terminar todas las pruebas de armas nucleares (pág. 882)

compromise/compromiso documento en el que cada lado cede en algunas de sus posiciones para poder llegar a un acuerdo (pág. 208)

Compromise of 1850/Compromiso de 1850 acuerdo con respecto a la esclavitud según el cual California se sumó a la Unión como estado libre, y se aprobó una estricta ley sobre esclavos fugitivos (pág. 465)

compulsory education/educación obligatoria requisito de que los niños fueran a la escuela hasta un cierto grado o una cierta edad (pág. 617)

concentration camp/campo de concentración campo de prisioneros civiles que se consideraban enemigos del Estado (pág. 776)

confederation/confederación liga de estados o naciones independientes (pág. 317)

Congress of Industrial Organizations/Congreso de Organizaciones Industriales (CIO) organización de trabajadores fundada en la década de 1930 para representar a los trabajadores de las industrias básicas de producción en masa (pág. 762)

conquistador/conquistador término que se refiere a los exploradores españoles que conquistaron en el nombre de España tierras en las Américas (pág. 74)

conservation/conservación protección de los recursos naturales (pág. 641)

Conservatives/conservadores durante la Reconstrucción, los blancos del Sur que se resistían al cambio (pág. 527)

consolidate/consolidar reunir, juntar (pág. 575)

constitution/constitución documento que establece las leyes, principios, organización y sistema de un gobierno (pág. 200)

Constitutional Convention/ Convención Constitucional reunión de los representantes de los estados realizada el 25 de mayo de 1787 para revisar los Artículos de la Confederación (pág. 206)

consumer/consumidor el que usa bienes y servicios (pág. 27)

containment/contención política que consistía en tratar de impedir la extensión de la influencia soviética más allá de donde ya existía (pág. 811)

continental divide/divisoria continental cadena de montañas que separa sistemas fluviales que corren en direcciones opuestas en un continente (pág. 309)

Contract With America/contrato con América paquete legislativo aprobado en1994 por los republicanos de la Cámara de Representantes que incluía el recorte de los programas de asistencia social, la reducción de la normativa medioambiental y la bajada de impuestos (pág. 875)

cooperative/cooperativa grupo de granjeros que contribuyen con dinero para comprar semillas o herramientas al por mayor (pág. 565)

Copperhead/Copperhead norteño que oponía el uso de la fuerza para mantener los estados del Sur dentro de la Unión (pág. 501)

corduroy road/camino de troncos camino hecho con troncos (pág. 339)

corollary/corolario añadidura a un principio enunciado anteriormente (pág. 678)

corporation/corporación negocio cuyos dueños son los inversionistas (pág. 580)

corral/corral recinto para animales (pág. 545)

"cottonocracy"/"algodocracia" sobrenombre dado a dueños de plantaciones ricos que hicieron su dinero con el algodón a mediados del siglo XIX (pág. 422)

counterculture/contracultura movimiento de protesta de la década de 1960 que rechazaba los valores y la cultura estadounidenses tradicionales (pág. 859)

coureur de bois/coureur de bois colonos franceses que cazaban animales por sus pieles (pág. 83)

cow town/pueblo vaquero asentamiento formado al final de una ruta de ganado (pág. 554)

creole/criollo persona de padres españoles nacida en las colonias españolas de América (págs. 78, 348)

Cuban missile crisis/crisis de los misiles en Cuba enfrentamiento de gran importancia en 1962 en el que Estados Unidos bloqueó el intento soviético de poner misiles atómicos en Cuba (pág. 823)

culture/cultura forma de vida de un pueblo (págs. 22, 40)

culture area/área cultural región en la que las personas tienen una forma de vida similar (pág. 42)

currency/moneda dinero circulante (pág. 202)

czar/zar emperador de Rusia (pág. 692)

D

D-Day/Día D 6 de junio de 1944, día de la invasión de Europa occidental por las potencias aliadas (pág. 792)

dame school/escuela de damas escuela privada dirigida por una mujer, generalmente en su propia casa (pág. 128)

Dayton Accord/Acuerdo de Dayton acuerdo de paz negociado en 1995 entre Bosnia, Croacia y Serbia (pág. 881)

debtor/deudor persona que no puede pagar el dinero que debe (págs. 116, 436)

Declaration of Independence/Declaración de Independencia documento de 1776 que declaraba que las 13 colonias formaban una nación independiente (pág. 175)

deficit spending/gasto deficitario práctica del gobierno de gastar más de lo que se recauda por impuestos (pág. 763)

demilitarized zone/zona desmilitarizada (DMZ) área en la que las fuerzas militares están prohibidas (pág. 818)

democratic/democrático que asegura que todas las personas tengan los mismos derechos (pág. 302)

department store/gran almacén tienda que ofrece al por menor una variedad de artículos organizados en departamentos separados (pág. 613)

deport/deportar expulsar de un país (pág. 737)

depression/depresión período en que la actividad comercial disminuye, los precios y los salarios bajan, y aumenta el desempleo (págs. 204, 373)

deregulation/desregulación reducción al control de las empresas (pág. 873)

détente/detente política de reducir las tensiones entre las superpotencias (pág. 833)

dictator/dictador gobernante que tiene poder y autoridad absolutos (pág. 386)

dime novel/novelas de diez centavos a finales del siglo XIX, libros de aventuras con tapa blanda y baratos (pág. 619)

direct democracy/democracia directa forma de gobierno según la cual los ciudadanos comunes tienen el poder de gobernar (pág. 57)

disarmament/desarme reducción de las fuerzas militares y el armamento (pág. 722)

discrimination/discriminación política que niega derechos igualitarios a ciertos grupos de personas (pág. 417)

dividend/dividendo parte de las ganancias de una corporación (pág. 580)

dollar diplomacy/diplomacia del dólar política del presidente Taft que consistía en tratar de crear fuertes lazos económicos con Latinoamérica (pág. 678)

domestic tranquility/tranquilidad interna orden y paz interna de una nación (pág. 249)

domino theory/teoría del dominó convencimiento de que si Vietnam del Sur sucumbía al comunismo, otros países cercanos seguirían el mismo camino (pág. 828)

"Double V" campaign/campaña "Doble V" campaña por los derechos civiles de los afroamericanos durante la Segunda Guerra Mundial (pág. 786)

downsizing/reducción de plantilla reducir el número de trabajadores (pág. 874)

draft/leva ley que obliga a las personas de cierta edad a alistarse en el servicio militar (págs. 502, 693, 829)

Dred Scott v. Sandford/Dred Scott versus Sandford un caso que llegó a la Corte Suprema en 1857 y puso en duda el poder federal con respecto a la esclavitud en los territorios (pág. 471)

Dust Bowl/Cuenca de Polvo región del centro de las Grandes Llanuras que sufrió una gran sequía en la década de 1930 (pág. 765)

E

e-commerce/comercio electrónico negocios y comercio por Internet (pág. 892)

Earth Summit/Cumbre de la Tierra reunión de los líderes mundiales en 1992 para dialogar acerca de los principales asuntos medioambientales (pág. 890)

economics/economía el estudio de cómo las personas manejan recursos limitados para satisfacer sus deseos y necesidades (pág. 26)

Eighteenth Amendment/Enmienda Decimoctava enmienda a la Constitución de Estados Unidos aprobada en 1917 que declaraba ilegal la venta de bebidas en el país (pág. 648)

electoral college/colegio electoral grupo de electores de cada estado que cada cuatro años vota para elegir al presidente y vicepresidente de Estados Unidos (pág. 255)

elevation/elevación altura por encima del nivel del mar (pág. 13)

emancipate/emancipar liberar (pág. 497)

Emancipation Proclamation/Proclama de Emancipación declaración de 1863 del presidente Lincoln que liberaba a los esclavos de la Confederación (pág. 497)

embargo/embargo prohibición de comerciar (pág. 314)

encomienda/encomienda tierra otorgada por el gobierno español a los colonos españoles; incluía el derecho a exigir trabajo o impuestos a los indígenas (pág. 78)

Spanish Glossary

Environmental Protection Agency/Agencia de Protección Medioambiental agencia del gobierno federal que tiene como cometido hacer cumplir la normativa medioambiental (pág. 890)

environmentalist/ecologista persona que lucha por reducir la polución y proteger el medio ambiente (pág. 889)

epidemic/epidemia dispersión rápida de una enfermedad contagiosa (pág. 702)

Equal Rights Amendment/Enmienda por la Igualdad de Derechos enmienda constitucional propuesta en 1923, que tenía como objetivo prohibir toda discriminación sexual; la enmienda nunca fue aprobada (pág. 726)

erosion/erosión desgaste gradual (pág. 13)

escalate/extender intensificar (pág. 828)

established church/iglesia oficial religión elegida por un Estado (pág. 94)

execute/ejecutar llevar a cabo (pág. 201)

executive branch/rama ejecutiva rama del gobierno que hace cumplir las leyes (pág. 208)

exile/exiliado persona forzada a abandonar su propio país (pág. 823)

expansionism/expansionismo política que consiste en extender los límites de una nación (pág. 660)

expatriate/expatriado persona que renuncia a su propio país y pasa a residir en el extranjero (pág. 731)

expedition/expedición largo viaje de exploración (pág. 308)

export/producto de exportación artículo comercial que se envía a mercados extranjeros (pág. 120)

extended family/familia extendida grupo familiar que incluye abuelos, padres, hijos, tías, tíos y primos (págs. 53, 425)

F

faction/facción grupo de oposición dentro de un partido (pág. 287)

factory system/sistema de fábricas método de producción que reunió en un mismo lugar trabajadores y maquinaria (pág. 331)

fad/novedad actividad o moda pasajera que se adopta con gran pasión por poco tiempo (pág. 730)

famine/hambruna severa escasez de alimentos (pág. 415)

Fascism/fascismo sistema político basado en el militarismo, el nacionalismo extremo y la lealtad ciega al Estado (pág. 774)

Federal Reserve Act/Ley de la Reserva Federal ley de 1913 que estableció un sistema de bancos federales y dio al gobierno el poder de controlar el suministro de dinero (pág. 643)

Federal Trade Commission (FTC)/Comisión Federal de Comercio (FTC) agencia del gobierno creada en 1914 para asegurar la competencia justa (pág. 643)

federalism/federalismo principio de la Constitución de Estados Unidos que establece la división de poderes entre el gobierno federal y los estados (pág. 251)

Federalist/federalista partidario de la Constitución quien estaba a favor de un gobierno federal o nacional fuerte (págs. 215, 289)

The Federalist Papers/Los Ensayos Federalistas ensayos escritos por los Federalistas James Madison, Alexander Hamilton y John Jay que apoyaban la ratificación de la Constitución (pág. 216)

feudalism/feudalismo sistema de gobierno en el que los señores regían sus propias tierras pero debían lealtad y servicio militar a un monarca (pág. 58)

Fifteenth Amendment/Enmienda Decimoquinta enmienda a la Constitución de Estados Unidos aprobada en 1869 que prohibe a los estados negar a los afroamericanos el derecho al voto por causa de su raza (pág. 524)

54th Massachusetts Regiment/regimiento 54° de Massachusetts unidad afroamericana del ejército de la Unión (pág. 499)

fireside chat/charla alrededor del fuego discurso por radio del presidente Franklin D. Roosevelt durante su presidencia (pág. 754)

First Amendment/Primera Enmienda enmienda a la Constitución de Estados Unidos que protege las libertades individuales básicas (pág. 260)

first global age/primera era global época a comienzos del siglo XV en la que el comercio y los viajes aumentaron notablemente (pág. 50)

flapper/flapper mujer joven que en la década de 1920 se revelaba contra los maneras tradicionales de pensar y actuar (pág. 731)

flatboat/carguero de poco fondo embarcación que se usa para transportar carga pesada en rutas acuáticas de tierra adentro (pág. 337)

Foraker Act/Ley de Foraker ley aprobada por el Congreso en 1900 bajo la cual Estados Unidos dio a los puertorriqueños una voz limitada en sus propios asuntos (pág. 674)

foreign policy/política exterior acciones de una nación en relación con otras naciones (pág. 285)

Fort Wagner/fuerte Wagner fuerte de Carolina del Sur objeto de un ataque en 1863 por parte del Regimiento 54° de Massachusetts (pág. 499)

forty-niner/persona del cuarenta y nueve una de los más de 80,000 personas que en 1849 se unieron a la fiebre del oro (pág. 400)

Founding Fathers/padres de la patria líderes que dieron los primeros pasos para la formación de Estados Unidos (pág. 211)

Fourteen Points/los catorce puntos los objetivos del presidente Wilson para los tiempos de paz después de la Primera Guerra Mundial (pág. 704)

Fourteenth Amendment/Enmienda Decimocuarta enmienda a la Constitución de Estados Unidos aprobada en 1868 que garantiza la protección igualitaria de las leyes (pág. 522)

free enterprise system/sistema de libre empresa sistema económico en el cual los negocios son de los ciudadanos privados, y ellos deciden qué producir, cuánto producir, dónde vender los productos y qué precios cobrar (págs. 28, 581)

free market/mercado libre sistema económico en el cual los bienes y servicios se intercambian con pocas restricciones (pág. 303)

Free-Soil party/partido del territorio libre partido antiesclavista fundado en 1848 en Estados Unidos, para mantener la esclavitud fuera de los territorios del oeste (pág. 462)

freedmen/libertos hombres y mujeres que habían sido esclavos (pág. 517)

Freedmen's Bureau/Oficina de Libertos agencia del gobierno de Estados Unidos fundada durante la Reconstrucción para ayudar a los libertos (pág. 517)

French and Indian War/guerra Franco-Indígena guerra ocurrida de 1754 a 1763 que acabó con el poder francés en América del Norte (pág.142)

frigate/fragata barco armado con muchos cañones que navega rápidamente (pág. 292)

fugitive/fugitivo persona que huye (pág. 464)

Fugitive Slave Act/Acta de los Esclavos Fugitivos ley de 1850 que exigía a todos los ciudadanos colaborar en la captura de esclavos fugitivos (pág. 465)

G

gauge/entrevía distancia entre las vías del tren (pág. 574)

general welfare/bienestar general bienestar de todos los ciudadanos de una nación (pág. 249)

"Gentlemen's Agreement"/"acuerdo entre caballeros" acuerdo de 1907

Spanish Glossary

entre Estados Unidos y Japón para limitar la inmigración japonesa (pág. 652)

gentry/alta burguesía la clase social más alta en las 13 colonias inglesas (pág. 126)

geography/geografía el estudio de las personas, su medio ambiente y sus recursos (pág. 4)

Gettysburg Address/discurso de Gettysburg discurso pronunciado en 1863 por el presidente Lincoln después de la batalla de Gettysburg (pág. 507)

Gilded Age/Época Dorada período en la historia estadounidense durante las últimas dos décadas del siglo XIX, marcado por la corrupción política y e derroche (pág. 630)

glacier/glaciar capa gruesa de hielo (pág. 36)

glasnost/_glasnost_ política de hablar abiertamente de los problemas de la Unión Soviética (pág. 835)

global warming/calentamiento global subida lenta pero ininterrumpida de la temperatura media de la Tierra (pág. 891)

Good Neighbor Policy/política de buena vecindad política del presidente Franklin Roosevelt que tenía como objetivo reforzar las relaciones de amistad con América Latina (pág. 777)

graduated income tax/impuesto sobre la renta escalonado impuesto sobre las ganancias que aplica porcentajes distintos según los diferentes niveles de renta (pág. 636)

grandfather clause/cláusula del abuelo ley que eximía a un votante de la prueba de alfabetización si su padre o su abuelo había sido elegible para votar el 1º de enero de 1867 (pág. 532)

Great Depression/Gran Depresión el peor período de decadencia económica de Estados Unidos; comenzó en 1929 (pág. 747)

Great White Fleet/Gran Flota Blanca nombre de los barcos de vapor de la marina de Estados Unidos, agrandados y modernizados, a principios del siglo XX (pág. 664)

guerrilla warfare/guerrillero uso de tácticas militares de ataque y fuga inmediata (págs. 192, 828)

Gulf of Tonkin Resolution/ Resolución del Golfo de Tonkín resolución aprobada por el Congreso en 1964 que autorizó la intervención militar en Vietnam (pág. 828)

H

habeas corpus/habeas corpus derecho por el cual no puede encarcelarse a ninguna persona a menos que se le acuse de haber cometido un crimen específico (págs. 213, 502)

Harlem Hell Fighters/luchadores infernales de Harlem unidad de infantería compuesta por afroamericanos que luchó junto con el ejército francés en la Primera Guerra Mundial (pág. 700)

Haymarket Riot/revuelta Haymarket mitin laboral que tuvo lugar en Chicago en 1886, encabezado por un grupo pequeño de anarquistas, terminó violentamente al explotar una bomba (pág. 592)

Holocaust/Holocausto masacre de judíos europeos por parte de los nazis antes durante la Segunda Guerra Mundial (pág. 799)

Hooverville/Hooverville conjunto de casuchas miserables donde vivían las personas que no tenían un hogar durante la Gran Depresión (pág. 750)

House of Representatives/Cámara de Representantes el mayor de los dos cuerpos que forman la rama legislativa del gobierno de Estados Unidos (pág. 252)

Hull House/casa Hull centro comunitario fundado en Chicago por la reformadora progresista Jane Addams en 1889 (pág. 610)

Hundred Days/los cien días los primeros 100 días de la presidencia de Franklin D. Roosevelt (pág. 754)

I

ILGWU/_ILGWU_ Sindicato Internacional de Trabajadoras de la Industria del Vestido, fundado en 1900 (pág. 593)

illegal alien/extranjero ilegal inmigrante que entra en un país sin autorización (pág. 895)

illiterate/analfabeto que no sabe leer ni escribir (pág. 694)

immigrant/inmigrante persona que se establece en otro país (pág. 266)

Immigration Reform and Control Act/Ley de Reforma y Control de la Inmigración ley que permitía que las personas que llegaron de forma ilegal a Estados Unidos antes de 1982 pudieran quedarse en el país y solicitar la residencia (pág. 895)

impeach/juicio político acusar formalmente de faltas serias a un representante político (págs. 257, 523)

imperialism/imperialismo política de los países poderosos que tratan de controlar los asuntos económicos y políticos de los países o regiones más débiles (pág. 662)

import/producto de importación artículo comercial que se ha introducido a un país (pág. 120)

impressment/leva práctica de forzar a las personas a que hagan el servicio militar (pág. 313)

inauguration/toma de mando ceremonia en la cual el presidente jura su cargo (pág. 278)

income tax/impuesto a los ingresos un impuesto al dinero que las personas ganan (pág. 502)

incriminate/incriminar presentar evidencias en contra de alguien (pág. 260)

indentured servant/sirviente por contrato persona que aceptaba trabajar sin pago por un tiempo a cambio de un pasaje a las colonias (pág. 126)

Indian New Deal/Nuevo Acuerdo Indígena leyes aprobadas en 1930 que dieron a las naciones de los indígenas un mayor control en sus propios asuntos (pág. 768)

indigo/índigo planta usada para hacer una valiosa tintura azul (pág. 115)

individualism/individualismo concepto que destaca la importancia de cada individuo (pág. 451)

Industrial Revolution/Revolución Industrial proceso gradual en el que las máquinas reemplazaron a las herramientas manuales (pág. 330)

inflation/inflación aumento de los precios y desvalorización del dinero (págs. 503, 565, 843)

infrastructure/infraestructura sistema de caminos, puentes y túneles (pág. 263)

initiative/iniciativa proceso por el cual los votantes pueden presentar un proyecto de ley directamente ante la legislación del estado (págs. 263, 636)

installment buying/compra a plazo comprar a crédito (pág. 720)

integration/integración mezcla de diversos grupos raciales o étnicos (pág. 850)

interchangeable parts/partes intercambiables partes o repuestos idénticos para herramientas o instrumentos hechos a máquina (pág. 332)

internal improvements/mejoras internas mejoras hechas a caminos, puentes y canales (pág. 346)

Internet/Internet ordenadores unidos de manera que los usuarios puedan acceder e intercambiar información (pág. 892)

interstate commerce/comercio interestatal negocio que se lleva a cabo cruzando los límites de dos o más estados (págs. 346, 632)

Interstate Commerce Commission (ICC)/Comisión de Comercio Interestatal (ICC) agencia del gobierno que vigila el comercio ferroviario (pág. 632)

intervention/intervención participación directa (pág. 351)

Intolerable Acts/Actas Intolerables leyes aprobadas en 1774 para castigar a Boston por la Fiesta del Té (pág. 157)

irrigation/irrigación riego de tierras áridas (pág. 6)

Islam/islam religión monoteísta fundada por el profeta Mahoma a principios del siglo VII (pág. 50)

island hopping/de isla en isla estrategia de los aliados durante la Segunda Guerra Mundial, que consistía en capturar islas ocupadas por los japoneses para obtener el control del Pacífico (pág. 796)

isolationism/aislacionismo política que consiste en tener poca relación con los asuntos políticos de las naciones extranjeras (págs. 660, 708)

isthmus/istmo estrecha franja de tierra que une dos áreas de terreno más extensas (págs. 11, 675)

J

jazz/*jazz* estilo musical que se desarrolló a partir del *blues*, el *ragtime* y otros estilos anteriores (pág. 731)

jerky/tasajo carne secada (pág. 545)

Jim Crow laws/leyes de Jim Crow leyes que separaban en los lugares públicos del Sur a las personas de diferentes razas (pág. 532)

judicial branch/rama judicial rama del gobierno que decide si las leyes se practican de manera justa (pág. 208)

judicial review/revisión judicial poder de la Corte Suprema para decidir si los actos de un presidente o las leyes aprobadas por el Congreso son constitucionales (pág. 305)

Judiciary Act/Acta Judicial ley de 1789 que creó la estructura de la Corte Suprema y estableció un sistema de cortes de distrito y cortes de circuito a nivel nacional (pág. 279)

jury duty/el deber de servir en un jurado obligación de todo ciudadano de servir en un jurado cuando se le llama (pág. 268)

K

kachina/kachina bailarín enmascarado que participaba en ceremonias religiosas de los indígenas del Sudoeste (pág. 47)

kaiser/*kaiser* título del emperador alemán entre 1871 y 1918 (pág. 688)

kamikaze/kamikaze piloto japonés entrenado durante la Segunda Guerra Mundial para estrellarse en un ataque suicida, generalmente contra un barco (pág. 797)

Kansas-Nebraska Act/Acta de Kansas-Nebraska ley de 1854 que estableció los territorios de Kansas y Nebraska, dando a los colonos el derecho de soberanía popular para decidir con respecto a la esclavitud (pág. 468)

Kellogg-Briand Pact/Pacto de Kellog-Briand tratado de 1928 que declaraba ilegal la guerra (pág. 722)

Khmer Rouge/Khmer Rojo partido comunista en Camboya que impuso un verdadero imperio de terror en los camboyanos (pág. 831)

kinship/parentesco cuando se tienen antepasados en común (pág. 53)

Knights of Labor/*Knights of Labor* organización laboral estadounidense fundada en 1869 para proteger los derechos de los trabajadores (pág. 591)

Ku Klux Klan/Ku Klux Klan sociedad secreta organizada en el Sur después de la Guerra Civil para afirmar la supremacía blanca por medio de la violencia (pág. 527)

L

laissez faire/*laissez faire* idea de que el gobierno debería tener una función mínimo en los asuntos económicos (pág. 303)

latitude/latitud distancia hacia el norte o el sur del ecuador (pág. 4)

lawsuit/demanda caso legal iniciado para dirimir una disputa entre personas o grupos (pág. 471)

League of Nations/Liga de las Naciones asociación de naciones formada después de la Primera Guerra Mundial bajo el plan de Los Catorce Puntos de Wilson (pág. 705)

League of the Iroquois/Liga de los Iroquois alianza de las cinco naciones de los iroquois (pág. 48)

League of Women Voters/Liga de Mujeres Votantes organización establecida en 1920 para garantizar los derechos de las mujeres (pág. 725)

legislative branch/rama legislativa rama del gobierno que aprueba las leyes (pág. 208)

legislature/legislatura grupo de personas que tiene el poder de hacer leyes (pág. 122)

Lend-Lease Act/Ley de Préstamo-Alquiler durante la Segunda Guerra Mundial, ley que permitió a Estados Unidos vender armas y equipamiento a Inglaterra (pág. 781)

libel/libelo acto de publicar afirmaciones que pueden dañar injustamente la reputación de una persona (pág. 130)

liberty/libertad independencia (pág. 249)

Liberty Bonds/bonos de la libertad bonos vendidos por el gobierno de Estados Unidos para recaudar dinero para la Primera Guerra Mundial (pág. 695)

limited government/gobierno limitado principio de la Constitución de Estados Unidos que establece que el gobierno sólo tiene los poderes que la constitución le otorga (pág. 250)

literacy test/prueba de alfabetización examen para determinar si una persona sabe leer y escribir; se usaba para restringir el derecho al voto (pág. 532)

local color/color local habla y costumbres de una región determinada (pág. 620)

local government/gobierno local gobierno del condado, distrito de condado, ciudad, pueblo, villa o distrito (pág. 263)

locomotive/locomotora máquina que arrastra un tren (pág. 409)

lode/filón veta rica en oro, plata u otro mineral valioso (pág. 547)

longitude/longitud distancia hacia el este o el oeste del primer meridiano (pág. 4)

Louisiana Purchase/Compra de Luisiana vasto territorio entre el río Mississippi y las Montañas Rocosas que se le compró a Francia en 1803 (pág. 308)

Lusitania* /*Lusitania barco de pasajeros inglés que fue torpedeado por un submarino alemán en 1915; 1,200 personas murieron incluyendo 128 estadounidenses (pág. 690)

lynch/linchar captura y ejecución ilegal de una persona por parte de una multitud (págs. 401, 649)

M

Magna Carta/Carta Magna documento británico de 1215 cuyas dos ideas básicas sostienen que incluso los monarcas tienen que obedecer la ley y que los ciudadanos tienen derechos básicos (págs. 90, 213)

mainstreaming/mainstreaming integración de los niños con necesidades especiales en clases normales (pág. 896)

majority/mayoría más de la mitad (pág. 362)

Manifest Destiny/destino manifiesto creencia que se diseminó en el siglo XIX que los estadounidenses tenían el derecho y la obligación de ocupar todo el continente, hasta el Pacífico (pág. 393)

manor/señorío distrito regido por un Señor que incluía su castillo y las tierras que lo rodeaban (pág. 58)

map projection/proyección cartográfica dibujo de la Tierra sobre una superficie plana (pág. 8)

Marbury v. Madison/Marbury versus Madison caso judicial de 1803 en el cual la Corte Suprema dictaminó que tenía el poder de decidir si las leyes aprobadas por el Congreso era constitucionales (pág. 305)

Spanish Glossary

Marshall Plan/plan Marshall plan estadounidense para ayudar a los países europeos a reconstruir sus economías después de la Segunda Guerra Mundial (pág. 812)

martial law/ley marcial gobierno de militares en vez de un gobierno electo (págs. 487, 834)

martyr/mártir persona que muere por sus creencias (pág. 476)

mass production/producción en masa proceso que consiste en hacer grandes cantidades de un producto, con gran rapidez y a bajo costo (pág. 588)

Mayflower Compact/acuerdo Mayflower acuerdo de 1620 para gobernar la colonia de Plymouth (pág. 95)

mediator/mediador agente que ayuda a las partes en conflicto a resolver sus diferencias (pág. 879)

mercantilism/mercantilismo teoría de que el poder económico de una nación provenía de mantener un estricto control sobre el comercio de las colonias (pág. 120)

mercenary/mercenario soldado que lucha exclusivamente por dinero, a menudo para un país extranjero (pág. 171)

merit/mérito habilidad (pág. 631)

mestizo/mestizo en las colonias españolas de las Américas, la persona que tiene mezcla indígena y española (pág. 78)

Mexican Cession/cesión mexicana territorio mexicano de California y Nuevo México que se entregó a Estados Unidos en 1848 (pág. 396)

middle class/clase media en las 13 colonias inglesas, la clase social que incluía artesanos cualificados, granjeros y algunos comerciantes (pág. 126)

migrant worker/trabajador itinerante persona que se traslada de una región a otra en busca de trabajo (págs. 766, 865)

militarism/militarismo política que consiste en reforzar las fuerzas armadas como preparación para la guerra (pág. 687)

militia/milicia ejército de ciudadanos que sirven como soldados en una emergencia (pág. 158)

minuteman/miliciano de la Guerra de Independencia voluntario de una milicia colonial que estaba siempre listo para luchar (pág. 159)

mission/misión colonia religiosa administrada por frailes y monjas católicas (pág. 78)

missionary/misionero persona que enseña sus creencias religiosas a otros (págs. 56, 84)

Missouri Compromise/compromiso de Missouri acuerdo, propuesto en 1819 por Henry Clay, para mantener igual el número de estados esclavistas y antiesclavistas (pág. 460)

Monitor/Monitor buque de guerra blindado de la Unión (pág. 492)

monopoly/monopolio compañía o agrupación que tiene control de toda o casi toda una industria (pág. 581)

Monroe Doctrine/Doctrina Monroe política exterior del presidente Monroe que prevenía a las naciones europeas de no intervenir en América Latina (pág. 351)

moral diplomacy/diplomacia moral política del presidente Wilson que consistía en condenar el imperialismo, extender la democracia y promover la paz (pág. 679)

Moral Majority/Mayoría Moral organización religiosa que apoyaba causas políticas conservadoras en la década de 1980 (pág. 873)

mountain man/hombre de montaña cazador que exploraba Oregón a principios del siglo XIX (pág. 381)

moving assembly line/cadena de ensamblaje en movimiento método de producción según el cual los trabajadores permanecen en un lugar mientras que los productos pasan frente a ellos en una cinta transportadora (pág. 588)

muckraker/muckraker periodista que ponía en evidencia la corrupción y otros problemas a finales del siglo XIX y principios del siglo XX (pág. 634)

mudslinging/detractar uso de insultos para atacar la reputación de un oponente (pág. 374)

Munich Conference/Conferencia de Munich reunión en 1938 entre los líderes de Inglaterra, Francia, Italia y Alemania en la que se acordó entregar a Hitler parte de Checoslovaquia (pág. 779)

mutualista/mutualista grupo de ayuda mutua de los estadounidenses de origen mexicano (pág. 651)

N

NAACP/NAACP (Asociación Nacional para el Avance de la Gente de Color) organización establecida para luchar por la igualdad de derechos de los afroamericanos (pág. 650)

National Aeronautics and Space Administration/Administración Nacional de la Aeronáutica y el Espacio (NASA) agencia gubernamental que dirige el programa espacial estadounidense (pág. 825)

national debt/deuda nacional cantidad total de dinero que un gobierno debe (págs. 280, 763)

National Labor Relations Act/Ley Nacional de Relaciones Laborales ley aprobada en 1935 que protege a los trabajadores de Estados Unidos de prácticas injustas por parte de sus patrones (pág. 761)

national park/parque nacional área que el gobierno federal reserva para que las personas la visiten (pág. 641)

National Recovery Administration/ Administración para la Recuperación Nacional agencia gubernamental establecida durante la Gran Depresión para asegurar el cumplimiento de nuevos códigos diseñados para estabilizar la industria (pág. 755)

National Woman Suffrage Association/Asociación Nacional para el Sufragio de la Mujer grupo fundado en 1869 para luchar por una enmienda constitucional que concediera a las mujeres el derecho al voto (pág. 645)

nationalism/nacionalismo orgullo excesivo en la propia nación (págs. 318, 686)

nativist/nativista persona a favor de que se limitara la immigración y Estados Unidos se reservara para los protestantes blancos nacidos en el país (págs. 416, 604, 738)

natural resources/recursos naturales materiales que los seres humanos toman del medio ambiente para sobrevivir y satisfacer sus necesidades (pág. 5)

natural rights/derechos naturales derechos que corresponden a todas las personas desde su nacimiento (pág. 175)

naturalize/naturalizarse proceso oficial para convertirse en ciudadano (pág. 265)

Navajo code-talkers/navajos que hablaban en código en la Segunda Guerra Mundial, soldados navajos que usaban su propio lenguaje para enviar por radio mensajes vitales para la campaña "de isla en isla" (pág. 796)

Nazi/nazi miembro del partido Nacional Socialista de Trabajadores Alemanes liderado por Adolf Hitler (pág. 775)

Nazi-Soviet Pact/pacto nazi-soviético acuerdo firmado entre Hitler y Stalin en 1939 por el cual los dos dictadores se comprometieron a no atacarse mutuamente (pág. 779)

network/red sistema de vías de ferrocarril que se comunican (pág. 575)

neutral/neutral que no toma partido en un conflicto (pág. 285)

Neutrality Acts/Leyes de Neutralidad leyes aprobadas por el Congreso en 1935 que prohibían la venta o préstamo de armas a los países que estuvieran en guerra (pág. 777)

New Deal/Nuevo Acuerdo programa del presidente Franklin D. Roosevelt para poner fin a la Gran Depresión (pág. 754)

New Freedom/nueva libertad programa del presidente Wilson para acabar con los *trusts* y restituir la competencia económica en Estados Unidos (pág. 643)

"New South"/"Nuevo Sur" término de fines de siglo XIX que describía el Sur cuando se esforzaba por expandir la economía a través de la industria (pág. 533)

Nineteenth Amendment/Enmienda Decimonovena enmienda a la Constitución de Estados Unidos que da a las mujeres el derecho al voto (págs. 261, 646)

nominating convention/convención de postulaciones reunión en la cual un partido político elige sus candidatos (pág. 364)

North American Free Trade Agreement/Tratado de Libre Comercio Norteamericano (TLC) tratado entre Estados Unidos, Canadá y México para eliminar gradualmente aranceles y otras barreras al comercio (pág. 889)

North Atlantic Treaty Organization/ Organización del Tratado del Atlántico Norte (OTAN) alianza constituida en 1949 por Estados Unidos y países de Europa occidental para combatir la agresión soviética (pág. 813)

northwest passage/pasaje noroeste pasaje de agua a través o alrededor de América del Norte (pág. 81)

nullification/anulación idea de que un estado tiene el derecho de anular o cancelar una ley federal que se considere inconstitucional (pág. 371)

Nuremberg Trials/juicios de Nuremberg en 1945 y 1946, juicios a los crímenes de guerra de los nazis (pág. 799)

O

on margin/con margen práctica que permite a las personas comprar acciones abonando una entrada del diez por ciento del valor total (pág. 747)

OPEC/OPEP (Organización de Países Exportadores de Petróleo) organización internacional que establece una política común para la venta de petróleo (pág. 884)

Open Door Policy/política de puertas abiertas política promulgada por el Secretario de Estado John Hay en 1899 que permitía a una nación comerciar con China en la esfera de influencia de cualquier otra nación (pág. 666)

Operation Overlord/operación Overlord nombre en código de la invasión de los aliados en Europa, ocurrida en 1944 (pág. 792)

Organization of American States/ Organización de Estados Americanos (OEA) organización internacional que promueve la paz y el progreso económico en las Américas (pág. 824)

override/invalidar no admitir, como cuando el Congreso decide no admitir el veto presidencial (pág. 257)

P

pacifist/pacifista persona que se opone a todas las guerras porque cree que todas las guerras son malignas (pág. 696)

Parliament/Parlamento en Inglaterra, asamblea representativa (pág. 90)

parochial/parroquial de la iglesia; usado a menudo para referirse a las escuelas auspiciadas por la iglesia (pág. 617)

patent/patente licencia para un nuevo invento (pág. 584)

patriotism/patriotismo sentimiento de amor y devoción hacia el propio país (pág. 266)

patronage/patronato práctica de otorgar puestos gubernamentales a los partidarios políticos (pág. 631)

patroon/patrón dueño de una gran propiedad en una colonia holandesa (pág. 109)

Peace Corps/Cuerpo de Paz organización del gobierno que envía voluntarios estadounidenses a países en desarrollo para dar asistencia técnica (pág. 824)

peninsulare/peninsular término que se refiere a un español que tenía una posición de poder en una colonia española (pág. 78)

pension/pensión suma de dinero que se paga a las personas regularmente después de jubilarse (pág. 760)

perjury/perjurio mentir bajo juramento (pág. 820)

persecution/persecución maltrato o castigo a un grupo de personas a causa de sus creencias (pág. 94)

Persian Gulf War/guerra del Golfo Pérsico guerra en 1991 en la que Estados Unidos y sus aliados en las Naciones Unidas expulsaron a las fuerzas invasoras de Iraq del contiguo territorio de Kuwait (pág. 885)

petition/petición solicitud formal firmada por un grupo de personas dirigida a alguien de mayor autoridad (pág. 149)

Pickett's Charge/ataque a Pickett ataque la Confederación como parte de la batalla de Gettysburg que fracasó (pág. 506)

pit house/casa subterránea casa de la región ártica cavada en la tierra y cubierta con madera y pieles (pág. 43)

plantation/plantación gran propiedad cultivada por muchos trabajadores (pág. 80)

Platt Amendment/Enmienda Platt enmienda de 1902 a la constitución cubana, que permitía a Estados Unidos intervenir en Cuba (pág. 673)

***Plessy v. Ferguson*/Plessy versus Ferguson** un caso legal de 1896 en el cual la Suprema Corte dictaminó que la segregación en las instalaciones públicas era legal si las instalaciones eran iguales (pág. 532)

PLO/OPL (Organización para la Liberación de Palestina) organización palestino-árabe fundada en 1964 con el fin de destruir a Israel, principalmente a través del uso de fuerza armada (pág. 884)

pogrom/*pogrom* en la Europa del este, ataque organizado a una comunidad judía (pág. 600)

polio/polio enfermedad infecciosa que inflama las células nerviosas de la base del cerebro y la columna vertebral, produciendo parálisis (pág. 752)

political boss/capo político político poderoso que controla el trabajo que se realiza localmente y exige sobornos a los negocios (pág. 633)

political science/ciencias políticas el estudio del gobierno (pág. 29)

poll tax/impuesto al voto impuesto que se requería antes de que las personas pudieran votar (pág. 532)

pool/mancomunidad sistema por el cual varias compañías de ferrocarril se ponen de acuerdo en repartirse el negocio de cierta área (pág. 576)

popular sovereignty/soberanía popular a mediados del siglo XIX, término que se refería a la idea de que cada territorio podía decidir por sí mismo si permitir la esclavitud (págs. 250, 462)

potlatch/*potlatch* cena ceremonial realizada por algunos indígenas de la costa noroeste para mostrar su riqueza (pág. 44)

Potsdam Declaration/Declaración de Potsdam mensaje enviado por los aliados a los japoneses en julio de 1945 pidiéndoles que se rindieran (pág. 798)

preamble/preámbulo introducción a una declaración, constitución u otro documento oficial (págs. 175, 248)

precedent/precedente acta o decisión que sirve de ejemplo a las que siguen (págs. 96, 278)

precipitation/precipitación agua que cae en forma de lluvia, cellisca, granizo o nieve (pág. 15)

predestination/predestinación
idea protestante según la cual Dios
decidía de antemano quiénes, después
de muertos, se salvarían (pág. 435)

presidio/presidio fuerte de las
colonias españolas donde vivían los
soldados (pág. 77)

primary election/elección primaria
elección en la que los votantes eligen los
candidatos de su partido para la elección general (pág. 635)

primary source/fuente original
información directa acerca de personas o sucesos (pág. 20)

productivity/productividad producción media por trabajador (pág. 845)

profiteer/aprovechador persona
que aprovecha una crisis para hacer
dinero (pág. 503)

Progressive/progresista reformista
de finales del siglo XIX y principios del
siglo XX que quería mejorar la calidad
de vida en Estados Unidos (pág. 634)

Prohibition/Ley Seca prohibición a la
fabricación, venta y transporte de
bebidas alcohólicas en todo el territorio
de Estados Unidos entre 1920 y 1933
(pág. 724)

propaganda/propaganda difusión
de ideas para apoyar una causa o perju-
dicar la causa opuesta (pág. 689)

**proprietary colony/colonia de
propietarios** colonia inglesa en la
cual el rey daba tierras a propietarios
a cambio de un pago anual (pág. 109)

protectorate/protectorado nación
cuya independencia está limitada por
el control de un país más poderoso
(pág. 673)

**Protestant Reformation/reforma
protestante** movimiento del siglo
XVI para reformar la iglesia católica
romana y que llevó a la creación de
muchas iglesias cristianas (pág. 83)

psychology/sicología el estudio
del modo de pensar y comportarse de
los seres humanos (pág. 30)

public interest/interés público lo
que es bueno para el pueblo (pág. 634)

public school/escuela pública
escuela financiada por los impuestos
(pág. 128)

public works/obras públicas
proyectos construidos por el gobierno
para uso público (pág. 750)

pueblo/pueblo ciudad de las colonias españolas; aldea de los anazasi
(págs. 41, 77)

pull factor/factor de atracción
condiciones que atraen a la gente a
mudarse a otra área (pág. 600)

**Pure Food and Drug Act/Ley de los
Alimentos y Medicamentos Puros**
ley de 1906 que exige a los fabricantes

de alimentos y medicamentos que
indiquen los ingredientes en los envases
(pág. 641)

push factor/factor de rechazo
condiciones que hacen que la gente se
vaya de sus lugares de origen (pág. 600)

Q

Quakers/cuáqueros reformistas
protestantes que creen en la igualdad
de todas las personas (pág. 110)

quipu/quipu artefacto hecho de cuer-
da o tiras con nudos que representaban
cantidades; usado por los incas para sus
registros y contabilidad (pág. 40)

quota system/sistema de cupos sistema que limita la inmigración permi-
tiendo que sólo un número determinado
de personas de cada país entre a Estados
Unidos (pág. 738)

R

racism/racismo creencia en la superi-
oridad de una raza con respecto a otra
(págs. 119, 662)

radical/radical persona que quiere
realizar cambios drásticos en la sociedad
(pág. 173)

**Radical Reconstruction/reconstruc-
ción radical** período que comenzó en
1867 cuando los Republicanos, que tenían
el control de ambas cámaras, se hicieron
cargo de la Reconstrucción (pág. 523)

**Radical Republican/republicano ra-
dical** en la época de la Reconstrucción,
miembro del Congreso que quería ase-
gurarse de que los libertos recibieran el
derecho a votar (pág. 522)

ragtime/ragtime música popular de
finales del siglo XIX, rítmica y alegre
(pág. 615)

ratify/ratificar aprobar (pág. 194)

rationing/racionamiento limitación
en la cantidad disponible para la venta
al público de ciertos artículos (pág. 785)

Reaganomics/reaganomics programa
económico del presidente Reagan que
bajó los impuestos, bajó los gastos federales en programas de asistencia social y
aumentó los gastos militares (pág. 873)

realist/realista escritor o pintor que
muestra la vida tal como es (pág. 620)

rebate/rebaja descuento (pág. 576)

recall/impugnación proceso por el
cual los votantes pueden destituir del
cargo a un funcionario electo (pág. 636)

recession/recesión disminución de la
actividad económica que es más leve
que una depresión (págs. 718, 874)

reconcentration/reconcentración
política de trasladar grandes cantidades
de personas a campos especiales con
intención militar o política (pág. 669)

Reconstruction/Reconstrucción
reconstrucción del Sur después de la
Guerra Civil (pág. 517)

**Reconstruction Act/Acta de la
Reconstrucción** ley de 1867 que
anuló los gobiernos de los estados del
Sur que se habían negado a ratificar la
Enmienda Decimocuarta (pág. 523)

referendum/referéndum proceso
por el cual las personas votan directamente con respecto a un proyecto de
ley (pág. 636)

refuge/refugio lugar donde se está
libre de persecuciones (pág. 399)

refugee/refugiado persona que
abandona su tierra natal en busca de
seguridad en otro lugar (pág. 895)

**relief program/programa de ayu-
das** programa del gobierno para ayudar
a los necesitados (pág. 750)

**religious tolerance/tolerancia
religiosa** deseo de permitir que
otros practiquen sus propias creencias
(pág. 104)

rendezvous/rendezvous encuentro
anual en el cual los hombres de montaña intercambiaban pieles (pág. 382)

**renewable resource/recurso reno-
vable** recurso que puede ser reem-
plazado rápidamente por la propia naturaleza (pág. 890)

reparations/reparaciones después
de una guerra, entregas de dinero por
parte de una nación vencida a la nación
vencedora para pagar por las pérdidas
sufridas durante la guerra (pág. 706)

repeal/revocar cancelar (págs. 150,
725)

**representative government/
gobierno representativo** sistema
político según el cual los votantes eligen a los representantes que dictarán
las leyes (pág. 90)

republic/república sistema de gobierno en el cual los ciudadanos eligen
representantes para que los gobiernen
(págs. 57, 211)

**Republican party/partido republi-
cano** partido político establecido en
1854 en Estados Unidos, con el fin de
mantener la esclavitud fuera de los territorios del oeste (pág. 473)

resident alien/extranjero residente
persona que vive en el país sin ser
ciudadano (pág. 266)

revival/reunión evangelista gran
encuentro religioso al aire libre (pág. 435)

**Roosevelt Corollary/corolario de
Roosevelt** declaración del presidente
Theodore Roosevelt según la cual
Estados Unidos tenía el derecho a inter-
venir en Latinoamérica para preservar la
ley y el orden (pág. 678)

**Rosie the Riveter/Rosie la
Remachadora** trabajadora de una

Spanish Glossary

fábrica ficticia que se convirtió en el símbolo de la contribución de las mujeres estadounidenses al esfuerzo que supuso la Segunda Guerra Mundial (pág. 785)

Rough Riders/jinetes rudos sobrenombre de la unidad organizada por Theodore Roosevelt durante la guerra entre España y Estados Unidos (pág. 672)

royal colony/colonia real colonia bajo el control directo de la corona inglesa (pág. 109)

rugged individualist/individualista recalcitrante persona que sigue en la vida su propio camino independiente (pág. 381)

S

sabotage/sabotaje destrucción secreta de propiedades o interrupción de la producción en una fábrica u otro lugar de trabajo (pág. 737)

sachem/*sachem* miembro del consejo tribal de jefes de la Liga de los Iroquois (pág. 48)

SALT Agreement/Tratado *SALT* (discursos sobre limitación de armas estratégicas) tratado firmado por Estados Unidos y la Unión Soviética para limitar el número de cabezas nucleares y misiles (pág. 833)

salvation/salvación vida eterna (pág. 56)

Salvation Army/Ejército de Salvación organización internacional de caridad (pág. 609)

sanctions/sanciones medidas diseñadas para obligar a un país a cambiar su política (pág. 880)

satellite nation/país satélite país dominado política y económicamente por otro más poderoso (pág. 811)

savanna/sabana región de pastos (pág. 52)

scalawag/*scalawag* blanco sureño que apoyaba a los Republicanos durante la Reconstrucción (pág. 526)

scapegoat/chivo expiatorio persona o grupo sobre el que se descargan las culpas de otros (pág. 775)

secede/separarse retirarse como miembro de un grupo (pág. 463)

Second Amendment/Segunda Enmienda enmienda a la Constitución de Estados Unidos que se refiere al derecho a tener armas (pág. 260)

secondary source/fuente secundaria relato de los hechos proporcionado por personas que no participaron directamente o presenciaron los hechos ocurridos (pág. 21)

sectionalism/seccionalismo lealtad a un estado o región antes que a todo el país (pág. 345)

sedition/sedición rebelión en contra de un gobierno (pág. 293)

segregation/segregación separación de las personas por razones de raza, etnia u otras características (págs. 532, 849)

Selective Service Act/Ley de Servicio Selectivo ley aprobada por el Congreso en 1917 que requería que todos los hombres de 21 a 30 años se inscribieran para el servicio militar (pág. 693)

self-determination/autodeterminación derecho de los grupos nacionales a tener su propio territorio y formas de gobierno (pág. 705)

self-sufficient/autosuficiente capaz de producir lo suficiente para satisfacer las necesidades propias (pág. 392)

Senate/Senado el menor de los dos cuerpos que constituyen la rama legislativa del gobierno de Estados Unidos (pág. 253)

Seneca Falls Convention/convención de Seneca Falls un encuentro de 1848 en el cual líderes del movimiento por los derechos femeninos reclamaron derechos igualitarios para la mujer (pág. 445)

separation of powers/separación de poderes principio según el cual los poderes del gobierno se dividen en ramas separadas (pág. 214)

settlement house/centro comunitario establecimiento organizado a finales del siglo XIX para ofrecer servicios a los pobres (pág. 609)

sharecropper/aparcero persona que alquila un terreno de otra persona y lo trabaja a cambio de parte de la cosecha (pág. 529)

Sherman Antitrust Act/Ley Antimonopolio de Sherman ley de 1890 que prohibía la formación de *trusts* y monopolios en Estados Unidos (págs. 582, 632)

siege/sitio cerco por parte del ejército de una ciudad o posición enemiga, seguido de bloqueo o bombardeo para obligarla a que se rinda (págs. 193, 387, 506)

silent majority/mayoría silenciosa término empleado para referirse a los estadounidenses que estaban preocupados por los disturbios de la década de 1960 pero no protestaban por ello públicamente (pág. 860)

sit-down strike/huelga en el lugar de trabajo huelga en la cual los obreros se niegan a salir del lugar donde trabajan hasta que se llegue a un acuerdo (pág. 762)

sit-in/sentada forma de protesta en la que la gente se sienta y se resiste a marcharse (pág. 862)

skyscraper/rascacielos edificio alto de muchos pisos sostenido por un armazón de acero de poco peso (pág. 612)

slave codes/códigos de la esclavitud leyes que controlaban la vida de los esclavos afroamericanos y les negaban los derechos básicos (págs. 119, 424)

smuggling/contrabando importar o exportar mercancías violando las leyes de comercio (pág. 314)

Social Gospel/evangelio social movimiento del protestantismo estadounidense de finales del siglo XIX que intentaba aplicar las enseñanzas de la Biblia a los problemas sociales (pág. 609)

social reform/reforma social intento organizado de mejorar lo que es injusto o imperfecto en la sociedad (pág. 434)

social sciences/ciencias sociales estudios que se refieren a la sociedad y a la conducta social (pág. 29)

Social Security Act/Ley de la Seguridad Social ley de 1935 que estableció un sistema de pensiones para personas mayores y el primer sistema nacional de seguro de desempleo (pág. 762)

Socialist/socialista persona que está a favor de que las propiedades pertenezcan a la comunidad y se compartan todas las ganancias (pág. 696)

Society of American Indians/ Sociedad de Indígenas Estadounidenses agrupación que luchaba por la justicia social y la participación de indígenas en la corriente social principal de Estados Unidos (pág. 653)

sociology/sociología estudio del comportamiento de las personas en grupos (pág. 30)

sod house/casa de tepe casa construida con tierra sujetada con raíces de hierbas (pág. 564)

sodbuster/*sodbuster* granjero de las Grandes Llanuras de a finales del siglo XIX (pág. 564)

Solidarity/Solidaridad sindicato independiente que desafió al gobierno comunista de Polonia (pág. 834)

soup kitchen/olla popular lugar donde se proporciona comida gratis o por un precio mínimo a los necesitados (pág. 750)

Spanish-American War/guerra Hispano-Americana guerra entre España y Estados Unidos en 1898, que tuvo como resultado que España cediera Puerto Rico, Filipinas y Guam a Estados Unidos, y otorgara la independencia a Cuba (pág. 671)

speculator/especulador alguien que invierte dinero en un negocio arriesgado con la esperanza de obtener grandes ganancias (pág. 280)

sphere of influence/esfera de influencia zona donde una nación tenía privilegios comerciales especiales (pág. 666)

Spanish Glossary   ★   **969**

Spanish Glossary

spinning jenny/hiladora de varios husos máquina inventada en 1764 que hilaba varios hilos al mismo tiempo (pág. 331)

spoils system/sistema de sinecuras práctica que recompensaba a los partidarios de un gobierno otorgándoles empleos en dicho gobierno (pág. 366)

Square Deal/acuerdo justo la promesa de Theodore Roosevelt durante su campaña de que todos los grupos tendrían las mismas oportunidades de éxito (pág. 640)

stagflation/estagflación combinación de alza de precios, alto desempleo y lento crecimiento económico (pág. 860)

stalemate/punto muerto empate en el cual ninguno de los lados es suficientemente fuerte como para derrotar al otro (pág. 688)

standard of living/nivel de vida índice basado en la cantidad de bienes, servicios y tiempo libre que tienen las personas (pág. 845)

Star Wars/guerra de las galaxias sistema armamentístico propuesto por el presidente Reagan con el objeto de destruir los misiles soviéticos desde el espacio (pág. 834)

states' rights/derechos de los estados el derecho de los estados a limitar el poder del gobierno federal (págs. 293, 370)

Statue of Liberty/estatua de la Libertad estatua monumental situada en la isla Liberty, en la bahía de Nueva York, que simboliza la esperanza y la libertad (pág. 602)

steerage/tercera clase en un barco, la zona hacinada en que viajan los pasajeros con los billetes más baratos (pág. 601)

stock/acción participación en la propiedad de una corporación (págs. 580, 720)

Strategic Arms Reduction Treaty/Tratado de Reducción de Armas Estratégicas (START) tratado firmado en 1991 por Estados Unidos y la Unión Soviética para reducir las armas nucleares (pág. 882)

strike/huelga acción, por parte de los trabajadores, de negarse a hacer su trabajo hasta que se acepten sus condiciones (pág. 414)

strikebreaker/rompehuelgas el que reemplaza a un trabajador que está de huelga (pág. 591)

subsidy/subsidio ayuda financiera o concesión de tierras por parte del gobierno (pág. 550)

suburb/suburbio área residencial en las afueras de una ciudad (págs. 613, 728, 845)

suffrage/sufragio derecho a votar (pág. 361)

suffragist/sufragista persona que lucho por conseguir el derecho al voto de las mujeres (pág. 646)

summit meeting/cumbre reunión entre los gobernantes de mayor rango de distintas naciones (pág. 835)

superpower/superpotencia país con suficiente fuerza militar, política y económica como para ejercer su influencia por todo el mundo (pág. 823)

Supreme Court/Corte Suprema corte de máxima autoridad de Estados Unidos, establecida por la Constitución (pág. 256)

surplus/superávit excedente; condición que se da cuando los ingresos superan a los gastos (págs. 37, 876)

sweatshop/taller del sudor fábrica donde la gente trabaja muchas horas en malas condiciones y por poco dinero (pág. 591)

T

tariff/tasa de importación impuesto que afecta a bienes extranjeros que se importan a un país (pág. 281)

Teapot Dome Scandal/escándalo *Teapot Dome* escándalo politico durante la administración del presidente Harding (pág. 719)

telegraph/telégrafo mecanismo para comunicarse que envía señales eléctricas por un cable (pág. 409)

temperance movement/movimiento por la temperancia campaña en contra del consumo de alcohol (pág. 436)

Ten Percent Plan/Plan del Diez Por Ciento plan del Lincoln que permitía que un estado del Sur formara un nuevo gobierno después de que el diez por ciento de sus votantes juraran lealtad a Estados Unidos (pág. 517)

tenement/apartamento de inquilinato pequeño apartamento en un barrio pobre de la ciudad (pág. 607)

Tennessee Valley Authority/Autoridad del Valle del Tennessee programa del Nuevo Acuerdo para la construcción de diques que controlaban las inundaciones y producían energía eléctrica a un precio económico (pág. 756)

tepee/tipi tienda construida con pieles de búfalo, estirada entre altos palos (pág. 545)

terrace/terraza amplio escalón de tierra que se cava en la ladera de una colina (pág. 40)

terrorism/terrorismo uso deliberado de actos arbitrarios de violencia con el fin de conseguir un determinado fin político (págs. 688, 886)

Tet Offensive/ofensiva *Tet* ataque orpresivo contra las fuerzas estadounidenses estacionadas en Vietnam en Año Nuevo vietnamita en 1968 (pág. 829)

Thanksgiving/Día de Acción de Gracias día al final de la temporada de cosecha que los peregrinos reservaban para dar gracias a Dios (pág. 97)

thematic map/mapa temático mapa sobre un tema específico, como población, recursos naturales o elecciones (pág. 9)

Thirteenth Amendment/Enmienda Decimotercera enmienda de 1865 a la Constitución de Estados Unidos que prohibe la esclavitud en toda la nación (pág. 519)

38th parallel/paralelo 38 línea divisoria entre Corea del Sur y Corea del Norte (pág. 816)

total war/guerra total guerra absoluta que afecta tanto a los civiles en sus casas como a los soldados en combate (pág. 508)

totalitarian state/estado totalitario país en el cual un único partido controla el gobierno y todos los aspectos de la vida de las personas (pág. 774)

town meeting/cabildo abierto reunión en Nueva Inglaterra durante la colonia donde los colonos discutían y votaban (pág. 107)

trade deficit/déficit comercial condición que se da cuando un país compra a otros países más bienes y servicios de los que vende (pág. 889)

trade union/gremio asociación de trabajadores de un mismo oficio formada para acceder a una paga mayor y a mejores condiciones de trabajo (págs. 414, 592)

traitor/traidor persona que traiciona a su país (pág. 175)

transatlantic/transatlántico a través del Atlántico (pág. 585)

transcendentalist/trascendentalista escritores de Nueva Inglaterra que creían que las verdades más importantes de la vida trascendían, o estaban más allá, de la razón humana (pág. 450)

transcontinental railroad/ferrocaril transcontinental ferrocarril que cruza un continente de costa a costa (pág. 549)

travois/*travois* trineo arrastrado por un perro o caballo (pág. 545)

treason/traición acciones contra el propio país (pág. 476)

Treaty of Brest-Litovsk/Tratado de Brest-Litovsk tratado de 1918 entre Rusia y Alemania que puso fin a la participación rusa en la Primera Guerra Mundial (pág. 699)

Treaty of Kanagawa/Tratado de Kanagawa tratado de 1854 entre Japón y Estados Unidos que abrió los puertos para el comercio estadounidense con Japón (pág. 661)

Spanish Glossary

Treaty of Versailles/Tratado de Versailles tratado firmado el 28 de junio de 1919 por Alemania y por los aliados; atribuía formalmente a Alemania y a sus aliados la responsabilidad por la guerra (pág. 706)

Triangle Fire/incendio de Triangle incendio de 1911 en la fábrica *Triangle Shirtwaist* de Nueva York, donde murieron casi 150 trabajadores (pág. 593)

triangular trade/comercio triangular ruta de comercio colonial entre Nueva Inglaterra, las Antillas y África (pág. 121)

tribe/tribu comunidad de personas que tienen las mismas costumbres, lenguaje y rituales (pág. 42)

tributary/tributario arroyo o río pequeño que desemboca en un río mayor (pág. 15)

tribute/tributo contribución de dinero (pág. 313)

Truman Doctrine/doctrina Truman política del presidente Truman de suministrar ayuda estadounidense a los países amenazados por la expansión comunista (pág. 811)

trust/trust grupo de corporaciones gobernadas por un solo consejo administrativo (pág. 581)

trustbuster/que lucha contra los trusts persona que desea disolver todos los *trust* (pág. 640)

turning point/momento decisivo momento histórico que indica un cambio fundamental (pág. 70)

turnpike/camino de peaje camino construido por una compañía privada que cobra un peaje por su uso (pág. 339)

Tuskegee Airmen/aviadores de Tuskegee pilotos afroamericanos de aviones de guerra entrenados en Tuskegee, Alabama, en la Segunda Guerra Mundial (pág. 787)

tutor/tutor maestro privado (pág. 128)

Twenty-sixth Amendment/Enmienda Vigesimosexta enmienda a la Constitución de Estados Unidos que redujo de 21 a 18 años la edad mínima requerida para votar (pág. 261)

U

U-boat/submarinos U-boat submarinos alemanes usados en la Primera y Segunda Guerra Mundial (pág. 690)

Uncle Tom's Cabin/La Cabaña del Tío Tom novela de Harriet Beecher Stowe en contra de la esclavitud y el Acta de Esclavos Fugitivos (pág. 466)

unconstitutional/inconstitucional que no está permitido por la Constitución (págs. 257, 288)

Underground Railroad/Ruta Clandestina red de abolicionistas negros y blancos que ayudaban en secreto a huir a los esclavos hacia la libertad en el norte de Estados Unidos o Canadá (pág. 441)

United Nations/Naciones Unidas organización mundial establecida en 1945 para proporcionar soluciones pacíficas a los conflictos internacionales (pág. 813)

urbanization/urbanización traslado de la población de las granjas a las ciudades (págs. 335, 606)

V

vaquero/vaquero término que se refiere a ganaderos mexicanos o hispanos (págs. 392, 553)

vaudeville/vaudeville espectáculo de variedades popularizado a finales del siglo XIX, que incluía comediantes, actuaciones de canto y baile, y acróbatas (pág. 615)

vertical integration/integración vertical práctica por la cual un solo fabricante controla todos los pasos necesarios para transformar la materia prima en productos terminados (pág. 579)

veto/veto rechazar, como cuando el presidente rechaza una ley que ha sido aprobada por el Congreso (pág. 257)

victory garden/huerta de la victoria durante la Segunda Guerra Mundial, huerta que se plantaba para combatir la escasez de alimentos en Estados Unidos (pág. 785)

Vietcong/Vietcong guerrilleros vietnamitas que se oponían al gobierno no comunista de Vietnam del Sur (pág. 828)

vigilante/vigilante alguien que se designa a sí mismo para hacer cumplir la ley (págs. 401, 549)

Virginia/Virginia buque de guerra blindado que usaron los Confederados para quebrar el bloqueo de la Unión (pág. 492)

W

Wade-Davis Bill/Proyecto de Wade-Davis plan de 1864 para la Reconstrucción que negaba el derecho al voto o el acceso a la función pública a quienes se habían ofrecido a luchar por la Confederación (pág. 517)

War Production Board/Junta de Producción de Guerra agencia del gobierno creada durante la Segunda Guerra Mundial para ayudar a las fábricas a producir materiales de guerra en lugar de bienes de consumo (pág. 785)

warmonger/belicista persona que fomenta la guerra (pág. 691)

Warsaw Pact/Pacto de Varsovia alianza militar de la Unión Soviética con otros países comunistas de Europa establecida en 1955 (pág. 814)

WCTU/WCTU (Asociación de las Mujeres Cristianas por la Abstinencia) grupo organizado en 1874 que luchó por la prohibición de la venta de bebidas alcohólicas en Estados Unidos (pág. 648)

weather/tiempo condición de la atmósfera terrestre en un lugar y momento determinado (pág. 15)

Whigs/Whigs miembros del viejo Partido Republicano Nacional, liderado por John Quincy Adams (pág. 363)

wholesale/venta al por mayor comprar o vender algo en grandes cantidades a precios reducidos (pág. 565)

Wilmot Proviso/Cláusula de Wilmot ley aprobada en 1846 que proscribía la esclavitud en todos los territorios ganados a México por Estados Unidos (pág. 461)

Wisconsin Idea/idea de Wisconsin serie de reformas progresistas introducidas a principios del siglo XX por el gobernador de Wisconsin Robert La Follette (pág. 635)

women's rights movement/movimiento por los derechos femeninos campaña organizada para obtener el derecho a la propiedad, la educación y otros derechos para la mujer (pág. 446)

writ of assistance/mandato de asistencia documento legal que permitía a los funcionarios de la aduana inglesa realizar la inspección de la carga de un barco sin tener que alegar razón alguna (pág. 150)

Y

yellow journalism/periodismo amarillo periodismo que publica noticias a menudo falsas o mal intencionadas y se apoya en artículos y titulares sensacionalistas (págs. 619, 670)

Young Men's Hebrew Association (YMHA)/Asociación Hebrea de Jóvenes (YMHA) organización fundada en Baltimore en 1845 para ofrecer servicios comunitarios en los barrios judíos (pág. 609)

Z

Zimmermann telegram/telegrama de Zimmermann telegrama enviado en 1917 por el secretario de asuntos exteriores de Alemania al ministro alemán en México, dándole órdenes de instigar a México a que atacara a Estados Unidos en caso de que éstos declarasen la guerra a Alemania (pág. 692)

Spanish Glossary

Index

Index

Index

Index

Index

Index

Index

Credits

Staff Credits

The people who made up *The American Nation* team—representing design services, editorial, editorial services, electronic publishing technology, manufacturing and inventory planning, market research, marketing services, online services and multimedia development, planning and budgeting, product planning, production services, project office, publishing processes, and rights and permissions—are listed below. Bold type denotes the core team members.

Ernest Albanese, Robert Aleman, Diane Alimena, **Margaret Antonini**, Rachel Avenia-Prol, Penelope Baker, Renée Beach, Rhett Conklin, Martha Conway, **Lisa DelGatto**, Marlies Dwyer, Libby Forsyth, Doreen Galbraith, Catalina Gavilanes, **Nancy Gilbert**, Evan Holstrom, **John Kingston**, Vicki Lamb, Mary Sue Langan, Carol Lavis, **Marian Manners**, Vickie Menanteaux, LaShonda Morris, Carrie O'Connor, James O'Neill, **Steven Palmé, Robert Prol, Maureen Raymond**, Bruce Rolff, Gerry Schrenk, Mildred Schulte, Melissa Shustyk, Annette Simmons, Robin Sullivan, Frank Tangredi.

Additional Credits

Greg Abroms, Susan Andariese, Rui Camarinha, John A. Carle, Orquidea Cepin, Lisa Ferrari, Jacki Hasko, Beth Hyslip, Helen Issackedes, Raegan Keida, Elizabeth Kiszonas, Steve Lewin, Kathleen Mercandetti, Art Mkrtchyan, Kenneth Myett, Jeremy Naidus, Xavier W. Niz, Ray Parenteau, Tamara Pellek, Andrew Roney, Robert Siek, Elaine Soares, Linda Westerhoff, Jeff Zoda.

Text Credits

Grateful acknowledgment is made to the following for copyrighted material

The Mother of Nations Excerpt from *The Mother of Nations* by Joseph Bruchac. Copyright © 1989 by Joseph Bruchac. Published by The Crossing Press, 1989. Reprinted by permission.

I Have A Dream *I Have A Dream* by Dr. Martin Luther King, Jr. Copyright © 1963 by Martin Luther King, Jr. Copyright renewed 1991 by Coretta Scott King. Reprinted by arrangement with The Heirs to the Estate of Martin Luther King, Jr., c/o Writer's House, Inc. as agent for the proprietor.

John D. Rockefeller, Sr., Poem Copyright © 1937 John D. Rockefeller, Sr.

The Little Rock Nine Excerpt from interview with Elizabeth Eckford, 1957. Copyright © 1957.

Note: Every effort has been made to locate the copyright owner of material used in this textbook. Omissions brought to our attention will be corrected in subsequent editions.

Map and Art Credits

Maps: Mapping Specialists Limited; **Art: 18–19** John Edwards & Associates; **Charts and Graphs:** Kathleen Mercandetti.

Photo Credits

Frequently cited sources are abbreviated as follows: GC, The Granger Collection, New York; AP, AP/Wide World Photos; CP, Culver Pictures, Inc.; LOC, Library of Congress; NWPA; North Wind Picture Archives; PR, Photo Researchers, Inc.; SS, SuperStock

Photo Research: Omni-Photo Communications, Inc.

Cover and Title Page: Richard Walker/Pearson Education/PH School. Drum: Collections of the Fort Ticonderoga Museum; **ii** *m.* Collections of the Fort Ticonderoga Museum; *t.* Richard Walker/ Pearson Education/PH School; **iv** Richard Walker/Pearson Education/PH School; **vi** *Attack at Battery Wagner* © 1993 Tom Lovell © 1993 The Greenwich Workshop, Inc. Courtesy of The Greenwich Workshop, Inc., Shelton CT; **vii** SS **viii** *t.* GC; *b.* National Museum of American History, Smithsonian Institution; **ix** *Drought Stricken Area*, (detail) 1934. Alexandre Hogue (1898–1994), Oil on canvas. Dallas Museum of Art, Texas, USA/The Bridgeman Art Library, London/New York; **x** *t.* National Organization for Women, © 1992; **xi** *b.* © 1989 North Wind Picture Archives; **xii** © CORBIS; **xiii** *t.* GC; *b.* Mark Wilson/Getty Images/ Liaison Agency **xvii** *t.* CP; *b.* Lianhe Zaobao Heng/Cartoonists & Writers Syndicate/ cartoonweb.com **xviii** GC **xxxvi** Chief Athore and Rene de Laudonniere. Gouache and metallic pigments on vellum, with traces of black chalk outlines, 27 June 1564. Jacques Le Moyne, Print Collection, Miriam and Ira D. Wallach Division of Art, Prints and Photographs, The New York Public Library, Astor, Lenox and Tilden Foundations; **R1** *Kindred Spirits*, Asher Brown Durand Oil on canvas, 1849. The Granger Collection, New York; **R2** The Granger Collection, New York; **R5** ©

Bettmann/CORBIS; **R6** The Granger Collection, New York; **R8** *l.* The Granger Collection, New York; *r.* Index Stock Imagery, Inc.; **R10** CORBIS **R11** Courtesy of The Bostonian Society, Old State House **R12** National Museum of American History, Smithsonian Institution, photo id: 95-\155/4 **R13** Doug Armand/Stone **456–457** Winslow Homer, *A Rainy Day in Camp*, 1871. The Metropolitan Museum of Art, Gift of Mrs. William F. Milton, 1923. (2377.1) Copyright ©2003 The Metropolitan Museum of Art; **458** *l.* Courtesy of the Illinois State Historical Library; *r.* Eastman Johnson, *A Ride for Liberty—the Fugitive Slaves*. The Brooklyn Museum; **459** *l.* GC; *r.* Ft. Sumter National Monument.; **460** The American Philosophical Society; **461** *b.l.* GC; *b.r.* GC; **463** GC; **464** GC; **467** *t.r.* Courtesy of the LOC; *m.* Courtesy of the LOC; *b.l.* ©Stock Montage, Inc.; **468** GC; **471** ©Bettmann/CORBIS; **473** National Portrait Gallery, Smithsonian Institution; **474** Currier & Ives, *The Right Man for the Right Place*, 1856. Lithograph on wove paper, 27 x 34 cm. Courtesy of the LOC; **477** *The Last Moments of John Brown*, Thomas Hovenden, The Metropolitan Museum of Art, Gift of Mr. & Mrs. Carl Stoeckel, 1897, (97.5), All Rights Reserved, The Metropolitan Museum of Art, NY; **478** Courtesy of the Illinois State Historical Library; **480** National Geographic Society; **481** GC; **483** GC; **484** ©1997 NWPA; **485** *l.* Courtesy of the LOC; *r.* CP; **486** West Point Museum Collections, United States Military Academy, West Point, New York; **489** ©Omni-Photo Communications, Inc.; **490** Smithsonian Institute; **494** Photograph by Mathew Brady. ©CORBIS; **495** ©2001 NWPA; **496** *Unidentified African-American Civil War soldier*. Tintype, unknown photographer, no date. Chicago Historical Society, ICHi-08068; **498** *Attack at Battery Wagner* © 1993 Tom Lovell © 1993 The Greenwich Workshop, Inc. Courtesy of The Greenwich Workshop, Inc., Shelton CT; **500** *Home Coming, 1865*, watercolor by William L. Sheppard. The Museum of the Confederacy, Richmond, Virginia. Copy Photography by Katherine Wetzel; *l.* Massachusetts Commandery, Military Order of the Loyal Legion and the U.S. Army Military History Institute; *t.l.* U.S. Army Military History Institute; *m.l.* U.S. Army Military History Institute; **501** *r.* ©Eric Kroll/Omni-Photo Communications, Inc.; **505** ©CORBIS; **506** GC; **511** Courtesy

of the LOC; **513** Photograph by Matthew Brady. CP; **514** *l.* CP; *r.* CP; *m. Upholstered walnut parlor rocking chair*. Used by President Abraham Lincoln at Ford's Theatre, Washington, DC, April 14, 1865. H: 10.00 x 106.68 cm., W: 36.625 in., L: 34.5 in. (29.1451.1). From the Collections of Henry Ford Museum and Greenfield Village, No. 11-A-35(A); **515** *l.* GC; *r.* GC; **516** ©Bern Keating; **517** GC; **518** Courtesy of Ford's Theatre, Washington, DC. Photo by Andrew Lautman; **521** AP Photo/Lou Krasky; **523** GC; **525** *t.* ©Copyright 2001 PhotoDisc, Inc.; *b.* ©Bettmann/CORBIS; **526** ©1994 NWPA; **527** GC; **528** GC; **530** SS; **532** ©1998 NWPA; **536** The National Portrait Gallery, Smithsonian Institution; **537** ©Copyright 2003 PhotoDisc, Inc.; **540–541** Peter Severin Kroyer (1851–1909), *The Biermeister & Main Steel Forge*. Statens Museum for Kunst, Copenhagen, Denmark/Bridgeman Art Library, London/SS; **542** *l.* GC; *r.* Image #:3273(3). Photo by: Lee Boltin. American Museum of Natural History Library; **543** GC; **544** Photo by I. G. Holmes, Panhandle-Plains Historical Society; **545** GC; **547** CP; **550** SS; **552** SS; **554** *l.* CP; *m.b.* SS; *m.t.* ©John Lei/Omni-Photo Communications, Inc.; *t.r.* Grace Davies/Omni-Photo Communications, Inc. *m.r.* ©Copyright 2003 PhotoDisc, Inc.; **557** SS; **558** ©Lawrence Migdale/Stock Boston; **559** GC; **562** GC; **563** GC; **565** ©CORBIS; **567** *b.* SS; *t.* ©1999 NWPA; **570** Permission granted by Troll Communications, LLC; **571** CP; **572** *l.* Courtesy of the LOC; *r.* GC; **573** *l.* GC; *r.* Courtesy Ford Motor Company; **574** CP/SS; **576** Courtesy of the LOC; **578** ©2001 NWPA; **579** GC; **583** *t.* GC; *b.* GC; *m.l.* GC; **584** ©Schenectady Museum; Hall of Electrical History Foundation/CORBIS; **585** CP; **586** *l.* National Park Service, U.S. Department of Interior, Edison National Historic Site; *inset* ©Breton Littlehales/ National Geographic Society; **588** From the collections of Henry Ford Museum & Greenfield Village; **590** CP; **591** Mary Kenney O'Sullivan, mid 1900s. Cabinet card by Purdy, Boston, Massachusetts. The Schlesinger Library, Radcliffe Institute, Harvard University; **593** ©CORBIS; **595** *t.r.* ©Bettmann /CORBIS; *l.* ©PR; *m.r.* Courtesy National Archives, photo no. 102-LH-1948; **597** *r.* Courtesy of the LOC; **598** *l.* GC; *r.* © Grace Davies/ Omni-Photo Communications, Inc.; **599** ©2001 NWPA; **600** ©Bettmann/CORBIS; **601** GC; **602** ©Kevin Fleming/CORBIS; **604** AP;

606 GC; 608 *l.* Brown Brothers; *r.* GC; 609 GC; 613 © NWPA; 614 *inset* CP; *l.* GC; 615 New York Public Library at Lincoln Center; 616 *b.* ©1989 NWPA; *t.* AP; 617 ©2001 NWPA; 618 *l.* GC; *r.* GC; 619 Brown Brothers; 620 GC; 626–627 *The Fourth of July* (detail), 1916, Frederick Childe Hassam (1859–1935)/Christie's Images; 628 *l.* ©1995 NWPA; *r.* Courtesy of the LOC; 629 *m.* ©1989 NWPA; *r.* Equity Management Inc./United States Postal Service; 630 © Richard Cheek for the Preservation Society of Newport County; 631 GC; 633 GC; 634 Courtesy of the LOC; 637 *m.t.* GC; *t.r. The Jungle* by Upton Sinclair. Cover of the 1995 Barnes and Noble Classics edition. Cover design by Tom McKeveny. Cover painting: Bill Jacklin, *Two Chimneys II*, 1986, private collection, courtesy of the artist; *m.l.* CP; *b.* GC; *inset The Epic of the Wheat: The Octopus:* A Story of California by Frank Norris. Cover of the 1994 Penguin Twentieth-Century Classics reissue edition. Cover painting: *His Private Car* by LeComte Stewart. Courtesy of The Museum of Church History and Art, Salt Lake City, Utah. Photograph © The Church of Jesus Christ of Latter Day Saints, 1985. All rights reserved; 637 *t.l.* Amereon, Limited; 638 GC; 639 *inset* National Museum of American History, Smithsonian Institution; *t.r.* Photo by R. Y. Young. Courtesy of the LOC; 640 *l.* CP; *r.* Silver Burdett Ginn; 642 *t.l.* GC; *inset* Courtesy of The New-York Historical Society; 644 CP; 645 ©CORBIS; 646 Sally Anderson-Bruce; 647 © Bettmann/CORBIS; 649 Courtesy of the Arizona Historical Society/ Tucson, accession number 69472; 650 Courtesy National Park Service, Museum Management Program and Tuskegee Institute National Historic Site. Photo by Eric Long; 652 Chinese Immigrants Harvesting at J. deBarth Short Vineyards, San Marino, CA. California Historical Society, San Francisco, FN-23451; 655 ©2001 NWPA; 656 GC; 657 Jacob Lawrence, Harriet Tubman Series, No. 1, (detail) 1939–40. "With sweat and toil and ignorance he consumes his life to pour the earnings into channels from which he does not drink."-Harriet Ward Beecher. Collection of Hampton University Museum, Hampton, Virginia. © Gwendolyn Knight Lawrence, courtesy of the Jacob and Gwendolyn Lawrence Foundation; 658 *m.* Courtesy National Archives, photo no. (RP0016); *r.* GC; *l.* ©Jeff Greenberg/ Omni-Photo Communications, Inc.; 659 GC; 660 © CORBIS; 661 American Naval vessel in a

Japanese harbour, 1861 (color woodcut) by Japanese School, (19th century). LOC, Washington, DC, USA/The Bridgeman Art Library, London/New York; 662 ©Jeff Greenberg/PR; 665 GC; 668 GC; 669 GC; 670 GC; 672 SS; 675 ©1996 NWPA; 676 GC; 678 GC; 681 *b.* ©Agence France Presse/ CORBIS; *b.r.* © David M. Schleser/ PR; *t.* GC; 683 CP; 684 *l.* GC; *r.* ©Bettmann/CORBIS; 685 *r.* © National Archives/PR; *l.* Courtesy of the LOC; 686 GC; 687 GC; 688 *l.* ©1989, FPG International LLC; 689 ©1999, Kerry Wetzel/FPG International LLC; 691 © CORBIS; 693 GC; 694 GC; 695 © 1988, FPG International LLC; 697 GC; 698 National Archives; 700 GC; ©Gamma Press US, Inc.; 701 AP; 703 *b.* © CORBIS; *t.r.* ©Jack Kurtz/Impact Visuals; *inset* Courtesy of the Veterans of Foreign Wars of the United States; *background image* ©PhotoDisc, Inc.; 704 National Portrait Gallery, Smithsonian Institution/Art Resource, NY; 705 Palace of Versailles, France/SS; 706 AP; 708 CP; 711 *r.* The Imperial War Museum, London, Louis Raemakers and *"In Belgium, Help"* 714–715 Alexandre Hogue (1898–1994), *Drought Stricken Area*, 1934 (detail) , Oil on canvas. Dallas Museum of Art, Texas, USA/The Bridgeman Art Library, London/New York; 716 *l.* Courtesy of the LOC; *r.* New York Stock Exchange Archives; 717 AP; 718 Warren Gamaliel Harding (detail) by Margaret Lindsay Williams (1887–1960). Oil on canvas. (Accession No. NPG66.21), 135.9 x 99.7 cm (53¹/₂ x 39¹/₄ in.) The National Portrait Gallery, Smithsonian Institution; 719 GC; 721 *l.* Courtesy of Spiegel; *r.* Brown Brothers; 723 GC; 724 CP; 725 Brown Brothers; 727 ©1999 FPG International LLC; 728 ©Robert Landau/CORBIS; 730 Photofest; 731 Photofest; 732 *inset* ©AP. Original art by C. K. Stevens; *b.* ©1999, Thompson/FPG International LLC; 735 *r.* CP; *m.l.* SS; *b.* SS; *l.* ©Janet Sommer/ Archive Photos; 736 Hulton Getty/Liaison Agency; 737 Collection of David J. and Janice L. Frent; 738 CP; 740 *t.* GC; *inset* From Black Moses: The Story of Marcus Garvey and the University Negro Improvement Association by E. David Cronon ©1955, 1969, Madison: University of Wisconsin Press. Used by permission of the publisher; 744 *r.* AP; *l.* GC; 745 *l.* ©1992 Photoworld/FPG International LLC; *r.* GC; 746 AP; 747 *inset* ©UPI-Bettmann/COR-BIS; ©Bettmann/CORBIS; 748 Isaac Soyer, *Employment Agency* (detail). Collection of Whitney Museum of American Art; 750 SS; 752 Franklin Delano Roosevelt

Library, Hyde Park, NY; 753 ©1999 FPG International LLC; 755 ©Sandy Felsenthal/CORBIS; 756 Courtesy of the LOC; 758 *t.r.* Tennessee Valley Authority; *r.* AP; *t.l.* Tennessee Valley Authority; 759 ©CORBIS; 760 GC; 762 ©Wally McNamee/CORBIS; 765 Courtesy National Archives 766 ©Bettmann/CORBIS; 767 GC; 768 GC; 771 Courtesy of the LOC; 772 *l.* GC; *r.* GC; 773 SS; 774 GC; 775 Collection Kharbine-Tapabor, Paris, France/The Bridgeman Art Library, London/New York; 776 *inset* ©Heinrich Hoffman/CORBIS; *t.* CP; 778 SS; 779 Courtesy National Archives, War and Conflict, #993, #1131; 781 From the book, *Dr. Seuss Goes to War: The World War II Editorial Cartoons of Theodor Seuss Geisel* by Richard H. Minear. Published in cooperation with the Dr. Seuss Collection at the University of California at San Diego; 782 ©H. K. Owen/ Black Star; 784 ©Hulton Getty/ Getty Images/Three Lions/Archive Photos; 785 Printed by permission of the Norman Rockwell Family Trust. Copyright ©2001, The Norman Rockwell Family Trust; 786 CP; 787 ©Bettmann/CORBIS; 789 *l.* AP; *r.* National Museum of American History, Smithsonian Institution; 790 ©Tria Giovan/ CORBIS; 792 ©Anthony Potter Collection/Hulton Getty/Archive Photos; 795 National D-Day Museum; 796 CP; 798 *r.* ©Mike Segar/Archive Photos; *l.* AP; *b.r.* Pete Souza/Liaison Agency; 802 ©Hulton Getty/Archive Photos; 803 ©Hulton Getty/Getty Images/ Anthony Potter Collection/Archive Photos; 806–807 Diana Ong, *4 The World.* SS; 808 *l.* ©Bettmann/ CORBIS; *r.* NASA; 809 *r.* AP; *l.* AP 810 ©Bettmann/CORBIS; 811 ©Bettmann/CORBIS; 812 CP; 815 GC; 816 GC; 817 GC; 818 SS; 819 AP 821 AP; 822 Michael Barson/Past Pefect; 823 ©Hulton Getty/MPI/Archive Photos; 824 CP; 826 *m.r.* ©Bettmann/CORBIS; *l.* NASA; *t.r.* ©NASA/Roger Ressmeyer/CORBIS; *m.b.* ©Roger Ressmeyer/CORBIS; 827 ©Bettmann/CORBIS; 830 SS; 832 AP Photo/Lutz Schmidt; 834 ©White House/Hulton Getty/ Archive Photos; 835 ©Hulton Getty/Archive Photos; 836 © COR-BIS; 839 ©LOC/CORBIS; 840 *l.* AP; *r.* AP; 841 ©Reuters NewMedia Inc./CORBIS; 842 "Two fine cars for the price of one!" Advertisement No. 7141-A, Prepared by J. Walter Thompson Company, 1953. Courtesy of Duke University, Hartman Center for Sales, Advertising & Marketing History, J. Walter Thompson Archives; 843 ©Frank Cancellare/ Bettmann/CORBIS; 844 ©Bettmann/CORBIS; 846 *l.* ©Bettmann/CORBIS; *r.* David

Young-Wolff/PictureQuest; 848 *t.l.* Photofest; *m.* ©NBC TV/Hulton Getty/Archive Photos; *b.l.* Photofest; *t.r.* ©Copyright 2001 PhotoDisc, Inc.; *inset* Archive Photos/ PictureQuest; 849 ©Bettmann/ CORBIS; 850 AP; 851 ©Bettmann/ CORBIS; 852 *l.* ©Bettmann/COR-BIS; *r.* ©Grey Villet/TimePix, Inc.; 853 *m.* ©Bettmann/CORBIS; *r.* ©Bettmann/CORBIS; 855 ©Bettmann/CORBIS; 856 AP; 857 ©CORBIS; 858 *inset* AP Photo/ Hattiesburg (MS) American, Joe Lovett; *t.* ©Hulton Getty/Archive Photos; 860 ©Bettmann/CORBIS; 862 AP Photo/Jackson (MS) Daily News, Fred Blackwell; 863 ©Flip Schulke/CORBIS; 864 *t.* Stock Boston; *inset* National Organization for Women, ©1992; 867 ©Philip Jon Bailey/Stock Boston; 870 *l.* ©Mike Mazzaschi/ Stock Boston; *r.* ©A. Ramey/ PhotoEdit; 871 ©2001 *The Record* (Bergen County, NJ) Thomas E. Franklin, staff photographer/ CORBIS/SABA; 872 National Museum of American History, Department of Social History, Political History Collection, Smithsonian Institution; 875 Lianhe Zaobao Heng/Cartoonists & Writers Syndicate/ cartoonweb.com; 878 ©Bob Daemmrich/Stock Boston; 879 ©Reuters/Christine Grunnet/ Archive Photos; 883 AP; 886 Mark Wilson/Getty Images/Liaison Agency; 888 ©David R. Austen/ Stock Boston; 890 ©AFP/Chris Wilkins/CORBIS; 891 ©Myrleen Ferguson Cate/PhotoEdit; 892 *l.* ©Owen Franken/Stock Boston; *t.r.* ©Michael Newman/PhotoEdit; *b.r.* ©1988 Peter L. Chapman/Stock Boston; *m.r.* ©Phyllis Ricardi/Stock Boston; 894 ©Michael Newman/ PhotoEdit; 895 © Reuters NewMedia Inc./CORBIS; 897 *r.* ©Bob Daemmrich/Stock Boston; 902 AP Photo/Dana Tynan; 903 ©1991 Robert Fried/Stock Boston; 906 *Washington Crossing the Delaware,* Emanuel Leutze, GC; 934–937: portrait nos.1, 2 ,4, 5, 6, 9, 10, 12, 14, 15, 18, 20, 21, 25, 26, 27, 35, National Portrait Gallery, Smithsonian Institution/Art Resource, NY; nos. 3, 7, 8, 9,11,13, 16, 17, 19, 22, 23, 24, 28, 29, 30, 31, 32, 33, 34, 36, 37, 38, 39, 40, 41, 42, White House Collection, copyright White House Historical Association; #43: © Bob Daemmrich/Stock, Boston, Inc./PictureQuest; *b.r.* GC; *b.* ©Peter Poulides/Stone/Getty Images

Credits